Differential
Psychology

Differential Psychology

Henry L. Minton
Frank W. Schneider

University of Windsor

Brooks/Cole Publishing Company

Monterey, California
A Division of Wadsworth, Inc.

Consulting Editors: *Lawrence S. Wrightsman
and Edward L. Walker*

Printed in the United States of America

10 9 8 7 6 5 4 3 2 1

Library of Congress Cataloging in Publication Data

Minton, Henry L
    Differential psychology.

    Includes bibliographical references and indexes.
    1. Difference (Psychology)   2. Personality.
3. Social groups. I. Schneider, Frank W., joint
author.   II. Title.
BF697.M54   155   79-14853
ISBN 0-8185-0353-X

Acquisition Editor: *C. Deborah Laughton*
Manuscript Editor: *Derek Gallagher*
Production Editor: *Marilu Uland*
Interior and Cover Design: *Katherine Minerva*
Illustrations: *Lori Heckelman*
Typesetting: *Continental Graphics, Los Angeles, California*

To Sheila and Gregory
Shari and Kimberly

Preface

This book provides an overview of the study of individual and group differences in psychological functioning. It is hoped that the reader will gain an understanding of the ways and the extent to which individuals and groups differ from one another as well as an understanding of the factors responsible for these differences.

A theme of this book is the interplay between society and the conceptualization and study of human differences. Differential psychology developed in an era in which division of labor and occupational specialization were dominant concerns of European and North American society. The time was therefore ripe for the acceptance and utilization of methods that could identify individual differences in ability level so that each person could be selected and, where necessary, appropriately trained for his or her most suitable vocational role. Differences in intelligence virtually defined the field when it began nearly a century ago. As we enter the 1980s, differential psychology has expanded far beyond its original emphasis, although intelligence remains an important area of investigation. Because of the changes occurring in Western society, the last two decades have been marked by an explosion of interest in sex differences, age differences, and race differences. The roles of heredity and environment as determinants of human variation—one of the oldest controversies in the study of human differences—continues to be an issue of major importance. In this book we present the current status of the study of human differences. Where relevant, classical investigations are referred to as a means of indicating how we have arrived at the research questions now being investigated. In light of our current knowledge and the impact of societal forces, we also sketch some future directions of differential psychology.

The book is organized into four parts. In Part 1 the reader is introduced to the origins and scope of differential psychology, basic concepts and methods, and the roles of heredity and environment as determinants of human variation. Part 2 concerns the major dimensions of individual differences—intelligence, school achievement, special aptitudes and abilities, personality, and interests and values. Part 3 deals with the major group differences—sex, age, social class, and race. In Part 4, the trends and implications of differential psychology are considered.

We believe that this book will prove to be a useful source for people interested in a variety of areas of psychology. Needless to say, it can serve as a textbook for undergraduate courses in the area of differential psychology. It could also be of value, however, as an ancillary text for undergraduate courses in personality, psychological testing, educational psychology, social psychology, and more specialized courses, such as those dealing with sex and race differences. The book can benefit graduate students in psychology and education as well as serve as a reference source for academic and professional psychologists, teachers, counselors, and academicians involved in teacher training and counseling education.

We wish to acknowledge and thank the following individuals for reading and helping to improve various sections of the book: Peter L. Burgher, Paul O. N. Hebert, Theodore Horvath, Wayne A. Lesko, Ann E. McCabe, Sheila G. Minton, Martin E. Morf, and Shari R. Schneider. We particularly want to express our gratitude to Allan R. Buss of the University of Calgary, Lawrence E. Jones of the University of Illinois at Urbana-Champaign, David V. Reynolds of the University of Windsor, Steven G. Vandenberg of the University of Colorado at Boulder, Edward L. Walker of the University of Michigan, and Lawrence S. Wrightsman of the University of Kansas, each of whom read the entire manuscript and provided many constructive criticisms and suggestions. Thanks go also to William H. Hicks, C. Deborah Laughton, Ron Munro, Marilu Uland, and the rest of the Brooks/Cole staff for their support and assistance from the seminal stages of the project to the completion of the final manuscript.

Some of the work on the book was carried out while the authors were on sabbatical leave from the University of Windsor. During this period Henry Minton received support from a University of Windsor Research Grant, and

Frank Schneider received support from a Canada Council Leave Fellowship Research Stipend. For generously making available a comfortable working atmosphere, Henry Minton expresses his appreciation to R. Leslie Reid, chairman, Kenneth T. Strongman, and other staff members of the Psychology Department, University of Exeter, and Frank Schneider conveys his appreciation to Robert E. Adamson, chairman, and other staff members of the Department of Psychology, Florida Atlantic University.

Several student assistants merit recognition and thanks for carrying out a variety of tasks related to conducting library research and compiling and editing reference materials. These individuals include Janet George, Priscilla Hoe, Ernst Hofmann, Michael Joschko, Helen Klein, Cynthia Lee, Valerie Melburg, and Ann Sprague. We also want to express our appreciation to the following people for helping to type various drafts of the manuscript: Irene Arseneau, Marjola Burdeshaw, Dorothy Desjardins, Lisa Gregg, Joyce Phillips, and Kathryn Tripp.

Henry L. Minton
Frank W. Schneider

Contents

9 **Interests and Values**   221

PART THREE   GROUP DIFFERENCES   263

10 **Sex Differences**   265

11 **Age Differences**   330

12 **Social Class Differences**   389

Differential
Psychology

Part One

Introduction

The Origins
of Differential Psychology

Shakespeare, an astute observer of the human psyche, illustrated through his characters a special sensitivity to individual and group differences. Hamlet, in order to convince his mother, the Queen, of his uncle's treachery, accentuates the differences between his uncle and his father:

Look here, upon this picture, and on this,
The counterfeit presentment of two brothers.
See what a grace was seated on this brow;
Hyperion's curls, the front of Jove himself,
An eye like Mars, to threaten and command,
A station like the herald Mercury . . . .
This was your husband. Look you now what follows:
Here is your husband, like a mildew'd ear,
Blasting his wholesome brother. Have you eyes?

Could you on this fair mountain leave to feed,
And batten on this moor? Ha! have you eyes?

Act III, Scene iv

Shylock in the *Merchant of Venice*, to justify his revenge, makes use of his identity as a Jew to demonstrate that he can experience the same emotions a Christian experiences:

> To bait fish withal, if it will feed nothing else, it will feed my revenge. He hath disgrac'd me, and hinder'd me half a million, laugh'd at my losses, mock'd at my gains, scorned my nation, thwarted my bargains, cool'd my friends, heated mine enemies, and what's his reason? I am a Jew. Hath not a Jew eyes, hath not a Jew hands, organs, dimensions, senses, affections, passions? . . .

> If you prick us, do we not bleed? if you tickle us do we not laugh, if you poison us do we not die, and if you wrong us, shall we not revenge? if we are like you in the rest, we will resemble you in that. If a Jew wrong a Christian, what is his humility? Revenge. If a Christian wrong a Jew, what should his sufferance be by Christian example? Why, revenge.

Act III, Scene i

The purpose of this book is to develop an understanding of the ways and extent to which individuals and groups of individuals differ from one another and to undertake an explanation of the factors responsible for the differences among individuals and groups. Differential psychology—the empirical study of individual and group differences—is primarily concerned with variability in psychological functioning. To the extent that they can be conceived as contributing to psychological differences, differences in physical structure and physiological functioning are also viewed as relevant areas of study. Thus, our focus in this book is on psychological differences rather than on physical differences, although we frequently look at the latter as possible determinants of psychological differences. Moreover, we will concentrate on variability among humans to the exclusion of variability among animals.

In this introductory chapter we will trace the origins of differential psychology and see how these early beginnings led to the emergence of a scientific study of human differences. A better appreciation of the issues and challenges of a field of study can be achieved if we have some perspective on its past. Let us begin with a look at the prescientific era of differential psychology.

EARLY ANTECEDENTS

The earliest roots of differential psychology go back to the ancient Chinese. Four thousand years ago the Chinese had instituted a relatively sophisticated program of assessing individual differences in occupational proficiency (DuBois, 1970). Civil-service officials were given oral examinations every third year to determine their competency for continuing in their present jobs or promotion to more responsible positions. By the time of the Han Dynasty (206 B.C. to 220 A.D.) written examinations had been introduced for civil servants working in such areas as geography, agriculture, civil law, and military affairs. The Chinese continued to utilize civil-service assessment programs well into the modern period. British diplomats and missionaries traveling in China during the 19th century returned with reports of the Chinese system, and, as a consequence, by the mid-19th century competitive examinations were introduced in the British civil service.

The ancient Greeks were also cognizant of individual differences. In *The Republic*, Plato stressed that the ideal state was based on the assignment of individuals to the tasks for which they were best suited. He proposed, for instance, an aptitude test for selecting those individuals most qualified for military careers. Aristotle in both his *Ethics* and *Politics* commented on group and individual differences. For example, he wrote about sex and racial differences in mental and moral characteristics. The physician Hippocrates developed a classification system of body build in which individuals could be typed or categorized as either long and thin or short and thick. Furthermore, based on Hippocrates' ideas, another physician, Galen, devised a four-category typology of temperament in which individuals could be typed as sanguine (hopeful). melancholic (sad), choleric (irascible), or phlegmatic (apathetic).

Interest in individual differences waned after the Greek and Roman periods. In European society during the Middle Ages the individual was viewed as inseparable from the group to which he or she belonged (Williams, 1961). As Fromm (1941) points out, "A person was identical with his role in society; he *was* a peasant, an artisan, a knight, and not *an individual* who *happened* to have this or that occupation" (pp. 41–42). By the time of the Renaissance, the rigid social structure of medieval society with its emphasis on group identity yielded to a capitalistic society based on individual economic initiative. Furthermore, the Protestant Reformation removed the central authority of the Church, forcing many individuals to face God alone. Thus, the emergence of capitalism and Protestantism marked the beginning of modern individualism—the belief that each person is a separate and, to some extent, self-sufficient entity (Buss & Poley, 1976; Fromm, 1941).

The cultural theme of individualism pervaded the capitalistic and Protestant countries of Western Europe from the 16th century onward. According to Buss (1976), individualism was most pronounced in 19th-century Britain, partly because of the emergence of a democratic political structure that stressed the liberal principles of individual freedom and equality. Another reason individualism flourished in 19th-century Britain was the growth of a capitalistic economy spurred by the Industrial Revolution. The modern capitalistic system produced greater division of labor and more occupational specialization. Buss (1976) comments: "For the first time in the history of man . . . individual differences ran rampant" (p. 54). Modern capitalism also set the stage for attempts at quantifying individual differences. Since measurement and quantification were used to determine prices, markets, profits, and losses, it followed that psychological characteristics might also be subject to measurement.

Within the milieu of British individualism we find the birthplace of a scientific differential psychology. Toward the end of the 19th century, Sir Francis Galton started his investigation of individual differences.

THE RISE OF DIFFERENTIAL PSYCHOLOGY

Galton, a brilliant and well-traveled British scholar, was influenced by the noted biologist Charles Darwin and attempted to apply Darwin's ideas about human evolution to the study of mental characteristics. Specifically, Galton believed that if physical characteristics are transmitted by heredity (as Darwin suggested) mental characteristics, such as intelligence, also might have a basis in heredity. In 1869, Galton published a book entitled *Hereditary Genius* in which he reported his investigation of the family histories of eminent British men. He found that outstanding achievements run along family lines and interpreted this finding as support for his thesis that differences in mental characteristics are hereditary. Galton's next step was to obtain direct measurements of mental characteristics. He set up an "anthropometric" laboratory at an international exhibition. This laboratory was later moved to a London museum. For a small fee visitors were physically measured and evaluated on a number of tasks including sensory discrimination and reaction time. (It's ironic how times have changed; now we often have to pay subjects for their participation in psychological studies.) Galton's major contribution to differential psychology was his development of quantitative methods of data analysis. He worked with distribution curves and introduced the concept of correlation, a statistical index of the degree of relationship between two variables (see Chapter 2). Galton's student Karl Pearson eventually developed what is currently known as the product/moment correlation coefficient.

Galton's measurements of sensory discrimination (for example, auditory and visual perceptiveness) and reaction time also marked the beginning of modern psychological testing. James McKeen Cattell, an American who had originally studied under Wilhelm Wundt, the German pioneer of experimental psychology, spent some time with Galton while in England. On his return to the United States, Cattell (1890) introduced the term *mental test* and was instrumental in generating the testing movement in psychology. The tests Cattell developed focused on the measurement of sensorimotor abilities. Like Galton, he believed that intelligence or general ability was based on the keenness of a person's sensory discrimination.

However, the Galton/Cattell approach to testing proved unsuccessful when used as a source of predicting academic achievement (see Chapter 4). In contrast, Alfred Binet, the French psychologist, developed a test of intelligence based on complex abilities, such as abstraction and memory. Binet's test, which first appeared in 1905, proved to be a successful predictor of individual differences in school performance and served as the prototype for future intelligence tests.

Binet also was a pioneer in defining the field of differential psychology. In 1895, Binet and his colleague Henri published an article entitled *La Psychologie Individuelle* (Binet & Henri, 1895). The article began: "We broach here a new subject, difficult and as yet very meagerly explored" (p. 411). Binet and Henri advanced two major goals for the new science: (1) the study of the nature and extent of individual differences in psychological processes and (2) the discovery of the interrelationships of mental processes within the individual in order to arrive at a classification of traits and ascertain which are the more basic functions. In 1900, the German psychologist William Stern published a book entitled *Über Psychologie der Individuellen Differenzen* (Stern, 1900). Stern characterized differential psychology in terms of three problems: (1) What is the nature and extent of differences in the psychological life of individuals and groups? (2) What factors determine or affect these differences? (3) How can the differences be manifested? For instance, can they be detected by indexes such as handwriting and facial conformation?

Thus, at the beginning of the 20th century, a new science of differential psychology was emerging. Curiously, from its beginning until quite recently differential psychology remained separated from experimental psychology.

THE TWO DISCIPLINES OF SCIENTIFIC PSYCHOLOGY

Experimental psychology had its beginning in 1879 when Wilhelm Wundt established the first psychological laboratory at Leipzig. The problems investigated by the early experimental psychologists were extensions of the concerns of those physiologists who were interested in behavioral phenomena. Thus, Wundt and his coworkers concentrated their efforts on investigating how stimulus variations affect sensory discrimination and reaction time. In contrast to Galton's work on sensory processes, Wundt and his followers were not interested in individual differences. In Wundt's laboratory any manifestation of individual differences among the respondents in studies of sensory discrimination or reaction time was attributed to error factors, such as chance or carelessness. Cattell's interest in individual differences as a bona fide psychological phenomenon was, therefore, not taken seriously at Leipzig.

The rather unsophisticated experimental procedures employed in Wundt's laboratory eventually yielded to the more rigorous experimental methods developed by Ivan P. Pavlov in Russia and John B. Watson in the United States. By the second decade of the 20th century, experimental psychology was rooted in a methodology based on the relationship between an independent variable (that is, the stimulus conditions manipulated by the experimenter) and its consequent effect on an objectively observed dependent variable. Only that which could be directly observed and studied under controlled laboratory conditions was deemed worthy of study by the new brand of experimental psychology—behaviorism.

In contrast to the experimental psychologists, investigators of individual differences did not conduct experiments. Rather, they relied on the correlational method involving the determination of the degree of relationship between naturally-occurring variables (for example, performance on measures of intelligence by soldiers with varying ethnic backgrounds). In addition, during the early decades of the 20th century, the pioneering differential psychologists, such as Lewis Terman, Henry Goddard, and Robert Yerkes, worked in an applied context (for example, an educational or military setting) rather than in the laboratory. Still another important distinction between the experimentalists and the differential specialists was the former group's emphasis on environmental determinants of observed behaviors and the latter group's emphasis on hereditary determinants of mental characteristics. The experimentalists believed that behaviors could be changed; the differential specialists believed that measured mental characteristics were relatively enduring and unchangeable.

In the years since World War II, a gradual rapprochement has been developing between the adherents of the experimental and differential approaches to psychology. This trend is keynoted by Lee J. Cronbach (1957, 1975), who advocates the simultaneous consideration of individual differences and the effects of experimental manipulation. For example, the academic achievement of high- and low-ability students can be measured (the differentialist's approach) and then studied in relation to various types of instructional methods (the experimentalist's approach). The consideration of the interaction between individual differences and the effects of varied experimental treatments will appear as a notable trend in our survey of various aspects of differential psychology.

DIFFERENTIAL PSYCHOLOGY AND CONTEMPORARY SOCIETY

The investigation of human differences, especially group differences, is an enterprise having considerable relevance to many social issues facing contemporary society. Consider the social significance of the following sample of questions asked by differential psychologists: Are there sex differences in occupational status, achievement motivation, nurturance, and mental illness? If so, what are the causes of the sex differences? Are there age differences among adults in intellectual ability, quality of vocational achievement, speed of response, and suicide rates, and, if so, what are the causes of the age differences? Are there race differences in intellectual performance, scholastic performance, aggression, and mental illness, and, if so, what are the causes of the race differences? Information that helps to provide valid answers to each of the above questions—namely, whether there are differences and why—can contribute significantly to our ability to make sound policy decisions concerning social, educational, and economic matters relevant to the groups in question. For instance, evidence bearing on whether older adults, relative to younger adults, show deficits in cognitive functioning, response speed, and quality of achievement has direct implications for age-related employment policies, including hiring, promotion, and retirement practices. Or the answer to the question of whether males or females differ in their levels of nurturance, and, if so, whether the difference is learned or biologically based clearly has implications for the roles of parents as caretakers for their children.

In determining the presence or absence of group differences, differential psychology provides another important social function—a means of assessing the accuracy of social stereotypes. Reliable information about the nature of group differences should aid in eradicating false stereotypic beliefs about social groups, and with the reduction of stereotypic views there should be a greater acceptance of the various groups of people that make up our society.

By definition the field of differential psychology, and consequently this book, focuses on how people, including groups of people, differ from one another. In all likelihood most readers will feel comfortable with the emphasis on differences, since in our everyday lives we continually make differentiations among people. Yet, in a book about human differences we may lose sight of the fact that, while people and groups of people differ from one another, they are also similar in many ways. That is, by concentrating on how people differ, we may be inclined to neglect how they are similar. And this neglect concerns us greatly. In the course of preparing this book we became increasingly sensitive to the potentially negative social implications of persistently focusing on existing differences among people, particularly members of different groups. By focusing on group differences, we carry the risk of reinforcing existing stereotypic beliefs about groups and thus potentially augmenting, rather than reducing, social barriers between groups. It is imperative to keep in mind that, while our purpose is to study human differences, people—both within groups and among groups—are more similar than they are different. As you will discover, we repeatedly make the point that, although research may show that two groups differ in terms of some psychological characteristic, the difference is an average one. With respect to the vast majority of characteristics that may differentiate two groups, there is a tremendous amount of overlap between the members of one group and those of the other group.

One final observation we wish to make is that our conception of differential psychology is a broad one. As we have defined the field, differential psychology encompasses not only the assessment of human differences but also the study of the determinants of human differences. According to this conceptualization, any activity relevant to the understanding of the origins of human differences falls under the purview of differential psychology. Therefore, a wide range of endeavors—from comparing members of certain groups on measures of personality to studying the possible hormonal underpinnings of sex differences in aggression to evaluating the effectiveness of school integration on reducing the Black/White achievement gap—may be viewed as within the scope of differential psychology.

PLAN OF THE BOOK

We begin in Part 1 with a consideration of the basic concepts and methods of differential psychology, followed by a discussion of the two basic determinants of variations among individuals and groups—heredity and environment. After these introductory chapters, we survey in Part 2 the major dimensions along which individuals vary—intelligence, school achievement, special aptitudes and abilities, personality characteristics, and motivational characteristics such as interests and values. When samples of an individual's behavioral repertoire are measured, we can place the individual at specific locations along the relevant dimensions. These locations on a dimension scaled from low to high levels of a given characteristic, such as intelligence, school achievement, and dependency, are viewed as representing relatively distinctive and enduring characteristics or "traits" of the individual. When we describe an individual and compare individuals with one another, we refer to such traits. For example, we might say that Bill is highly intelligent, a good student, excels in musical ability, has a friendly and charming personality, and is interested in camping and outdoor activities. Larry, on the other hand, is of average intelligence, a fair student, very independent, rather introverted, athletically inclined, and an avid sports fan.

In Part 3 we look at the primary ways in which individuals are grouped together—sex, age, social class, and race. The study of such group differences provides insights about the sources of individual differences. For instance, Betty Wilson, a 25-year-old Black female who was brought up in lower-class surroundings and has achieved a middle-class level of income and occupation, may be a very different person than Carlton Bradshaw III, a middle-aged White male who was reared in upper-class surroundings and has maintained his upper-class status. Largely because of her social-class background and her sexual, racial, and generational identities, Betty Wilson is a highly achievement-oriented person actively engaged in the women's liberation movement and civil-rights activities. In contrast, Carlton Bradshaw III, because of his social background and group ties, is greatly involved in corporate affairs, actively interested in philanthropic endeavors, and politically conservative. Of course, as we noted, we must be careful not to draw stereotyped scripts about people, simply because they belong to this or that group. Group categorizations only suggest certain probabilities about individual characteristics.

We conclude in Part 4 with an examination of some of the current directions in differential psychology and their social implications. For example, racial differences in school achievement and sex differences in occupational achievement challenge our traditional belief that American society is based on equality. It is to be hoped that the study of differential psychology can raise our consciousness about issues of human rights in our society.

REFERENCES

Binet, A., & Henri, V. La psychologie individuelle. *Année Psychologique*, 1895, *2*, 411–465.

Buss, A. R. Galton and the birth of differential psychology and eugenics: Social, political, and economic forces. *Journal of the History of the Behavioral Sciences*, 1976, *12*, 47–58.

Buss, A. R., & Poley, W. *Individual differences: Traits and factors.* New York: Gardner Press, 1976.

Cattell, J. McK. Mental tests and measurements. *Mind*, 1890, *15*, 373–380.

Cronbach, L. J. The two disciplines of scientific psychology. *American Psychologist*, 1957, *12*, 671–684.

Cronbach, L. J. Beyond the two disciplines of scientific psychology. *American Psychologist*, 1975, *30*, 116–127.

DuBois, P. H. *A history of psychological testing.* Boston: Allyn & Bacon, 1970.

Fromm, E. *Escape from freedom.* New York: Rinehart, 1941.

Galton, F. *Hereditary genius: An inquiry into its laws and consequences.* London: Macmillan, 1869.

Stern, W. *Über Psychologie der individuellen Differenzen (Ideen zur einer "Differentielle Psychologie").* Leipzig: Barth, 1900.

Williams, R. *The long revolution.* London: Chatto & Windus, 1961.

Basic Concepts
and Research Methods

We are concerned with human variability—the study of individual and group differences. It does not require a great deal of perceptiveness to recognize the extent to which variation characterizes human beings. Take at random a small group of people, and differences will exist on virtually every biological and psychological characteristic we may choose to measure. Such characteristics include, for example, body weight and height, amount of sugar and calcium in the blood, respiratory rate, pulse rate, size and shape of body organs, chemical composition of saliva, excretory patterns, reaction time, visual and auditory acuity, as well as the various aspects of psychological functioning with which we are primarily concerned—intelligence, achievement, aptitudes, abilities, personality, interests, and values. However, as animal lovers are well aware, differences among individuals are by no means confined to human beings. In fact, individual variability cuts across all species, from the most complex animals to the simplest one-celled organisms. For instance, it was early demonstrated that single-celled protozoa vary greatly in how quickly they learn an elementary form of conditioned response (Razran, 1933).

An understanding of the basic concepts and methods relevant to the investigation of individual and group differences is *essential* to an understanding of the data and interpretations presented in this text. In this chapter we will first consider the techniques that differential psychology uses in describing the manner in which human characteristics vary. Then we will consider the basic research strategies employed in the investigation of individual and group differences. Readers with different backgrounds will read this book. For some it will be their first introduction to many of the concepts and methods. For others some of the material may overlap with information acquired in other courses, such as introductory statistics and psychological testing. To this second group of readers we suggest that a careful reading may serve as a helpful review. Also, because there is some variation in the difficulty level of the material, we believe that most readers will come across information they have not previously encountered.

SCALES OF MEASUREMENT

In order for us to study the variation among people on a given characteristic, we must be able to measure that characteristic. Most biological characteristics are amenable to reasonably precise measurement by objective, physical measuring instruments. We can, for example, accurately record a person's height, pulse rate, and lung capacity.

Physical measuring instruments, such as those that measure length, weight, and volume, provide data at a ratio-scale level. A *ratio scale* has an absolute zero point, signifying the complete absence of the variable. It comprises equal units (intervals) from the zero point along the whole length of the scale. For example, the difference between the second and third inch on a ruler is identical to the difference between the eighth and ninth inch. With this kind of scale we can meaningfully speak in terms of ratios. If a husband and wife weigh 200 and 100 pounds, respectively, it is appropriate to say that he is two times as heavy as she is.

Difficulties arise, however, when we try to measure psychological variables. For one thing, most psychological variables cannot be measured directly. Instead, they are measured indirectly; that is, we infer them from some behavior(s) displayed by individuals. For instance, people's levels of anxiety might be inferred from the kinds of items they endorse on an anxiety questionnaire, from the amount they fidget in their seats, from the number of errors they make on a simple arithmetic task, or from the amount of perspiration on the palms of their hands. As in the measurement of biological variables, our goal in measuring a psychological variable is to derive a number that reflects the extent to which the variable in question is characteristic of the individual. However, unlike the measurement of biological characteristics, psychological measurement generally does not provide ratio data. Measures of psychological variables, such as memory, intelligence, dependency, and achievement motivation, yield data at either the interval-scale level or the less precise ordinal-scale level.

Like a ratio scale, an *interval scale* conveys information about order. That is, if a person is assigned a higher score than another person, we know that the first person possesses more of the characteristic in question than does the second person. Also, like a ratio scale, an interval scale consists of equal units (intervals), so we have information about the magnitude of the difference between people receiving different scores. However, unlike a ratio scale, an interval scale has no zero point. Therefore, if a person's score on a psychological measure is twice (or three times) as high as another person's score, we simply cannot conclude that the first person possesses twice (or three times) as much of the characteristic as the second person. For example, even if we can assume that our measures of IQ are on an interval scale, we cannot say that a person with an IQ of 140 is twice as intelligent as one with an IQ of 70. This limitation of psychological measurement is important to keep in mind when we compare the standing of different individuals on various individual-difference variables.

An *ordinal scale* is less precise than an interval scale in that it only indicates the relative order of individuals with respect to the variable of interest; it does not provide information about the actual magnitude of differences between scores. For instance, if John is more aggressive than Susan but less aggressive than Janice, then John would be assigned a higher score on aggressiveness than Susan and a lower score than Janice; but, because there is no requirement that the intervals be equal, we would not know how much more aggressive than Susan and how much less aggressive than Janice he is.

We should also note that *nominal scales* typically are included in a consideration of scales of measurement. A nominal scale is used when variables are qualitative or categorical. Objects (for example, people) are placed into categories so that those in the same category are equivalent or nearly equivalent in terms of some attribute or property. For instance, the following are commonly treated as nominal characteristics: sex, race, religion, marital status, profession, and college major. Actually, the term *nominal scale* hardly deserves to be discussed under the topic of measurement, because, as they are commonly used, nominal variables are not quantitative—that is, they do not have any numerical values associated with them in any natural way. We may assign numbers to the various categories (for example, a 0 to male and a 1 to female), but this is merely for purposes of identification, and the numbers are not intended to impart quantitative information (for example, regarding order or size).

To conclude our brief discussion of scales of measurement, we wish to point out, as Tyler (1965) did, that the reliance on nonratio scales prevents us from answering certain questions relevant to the field of differential psychology. For instance, we cannot ascertain whether the variation among people on a certain trait, such as intelligence, is greater or smaller than the variation on other traits, such as memory, achievement motivation, and mechanical aptitude.

DESCRIPTION OF HUMAN VARIATION

Until this point we have been referring to a person's score on a particular individual-difference variable without acknowledging that, in the absence of additional information, such a score is uninterpretable. For one thing, we have no way of knowing the position of the individual who has been assigned the score in relationship to other people with whom we might wish to compare him or her. If a student correctly answers 23 questions on a 50-item psychology exam, is that good or bad? That's hard to answer unless we know how many questions other students are able to answer. A raw score (score on the psychological measure) is meaningful only when considered in the context of the scores of some comparison group.

Frequency Distributions

A frequency distribution is a technique used to organize and summarize a group of people's scores on a variable, thus providing a greater understanding about the meaning of a given person's raw score, as well as a better perspective on the group as a whole. Specifically, a frequency distribution is a table in which all of the score units are listed in one column and the number of persons receiving each score is presented in a second column. When there is a large number of possible scores to which individuals may be assigned, the scores usually are grouped into specified ranges, called *class intervals.* Such a grouped frequency distribution is illustrated in Table 2-1, which shows the Scholastic Aptitude Test—Verbal scores of students in a freshman class at a large American university. The left column shows the possible scores grouped into 12 class intervals of 50 points each. Opposite each class interval, in the right column, is a figure corresponding to the number (frequency) of students who received one of the scores in that interval. For instance, five students scored very high, somewhere between 750 and 799 points, whereas one student managed to score only between 200 and 249; the largest group, 330 students, scored between 500 and 549.

To further facilitate our understanding of the distribution of the scores in Table 2-1, such scores can be portrayed graphically, as shown in Figure 2-1. The class intervals are presented along the horizontal axis, and the number of students in each class interval is indicated by the vertical axis. Two ways of plotting the frequency distribution are illustrated. In the *histogram,* columns are erected to indicate the frequency of scores for the various class intervals, each column being centered over the midpoint of its class interval. In the *polygon,* a point is placed above the center of each class interval at a level corresponding with the appropriate frequency, and the successive points are connected by straight lines.

By plotting a frequency distribution in graphic form, not only can we gain a better impression of how an individual with a given score compares in relation to the entire group, but the "shape" of the distribution is brought into sharper focus. The distribution in Figure 2-1 resembles what is commonly referred to as a *normal curve.* A normal curve is normal in a mathematical

Table 2-1. Frequency Distribution of Scholastic Aptitude Test—Verbal Scores of 1450 University Students

Class Interval	Frequency
750–799	5
700–749	55
650–699	119
600–649	223
550–599	291
500–549	330
450–499	257
400–449	128
350–399	34
300–349	5
250–299	2
200–249	1
	Total = 1450

Adapted from *Statistical Methods in Education and Psychology,* by G. V. Glass and J. C. Stanley. © 1970. Used by permission of Prentice-Hall, Inc., Englewood Cliffs, New Jersey.

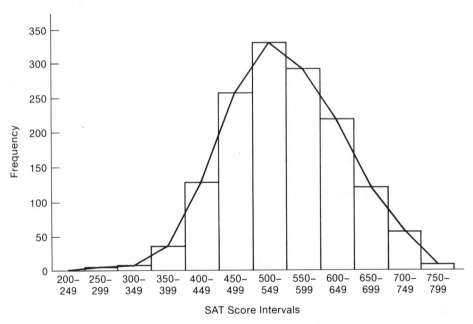

Figure 2-1. Frequency polygon and histogram of Scholastic Aptitude Test—Verbal scores of 1450 university students; data are from Table 2-1.

sense, not a psychological sense. Strictly speaking, for a distribution to be normal, it must meet a specific set of mathematical criteria. Two mathematically derived normal curves are presented in Figure 2-2. As Figure 2-2 suggests, a normal curve is bilaterally symmetrical; that is, each half is the mirror opposite of the other. Also, the high point is in the center, and it falls off in both

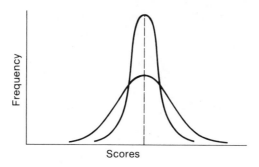

Figure 2-2. Two normal distributions.

directions, gradually approaching the baseline. Thus, if a variable, such as intelligence, shows a normal distribution, the highest frequency of people is at the center, and the frequencies decline as the distance from the center increases, with only an extremely small proportion located on the extremes.

While it is unlikely that many distributions in nature fit a normal curve perfectly, many biological and anatomical variables do assume distributions that closely approximate the properties of a normal curve. Also, it is likely that many psychological characteristics approximate a normal distribution (Anastasi, 1958). However, not all distributions of individual-difference variables necessarily approximate the bell-shaped normal curve. There are several basic ways in which distributions can diverge from "normality." A skewed distribution is one in which the peak is located to one side of the center and the number of individuals tapers off toward the opposite end of the distribution. Attitudes are one class of psychological variables likely to form skewed distributions. For instance, the vast majority of people will hold positive attitudes toward their countries and negative attitudes toward crime; as a result, their attitude scores will cluster at the corresponding positive and negative ends of the distribution of attitudes. All of the distributions in Figure 2-3, except for the one for "enlisted men–literate," may be described as skewed.

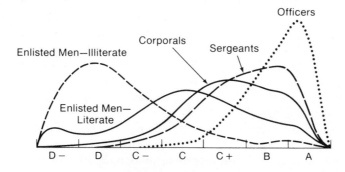

Figure 2-3. Distribution of intelligence test scores of various Army groups, where A = highest intelligence and D– = lowest intelligence. Adapted from *Army Mental Tests*, by C. S. Yoakum and R. M. Yerkes. Copyright © 1920 by Holt, Rinehart and Winston. Used by permission.

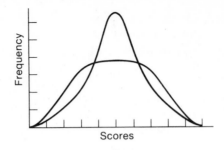

Figure 2-4. A peaked distribution and a relatively flat distribution.

Distributions also may differ from normality in terms of their degree of flatness or peakedness. In a distribution that is flatter than a normal distribution, a smaller proportion of people are clustered in the center, and there is little variation in the frequencies at any point in the distribution. In a more peaked distribution, more people are located around the center point than in a normal distribution. Figure 2-4 depicts a curve that is more peaked and one that is flatter than the theoretical normal curve. Distributions also may have more than one peak or mode. An example of such a multimodal curve (more accurately, a bimodal curve) is shown in Figure 2-5.

Figure 2-5. A bimodal distribution.

Factors Influencing the Shape of Distributions. Several years ago Anastasi (1958) delineated a number of factors that can modify the shape of a distribution. As you read about a few of these factors, keep in mind that, because of their existence, it is virtually impossible to determine, at least for the present, the actual (natural) distribution of psychological characteristics in the general population. One factor is sampling. The shape of a frequency distribution may vary considerably because of the composition of the sample. A good illustration of this appears in Figure 2-3, which shows a marked variation in the frequency distributions of intelligence-test scores of several categories of Army personnel. An erroneous impression of the overall frequency distribution of intelligence-test scores could be formed if some of the categories in Figure 2-3 were disproportionately represented in a sampling of Army personnel.

A second factor influencing the shape of frequency distributions is the measuring instrument. An important feature of an instrument that is used to measure some aspect of an individual's ability is the range of difficulty covered.

If the range is restricted, so that it does not include sufficiently difficult or sufficiently easy items for the population under consideration, then a skewed distribution may erroneously result. For instance, as Figure 2-3 indicates, the intelligence test apparently was too easy for the group of officers and too difficult for those enlisted men who were illiterate. For the former group a test including more difficult items and for the latter group one with easier items would, in all likelihood, have yielded much less skewed distributions.

Therefore, the nature of the measuring instrument may play an important role in determining the shape of a frequency distribution. In fact, quite often the content of instruments is deliberately manipulated by test developers to yield a distribution that approximates the normal curve. This is called *normalizing* and is carried out because there are certain mathematical or statistical advantages to having normally distributed data. Because of the confounding factors discussed above (as well as additional ones not discussed here) and because the composition of most tests is adjusted to produce a normal distribution, it makes little sense to rely on such tests as indexes of the natural distribution of psychological traits. For the time being then, it is not possible to establish whether most psychological characteristics are normally distributed or not, although, as with many biological characteristics, it is a good bet that many are (see Anastasi, 1958, for a more thorough examination of these issues).

Continuous Distributions. Although the exact shape of the distributions of psychological characteristics is uncertain, most evidence indicates that psychological characteristics (as well as biological ones) are continuous variables. A *continuous variable* is one that can take on any value, from the lowest possible amount of the variable to the highest. For instance, length is a continuous variable. An object can be 2 feet, 1 inch long or 2 feet, 2 inches long or any conceivable amount in between. A continuous variable may be contrasted to a *discrete variable*, which can assume only certain values and none in between. The number of rooms in a building or the number of courses taken by a student are examples of discrete variables.

Thus most psychological characteristics may be seen as falling on a continuous distribution—a distribution in which there are no gaps or breaks. In other words, there are no sharp, qualitative differences among people; the differences are quantitative—a matter of degree. A good example of the failure to recognize the continuous nature of a distribution, and one that is familiar to many students, occurs when school policy prescribes the assignment of a limited set of grades, such as A, B, C, D, and F. This forced grading system masks the fact that the differences in the performances of the students are a matter of degree. This is keenly felt by the B student whose performance was just a shade lower than that of the student who barely earned an A and quite a bit higher than that of the student who just squeezed into the B category.

The recognition that psychological characteristics are continuous has led to an emphasis in differential psychology on psychological traits rather than psychological types. A *typological approach* suggests that people can be divided neatly into qualitatively distinct categories, usually two of them, such as introverts versus extroverts and dominant versus submissive. The *trait approach* assumes that the differences among people are only a matter of degree, with many people falling at all of the points separating the extremes of introversion/ extroversion or of dominance/submission. However, while interest in a typological approach had waned for some years, it appears that typology is making a comeback in psychology (Carlson, 1972). We might also point out that types do not necessarily preclude traits. Rather, an integration of the two is possible in that some researchers conceive of a type as representing an interrelated constellation of traits. We discuss the notion of personality types in Chapter 8 and that of interest types in Chapter 9.

Descriptive Statistics

As we have seen, a frequency distribution is one way of organizing and summarizing the measurements taken on a large number of people. Certain descriptive statistics may be used to further summarize the data. A *descriptive statistic* is a single number used to characterize (describe) some aspect of a distribution of scores. We will consider only three kinds of descriptive statistics: measures of central tendency, of variability, and of correlation.

Central Tendency. Measures of central tendency are designed to specify the score that is most representative of a distribution of scores. The *mean* is perhaps the most familiar and commonly used measure of central tendency. The mean is the same as the arithmetic average and is derived by summing all of the scores and dividing by the total number of scores. The *mode* refers to the score that occurs with the greatest frequency. In a grouped frequency distribution the mode falls at the midpoint of the class interval having the greatest frequency. (Recall that some distributions are viewed as having more than one mode; that is, they are multimodal.) The *median* is the score that divides the distribution into halves, so that 50% of the sample falls above the median and 50% below it. In a normal distribution the mean, median, and mode all fall at exactly the same point, the very middle of the distribution. On the other hand, for many distributions the three kinds of central tendency fall at different points. For instance, in the skewed distribution of scores for the officers in Figure 2-3, the mode would be on the far right at the peak of the distribution, the median would be a little to the left of the mode, and the mean would be to the left of the median.

Variability. An index of central tendency by itself does not provide a sufficient description of a distribution of scores. It is also important to have an index of a distribution's degree of variability—how dispersed or scattered the scores are. In point of fact, the variability is the most central concept of differential psychology—the degree to which individual scores are dispersed around the central tendency. The data in Figure 2-6 show how the variability may differ from one group to another. Figure 2-6 shows the scores of six age groups of men on Raven's Progressive Matrices Test, a perceptual-reasoning

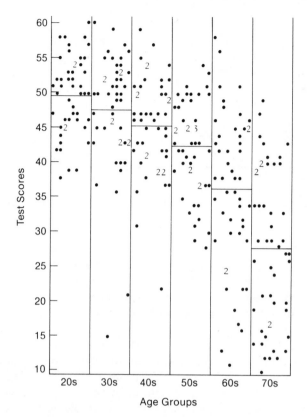

Figure 2-6. Distributions of six age groups of men on the Progressive Matrices Test. Means are depicted by horizontal lines. Adapted from *Age and Function,* by A. Heron and S. M. Chown. Copyright 1967 by Churchill Livingston, Edinburgh. Used by permission.

measure of intelligence. Each dot represents the score of one individual whose exact age can be ascertained by reference to its position on the scale below. A "2" or "3" appears in the figure when two or three people of the same age receive the same score. We can see that the mean scores decrease from the younger to the older age groups. On the other hand, the variability in scores seems to increase with age. Notice how in the youngest groups the preponderance of scores cluster within the relatively narrow 36-to-60 range, whereas in the two oldest groups the scores are scattered over a much broader range.

In Figure 2-6 the younger and older groups differ in both their means and variabilities. It is also entirely possible for two groups to possess different means but similar variabilities, be similar in both their means and variabilities, or have similar means but different variabilities. An illustration of the latter instance is shown graphically in Figure 2-7 (see also Figure 2-2).

When we wish to compare the variability of two groups, the most useful measure is the *standard deviation*, which is roughly equivalent to the average

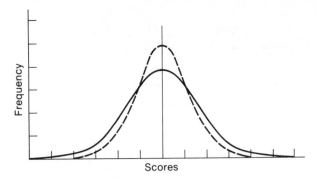

Figure 2-7. Frequency distributions with the same mean but different variabilities.

amount by which scores in a distribution vary from the mean. In Figure 2-7 the distribution with the widest spread of scores would have the largest standard deviation. To calculate the standard deviation, one first calculates the difference between each score and the mean. Then these differences are squared, the squares are averaged, and lastly the square root of the resulting average is taken.[1]

The standard deviation serves as another important source of information when the distribution of scores is normal or approximately normal. If a normal distribution is divided into bands that are one standard-deviation wide, then a fixed percentage of scores falls within each band. This relationship can be seen in Figure 2-8, which shows a normal curve sliced into sections corresponding to standard deviations (designated by the symbol σ). We can see that 34.13% of the cases fall in the area between the mean and one standard deviation below the mean and that another 34.13% fall between the mean and one standard deviation above it. Thus, slightly over two-thirds (68.26%) of all cases occur within one standard deviation of the mean. Further inspection indicates that all but a tiny percentage (.26%) of the cases fall within three standard deviations of the mean. What should be stressed is that the same relationships hold for any set of scores that are normally distributed. For instance, the standard deviation of the general population on the Wechsler intelligence tests is 15. This is noted on the bottom line of Figure 2-8. As we can see, 68.26% of people have IQ scores in the 85-to-115 range—that is, from one standard deviation below the mean to one standard deviation above it (see Chapter 4 for a discussion of IQ scores).

The standard deviation is the preferred index when we simply wish to describe the amount of variation in a set of scores. The *variance,* which is the standard deviation squared, is used when we wish to estimate the extent

---

[1]Standard deviation = $\sqrt{\dfrac{\Sigma(X - M)^2}{N}}$, where X = a raw score, M = the mean, and N = the total number of cases (scores). The Σ tells us to sum all of the squared deviations from the mean; that is, sum all of the $(X - M)^2$'s.

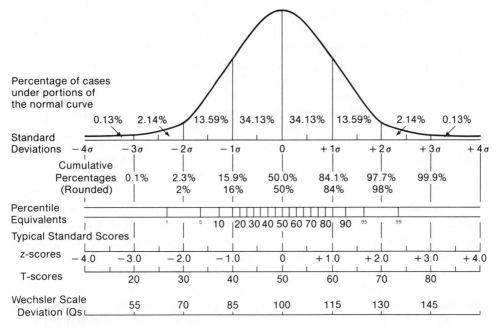

Percentage of cases
under portions of
the normal curve

| 0.13% | 2.14% | 13.59% | 34.13% | 34.13% | 13.59% | 2.14% | 0.13% |

Standard
Deviations -4σ -3σ -2σ -1σ 0 $+1\sigma$ $+2\sigma$ $+3\sigma$ $+4\sigma$

Cumulative
Percentages   0.1%   2.3%   15.9%   50.0%   84.1%   97.7%   99.9%
(Rounded)   2%   16%   50%   84%   98%

Percentile
Equivalents   1   5   10   20 30 40 50 60 70 80   90   95   99

Typical Standard Scores

z-scores -4.0 -3.0 -2.0 -1.0 0 $+1.0$ $+2.0$ $+3.0$ $+4.0$

T-scores   20   30   40   50   60   70   80

Wechsler Scale   55   70   85   100   115   130   145
Deviation IQs

Figure 2-8. Normal curve and related scores. Adapted from *Test Service Bulletin 48: Methods of Expressing Test Scores*, H. G. Seashore, Ed. Copyright 1955 by The Psychological Corporation, New York, N.Y. Used by permission.

to which each factor of a set of factors contributes to the existing variability of scores. In other words, if it can be shown that certain variables *X*, *Y*, and *Z* can account for the fact that people differ from one another on some characteristic, we may want to determine what proportion of the variation is associated with each of the three variables. For example, we might be interested in studying how much a knowledge of students' scores on a general intelligence test and a measure of achievement motivation help to account for the variation in the grade-point averages of students in a high school class. Suppose that our analysis indicates that intelligence-test performance accounts for 45% of the variance in the students' grade-point averages and achievement-motivation scores for 20% of the variance. This would mean that almost half (45%) of the variability (individual differences) in school grades is associated with the fact that students differ in how well they do on intelligence tests (and, by implication, in their levels of intelligence) and 20% of the variability is related to the students' measured levels of achievement motivation. The remaining 35% of the variance is attributable to additional, unmeasured factors.

One problem that is commonly faced by workers in the field of differential psychology is that the raw scores derived from different measuring instruments are not directly comparable. A person may earn a score of 74 on a mathematics test and a score of 44 on a mechanical-aptitude test. However, without more information, we have no idea which of the two scores is better, because the scores usually are expressed in different units. The use of *standard scores* permits us to get around this problem and thus compare directly a person's relative standing on several individual-difference variables. A standard score merely specifies how many standard-deviation units a given score is above or below the group mean.

One kind of standard score, the z score, does this directly. The z score refers to the number of standard deviations an individual's score is above or below the mean of a distribution. The correspondence between z scores and standard-deviation units is illustrated in Figure 2-8. Notice, for example, that, if $z = -1.0$, the score is exactly one standard deviation below the mean, whereas, if $z = +2.5$, a score is two-and-a-half standard deviations above the mean. Another standard score, the *T*-score, avoids the awkwardness of using negative values and decimals by arbitrarily setting the mean at 50 and standard deviation at 10 (see Figure 2-8). Here scores of 40 and 60 are one standard deviation below and above the mean, respectively. To relate these standard scores to performance on the Wechsler tests (see Figure 2-8), an IQ of 70 would have a z score of –2.0 and a *T*-score of 30.

Figure 2-8 also shows how a normal curve may be broken down into percentile equivalents. A given percentile designates the percentage of scores that fall below that point in a distribution of scores. For instance, if a person's score is at the 18th percentile, 18% of the comparison group have lower scores. When a distribution is normal, the 50th percentile is equal to the mean, median, and mode. However, with other distributions, we can be certain only that the 50th percentile is the same as the median (recall that the median is the point separating the top and bottom 50%). We have explained the meaning of standard scores and percentiles because this book often presents data in such format.

Correlation. The term *correlation* refers to the degree of linear (straight-line) relationship between two sets of variables, which we will designate as X and Y. The extent of relationship is expressed in terms of a mathematically derived *correlation coefficient.* The Pearson product/moment correlation coefficient (typically designated as r) is the most commonly used index of correlation. We can use a correlation coefficient to determine for a group of individuals the relationship between their standing on variable X and their standing on variable Y, such as the correlation between the group's scores on a measure of general ability and their school grades or between their scores on a measure of affiliation motivation (desire to develop many close interpersonal relationships) and the amount of time spent doing homework. Correlation coefficients are also used to measure the degree of relationship between the standing of members of two groups with respect to a single variable, such as between the social adjustment of pairs of twins or between the occupational values of fathers and sons.

A correlation coefficient can range from +1.00 to –1.00—that is, from a perfect positive correlation through zero correlation to a perfect negative correlation. A +1.00 correlation implies that the person who receives the highest score on variable X (for example, general ability) also receives the highest score on variable *Y* (for example, school grades); the person who is second highest on *X* is also second highest on *Y;* and so on. A –1.00 correlation means that an individual's position on variable *X* is directly opposite to his or her position on *Y;* if the individual has the highest score on *X* (for example, affiliation motivation), he or she has the lowest score on *Y* (for example, time spent studying); and so forth. A zero correlation signifies the complete absence of a relationship; knowledge of one's score on *X* provides no information whatsoever about his or her score on *Y*. In reality, perfect positive and negative correlations between psychological variables very rarely, if ever, occur.

A less-than-perfect correlation means that there is a *tendency* for high scores on *X* to correspond with high scores on *Y* (with a positive correlation) or for high scores on *X* to correspond with low scores on *Y* (with a negative correlation). There are, however, exceptions to this tendency. The strength of the tendency for such correspondence varies directly with the magnitude of the correlation coefficient. For two variables that are correlated, one can easily calculate the percentage of the variance in one of the variables that is accounted for by the other variable—just square the correlation coefficient. Thus, it is clear why correlations in the range of .20 to .39 are often considered low; with a correlation of .39, only 15.21% ($.39 \times .39$) of the variance is accounted for.

The frequency distribution and related descriptive statistics—including indexes of central tendency, variability, and correlation—are essential tools for the descriptive appraisal of a set of scores or relationships between scores (in the case of correlation) on some individual difference variable(s). But research in differential psychology goes beyond mere description to an application of another kind of statistics, inferential statistics. Inferential statistics enable us to estimate the level of confidence we may have in the conclusions we can make concerning the nature and origins of human differences.

Inferential Statistics

One problem common to all social scientists is that they rarely have the opportunity to measure the behavior of *all* of the individuals in whom they are interested. For instance, a psychologist who wants to study the attitudes of a given population (such as the attitudes of American Catholics concerning birth control) cannot hope to measure the attitudes of the entire group of people (all adult Catholics living in the United States). What the researcher inevitably does is to restrict his or her investigation to a subset (sample) of the overall population and hope that the findings accurately depict the attitudes of the population. This is where the role of inferential statistics comes in. *Inferential statistics* are techniques that make it possible to draw inferences (conclusions) about a population on the basis of information collected on a sample of people from the population.

We will use correlational evidence to illustrate the meaning of inferential statistics. Suppose that we take a random sample of 20 students at a university and find a correlation of .45 between their grade-point averages in high school and their grade-point averages in college. If we are interested only in the correlation for that particular sample of 20 students, then .45 is an accurate indication of the relationship between high school grades and college grades. Usually, however, we wish to generalize—to make a statement about the nature of the relationship in the larger population of college students, perhaps all students at the particular college or college students in general. Obviously we cannot automatically assume that the correlation in the population is identical to the one in the sample of 20 students. A sample, especially a relatively small one, might yield a correlation as high as .45, or higher, just on the basis of chance. That is, in drawing our sample we by chance happened to pick people whose high school and college grade-point averages were correlated when in fact a zero correlation exists in the overall population (of course, a zero correlation is an unlikely eventuality in this particular instance).

We use a test of *statistical significance* to determine the *probability* that a correlation of that magnitude (that is, .45) could have resulted solely from the operation of chance in the selection of the sample from the larger population. We ask the question: If in the total population the correlation between the two variables is zero, what is the probability that a correlation as high as .45 could have resulted strictly on the basis of an error (accident) in sampling? The standard and generally accepted probability levels are .05 and .01. A correlation for a given sample that is statistically significant at the .05 level indicates that the probability is only 5 out of 100 (for the .01 level, 1 out of 100) that the population correlation is zero; or said in a different way, there is a 95% probability (for the .01 level, 99%) that the population correlation is greater than zero. The .45 correlation in our example is said to be "statistically significant" at the .05 level. Thus, we feel fairly confident that high school grades and college grades are actually related, not just in our sample of 20 students but in the population as well. We should note that a negative correlation of the same magnitude (namely, −.45) would be equally significant.

It is also important to recognize that, as the size of the sample increases, the magnitude of a correlation needed for significance declines because the possibility of chance fluctuation lessens. Thus, for a sample of 100, a correlation as small as .20 is significant at the .05 level; for a sample of 500 an even smaller correlation of .09 is significant. These correlations are statistically significant but probably of little value psychologically. Recall that a correlation of .20 indicates that variable X accounts for a very small proportion of the variance in Y—only 4% (.20 × .20 = .04).

Measures of statistical significance may also be applied to estimate the probability that two or more groups differ with respect to the sizes of their variances or their central tendencies. In a later section we will consider the meaning of statistically significant differences between the means of groups.

CORRELATIONAL RESEARCH

The correlation coefficient has proved to be a useful research tool in differential psychology. We will briefly explore three of its major uses: (1) as a measure of reliability, (2) as an index of validity, and (3) as a basis for factor analysis.

Reliability

In order for a measuring instrument to be of value, it must be reliable. The determination of reliability involves calculating a correlation between two sets of responses made by respondents to a given measuring instrument. An index of reliability indicates the degree of consistency from one measurement to another. There are several types of reliability. We will consider two major classes: those reflecting internal consistency—consistency between items—and those reflecting temporal stability—consistency across time on the same set of items.

One index of internal consistency is *split-half reliability*. In split-half reliability a measuring instrument is administered once and then divided in half (for example, into odd and even items) to determine the correlation between the scores on the two halves. A more general and preferable measure of internal consistency is known as *coefficient alpha*.[2] Coefficient alpha reflects the degree of response consistency across all of the items of an instrument—that is, the homogeneity or interrelatedness of the items. The more homogeneous the content (for example, a measure containing only questions pertaining to mathematics, not to a mixture of skills), the greater the internal consistency is. The more familiar split-half reliability coefficient is actually a special case of coefficient alpha. Coefficient alpha represents the mean of all possible split-half reliability coefficients resulting from different "splittings" of the items of the instrument.

A well-known index of reliability is test-retest reliability, which is calculated in order to estimate the temporal stability of an instrument. *Test-retest reliability* refers to the correlation between a group's scores on a measuring instrument on one occasion and their scores on the same instrument at a later occasion. Although high test-retest reliability obviously is desirable, high (as well as low) reliability coefficients present difficulties of interpretation. If the interval between administrations is short, the ability to recall one's responses on the first occasion may inappropriately inflate the amount of consistency displayed by the respondents. On the other hand, a low test-retest correlation, particularly if the interval is longer than a few weeks, may suggest that the instrument is unreliable. Or (especially if the interval is greater than a few weeks) it may reflect the fact that the respondents have experienced an actual change in their standing on the variable in question. For these and other reasons, test-retest correlations are recognized as possessing limited usefulness. One way of circumventing some of the problems associated with test-retest reliability is to use a measure of alternate-forms reliability. *Alternate-forms reliability* involves calculating the correlation between scores obtained on parallel forms (that is, different sets of items covering the same content) of a measuring instrument. Each form is administered separately within a short time interval (for example, a few days). By using different forms, a respondent's performance on the second form cannot be influenced by memory of the specific content of the first form.

[2]See textbooks on testing (for example, Anastasi, 1976) for formulas used in calculating coefficient alpha.

Validity

The correlational method is also very useful in helping to answer the most important question about a psychological test: "Is the test valid?" By valid we mean that the test measures what it was designed to measure. For example, a test purported to measure mechanical aptitude is valid if it does, in fact, evaluate one's mechanical aptitude. For the most part, in order for a measure to be valid, it must meet the previously mentioned criteria of reliability. For example, if the alternate-forms reliability of a test is low (that is, low correlation between two forms), we would not know which form of the test, if either, is an accurate measure of the trait in question.

Three general categories of validity may be distinguished: content, criterion-related, and construct (*Standards for Educational and Psychological Tests*, 1974). Although we will discuss each kind of validity separately, they are interrelated, and we typically should consider all three when examining the validity of a measuring instrument.

An instrument has *content validity* if its content (items) adequately samples the behavior domain or subject matter of the variable being measured. The correlational method is not typically used in the determination of content validity. However, it is central to the establishment of both criterion-related and construct validity, and, when used so, the resulting correlation is called a *validity coefficient. Criterion-related* validity indicates the extent to which scores on a test are correlated with values of an external variable (behavior) that is viewed as a direct indicator of the variable the test purports to measure. The test score and criterion measure (that is, the external variable) may be taken at (about) the same time or may be separated by some period of time. In the former instance, we usually speak of *concurrent validity* and in the latter of *predictive validity*. The two, however, are more appropriately distinguished on the basis of the purpose of the testing than the time interval per se (Anastasi, 1976).

We are interested in concurrent validity when the objective of testing is the assessment of current status. For example, scores on a test designed to measure neuroticism can be correlated with evaluations of neuroticism based on an extensive psychiatric examination. If the correlation is high, then the neuroticism scale may suffice as a convenient substitute for the lengthier examination. Predictive validity is relevant when scores on a test are to be relied on to predict future performance. For example, academic aptitude tests, like the Scholastic Aptitude Test and Graduate Record Examination, are frequently used by university administrators to predict which students will be most successful in undergraduate school and graduate school, respectively. The predictive validity of these tests may be evaluated by correlating test scores with indexes of academic success (such as grades and graduation rates).

The meaning of *construct validity* is a bit harder to explain. It is concerned with the extent to which a test is a measure of a theoretical construct. Essentially, assessing a test's construct validity involves checking on the theory underlying the trait in question (that is, the theoretical construct). Based on the theory, hypotheses are derived regarding the behavior of people scoring at various levels of the test. Confirming the hypotheses by research provides support for the construct validity of the test.

Construct validation is a gradual process, based on the accumulation of several kinds of evidence. For example, one method entails testing for differences between categories of people who on theoretical grounds should differ in their standing on the trait. For instance, older children should on the average earn higher scores than younger children on a test designed to measure social maturity. Another example is that males might be predicted to receive higher scores than females on a measure of physical aggressiveness. Construct validation may also entail experimentally exposing subjects to conditions that should induce changes in their standing on the trait in question. For example, we could compare responses to an anxiety scale of subjects who have and have not been subjected to an anxiety-arousing situation. Evidence for the construct validity of the anxiety scale would be found if the former group scored higher than the latter group. Research involving testing for group differences and experimental manipulations will be considered further in the following sections of the chapter.

Correlational evidence may also be used to appraise construct validity. A newly developed test may be correlated with another test that is assumed to measure the same variable. Group tests of intelligence often are validated by being correlated with individual intelligence tests, such as the Stanford-Binet or the Wechsler tests. Also, it is usually necessary to demonstrate low correlations with certain other tests that are *not* supposed to measure the same variable in order to feel confident that scores on the test don't reflect the influence of irrelevant factors. Tests of musical aptitude and clerical aptitude, for instance, should not correlate with general intelligence tests and measures of reading comprehension; otherwise a person's performance may, at least partially, reflect his ranking on those factors, instead of his musical or clerical aptitude (Anastasi, 1976).

Factor Analysis

The construct validity of a test also may be studied by a statistical procedure known as *factor analysis*. Factor analysis is a method for simplifying a large number of psychological variables by relating them to a relatively small number of factors or traits. The basic procedure is to administer a number of measures to a group of people and find the correlations among all of the measures. Then certain statistical analyses are applied to this set of intercorrelations in order to determine the common factors that can account for the observed relationships among the measures and the extent to which each factor is measured by each of the measures.

What follows is a simplified description of factor analysis (taken from Guilford, 1959). A factor analytic study of some 70 personality tests was carried out by Guilford and Zimmerman (1956). For explanatory purposes, we will

Table 2-2. Intercorrelations of Scores from Five Short Personality Tests

Personality-Test Number					*Personality-Test Number and Name*
1	2	3	4	5	
—	.56	.38	.11	−.19	1. Liking for social affairs
	—	.32	−.07	.06	2. Gregariousness
		—	.36	.22	3. Lack of fear of social contacts
			—	.49	4. Self-defense
				—	5. Maintaining one's rights

Adapted from *Personality*, by J. P. Guilford. Copyright 1959 by McGraw-Hill, Inc. Used by permission of McGraw-Hill Book Company.

restrict our attention to the results regarding five of the measures. The name of each test is listed below along with a sample item that may help to convey the meaning of the trait being measured.

1. Liking for social affairs
   Item: Do you like to have many social engagements?
2. Gregariousness
   Item: Do you prefer to work with others rather than to work alone?
3. Lack of fear of social contacts
   Item: Have you ever hesitated about applying for a job in person?
4. Self-defense
   Item: Are you rather good at bluffing when you find yourself in difficulty?
5. Maintaining one's rights
   Item: Do you ever protest to a waiter or clerk when you think that you have been overcharged [Guilford, 1959, pp. 94–95]?

The intercorrelations of the five tests, based on a sample of 213 college students, are presented in Table 2-2.

Inspection of the correlations suggests that the tests showing the highest relationship to each other are 1 and 2 (liking for social affairs and gregariousness) and 4 and 5 (self-defense and maintaining one's rights). In addition, each of Tests 1 and 2 shows a very low correlation with each of Tests 4 and 5. This pattern of correlations suggests that Tests 1 and 2 may be measuring the same personality trait, one different from that measured by Tests 4 and 5. Thus, we might expect two separate factors to emerge from the factor analysis. Test 3 is moderately correlated with each of the four other tests, suggesting it may be found to be related to both factors.

The end result of a factor analysis (a detailed explanation of which is beyond the scope of this book) is a factor matrix as presented in Table 2-3. This table shows the "loading" of each factor on each of the five personality tests. A loading of a factor on a test can be regarded as the test's correlation with the factor. The four factors in Table 2-3 actually were derived from the overall analysis of the 70 tests used by Guilford and Zimmerman (recall that we are discussing only part of their analysis), and, as will be seen, we will draw upon the overall analysis for some of our interpretation and labeling

Table 2-3. Factor Matrix Showing Correlations of the Five Personality Tests with the Underlying Factors (Primary Traits)

Personality Test	Factor Loadings			
	S	A	I	N
1. Liking for social affairs	.77	.04	.15	-.07
2. Gregariousness	.45	.29	.19	-.20
3. Lack of fear of social contacts	.29	.40	.46	.24
4. Self-defense	-.06	.74	.22	.37
5. Maintaining one's rights	.02	.46	.09	.25

Adapted from *Personality,* by J. P. Guilford. Copyright 1959 by McGraw-Hill, Inc. Used by permission of McGraw-Hill Book Company.

of the factors. The process of interpreting and labeling factors calls for psychological insight rather than mathematical skill. This procedure involves examining the various tests on which a given factor loads highly and trying to discover the psychological quality or process they seem to have in common. In our example, factor S is most strongly related to Tests 1 and 2, both of which seem to reflect a sociability trait; thus it is identified as factor S (for sociability). Factor A loads quite highly on Test 4 and moderately highly with Tests 3 and 5. Based on these relationships we would be inclined to interpret the factor as reflecting something like standing up for one's self. However, consideration of the loadings of other tests included in the larger battery (not shown in Table 2-3) led to an interpretation of self-assertion; hence it was called factor A (for ascendence). The remaining two factors related to our five tests were designated as factor I (for inferiority) and factor N (for nervousness).

Therefore, it should be clear from the factor loadings in Table 2-3 that a given test may be related to more than a single factor; in other words, several factors may contribute to the scores people receive on a test. For instance, the total variance in Test 4 was 55% attributable to factor A, 5% to factor I, 14% to factor N, and 26% to unknown sources.

To the extent that a test is strongly related to only one factor, our confidence that the test measures a single trait increases. This returns us to the issue of construct validity. Assume, for instance, that a vocabulary test is viewed as a measure of verbal comprehension, and, when factor analyzed along with a battery of ability tests, it loads on the same factor as other measures that also are conceived as reflecting verbal comprehension. The correlation of the vocabulary test with that factor is known as its *factorial validity,* which in this instance may be viewed as an index of the test's construct validity.

Actually, a very common problem in studying individual and group differences is that many traits that are initially thought to be *unidimensional* turn out to be *multidimensional.* As we will discover, for instance, such traits as intelligence, dependency, and rigidity apparently are not unitary constructs and may be broken down into two or more separate traits. Factor analysis of a group of measures purported to be indicators of a given trait may help in determining whether the indicators can be accounted for by a single factor (that is, they are measuring one common trait) or by more than one factor (that is, we are dealing with a multidimensional construct).

RESEARCH ON GROUP DIFFERENCES

In addition to studying the major psychological dimensions along which individuals vary, differential psychology investigates group differences. Traditionally, the focus of differential psychology has been on differences relevant to four categorizations of people—sex, age, social class, and race—and these are the ones considered in this book. However, we should keep in mind that any socially or psychologically meaningful way of assigning people to different groups falls within the purview of differential psychology. We could study, for instance, cross-national differences (for example, between Americans and Canadians), differences based on religion (for example, between Catholics, Jews, and Protestants), differences based on order of birth (for example, between first borns and later borns), differences based on marital status (for example, between single, married, and divorced people), and differences based on sexual orientation (for example, between heterosexuals, bisexuals, and homosexuals).

The general research strategy in the investigation of group differences first involves drawing a sample from each of the populations under consideration. Then we measure one or more variables of interest from each member of the samples and perform a statistical test to determine whether the central tendencies (usually the means) of the samples are statistically different from each other.[3] We might, for example, compare the scores of a sample of 20-year-olds and a sample of 60-year-olds on a scale of risk-taking or compare the occupational aspirations of samples of Black and White Americans.

The meaning of statistical significance in making group comparisons is the same as with a correlation coefficient. It is an index of the probability that the results could have occurred as a result of a chance error in sampling. If there were a statistically significant difference (for example, at the .05 level) between the mean risk-taking scores of the 20- and 60-year-olds, it would mean that the probability is very small (for example, 5%) that the mean levels of riskiness of the larger populations of 20- and 60-year-olds are the same.

As with correlational research, the probability of finding statistical significance increases as the sample size increases. Furthermore, if our samples are quite large, two groups may show a statistically significant difference between their means; yet the absolute or actual difference may be very small and of little theoretical or practical value. For instance, Schneider and Coutts (1977) found that, of 1000 high school students in grade 12, girls had lower self-concepts of school ability than boys. However, the means for the girls and boys

---

[3]The various statistical tests employed in testing for differences in central tendency may be found in any of the many introductory statistics textbooks.

were 14.50 and 15.57, respectively, on a scale that ranged from 4 to 20. Is an absolute difference of 1.07 between the sexes really of very much educational significance, practically speaking? Probably not, because there was extensive overlap between the two distributions of scores. A great many boys had scores that fell below the mean for the girls and, conversely, many girls scored above the mean for the boys.

The above example underscores an especially important point in the study of group differences. While statistically significant differences between groups frequently are found, in the vast majority of cases there is a large amount of overlap. Such overlap is aptly exemplified in a comparison of scores of the various age groups in Figure 2-6. Notice, for instance, that although the 20-year-olds have the highest mean score, many members of the other age groups score higher than the average 20-year-old. This is true especially of the middle-aged groups. In addition, despite the large difference between the means of the oldest group and youngest group, some of the former do better than some of the latter. Thus, we normally find that the variability between two differing groups (difference between their means) is much smaller than the variability within each group.

Methodological Problems in Comparing Groups

Although determining whether or not there is a difference between groups would seem to be a relatively straightforward matter, a researcher has to be aware of a number of potential methodological pitfalls, a few of which we will mention.

Representative Sampling. One of the most difficult problems in research on group differences is insuring that the people included in the samples are typical or representative of the populations about which inferences are to be made. If we want to compare the intelligence of American lower-class and middle-class children or the conforming tendencies of American male and female adults, how can we find samples that are representative of those groups? Ideally we would try to obtain a *random sample* of each group. Random sampling occurs when all members of the larger population have an equal likelihood of being included in the sample. In the example of studying social-class differences in intelligence, random sampling of lower-class children would be the equivalent of picking the names of the sample members out of a gigantic hat containing the names of all lower-class children in the United States.

Obviously, practical considerations prevent the use of random sampling procedures, particularly if the objective is making inferences about the overall population of a society. Typically samples are selected from people who are available to the researcher. A convenient source of subjects, hence a very commonly used one, is the school system, from the preschool level through graduate and adult education. However, the likelihood of obtaining a representative sample lessens when a sample is younger or older than the age span covered by compulsory education (Tyler, 1965). Compulsory education laws insure that practically all children aged 6 to 16 attend school, whereas those who attend earlier (for example, preschool) and later than 6 to 16 (for example, late high school and university) are apt to be a more select, less representative, group.

The problem of *self-selection*—where inclusion in a research sample is in the hands of potential subjects (in the case of children, their guardians) instead of the researcher—is particularly problematic. For instance, many conclusions about sex differences have been based primarily on studies of college students who are majoring in the social sciences and who volunteer to participate in research. Most of us would find it easy to argue that such college students necessarily are not representative of males and females in the college population, much less of males and females in society as a whole.

As we will see in Chapter 11, self-selection is particularly troublesome in the study of adult age differences. In cross-sectional research (in which people of different ages are compared), there is a tendency, particularly among the older age groups, for the better educated, more intelligent person to volunteer to participate in research. In longitudinal research (in which the behavior of the same group of people is measured at specified intervals over a span of years), a tendency exists for the less educated, less intelligent individual to drop out at later stages of the research program. Consequently, regardless of the method used to study age differences, there is a selection bias against the discovery of an age-related decrement in intellectual functioning. We should recognize that the importance of representative sampling is not peculiar to the study of group differences but pertains to any research strategy in which the goal is to make inferences from sample data to a larger population, including both correlational research and experimental research (discussed in the following section).

Simply being aware of the representativeness problem should alert the careful researcher to refrain from recklessly generalizing beyond his or her sample data. Moreover, some explicit steps can be taken to minimize the possibility of drawing erroneous conclusions. One is to see if the same results can be replicated in a number of different samples, all of which are assumed to represent the larger population.

Extraneous Variables. Frequently a statistically significant difference between groups is found that partially or entirely is due to the fact that the groups differ on one or more variables that are not inherent to a conceptual distinction between the groups. If the influence of such an extraneous variable is eliminated, then the difference between the groups is reduced or eliminated. To avoid the possible confounding influence of such an extraneous variable, the members of the samples may either be matched on the variable or the variable may be held constant by statistical means. For instance, investigators interested in comparing the intelligence test scores of different age groups must take heed of the fact that older groups often have had less formal education than the younger groups. Thus, possible age differences in measured intelligence might be due to age differences in amount of education (the extraneous variable) rather than to the aging process per se. One way of handling the possible confounding role of education is to have the investigators match the different age groups in terms of their mean educational level. The existing educational differences could also be controlled statistically. This means that the intelligence of the age groups could be compared while the influence of education has been removed by statistical procedures.

Suitability of Measures. Another potential problem in making comparisons among different groups is that the measuring instrument may not be equally suitable for all the groups (Tyler, 1965). A children's intelligence test that is composed of items that are familiar to White middle-class children would be rather inappropriate for use with children who have not shared the same kinds of cultural experience. Erroneous conclusions may therefore be reached if such a test is used in a comparison of White and Black children or of middle- and lower-class children.

Investigator Bias. Investigator bias occurs when the investigator's desires and/or expectations systematically influence the results of the research in a self-confirming way. Investigator bias is a problem that plagues all kinds of research. In the case of research on group differences, investigators, for any of a variety of reasons, may anticipate that groups differ on a given characteristic and behave in a way that increases the likelihood that their expectation will be confirmed. The expectancy can conceivably bias the data in several ways. For instance, investigators may wittingly or unwittingly (1) select samples or measuring instruments likely to provide data congruent with their expectations, (2) convey by verbal or nonverbal cues their expectations to the subjects, who in turn, modify their behavior in line with those expectations, (3) differentially reinforce subjects' behaviors so as to confirm their expectations, (4) make systematic errors during the scoring, recording, and/or analyses of the data, and (5) interpret not altogether unambiguous results in accordance with their expectations.

Because the investigator often cannot be blind as to the group identity of the subjects, the study of group differences seems especially vulnerable to pitfalls of investigator bias. Moreover, it is an area of study that is open to the intrusive influence of social stereotypes. It would be a rare researcher, indeed, whose assumptions about group differences—racial, social class, sex, or age differences—remained completely unaffected by the prevailing social stereotypes about these groups. Even for the most objective researchers, the possibility remains that stereotypes creep into some phase of their research effort.

Needless to say, the way writers, including authors of psychology textbooks, depict, organize, and interpret the material they present to their readers is bound to be influenced to some extent by their own unique backgrounds and perspectives. Therefore, with regard to the present endeavor, although we have tried to provide an objective representation of the existing evidence concerning group differences, a careful reader is encouraged to keep in mind the particular backgrounds of your authors. When reading Chapter 10 on sex differences, remember that we are male, Chapter 11 on age differences that we are middle aged, Chapter 12 on social class differences that we were brought up in middle-class American families (Henry Minton in New York City and Frank Schneider in a small Connecticut town), and Chapter 13 on race differences that we are White.

An illustration of the possible confounding influence of social stereotypes stems from a review of sex difference by Maccoby and Jacklin (1974). These writers have observed that stereotypical differences between males and females on such traits as dependency and activity level tend to be found when ratings by observers are employed (for example, when children's behaviors are rated by parents and teachers), but much less commonly found with more objective measures (such as making simple frequency counts of relatively unambiguous classes of behavior). Maccoby and Jacklin attribute the difference in results to the rating method's greater susceptibility to the encroachment of sex-role stereotypes.

Also, in writing about the controversy over whether intelligence declines or not with advancement of age, Horn and Donaldson (1976) warn the scientific community of a natural and powerful human bias against the intellectual decrement hypothesis:

> Consider why the position . . . [that there is minimal intellectual decline] so often seems to have gone uncontested when presented in professional meetings and as prologues to articles. . . . there are reasons largely unrelated to evidence (scientific or otherwise) that predispose one to rather easily accept the . . . [idea that decline is a myth] and to reject the counterarguments and evidence. There are powerful reasons for wanting to believe that intellectual decrement does not occur. . . . Humans have a well-developed ability for wishful thinking, and most humans who derive their livelihood and status from exercise of their intellectual abilities have a strong wish that these abilities will not wane. This includes most people who do research on aging. Most of us do not desire to see our friends and loved ones lose qualities that we have most admired and liked, and these qualities often include their abilities. The audience for abilities research is thus set to hear what it wants to hear, and what it wants to hear is that intelligence does not decline with age. Researchers operate under a variety of subtle pressures to give this audience what it wants. This not only shapes the nature of research—the choice of variables and methods of analysis, for example—but also the interpretations given to results [p. 702].

EXPERIMENTAL RESEARCH

Both correlational research and research on group differences are non-manipulative—the variables of interest are measured as they exist in nature. Experimental research, on the other hand, involves the manipulation of variables.

In essence, experimental research consists of two steps: The investigator arranges for a group of subjects to be exposed to a treatment condition; that is, the investigator manipulates (regulates) the subjects' environment. Then the investigator measures an aspect of the subjects' behavior that is expected to be influenced by the treatment condition. We typically refer to the treatment condition as the *independent variable* and the behavior being measured as the *dependent variable*. In the simplest kind of experiment, the behavior of this group of subjects, the *experimental group*, is compared with that of a *control group*, which consists of subjects who are not exposed to the treatment condition. If a statistically significant difference is found between the behavior of the experimental group and the control group, the investigator's confidence that the treatment condition influenced the behavior of the experimental group is increased.

Many experiments involve a number of experimental groups and control groups, plus the manipulation of several independent variables. Nevertheless, regardless of its degree of complexity, a properly conducted experiment requires that the only difference between the groups under comparison—the experimental group(s) and control group(s)—is in terms of their exposure (or nonexposure) to the independent variable. All other variables that might conceivably influence the dependent variable should be controlled by the investigator. There are two major ways of achieving such control. One is to insure that, with the exception of the independent variable, the experimental context is exactly the same for subjects in the experimental group(s) and control group(s). The other is the random assignment of subjects to the various groups in order to minimize the chance of sampling error. This reduces the possibility that there are differences between the groups in terms of certain individual difference variables (for example, differences in intelligence or personality) that conceivably might be related to the dependent variable(s) and, thus, might spuriously produce differences (or similarities) among the groups.

The primary advantage of an experimental study over a correlational study is the greater certainty with which one can make inferences about the direction of causation. In a well-executed experiment (that is, one in which extraneous variables have been successfully controlled), we know that the independent variable is the cause, and the dependent variable is the effect. Clearly the dependent variable is not the cause of the independent variable because the independent variable preceded it in time, and, besides, the independent variable was caused (manipulated) by the investigator. However, in a correlational study a relationship between two variables may be established, but it is generally much harder to make conclusions about whether one variable is the cause or the effect of the other. For instance, if we find that social-class level and intelligence-test performance are positively correlated, it is difficult to know whether (1) the conditions related to one's social class are, in fact, responsible for a person's intelligence score; (2) one's level of intelligence accounts for how successfully one can climb the social-class ladder; or (3) a third variable, such as the amount of formal education one has achieved, is responsible for the relationship between social class and intelligence (that is, lack of education may be responsible for both inferior socioeconomic status and low intelligence scores).

These comments are not intended to imply that correlational evidence cannot shed any light on questions related to cause and effect. For one thing, while correlations may not directly establish a causal connection between variables, they may furnish strong clues to the direction of causality. Perhaps the best known example of this occurred in the early 1960s when medical researchers relied primarily on correlational evidence to conclude that cigarette smoking is a cause of lung cancer. Moreover, there are several more sophisticated correlational procedures that may be used to gain a better understanding of the direction of causality among correlated variables. These include, for instance, partial correlations, multiple regression, cross-lagged correlations, and path analysis. An interesting application of these techniques has been carried out by Eron, Huesmann, Letkowitz, and Walder (1972), who used them to demonstrate the existence of a "probable causative influence" of viewing television violence on the viewers' subsequent levels of aggressiveness.

However, notwithstanding the value of correlational research and the other research strategies we have reviewed, experimental research is especially suitable to the fulfillment of what is probably the most important objective in the study of human differences—the investigation of the causes of behavioral differences among people and among groups of people. The basic strategy involves effecting an alteration in the conditions experienced by subjects in order to ascertain whether such changes reduce or enhance the existing differences among people.

A well-known example is the social intervention research that is directed at establishing whether or not improved environmental conditions ("environmental enrichment") can facilitate the intellectual development of the so-called disadvantaged child. Thus, for example, some preschool children (the experimental group) may be enrolled in a special educational program, whereas other, equally disadvantaged children (the control group) are left to develop under naturally occurring circumstances. If only the experimental group displays a significant improvement or if they manifest greater improvement than the control group that also improves, this supports an environmental deprivation explanation of individual and group differences in intellectual development.

While intervention research carried out in the natural environment is of great value in our efforts to discover the factors contributing to human variability, by its very nature it is less methodologically rigorous than research conducted in a laboratory setting. A particularly troublesome feature of research conducted in the field is the inability to impose adequate control over potentially confounding environmental factors, such as the family environment to which the child must return after his or her involvement in the intervention program. Laboratory research does permit the investigator to have much greater control over relevant environmental factors. However, the increased control usually is accompanied by at least some loss in realism and, thus, probably a loss in the generalizability of potential findings.

An excellent illustration of a laboratory investigation of the causes of human differences is a series of studies by Klein (Klein, 1972; Klein & Birren,

1973). Klein was interested in whether or not there are age differences among adults in the tendency to conform to the opinions of others. He first designed a series of experiments in which young and old adults were given a task in which they had to make various kinds of judgments. For example, in one case they had to evaluate which of two disks was smaller and in a second case they had to decide on the solutions to arithmetic problems. In each instance, on certain judgment trials the subjects received fictitious information about the opinions of other participating subjects. The subjects were viewed as conforming if they expressed agreement with the other people when the others were wrong. Across all kinds of judgment situations, the older adults tended to conform more than the younger adults, and, as the difficulty level of judgments increased, the older people showed even more conformity than the younger people.

It is important to note here that although this was an experimental investigation (the experimenter manipulated the treatment conditions and subjects were randomly assigned), the results tell us only that age differences in conformity exist and little, if anything, about the causes of these differences. (As we will explain in Chapter 11, the concept of age itself has negligible explanatory value.) A possible causal factor in the age differences was not manipulated. However, in a follow-up experiment Klein endeavored to manipulate a variable that he felt might account for the age difference. He hypothesized that feelings of low self-competence underlie the heightened conformity of the older persons. Thus, he manipulated the situation in order to vary the subjects' perception of their own levels of competence. After practicing alone on two judgmental tasks, the subjects were given no feedback about their level of competence or they were either informed that they were better than all of those whom already had been tested or told that they were worse than them. The behavior of the subjects in the subsequent conformity phase of the experiment suggested that perceived self-competence is an important cause of the greater conformity of older persons—there was no significant difference in conformity between the old and young groups who were led to have confidence in their levels of ability.

In conclusion, the major advantage of experimental research over other modes of research is that it is generally a more effective tool for enhancing our understanding of the reasons for existing individual and group differences. The other research procedures we have discussed—frequency distributions, correlational studies, and group difference studies—are particularly useful in providing information about the existing status of human variability but, for the most part, shed little light on the causes. However, as we have noted, recent years have witnessed the development of certain correlation-based procedures that do permit stronger inferences about the direction of causality. Of course, progress in the exploration of human variation necessarily requires a combination of all the research strategies. Once the nature and extent of individual and group differences have been adequately documented, research is undertaken to discover the factors accounting for the differences. As we proceed with the study of differential psychology, it will become increasingly apparent that far more is known about the existence of individual and group differences than about the causes.

SUMMARY

Individual variability is characteristic of all species, from the simplest one-celled organisms to the most complex of animals, human beings. Whereas biological measurement provides data at a ratio-scale level, psychological measurement tends to be much less precise, usually providing data at either an ordinal-scale level or interval-scale level.

Several techniques are used in the description of human variation. A frequency distribution is a table that helps to organize a group of people's scores on a variable. Frequency distributions often are presented graphically in the form of a polygram or histogram. The shape of many distributions of biological variables seems to approximate a bell-shaped normal curve. It is reasonable to assume that many distributions of psychological variables also resemble a normal curve, but the inadequacy of our current measuring instruments precludes definitive statements about the form of such distributions. We can feel fairly confident that psychological characteristics are continuous variables, that is, those that can assume any value of the variable from the lowest possible amount to the highest. Recognition of the continuous nature of psychological variables has led to an emphasis on traits rather than types.

Descriptive statistics, such as measures of central tendency, variability, and correlation, also represent ways of summarizing measurements taken on a large number of people. Measures of central tendency—the mean, median, and mode—signify a score that is most representative of a distribution of scores. One measure of variability, the standard deviation, is commonly used to provide an index of the degree of variability in a distribution of scores. A second measure, the variance, is useful in expressing the extent to which a factor accounts for the existing variability of scores. Correlation, another descriptive statistic, refers to the degree of association between two sets of variables.

Inferential statistics are techniques that make it possible to draw inferences about a population on the basis of data taken on a sample from the population. Inferential statistics rely on a test of statistical significance to determine the degree of confidence the researcher can have that the research finding is not merely a result of an error in sampling.

Correlational research has several important uses. A correlation coefficient may be used as an index of reliability—the degree of consistency from one measurement to another. The major types of reliability include split-half, coefficient alpha, test-retest, and alternate forms. The correlational method is useful in determining how valid a test is. A test is valid if it measures what it is purported to measure. Correlation coefficients are especially useful in the assessment of criterion-related validity and construct validity. The correlational method also forms the basis of factor analysis, a statistical procedure used to relate a large number of variables to a relatively small set of factors (traits). Factor analysis is particularly helpful in determining whether a test is measuring a single trait (that is, is unidimensional) or two or more traits (that is, is multidimensional).

Another major concern of differential psychology is the study of group differences. This research strategy entails drawing a sample from each of the populations of interest, measuring the relevant psychological variable(s), and performing a statistical test in order to determine if the central tendencies of the samples are statistically different from each other. The attainment of representative sampling, control of extraneous variables, application of measures suitable for all the groups, and avoidance of investigator bias are some of the methodological problems relevant to the study of group differences.

Experimental research essentially entails exposing a group of subjects to an environmental stimulus (the independent variable) and then measuring each subject's behavioral response (the dependent variable). The subject's responses are compared with those of a control group, that is, subjects who were not exposed to the independent variable. In contrast to using the correlational method, the investigator who properly applies the experimental method is generally in a better position to infer the direction of causality. Because of this, the experimental method is particularly suitable for studying the causes of individual and group differences.

REFERENCES

Anastasi, A. *Differential psychology* (3rd ed.). New York: Macmillan, 1958.

Anastasi, A. *Psychological testing* (4th ed.). New York: Macmillan, 1976.

Carlson, R. Understanding women: Implications for personality theory and research. *Journal of Social Issues*, 1972, *28*(2), 17–32.

Eron, L. D., Huesmann, L. R., Lefkowitz, M. M., & Walder, L. O. Does television violence cause aggression? *American Psychologist*, 1972, *27*, 253–263.

Glass, G. V., & Stanley, J. C. *Statistical methods in education and psychology.* Englewood Cliffs, N.J.: Prentice-Hall, 1970.

Guilford, J. P. *Personality.* New York: McGraw-Hill, 1959.

Guilford, J. P., & Zimmerman, W. S. Fourteen dimensions of temperament. *Psychological Monographs*, 1956, *70* (10, Whole No. 417), 1–26.

Heron, A., & Chown, S. *Age and function.* Boston: Little, Brown, 1967.

Horn, J. L., & Donaldson, G. On the myth of intellectual decline in adulthood. *American Psychologist*, 1976, *31*, 701–719.

Klein, R. L. Age, sex and task difficulty as predictors of social conformity. *Journal of Gerontology*, 1972, *27*, 229–236.

Klein, R. L., & Birren, J. E. Age, perceived self-competence, and conformity: A partial explanation. Proceedings, 81st Annual Convention, American Psychological Association, 1973, 775–776.

Maccoby, E. M., & Jacklin, C. N. *The psychology of sex differences.* Stanford, Calif.: Stanford University Press, 1974.

Razran, G. H. S. Conditional responses in animals other than dogs. *Psychological Bulletin*, 1933, *30*, 261–324.

Schneider, F. W., & Coutts, L. M. *Educational orientation of students in coeducational and single-sex high schools.* Report to Canada Council (S73–1887), June, 1977.

Standards for educational and psychological tests. Washington, D.C.: American Psychological Association, 1974.

Test Service Bulletin Number 48. New York: The Psychological Corporation, 1955.

Tyler, L. E. *The psychology of human differences* (3rd ed.). New York: Appleton-Century-Crofts, 1965.

Yoakum, C. S., & Yerkes, R. M. (Eds.). *Army mental tests.* New York: Holt, 1920.

3

Heredity
and Environment

In this book we are concerned with the manifold ways in which people differ as individuals and as representatives of groups. But before we consider the variation among people and groups of people, it is important to give some attention to why there are such differences. When we think about the causes of human differences, we usually break them down into two broad categories: hereditary factors and environmental factors.

Let us ask you a question. Which is more important, heredity or environment? This question, or some variation of it, has on several occasions been asked of us, and it may very well have been posed to you—if not by someone else, perhaps by you yourself. Eventually every student of human behavior must come to grips with how he or she stands on the role of heredity and environment in the etiology (causation) of behavior. And clearly it is a question we should not take lightly. As we will discover, the position we assume may be tied directly to our social and political beliefs; moreover, our position undoubtedly affects the way we react to policy recommendations regarding the enactment of various social and educational programs. For example, government sponsored educational enrichment programs are based on the assumption that environmental influences play an important role in the development of intellectual ability. A strong hereditarian would argue against the effectiveness of such programs, and, consequently, against public funding of them.

Indeed, you may balk at responding to the question about your stance on the role of heredity and environment and insist that your view does not fit neatly into one camp or the other. You may contend that, if anything, you are an eclectic, favoring an approach that recognizes the joint contributions of heredity and environment. Yet at the same time you may be aware that there is something socially unacceptable about advocating the hereditarian viewpoint in favor of the environmental viewpoint. In fact, you may even feel a bit wary about publicly acknowledging the possible merit of the hereditarian approach lest you risk verbal onslaught from your contemporaries. For many the heredity/environment controversy (often called the "nature/nurture" issue) is an emotion laden topic. Why is this so? Before we explore precisely what is meant by the terms heredity and environment, let us review the development of the controversy during this century.

DEVELOPMENT OF THE NATURE/NURTURE CONTROVERSY

In the early part of the present century the nature/nurture controversy began to intensify. At first the hereditarians, strongly influenced by Darwin (1859), Mendel (1866), and Galton (1869), held the upper hand. According to Haller (1968) most authorities were convinced that mental illness, mental retardation, and crime were primarily rooted in heredity. In addition, the hereditarian thesis was readily embraced by the advocates of racist doctrines. The belief that various branches of the Nordic races of Northern Europe were innately superior to other races and, consequently, were primarily responsible for the major accomplishments of mankind had been cogently voiced in the 1850s by the French historian, Joseph Arthur de Gobineau, in his *Essay on the Inequality of Human Races* (cited in Cancro, 1971) and later in the United States by Madison Grant in *The Passing of the Great Race* (1916). As Haller (1968) notes, Grant's highly racist, particularly anti-Semitic, book was favorably received by much of the scientific community. For instance, at the time it was acclaimed as a "work of solid merit" by the magazine *Science*. The uncritical interpretation of the findings of early investigations of measured intelligence (see Chapter 5) gave added impetus to the racist dogma. This research indicated that those groups thought to be inferior actually performed at an inferior level on measures of intelligence. In the newly emerging discipline of psychology the hereditarian position was associated closely with William McDougall's (1908) theory of instincts. McDougall's position was that all social interaction is based on inherited patterns of behavior known as instincts.

The hereditarian doctrine had considerable impact on social and political thought in America during the early 1900s. Haller says "many prestigious biologists, social scientists, and publicists drew specifically 'conservative' and elitist conclusions from hereditary interpretations of human behavior" (pp. 217–218). For example, at a national conference of social workers, America's most prominent human geneticist, Charles B. Davenport (1912), argued the futility of carrying out social reform, including the improvement of education. Furthermore, in his 1921 book, *Is America Safe for Democracy?*, McDougall, who at the time was chairman of Harvard's psychology department, warned his readers about the possible deterioration of the genetic stock of America caused by the disproportionately high birth rate among the lower classes (the "inferior half") and thus America's eventual decay and downfall. To prevent this from happening McDougall urged that a castelike system must be established. Among its features would be that married couples from the "intrinsically better half of the population" would be subsidized for each offspring they bore, interbreeding among the least fit (for example, the mentally retarded) would be prevented, and family histories would be registered to insure that intermarriage among the superior and inferior halves could be minimized.

In the political sphere, hereditarian "reform" culminated in the 1920s with the enactment by the U.S. Congress of laws sharply restricting the immigration of national groups presumed to be genetically inferior, most notably those from Southern and Eastern Europe. Also, by 1931 many states had passed laws (which rarely were implemented) requiring the sterilization of certain "unfit" groups, including criminals, the mentally retarded, and the mentally ill (see Kamin, 1974).

As we have noted, the doctrine of racial inferiority is readily endorsed by proponents of racist doctrines, especially those whose goals are to subjugate or enslave other peoples. The doctrine was used as a major justification for slavery and the subsequent oppression of Black people in America and for the Nazi German plan to advance the "master race" by committing genocide. Because of its regrettable association with such unconscionable policies it is easy to see why there emerged a growing distrust for the field of genetics. The peak of academic opposition to hereditarian thought occurred in the 1930s, largely in response to Nazism, with many professional associations issuing official pronouncements against racism and the scientific validity of Nazi doctrines (Haller, 1968). By 1940 the academic climate concerning the heredity/environment issue was almost opposite to that which had prevailed just two decades or so earlier, now leaning rather heavily on the latter side of the debate.

There were other factors contributing to the disenchantment with hereditarian thought. As several writers have observed, much of the nature/nurture controversy has involved *ideological* rather than scientific considerations (for example, Haller, 1968; Elias, 1973). Not only was the hereditarian position distorted on the behalf of racist dogma, but the thesis that a person's psychological characteristics are predetermined by his or her heredity was viewed by many as contradicting the American democratic ideal that all men are created equal. American democratic philosophy is heavily influenced by John Locke's notion of a "tabula rasa" (clean slate), namely, that infants are born free of any innate tendencies, and the course of their development into adulthood is determined entirely by their experiences with their environments. Thus, with the constitutionally guaranteed freedoms and the proper environmental conditions, every person can be the equal of others, and there is no justification for the dominance of some over others purely on the basis of genetic differences.

In addition to ideology, several intellectual developments began to herald the decline of hereditarianism (Haller, 1968). For instance, soon after World War I mental testers began to admit that they initially had overestimated the extent to which mental retardation is grounded in heredity; they acknowledged the role of sociocultural influences on tested intelligence. Anthropologists increasingly emphasized the concept of cultural relativism—that differences between groups of people are largely traceable to cultural differences in socialization. In psychology, McDougall's (1908) instinct theory was attacked by behaviorists (see below) and others as circular and redundant. Because genetic determinants of behavior were confused with instincts, the growing disenchantment with the latter facilitated the rejection of the genetic approach.

Environmentalism probably was given its biggest boost by the rise of John B. Watson's (1930/1959) behaviorism, which epitomized the extreme environmentalist reaction. Watson endorsed Locke's tabula rasa when he made his now famous challenge:

> Give me a dozen healthy infants, well-formed, and my own specified world to bring them up in and I'll guarantee to take any one at random and train him to become any type of specialist I might select—doctor, lawyer, artist, merchant-chief and, yes, even beggar-man and thief, regardless of his talents, penchants, tendencies, abilities, vocations, and race of his ancestors. I am going beyond my facts and I admit it, but so have the advocates of the contrary and they have been doing it for many thousands of years [p. 104].

We should point out that the last sentence rarely is quoted, and it may signify, as Woodworth (1948) has suggested, that Watson's intent was, at least in part, "to shake people out of their complacent acceptance of traditional views" (p. 92). Moreover, McClearn and DeFries (1973) state, "For whatever reason Watson sought to exorcise genetics from psychology, he succeeded to a remarkable degree, and the position taken in his book entitled *Behaviorism* soon became the 'traditional view' that was 'complacently accepted' by the majority of psychologists" (p. 31).

Thus, during the middle period of this century a schism existed between social science and behavior genetics (the study of genetic contributions to behavior). While intellectual (scientific) reasons were partially responsible for the estrangement between the two, most observers believe that the major cause was ideological in nature. Social scientists had a vested interest in backing environmentalism, and this interest was largely rooted in their traditionally liberal values. As Tyler (1965) has observed, hereditarians typically have been conservative, sharing a pessimism about the possibility of "improving" people by changing their social, educational, and economic conditions, whereas environmentalists by tradition are liberal, being far more optimistic about the potentially beneficial effects of environmental change.

During the 1940s, 1950s, and most of the 1960s environmentalism was so firmly entrenched in the social sciences that the nature/nurture issue remained relatively dormant. While most social scientists claimed to hold an intermediate position—both heredity and environment influence human variability—the vast majority was much closer to the environmental position. However, in 1969 the controversy suddenly was reignited when Arthur Jensen, a reputable educational psychologist, picked up the banner for heredity. Jensen (1969) argues persuasively that most of the variation in intelligence is due to the influence of heredity rather than environment, and, consequently, average differences in intelligence between various ethnic and racial groups are not for the most part caused by environmental factors, as most mainstream social scientists preferred to assume. In Chapter 5 we will examine Jensen's position and that of his critics concerning the determinants of intelligence. The point we want to make here is how volatile the nature/nurture debate continues to be. Jensen's article produced a storm of protest both in public and scientific circles, and, in fact, he and others who publicly agreed with him have been subjected to a large amount of personal abuse.[1]

The 1970s witnessed the development of the discipline of *sociobiology,* which has added a new and provocative dimension to the nature/nurture question (see Wilson, 1975). Sociobiologists view their discipline as the culmination of the Darwinian revolution. Their thesis is that in the evolutionary process, the genes are the units of selection, not the individual as Darwin had believed. That is, genes are engaged in the struggle for survival, and behavior that serves to perpetuate our genetic material will be favored in evolution (that is, will be likely to evolve). Thus, sociobiology can account for altruistic behavior that from the Darwinian perspective should have been selected out because it reduces the organism's survival chances. We help our relatives even at the risk of death (for example, a parent rushes into a flame engulfed house to save a child) because in so doing our genes' chances of survival are increased. Sociobiologists do acknowledge the role of the environment, positing that, in contrast to lower species, human social behavior is mainly regulated by facultative genes—genes whose effects can be moderated by environmental influences. Sociobiology is too recent a development to confidently gauge its scientific promise. Yet, not surprisingly, it has come under severe criticism for its inflammatory potential, including the argument that it may be used to support the superiority of some groups over others, for example males over females and Whites over Nonwhites (Sociobiology: A New Theory of Behavior, 1977).

In conclusion, it is apparent that the position taken by many people on the nature/nurture controversy is based more on emotion than on reason.

---

[1]In one instance, the British psychologist H. J. Eysenck was physically assaulted as he gave a speech at the London School of Economics (Loehlin, Lindzey, & Spuhler, 1975).

Nevertheless, there is no doubt that advancements made in the field of behavior genetics impressively demonstrate that heredity (as well as environment) plays an extremely important role in the etiology of human differences. Human variation is due to both heredity and environment. Now let us examine what is meant by the terms heredity and environment and how the two jointly interact to determine behavior.

NATURE OF HEREDITY

As recently as the 17th century the preformist theory of the origin of life was widely accepted among biologists. According to this theory, a pre-formed miniature person resided in the gamete (reproductive cell) and merely had to develop in the uterus. A point of contention did center, however, on whether a prefabricated person was contained in the female gamete (egg) or male gamete (sperm). The improvement of the microscope and other scientific techniques during the 18th and 19th centuries led to the recognition that there is no spontaneous generation of life in the gametes; rather, a new human life begins with the uniting of a sperm and egg. Yet, although this process of fertilization had been determined, the process of heredity, the manner in which parental characteristics are transmitted to their offspring, had not been. According to one widely held misconception, the "blood theory," trait-carrying factors were contained in the blood of the parents and were somehow transferred into the zygote (the fertilized egg). Consider the many idioms reflecting this idea that have persisted in our language, including, for example, "half-blooded," "blood-brothers," and "he has bad blood."

Today, of course, we know that one's heredity is fixed at conception and that inherited characteristics are transmitted by *genes*. Genes are carried on *chromosomes*, and each chromosome may have as many as 1200 or so genes. Chromosomes are threadlike structures found in the nucleus of every body cell. During one stage of cell division, they condense to take on the familiar X-like shape. They are made of proteins and a nucleic acid commonly referred to as DNA (*deoxyribonucleic acid*). DNA is the chemical material of which genes are made; in fact, a gene may be conceived as a segment of a molecular chain of DNA. A major, Nobel prize winning breakthrough in understanding genetic transmission came in the early 1950s when J. D. Watson and Crick (1953) proposed a model of the chemical and physical nature of the DNA molecule. The model is pictorially illustrated in Figure 3-1.

According to the model, a DNA molecule has a double-stranded helical structure (the "double helix") that gives the appearance of a twisted ladder (or circular stairway). The sides (strands) of the ladder consist of phosphorus and sugar molecules, and each rung is comprised of two of four nitrogeneous bases, adenine, thymine, guanine, and cytosine, called A, T, G, and C for short (see Figure 3-1). Adenine is always paired with thymine and guanine with cytosine. The rungs (paired nitrogeneous bases) may be arranged in any order (for example, AT, GC, TA, AT, CG, CG, AT, CG, GC), and a single gene may

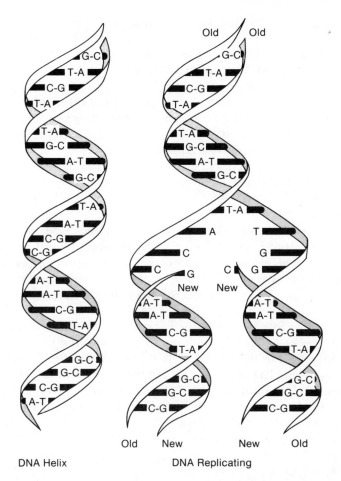

Old Old

New New

Old New New Old

DNA Helix   DNA Replicating

Figure 3-1. Diagram of the DNA double helix and DNA replicating. The sides (strands) of the "twisted ladder" are joined by weak interactions between the nitrogeneous bases adenine (A), thymine (T), cytosine (C), and guanine (G). From *Genetics of Man*, by F. C. Fraser and J. J. Nora. Copyright 1975 by Lea & Febiger. Reprinted by permission.

be comprised of a segment of DNA that is perhaps 2000 rungs long. The variable component of DNA, that which changes from individual to individual, is the sequence and number of the pairs of nitrogeneous bases. The order of these pairs of bases determines the genetic code of the organism. This code carries the instructions for the replication of the DNA prior to cell division (see below), thus providing for the transfer of genetic information from cell to cell, and it carries instructions for the formation of proteins within the cells of the body. Proteins are organic compounds that not only make up much of the substance of our body tissues (for example, blood, nerves, and skin) but, in the form of enzymes, determine the metabolic reactions that occur in a cell. In other

words, proteins determine the structure and function of cells, and, consequently, the structure and function of the organism. The genetic information
incorporated in the DNA is transmitted to the protein production sites, the
ribosomes, by another nucleic acid, RNA (ribonucleic acid).

At this point it is useful to distinguish between one's genotype and one's
phenotype. *Genotype* refers to our actual genetic constitution (gene makeup),
whereas *phenotype* refers to our observable characteristics (for example, height,
blood type, and running speed). As the preceding paragraph suggests, we do
not directly inherit our phenotype. That is, technically it is not correct to say
that we inherit a particular characteristic such as blue eyes. Rather we inherit
genes (a set of chemical instructions) that interact with the biochemical environment to produce proteins that, assuming all goes well, cause the eyes to
have a blue color.

Each human possesses 23 pairs of chromosomes (see Figure 3-2). One
chromosome from each pair is contributed by each parent at the time of
conception. Moreover, every body cell contains a precise copy of the 23 pairs
of chromosomes that were formed at conception. Once a sperm has fertilized
the egg, a process of cell reproduction, known as *mitosis*, begins. During mitosis
each of the 46 chromosomes in a cell first doubles by splitting lengthwise;
then the cell divides into two cells, each containing an identical set of chromosomes. These two cells likewise undergo mitosis, and the process is repeated
over and over until the trillions of cells that comprise the mature organism
have been produced. The genetic code contained in DNA directs the process
of cell division and accounts for the development of the diverse types of cells
required for the development of an organism. Developmental genetics is the
subspecialty that studies the processes of differentiation that cause one cell
to become a neuron, another a red blood cell, another a muscle fiber cell,
and so on.

The sperm and egg are produced by a special kind of cell division called
meiosis. As with mitosis, meiosis begins with the chromosomes duplicating
themselves; however, the ensuing cell divisions result in the production of four
cells, instead of two. Each gamete contains only one member of each chromosome pair, that is, a total of 23 chromosomes instead of the 46 found in other
body cells. Thus, when the sperm fertilizes the ovum (producing the fertilized
egg or zygote), 23 chromosomes from the male pair up with the 23 from the
female, creating the normal human complement of 46 chromosomes.

When during meiosis the 46 chromosomes divide into the two sets of 23
chromosomes, it is a random event which chromosome of each pair goes into
a particular gamete. This principle of *random assortment* is an especially
important feature of the genetic process because it insures that there is an
enormous amount of genetic variability among the offspring, and genetic variability is essential to the process of evolution. The total possible number of
gametes that a member of a species can produce is 2^n (where n is the number
of chromosome pairs). For example, a species with two pairs of chromosomes
AA' and BB' can produce four (2^2) possible combinations: AB, AB', A'B, and
A'B'. When $n = 23$, as in humans, the number of gamete types = 8,388,608.

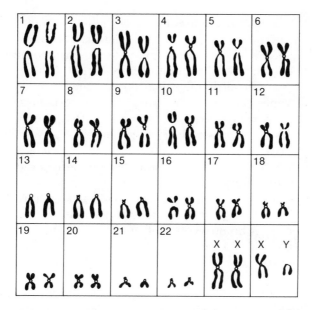

Figure 3-2. The 23 chromosome pairs of a normal human female gamete. The last area shows the XY pair of a normal male. From *Fundamentals of Child Development* (2nd Ed.), by Harry Munsinger. Copyright © 1971, 1975 by Holt, Rinehart and Winston. Reprinted by permission of Holt, Rinehart and Winston.

Then when we consider that both parents contribute 23 chromosomes, the possible number of combinations of chromosomes from this process alone is approximately 70 trillion ($2^{23} \times 2^{23}$).

Another process occurring during meiosis, called *crossing over*, further amplifies the potential genetic variability of offspring. Two chromosomes that constitute a pair are comparable part by part. In other words, for each gene or segment on the chromosome of maternal origin there is a corresponding gene or segment on the chromosome of paternal origin. Crossing over occurs when the two chromosomes exchange portions of their genetic material. Because such exchanges tend to occur for several sections of each chromosome, all possible combinations of genes can eventuate. The possible number of different combinations of genes due to crossing over is infinitely large. Thus, when we consider the combined effects of random assortment and crossing over, it is extremely unlikely, with one exception, that two individuals ever will be genetically identical; one estimate is that the chances are 1 out of 1 followed by 9031 zeroes (Pfeiffer, 1969). The one exception, of course, is the case of *identical twins* (monozygotic twins). Identical twins occur when the single zygote (thus the term monozygote) separates into equal cells, each with exactly the same genetic structure. In the United States a pair of identical twins occurs about 4 times in 1000 live births (Public Health Service, 1967). The more common (about 6 pairs per 1000) kind of twin is the *fraternal twin* (dizygotic twin). These are the consequence of the fertilization of two separate eggs and, as such, are no more genetically similar than ordinary siblings.

The combination of the maternal and paternal chromosomes at the time of conception results in two genes that occupy corresponding loci (positions) on the chromosomes, and it is these genes that determine a particular trait. In most pairs of genes (that is, genes occupying corresponding loci) the two genes are the same, carrying instructions common to all human beings. They specify that we have arms instead of wings, hands that permit us to grasp objects, and so forth. Some genes carry instructions that are less universal, for example, those that determine the skin color of various racial groups. Still others provide for individual differences within a given population group.

If two genes at a particular locus are identical, the individual is said to be *homozygous* for this locus; if they are different, the individual is *heterozygous*. When a person is homozygous with respect to a particular locus, then his or her phenotype will directly reflect the genotype. For example, if a person is homozygous for the gene determining brown eye color (BR BR), then his or her eyes will, in fact, be brown. In the case of a person who is heterozygous, the picture is somewhat more complicated. For example, if one gene prescribes brown eyes, whereas the other prescribes blue eyes (BR BL), the resulting eye color will depend on which gene is *dominant* and which is *recessive*. In this particular instance, brown is dominant, and the resulting eye color is brown. A recessive gene can manifest itself only when matched with another recessive gene. Therefore, for a person to have blue eyes, both of his or her genes must carry the code for blue (BL BL).

Table 3-1 further illustrates the transmission of dominant and recessive characteristics. The left-hand column shows all possible combinations of brown-eyed and blue-eyed parents. The possible gametes from each parent are presented in the next column along with the possible pairings of gametes. For example, if both parents are heterozygotes (BR BL), as a consequence of meiosis, half of their gametes will carry the BR gene and half the BL gene. Because these gametes will combine randomly in forming a zygote, the mating of such heterozygotes will yield offspring of three different genotypes, BR BR, BR BL, and BL BL in the ratio of 1:2:1 (see the third column). Notice that only half of the offspring will have the same BR BL genotype as their parents. However, three-fourths of the offspring will have the same phenotype (brown eyes) as their parents (see the fourth column). It is important to note that although we may not phenotypically manifest a particular recessive characteristic, we may carry the gene for it and transmit it to our children. Some common recessive and dominant traits are presented in Table 3-2. Gregor Mendel, the father of genetics, relied on similar observations in developing his famous laws of heredity. His ideas were based on the predictability of the ratios of phenotypes when pea plants of differing physical characteristics (for example, color and size) were crossed.

An understanding of the transmission of recessive traits helps us to appreciate the risks involved in *consanguineous* matings (matings of related people). Most abnormalities of a genetic origin are transmitted by a recessive gene.

Table 3-1. Expected Ratio of Genotypes and Phenotypes for Offspring of Various Combinations of Matings Involving Parents Having Brown Eyes (BR) and Those Having Blue Eyes (BL)

Parents	Gametes	Expected Offspring Ratios	
		Genotypes	Phenotypes
BR BR × BR BR	BR BR BR ┌ BR BR │ BR BR ┐ BR └ BR BR │ BR BR ┘	All BR BR	All Brown
BR BR × BR BL	BR BL BR ┌ BR BR │ BR BL ┐ BR └ BR BR │ BR BL ┘	½ BR BR ½ BR BL	All Brown
BR BR × BL BL	BL BL BR ┌ BR BL │ BR BL ┐ BR └ BR BL │ BR BL ┘	All BR BL	All Brown
BR BL × BR BL	BR BL BR ┌ BR BR │ BR BL ┐ BL └ BR BL │ BL BL ┘	¼ BR BR ½ BR BL ¼ BL BL	¾ Brown ¼ Blue
BR BL × BL BL	BL BL BR ┌ BR BL │ BR BL ┐ BL └ BL BL │ BL BL ┘	½ BR BL ½ BL BL	½ Brown ½ Blue
BL BL × BL BL	BL BL BL ┌ BL BL │ BL BL ┐ BL └ BL BL │ BL BL ┘	All BL BL	All Blue

If a recessive gene is uncommon, as is the case with most genes that produce abnormalities, the chance of mating a male and female who possess the recessive gene (that is, are either heterozygous or homozygous for the abnormal trait) is much greater if they are related than unrelated. This is because relatives may have inherited the recessive gene from a common ancestor. Research (for example, Adams & Neel, 1967) does indicate a higher incidence of genetic defects and infant mortality in the offspring of consanguineous marriages. Highly inbred populations, such as the Amish, who for religious reasons discourage marriages with outsiders, have been found to show an above average number of genetic defects in their young. One study of Amish communities showed that such abnormalities include certain kinds of dwarfism, anemia, hemophilia, and muscular dystrophy (McKusick, Hosteter, Egeland, & Eldridge, 1964).

We have yet to discuss the process by which a person's sex is determined. Whereas both sexes possess 23 pairs of chromosomes, only in the female are all 23 pairs said to be homologous. *Homologous* chromosomes are pairs of

Table 3-2. Some Dominant and Recessive Characteristics

Dominant Characteristics	*Recessive Characteristics*
Brown eyes	Blue eyes
Dark or brunette hair	Light, blond, or red hair
Curly hair	Straight hair
Freckles	No freckles
Dimples	No dimples
Free earlobes	Attached earlobes
Normal color vision	Color blindness: Red/green
Normal sight	Myopia (nearsightedness)
Normal hearing	Congenital deafness
Normal coloring	Albinism (lack of pigment)
Normal sensitivity to poison ivy	Hypersusceptibility to poison ivy
Normal blood	Hemophilia (lack of blood clotting)
Normal metabolism	Phenylketonuria

chromosomes that carry the same gene loci and are generally alike in size and shape. In a male 22 chromosome pairs are homologous; one pair isn't. These are his sex chromosomes. One of the pair is the *X chromosome,* and the second is the much smaller *Y chromosome.* Females lack a Y chromosome, possessing two X chromosomes instead of an XY pair. It is the Y chromosome that carries the genetic code for maleness; this means that the father's chromosome determines a child's sex. Since the sex chromosomes undergo the same meiotic process as the other 22 chromosome pairs, there is a theoretically equal probability that an XX and an XY chromosome pair will result at fertilization.[2] A zygote with the XX combination will develop into a female, whereas one with an XY combination will become a male.

Genes carried on only one of the sex chromosomes (either the X or Y) are said to be *sex linked.* However, because many more genes occur on the X chromosome, the vast majority of sex-linked traits are X-linked rather than Y-linked. In the male a trait associated with an X-linked gene will always be expressed. However, because a female has two X chromosomes, whether an X-linked characteristic is expressed will depend on whether the gene determining it is dominant or recessive. It should be apparent then that X-linked recessive traits are more commonly expressed in males than females. Females will express such a trait only if both genes carry the instructions for it (that is, only if both of their genes are recessive).

A good example of an X-linked recessive characteristic is color-blindness, a trait that coincidentally both of the authors possess. Figure 3-3 shows the ways color-blindness apparently was transmitted from our mothers to us. Note that although the example shows the father to be color-blind, the male offspring

---

[2]A slightly higher proportion of sperm with Y chromosomes than those with X chromosomes are successful in fertilizing the egg. Therefore more boys than girls are born (in the United States, the ratio is 106:100); however, the discrepancy eventually is eliminated (by age 18) and reversed because the mortality rate of males exceeds that of females. By age 57 the ratio is 90:100 and by age 87 it is 50:100 (Lerner, 1968).

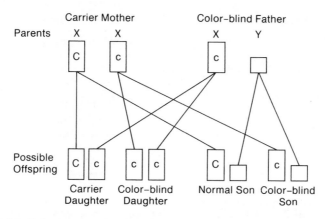

Figure 3-3. Inheritance of color-blindness, a sex-linked trait. C, the gene for normal color vision, is dominant over c, the gene for color-blindness.

of a carrier mother can possess the characteristic even when the father has normal color vision.

Another X-linked recessive characteristic is hemophilia, a disease that prevents normal blood clotting. Interestingly, analysis of pedigree charts, which are used to follow the transmission of an inherited condition across generations, reveals that hemophilia existed among the royal families of Europe (Pai, 1974). The original carrier has been traced to Queen Victoria of England who apparently was conceived by a gamete carrying a gene for hemophilia. We should note, however, that with respect to the current British royal family, the gene for hemophilia was not passed on to their immediate ancestors, meaning that they cannot transmit the condition to future generations. More than 120 traits in humans have now been identified as sex linked (Gardner, 1972). In addition to hemophilia and color-blindness, some other important and distinctive traits are juvenile glaucoma (hardening of the eyeball), juvenile muscular dystrophy (degeneration of certain muscles), optic atrophy (degeneration of the optic nerve), albinism, nearsightedness, and one type of night blindness.

A few final observations about genetics are in order. The preceding discussion may lead one to assume that the typical inherited characteristic is the end result of the action of a single pair of genes. However, the hereditary process normally is not that simple. Most structural and behavioral traits are determined by a constellation of genes that interact to produce a particular phenotype. This is referred to as *polygenic inheritance.* Genes in a polygenic system may occur on different chromosomes, and the contribution of each pair tends to be small and cumulative instead of all-or-none as in the case of traits determined by a single pair of genes (for example, albinism). Polygenic characteristics usually show continuous variation on a quantitative dimension. For example, height and intelligence are polygenic traits.

In Table 3-3 is a hypothetical example of the multigenetic determination of intellectual ability. Suppose that nine gene pairs influence intellectual potential. (Of course, the actual number is likely to be much larger.) Moreover,

Table 3-3. A Hypothetical Case of Multiple Gene Determination of a Trait*

Gene Pair	Father's Genes	Mother's Genes
1	bright-bright	bright-dull
2	bright-bright	bright-bright
3	bright-dull	dull-dull
4	bright-dull	dull-dull
5	bright-dull	bright-dull
6	dull-dull	bright-bright
7	bright-dull	dull-dull
8	dull-dull	bright-dull
9	dull-dull	bright-dull

Each parent can contribute only one gene out of any gene pair. Possible contributions include the following combinations.

Offspring 1		*Offspring 2*	
Offspring Gene Pair	*Father-Mother*	*Offspring Gene Pair*	*Father-Mother*
1	bright-dull	1	bright-dull
2	bright-bright	2	bright-bright
3	bright-dull	3	dull-dull
4	bright-dull	4	dull-dull
5	bright-bright	5	dull-dull
6	dull-bright	6	dull-bright
7	bright-dull	7	dull-dull
8	dull-bright	8	dull-dull
9	dull-bright	9	dull-dull

This offspring has nine of nine pairs of genes with one or more bright genes in the pair. The offspring, then, is brighter than either parent.	This offspring, on the other hand, has only three gene pairs disposing toward brightness and six double recessive pairs of genes disposing toward dullness. The offspring, then, is less able than both parents.

*For present purposes bright genes are designated as dominant.
From *Child Psychology: Behavior and Development* (3rd ed.), by R. C. Johnson and G. R. Medinnus. Copyright 1974 by John Wiley & Sons, Inc. Reprinted by permission.

imagine that each pair consists of only two possible genes; one indicates brightness and is dominant, and the second indicates dullness and is recessive. Offspring with many different genetic endowments are possible. Two possibilities are presented in Table 3-3. One can see how the intellectual level of a child can differ markedly from that of his or her parents.

There are still other phenomena that confuse the genetic picture. For example, genes are likely to have multiple effects, contributing to many different characteristics. Also, in the case of some traits, the dominant gene is not completely dominant (called *incomplete dominance*) over the other gene, resulting in a phenotype that is intermediate between that of homozygous dominant and homozygous recessive individuals. Another phenomenon occurs when genes at one locus influence (for example, mask) the expression of another pair of genes (called *epistasis*).

THE INFLUENCE OF HEREDITY ON BEHAVIOR

The answer to the question "How does heredity influence behavior?" is not a simple one. When we earlier considered the relationship between the individual's genotype and his phenotype we noted that our genes do not directly determine our traits. Rather, we pointed out that how the genetic code is enacted depends to a considerable extent on the complex interaction between the genetic instructions and the biochemical environment of the cell. Essentially, what we are saying is that one's phenotype cannot be predicted strictly on the basis of one's genotype. However, in the case of many structural (anatomical, physiological, and biochemical) characteristics the effect of heredity is pretty much a direct one. Such characteristics include those anatomical features that uniquely define the human species and certain physiological and biochemical attributes, including sex, eye color, and blood type. For these characteristics, given a specific genotype the possible range of variation is quite restricted. On the other hand, the genotype-expression relationship is much less direct with respect to some biological traits. A good example is body weight. Because of the role of such factors as quantity of food intake and exercise there is considerably more room for phenotypic variation given one's genetic predisposition.

Anne Anastasi (1958, 1973) has made similar observations in delineating some of the ways heredity can influence our behavioral or psychological attributes. In fact she suggests that the influence of heredity on behavior is indirect:

> No psychological trait is inherited as such. Through its control of the development of physical structures such as eyes, hands, or nervous system, heredity sets limits for behavior development. If some essential chemical is lacking in one of the genes, or if there is an imbalance in the proportion of different substances, a seriously defective organism may result, with stunted body and severely retarded intelligence. In such individuals, some of the minimum physical prerequisites for normal intellectual growth are lacking. Except in the case of such pathological deviants, however, heredity sets very broad limits for behavior development. Within these limits, what the individual actually becomes depends upon his environment [Anastasi, 1973, p. 4].

Therefore, according to Anastasi, heredity affects behavior indirectly through one's structural makeup, and, therefore, the mechanisms whereby heredity influences behavior necessarily fall along a *continuum of indirectness*. At one end of the continuum (the less indirect end), she includes, for instance, the kind of mental retardation that results from cerebral deficits accompanying hereditary metabolic disorders, such as phenylketonuria (PKU). An example of a more indirect influence is a case of mental retardation that is associated with hereditary deafness. In this instance, there is not a deficiency in intellectual potential; instead retardation results from the fact that deafness may interfere with the individual's normal social and educational opportunities.

On the most indirect end of the continuum Anastasi refers to those behavioral traits that develop as a function of the individual's incorporation of social stereotypes about largely hereditarily based physical characteristics. Our culture is pervaded with stereotypes regarding such biological attributes as sex, race, body shape, height, physical attractiveness, and physical disability. Social psychological research suggests that people use such stereotypes as guides for the way they interact with others, and that expectations based on such stereotypes often become self-fulfilling prophecies—individuals who are the targets of the stereotypes (for example, stereotypes that characterize members of a particular social class as below average in intelligence) tend to adapt their behaviors and/or self images to conform to them.

As the above examples imply, as the hereditary influence becomes more and more indirect, the possible variation in behavioral outcomes likewise increases because of the heightened influence of environmental variables. It is important to note that Anastasi was unable to consider hereditary influences on behavior without at the same time referring to the environment. Heredity and environment are inextricably tied together in the determination of individual differences. Whereas our genotype provides our potential, our environment determines the manner and extent to which that potential will be fulfilled.

In a short while we will take a look at the nature of environment and the importance of the interactive relationship between heredity and environment. First, however, let's consider how behavior geneticists go about ascertaining whether or not a behavioral trait has a hereditary basis to it. For illustrative purposes we will take a look at research on the genetics of criminality.

INVESTIGATING THE INFLUENCE OF HEREDITY: GENETICS AND CRIMINALITY

David Rosenthal (1975) has analyzed the evidence concerning heredity and criminal behavior. He distinguishes among three kinds of research strategy: family studies, twin studies, and adoption studies.

Family Studies

In a family study the investigator first selects a group of individuals who display the trait in question and a group that doesn't express the trait. Then he looks at the distribution of the trait among relatives of the members of the two groups. If the relatives of the group possessing the trait show a greater incidence of the trait, a genetic basis is suggested. Using this approach we typically find that the relatives of people who engage in antisocial (criminal or delinquent) behavior display an above normal level of criminality (for example, Robins, 1966). However, as you already may have surmised, family studies are fraught with a major pitfall. Because relatives not only share a common heredity but also a common environment (that is, a wide range of social experiences), it is extremely difficult, if not impossible, to rule out the possibility of environmental influences and to tie a specific trait, such as criminality, to heredity. We should note here that the fact that there often is an interrelationship between one's heredity and one's environment (that is, a "good" environment tends to accompany "good" genes) is a serious obstacle for investigators who seek to disentangle the effects of one from the other. Because of this problem, investigators tend to rely on either twin studies or adoption studies.

Twin Studies

In the most common type of twin study, the *concordance rates* of identical and same-sex fraternal twins are compared. A pair of twins is said to be concordant to the extent that they are similar with respect to a given trait. The genetic contribution to the trait is considered to be a reflection of the degree to which the concordance rates of the identical twins exceed those of the fraternal twins. The underlying rationale is that whereas identical twins are assumed to possess the same genetic endowment, fraternal twins have, on the average, 50% of their genes in common. Because both members of each pair of twins come from the same environment, environment is considered to be a constant factor, and any difference in concordance rates between identical and fraternal twins must result from genetic factors.

Table 3-4 presents the results of eight investigations conducted in different areas of the world. Criminality in these cases refers to people who have been convicted and incarcerated. Although the sample sizes are quite small in a few of the studies, the concordance rates for the identical twins are consistently higher than those for the fraternal twins, with the average rate being 54.4% and 21%, respectively. However, while these figures are consistent with the idea that hereditary factors are in part responsible for the expression of criminal behavior, they cannot be interpreted unquestionably as such. For one thing, we may question the assumption that the degree of common social experiences (environmental conditions) is the same for both types of twins. There is evidence that the routine activities of identical twins are more similar than those of fraternal twins and that parents tend to treat identical twins more alike than they do fraternal twins (Bronfenbrenner, 1975).[3] As Rosenthal suggests, identical

---

[3]An important question pertaining to the extent to which identical twins are treated more alike than fraternal twins is whether (1) the different genotypes of fraternal twins lead to greater variation in their behavior than that which occurs in genetically alike twins, and parents respond in accordance with actual behavioral differences or (2) parents react in accordance with preconceived notions that identical twins are more similar and, consequently, treat them alike. Support for the first alternative comes from an analysis by Lytton (1977) who concludes "parents respond to, rather than create, differences between the twins" (p. 459).

Table 3-4. Concordance Rates from Twin Studies of Criminality

Study	Location	Identical			Fraternal (Same-Sex Twins Only)		
		Total Pairs	Pairs Concordant	Percent Concordant	Total Pairs	Pairs Concordant	Percent Concordant
Lange (1929)	Bavaria	13	10	77	17	2	12
Legras (1932)	Holland	4	4	100	5	1	20
Rosanoff (1934)	United States	37	25	68	28	5	18
Stumpfl (1936)	Germany	18	11	61	19	7	37
Kranz (1936)	Prussia	32	21	66	43	23	54
Borgström (1939)	Finland	4	3	75	5	2	40
Yoshimasu (1961)	Japan	28	17	61	18	2	11
Christiansen (1968)	Denmark	81	27	33	137	15	11
Total		217	118	54.4	272	57	21.0

Adapted from "Heredity in Criminality," by D. Rosenthal, *Criminal Justice & Behavior*, 1975, 2, 3–21. Copyright 1975 by Sage Publications, Inc. Used by permission.

twins may have a stronger mutual identification that might lead them to have more interests in common and to engage in more similar kinds of activities. The role of environmental influences also is indicated by the finding that when the concordance rates among opposite-sex twins are considered they are not as high as the rates of same-sex twins (Crowe, 1974). The higher concordance rates among twins of the same sex presumably are due to the fact that twin boys or twin girls have more experiences in common than do twins of the opposite sex. For your interest, concordance rates regarding a number of characteristics are listed in Figure 3-4. Notice that some conditions show a relatively strong genetic component (for example, beginning of walking and hair color), whereas others do not (for example, beginning of sitting up and handedness).

The other major kind of twin study is one that involves the comparison of identical twins who were reared in the same home with identical twins who were separated soon after birth and reared in different adoptive homes. If genetic factors are predominantly responsible for the development of a trait, then the correlation for identical twins raised in different home environments should be very high, in fact just as (or almost as) high as the correlation for identical twins reared in the same home. This research design is superior to the study of fraternal and identical twins in that it does not confound heredity and environment. Unfortunately, instances involving the separation of identical twins occur rarely, thus reducing the feasibility of conducting this kind of investigation. As Rosenthal's review suggests, apparently no such study of criminality has been reported.

Adoption Studies

The adoption study also represents a more effective means of disentangling environmental and hereditary factors. Using the adoption method, an investigator is in a better position to ascertain if, in fact, heredity has an influence on the development of criminal behavior. This method involves studying infants who have been separated from their natural (biological) parents and placed with adoptive parents. In the case of criminality, the objective is to determine whether a person who has a criminal natural parent but who is brought up by noncriminal adoptive or foster parents shows a greater propensity toward antisocial behavior than offspring of noncriminal natural parents who also are placed with noncriminal adoptive or foster parents. If this is the case, then heredity is implicated.

Data from two adoption studies do indicate more criminal behavior among the offspring of the criminal parents (Crowe, 1972; Hutchings & Mednick, 1975). Crowe (1972) checked the arrest records of 104 people who as babies had been given up for adoption. The mothers of 52 of them, the experimental subjects, had been inmates in a women's reformatory at the time of birth. A significantly greater amount of antisocial activity characterized the experimental group over the control group. The offspring of the criminal offenders had more arrest records (8 versus 2), more total arrests (18 versus 2), and more traffic convictions (37 versus 21). Hutchings and Mednick (1975)

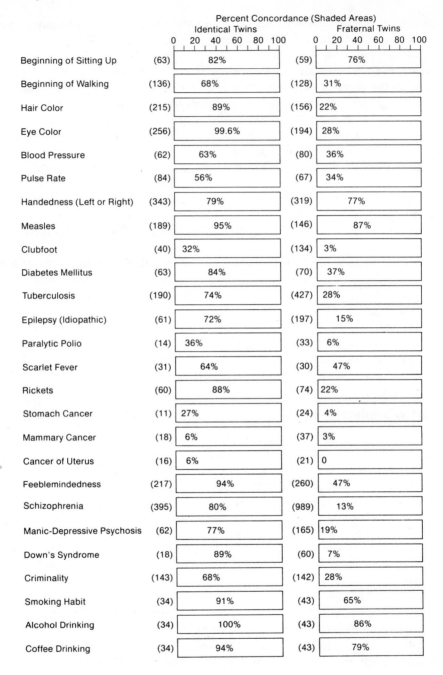

Figure 3-4. Percentage of concordance (shaded areas) among identical and fraternal twins for various traits. Figures in parentheses indicate number of twin pairs on which data are based. From *Genetics*, by M. W. Strickberger. Copyright © 1968 by Monroe W. Strickberger. Reprinted by permission of Macmillan Publishing Co., Inc.

Table 3-5. Rate of Criminality (Percentage with Criminal Records) of Natural and Adoptive Fathers of Criminal and Noncriminal Adoptees

	Fathers	
Adoptees	*Natural*	*Adoptive*
Criminal	49%	23%
Noncriminal	28%	10%

Data from "Registered Criminality in the Adoptive and Biological Parents of Registered Male Criminal Adoptees," by B. Hutchings and S. A. Mednick. In R. R. Fieve, D. Rosenthal, and H. Brill (Eds.), *Genetic Research in Psychiatry*. Baltimore: Johns Hopkins University Press, 1975.

conducted their study in Denmark. They selected 143 adoptees who had criminal records and 143 noncriminal adoptees. As shown in Table 3-5, it was found that a higher percentage of the natural fathers of the criminal adoptees (49%) had criminal records than the natural fathers of the noncriminal adoptees (28%).[4]

On the basis of the above evidence it appears that hereditary factors do contribute to the development of criminality. However, Rosenthal is careful to point out that it is unlikely that there is a single gene locus underlying all criminal behavior. Rather he favors a polygenic explanation, citing a number of examples of individual difference variables that are both genetically influenced and that may predispose one to crime. Relative to the general population, criminals tend to have a higher incidence of EEG abnormalities (often associated with poor impulse control), lower IQs, and muscular or mesomorphic body builds (see Chapter 8). All of these factors are thought to have some genetic component and may predispose one to engage in criminal activities. Also many crimes are committed by people who are psychotic or borderline psychotic or by people who are under the influence of alcohol or drugs. These characteristics likewise may have hereditary underpinnings. Rosenthal's exposition underscores a very important point, one that merits reiterating. Most probably all behavioral characteristics that have some genetic origin, including criminality, are the reflection of polygenic inheritance.

As mentioned, it is difficult to isolate the effects of heredity and environment. This was demonstrated in our review of the strategies used in the investigation of the genetics of criminal behavior. Let us now explore the meaning of environment.

NATURE OF ENVIRONMENT

Many of us have a tendency to think of our environment as comprising those physical stimuli and social psychological stimuli that are external to our persons. When viewed in this manner, our environment consists of such diverse

[4]The probable influence of the environment also is apparent in Table 3-5. Notice that there was a higher rate of criminality among the adoptive fathers of the criminal adoptees than the adoptive fathers of the noncriminal adoptees.

things as this book, the weather, the overt behavior of people around us, the child-rearing practices of our parents, the media, the values and norms of our culture, and so forth. However, for the purposes of examining the contribution of environment to the development of individual and group differences, an even broader conceptualization is needed. Actually we would not be incorrect in saying that the environment is everything that is nongenetic. Yet, while that may be true, it does not help us to conceptualize environment in a meaningful way. One useful way of viewing environment is to distinguish between intraorganic conditions and extraorganic conditions (Munn, 1965). *Intraorganic conditions* may be broken down further into intercellular and intracellular.

Intercellular conditions include such factors as the cells that surround a given cell and hormones that are secreted by the endocrine glands and carried in the blood. During the development of the organism, cells possessing the same genes may develop markedly different structures as a result of variations in the intercellular environment. For instance, animal research indicates that transplantation of cells from one part of an embryo (for example, the skin) to another part (for example, the brain) alters the course of the cells' development (that is, so that the cells become brain cells). The *intracellular* environment involves those materials, especially the cytoplasm, that surround the chromosomes. As noted earlier, genes interact with the biochemical environment of the cell to create the proteins that determine the structure and function of the cell. Furthermore, it seems that the same genetic material will produce different structures if the intracellular environment is varied (Munn, 1965).

However, although not necessarily more relevant to the study of human differences, *extraorganic conditions* (that is, environmental factors external to the individual) generally have received more attention than have intraorganic conditions. Such factors may be divided into prenatal, perinatal, and postnatal influences. For the unborn child to undergo normal growth and development it needs a healthy *prenatal* or intrauterine environment. Unfortunately there are many environmental agents that can adversely affect the embryo or fetus. For example, some kinds of drugs have been discovered to severely harm the growing fetus when taken by the mother. You may have heard about the tragedy that occurred to expectant mothers who during the 1960s took thalidomide, a nausea preventative and sleeping pill. Women who took this drug during early pregnancy often had children who, if not stillborn, suffered gross physical deformities such as very small, useless arms.

The mother's diet is another environmental influence that has been directly related to the health of the fetus. For instance, the probability of spontaneous abortions, premature births, stillbirths, and major deformities significantly increases when the maternal diet is nutritionally deficient (Knobloch & Pasamanick, 1966). Some other environmental conditions that may seriously impair the prenatal development of a child are radiation, poisons, oxygen deficit, infectious diseases in the mother (for example, German measles), incompatibility of Rh blood factors, and quite possibly maternal emotional stress, smoking, and alcohol consumption. It is quite apparent that the prenatal environment plays a critical role in the development of the organism. We should note that *perinatal* problems—those occurring during the birth process—also may have extremely harmful effects on the infant. The potentially profound impact of prenatal and perinatal factors underscores the difficulty that may be encountered in determining the causes of a congenital (existing at birth) characteristic. In the past it was customary to attribute congenital defects to bad heredity. However, as we have indicated, to do so may be to ignore prenatal or perinatal environmental influences.

Notwithstanding the possible intrusion of the aforementioned disruptive factors, the prenatal environment usually is relatively constant from individual to individual. This certainly is the case when compared with the *postnatal* environment, which as you know may vary greatly from one person to another. Another means of classifying environmental influences has been proposed by Anastasi (1973) who, incidentally, says "psychologically, the individual's environment comprises the sum total of the stimulation he receives from conception to death" (p. 6). One category of environmental conditions includes those factors that affect behavior through their physical (organic) impact on the organism; a second category includes those conditions that immediately and directly induce a change in the individual's behavior.

As with heredity, Anastasi conceives of environmental influences of an organic nature (the first category) as being represented along a continuum of indirectness with regard to their relation to behavior. For instance, on the least indirect end of the continuum would be a state of mental retardation caused by pre- or postnatal nutritional deficiencies or by cerebral birth injury. A more indirect influence might involve severe motor or speech dysfunctioning in which there is no damage to the higher neural centers. This can occur with, for example, cerebral palsy. In such a case, individuals may possess the potential for normal or even superior cognitive development, but because of the reduction of educational and social opportunities resulting from their physical handicaps, their intellectual growth is retarded. Anastasi illustrates the most indirect end of the continuum with an environmental parallel of the behavioral consequences of being the target of stereotypes based on one's biological characteristics having a hereditary origin. A person who is overweight primarily because of overeating will be subjected to the same stereotypes as one whose weight problem has a stronger genetic basis.

Anastasi's second category of environmental factors, those directly inducing behavioral change, essentially entails all those aspects of a person's sociocultural milieu that shape his or her behavior. Under this category, which is generally referred to as the social environment, fall those influences deriving from such diverse factors as one's home upbringing, social-class membership, formal education, religious upbringing, peer group relationships, social stereotypes, and exposure to mass media. As we are well aware, people, certainly to a far greater extent than animals, are especially sensitive to socialization influences. The extent of such influences is evident if we consider that many presumably "universal" (thus largely hereditary) human characteristics are much less common than was once believed and that human behavior varies greatly from culture to culture. Munn (1965), for instance, notes that aggressiveness was at one time believed to be strongly rooted in all societies (for example, McDougall proposed an "instinct of pugnacity"), but that cross-cultural evidence indicates marked aggressiveness is characteristic of some societies, whereas aggressiveness of any form is virtually absent in other societies.

Let us return momentarily to the causes of criminality. In his review of heredity in antisocial behavior, Rosenthal (1975) readily acknowledges the importance of environmental influences:

> The implication of a genetic basis underlying some criminality does not mean that an individual harboring the genotype must at some time commit a crime. Rather it is felt that most crime arises because of environmental and psychological influences, and that sociocultural factors in modern society primarily underlie the current crime wave [p. 19].

Thus, as Rosenthal points out, a genetic explanation cannot account for the burgeoning crime rate in American society. Unmistakably, the rate of crime is not caused by changes in the genotype of a population. Rather many social-environmental variables are obviously at work. Such variables include early emotional deprivation, parental rejection, broken families, and low economic status (Crowe, 1974).

At the risk of repetition, we reaffirm the very important observation that, whereas for illustrative purposes hereditary and environmental influences often are treated separately, it is much more appropriate to consider them jointly. Virtually all of our biological and behavioral traits are produced by the interaction of genetic and environmental factors.

INTERACTION BETWEEN HEREDITY AND ENVIRONMENT

In the early part of this century the nature/nurture controversy centered on the question of whether heredity or environment is responsible for individual differences in a given behavioral trait. That aspect of the controversy—whether heredity or environment is responsible for the variation in behavior—is now a dead issue as Anastasi pointed out in her classic 1958 article, "Heredity, Environment, and the Question 'How?'" Today we recognize that the development of any trait involves both environmental and genetic factors.

In its more contemporary form, the nature/nurture controversy focuses on the "heritability" of traits. Now, the question is not whether heredity or environment is responsible for the development of a trait, but what is the proportional contribution of heredity and environment. Thus, a common goal is to calculate an "estimate of heritability" that represents the proportion of the variation in a trait that is due to heredity. The most widely publicized aspect of this controversy focuses on the relative contributions of heredity and environment to general intelligence (this will be considered in detail in Chapter 5).

The question pertaining to the relative contributions of heredity and environment turns out to be more complex than it may appear on the surface.

Anastasi (1958, 1973), as well as many modern behavior geneticists (for example, Gottesman, 1968; Thompson, 1968), maintains that attempts to determine the proportional contributions of heredity and environment are futile because they are based on the assumption that heredity and environment work in an additive fashion to determine a trait (that is, trait X = 40% heredity + 60% environment). Instead there is ample evidence that heredity and environment operate in an interactive manner in determining traits—the influence of each depends on the contribution of the other. In other words, the proportional contribution of heredity to the observed variation of a trait varies, depending on the environmental conditions; likewise, the proportional contribution of environment depends on the genetic endowment of the organism.

We already have referred to the interaction between heredity and environment at a molecular level. The interactionist viewpoint also is readily applicable on a molar level. To illustrate, consider again the etiology of criminal behavior. If we have an environment that is fairly uniform in terms of those social and economic factors conducive to the development of criminal behavior, then individual differences in criminality will be largely determined by hereditary factors and conversely little determined by environmental factors. In other words, if all members of a society experience very similar environmental conditions, then differences among them in criminal behavior could be due only minimally to the environment; thus, most of the differences would have to result from differences in their genetic makeup. On the other hand, the relative contribution of heredity declines as environmental uniformity decreases and as individuals experience differential exposure to the environmental conditions that facilitate criminality.

In the previously mentioned adoption study on criminality carried out by Crowe (1972), there is suggestive evidence of the interactive effects of heredity and environment. Crowe (1974) reports in a later paper that the development of criminality was directly associated with the experience of an unfavorable environmental circumstance during infancy, namely the length of time spent in temporary care (for example, orphanages). However, the pattern of results indicated that antisocial behavior occurred in only one subgroup, those experimental subjects (that is, those whose mothers were reformatory inmates) who had experienced the adverse environmental condition of temporary care. It tended not to emerge in the other experimental subjects who had not been subjected to this condition nor in any of the control subjects, including those who had been exposed to the unfavorable condition as well as those who had not. Thus, Crowe's data suggest an interaction between heredity and environment—whether or not the criminal genotype was manifested in the individual's social behavior (phenotype) depended on whether certain environmental circumstances were present. If the adverse conditions had not been present, the criminal genotype would not have been manifested.

What we are suggesting, then, is that *heritability is not a constant property of a particular trait.* Rather it varies as a function of the genotypic nature of the population in question and the specific range of environmental conditions. The heritability of certain physical defects (for example, blindness) has increased markedly over the last century because of the elimination of some of the potential environmental causes (in the case of blindness, smallpox and other communicable diseases). Similarly, the heritability of IQ scores would be expected to increase as both the less privileged and more privileged groups are provided with more equivalent educational and socioeconomic opportunities.

The above examples indicate that the heritability estimate varies as a function of variations in the range of relevant hereditary and environmental factors. Consequently, as Anastasi (1973) notes, we cannot obtain a *generalized* estimate of the proportional contributions of heredity and environment because every estimate is based on a sample from a specific population and set of environmental conditions. Furthermore, a heritability estimate is a population statistic, meaning that we have to be careful about inferring from it anything about the determinants of an individual's traits. For example, in some cultures heredity might be estimated to account for 80% of the variation among people in the incidence of criminal behavior; however, the criminal activity of a specific person might be the consequence of predominantly environmental pressures.

The following statement by Robert Cancro (1971) very nicely summarizes our view of the nature/nurture issue:

> Both the genetic and environmental contributions are equally important because they are both indispensable. The gene can only express itself in an environment, and an environment can only evoke the genotype that is present. In this sense it may be very misleading to speak of one or the other as more important, even in theoretical terms. This statement should not be misunderstood to mean that we cannot look at a population at a given moment in time and say that the variation in the trait measured is determined more by the genes or the environment. It does mean, however, that we must generalize very carefully from such a finding. With a different population or a radically different environment the results might be totally different. Perhaps the clearest way of presenting the value and the limitation of this approach is by recognizing that a heritability measure is only useful as long as the environment is relatively constant [p. 60].[5]

Lastly, we agree with Tyler (1965) who suggests that the most important information we can obtain about a characteristic is not the proportional contribution of heredity and environment but how amenable it is to change and precisely how change can be affected. In this context, we should emphasize the importance of avoiding the assumption that traits that are strongly influenced by genetic factors are immutable (show a lack of responsiveness to environmental change), whereas characteristics with a strong environmental component are easily modifiable. Clearly *genetic* does not automatically imply a low level of modifiability, nor does *environmental* necessarily signify that a trait is readily changeable. For example, the genetically based metabolic

---

[5]From *Intelligence: Genetic and Environmental Influences*, by R. Cancro. Copyright 1971 by Grune & Stratton, Inc. Reprinted by permission.

disorder, PKU, can often be prevented by special dietary treatment, whereas anyone whose job deals with inducing positive behavior change, including social workers, psychotherapists, educators, and correction officers, is keenly aware of the rigidity of many acquired dispositions.

SUMMARY

Heredity refers to the process by which physical and psychological characteristics are transmitted from parents to offspring. The basic units of heredity are genes carried on chromosomes found in every body cell. Genes are composed of deoxyribonucleic acid (DNA). A DNA molecule has the shape of a twisted ladder, each "rung" of which consists of two of four nitrogeneous bases. It is the order and number of these pairs of bases that determine the genetic code (that is, instructions) for the development of the organism. Such processes as random assortment and crossing over guarantee that there is a tremendous amount of genetic variability among the offspring of two parents, the only exception being the case of identical twins, who have the same gene makeup because they come from the same fertilized egg. Most human characteristics are influenced by a number of genes, actually pairs of genes, rather than a single pair of genes.

Three of the commonly used methods for investigating whether or not a behavioral trait has a genetic basis are family studies, twin studies, and adoption studies. The adoption study and the study of identical twins reared apart versus together show the most promise because they enable the investigator to separate the effects of genetic factors from environmental factors.

The environment consists of all those stimuli to which the organism responds. We may distinguish between intraorganic environmental conditions and extraorganic conditions. The former may be further subdivided into intracellular and intercellular conditions and the latter into prenatal, perinatal, and postnatal conditions.

During the early part of this century, the social sciences were plagued by the so-called "nature/nurture controversy," a debate over whether heredity or environment is responsible for individual and group differences. As a historical overview indicates, it appears that the two sides of the debate were taken as much, if not more, on the basis of ideological reasons than scientific reasons. Today, it is recognized that virtually every human characteristic is influenced by both environment and heredity. In its contemporary form the nature/nurture issue centers on which factor—heredity or environment—contributes the most to the variation in given traits. However, it is now recognized that heredity and environment operate in an interactive manner; that is, the influence of one depends on the contribution of the other. It is the thesis of many contemporary behavior geneticists that it is futile to seek a generalized estimate of the proportional contribution of heredity and environment to a given trait because the contribution of each will vary with changes in the contribution of the other.

REFERENCES

Adams, M. S., & Neel, J. V. Children of incest. *Pediatrics,* 1967, *40,* 55–63.

Anastasi, A. Heredity, environment, and the question "How?" *Psychological Review,* 1958, *65,* 197–208.

Anastasi, A. *Common fallacies about heredity, environment, and human behavior.* Iowa City: American College Testing Program, 1973.

Bronfenbrenner, U. Nature with nurture: A reinterpretation of the evidence. In A. Montagu (Ed.), *Race and IQ.* New York: Oxford, 1975.

Cancro, R. Genetic contributions to individual differences in intelligence: An introduction. In R. Cancro (Ed.), *Intelligence: Genetic and environmental influences.* New York: Grune & Stratton, 1971.

Crowe, R. R. The adopted offspring of women criminal offenders: A study of their arrest records. *Archives of General Psychiatry,* 1972, *27,* 600–603.

Crowe, R. R. An adoption study of antisocial personality. *Archives of General Psychiatry,* 1974, *31,* 785–791.

Darwin, C. *On the origin of species by means of natural selection, or the preservation of favoured races in the struggle for life.* London: Murray, 1859.

Davenport, C. B. *Eugenics and charity.* Proceedings of the 39th National Conference of Charities and Corrections, 1912.

Elias, M. F. Disciplinary barriers to progress in behavior genetics: Defensive reactions to bits and pieces. *Human Development,* 1973, *16,* 119–132.

Fraser, F. C., & Nora, J. J. *Genetics of man.* Philadelphia: Lea & Febiger, 1975.

Galton, F. *Hereditary genius: An inquiry into its laws and consequences.* London: Macmillan, 1869.

Gardner, E. J. *Principles of genetics.* New York: Wiley, 1972.

Gottesman, I. I. Beyond the fringe-personality and psychopathology. In D. C. Glass (Ed.), *Genetics.* New York: Rockefeller University Press, 1968.

Grant, M. *The passing of the great race.* New York: Scribner's, 1916.

Haller, M. H. Social science and genetics: A historical perspective. In D. C. Glass (Ed.), *Genetics.* New York: Rockefeller University Press, 1968.

Hutchings, B., & Mednick, S. A. Registered criminality in the adoptive and biological parents of registered male criminal adoptees. In R. R. Fieve, D. Rosenthal, & H. Brill (Eds.), *Genetic research in psychiatry.* Baltimore: Johns Hopkins University Press, 1975.

Jensen, A. R. How much can we boost IQ and scholastic achievement? *Harvard Educational Review,* 1969, *39,* 1–123.

Johnson, R. C., & Medinnus, G. R. *Child psychology: Behavior and development.* New York: Wiley, 1974.

Kamin, L. J. *The science and politics of IQ.* Potomac, Md.: Erlbaum, 1974.

Knobloch, H., & Pasamanick, B. Prospective studies on the epidemiology of reproductive casualty: Methods, findings, and some implications. *Merrill-Palmer Quarterly of Behavior and Development,* 1966, *12,* 27–43.

Lerner, I. M. *Heredity, evolution and society.* San Francisco: Freeman, 1968.

Loehlin, J. C., Lindzey, G., & Spuhler, J. *Race differences in intelligence.* San Francisco: Freeman, 1975.

Lytton, H. Do parents create, or respond to, differences in twins? *Developmental Psychology,* 1977, *13,* 456–459.

McClearn, G. E., & DeFries, J. C. *Introduction to behavioral genetics.* San Francisco: Freeman, 1973.

McDougall, W. *Introduction to social psychology.* Boston: Luce, 1908.

McDougall, W. *Is America safe for democracy?* New York: Scribner's, 1921.

McKusick, V. A., Hosteter, J. A., Egeland, J. A., & Eldridge, R. The distribution of certain genes in the old order Amish. *Cold Spring Harbor Symposium of Quantitative Biology*, 1964, *29*, 99–114.

Mendel, G. J. Versuche über pflanzen-hybriden. *Verhandlungen des Naturforschunden Vereines in Brünn*, 1866, *4*, 3–47.

Munn, N. *The evolution and growth of human behavior.* Boston: Houghton Mifflin, 1965.

Munsinger, H. *Fundamentals of child development* (2nd ed.). New York: Holt, Rinehart & Winston, 1975.

Pai, A. C. *Foundations of genetics: A science for society.* New York: McGraw-Hill, 1974.

Pfeiffer, J. (Ed.). *The cell.* New York: Time-Life Books, 1969.

Public Health Service. *Multiple births United States—1964.* Publication No. 1000, Series 21, No. 14. Rockville, Md.: National Center for Health Statistics, 1967.

Robins, L. N. *Deviant children grown up.* Baltimore: Williams & Wilkins, 1966.

Rosenthal, D. Heredity in criminality. *Criminal Justice and Behavior*, 1975, *2*, 3–21.

Sheppard, W. C., & Willoughby, R. H. *Child behavior: Learning and development.* Chicago: Rand McNally, 1975.

Sociobiology: A new theory of behavior. *Time*, August 1, 1977, pp. 36–41.

Strickberger, M. W. *Genetics.* New York: Macmillan, 1968.

Thompson, W. R. Genetics and social behavior. In D. C. Glass (Ed.), *Genetics*. New York: Rockefeller University Press, 1968.

Tyler, L. E. *The psychology of human differences* (3rd ed.). New York: Appleton-Century-Crofts, 1965.

Watson, J. B. *Behaviorism.* Chicago: University of Chicago Press, 1959. (Originally published, 1930)

Watson, J. D., & Crick, F. H. C. Molecular structure of nucleic acids: A structure for deoxyribose nucleic acid. *Nature*, 1953, *171*, 737–738.

Wilson, E. O. *Sociobiology: The new synthesis.* Cambridge, Mass.: Harvard University Press, 1975.

Woodworth, R. S. *Contemporary schools of psychology.* New York: Ronald Press, 1948.

Part Two

Individual Differences

The Nature of
Intelligence

4

The study of individual differences in intelligence represents the earliest area of inquiry in differential psychology. Over the years intelligence has continued to be a topic of major interest, both in terms of scientific study and practical utility. To gain a perspective on the current status of the study of intelligence, we begin with a look at how this characteristic was first investigated. Then we consider the way in which intelligence is measured and defined, and how useful intelligence tests are in the prediction of achievement. At the end of the chapter we return to the task of trying to conceptualize the nature of intelligence, and consider whether intelligence is a unitary or a multidimensional trait as well as its relationship to brain functioning and stages of development. We will reserve a separate chapter (Chapter 5) to consider the extensive literature on intelligence and the heredity/environment issue.

THE ORIGINS OF STUDYING INTELLIGENCE

Recognition of the phenomenon that individuals differ in intellectual ability probably had its origins in the earliest of civilizations. However, the first known scientific inquiry into intelligence dates back only a little more than a century. In 1869, Sir Francis Galton published his book, *Hereditary Genius: An Inquiry into Its Laws and Consequences*. Galton's thesis (mentioned in Chapter 1) about the nature of exceptionally high ability—which is what he meant by "genius"—is reflected in the statement that appeared in the preface to his book.

> The idea of investigating the subject of hereditary genius occurred to me during the course of a purely ethnological inquiry, into the mental peculiarities of different races; when the fact, that characteristics cling to families, was so frequently forced on my notice as to induce me to pay especial attention to that branch of the subject. I began by thinking over the dispositions and achievements of my contemporaries at school, at college, and in after [later] life, and was surprised to find how frequently ability seemed to go by descent. Then I made a cursory examination into the kindred of about four hundred illustrious men of all periods of history, and the results were such, in my own opinion, as completely to establish the theory that genius was hereditary, under limitations that required to be investigated [Galton, 1869, p. v].

From such preliminary data, Galton went on to expand his investigation by tracing the genealogy of eminent British men in various fields of endeavor, including law, politics, science, and the arts. Based on his survey, Galton found that exceptional ability did indeed run in families and, hence, concluded that such ability is inherited. Of course, what Galton overlooked was the possible influence of environmental factors, such as the opportunities, status, and the social connections that are derived from being the progeny of an illustrious man.

Galton's conclusion regarding the hereditary basis of intelligence is not surprising when one realizes that just ten years prior to the appearance of his book, Charles Darwin, who was Galton's cousin, had produced his treatise, the *Origin of Species*. Darwin's theory of evolution was to have a profound influence on scientific and philosophical thought. Galton's view of genius as an inherited characteristic was a logical extension of Darwin's view of evolution as the survival of inherited characteristics.

Galton was not content to restrict his study of mental ability to a genealogical examination of men who were reputed to have exceptionally high ability. He was particularly interested in obtaining direct evidence of such ability and reasoned that intellectual differences are reflected in measures of sensory discrimination. In his book, *Inquiries into Human Faculty and Its Development*, Galton (1883) explained his choice of sensory sensitivity as a measure of intelligence:

The only information that reaches us concerning outward events appears to pass through the avenue of our senses; and the more perceptive the senses are of difference, the larger is the field upon which our judgment and intelligence can act. . . . Two persons may be equally able just to hear the same faint sound, and they may equally begin to be pained by the same loud sound, and yet they may differ as to the number of intermediate grades of sensation. The grades will be less numerous as the organization is of a lower order, and the keenest sensation possible to it will in consequence be less intense. . . . The discriminative faculty of idiots is curiously low; they hardly distinguish between heat and cold, and their sense of pain is so obtuse that some of the more idiotic seem hardly to know what it is. . . . The trials I have as yet made on the sensitivity of different persons confirms the reasonable expectation that it would on the whole be highest among the intellectually ablest [pp. 27–29].

Galton, in line with his view of intelligence, devised a series of methods to measure sensory and motor functioning. For example, he developed a test of weight discrimination to assess kinesthetic sensitivity, a questionnaire (probably the first use of such a method) to measure mental imagery, and a whistle (which was to become known as the "Galton Whistle") to detect the upper limits of audible pitch. Galton used these methods in his anthropometric laboratory, later moved to the South Kensington Museum in London, where the characteristics of large numbers of individuals were assessed under standardized conditions.

As noted, Galton's goal in utilizing his sensory and motor tests was to be able to identify those individuals who were the most intelligent. Moreover, consistent with his assumption that intelligence is an inherited characteristic, once the most intelligent individuals were identified, it would be possible to embark on a program of selectively mating these individuals in order to improve the quality of future generations. Galton coined the term *eugenics* to refer to this program. However, because the results of his testing program showed that individuals generally do not perform consistently across various sensory and motor tasks, Galton was not successful in achieving his goal of identifying the highly intelligent in this way.

An attempt to carry on Galton's pioneering work with sensory-motor tests was undertaken by James McKeen Cattell, an American psychologist, who had studied briefly with Galton after working with Wundt. Cattell (1890) introduced the term *mental test* and expanded the Galton measures. During the mid-1890s, Cattell (see Cattell & Farrand, 1896) administered his battery of mental tests to entering first-year students at Columbia University with the expectation that the tests would be accurate predictors of scholastic achievement. However, a devastating blow to Cattell's mental test movement came from a study by Wissler (1901). Wissler, a member of Cattell's laboratory at Columbia, found negligible correlations among the various mental tests, indicating that the tests were not measuring a unitary dimension of intelligence. Furthermore, performance on Cattell's tests was negligibly correlated with college standing, a primary criterion for establishing the validity of the measures. Thus, such tests as reaction time, naming colors, and auditory memory were not the kind of indexes that Galton and Cattell had hoped would be useful in the identification of the most intelligent individuals. Indeed, it appeared that only a few decades after Galton's pioneering ideas, the measurement of intelligence had reached a dead end. But, fortunately, during the same decade that Cattell was developing his mental tests, Alfred Binet in France was beginning to develop a more fruitful approach to the conceptualization and measurement of intelligence.

Binet was the most notable French psychologist of his generation. He was initially interested in the nature of hypnotic phenomena, and this interest developed into a more general consideration of complex mental functions. In 1894 Binet and his student, Victor Henri, began to employ a variety of tests for the purpose of identifying individual differences among school children. The next year, in an important paper that charted the course of their work, Binet and Henri (1895) proposed that individual differences could be identified only by the use of tests that assessed complex processes, such as memory, imagination, attention, comprehension, and aesthetic appreciation. Binet and Henri, therefore, were in strong disagreement with the Galton/Cattell approach to mental testing, which stressed simple sensorimotor functions.

In 1904 Binet was appointed by the French Minister of Public Instruction to a commission concerned with the problem of retardation among public school children in Paris. As a result of this appointment, Binet and his new junior collaborator, Theodore Simon, constructed a scale that yielded an overall index of intellectual functioning (Binet & Simon, 1905). This scale consisted of a variety of different tests that assessed the kinds of complex mental processes that Binet and Henri (1895) had proposed. Soon afterwards, Binet and Simon (1908) revised their 1905 scale by grouping the tests into age levels. For example, the tests that were categorized for the 7-year level were tests that normal 7-year-old children could pass. Another innovation in the 1908 revision was the use of an index, called the *mental age,* that refers to the age group that a child's test performance is equivalent to. For example, if a 6-year-old child can pass all of the tests at the 8-year level and half of the tests at the 9-year level, his or her mental age is 8½. Thus, the mental age index made it possible to indicate how retarded or advanced a child's intellectual functioning is by noting the difference between the child's chronological and mental ages. The Binet/Simon scales were revised once again in 1911, just prior to Binet's untimely death at the age of 54.

Binet's work in France did not go unnoticed elsewhere. The most influential advocate and translator of Binet's work was Henry Goddard, an American psychologist who was the director of the well-known Vineland Training School for the retarded. Several other translations and adaptations appeared in the United States during the next decade. By far the most influential one was the scale developed by Lewis Terman (1916) at Stanford University, which became known as the Stanford-Binet scale. An important feature introduced in the Stanford-Binet was the *Intelligence Quotient* or IQ. A person's IQ is his or her mental age divided by his or her chronological age, and multiplied by 100 to eliminate decimals. For instance, if a child's mental and chronological ages are equivalent, his or her IQ would be 100. An IQ of 100 represents average performance. When mental age exceeds chronological age, the IQ will be greater than 100 and reflects accelerated performance. When the mental age is below the chronological age, the IQ will be lower than 100 and reflects retarded performance.

The Stanford-Binet became the first widely used measure of intelligence in the United States and greatly influenced the development of subsequent tests. It is still in widespread use, although one early recognized limitation of the Stanford-Binet is that it can be administered to only one person at a time. With the advent of the First World War, there was a demand by the armed forces for large-scale testing. A committee of psychologists, including Terman, was appointed, and the committee was responsible for the development of the first tests of intelligence for group administration (the Army Alpha and the Army Beta tests).

THE MEASUREMENT AND DEFINITION OF INTELLIGENCE

As we have seen, intelligence can be measured by individual or group tests. Among the individual tests, the Stanford-Binet, which is primarily designed for assessing children, has gone through several revisions (the 1960 revision is the most recent). Other individual tests were developed by David Wechsler. The first Wechsler scale, the Wechsler-Bellevue Intelligence Scale, was specifically developed to assess adults (Wechsler, 1939). The Wechsler-Bellevue was subsequently revised in 1955 and retitled the Wechsler Adult Intelligence Scale (WAIS). In 1950 the first Wechsler test for children appeared—the Wechsler Intelligence Scale for Children (WISC). The group intelligence tests, such as the Otis and Henmon-Nelson, differ from the individual tests in the type of item response; that is, group tests are composed of multiple-choice items, whereas individual tests consist of open-ended questions. However, all intelligence tests tend to be similar in content. To give you an idea of the content covered in intelligence tests, brief descriptions of the 11 subtests included in the WAIS are shown in Table 4-1.

Intelligence tests are typically scored in terms of a total IQ score. Note in Table 4-1 that the subtests in the WAIS are organized into verbal and performance or nonverbal scales. (This is also true for the other Wechsler tests.) The Wechsler tests provide separate IQ scores for verbal ability and performance ability as well as a total IQ score that essentially represents a combination of the two.

IQ scores on intelligence tests are now based on standard scores rather than on the ratio of mental age to chronological age. The latest revision of the Stanford-Binet involved replacing the ratio IQ with the standard score version, and the Wechsler tests utilized the standard IQ scores from the beginning. Recall from Chapter 2 that a standard score is based on the standard deviation. The IQ in the form of a standard score is therefore called the *deviation IQ*. A deviation IQ always has a mean of 100. The standard deviation

Table 4-1. Description of Subtests on the Wechsler Adult Intelligence Scale

Verbal Scale

1. *Information:* Twenty-nine questions covering a wide variety of information that adults have presumably had an opportunity to acquire in our culture. An effort was made to avoid specialized or academic knowledge. It might be added that questions of general information have been used for a long time in informal psychiatric examinations to establish the individual's intellectual level and his practical orientation.
2. *Comprehension:* Fourteen items, in each of which the examinee explains what should be done under certain circumstances, why certain practices are followed, the meaning of proverbs, and so on. The subtest is designed to measure practical judgment and common sense.
3. *Arithmetic:* Fourteen problems similar to those encountered in elementary school arithmetic. Each problem is orally presented and is to be solved without the use of paper and pencil.
4. *Similarities:* Thirteen items requiring the subject to say in what way two things are alike.
5. *Digit Span:* Orally presented lists of three to nine digits are to be orally reproduced. In the second part, the examinee must reproduce lists of two to eight digits backwards.
6. *Vocabulary:* Forty words of increasing difficulty are presented both orally and visually. The examinee is asked what each word means.

Performance Scale

7. *Digit Symbol:* This is a version of the familiar code-substitution test that has often been included in nonlanguage intelligence scales. The key contains nine symbols paired with the nine digits. With this key before him, the examinee has ninety seconds to fill in as many symbols as he can under the numbers on the answer sheet.
8. *Picture Completion:* Twenty-one cards, each containing a picture from which some part is missing. Examinee must tell what is missing from each picture.
9. *Block Design:* This subtest uses a set of cards containing designs in red and white and a set of identical one-inch blocks whose sides are painted red, white, and red-and-white. The examinee is shown one design at a time, which he must reproduce by choosing and assembling the proper blocks.
10. *Picture Arrangement:* Each item consists of a set of cards containing pictures to be rearranged in the proper sequence so as to tell a story.
11. *Object Assembly:* In each of the four parts of this subtest, cutouts are to be assembled to make a flat picture of a familiar object.

Adapted from *Psychological Testing* (4th Ed.), by A. Anastasi. Copyright © 1976 by Anne Anastasi. Used by permission of Macmillan Publishing Co., Inc.

varies somewhat from test to test. On the Wechsler tests the standard deviation is 15, and on the Stanford-Binet it is 16. Thus, a total IQ of 115 on the WISC represents performance that is one standard deviation above the mean. The advantage of the deviation IQ over the ratio IQ is that, with the former but not necessarily the latter, the standard deviation is equivalent for different age groups. Therefore, a 10-year-old with a WISC IQ (that is, a deviation IQ) of 115 is one standard deviation above the mean of his or her age group,

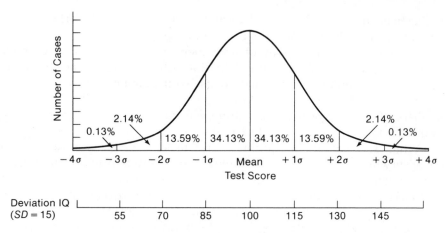

Figure 4-1. Relationship between deviation IQ and test scores in a normal distribution. Adapted from *Psychological Testing* (4th Ed.), by A. Anastasi. Copyright © 1976 by Anne Anastasi. Used by permission of Macmillan Publishing Co., Inc.

and the same holds for a 12-year-old with a WISC IQ of 115. Figure 4-1 illustrates how the deviation IQ relates to a normal distribution.

An inspection of Figure 4-1 also gives us an indication of how IQ scores are distributed in the general population. Two standard deviation units below and above the mean (the lower and upper 2.14%) are generally viewed as the cutoff points for the extreme ranges of IQ. Thus, mental retardation is defined in terms of IQs that are two or more standard deviation units below the mean (for example, 70 or below on the Wechsler scales). Within the range of mental retardation the following distinctions are made: (1) mild retardation, between 2 and 3 standard deviation units below the mean; (2) moderate retardation, between 3 and 4 standard deviation units below the mean; (3) severe retardation, between 4 and 5 standard deviation units below the mean; and, (4) profound retardation, greater than 5 standard deviation units below the mean (Grossman, 1973). There is no generally accepted classification scheme within the superior range of IQ (Anastasi, 1976).

A question that arises out of the measurement of intelligence concerns the extent to which intelligence tests reflect the definition of what intelligence is. This question has been a subject of debate going back to the period just after the First World War when the intelligence testing movement had become well established. Some psychologists, most notably Boring (1923), took the position that intelligence is what intelligence tests measure. Others were more interested in trying to relate intelligence tests to a definition of what the concept of intelligence represents. However, considerable uncertainty was expressed about how to conceptualize intelligence. Indicative of this problem was what transpired at a symposium held in 1921.[1] Fourteen leading investigators of

[1]Portions of the symposium are reprinted in Tyler (1969).

intelligence, including Terman, Thorndike, Thurstone, and Yerkes, were invited to discuss their conceptions of "intelligence" and how it could best be measured. Little in the way of agreement was contained in the opinions of the 14 participants. Among the definitions offered were some that emphasized abstract thinking, some that focused on adaptability to new circumstances, and some that considered intelligence to be the ability to learn. The members of the symposium also disagreed concerning whether intelligence is a unitary trait or an average of several separate abilities.

While the definitional problem still needed to be resolved, the psychologists who were working with intelligence tests were primarily interested in the pragmatics of what the tests could actually predict. What were the test developers trying to measure? It was generally agreed that intelligence tests should predict school success. Binet's objective in developing his scales was to identify mentally retarded children—children who were unable to profit from the standard curriculum of the French public schools. Terman's goal was to go beyond the identification of mental retardation. He adapted Binet's test so that it could differentiate among the intellectual levels in the normal population. In order to do this, Terman increased the difficulty of the Binet items so that noticeable differences emerged among normal children at each age level. It was then possible to determine the success of the Stanford-Binet as a predictor of school success for the normal population.

In our consideration of individual differences in intelligence, it is critical to make a distinction between the concept of intelligence and measures of intelligence. This distinction is necessary, because, as we have seen, intelligence tests were developed from the standpoint of predictive validity. That is, the tests are designed to measure skills and abilities that are required for school success and success in later life. However, what intelligence tests in fact measure may be only a subset of the kinds of things that are referred to in traditional definitions of intelligence. For example, does doing well on intelligence-test items, such as those described in Table 4-1, mean that one will be able to adapt easily to new circumstances? As yet we don't have any clear answer to such a question. Adaptability to novel situations is not typically a skill covered in school curricula, and so it has not served as a criterion with which intelligence measures have been compared. At this point, it seems best to define what intelligence tests measure simply as a readiness to profit from the formal school learning experience. It is possible that future work may determine whether the tests measure other aspects of the concept of intelligence.

INTELLIGENCE AND ACHIEVEMENT

As we have indicated, intelligence tests were originally developed to predict successful performance in school. Therefore, it is not surprising that the common criterion used to establish the predictive validity of IQ tests has been success in school. Another common criterion is the IQ tests' ability to predict occupational achievement. Finally, since definitions of intelligence often include the notion of learning ability, IQ test performance has been studied in relation to measures of learning.

Intelligence and School Achievement

In general, performance on intelligence tests and school grades show a moderately high relationship to each other. Both individual and group tests correlate about .50 with school marks (Tyler, 1965). Some qualifications need to be added to this overall finding. One is that verbal tests tend to correlate more highly with school grades than nonverbal or performance tests. Another qualification is that predictions of grades over short periods of time are more accurate than predictions of grades over long periods of time. Moreover, grades in some school subjects (for example, English and science) are more closely related to IQ scores than grades in other subjects (for example, geometry, music, and art). Despite these differences, there is a general consistency in the magnitude of the correlations between intelligence-test scores and school grades. This kind of consistency provides impressive evidence that performance on intelligence tests does reflect a general intellectual factor which serves as the basis for success in school (see Chapter 6 for an extended discussion of the prediction of school achievement).

When intelligence tests are related to tests of school achievement, the correlations are somewhat higher than they are in the case of school grades. This is especially true with group intelligence tests, which correlate as high as .80 with standardized measures of school achievement (Tyler, 1965). The higher correlations for group than for individual IQ tests are most likely due to the greater dependence of the group tests on reading skill. Intelligence-test scores have also been evaluated in terms of their success in predicting long-term academic progress. A number of studies have shown a relationship between scores on intelligence tests given in grade school and the amount of education eventually completed (Tyler, 1965). For example, among high school students those who drop out at the ninth-grade level score lower than those who complete the twelfth grade. In addition, students who attend college score higher than those who stop after completing high school.

The consistent evidence of a relationship between tested intelligence and indexes of school achievement confirms our previously mentioned conclusion that IQ tests measure the readiness to profit from the formal school learning experience. This readiness is based on a relatively broad area of learning that has been acquired from informal learning experiences, such as being read to by parents and playing with a variety of toys and games. In contrast, an achievement test assesses the specific knowledge and skills taught in school (see Chapter 6). If one has been able to acquire a wide range of skills as reflected by a high score on an intelligence test, the evidence suggests that the probability is high that one will be successful in acquiring the specific skills taught in school.

A study by Crano, Kenny, and Campbell (1972) provides some clarification on the direction of causation between intelligence and school achievement. These investigators worked with a large-scale sample of suburban school children who had been given both intelligence and achievement tests in grades 4 and 6. The results showed that the correlation of .73 between grade 4 intelligence and grade 6 achievement was significantly higher than the correlation of .70 between grade 4 achievement and grade 6 intelligence. (Although the correlations are close in size, the difference is statistically significant because of the large sample size of 3994.) These results indicate that intelligence-test performance can better predict future achievement-test performance than achievement-test performance can predict future intelligence-test performance. Such a result is consistent with the notion that tested intelligence reflects a readiness to profit from the formal school instruction to be provided at a future time. We should add that the high correlation between grade 4 achievement and grade 6 intelligence also means that intelligence-test performance later on in school is influenced by previous exposure to school instruction.

An important issue in considering the relationship between tested intelligence and school achievement is the influence of social class. It appears that both intelligence-test performance and school achievement are largely affected by socioeconomic background factors (Cronin, Daniels, Hurley, Kroch, & Webber, 1975). Therefore, there is reason to believe that the demonstrated relationship between IQ and school success can for the most part be accounted for by socioeconomic status and the attitudes that are associated with such status. If a student comes from an upper-class background, he or she is more likely to do well on an intelligence test and in school performance than a student who comes from a lower-class background. In fact, the developers of intelligence tests biased their tests against the lower social classes. For example, in developing the Stanford-Binet, Terman used correlations between test performance and social class as a means of establishing the validity of his test. His confidence in the validity of the Stanford-Binet was increased by the evidence that high test scores were associated with high social-class standing.

The developers of intelligence tests, however, should not really be faulted for building a social-class bias into their tests. They were trying to predict school success, which itself is an important consequence of social-class background. It should also be noted that although there is a bias in IQ tests in favor of middle- and upper-class children, the bias may not be as great as some believe it to be. Many children from low social-class backgrounds score exceptionally well on IQ tests (McCall, 1975; see also Chapter 12).

Intelligence and Occupational Achievement

As was true in the case of school achievement, intelligence tests generally show a consistent and moderately high relationship with indexes of occupational achievement (Tyler, 1965). The criterion of occupational achievement most often used has been a ranking of the prestige value of occupations in which professional jobs rank at the top and unskilled jobs at the bottom. In a study by Ball (1938), ratings on a standardized scale of occupational status were obtained for a sample of about 200 men who had taken a group intelligence test when they were children. The time interval between the testing and the measure of status was 14 years in some cases and 19 years in other cases. For the group with a 14-year interval, the correlation between IQ and occupational status was .57, whereas for the group with a 19-year interval the correlation was .71. The higher correlation for the latter group, which was the older group, suggests that with time there is a tendency towards achieving a closer correspondence between occupational status and tested intelligence. The results of other studies have also demonstrated a relationship between tested intelligence and occupational status (see Chapter 12). Nevertheless, it should be noted that a great deal of IQ variability exists within occupational groups, so that many unskilled workers score just as high as professionals (Tyler, 1965).

The relationship between measured intelligence and occupational status most likely reflects the same social-class bias we commented on with respect to school achievement. It has been argued that social-class background is the primary determinant of occupational status (Cronin et al., 1975; McClelland, 1973). Therefore, in contrast to a lower-class background, a middle or upper social-class background makes it more likely that a child will perform well on an intelligence test, go on to do well in school, and eventually take advantage of the opportunities for higher education—all of which should finally result in being able to achieve a high level of occupational status.

In addition to occupational prestige, a variety of other indexes of occupational achievement have been studied in relation to intelligence, including income, career accomplishment, and vocational job competence. With respect to income, evidence from one study indicated that, among individuals with some college education, those who as children scored in the top 10% on an intelligence test earned higher incomes than those who scored lower in intelligence (Tyler, 1974). As for career accomplishment, follow-up studies of Terman's (1925) classic investigation of gifted children (they had an IQ of at least 140) have shown that as adults (with an average age of 50) this group attained high levels of accomplishment. For instance, some were listed in *Who's Who in America* and others held important administrative positions. This was more true of men than of women, because the majority of women in the sample were homemakers (Oden, 1968; Terman & Oden, 1959).

The research relating intelligence-test performance and job competence within given occupations is rather dated (most of the studies were carried out in the 1920s) and based mainly on clerical, sales, and factory jobs (Brody & Brody, 1976). The general lack of recent data and the emphasis on jobs at the lower levels of occupational status probably reflects the difficulties of trying to assess job competence at higher levels. Ratings by supervisors of on-the-job performance are most typically used as measures of job competence, but such ratings are subject to biases, such as tendencies on the rater's part to be too lenient or too severe in making his or her ratings. Furthermore, for high-prestige occupations, such as professional and managerial jobs, ratings by supervisors are often inappropriate because professionals and managers direct much of their own work. Consequently, we have a problem of deciding what the level of good job performance is for such occupational groups as lawyers, physicians, and business executives. Still another problem in evaluating job performance for high-prestige occupations is the fact that individuals who enter these occupations have been highly selected on the basis of their ability; that is, they are primarily representative of the upper range of intelligence in the general population. Thus, we don't have the opportunity to determine whether or not individuals who obtain low scores on intelligence tests could be successful in occupations such as medicine or law.

With the limitations we have noted, the results show that for low-status jobs, such as those involved in doing factory work, little relationship exists between intelligence-test scores and success on the job—a finding that is not unexpected in view of the routine nature of most of these jobs and their lack of intellectual challenge. For some middle-status jobs, most notably clerical jobs, correlations between test scores and job competence tend to be fairly high (around .45). On the other hand, middle-status jobs involving sales show negligible relationships with intelligence, suggesting that sales competence is based on nonintellective characteristics, perhaps, for example, being assertive and outgoing. The few studies of high-prestige occupations, in which the criterion consisted of ratings by colleagues, also show negligible relationships between intelligence-test scores and indexes of job effectiveness. As noted, the restricted range of ability for high-prestige occupations makes it difficult to test the predictive validity of intelligence tests for these groups.

In summary, people who score high on intelligence tests are more likely to attain higher status jobs, earn a higher income, and achieve higher levels of career accomplishment than people who score relatively low on intelligence tests. On the other hand, intelligence-test performance generally shows little relationship to job competence. The major exception is with clerical jobs, in which intelligence-test scores are predictive of the level of competence.

Intelligence and Learning Ability

Because intelligence tests have been shown to predict school success and those aspects of occupational status that are dependent on school success, it seems reasonable to infer that intelligence tests measure one aspect of a person's ability to learn. Yet, it is not exactly clear what an ability to learn really means. Does it mean the rate at which a person can learn something, or the amount that he or she can learn? Perhaps it refers to differences in the way in which things are learned? Several investigators have attempted to clarify the aspects of learning that are being assessed by intelligence tests.

In a series of studies, Woodrow (1938, 1939, 1940) investigated the relationship between performance on intelligence tests and the *rate at which material is learned.* Students were given a number of practice sessions on several tasks, such as adding numbers and the use of digits as symbols. Intelligence tests were administered before and after the series of practice sessions. No significant relationship was found between tested intelligence and rate of learning for any of the learning tasks. Further evidence of a lack of association between intelligence and rate of learning is contained in research on programmed learning, that is, learning material through the use of automated teaching devices such as "teaching machines" (Tyler, 1965). It seems quite clear, then, that, at least with relatively simple tasks such as those used by Woodrow and in programmed learning, intelligence-test performance is not related to the rate at which one learns.

The relationship between intelligence and the *amount of learning* depends on the complexity of the material. While studies of programmed learning generally indicate no relationship between IQ and how much material has been learned, other evidence shows that a relationship does appear when complex material is presented to individuals representing different levels of intelligence (Tyler, 1965). Apparently, when the material is complex there are limits as to what can be taught to individuals below some minimal level of intelligence. For example, in one study, a program of molecular physics was presented to first graders. The extent to which this material was learned was clearly associated with tested intelligence.

Another way of looking at the role of task complexity is dealt with in a study by Tilton (1949). Tilton was interested in looking at learning ability in terms of being able to progress from simple to more complex tasks. He pointed out that this is a much more realistic measure of learning ability than measures that are limited to the effect of practice on simple tasks. In order to assess the learning of complex material, Tilton measured the improvement in the scores obtained by seventh-grade students on a history test during an 11-week period of history instruction. After eliminating the easier items on the test (those initially answered by at least 45% of the group), he found a correlation of .49 between IQ level and the gains made on the history test. Those students who had higher IQs were able to master the more difficult material.

What emerges from the research on measured intelligence and indexes of learning is that when difficult and complex material is presented to learners, intelligence level does predict fairly successfully who the better learners will be. Research also suggests that there may be differences in *the way in which learning occurs* in bright and less intelligent individuals. Osler and Fivel (1961) studied the performance of intellectually average and superior children on tasks involving the learning of concepts. With groups of 6-, 10-, and 14-year-old children, they found that the high-IQ children were more adept at learning concepts. This was interpreted as indicating that, unlike children of lower ability, highly intelligent children use a process of hypothesis formation and testing; that is, in learning a concept, they identify what the problem is and then go about solving it. A follow-up study by Osler and Weiss (1962) replicated the original findings and also added a condition in which explicit instructions were given that spelled out the nature of the problem. Such instruction eliminated the need on the part of the children to identify the problem. Under these conditions, no differences were found in the problem-solving ability of the average and superior children. Apparently, highly intelligent children are better able than other children to formulate the nature of a problem; however, once the problem is defined, children with average and superior intelligence scores are equally proficient at problem solving.

That the manner or style of learning differs between high-IQ and low-IQ individuals is also suggested by Whimbey (1976). He reports that college students with high IQ scores tend to use a sequential-reasoning process; that is, if they are confused at first they try to work out the problem step-by-step until they come up with the right answer. In contrast, students with lower IQs are almost completely passive in their thinking, and show little reliance on reasoning as a method of solving problems. They spend little time considering a problem, but rather choose an answer on the basis of a few clues or an initial impression. In conclusion, style of learning in terms of hypothesis formation and reasoning skills seems to be reflected in measured intelligence. Indeed, if reasoning skills are emphasized by parents in bringing up their children, such an emphasis is more likely to appear at the higher levels of socioeconomic status. When we conclude that social-class background is a significant contributor to the relationship between intelligence-test scores and school and occupational achievement, it seems very likely that a part of that background is the learning style to which one is exposed.

ISSUES IN CONCEPTUALIZING INTELLIGENCE

Up to this point our focus has been on general measures of intelligence. As we have seen, these standard measures of intelligence do not necessarily encompass all of the aspects that definitions of intelligence have included. Intelligence tests seem to be heavily weighted with the skills required for scholastic success. In this section, we shall consider some issues related to the conceptualization of intelligence. These issues deal with the following: (1) the varieties of intelligence, (2) the physiological basis of intelligence, and (3) the possibility of qualitative changes in intelligence during the early years of development.

Varieties of Intelligence

When intelligence tests were first developed, there was recognition that individuals would have varying strengths and weaknesses across the several kinds of skills assessed by these tests. However, it was the pragmatics of having to differentiate the overall level of intellectual functioning among school children that led Binet to introduce a single score or index of intelligence. When the Wechsler tests were introduced, an innovation in scoring was included so that, in addition to the total IQ, separate IQs could be obtained for the verbal and the performance subtests. Wechsler (1950) reported a correlation of .67 between the verbal and performance halves of the Wechsler-Bellevue test for adults. Correlations of similar magnitude have been reported for various age groups on the Wechsler Intelligence Scale for Children. The size of these correlations indicates that the verbal and performance aspects of measured intelligence are not identical, although it also shows that there is much that is common between the two. Such correlational evidence then suggests that intelligence is not a unidimensional characteristic. Rather, intelligence seems to consist of at least two partially related kinds of ability.

Other evidence suggesting that intelligence is not unidimensional comes from reports of uneven performance across measured abilities. There have been several case studies of mentally retarded individuals who display an unusually high level of skill on certain tasks, but otherwise perform within the range of mental retardation (for example, Anastasi & Levee, 1959; Scheerer, Rothmann, & Goldstein, 1945). Individuals manifesting such marked unevenness have been referred to as "idiots savants." For example, in one case a young man became an accomplished pianist and composer despite having a tested IQ of 70. In another case an eleven-year-old boy had unusual numerical skills as well as good musical aptitude, but had an IQ of only 50.

Still other evidence suggesting the multidimensionality of intelligence is the differential rates of decline on the various subtests of the Wechsler scales (Wechsler, 1950). Beyond the ages of 45 to 50 the means on verbal subtests generally hold up more than those on performance subtests. If intelligence is a unitary trait, we would expect that both of these abilities would decline at the same rate.

To obtain a complete perspective of the dimensional makeup of intelligence, it is necessary to gather a great deal of correlational evidence. The various kinds of items that are included in intelligence tests need to be intercorrelated with one another so that combinations or clusters of items can be identified. Such item-clusters would be based on sets of items that correlate highly with one another and show low correlations with other kinds of items. These clusters would then indicate the kinds of relatively separate dimensions that contribute to the total makeup of intelligence. The mathematical technique of *factor analysis* (see Chapter 2) serves the purpose of identifying the dimensions or factors that can emerge from a set of item correlations.

Let us now consider the factor analytic investigations that have been carried out with respect to intelligence. Historically, factor analysis was first developed in Britain, and we will therefore initially consider the British approach. Then we will look at the approach that was adopted by American psychologists when they started their factor analytic work on intelligence.

Spearman and the British Approach. The originator of the factor analytic method was the British psychologist Charles Spearman. Spearman (1904) conceived of intelligence as being composed of two kinds of factors. Underlying all of the various types of intellectual activity was a common factor that he called general intelligence or "g." In addition, each type of intellectual task had a unique component that he labeled a specific factor or "s." In his book *The Abilities of Man,* Spearman (1927) presented data to support his two-factor conceptualization of intelligence. He concluded from his correlational analyses of a variety of tests that what was common to the tests was the factor of "g." He also concluded that "g" was most directly measured by items that required the use of reasoning, that is, where the individual was called upon to determine the relationship between two things.

Spearman's work was developed further by Burt (1940). Burt went beyond the two-factor approach of Spearman by introducing the notion that there were intermediate factors between the common factor of general intelligence ("g") and the task-specific factors ("s"). These intermediate or group factors represented the distinction between verbal and nonverbal abilities. Evidence in support of these group factors was presented by Burt (1949) and Vernon (1950). Both Burt and Vernon conceptualized the structure of intelligence in terms of a hierarchical model. This model is illustrated by Vernon's diagram shown in Figure 4-2. At the top of the hierarchy is the most general source of variation, the general intelligence factor or "g." Next, in descending order are the two major group factors identified as verbal/educational ("v:ed") and spatial/mechanical ("k:m"). These two factors contribute much of the variance to verbal and nonverbal tasks, respectively. Within each of the two major group factors are further differentiations. The verbal/educational factor is broken down into its verbal and educational components, while the spatial/mechanical factor is broken down into its spatial and mechanical components. Further differentiations within these components constitute the specific factors (Spearman's "s") inherent in the tasks utilized. Not all of the factors in the Vernon hierarchical model will necessarily appear in a given factor analysis of intelligence tests. The emerging factors will depend on the kinds of tests included. If primarily tests that emphasize verbal tasks are included in a factor analysis, most of the variance will be accounted for by the "g" and "v:ed" factors.

The British approach emphasizes the general intelligence and major group factors. The more narrow factors at the lower levels of the hierarchy are seen as important sources of variance only when specific predictions about job performance are needed or if one is interested in research about narrow kinds of abilities.

Thurstone's "Primary Mental Abilities." The leading developer of factor analytic techniques in America was L. L. Thurstone. Starting in the 1930s, Thurstone developed a particular factor analytic solution that identified a group of separate factors all of which were at the same level of generality. This was in contrast with the type of solution used by the British investigators, which produced a hierarchical set of factors of ascending generality.

Thurstone (1938) gathered evidence to test out his views on intelligence by administering a battery of 56 different kinds of ability tests to a sample of 240 volunteer college students. Nine factors emerged from the factor analysis of the tests. Thurstone called them the "primary mental abilities." A subsequent study was conducted by Thurstone and Thurstone with a sample of 1154 eighth-grade children and a similar battery of tests (L. L. Thurstone & T. G. Thurstone, 1941). In this study seven of the original nine factors were replicated, thus providing support for the generality of most of the factors across different

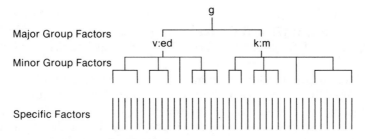

Figure 4-2. Diagram illustrating hierarchical structure of human abilities. From *The Structure of Human Abilities,* by P. E. Vernon. Copyright 1950 by Methuen & Co., Ltd. Reprinted by permission.

age groups. Further confirmation was indicated in a study that identified six of the primary factors for a sample of kindergarten children (T. G. Thurstone, 1941).

The seven primary ability factors identified for both the college students and the eighth-graders were as follows:

S. *Space:* Facility in spatial and visual imagery.
P. *Perceptual Speed:* Quick and accurate noting of visual details.
N. *Number:* Speed and accuracy in making arithmetic computations.
V. *Verbal Meaning:* Understanding of ideas and meanings of words.
W. *Word Fluency:* Speed in manipulating single and isolated words.
M. *Memory:* Facility in rote memory of words, numbers, letters, and other materials.
I. *Inductive Reasoning:* Ability to abstract a rule common to a set of particulars.

Subsequent investigations of the Thurstone factors by other researchers have most clearly confirmed the Space, Number, Verbal Meaning, and Memory factors. The identity of the Perceptual Speed and Inductive Reasoning factors is particularly unclear. As Tyler (1965) has observed, the low intercorrelations among the tests contributing to each of these two factors found in the original studies suggests the presence of several factors of both perception and reasoning.

Guilford's "Structure of Intellect." One of the trends of factor analytic research in abilities during the 1940s was to narrow the scope of the kinds of tests included in a given factor analysis. Instead of using a wide variety of tests as Thurstone had done, some investigators chose test batteries consisting of tests that were fairly similar to one another. The results of such investigations frequently identified several factors in an ability area where Thurstone had identified only one or two factors. For example, Carroll (1941) demonstrated the existence of nine verbal factors, whereas Thurstone had reported only two.

The most systematic and ambitious program of research along the lines of identifying more specific group factors was the work of Guilford and his associates. Guilford's preliminary work was carried out with the Army Air Force (Guilford & Lacey, 1947), and the results of his subsequent research program at the University of Southern California have been summarized in two books (Guilford, 1967; Guilford & Hoepfner, 1971).

In order to provide a framework for the increasing number of factors being identified in his research, Guilford developed his structure-of-intellect model. This model is based on three dimensions or categories, as shown in Figure 4-3. At the top of the cube in Figure 4-3 is the mode of categorizing mental abilities based on the *operations* utilized by an individual as he or she processes information. Guilford identified five types or classes of operations: (1) cognition (awareness, recognition), (2) memory (retention), (3) divergent production (generating information and arriving at various solutions to a problem), (4) convergent production (processing information in a way that leads to the one right answer), and (5) evaluation (making comparisons according to a criterion).

At the bottom of the cube is the dimension based on the *contents* or material presented to the individual as he or she processes information. There are four classes of contents: (1) figural (shapes, colors, sizes), (2) symbolic (signs, codes), (3) semantic (meaningful words), and (4) behavioral (information processed about the behavior of other people).

Along the vertical axis of the cube is the dimension based on the *products* or the kinds of answers a person is asked to produce. There are six kinds of products: (1) units (things, wholes), (2) classes (sets of units), (3) relations (relations between units), (4) systems (arrangements of units, sequences), (5) transformations (shifts in meaning), and (6) implications (inferences, foresights).

Guilford's structure-of-intellect model allows for the possibility of 120 factors, which are based on the total number of combinations of operations, contents, and products ($5 \times 4 \times 6$). In Guilford's research almost all of these factors have been identified. However, there are some areas where the kinds of tests that might lead to the identification of factors have not as yet been developed. This gap is particularly apparent in the behavioral type of contents that reflects what is generally thought of as social intelligence. Guilford (1967) reports very few factors involving behavioral abilities.

Perhaps the most interesting factors to emerge from Guilford's work are those involving divergent production. Traditional intelligence tests have been based on questions involving only one right answer. In tests that have high loadings on divergent production, the task is to generate a variety of solutions to a given problem. Divergent production, therefore, seems to reflect the kind of ability that has generally been associated with creativity (see Chapter 7 for a discussion of creativity).

Second-Order Factors. The identification of various primary abilities or group factors has led some factor analytic researchers to consider the possibility that such factors are not completely independent of one another. The procedure that can be utilized to study the possible interrelation among group

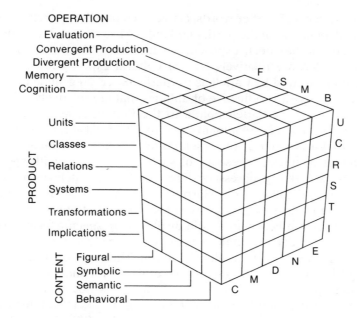

OPERATION
Evaluation
Convergent Production
Divergent Production
Memory
Cognition

Units
Classes
Relations
Systems
Transformations
Implications

PRODUCT

CONTENT
Figural
Symbolic
Semantic
Behavioral

Figure 4-3. Guilford's structure-of-intellect model. From *The Nature of Human Intelligence*, by J. P. Guilford. Copyright 1967 by McGraw-Hill, Inc. Reprinted by permission of McGraw-Hill Book Company.

factors involves obtaining scores on each of the factors in question, intercorrelating these scores, and then factor analyzing the correlation matrix. What such a procedure amounts to is a factor analysis of factors, with the result that any factors that emerge are "second-order" factors reflecting what is common to a set of primary or group factors. Thurstone (1944) noted that the identification of a second-order factor from a set of primary factors would support both Spearman's notion of a general intelligence or "g" factor and his own conception of intelligence as a set of primary mental abilities. The "g" factor, a second-order factor, would reflect what was common among the primary mental abilities. However, factor analytic studies of primary factors produced more than one second-order factor. For example, Rimoldi (1948, 1951) reported three second-order factors in an analysis of a large number of tests given to Argentine school children.

One program of research that has rather consistently identified a set of second-order factors is the work of R. B. Cattell and his associates. In Cattell's (1971) factor analytic research with test batteries that include the Thurstone tests of primary mental abilities, two second-order factors have emerged. Cattell views these two factors as different aspects of general intelligence. One factor is designated *crystallized intelligence* and the other *fluid intelligence*. The crystallized-intelligence factor is predominantly made up of tests reflecting verbal, numerical, and reasoning skills; the fluid-intelligence factor loads most highly on tests of abstract and relational skills that seem to be relatively independent of previous experience. In other words, crystallized intelligence reflects abilities that are more dependent on the particular kinds of learning and training experiences to which one has been exposed. On the other hand, fluid intelligence reflects abilities that are relatively free of cultural experiences. Fluid intelligence is therefore viewed by Cattell as primarily based on genetic endowment. Furthermore, because it is reflective of abilities that are relatively independent from cultural influences, Cattell points to the fluid-intelligence factor as an appropriate basis for the development of culture-fair tests of intelligence.[2]

An issue that arises out of the research on second-order factors of intelligence is whether or not the presence of such factors varies with age. Garrett (1946) hypothesized that progressive differentiation of intelligence occurs as people age. It would follow from Garrett's hypothesis that the second-order factors should show up to a greater extent in samples of young children than in samples of older subjects who should display more specific factors. Garrett's research provided evidence that there is more of a "g" factor (the second-order factor) in younger children than older children. This was because the correlations among Thurstone's group factors were higher for the younger subjects. However, subsequent research indicated that age is not necessarily related to how extensive the general intelligence factor is. Curtis (1949) demonstrated that general intelligence varies as a function of the difficulty level of tests. His study included samples of 9-year-old boys and 12-year-old boys. Each group was given a series of tests selected to measure some of Thurstone's primary factors as well as "g." The results showed that there were no age differences on the "g" factor. However, it was found that the easier tests produced a larger general intelligence factor than the difficult tests. Thus, the variable of test difficulty may account for the age differences in the general intelligence factor reported by Garrett and others, since the easier tests that reflect more "g" are more likely to be included in the tests given to younger subjects.

In sum, it is our opinion that the results of the factor analytic research in intelligence can best be interpreted in terms of the kind of hierarchical model first proposed by the British investigators (see Figure 4-2). At the lowest level we have the task-specific factors. At the next level of generality, the minor group factors, we can place Thurstone's primary mental abilities and Guilford's structure-of-intellect factors.[3] Moving up to the next level, the major group factors, we can place Cattell's crystallized-intelligence and fluid-intelligence factors. Recall these are second-order factors that emerged from factor analyses of test batteries that included Thurstone's tests of primary mental abilities. Vernon's distinction between verbal/educational and spatial/mechanical factors seems to roughly parallel Cattell's crystallized and fluid factors. Finally,

[2]Another conceptualization of second-order factors has been proposed by Jensen (1969), who distinguishes between associative learning and conceptual learning. Because this distinction is viewed as a reflection of social-class differences, we will consider it in Chapter 12.

[3]Guilford (1972) points out that some of Thurstone's factors are similar to particular factors identified in Guilford's own research. The differences in the factor-analytic results reported by these two investigators are due to the fact that in each ability area Guilford used a greater variety and number of tests than Thurstone had used. Consequently, Guilford was able to identify many more factors than Thurstone.

at the top of the hierarchical model we can place "g," the general intelligence factor. Cattell (1971) has factor analyzed his second-order factors and found one third-order factor (that is, a factor that emerges from factor analyzing second-order factors). This third-order factor was identified as the general intelligence factor, "g."

Standard intelligence tests that yield one overall index, such as the Binet and Wechsler scales, have high loadings on the crystallized-intelligence factor (or verbal/educational factor) as well as on "g." If we have measures that reflect general intelligence factors and a major group factor such as crystallized intelligence, the issue arises as to why we need measures of more specific or differentiated intelligence factors. Performance on these more specific factors, such as Thurstone's and Guilford's factors, should be more useful than an overall IQ score if we want to make more specific predictions about particular kinds of success. In other words, specific and minor group factors should be useful in counseling a student about curriculum choices or in guiding a worker toward appropriate job selection. For example, if a person obtains high scores on measures of spatial ability, it would seem reasonable for a vocational counselor to recommend a training program in areas such as art, design, and photography. Another advantage of identifying special ability factors (that is, factors other than "g" and the major group factors, such as crystallized intelligence) is that certain types of ability measures may emerge that have not been part of measures of general intelligence. An excellent example is Guilford's identification of divergent-production abilities, which have stimulated assessment and research in the area of creativity.

The Validity of Intelligence Factors. If we can assume that intelligence factors other than "g" have appropriate functions, we need to evaluate how valid they actually are. As we noted in Chapter 2, in order to assess the validity of any measurement, we first have to determine if the measurement is reliable. In the case of measures of intelligence factors, an index of reliability is whether or not the same factors can be identified for different samples—that is, whether or not factors first identified in one sample can be replicated for other samples. Reviews of the research on the kinds of factors identified by Thurstone and Guilford have generally indicated that such factors are consistently found across different age levels and different cultures (French, 1951; Horn, 1976). There still may be, however, a problem with Guilford's factor structure, since other investigators have not consistently replicated his results (Horn, 1976). A considerable degree of subjective judgment on the part of the investigator appears to be involved in producing a factor structure according to Guilford's three-dimensional model.

We see, then, that there is some support for the reliability of special ability factors. What does the evidence indicate regarding the validity of special ability factors? To test the validity of these factors we try to determine how successful they are as predictors of relevant criteria. Reviews of research on the predictive validity of the Thurstone and Guilford factors indicate that generally the degree of predictability is not very good (Brody & Brody, 1976; Butcher, 1968; Tyler, 1965).

In the case of Thurstone's factors the verbal and reasoning factors have produced moderately high correlations with school grades in most courses, but the other ability factors have generally demonstrated little predictive value. For example, in one study with high school students (Shaw, 1949), the numerical factor correlated more highly with measures of writing correctness (.43) than with quantitative thinking (.32) or science (.19)—subject areas we would expect to be especially related to numerical ability. The limited data relating the Thurstone factors to vocational criteria have not demonstrated predictive validity. Thus, in the example we gave earlier, there is no evidence as yet to support our expectation that Thurstone's spatial ability factor would be predictive of success in careers such as art or photography. With respect to Guilford's factors, it is quite possible that they are too narrow to be of much practical use except, perhaps, in predicting narrow criteria. Thus, according to Varela (1971), the Guilford factors are useful in predicting such specific job skills as ability to plan and social sensitivity in working with others.

In summary, then, intelligence factors have their place in predicting specific criteria. However, the empirical support for such a function is at present rather limited. We should mention that some factor-analytic research on special abilities has been specifically carried out for the purpose of predicting vocational criteria, and we will consider this in Chapter 7.

The Physiological Basis of Intelligence

What is the relationship between intelligence and the way in which the brain functions? The answer to this kind of question will give us some insight into the physiological basis of intelligence. Most of the investigations of brain functioning in relation to intelligence have been based on people who have suffered brain injury.

Psychologists who have worked with brain-injured individuals have pointed out that standard measures of intelligence, such as the Binet or Wechsler scales, do not necessarily reflect the presence of known neurological abnormalities. For example, Hebb (1939) demonstrated that the IQ may not be changed and may be within the normal range with the major part of the frontal areas of the cortex absent. Observations of this kind led Halstead (1947, 1951) to make a distinction between psychometric intelligence (as measured by standard IQ tests) and "biological intelligence." Halstead studied the behavioral effects of surgical lesions in the frontal areas of humans and animals and noted that there were certain recurrent forms of behavior that distinguished these subjects from normal subjects. Based on factor analyses of correlational data obtained from both brain-injured and normal groups, Halstead identified four factors. These four factors or components of biological intelligence were: (1) ability to categorize and form concepts; (2) cerebral power, which is reflected in flicker-fusion tests where individuals high in the factor make better discriminations between a steady and an unsteady light than those low on the factor; (3) direction or modality, which refers to the special talents through which intelligence is manifested (for example, a brain-injured person who can only understand words when they are orally transmitted because he or she has lost the ability to recognize printed words); and (4) the memory or organized experience of the individual. The brain-injured subjects, as opposed to the normal subjects, performed at a lower level on indexes reflecting these factors.

The "ability to categorize" component of Halstead's biological intelligence is similar to the characteristic of abstract ability that Goldstein and Scheerer (1941) identified in their work with brain-injured individuals. Goldstein and Scheerer developed special sorting tests and found that brain-injured individuals were generally unable to sort objects into categories—they manifested a deficiency in the ability to abstract. What these individuals did do in the sorting tasks was to operate at a concrete level; that is, they were unable to place objects together on the basis of an attribute common to a given category. For instance, they might group paper and pencil together because they had used these objects together at one time, but they could not group objects according to some common attribute such as color, size, or shape.

While the work of Halstead and of Goldstein and Scheerer emphasized the behavior of brain-injured individuals, it has implications for a generalized conception of what intelligence includes. As in the case of the factor analytic work with psychometric measures of intelligence, several components of intelligence emerge from the physiological research. However, this research suggests a somewhat different structural makeup of intelligence—a makeup that includes abstract ability, the power one can apply to a problem, the specialized ways in which intelligence is expressed, and the extent of the memories one possesses. The last three have not been typically identified in factor analyses of standard intelligence tests.

While the biologically based measures have identified some aspects of intellectual functioning not commonly identified by factor analyses of intelligence tests, research also exists demonstrating a parallel between brain functioning and factors derived from intelligence tests. Investigations show that damage to the left cerebral hemisphere seriously impairs verbal abilities, while damage to the right cerebral hemisphere seriously impairs spatial abilities (for example, Milner, 1971; Warrington & Taylor, 1973). Such results lead to the conclusion that the left hemisphere is the center for verbal abilities, while the right hemisphere is the center for spatial abilities. Recall from our discussion of intelligence factors that two commonly identified major group factors are verbal/educational and spatial/mechanical.

Another approach to the physiological basis of intelligence has been to theorize about the neurophysiological processes involved in thinking. Some years ago Hebb (1949) proposed the notion of "autonomous central processes," referring to central processes that are relatively independent of external stimulation or direct stimulus control. Such processes are viewed as underlying various thinking or cognitive activities, such as perception, attention, and imagination. Because these cognitive activities are involved in intelligence, it follows that the autonomous central processes may account for intelligence. The autonomous central processes are presumably located in the associative areas of the brain—that is, all areas of the neocortex that are not primary sensory or motor areas. According to Hebb, the potential of any organism for complex problem solving or intelligent behavior is a function of the size of the associative areas relative to the size of the motor and sensory areas of the cortex. In humans, the ratio of associative areas to sensory-motor areas is high relative to the ratio in lower animals.

What is particularly significant about Hebb's view of the physiological basis of intelligence is his conception of the brain (more specifically, the cortex) as an ongoing active system ready to process and store incoming information that can then be utilized in various problem-solving activities. Hebb's conception of cortical functioning is suggestive of the way in which an electronic computer functions. Indeed, starting in the late 1950s, a number of psychologists developed conceptions of brain functioning that were specifically modeled on computer processing. For example, Newell, Shaw, and Simon (1958) view brain functioning as "an information-processing system with large storage capacity that holds, among other things, complex strategies (programs) that may be evoked by stimuli. The stimulus determines what strategy or strategies will be evoked" (p. 163). Butcher (1968) comments on the implications that such computer-based models of brain functioning have for a conceptualization of intelligence, as follows:

> It is quite likely that individual differences in ability may come to be described in something more like computer-language. If the analogies . . . between machine and human intelligence are not entirely misleading . . . the appropriate components into which human intelligence should be analyzed and most effectively described will be such variables as capacity of working store, speed of basic operations, speed of access to store, sophistication of programming language, number and variety of standard programmes on file, and so on [p. 147].

Developmental Stages of Intelligence

The Swiss psychologist Jean Piaget (1947) conceives of intelligence as a phenomenon that involves *qualitative* changes during the early developmental years. According to Piaget, the nature of intellectual functioning at one level of development may be quite different than at another level of development. He is therefore interested in identifying age group differences in intellectual functioning. Essentially, Piaget conceives of intelligence as composed of a series of developmental stages, each stage being qualitatively distinct. The progression from stage to stage is based on two basic intellectual functions. These two functions are *assimilation* and *accommodation*. Assimilation involves the way in which the infant or child incorporates his or her experiences with the environment, while accommodation involves the way in which the infant or child modifies what he or she has already assimilated in order to respond to the impact of the environment. These functions represent two complementary aspects of adaptation to the environment, and Piaget assumes that they are inherent in the infant.

The intellectual functions of assimilation and accommodation are continually being manifested in the child's engagement with the environment. The child's intellectual development, then, is marked by a step-by-step process of learning about the environment—what has been previously acquired is utilized in solving current problems, and once a problem is solved it can in turn be utilized in future problem-solving activities. According to Piaget, this step-by-step or hierarchical process of intellectual development undergoes qualitative changes, which are reflected in several stages from birth to adolescence. Piaget's scheme of the stages of intellectual development is based on his observations and experiments with children in various problem-solving situations. The following four stages of intellectual development have been identified: (1) sensory-motor operations, lasting from birth to 18 months or 2 years; (2) preoperational representations, extending until approximately 7 years of age; (3) concrete operations, lasting until the age of 11 or 12; and (4) formal operations, beginning at age 11 or 12 and usually completed by about 15 years of age.

Let's briefly look at each of these stages. In the first stage (sensory-motor), the child develops a sense of separateness from his or her external world by learning that personally initiated actions can bring about intended effects, such as purposely rolling a ball to knock down a tower of building blocks. In the second stage (preoperational representations), the child learns to make symbolic representations; that is, one object can stand for another—a box can represent a house. In the third stage (concrete operations), the child learns to perform according to principles of logic, even though unable to verbalize these, such as "reversibility," which means that a verbal principle or mathematical expression is capable of being returned to its point of origin ($2 + 4 = 6$, and $6 - 4 = 2$). In the final stage (formal operations), the adolescent is able to achieve the level of adult reasoning through the use of formal operations. These formal operations are based on logical properties, but unlike the phase of concrete operations, the adolescent can reveal such operations without having to manipulate concrete objects.

Hunt (1961) has pointed out that Piaget's hierarchical conception of intelligence shares much in common with the computer-based models of brain functioning. Both approaches view intelligence as a product of central processes, and central processes are viewed as changing with experience. Consistent with Piaget, Hebb and Newell, Shaw, and Simon conceive of problem-solving strategies as hierarchically arranged. Hunt also points out a similarity between Piaget's hierarchical conception and the British factor analysts' hierarchical factor structure. Piaget's notion of successive points of transition in the development of intelligence implies that qualitative changes are occurring along a single dimension of general intelligence as reflected in Spearman's "g" at the apex of the hierarchical factor structure. Along similar lines, Eysenck (1973/1975) has indicated that Piaget-type test items do, in fact, have very high "g" loadings; and therefore, the Piaget-type measures provide support for the hierarchical factor model.

The Piagetian approach to assessing intellectual performance is based on selected tasks that reflect the various criteria associated with a given stage of development. Such an approach does not provide an overall estimate or a pattern of subscores for an individual's level of intelligence. However, there have been some attempts to develop test batteries for infants and children aimed at giving an overall assessment of Piagetian intellectual development (Hunt & Kirk, 1971; Tuddenham, 1970; Uzgiris, 1976). These measures, consisting of scales based on Piaget's observations, make it possible to identify a child's level of acquisition within particular sequences of development. Hopefully, knowing the identity of levels of development, it will become possible to compare the ages at which children with different backgrounds of experience achieve such levels. Educational programming can then be adjusted to the level at which the child is currently functioning, with the goal of eventually facilitating the child's progression along the landmarks of intellectual development. It remains to be seen how effective these Piagetian approaches to measuring intelligence will be. Any methods of assessment generated by Piaget's conception of intelligence will cast a different focus on what is being measured. Instead of the traditional focus on how much intelligence one has, the Piagetian measure will reflect the stage of intellectual development at which one is functioning.

SUMMARY

The scientific study of intelligence began with the work of Sir Francis Galton. Galton assumed that intelligence was an inherited characteristic, and he attempted to assess individual differences in mental ability on the basis of sensory-motor tests. James McKeen Cattell carried on Galton's work, but neither Galton nor Cattell was able to demonstrate any predictive validity with sensory-motor measures. The first successful measure of intellectual differences was developed by the French psychologist Alfred Binet. Binet's scale of intelligence consisted of a variety of tests that assessed complex mental processes. These tests were arranged in age levels, and a child's level of success was represented by a mental age. The Binet scale was eventually translated and adapted by several American psychologists. The most successful adaptation was the Stanford-Binet developed by Lewis Terman. The Stanford-Binet made use of the Intelligence Quotient or IQ—that is, the ratio between mental age and chronological age. The first group tests of intelligence appeared shortly after the introduction of the Stanford-Binet. As intelligence tests were being developed, more attention was given to defining the concept of intelligence. However, since the tests focused on predicting school success, the tests appeared to be only measuring a subset of the kinds of things that definitions of intelligence were referring to.

Intelligence tests have generally been successful in predicting school achievement as well as occupational achievement. However, in both areas of prediction there seems to be a social-class bias at work. An individual with a middle or upper social-class background has had the kinds of experiences that will enable him or her to perform well on an intelligence test. The same background experience will also enable such a person to do well in school, which in turn will increase the probability of attaining a high level of occupational achievement. Measured intelligence has also been used as a predictor of success in learning. The research indicates that when difficult and complex material is presented to learners, intelligence level does predict fairly successfully who the better learners will be. Research also indicates that the manner or style of learning differs between high-IQ and low-IQ individuals. There is thus the suggestion that social-class differences in intelligence-test performance may be due to differences in the kind of learning style one has been exposed to.

Some areas of investigation have led to attempts at clarifying the conceptualization of intelligence. Through the use of factor analysis, it has been possible to gain an understanding of the structure of intelligence. Several dimensions or factors of intelligence have been identified. These factors appear to be arranged in a hierarchical structure, with the more general factors at the top of the hierarchy. The traditional measures of intelligence, such as the Binet and Wechsler scales, seem to be based primarily on the more general factors. Measures that have been devised as indexes of the more specific factors are useful for making predictions about particular kinds of success, such as academic programming or job selection. The physiological basis of intelligence has been conceived in terms of a computer-based model of brain functioning. The view that intelligence undergoes qualitative changes as a function of development during the childhood and adolescent years has been proposed by Piaget. This developmental approach to conceptualizing intelligence has led to new methods of assessment.

REFERENCES

Anastasi, A. *Psychological testing* (4th ed.). New York: Macmillan, 1976.

Anastasi, A., & Levee, R. F. Intellectual defect and musical talent. *American Journal of Mental Deficiency,* 1959, *64,* 695–703.

Ball, R. S. The predictability of occupational level from intelligence. *Journal of Consulting Psychology,* 1938, *2,* 184–186.

Binet, A., & Henri, V. La psychologie individuelle. *Année Psychologique,* 1895, *2,* 411–465.

Binet, A., & Simon, T. Méthodes nouvelles pour le diagnostic du niveau intellectuel des anormaux. *Année Psychologique,* 1905, *11,* 191–244.

Binet, A., & Simon, T. Le dévelopment de l'intelligence chez les jeunes enfants. *Année Psychologique,* 1908, *14,* 1–90.

Boring, E. G. Intelligence as the tests test it. *New Republic,* 1923, *35,* 35–37.

Brody, E. B., & Brody, N. *Intelligence: Nature, determinants, and consequences.* New York: Academic Press, 1976.

Burt, C. *The factors of the mind.* London: University of London Press, 1940.

Burt, C. The structure of the mind: A review of the results of factor analysis. *British Journal of Educational Psychology,* 1949, *19,* 100–111, 176–199.

Butcher, H. J. *Human intelligence: Its nature and assessment.* London: Methuen, 1968.

Carroll, J. B. A factor analysis of verbal abilities. *Psychometrika,* 1941, *6,* 279–308.

Cattell, J. McK. Mental tests and measurements. *Mind,* 1890, *15,* 373–380.

Cattell, J. McK., & Farrand, L. Physical and mental measurements of the students of Columbia University. *Psychological Review*, 1896, *3*, 618–648.

Cattell, R. B. The structure of intelligence in relation to the nature/nurture controversy. In R. Cancro (Ed.), *Intelligence: Genetic and environmental influences*. New York: Grune & Stratton, 1971.

Crano, W. D., Kenny, D. A., & Campbell, D. T. Does intelligence cause achievement?: A cross-lagged panel analysis. *Journal of Educational Psychology*, 1972, *63*, 258–275.

Cronin, J., Daniels, N., Hurley, A., Kroch, A., & Webber, R. Race, class, and intelligence: A critical look at the IQ controversy. *International Journal of Mental Health*, 1975, *3*(4), 46–132.

Curtis, H. A. A study of the relative effects of age and of test difficulty upon factor patterns. *Genetic Psychology Monographs*, 1949, *40*, 99–148.

Eysenck, H. J. *The inequality of man*. San Diego: EdITS, 1975. (Originally published, 1973)

French, J. W. *The description of aptitude and achievement tests in terms of rotated factors*. Chicago: University of Chicago Press, 1951.

Galton, F. *Hereditary genius: An inquiry into its laws and consequence*. London: Macmillan, 1869.

Galton, F. *Inquiries into human faculty and its development*. London: Macmillan, 1883.

Garrett, H. E. A developmental theory of intelligence. *American Psychologist*, 1946, *1*, 372–378.

Goldstein, K., & Scheerer, M. Abstract and concrete behavior: An experimental study with special tests. *Psychological Monographs*, 1941, *53*(2, Whole No. 239).

Grossman, H. (Ed.). *Manual on terminology and classification in mental retardation* (1973 revision). Washington, D.C.: American Association on Mental Deficiency, 1973.

Guilford, J. P. *The nature of human intelligence*. New York: McGraw-Hill, 1967.

Guilford, J. P. Thurstone's primary mental abilities and structure-of-intellect abilities. *Psychological Bulletin*, 1972, *77*, 129–143.

Guilford, J. P., & Hoepfner, R. *The analysis of intelligence*. New York: McGraw-Hill, 1971.

Guilford, J. P., & Lacey, J. I. *Printed classification tests*. (Army Air Forces Aviation Psychology Program Research Reports, No. 5) Washington, D.C.: U.S. Government Printing Office, 1947.

Halstead, W. C. *Brain and intelligence*. Chicago: University of Chicago Press, 1947.

Halstead, W. C. Biological intelligence. *Journal of Personality*, 1951, *20*, 118–130.

Hebb, D. O. Intelligence in man after large removals of cerebral tissue: Report of four left frontal lobe cases. *Journal of Genetic Psychology*, 1939, *21*, 73–87.

Hebb, D. O. *The organization of behavior*. New York: Wiley, 1949.

Horn, J. L. Human abilities: A review of research and theory in the early 1970's. In M. R. Rosenzweig & L. W. Porter (Eds.), *Annual Review of Psychology* (Vol. 27). Palo Alto, Calif.: Annual Review, 1976.

Hunt, J. McV. *Intelligence and experience*. New York: Ronald, 1961.

Hunt, J. McV., & Kirk, G. E. Social aspects of intelligence: Evidence and issues. In R. Cancro (Ed.), *Intelligence: Genetic and environmental influences*. New York: Grune & Stratton, 1971.

Jensen, A. R. How much can we boost IQ and scholastic achievement? *Harvard Educational Review*, 1969, *39*, 1–123.

McCall, R. B. *Intelligence and heredity*. Homewood, Ill.: Learning Systems, 1975.

McClelland, D. C. Testing for competence rather than for "Intelligence." *American Psychologist*, 1973, *28*, 1–14.

Milner, B. Interhemispheric differences in the localization of psychological processes in men. *British Medical Journal,* 1971, *27,* 272–277.

Newell, A., Shaw, J. C., & Simon, H. A. Elements of a theory of human problem solving. *Psychological Review,* 1958, *65,* 151–166.

Oden, M. H. The fulfillment of promise: 40-year follow-up of the Terman gifted group. *Genetic Psychology Monographs,* 1968, *77,* 3–93.

Osler, S. F., & Fivel, M. W. Concept attainment: I. The role of age and intelligence in concept attainment by induction. *Journal of Experimental Psychology,* 1961, *62,* 1–8.

Osler, S. F., & Weiss, S. R. Studies in concept attainment: Effect of instruction at two levels of intelligence. *Journal of Experimental Psychology,* 1962, *63,* 528–533.

Piaget, J. [*The psychology of intelligence*] (M. Piercy & D. E. Berlyne, Trans.). Paterson, N. J.: Littlefield, Adams, 1960. (Originally published, 1947)

Rimoldi, H. J. A. Study of some factors related to intelligence. *Psychometrika,* 1948, *13,* 27–46.

Rimoldi, H. J. A. The central intellective factor. *Psychometrika,* 1951, *16,* 75–101.

Scheerer, M., Rothmann, E., & Goldstein, K. A case of "Idiot Savant": An experimental study of personality organization. *Psychological Monographs,* 1945, *58*(4, Whole No. 269).

Shaw, D. G. A study of the relationships between Thurstone Primary Mental Abilities and high school achievement. *Journal of Educational Psychology,* 1949, *40,* 239–249.

Spearman, C. "General intelligence," objectively determined and measured. *American Journal of Psychology,* 1904, *15,* 201–292.

Spearman, C. *The abilities of man.* New York: Macmillan, 1927.

Terman, L. M. *The measurement of intelligence.* Boston: Houghton Mifflin, 1916.

Terman, L. M. (Ed.). *Genetic studies of genius. Volume I. Mental and physical traits of a thousand gifted children.* Stanford, Calif.: Stanford University Press, 1925.

Terman, L. M., & Oden, M. H. *The gifted group at mid-life.* Stanford, Calif.: Stanford University Press, 1959.

Thurstone, L. L. Primary mental abilities. *Psychometric Monographs,* 1938, No. 1.

Thurstone, L. L. Second-order factors. *Psychometrika,* 1944, *9,* 71–100.

Thurstone, L. L., & Thurstone, T. G. Factorial studies of intelligence. *Psychometric Monographs,* 1941, No. 2.

Thurstone, T. G. Primary mental abilities of children. *Educational and Psychological Measurement,* 1941, *1,* 105–116.

Tilton, J. W. Intelligence test scores as indicative of ability to learn. *Educational and Psychological Measurement,* 1949, *9,* 291–296.

Tuddenham, R. D. A "Piagetian" test of cognitive development. In W. B. Dockrell (Ed.), *On intelligence.* Toronto: The Ontario Institute for Studies in Education, 1970.

Tyler, L. E. *The psychology of human differences* (3rd ed.). New York: Appleton-Century-Crofts, 1965.

Tyler, L. E. (Ed.). *Intelligence: Some recurring issues.* New York: Van Nostrand Reinhold, 1969.

Tyler, L. E. *Individual differences: Abilities and motivational directions.* New York: Appleton-Century-Crofts, 1974.

Uzgiris, I. C. Organization of sensorimotor intelligence. In M. Lewis (Ed.), *Origins of intelligence.* New York: Plenum, 1976.

Varela, J. A. *Psychological solutions to social problems: An introduction to social technology.* New York: Academic Press, 1971.

Vernon, P. E. *The structure of human abilities.* London: Methuen, 1950.

Warrington, E., & Taylor, A. The contribution of the right parietal lobe to object recognition. *Cortex,* 1973, *9,* 152–164.

Wechsler, D. *The measurement of adult intelligence.* Baltimore: Williams & Wilkins, 1939.

Wechsler, D. *The measurement of adult intelligence* (3rd ed.). Baltimore: Williams & Wilkins, 1950.

Whimbey, A. Getting ready for the tester: You can learn to raise your IQ score. *Psychology Today,* 1976, *9*(8), 27–29, 84–85.

Wissler, C. The correlation of mental and physical tests. *Psychological Review Monograph Supplements,* 1901, *3*(6, Whole No. 16).

Woodrow, H. The effect of practice on groups of different initial ability. *Journal of Educational Psychology,* 1938, *29,* 268–278.

Woodrow, H. Factors in improvement with practice. *Journal of Psychology,* 1939, *7,* 55–70.

Woodrow, H. Interrelations of measures of learning. *Journal of Psychology,* 1940, *10,* 49–73.

5

Intelligence and the Heredity/Environment Issue

In the early stages of the development of psychology, it was not uncommon to find the expression of extreme views about the roles of heredity and environment (see Chapter 3). A well-known example of the hereditarian argument was Henry Goddard's (1912) study of the Kallikak family. Goddard traced the lines of descent starting from the union of Martin Kallikak with two different women at the time of the American Revolution. One line, based on Kallikak's mating with a mentally retarded girl, showed a high incidence of mentally retarded and socially deviant individuals. The other line, based on descendents of Kallikak and his lawful wife, was marked by a virtual absence of abnormality. Goddard concluded that the high rate of abnormality among the descendants of Kallikak and the mentally retarded girl was due to the passing on of her "poor" genes from one generation to the next. Of course, an equally plausible interpretation was that "poor" environments, not "poor" genes, were passed on from one generation to the next.

As noted in Chapter 3, with the growth of knowledge about the contributions of heredity and environment, there has been the general acceptance that both sets of determinants need to be considered. Nevertheless, there is presently much controversy over the relative impact of hereditary and environmental determinants. Before reviewing the research on intelligence and the nature/nurture issue, we will consider how the relative contribution of heredity and environment can be assessed.

THE RELATIVE CONTRIBUTIONS OF HEREDITY AND ENVIRONMENT

A number of attempts have been made to arrive at quantitative estimates regarding the relative contributions of heredity and environment to measured differences in intelligence. Jensen (1969), on the basis of his review of the evidence, concludes that intelligence, as measured by IQ tests, is about 80% determined by heredity. Other reported percentages of hereditary determination have included Burt's (1958) range of 77 to 88%, Newman, Freeman, and Holzinger's (1937) range of 65 to 80%, Burks's (1928) 66%, Woodworth's (1941) 60%, and Jencks et al.'s (1972) 45%. How are such percentages arrived at? Why is there disagreement among the reported percentages? Is it meaningful to account for the contributions of heredity and environment in quantitative terms? To answer these questions, we first have to consider what these estimates of hereditary determination actually mean. Recall from Chapter 3 that the term commonly used to refer to such estimates is *heritability.*

Heritability refers to the ratio of genetic or genotypic variance to the total observed or phenotypic variance in a particular trait for a given population. A heritability index (h^2) can therefore be defined by the following formula[1]:

$$h^2 = \frac{\sigma^2 \text{ Genetic}}{\sigma^2 \text{ Total}}$$

In the case of intelligence as measured by an IQ test, we can obtain a distribution of test scores for a given population, such as American elementary school children. What we want to determine is how much of the variation (that is, individual differences) in test scores is due to the genetic variance of the population. It is important to point out that the differences in the magnitude of reported heritability estimates reflect differences in the specific formulas used by various investigators to determine such estimates as well as differences in the samples from the given population that are used to derive the estimates.

As indicated in Chapter 3, controversy exists about how meaningfully an index of heritability can be applied to a psychological characteristic such as human intelligence. Proponents of using heritability estimates, including Jensen (1969), Herrnstein (1973), and Eysenck (1973/1975), believe that these estimates

---

[1]An extended discussion of various formulas that are used to estimate heritability is contained in Loehlin, Lindzey, and Spuhler (1975, Appendix G).

are valid indicators of the genetic contribution to intelligence. Therefore, when Jensen concludes that the heritability for intelligence as measured by IQ tests is .80, he believes that this definitely indicates that individual differences in intelligence are predominantly based on genetic rather than environmental factors. On the other hand, critics of applying heritability estimates to intelligence argue that heritability provides deceptive and, perhaps, even trivial information and is not at all a valid indicator of the genetic contribution (for example, Block & Dworkin, 1974; Hirsch, 1971, 1975; Hunt, 1961; Lewontin, 1974).

As we pointed out in Chapter 3, heritability is not a constant property of a particular trait, and this includes intelligence. Hirsch (1975) states that "heritability, an average statistic and *population* measure, provides no information about how a given *individual* might have developed under conditions different from those under which he (she, or it) actually did develop" (p. 23). What Hirsch is suggesting is that it is entirely possible that, in cases where a high heritability has been reported for a given population under a particular set of environmental conditions, if individuals from the same kind of population were exposed to different environmental conditions they would develop considerably different phenotypes from those developed in the original environments. An excellent example is tuberculosis, which at one time had high heritability but now has an extremely small heritability because the bacillus leading to the disease has been virtually eliminated. Thus, in the case of intelligence, a heritability estimate of .80 does not actually tell us anything about the *possibility* of our being able to modify intelligence under different environmental conditions than those already sampled. As we will see when we review the evidence in the next section, the range of environments that have been sampled in the existing studies of heritability in intelligence is quite limited. We therefore don't know what the heritability would be for different sets of environmental conditions.

Another limitation of the heritability index is that it is based on the assumption that hereditary and environmental factors are uncorrelated with one another. Independence between heredity and environment can be achieved when dealing with plants and animals—heritability estimates were originally developed for plant and animal breeders—because it is possible for the investigator to control all of the conditions. However, with respect to most human characteristics, it is not possible to achieve such independence. In the case of intelligence, it is clear that there is a correlation between environment and heredity that makes it hard to separate out what is due to each determinant. Parents who pass along "good" genes are also likely to pass along "good" environments. In other words, parents who have high IQs not only transmit to their children the genotype for high intelligence but also provide them with an intellectually stimulating environment.

In light of the above arguments, is there any value in obtaining heritability estimates with respect to human intelligence? Because of the correlation between heredity and environment, heritability estimates can provide only rough approximations of the proportionality of genetic to total variance. At best, heritability estimates can afford some indication of the effects that might be expected from various types of environmental intervention programs (Loehlin et al., 1975; Scarr-Salapatek, 1971). Scarr-Salapatek (1971) gives the following examples:

> If, for example, IQ tests, which predict well to achievements in the larger society, show low heritabilities in a population, then it is probable that simply providing better environments which now exist will improve average performance in that population. If h^2 [heritability] is high but environments sampled in that population are largely unfavorable, then (again) simple environmental improvement will probably change the mean phenotypic level. If h^2 is high and the environments sampled are largely favorable, then novel environmental manipulations are probably required to change phenotypes, and eugenic programs may be advocated [pp. 1227–1228].

Let us proceed to an examination of the kinds of hereditary and environmental factors that have a bearing on individual differences in intelligence. The contributions of heredity and environment to group differences in intelligence, such as sex, social class, and race, will be considered in the chapters within Part 3.

HEREDITARY INFLUENCES

The research on the contribution of hereditary factors to the development of intelligence can be reviewed on the basis of two general types of study (Vandenberg, 1971). One group involves investigations of related individuals including twin studies and adoption studies. This type of research is characterized by a comparison of the similarity in IQ scores of groups that differ in the degree to which they are genetically related. A second group of investigations involves studies of genetic abnormalities and includes studies of the effects of inbreeding, defective genes, and chromosomal anomalies. We will first review the studies of genetically related individuals.

Biological Relatedness

A survey by Erlenmeyer-Kimling and Jarvik (1963) summarizes 52 studies of the correlations between the tested intelligence of individuals varying in the degree to which they are genetically related. The range is from those who are completely unrelated genetically to those who show identical genotypes (identical twins). The results of this survey are shown in Figure 5-1. The dark circles in the figure represent the correlation coefficients obtained in each study; the horizontal lines indicate the ranges of the correlations for each category of relatedness; and the vertical lines indicate the medians of these values.

Inspection of Figure 5-1 indicates that the more genetically similar paired individuals are, the more similar their IQs are. For example, the correlations are highest for identical twins (who have identical genotypes) and lowest for

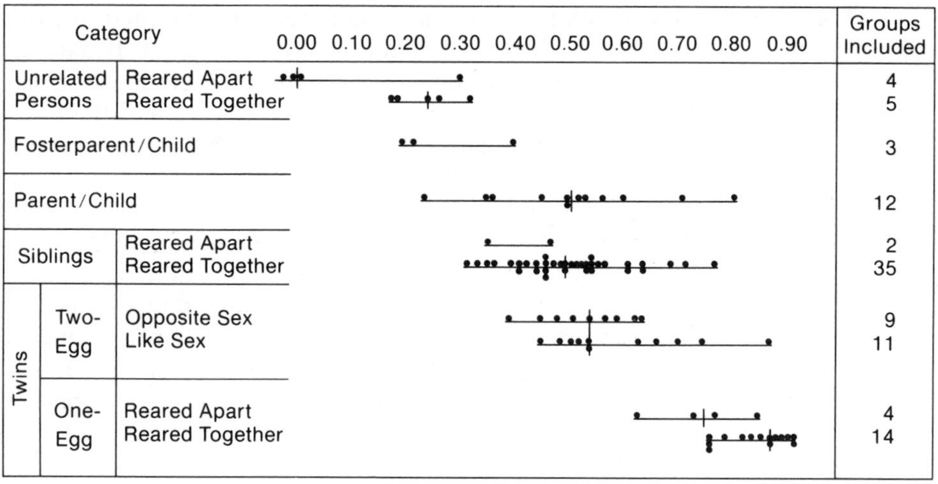

Category		0.00 0.10 0.20 0.30 0.40 0.50 0.60 0.70 0.80 0.90	Groups Included
Unrelated Persons	Reared Apart		4
	Reared Together		5
Fosterparent/Child			3
Parent/Child			12
Siblings	Reared Apart		2
	Reared Together		35
Twins — Two-Egg	Opposite Sex		9
	Like Sex		11
Twins — One-Egg	Reared Apart		4
	Reared Together		14

Figure 5-1. Correlations between IQs of paired individuals of genetic relations ranging from none to complete. From "Genetics and Intelligence: A Review," by L. Erlenmeyer-Kimling and L. F. Jarvik, *Science*, 1963, *142*, 1477–1479. Copyright 1963 by the American Association for the Advancement of Science. Reprinted by permission.

unrelated persons (including fosterparent/child pairs). Paired individuals who are about 50% genetically similar (that is, parent/child pairs, siblings, and fraternal twins) have correlations that generally fall between the high correlations for identical twins and the low correlations for pairs of unrelated persons. The fact that correlations between IQs of paired individuals vary directly with the degree of genetic relatedness supports the importance of heredity as a determinant of individual differences in tested intelligence. However, one could argue that Figure 5-1 also shows that environmental influences can affect tested intelligence, because as we go from the top to the bottom of the figure there is an increasing environmental similarity that parallels the increase in the level of correlations.

Let us examine some of the specific types of studies shown in Figure 5-1.[2] First, we will take a look at adoption studies (that is, studies involving adoptive parent/child or fosterparent/child correlations). Then, we will consider studies comparing identical twins who have been reared together with identical twins who have been reared apart, and finally, we will turn our attention to studies comparing identical twins reared together and fraternal twins reared together.

---

[2]We should note that some of the studies we will consider have appeared since the Erlenmeyer-Kimling and Jarvik (1963) survey. Furthermore, on some occasions different correlation coefficients have been reported for the same study. This is because secondary sources have sometimes involved the reanalysis of the original data. Erlenmeyer-Kimling and Jarvik in their review included some of these recomputed correlations. The correlations we will be reporting are from the original sources.

Adoption Studies. Situations in which children are adopted provide opportunities to separate the effects of heredity and environment. If data are available for both adoptive parents and natural parents, a comparison can be made between the effect of environment in the former case and the effect of heredity in the latter case. That is, any correlation between adopted children and their adoptive parents is necessarily due to environmental influences because they are not genetically related. On the other hand, any correlation between adopted children and their natural parents, assuming adopted children are separated from their natural parents in early infancy and that the prenatal period can be regarded as relatively unimportant, is due to hereditary influences because the natural parents have had virtually no environmental influence upon their children. Munsinger (1975a) has reviewed the research on adopted children's tested intelligence and cites several studies that were published between 1922 and 1949. Because no further research was published until 1971, we will divide our consideration of these studies into those reported during the earlier period and those reported during the more recent period.

Among the early studies, only three involved rather well-controlled comparisons of tested intelligence between adoptive parent/child and natural parent/child pairs. The first study was carried out by Burks (1928) and entailed a comparison of 214 adopted children and their adoptive parents with a control group of 105 children and their natural parents with whom they were living. All of the adopted children were adopted before the age of 12 months. The second study, by Leahy (1935), involved a comparison of 194 adopted children who had been adopted before the age of 6 months and an equal number of control children. In both the Burks and Leahy studies, the adopted and control children were matched for sex, age, and father's occupational level. The third study, by Skodak and Skeels (1949), involved both the natural and adoptive parents of a sample of adopted children.

We will first report the major results of the Burks and Leahy studies. In the Burks study, the Stanford-Binet was given to both children and parents, whereas in the Leahy study the Stanford-Binet was given to the children and the Otis group test to the parents. The parent/child correlations for both of these studies are presented in Table 5-1. As the table indicates, the fact that the correlations between the control children and their natural parents are greater than those between the adopted children and their adoptive parents readily suggests that the effect of environment does not exert as much influence on tested intelligence as does the effect of heredity. There are some confounding factors, however, that need to be considered in interpreting the correlations in the Burks and Leahy studies. One problem in both of these studies is the fact that although each investigator took great care in matching the adopted and control groups on relevant background factors, the two groups were not actually comparable (Kamin, 1974). In both studies, the adoptive homes were significantly superior to the control homes in environmental status, including cultural level and income level. In the Burks study the adoptive parents were significantly older than the control parents. These differences between the home environments of the adopted and control groups could have had some influence

Table 5-1. Correlations between Parents and Adopted
and Control Children

	Parent/Child Correlation	
	IQ of Adopted Children	IQ of Control Children
Mother's IQ		
Burks (1928)	.23	.57
Leahy (1935)	.24	.51
Father's IQ		
Burks (1928)	.09	.55
Leahy (1935)	.19	.51

on the correlational results of the two studies. Furthermore, in Leahy's study the adoptive homes were more uniform in environment than the control homes. Such a restricted range in adoptive-home characteristics could contribute to the lower correlation found for the adopted group, because a restricted range tends to lower correlation coefficients.

In the Skodak and Skeels (1949) study, comparisons were made between the natural parent/child and adoptive parent/child correlations for a group of 100 adopted children who were followed over a period of 13 years and given administrations of the Stanford-Binet at the average ages of 2, 4, 7, and 13. The children were separated from their natural parents by the age of 6 months. Binet IQs were also available for 63 of the natural mothers. When the children were tested at age 13, the correlation between the natural mothers' IQ and the children's IQ was .44, and the correlation between the natural mothers' education in years and the children's IQ was .32. For the adoptive parents, IQ data were not available, so only the level of education was used as an index of intelligence. The correlations between the children's IQs and the education of their adoptive mothers and fathers were .02 and .00, respectively. These findings showing a significantly higher correlation for the natural parent/child pairs than for the adoptive parent/child pairs are consistent with the results of the Burks and Leahy studies. In the Skodak and Skeels study, the differences are even more striking because of the absence of any relationship for the adoptive parent/child pairs.

However, as in the case of the two previous studies, Skodak and Skeels's results need to be interpreted with caution. Indeed, two divergent interpretations have been offered. On the one hand, Skodak and Skeels took the position that the moderate correlation between adopted children and their natural parents might be a reflection of selective placement. In support of this interpretation, they presented evidence indicating that the children of more intelligent and better-educated mothers were placed in better adoptive homes than the children of less intelligent and more poorly educated mothers. Thus the moderate correlation reported for the natural parent/child pairs could have been due to the effects of the adoptive environments. Honzik (1957), however, interpreted the results as supporting the hereditarian point of view, because she noted that at each age the correlations between adopted children's IQs and natural parents' IQs were similar in magnitude to those obtained in her own study in which children were reared with their own parents.

Skodak and Skeels also presented data on the mean IQs of their subjects. The mean IQ for the sample of adopted children tested at age 13 was 117, which was 20 points higher than the average IQ of their natural mothers.[3] On the basis of this 20-point difference, Skodak and Skeels concluded that the adoptive-home environment provided the opportunity for the adopted children to significantly surpass the intellectual level of their natural parents. Thus, the results of the Skodak and Skeels study suggest that environment, as well as heredity, is an important factor in the development of intelligence.

Among the studies conducted in the 1970s, three provide data from well-controlled comparisons of adoptive parent/child and natural parent/child pairs. As with the Skodak and Skeels study, data were available for both the adopted children's natural and adoptive parents. In the first study, Munsinger (1975b) used samples of 20 Chicano and 21 Anglo families. All of the children in both samples were placed for adoption before 6 months of age. The Lorge-Thorndike test, a group intelligence test, was administered to the children, whose average age at the time of testing was 8.5 years. The results for the two ethnic groups were very similar, so it was possible to report correlations for the total group of 41 families. The correlation between the adoptive midparent (average of mother and father) education/social status (the parents' IQs were not available) and their adopted children's IQ was –.14, whereas the correlation between the biological midparent's education/social status and their children's IQ was .70. Unlike some of the earlier studies, there was no evidence of any significant selective placement. The only apparent limitation is the rather small sample size. Nevertheless, in this study, the correlational data clearly suggest that genetic factors have a stronger effect than environmental factors on adopted children's IQs.

In another study, Horn, Loehlin, and Willerman (1975) worked with a sample of 146 families. As in the Munsinger study, there was no evidence of a selective placement bias. The children, who were separated from their biological mothers at birth, were tested with the Wechsler Intelligence Scale for Children, and the adults were tested with the Beta form of the Army Group Examination. The correlation between the biological mothers' IQs and the children's IQs was .32. In the case of the adoptive parents, the correlation between the

---

[3]Recall that the correlation between the children's IQ and the natural mothers' IQ was .44. It is statistically possible to have a large mean difference, as seen in the 20-point difference between mean IQs of the children and their natural mothers, and still have a relatively high correlation between the distributions of two groups. This is because the correlation coefficient represents the degree of correspondence in the rank ordering of scores across two distributions. Therefore, the rank ordering of one set of scores could correspond perfectly with the rank ordering of a second set of scores, while the mean of the second set could be much higher than the mean of the first set.

mothers' IQs and the children's IQs was .15, and the correlation between the fathers' IQs and the children's IQs was .09. The results of this study suggest an influence of heredity and a negligible effect of environment.

The third recent study was by Scarr and Weinberg (1976), and the results are reported in terms of means. This investigation was based on a sample of 101 White families who adopted Black children and in some cases also adopted children of other races. The 101 families included 321 children 4 years of age and older: 145 were natural and 176 were adopted, of whom 130 were Black, 25 White, and 21 either Asian or Native American. All of these children were given an intelligence test (either the Binet or one of the Wechsler scales), and the Wechsler Adult Intelligence Scale was given to their parents. The results showed that the typical adopted child in these families, regardless of race, scored at least at the average IQ for the general population. However, the child's age at the time of adoption and his or her experiences before being placed with the new family were strongly related to his or her later IQ. The earlier children were adopted, the fewer disruptions in their lives, and the better the care they received in the first few years, the higher their later IQ scores were likely to be. The White adopted children, who were placed earlier than any other group, had a mean IQ of 111. The mean IQ for the Black children was 106, whereas the Asian and Native American children, who were adopted later than any other group, scored at the national average of 100. The mean IQ for the sample of natural children was 117, which was slightly below the mean IQs reported for their parents (118 for the mothers and 121 for the fathers). For the Black children, the estimated mean IQ of their natural parents, based on educational and occupational level, was 90. The IQ of 106, then, for the Black children was considerably above the level of their natural parents, and slightly closer to that of their adoptive parents. Because early adoption was related to higher IQ, the investigators also reported data for those children who were adopted at an early age. The average IQ for such a sample of 99 Black children was 110, reflecting a greater similarity to the average level of their adoptive parents than to their natural parents. Thus, the findings from this study, which are based on mean IQ levels, provide evidence supportive of the appreciable influence of the adoptive-home environment on tested intelligence.

In sum, the results of the adoption studies indicate the importance of both heredity and environment. The evidence for heredity stems from the generally moderate correlation between the IQs of the natural parents and the adopted children. The role of the environment is indicated by the mean data, which show that the IQs of adopted children can be appreciably influenced by adoptive home placement.

Identical Twins Reared Together and Reared Apart. A condition in which identical twins have been reared apart from each other provides a unique opportunity to examine the effects of different environments while heredity is held constant. If environmental effects are important and separated twins are not selectively placed, the correlation for separated twins should be much lower than for twins reared together; otherwise heredity is the more critical factor. Four studies have been concerned with the similarities of tested intelligence among pairs of identical twins who were separated at an early age and raised apart. In three of these investigations, data were also gathered on pairs of identical twins who were reared together. The results of the four studies are presented in Table 5-2. They appear to offer strong support for a genetic interpretation. The correlations for identical twins reared apart are all high, which would seem to indicate that the effect of being raised in different environments played a negligible role in the development of intelligence. Furthermore, the correlations for identical twins reared together tend to be only slightly higher than the correlations for identical twins reared apart. A wider discrepancy between these two sets of correlations would be expected if environmental factors make a significant contribution. Indeed, this is the conclusion reached by Jensen (1969) and Herrnstein (1973).

However, before reaching final conclusions about the implications of the results of these twin studies, it is important to consider some of the details of each of the studies. The investigation by Newman, Freeman, and Holzinger (1937) was the only study in this group of investigations that was carried out in the United States. The sample of twins raised apart consisted of 19 pairs, most of whom had been separated by the age of 12 months. All of the twins had continued to live apart, although in one or two cases they had corresponded or occasionally visited each other. At the time their intelligence was measured (Stanford-Binet), the twins ranged in age from 11 to 59 years. A particularly important part of this study was the analysis of the degree to which the environments of the members of each twin pair had differed. A summary of these differences is shown in Table 5-3. As the table indicates, the variation in environments for each set of twins was based on differences in (1) years of schooling, (2) educational advantages, and (3) social advantages. The numbers in the last column refer to the difference between the IQs of the two twins. A positive number signifies that the twin with more education also had the higher IQ, whereas a negative number means the more poorly educated twin was higher in IQ. In general the IQ differences favor the twin with the better education. It is noteworthy to compare the top five cases in the table with the remaining cases, because this first group includes the only instances wherein an appreciable difference in the amount of education existed. For the first five cases the mean IQ difference is 16 points in favor of the better-educated twin, whereas for the remaining cases the mean IQ difference is 4 points in favor of the better-educated twin. Thus, these results clearly indicate that an environmental factor, amount of schooling, did have an appreciable effect on the level of intelligence attained by the twins—an effect that is masked by considering only the correlation of .67 for the 19 cases of twins reared apart.

Other data presented in Table 5-3 are consistent with the results on amount of schooling. In the Newman, Freeman, and Holzinger study, the investigators used five judges to rate the degree of intrapair difference in both

Table 5-2. IQ Correlations of Identical Twins Reared Apart and Identical Twins Reared Together

| Study | Identical Twins Apart | | Identical Twins Together | |
	Correlation	Number of Pairs	Correlation	Number of Pairs
Newman et al. (1937)	.67	19	.91	50
Burt (1966)*	.86	53	.92	95
Shields (1962)	.77	37	.76	34
Juel-Nielsen (1965)	.62	12	(not studied)	

*The correlations reported are based on an individual intelligence test. The study also included a group intelligence test.

educational and social advantages. These ratings were based on the case materials gathered for each twin pair. A correlation of .79 was obtained between the differences in educational advantages and the IQ difference within each pair of twins, and a correlation of .51 was obtained for the differences in social advantages and IQ differences. It is also important to note that the types of homes in which pairs of twins were placed were generally similar to one another. In fact, in some instances the twins were placed with relatives. Nevertheless, even with a restricted degree of variability in environments, the data do indicate that educational and social differences did have an effect on tested intelligence.

The research by Burt (1966) was carried out in England. The 53 pairs of twins reared apart were obtained largely from schools in London, and all were separated by the age of 6 months. According to Burt the separated twins were spread over a wide range of environments in terms of socioeconomic level. In fact, because Burt's study did involve a wide range of environmental conditions, as well as a relatively large number of twin pairs, it has been cited frequently as providing the most definitive data on identical twins reared apart versus reared together. However, in tracing the data, which Burt published in a series of papers, Kamin (1974) points out that often contradictory data were reported for the same study. Furthermore, there is considerable ambiguity about how the IQ scores were obtained. Such questionable data make the Burt study virtually useless as a source of information about the role of heredity and environment.[4]

[4]During the writing of this book, much controversy has arisen over the scientific integrity of Sir Cyril Burt. Burt, who died in 1971, was considered the leading figure in Britain in the field of mental measurement for nearly 60 years (Vernon, 1979). It now seems apparent, based on a detailed analysis of some of Burt's IQ data (see Dorfman, 1978), that Burt was guilty of fabricating data. Other evidence leading to the conclusion that Burt perpetrated systematic fraud is contained in a biographical analysis being prepared by Leslie S. Hearnshaw (cited by Vernon, 1979).

Table 5-3. Individual Data on Identical Twins Reared Apart in the Newman, Freeman, and Holzinger Study

Case Number	Sex	Age at Separation	Age at Testing	Environmental Differences			Twin Difference in IQ
				In Years of Schooling	In Estimated Educational Advantages*	In Estimated Social Advantages*	
11	F	18 mo.	35	14	37	25	24
2	F	18 mo.	27	10	32	14	12
18	M	1 yr.	27	4	28	31	19
4	F	5 mo.	29	4	22	15	17
12	F	18 mo.	29	5	19	13	7
1	F	18 mo.	19	1	15	27	12
17	M	2 yr.	14	0	15	15	10
8	F	3 mo.	15	1	14	32	15
3	M	2 mo.	23	1	12	15	-2
14	F	6 mo.	39	0	12	15	-1
5	F	14 mo.	38	1	11	26	4
13	M	1 mo.	19	0	11	13	1
10	F	1 yr.	12	1	10	15	5
15	M	1 yr.	26	2	9	7	1
7	M	1 mo.	13	0	9	27	-1
19	F	6 yr.	41	0	9	14	-9
16	F	2 yr.	11	0	8	12	2
6	F	3 yr.	59	0	7	10	8
9	M	1 mo.	19	0	7	14	6

*Ratings are on a scale of 50 points; the higher the rating, the greater the estimated environmental difference between the twins.

Adapted from "Heredity and Environment: A Critical Survey of Recently Published Material on Twins and Foster Children," by R. S. Woodworth, *Social Science Research Council Bulletin No. 47.* Copyright 1941 by the Social Science Research Council. Used by permission.

The Shields (1962) study was also carried out in England. When tested, the 37 twin pairs who were raised apart were mostly adults, and most had been separated before 6 months of age. The reported IQ correlations of .77 for twins reared apart and .75 for twins reared together are based on a variety of intelligence tests. Shields provided detailed information about the kinds of environments in which the twins were raised. This information indicates that although reared apart, there tended to be a close similarity in the environments of the twin pairs. Moreover, in several cases, the twins were brought up in physical proximity to one another and reared in related branches of their parents' families. The sample of twins reared apart in this study, therefore, really does not constitute a condition in which twins are separated at young ages and raised in substantially different environments.

The final study in this group was conducted in Denmark by Juel-Nielsen (1965) and considered only twins who were raised apart. Most of the 12 twin pairs were separated before 12 months. The descriptions of the environments the twins were raised in suggest that, as in the Shields study, the twins did not grow up in truly separate environments (Kamin, 1974).

What conclusions can be drawn from these identical twin studies? First, it is apparent that heredity is important. The IQ correlations are high for identical twins, whether reared apart or together. Furthermore, the correlations for twins reared apart are nearly as high as the correlations for twins reared together. However, the correlations for twins reared apart may well be spuriously high because in some instances members of twin pairs have been reared in proximity with one another and brought up in related families. When environments differ in terms of educational and social advantages, evidence indicates that these environmental variations do influence IQ scores.

Comparisons of Identical and Fraternal Twins. Recall that comparisons between identical and fraternal twins allow us to look at the degree of similarity between individuals with the same environment and heredity (identical twins) versus the degree of similarity between individuals with the same environment but about 50% shared heredity (fraternal twins). Evidence of the influence of heredity is demonstrated by a greater degree of similarity among identical twin pairs than among fraternal twin pairs.

As the summary in Figure 5-1 reveals, higher correlations generally are found for identical twins than for fraternal twins. The median correlation for identical twins raised together is .89, while the median correlation for both same-sex and opposite-sex fraternal twins is .56. These results are therefore consistent with a genetic interpretation.

In addition to the above studies, all of which dealt with measures of general intelligence, an investigation by Vandenberg (1962) provides evidence that some of the more specific abilities are also significantly influenced by heredity. Thurstone's measures of primary mental abilities (see Chapter 4) were administered to samples of identical and fraternal twins. Significantly greater similarity was found for identical twins than for fraternal twins on the subtest measures of numerical, verbal, word fluency, and spatial abilities, but not for the reasoning and memory abilities.

Environmental factors, however, may also contribute to the finding of greater similarity for identical twins on measures of intelligence and special abilities. As noted in Chapter 3, it appears that identical twins are treated more alike than are fraternal twins (Bronfenbrenner, 1975; Scarr, 1969; R. T. Smith, 1965). For instance, parents are more likely to minimize differences between identical twins than differences between fraternal twins. In sum it seems that both genetic and environmental factors are involved in the intelligence- and ability-test differences between identical and fraternal twins.

Genetic Abnormalities

Investigations of genetic abnormalities involve an analysis of the effects of inbreeding, defective genes, and chromosomal abnormalities. In investigating *inbreeding* we are interested in how the intelligence of offspring is affected by the mating of two genetically related individuals. We pointed out in Chapter 3 that inbreeding generally increases the incidence of birth defects because of the increased probability that defective genes will be passed on from the parents to their children. While all individuals carry a number of defective genes in their chromosomes, such genes are usually recessive, and therefore it is unlikely that they will be passed on to offspring. However, in the case of parents who are genetically related, there is an increased probability that defective recessive genes will be paired in the offspring, thus having an effect on the offspring's phenotype.

Research demonstrates that inbreeding does tend to depress intelligence. The most extensive study was carried out in Japan after World War II by Schull and Neel (1965). These investigators studied the offspring of marriages of first cousins, first cousins once removed, and second cousins. In Japan approximately 5% of all marriages are between first cousins. The children of the marriages between cousins were compared with a control group of children from unrelated marriages. A Japanese version of the Wechsler Intelligence Scale for Children (WISC) was used. The results indicated that consanguinity (matings of related individuals) depressed WISC IQs by an average of about 5 IQ points.

Data are also available concerning the effect of inbreeding on the intelligence of offspring from incestuous matings (Vandenberg, 1971). In one study of 13 offspring of father/daughter and brother/sister unions, 3 children died of rare diseases by the time they were 4 years old. Of the remaining 10 children, who ranged in age from 4 to 6 years, 5 were retarded. In another study, children from incestuous matings had a mean IQ of 75, whereas a group of control children had a mean IQ of 102.

Defective genes can affect intelligence even when inbreeding is not involved. Vandenberg (1971) reports that as many as 50 different single genes have been connected with rare diseases that produce mental retardation. The best known example of such a gene-connected disease is phenylketonuria (PKU), a recessive condition with a very low rate of occurrence (between 1 per 10,000 and 1 per 40,000 in most Caucasian populations). In PKU severe retardation occurs because the liver does not produce the enzyme needed for the normal development of the young brain. Once the enzyme deficiency is identified, intellectual functioning can be kept from deteriorating by the introduction of a special diet. Prevention of mental retardation caused by PKU is now possible through screening procedures for newborn infants and through appropriate dietary intervention.

Intelligence also can be affected by *chromosomal abnormalities*— deviations in the normal number of 46 chromosomes. One example of this is a form of mental retardation known as Down's syndrome, or Mongolism as it was formerly called. Down's syndrome is caused by the presence of an extra autosome (one of the chromosomes that does not determine sex). There are also some individuals who have an abnormal number of sex chromosomes. Recall that males have one X and one Y chromosome, while females have two X chromosomes. Occasionally, an individual has only one X chromosome. This condition is known as Turner's syndrome, and such individuals are designated XO. While phenotypically similar to a normal female, an XO female will be infertile and have physically underdeveloped sexual characteristics. XO females usually score low on performance subtests of intelligence scales, although their performance on verbal subtests is about average. Another type of sex chromosome abnormality occurs in males who have an extra Y chromosome. Vandenberg (1971) reports that these XYY males show only mild retardation.

Conclusions

We have surveyed the kinds of evidence that can shed some light on the role of heredity in determining intelligence. Two kinds of studies are available, one type dealing with comparisons of tested intelligence among biologically related individuals and the other dealing with genetic abnormalities. With respect to the first kind of study, there is some disagreement regarding the appropriate interpretation of the results. The position taken by Jensen (1969) and Herrnstein (1973) is that the comparisons of tested intelligence among biologically related individuals provide clear support for the predominance of heredity over environment. On the other hand, Kamin (1974) argues that the serious methodological flaws intrinsic to many of the studies that have been carried out, particularly the early studies of adopted children and the studies of twins raised apart, make it difficult to place any confidence in the interpretation that individual differences in intelligence are primarily due to heredity. We believe that the safest conclusion at this point is that the overall evidence indicates that both hereditary and environmental factors are important. The second kind of study—the investigation of genetic abnormalities—appears to be a promising approach to learning more of the specifics of genetic contributions to intelligence. These investigations, while few in number, point to the role of heredity in the development of intelligence by indicating that genetic abnormalities tend to lower intelligence-test performance.

ENVIRONMENTAL INFLUENCES

We have already noted in our review of studies involving genetically related individuals that environmental factors have an effect on tested intelligence. There is also other evidence bearing on the relationship between environmental factors and intelligence. First, we will look at "longitudinal" studies in which individuals are given repeated tests of intelligence over a period of several years and see what role environmental factors play in accounting for any changes in test performance. Next, we will consider the effect of different kinds of environmental conditions: those that appear to be deficient in intellectual stimulation (environmental deprivation) and those that appear to provide high levels of intellectual stimulation (environmental enrichment). With respect to both longitudinal data and varieties of environmental conditions, our concern is with the nature of the social environment. Finally, there are also environmental factors of a biological nature that may affect intelligence, such as nutrition and conditions connected with birth.

Longitudinal Studies

Evidence pertinent to the degree of stability of tested intelligence has been determined by comparing IQs that have been obtained at two or more ages on a given sample of individuals.[5] The general results of longitudinal studies involving test-retest correlations of intelligence-test scores have been very consistent (Bloom, 1964). For example, in the Berkeley Growth Study (Bayley, 1949) a sample of 40 children were given several intelligence tests within their first year and then followed up until they reached age 18. Correlations between IQs obtained during infancy (the first year) and IQs at age 18 were negligible. The correlation between IQs at ages 3 and 18 was .50, and between ages 6 and 18, .80. After age 6, the correlations with age 18 remained above .80, and by age 15 reached as high as approximately .96.

The test-retest results reported in the Berkeley Growth Study, as well as the similar results reported in other longitudinal studies (see Bloom, 1964), have been interpreted as indicating that on the average tested intelligence is very stable from age 6 onward. On the other hand, below age 3 the IQ is a very poor predictor of later IQ. The negligible relationship between infant

[5] In this section we shall limit our consideration of longitudinal data to childhood and adolescence. Longitudinal data with respect to adulthood and old age will be considered in Chapter 11.

tests and those given at later ages seems to reflect differences in what is being measured at early and later ages. The infant tests, unlike later tests, are greatly influenced by physical and motor development. The infant tests also are intended for use with children who have not developed language, whereas later tests assume the individual being tested understands language (Brody & Brody, 1976).

Even with the high test-retest correlations starting at age 6, it is possible that large shifts in IQ can occur in individual cases. For instance, Honzik, McFarlane, and Allen (1948) found in a sample of 222 children that individual IQ changes of as much as 50 points (somewhat over 3 standard deviations) occurred during the school years. They further reported that changes of 30 or more IQ points occurred in 9% of their sample of 222 children, and changes of 20 or more points occurred in 37% of their sample. One factor that possibly could account for such reported changes in IQ scores over age is the effect of repeated testing, that is, subjects should be able to improve their test performance with increased exposure to testing. However, evidence has demonstrated that repeated testing does not, in fact, have a significant effect on increases in IQ scores (Freeman & Flory, 1937; Moriarty, 1966). In both these studies new subjects were introduced during the course of the testing programs, and no differences were found between experienced and nonexperienced subjects.

The most extensive investigation of individual patterns of IQ change over age has been conducted in a series of studies at the Fels Research Institute (McCall, Appelbaum, & Hogarty, 1973; Sontag, Baker, & Nelson, 1958). In the more recent study 80 middle-class children were given 17 IQ tests between the ages of 2½ and 17 (McCall et al., 1973). The same IQ test, the Stanford-Binet, was used in each of the administrations. McCall and his associates reported that these children changed, on the average, 28.5 IQ points during the 2½- to 17-year-old period and that one in seven showed shifts of more than 40 points. As the sample consisted of both siblings and unrelated children, it is of interest to note that the results showed that while siblings were more similar in their IQ scores, the fluctuating pattern of developmental change was not more similar for siblings than for unrelated children.

Based on an analysis of the developmental profiles, 67 out of the 80 subjects could be clustered into one of five groups that represented different patterns of IQ change over age. The mean IQ over age for each of the five IQ clusters is shown in Figure 5-2. The largest profile group (*group 1*) reflected a slightly rising pattern throughout childhood. The four other profile groups were as follows: *group 2*, a sharp decline between ages 4 and 6, then a slight recovery until age 14 when a downward trend again appeared; *group 3*, a sharp decline between ages 4 and 6, followed by a stable pattern between ages 6 and 14 and an upswing after age 14; *group 4*, an increase until age 8 and then a sharp decline starting at age 10; and *group 5*, similar to group 4 but with less of a subsequent decline after age 10. Overall, when major shifts occurred they took place when the children were at age 6 or when they were age 10.

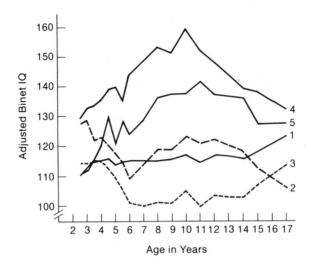

Figure 5-2. Mean IQ (adjusted for differences between Binet revisions) over age for the five IQ clusters. From "Developmental Changes in Mental Performance," by R. B. McCall, M. L. Appelbaum, and P. S. Hogarty, *Monographs of the Society for Research in Child Development*, 1973, *38*(3), Serial No. 150. Copyright 1973 by the Society for Research in Child Development. Reprinted by permission.

We can conclude from the results of longitudinal studies that tested intelligence does in some cases remain relatively stable or constant by age 6. However, the evidence from a series of repeated test administrations also demonstrates that a variety of developmental patterns emerges. How can we account for age-related changes in IQ? The study by McCall et al. suggests that such changes are related to environmental events, because relationships were found between parental behaviors and the particular developmental pattern of the child. Children who showed predominantly declining IQ patterns in the preschool years tended to come from homes in which parents provided little encouragement for intellectual tasks. On the other hand, children showing increases in IQ until about age 8 came from homes in which parents directly attempted to accelerate their children's mastery of intellectual skills.

Environmental Deprivation

One kind of situation involving environmental deprivation is the *rearing of children in institutions,* such as orphanages, where there may be little opportunity for them to receive personal attention. Several investigators have looked at the effect of such institutional life on intellectual functioning. For example, Goldfarb (1943) compared children remaining in orphanages for the first three years with those adopted immediately after birth. The results showed that 37.5% of the orphanage children were classified as mentally retarded, whereas only 7.5% of the adopted children were so classified. Goldfarb concluded that these differences were due to the lack of intellectual stimulation experienced by the institutionalized children. In another study, Goldfarb (1947) compared two groups of adolescents who were adopted. One group had been adopted immediately after birth; the other group was raised during the infancy period in an orphanage. A marked contrast was found between the two groups in terms of their approach to problem solving. The group that spent the infancy period in an orphanage group approached the problems more concretely, while the other group utilized a more abstract approach.

Other studies of children reared in institutional environments also generally point to the negative effect such environments have on intellectual development (for example, Dennis & Najarian, 1957; Spitz, 1945). The specific time at which the child is exposed to the deprived conditions of institutional life seems to be a particularly critical factor. In a review of the studies on the effect of institutionalization, Yarrow (1961) concluded that the greatest vulnerability to intellectual impairment takes place when deprivation occurs between the ages of 3 and 12 months.

Another kind of situation that involves environmental deprivation is *social isolation.* As we might expect, the results of studies that have involved children raised in socially isolated communities generally show that such conditions are related to some impairment in intellectual functioning. The earliest study of this kind was Gordon's (1923) report of the canal boat children of England. These children attended school only about 5% of the school year, and their parents were illiterate. Their mean Stanford-Binet IQ was 70, and there was a noted decline in IQ with age. In a related study, Gordon reported on a group of Gypsy children in England who attended school an average of 35% of the year. The mean IQ for this sample was 75. During the 1930s, a number of studies were carried out in the isolated mountain areas of eastern Kentucky and Tennessee (Ascher, 1935; Sherman & Key, 1932; Wheeler, 1932). The results generally showed that the children in these isolated communities had lower-than-average IQs, especially when their IQs were based on verbal as opposed to nonverbal tests. As in the English studies, IQ declined with age.

One other condition of environmental deprivation has recently drawn attention. Zajonc and Markus (1975) have attempted to explain two interrelated sets of findings: One is that there is a negative relationship (correlations of around –.25) between the *size of a child's family* and his or her IQ, and this relationship holds even when social class is controlled. The second finding is that intelligence declines with *birth order;* that is, first-born children tend to have higher IQs than second-born children who have higher IQs than third-born children, and so on. Both of these trends are illustrated in Figure 5-3, which is based on data collected by Belmont and Marolla (1973) with a sample of close to 400,000 Dutch 19-year-old men who were given the Raven Progressive Matrices, a nonverbal intelligence test that is relatively free of cultural bias. Zajonc and Markus interpret these results as a reflection of the decreasing opportunities a child has for receiving parental intellectual stimulation the higher his or her birth order and the larger the number of siblings. This is an interesting interpretation of the data and consistent with other evidence we have reviewed that shows that lowered intelligence-test performance is associated with conditions of environmental deprivation. In the case of only children, whose mean IQ is lower than would be expected on the basis of family size (see "j = 1" in Figure 5-3), Zajonc and Markus point out that such children are at a disadvantage compared with children who have younger siblings because only children are deprived of being able to teach younger children in the family.[6] Similarly, last-born children are also deprived of a teaching role, which would explain the substantially larger drop in mean IQ for last-born children than the decline between other adjacent siblings (see Figure 5-3).

Zajonc and Markus also suggest that intelligence does not necessarily have to decline with birth order. If siblings are spaced far apart there would be less competition for parental attention than if they are close in age. Consistent with this hypothesis about the spacing of children are data comparing the intelligence-test performance of twins and singletons. The mean intelligence-test scores of twins are lower than those of singletons, and furthermore the mean intelligence-test scores of triplets are lower than those of twins (Record, McKeown, & Edwards, 1970). No data are as yet available with respect to IQ and spacing among single-birth siblings.

Environmental Enrichment

With conditions of environmental enrichment, we should expect the facilitation of intellectual development. This was the hypothesis of the research group at the University of Iowa in the 1930s. More specifically, these investigators predicted that children who were exposed to a nursery-school program would show resultant increases in IQ. A comparison of IQ changes was first made from fall to spring when the nursery school was in session, and an average gain of 6.6 IQ points occurred during this period (Wellman, 1940). A small loss took place during the subsequent spring-to-fall period. However, a further gain of 3.8 points occurred for those children who remained in the nursery school during the second year. Some children also continued for a third year, but by this point further gains were minimal, and it appeared that the children had reached a point of diminishing returns. Another source of comparison was provided by contrasting the preschool group of children with a nonpreschool group of children who were matched for age and IQ. A significant difference was found. Between the fall and spring testing, the preschool group gained 7.0 points, while the nonpreschool group lost 3.9 points.

The Iowa researchers interpreted the above findings as supporting their hypothesis that it is possible to raise IQ as a result of enrichment provided by a nursery-school program. However, a problem with the Iowa study lay in the sampling of the preschool and nonpreschool groups. In comparing these

---

[6]The data with respect to only children need to be accepted with caution. Other evidence shows that only children exceed other first-born children on intellectual-test performance (Scottish Council for Research in Education, 1949).

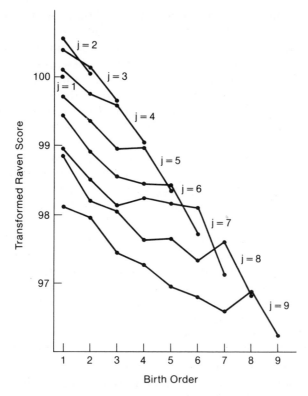

Figure 5-3. Average transformed Raven scores as a function of birth order and family size (j), recalculated from Belmont and Marolla (1973). From "Birth Order and Intellectual Development," by R. B. Zajonc and G. B. Markus, *Psychological Review*, 1975, *82*, 74–88. Copyright 1975 by the American Psychological Association. Reprinted by permission.

two groups, the investigators failed to take into consideration factors that might have differentially influenced the makeup of the groups. For instance, it may be that parents who chose to enroll their children in nursery schools were more sensitive to the intellectual needs of their children and also provided a more intellectually stimulating home environment than parents who chose not to enroll their children in nursery school. In other words, sampling bias resulting from self-selection may have occurred (see Chapter 2). Thus, the results of the Iowa study that showed an increase in IQ for the preschool group and a decrease for the nonpreschool group may have been due to a lack of comparability of the two groups. As we noted in Chapter 2, to avoid sampling bias it is necessary to randomly select and assign individuals to different treatment groups.

Several other investigations of the effect of nursery school on IQ were reported around the same time as the Iowa study, and these studies (for example, Jones & Jorgensen, 1940) showed no significant changes in IQ. It is important to recognize that in these and other investigations the children who attended nursery school were generally the offspring of university faculty or students. We should not really expect nursery school to have an appreciable effect on the intellectual development of such already "advantaged" children. On the other hand, for children of culturally deprived environments, preschool exposure might prove to be a very significant factor. During the 1960s, a concentrated effort was made to implement and evaluate the effects of preschool experiences on children from culturally deprived environments. Later on in this section we will look at two examples of research with lower-class preschool children.

Other members of the Iowa research group, Skeels and Dye (1939), investigated the effect of transferring a group of children from an orphanage to an institution for the mentally retarded. Such an unorthodox procedure was suggested by the marked changes that were observed after two baby girls had been committed to the institution for the mentally retarded. These babies had originally been admitted to the orphanage at the ages of 13 and 16 months, respectively. Because both had measured IQs of 46 and were retarded in their physical development, an institution for the mentally retarded was deemed a more appropriate placement. At the time of transfer, one girl was 15 months old and the other was 18 months. In the institution, the two little girls were placed on a ward with adult female retardates. After six months the younger girl's IQ had increased to 77 and the older girl's IQ to 87. Subsequent testings over a two-year period indicated that they were performing within the average range. To account for these changes, the nature of the ward environment was examined. It was noted that the two children received a great deal of individual attention from both the older inmates on the ward and the ward attendants.

In the actual study reported by Skeels and Dye, an experimental group of 13 children with a median age of 16½ months was transferred from the orphanage to the institution for the mentally retarded. This group was compared with a control group of 12 children who remained in the orphanage. Just prior to transfer, the experimental group had an average IQ of 64 with a range of 36 to 89, and the control group an average of 87 with a range of 50 to 103. After intervals ranging from 6 months to 4 years, all of the 13 experimental children showed increases in tested IQ, ranging from 7 to 58 points. For the 12 control children, only one showed an increase and this increase was just 2 points. The other control children displayed IQ decrements ranging from 8 to 45 points. Skeels and Dye interpreted these findings as demonstrating the impact the environment can have on tested intelligence. However, it is also possible that the obtained differences for the two groups could have been due to the effect of statistical regression; that is, the movement of scores towards the mean for the combined groups over repeated testings, because of chance factors. Consistent with this statistical rationale, we would expect the experimental group with the lower initial IQ to show an increase over subsequent testings and the control group with the higher initial IQ to show a decrease over subsequent testings.

Fortunately, further data are available that clarify the Skeels/Dye study. Skeels (1966) conducted a follow-up of the subjects in the original study by surveying their accomplishments 21 years later. He found that 11 of the 13 experimental children who were placed in the institution for the mentally retarded had later been placed in foster homes. The 12 control children who were in the orphanage remained in the institutionalized setting for a longer period of time than the majority of the experimental children. As adults there were rather striking differences between the two groups. The members of the experimental group were self-supporting, with occupations ranging from domestic to professional. They had completed an average of 12 years of education. Eleven had married and all of their children were of normal intelligence. On the other hand, the 11 surviving members of the control group (one was deceased at the time of the follow-up) included four who were institutionalized. The seven who were employed had on the average a lower level of occupation than the members of the experimental group. The mean educational level of the control group was at the third grade, and only two members had married. The differences between these two groups definitely suggest the significant impact that early environmental factors can have on intellectual development. It should be pointed out, however, that the control children who stayed in the orphanage were probably not representative of an orphanage population because many of the children in the orphanage were eventually placed in foster homes or even adopted.

The effect of elementary school and high school education on tested intelligence has been investigated in several studies. Lorge (1945) retested 131 men who had been tested 20 years earlier while in the eighth grade of New York City public schools. The subjects were categorized according to their initial IQ scores. The results showed that when initial intelligence level was the same, the final scores varied as a function of the amount of schooling. Those who had gone to college had significantly higher scores than those who had dropped out of high school. A similar study with a larger sample was carried out by Husen (1951) in Sweden. In this study, 722 young men were given intelligence tests at the time of their induction into military service. Their test performance was compared with the results of a previous testing carried out 10 years earlier when they were in the third grade. As in the Lorge study, the results of the final testing showed that higher scores were associated with amount of schooling. The group of subjects that had stopped their schooling after the compulsory 7 years of primary school showed an average decrease of 1.2 IQ points, while the group that had completed 12–13 years of school had an average increase of 11 IQ points.

Evidence from a number of other studies suggests that improvements in the quality of education, as well as other community improvements, can result in an upward shift in intelligence-test performance. We referred earlier to a study by Wheeler (1932) which showed that children in the mountain regions of Eastern Tennessee scored in the lower-than-average range of intelligence. Wheeler (1942) returned 10 years later and tested another sample of children. During the 10-year interval considerable social, economic, and educational improvements had taken place. Consistent with these environmental changes, the second sample obtained higher scores than the first sample, and this difference occurred for all of the age groups (6 through 18). The median IQ in the first sample was 82, whereas in the second sample it was 93. Studies by S. Smith (1942) in Hawaii and Finch (1946) in two midwestern states have reported similar increments in tested intelligence as community and educational improvements have occurred.

In general, the various investigations of the effect of education on tested intelligence do not directly indicate that it is the amount or quality of schooling per se that is related to increases in IQ. It may be that the IQ changes are due to other kinds of environmental stimulants, such as family attitudes, increased vocational opportunities, or community progress. Evidence that a stimulating family environment can lead to gains in tested intelligence comes from a study by Levenstein (1970). A within-the-home intervention program for 2-year-old children was carried out for a group of lower-working-class families who lived in a public housing project. Other families, which were equated with the experimental group for social class and housing, were used as a source of comparison. The intervention program consisted of a 7-month series of semiweekly visits to the home of the experimental group. Each half-hour visit was made by a social worker or trained nonprofessional who provided educational toys and books. The visitors also encouraged the mothers to interact with their children using the educational materials. The mean IQ of the experimental children increased from 85 at the beginning of the intervention program to 102 at the end. On the other hand, the control group had an initial mean IQ of 92 (which was not significantly different from the initial mean IQ of the experimental group) and a subsequent mean IQ of 94. Thus, unlike the experimental group, the control group showed no meaningful change in intelligence-test performance. Levenstein further indicates, in an unpublished report summarized by Cronin, Daniels, Hurley, Kroch, and Webber (1975), that these group differences held up during the two-year period following the completion of the program.

Another family-intervention study, carried out by Heber, Garber, Herrington, Hoffman, and Falender (1972), also demonstrates the facilitative effect of this kind of environmental enrichment on intellectual development. This study, known as the Milwaukee Project, has produced a 30-point IQ difference between an experimental group and a control group of preschool children. At the start of the study, the investigators selected 40 families with newborn infants from the lowest income area of Milwaukee. In each of these families, the mother scored less than 75 on the Wechsler Adult Intelligence Scale. The infants were randomly assigned to either an experimental group or a control group. In the experimental group, the mothers were first exposed to adult education classes in reading and arithmetic and then to a training program that dealt with nursing skills, homemaking skills, and child-rearing practices. The intervention program started when the infants were 3 months old and continued until the children entered public school at age 6. During this period, each child received five-day-a-week care and cognitive training at a preschool learning center from specially trained residents in the neighborhood. Between 12 months and 30 months, the control group showed a progressive decline in IQ. After 30 months the control group averaged around an IQ of 95. On the other hand, the experimental group had a gradual rise in IQ starting at 12 months and by 36 months averaged around an IQ of 125. The results thus showed that by age 3, the experimental group was approximately 30 IQ points higher than the control group. These results provide impressive evidence for the effectiveness of family-intervention programs, and it will be important to see if the gains made by the experimental group are maintained during the school years. In Chapter 13 we will consider the overall results of intervention studies with disadvantaged children.

In general, evidence does indicate that environmental enrichment can have a marked effect on intellectual development. This is especially illustrated in the Skeels (1966) study with institutionalized children, and the family-intervention studies by Levenstein (1970) and Heber et al. (1972). These studies also suggest that to be effective enrichment programs must be comprehensive; that is, at the very least they should involve the parents or parent-substitutes as well as the children.

Biological Factors

It is reasonable to expect that the biological environment can affect intellectual development. Specifically, complications during pregnancy and delivery as well as conditions of malnutrition (which we will consider in the next paragraph) could result in retarded intellectual functioning. Difficulties during the period of gestation often lead to low birth weight, and low birth weight has been studied in relation to intelligence. Infants with low birth weight include those who are born prematurely or those who are below normal birth weight even though born at or near the 9-month gestation period. A difficulty with estimating the effect of low birth weight on intelligence is the high relationship between birth weight and social class; that is, low birth weight is more prevalent among the lower classes. When social class is controlled, evidence indicates that the mean IQ is lowered for children having birth weights under 3 pounds (Jensen, 1969). However, this depressed effect among low birth weight children is apparently only of short duration. With the exception of extreme cases (IQs below 50), the effect of low birth weight has little relationship to children's IQs by the time they reach school age.

Early nutritional deprivation can have an adverse effect on the development of the brain in humans (Brody & Brody, 1976). Therefore, when malnutrition occurs in very young children, we should expect to find retarded intellectual functioning. Some support for such an expectation is indicated in studies conducted in South Africa and India. However, it is not apparent in these studies whether the lower intelligence was due to the effect of severe malnutrition or to the effect of the social deprivation to which the children also were exposed. Furthermore, such studies are based on extremely impoverished populations, and thus may not provide very much information about the relationship between nutrition and intelligence in the population of North

America. Investigations based on American samples have compared the intelligence of children from two groups of mothers: low-social-class mothers who received nutritional supplements during pregnancy and matched groups of mothers who were not given such supplements during pregnancy (see Brody & Brody, 1976). The results of the investigations have been mixed. For example, one study involving groups of Black mothers in an urban area showed a small but significant increase in the Binet IQs of the children of the mothers given a nutritional supplement. However, when the study was repeated in a rural setting with White mothers no significant effect was demonstrated for such a group of children. In reviewing the evidence on nutrition and intelligence, Brody and Brody (1976) conclude: "there is little available evidence at present that suggests that nutritional factors will account for any, or for any appreciable, variance in intelligence test scores in a representative sample of the U.S. population" (p. 157).

Conclusions

From our consideration of the role of environmental factors, it is apparent that the environment can have a significant effect on the development of intelligence. Conditions of environmental deprivation lead to lowered intellectual functioning, and, as seen in the Skeels study with the sample of orphanage children, these effects can continue into the adult years. When conditions of deprivation are modified in the direction of environmental enrichment, evidence indicates that intellectual functioning can be improved. In his comments on the role of environmental factors, Jensen (1969) acknowledges that the social environment can significantly affect intellectual functioning; however, he feels that environmental influences are limited to rather extreme situations of deprivation. The evidence that we have reviewed from studies of institutionalized children and poor families is consistent with Jensen's conclusion. Nevertheless, there is also some suggestion that environmental factors can play a critical role within the so-called "normal" kinds of conditions in which children are raised. The study of developmental changes in intelligence by McCall and associates points to the importance that specific environmental events, such as parental encouragement, can have on the intellectual development of middle-class children.

THE APPROPRIATE QUESTION

Two decades ago Anastasi (1958) wrote a paper entitled, "Heredity, Environment, and the Question 'How?'" (see Chapter 3). Her major point was that the historical "either/or" formulation with respect to heredity and environment, and the efforts to determine the proportional contribution of hereditary and environmental factors, were the wrong issues to pursue. They were wrong because hereditary and environmental factors interact with one another—the proportional contribution of heredity to the variance of a given trait, such as intelligence, will vary under different environmental conditions. For example, if environmental conditions are fairly uniform for a given population, the environmental component of the total IQ variance will be relatively low and the genetic component will be relatively high, resulting in a high heritability estimate. As environmental variability increases the relative contribution of heredity decreases. Since Anastasi published her article, some of the same questions are still being asked. It is true that we have moved away from a simple "either/or" argument (which Anastasi indicated was already a dead issue in 1958), but the question of proportional contribution is still being debated. According to Anastasi the important question to ask is not *which* factor accounts for individual differences in a trait or *how much* each factor contributes to individual differences, but rather *how* heredity and environment influence the development of behavioral differences. In a similar vein, Tyler (1965) suggests that the most important information we can obtain about a characteristic is not the proportional contribution of heredity and environment, but how amenable it is to change and precisely how change can be effected.

In our review of intelligence and the heredity/environment issue we have seen that both heredity and environment influence the development of individual differences in intelligence. We have also noted that intelligence-test performance is amenable to change. Probably the biggest challenge still facing us, as suggested by Anastasi and Tyler, is coming to an understanding of precisely how change in intellectual functioning can be effected.

SUMMARY

With the appearance of the first intelligence tests, considerable controversy arose over whether intelligence was primarily an inherited or an acquired trait. The early arguments on the nature/nurture issue were typically at one extreme or the other. There is currently a general acceptance that both sets of determinants need to be considered. Nevertheless, much controversy exists over the relative impact of hereditary and environmental determinants. The proportion of the hereditary variance to the total variance of intelligence-test scores for a given population is referred to as the heritability of intelligence. Various indexes of heritability have been presented, but several questions have been raised as to the applicability of heritability with respect to human intelligence. Rather than trying to determine the proportional contribution of hereditary and environmental factors, the more appropriate question is how both hereditary and environmental factors operate to produce differences in intelligence.

Evidence on the role of heredity is based on studies comparing tested intelligence among genetically related individuals and studies of genetic abnormalities. The results of studies of IQ comparisons among genetically related individuals indicate that heredity is a significant influence. However, these studies also demonstrate that environmental factors are important. The investigation of genetic abnormalities indicates that these factors tend to lower intelligence-test performance.

In addition to studies of genetically related individuals, evidence of environmental influences is based on longitudinal studies of changes in tested intelligence for given individuals, the effects of deprivation and enrichment in the social environment, and the effect of biological factors such as nutrition and birth weight. The overall results of studies of the role of environmental factors indicate that the social environment can have a significant effect on the development of intelligence. On the other hand, biological factors, such as nutrition and birth weight, appear to have little relationship to differences in intelligence.

REFERENCES

Anastasi, A. Heredity, environment, and the question "How?" *Psychological Review,* 1958, *65,* 197–208.

Ascher, E. J. The inadequacy of current intelligence tests for testing Kentucky mountain children. *Journal of Genetic Psychology,* 1935, *46,* 480–486.

Bayley, N. Consistency and variability in the growth of intelligence from birth to eighteen years. *Journal of Genetic Psychology,* 1949, 75, 165–196.

Belmont, L., & Marolla, F. A. Birth order, family size, and intelligence. *Science,* 1973, *182,* 1096–1101.

Block, N. J., & Dworkin, G. IQ, heritability, and inequality, Part 2. *Philosophy and Public Affairs,* 1974, *4,* 40–90.

Bloom, B. S. *Stability and change in human characteristics.* New York: Wiley, 1964.

Brody, E. B., & Brody, N. *Intelligence: Nature, determinants, and consequences.* New York: Academic Press, 1976.

Bronfenbrenner, U. Nature with nurture: A reinterpretation of the evidence. In A. Montagu (Ed.), *Race and IQ.* New York: Oxford University Press, 1975.

Burks, B. S. The relative influence of nature and nurture upon mental development: A comparative study of foster parent-foster child resemblance and true parent-true child resemblance. *Yearbook of the National Society for the Study of Education,* 1928, *27*(1), 219–316.

Burt, C. The inheritance of mental ability. *American Psychologist,* 1958, *13,* 1–15.

Burt, C. The genetic determination of differences in intelligence: A study of monozygotic twins reared together and apart. *British Journal of Psychology,* 1966, *57,* 137–153.

Cronin, J., Daniels, N., Hurley, A., Kroch, A., & Webber, R. Race, class, and intelligence: A critical look at the IQ controversy. *International Journal of Mental Health,* 1975, *3*(4), 46–132.

Dennis, W., & Najarian, P. Infant development under environmental handicap. *Psychological Monographs,* 1957, *71*(7, Whole No. 436).

Dorfman, D. D. The Cyril Burt question: New findings. *Science,* 1978, *201,* 1177–1186.

Erlenmeyer-Kimling, L., & Jarvik, L. F. Genetics and intelligence: A review. *Science,* 1963, *142,* 1477–1479.

Eysenck, H. J. *The inequality of man.* San Diego: EdITS, 1975. (Originally published, 1973)

Finch, F. H. Enrollment increases and changes in the mental level of the high school population. *Applied Psychology Monographs,* 1946, No. 10.

Freeman, F. N., & Flory, C. D. Growth in the intellectual ability as measured by repeated tests. *Monographs of the Society for Research in Child Development*, 1937, *2*(2, Serial No. 9).

Goddard, H. H. *The Kallikak family: A study in the heredity of feeblemindedness.* New York: Macmillan, 1912.

Goldfarb, W. Infant rearing and problem behavior. *American Journal of Orthopsychiatry*, 1943, *13*, 249–265.

Goldfarb, W. Variations in adolescent adjustment of institutionally reared children. *American Journal of Orthopsychiatry*, 1947, *17*, 449–457.

Gordon, H. *Mental and scholastic tests among retarded children.* London: Board of Education Pamphlet No. 44, 1923.

Heber, R., Garber, H., Herrington, S., Hoffman, C., & Falender, C. *Rehabilitation of families at risk for mental retardation.* Progress report, December 1972, Rehabilitation Research and Training Center in Mental Retardation, University of Wisconsin, Madison, Wisconsin.

Herrnstein, R. J. *IQ in the meritocracy.* Boston: Atlantic Monthly Press, 1973.

Hirsch, J. Behavior-genetic analysis and its biosocial consequences. In R. Cancro (Ed.), *Intelligence: Genetic and environmental influences.* New York: Grune & Stratton, 1971.

Hirsch, J. Jensenism: The bankruptcy of "science" without scholarship. *Educational Theory*, 1975, *25*, 3–27.

Honzik, M. P. Developmental studies of parent-child resemblance in intelligence. *Child Development*, 1957, *28*, 215–228.

Honzik, M. P., McFarlane, J. W., & Allen, L. The stability of mental test performance between two and eighteen years. *Journal of Experimental Education*, 1948, *17*, 309–324.

Horn, J. M., Loehlin, J. C., & Willerman, L. *The Texas Adoption Project.* Paper presented at the meeting of the Behavior Genetics Association, Austin, Texas, March 1975.

Hunt, J. McV. *Intelligence and experience.* New York: Ronald, 1961.

Husen, T. The influence of schooling upon IQ. *Theoria*, 1951, *17*, 61–88.

Jencks, C., Smith, M., Acland, H., Bane, M. J., Cohen, D., Gintis, H., Heynes, B., & Michelson, S. *Inequality: A reassessment of the effect of family and schooling in America.* New York: Basic Books, 1972.

Jensen, A. R. How much can we boost IQ and scholastic achievement? *Harvard Educational Review*, 1969, *39*, 1–123.

Jones, H. E., & Jorgensen, A. P. Mental growth as related to nursery-school attendance. *Yearbook of the National Society for the Study of Education*, 1940, *39*(2), 207–222.

Juel-Nielsen, N. Individual and environment: A psychiatric-psychological investigation of monozygotic twins reared apart. *Acta Psychiatrica et Neurologica Scandinavica*, 1965, (Monograph Supplement, 183).

Kamin, L. J. *The science and politics of IQ.* Potomac, Md.: Lawrence Erlbaum Associates, 1974.

Leahy, A. M. Nature-nurture and intelligence. *Genetic Psychology Monographs*, 1935, *17*, 235–308.

Levenstein, P. Cognitive growth in preschoolers through verbal interaction with mothers. *American Journal of Orthopsychiatry*, 1970, *40*, 426–432.

Lewontin, R. C. The analysis of variance and the analysis of causes. *American Journal of Human Genetics*, 1974, *26*, 400–411.

Loehlin, J. C., Lindzey, G., & Spuhler, J. N. *Race differences in intelligence.* San Francisco: Freeman, 1975.

Lorge, I. Schooling makes a difference. *Teachers College Record,* 1945, *46,* 483–492.

McCall, R. B., Appelbaum, M. L., & Hogarty, P. S. Developmental changes in mental performance. *Monographs of the Society for Research in Child Development,* 1973, *38*(3, Serial No. 150).

Moriarty, A. E. *Constancy and IQ change: A clinical view of relationships between tested intelligence and personality.* Springfield, Ill.: Charles C. Thomas, 1966.

Munsinger, H. The adopted child's IQ: A critical review. *Psychological Bulletin,* 1975, *82,* 623–659. (a)

Munsinger, H. Children's resemblance to their biological and adopting parents in two ethnic groups. *Behavior Genetics,* 1975, *5,* 239–254. (b)

Newman, H. H., Freeman, F. N., & Holzinger, K. J. *Twins: A study of heredity and environment.* Chicago: University of Chicago Press, 1937.

Record, R. G., McKeown, T., & Edwards, J. H. An investigation of the differences in measured intelligence between twins and single births. *Annals of the Human Genetic Society,* 1970, *34,* 11–20.

Scarr, S. Environmental bias in twin studies. In M. Manosevitz, G. Lindzey, & D. D. Thiessen (Eds.), *Behavioral genetics: Method and research.* New York: Appleton-Century-Crofts, 1969.

Scarr, S., & Weinberg, R. A. IQ test performance of black children adopted by white families. *American Psychologist,* 1976, *31,* 726–739.

Scarr-Salapatek, S. Unknowns in the IQ equation. *Science,* 1971, *174,* 1223–1228.

Schull, W. J., & Neel, J. V. *The effects of inbreeding on Japanese children.* New York: Harper & Row, 1965.

Scottish Council for Research in Education. *The trend of Scottish intelligence.* London: University of London Press, 1949.

Sherman, M., & Key, C. B. The intelligence of isolated mountain children. *Child Development,* 1932, *3,* 279–290.

Shields, J. *Monozygotic twins brought up apart and brought up together.* London: Oxford University Press, 1962.

Skeels, H. M. Adult states of children with contrasting early life experiences. *Monographs of the Society for Research in Child Development,* 1966, *31*(3, Serial No. 105).

Skeels, H. M., & Dye, H. B. A study of the effects of differential stimulation of mentally retarded children. *Proceedings of the American Association of Mental Deficiency,* 1939, *44,* 114–136.

Skodak, M., & Skeels, H. M. A final follow-up study of one hundred adopted children. *Journal of Genetic Psychology,* 1949, *75,* 85–125.

Smith, R. T. A comparison of socioenvironmental factors in monozygotic and dyzygotic twins, testing an assumption. In S. G. Vandenberg (Ed.), *Methods and goals in human behavior genetics.* New York: Academic Press, 1965.

Smith, S. Language and non-verbal test performance of racial groups in Honolulu before and after a 14-year interval. *Journal of General Psychology,* 1942, *26,* 51–93.

Sontag, L. W., Baker, C. T., & Nelson, V. L. Mental growth and personality development: A longitudinal study. *Monographs of the Society for Research in Child Development,* 1958, *23*(2, Serial No. 68).

Spitz, R. A. Hospitalism: An inquiry into the genesis of psychiatric conditions in early childhood. *Psychoanalytic Study of the Child,* 1945, *1,* 53–74, 113–117.

Tyler, L. E. *The psychology of human differences* (3rd ed.). New York: Appleton-Century-Crofts, 1965.

Vandenberg, S. G. The hereditary abilities study: Hereditary components in a psychological test battery. *American Journal of Human Genetics,* 1962, *14,* 220–237.

Vandenberg, S. G. What do we know today about the inheritance of intelligence and how do we know it? In R. Cancro (Ed.), *Intelligence: Genetic and environmental influences.* New York: Grune & Stratton, 1971.

Vernon, P. E. *Intelligence: Heredity and environment.* San Francisco: Freeman, 1979.

Wellman, B. L. Iowa studies of the effects of schooling. *Yearbook of the National Society for the Study of Education,* 1940, *39*(2), 377–399.

Wheeler, L. R. The intelligence of East Tennessee children. *Journal of Educational Psychology,* 1932, *23,* 351–370.

Wheeler, L. R. A comparative study of the intelligence of East Tennessee mountain children. *Journal of Educational Psychology,* 1942, *33,* 321–334.

Woodworth, R. S. *Heredity and environment: A critical survey of recently published material on twins and foster children.* New York: Social Science Research Council Bulletin, 1941, No. 47.

Yarrow, L. J. Maternal deprivation: Toward an empirical and conceptual reevaluation. *Psychological Bulletin,* 1961, *58,* 459–490.

Zajonc, R. B., & Markus, G. B. Birth order and intellectual development. *Psychological Review,* 1975, *82,* 74–88.

School Achievement 6

In modern society a major purpose of education is to provide the necessary training and credentials for economic and social success. Doubts have often been raised as to whether our schools are in fact accomplishing this goal. Clearly some children are far more successful than others in acquiring the prerequisite skills and credentials. In this chapter we explore three questions about school achievement: (1) How do we measure individual differences in school achievement? (2) How can we predict such differences? (3) To what extent is success in later life related to school achievement?

MEASURING SCHOOL ACHIEVEMENT

Standardized Achievement Tests

School achievement can be assessed by the grades that teachers assign or by the use of achievement tests. The problem with teacher-assigned grades and teacher-made tests is that standards of achievement can vary from teacher to teacher as well as from school to school, therefore reducing the comparability of the measured achievement of students in different settings. Standardized achievement tests are designed to overcome the problem of varying standards. Such tests are constructed by test publishers for use in a wide variety of schools. The content covered is usually broad and the norms are generally based on national samples. Standardized tests are therefore useful in assessing an individual student, class, or school system within the context of a wider population. These tests can also serve as a basis for measuring academic growth over a period of several years. A disadvantage of standardized tests is that they cannot be adapted to special local needs, such as curriculum differences in different school systems. Furthermore, such tests are inappropriate for students whose social backgrounds are at variance with those of the sample the test norms are based on, as would be the case if students with a bilingual background were compared with a normative sample of students who spoke only English.

As we noted in Chapter 4, achievement tests differ from ability tests. Achievement tests measure the results of specific learning experiences, such as school instruction in particular subject areas; ability tests measure the results of more general learning experiences, such as the knowledge we acquire by listening to our parents, reading books, and watching television, as well as what we generally learn in school. Like measures of ability, achievement tests may survey several content areas or be limited to a specific content area. Unlike measures of ability, achievement-test content is based on specific coverage in the school curriculum or training syllabus.

Before the days of standardized tests, teachers and pupils were undoubtedly aware of individual differences in school achievement. However, without any standard of comparison, gauging individual differences was difficult. Were differences within a classroom due to limitations of the teacher, limitations of certain pupils, or both? Did different teachers and school administrators have different standards? Practical questions such as these became increasingly relevant in the United States during the latter half of the 19th century as the school population was rapidly expanding.

With the expansion of the school population, more and more schools began to be organized by grade (see Levine, 1976), as even rural schools were gradually consolidated. An examining procedure was needed to determine whether children were ready to be promoted from grade to grade. In order to meet this need, some school systems began to administer standard examinations across all of their schools. However, whereas the exams were standardized, the scoring was still left up to the individual teachers, and in many instances the scoring was found to be unreliable. Standardized achievement tests with norms based on the average scores for each grade were developed to overcome such problems. The practice of separating students into grade levels was not the only historical factor underlying the development of standardized achievement tests. Levine (1976) points out that achievement tests proved useful in resolving arguments about the effectiveness of the schools. Various political-interest groups, such as the upper-class establishment and big-city bosses, could point to test results to bolster their particular positions about whether the schools were meeting the needs of their special constituencies.

One of the first examples of a graded achievement test was an arithmetic test used in the New York City schools in 1911. The arithmetic test was a speed test with a standard set of items, and the results of the test administration showed a consistent grade-by-grade improvement. Standardized achievement tests came into wide use during the 1920s. The Stanford Achievement Test, published in 1923, was the first standardized achievement test battery for elementary school children. Two years later, a test battery for secondary students appeared—the Iowa High School Content Examination.

While standardized achievement tests have been widely accepted for many years, they have not been free from criticism (see Carver, 1974; Hoffman, 1962; Levine, 1976). One issue revolves around the fact that the tests have been primarily developed to assess the acquisition and utilization of knowledge (the so-called "cognitive domain" of educational objectives); whereas, they have largely been unrelated to "affective" goals, such as the development of empathy, social competence, and humaritarian values (see Krathwohl & Payne, 1971).

Another issue in achievement testing is whether or not tests should serve the traditional function of identifying individual differences. Some workers argue that rather than comparing an individual in relation to a normative group, achievement tests should be used primarily to assess mastery of a particular realm of knowledge (Bloom, 1974). For instance, a student might be considered to have attained mastery when he or she was able to get 80% to 90% correct responses. Differences between students would exist only in terms of the amount of time spent in acquiring mastery.

When tests are used to assess mastery, they are referred to as "criterion-referenced" tests; when tests are used to assess individual differences, they are referred to as "norm-referenced" tests. However, according to Carver (1974) these two functions of achievement tests are not incompatible with each other. Rather than argue for one over the other, we can consider a given achievement test as serving both functions. In many situations meaningful information may be obtained by using both criterion-referenced and norm-referenced scores. For example, on a given test of reading comprehension, it may be desirable to know how much material a student has mastered as well as how he or she compares with other students in the same grade.

The Range of Individual Differences

The extent of individual differences in school achievement can best be illustrated by looking at the norms for standardized achievement tests. Selected percentile norms for individuals on the Sequential Tests of Educational Progress (STEP) (1971) are presented in Tables 6-1, 6-2, and 6-3. These norms are based on a large-scale sample of students who were chosen to be representative of the student population of the United States.

Table 6-1. Percentile Norms for Sequential Tests of Educational Progress (STEP) in Reading, Form 4A

Percentile Ranks	Raw Scores*		
	Grade 3 Spring-Grade 4 Fall	Grade 4 Spring-Grade 5 Fall	Grade 5 Spring-Grade 6 Fall
99	50	55	57
90	40	48	52
75	33	42	48
50	25	32	39
25	19	24	29
10	15	18	21
1	10	12	13

*The number of items correct out of a total of 60 items.
Adapted from *Sequential Tests of Educational Progress: Handbook for STEP Series II.*

In Table 6-1 the raw-score equivalents for percentile ranks are shown for the Reading subtest for three elementary school grade levels. Looking at the extreme percentile ranks within the grade 3-4 level we find that students at the 99th percentile have mastered 83% of the content they were tested on (50 items correct out of a total of 60 items), in contrast with students at the 10th percentile who have mastered only 17% of what they were tested on (10 items correct out of 60). Similar contrasts exist at grades 4-5 and 5-6. A wide difference exists even within the middle range; that is, the range between the 25th and 75th percentiles. For example, at the grade 3-4 level students at the 75th percentile have mastered 55% of the material, while students at the 25th percentile have mastered only 32% of the material. Table 6-1 also illustrates the progress in reading achievement accomplished across the three elementary grade levels. On the same test a fifth-grader with a percentile rank of 50 has a mastery level of 65%, while a third-grader with the same percentile rank has a mastery level of 42%. One other comparison in Table 6-1 is worth noting. Some children in lower grades score higher on reading achievement than those in upper grades. For example, there are children in grade 3-4 (those at the 99th percentile) who score higher than 75% of the grade 5-6 children (those at or below the 75th percentile).

Table 6-2 shows the percentile norms for high school students on the English Expression subtest, and Table 6-3 shows the percentile norms for college students on the Basic Concepts of Mathematics subtest. At both of these levels, as we saw with the elementary school samples, a wide range of individual differences exists within each grade. At the college level, however, the differences between grades are not quite as large as at the elementary and high school levels.

Individual differences in achievement among students have not traditionally been translated into an emphasis on tailoring instruction to meet the individual achievement level of the student. On the contrary, public education

Table 6-2. Percentile Norms for Sequential Tests of Educational Progress (STEP) in English Expression, Form 2A

	Raw Scores*			
Percentile Ranks	*Grade 9 Spring-Grade 10 Fall*	*Grade 10 Spring-Grade 11 Fall*	*Grade 11 Spring-Grade 12 Fall*	*Grade 12 Spring*
99	54	57	59	61
90	45	49	52	54
75	39	42	46	49
50	31	34	38	41
25	25	27	30	32
10	19	21	24	26
1	13	14	15	17

*The number of items correct out of a total of 65 items.

Adapted from *Sequential Tests of Educational Progress: Handbook for STEP Series II.* Copyright © 1971 by Educational Testing Service. All rights reserved. Used by permission.

Table 6-3. Percentile Norms for Sequential Tests of Educational Progress
(STEP) in Mathematics Basic Concepts, Form 1A

	Raw Scores*	
Percentile Ranks	*College Freshmen (Grade 13 Fall)*	*College Sophomores (Grade 14 Spring)*
99	48	48
90	42	43
75	35	38
50	28	30
25	21	24
10	17	20
1	11	13

*The number of items correct out of a total of 50 items.

Adapted from *Sequential Tests of Educational Progress: Handbook for STEP Series II.* Copyright © 1971 by Educational Testing Service. All rights reserved. Used by permission.

has generally been directed at the "class" as a whole or at the "average student" (Ausubel & Robinson, 1969). Within the past two decades increasing attention has been given to the development of programs geared to achievement and ability differences among students. Some of these programs include increasing the number of special classes for slow learners, gifted students, and students with special learning problems, grouping students according to their abilities and interests, and employing individualized learning aids, such as language labs and programmed instruction.

Assessing the Quality of Education

Considerable controversy has existed and continues to exist about the effectiveness of American public education (see Kline, 1974). Are our present-day students learning more than previous generations of students or are they learning less? A few investigations have involved comparing performance of different generations of American school children who were administered the same achievement tests. For example, in 1905, ninth-grade students in Springfield, Massachusetts, were superior in spelling, arithmetic, geography, and penmanship to a group of students who had taken the same examinations in the same school in 1846 (Levine, 1976). More recently, grade school children in Evanston, Illinois, tested between 1952 and 1954 were superior in reading achievement to a 1932-34 group of Evanston children (Miller, 1956). In New York City, between 1966 and 1970, third-graders showed a steady decline in reading and math test scores, but this trend was followed by a marked improvement in 1971 and 1972 (Tavris, 1976). Unfortunately, as you might have noted, it is difficult to compare these studies because they varied with respect to the generations that were compared, the tests that were used, and the locales surveyed. In addition, earlier studies may have been based on more selected samples.

In order to provide a standard for *comparing achievement at different times,* a nationwide program was planned in 1964 (Tyler, Merwin, & Ebel, 1966). This project, called the National Assessment of Educational Progress (NAEP), involves the administration of a test battery representing ten content areas: Literature, Science, Social Studies, Writing, Citizenship, Music, Mathematics, Reading, Art, and Vocational Education. Part of the testing program was first begun in 1969. The tests are given to four age groups: 9, 13, 17, and 26-35. Each person tested takes only parts of the test battery. The major goal of the National Assessment is to measure whether the quality of education changes across long time intervals. Therefore, the goal is to administer the test battery every several years with a new sample composed of the same four age levels. Results are given for each age group and each content area, and summarized according to geographic region, size and type of community, sex, race, and the educational background of parents. Reports on the first assessment provide valuable information about the achievement level of students of various ages (see Justus, 1973). Little data are as yet available on repeated assessments, although the second assessment has been completed for science. The results indicate that over the decade covered, science knowledge declined slightly (about 2% decrease in average performance). This decline occurred in schools across virtually all types of socioeconomic communities (Beshoar, 1975; Tolman, 1976). However, evidence from another program of research based on a comparison between the 1965-66 and 1975-76 mean scores of the College Board subject-matter tests in science (Biology, Chemistry, Physics, and Mathematics I) indicates that there has been a slight positive trend in science achievement (Tolman, 1976). Thus, until we have more data on the National Assessment and other testing programs, it is difficult to draw any definitive conclusions about trends in student achievement.

It is relevant at this point to refer to the reports of a decline in scores (about one-third of a standard deviation) over the past decade on two general ability tests used for college admissions—the Scholastic Aptitude Test (SAT) and the American College Testing Program (ACT) (see Tolman, 1976). These tests assess verbal and mathematical abilities, rather than the specific content of high school instruction, which is assessed by achievement tests. Nevertheless, because general ability tests are highly correlated with standardized achievement tests (see Chapter 4), the decline in SAT and ACT scores has been interpreted as reflecting a decline in the quality of our education. Yet, as Tolman (1976) comments, it is not clear that the decline in these scores is caused by changes in the schools. Several researchers point to societal influences, such as the relinquished authority of parents over children, family size and spacing of children, divorce, the Women's Liberation movement, and drugs, as possible major determinants of the decline in the college admission tests (Harris, 1976; Walberg, 1976; Zajonc, 1976).

Cross-national comparisons of school achievement can also provide some basis for evaluating the effectiveness of American public education. The International Study of Educational Achievement has involved a series of studies of achievement in mathematics, science, literature, reading, English as a second language, French as a second language, and civic competence (Comber & Keeves, 1973; Husen, 1967; Purves, 1973; Thorndike, 1973). When compared with high school seniors from other countries, such as England and Japan, American high school seniors scored relatively low on mathematics, science, and reading comprehension tests. Such findings, however, need to be carefully interpreted. One problem is that differences in curricular emphasis exist across countries. Another problem is sampling differences. For example, at the time data for the international study were gathered 70% of American children of high-school-senior age were in school, compared with 57% in Japan and 12% in England (Carnett, 1967). Sampling bias is less of a problem when we look at the data for 13-year-olds, because all of the countries sampled required school attendance for this age group. In the mathematics study, involving 12 different countries, American 13-year-olds ranked tenth (Husen, 1967). However, we must also recognize that differences in curricular emphasis may account in part for the low standing of American students. Teachers from the U.S. ranked seventh out of eight countries in reporting that the topics tested had, in fact, been taught to the students.

Another issue about the effectiveness of American public education concerns equality of opportunities for educational achievement among all segments of the school population. We will consider this topic in the chapters on sex, social class, and race differences (see Chapters 10, 12, and 13).

PREDICTING SCHOOL ACHIEVEMENT

What kinds of individual characteristics as well as factors in the school environment account for the variation in school achievement? Why do some students achieve so much more than others? A considerable amount of research has been undertaken to identify those variables that are effective predictors of school achievement. Despite this effort, our ability to make accurate predictions about an individual's probable degree of academic success is quite limited. Yet, such practical needs as selecting students for higher education, technical training, and special education programs suggest the importance of knowledge about prediction. We shall first consider ability variables as predictors of school achievement, then motivational and personality variables, and finally, situational variables.

Ability Variables

Studies that use ability measures to predict scholastic achievement show considerable variation in design. We shall follow the organizational scheme used by Lavin (1965) in his extensive summary of the research in this area (see Figure 6-1). With respect to both the criteria of school achievement and the ability predictors, a distinction can be made between the use of a single global index and one or more specific indexes. This global-specific distinction leads to a classification of four types of studies relating ability and school

Predictor   Criterion

                            Global   Specific

	Global	Specific
Global	General ability measure used to predict grade-point average or overall achievement-test score. (A)	General ability measure used to predict specific course grades or achievement-test scores in specific subjects. (B)
Specific	Specific ability dimensions used to predict grade-point average or overall achievement-test score. (C)	Specific ability dimensions used to predict specific course grades or achievement-test scores in specific subjects. (D)

Figure 6-1. Types of studies relating ability and school achievement. Adapted from *The Prediction of Academic Performance: A Theoretical Analysis and Review of Research,* by David E. Lavin. © 1965 Russell Sage Foundation, New York. Used by permission of Basic Books, Inc.

achievement. Cell A refers to a study in which an index of general ability (for example, the total score on an intelligence test) is used to predict a global index of academic performance (for example, the total score on an achievement-test battery or an overall grade-point average). In cell B, a global ability measure is used to predict achievement in specific subjects (for example, science, history, mathematics). Cell C represents studies that use measures of specific abilities (for example, scores on a test battery like the Primary Mental Abilities tests) to predict a global measure of achievement. Cell D refers to the use of specific ability measures to predict achievement in specific subjects.

Cell A studies reveal that the correlations between performance on general ability tests and overall school grades average about .50 with a range that generally falls between .40 and .60 (see Anastasi, 1976; Lavin, 1965; Tyler, 1965). This variation reflects the fact that correlations between general ability tests and overall school grades are lower for groups with a more restricted range of ability. Thus, the lowest correlations are obtained at the graduate level, whereas the highest are at the high school level, with the college level falling in between. Data for grade school students are too scarce to allow a meaningful generalization. As noted in Chapter 4, correlations between performance on general ability tests and achievement tests are somewhat higher than those between general ability tests and grades. The correlations between general ability measures and total scores on achievement-test batteries average about .70.

Cell B studies, which use a global measure of ability to predict achievement in specific subject areas, have rarely been carried out. Tyler (1965) reports a large-scale study done with high school students. In that study general ability correlated highly with achievement test scores in English (.74), somewhat lower with scores in algebra (.68), and lowest with scores in the sciences and social studies (an average of about .50). Other studies have shown negligible relationships between general ability measures and achievement-test scores in music and the arts (Tyler, 1965).

Cell C studies, utilizing several measures of specific ability (often an index of previous achievement, such as grades, is added) to predict an overall index of academic performance, tend to show higher correlations than studies using a single index of general ability (Cell A studies). Most of these studies have been carried out at the college level. Correlations between college grade-point average and batteries of ability tests or of combinations of such tests and previous academic record fall mostly between .55 and .65 (Chissom & Lanier, 1975; Larson & Scontrino, 1976; Lavin, 1965). In general, the best single predictor within these combinations is the high school average or high school rank. Therefore, previous grades are better predictors than batteries containing measures of specific abilities. At the graduate school level, a study by Willingham (1974) indicates that a combination of undergraduate grade-point average and one or more Graduate Record Examination scores (a general ability battery used for graduate school selection) correlated mostly between .40 and .45 for various graduate school criteria and for different fields. As indicated before, the somewhat lower correlations found at the graduate school level than at the college level probably reflect the more select (and therefore narrower) range of ability among graduate school applicants.

Cell D studies, involving the use of several specific ability measures to predict achievement in specific subjects, do not produce consistent results (Lavin, 1965). Some studies show that the most effective predictive variables of grades in specific courses are the parallel content areas of the predictive tests. For example, measures of verbal ability are the best predictors of grades in English and foreign languages, while quantitative ability measures are the best predictors of mathematics grades. However, other studies indicate that these multifactor tests of abilities add little to the prediction of performance in particular courses beyond what a general ability test will predict. The inconsistency in results appears to be due to the variation from study to study in the content of the predictive batteries and the kind of criteria used (grades in specific courses or overall performance in different curricula, such as liberal arts and engineering).

In sum, there has been more success in predicting overall school achievement than achievement in specific content areas, and predictability is better with a battery of ability measures than with a single index of ability. Ability tests correlate more highly with achievement tests than with grades. The best predictor of grades are the grades one has previously attained. Most of the ability/achievement correlations range from about .50 to .65, which means that measures of ability generally account for 25% to 40% of the variation in school achievement. As Lavin (1965) points out, no other single type of predictor accounts for this much variation, yet more than half still remains unexplained. We now turn to a consideration of the relevant nonintellective variables.

Motivational and Personality Variables

A wide variety of motivational and personality variables have been considered in relation to school achievement. The distinction between motivational and personality characteristics is relative rather than absolute (Butcher, 1968; Cattell, 1971; see also Chapter 8). Motivational variables, such as motives, interests, attitudes, expectancies, and goal-seeking behaviors, tend to be more changeable than personality variables. Motivational characteristics that have been used as predictors of academic performance include study habits, attitudes toward study, degree of interest in different content areas, achievement motivation, expectancy of success, and anxiety. The more frequent personality predictors include introversion/extroversion, self-concept, and level of adjustment.

Two basic methods of analysis are used in studies of motivational and personality factors: the correlational method and the use of contrasting groups (Lavin, 1965). In a correlational study, the investigator assesses the degree of relationship between the motivational/personality variable and academic performance. In such studies, ability is statistically controlled, therefore the motivational/personality variable can be studied independent of ability. Studies using the contrasting groups method examine possible motivational/personality differences between groups composed of high and low achievers or under- and overachievers. The terms *overachiever* and *underachiever* refer to students whose academic performance exceeds (overachiever) or falls below (underachiever) the level that would be predicted from measures of their intellectual ability.[1]

Most studies involve the use of a single motivational or personality variable to predict school achievement. After reviewing findings of such studies, we will consider the results of studies that have used a battery of motivational and personality predictors.

Study Habits and Attitudes toward Study. The studies indicate that students who have good study habits tend to achieve better (Lavin, 1965). In addition, positive attitudes toward school, such as beliefs in the value of intellectual activities and of education in general, are positively related to performance.

Interests. In general, measures of interests in specific content areas are useful for predicting performance in parallel course areas (Lavin, 1965). For example, a student who expresses considerable interest in the science area should obtain high grades in science courses. Moreover, among college students, those who are certain of their occupational choice or who have definitely chosen a major field of study are more likely to attain higher grades than students who are less sure of their goals.

---

[1]As Lavin (1965) points out, these labels are unfortunate, because ability measures alone can account for only a part of the variation in academic performance. Thus, over- and underachievement actually refer to the inaccuracy involved in predicting academic performance from ability measures alone.

Achievement Motivation. The concept of achievement motivation refers to an individual's need to perform according to a high standard of excellence and is measured either through the use of projective techniques or by self-report questionnaires (see Chapter 8). The most commonly used projective measure is the story-telling method developed by McClelland, Atkinson, Clark, and Lowell (1953). In this procedure an individual is presented with four cards selected from the Thematic Apperception Test and asked to tell a story in response to each card. The stories are scored according to the frequency of achievement themes. Questionnaire measures of achievement motivation appear in many multidimensional personality inventories, such as the Edwards Personal Preference Schedule (Edwards, 1953) and the Personality Research Form (Jackson, 1967).

The results of studies using projective measures of achievement motivation are very inconsistent (Klinger, 1966; Lavin, 1965). Some studies show that projective measures are positively related to school-achievement performance, while others show no relationship. This inconsistency appears to stem from the low reliability of such measures (Entwisle, 1972). On the other hand, questionnaire measures of achievement motivation show consistent and positive relationships with academic performance, though these relationships are not very strong (Harper, 1975; Lavin, 1965). Lavin concluded that aside from the problem of the low reliability of projective measures, achievement motivation is not likely to be highly correlated with academic performance because it appears to be a multidimensional concept. Thus, some facets of achievement motivation may be useful predictors, while others may be irrelevant to school achievement. Some specific aspects of achievement motivation have been identified in recent research, such as fear of success and task versus person orientation. However, since these variables are especially pertinent to sex differences, we will consider them in Chapter 10.

Expectancy of Success. When students are asked to estimate how successfully they will perform in school, consistent positive correlations are found between stated expectancy and quality of performance (Crandall, 1969). When the expectancy is specific to the particular area in which grades are obtained, the correlations are very high (in the .80s). When the expectancy estimates are given for general competence, the correlations are lower (in the .30s). The relationship between expectancy and actual performance probably reflects an interdependence between the two; high expectancies lead to better performance and high quality of performance leads to higher expectancies (Kagan & Kogan, 1970).

Crandall and her associates (Crandall, Katkovsky, & Crandall, 1965) have also considered a generalized expectancy variable dealing with children's attribution of responsibility for the quality of their performance. By the use of the Intellectual Achievement Responsibility Questionnaire, a student indicates whether his or her good or poor grades are due to personal effort (internal attribution) or to environmental factors such as chance or fate (external attribution). Grade school and high school students who attribute their successes and failures to personal effort obtain higher grades or have better achievement-test performance than students who give an external attribution (Clifford & Cleary, 1972; McGhee & Crandall, 1968; Messer, 1972).

Anxiety. Two types of anxiety have been considered in relation to school achievement. The first deals with generalized feelings of anxiety and is most frequently assessed by the Taylor Manifest Anxiety Scale. The second kind is anxiety that is specific to testing situations. Whereas measures of general anxiety have not proved very useful in predicting school achievement, somewhat more consistent results have been found with measures of test-taking anxiety (Hill & Sarason, 1966; Lavin, 1965). Students who report experiencing test-taking anxiety seem to do poorer academically than those who do not experience test anxiety, although the relationship is not very strong. Evidence also suggests that, for adolescents, anxiety over peer rejection may interfere with school performance (Coleman, 1961; Phillips, Hindsman, & McGuire, 1960). Of course it is not clear from these correlational studies of anxiety and school performance what the direction of the relationship is.

Adjustment and Other Personality Variables. A number of studies with college students have been concerned with the relationship between adjustment and academic performance. Most of these studies have used the Minnesota Multiphasic Personality Inventory (MMPI), which measures a number of personality dimensions having pathological significance. Generally the results show that the MMPI is unrelated to academic performance (Lavin, 1965). Some studies have used projective techniques, most notably the Rorschach Test, to derive indexes of adjustment. As with the MMPI, the Rorschach is a poor instrument for predicting college grades (Lavin, 1965).

Measures of self-concept have been used as predictors, and the findings indicate that a positive self-image is associated with higher academic performance (Lavin, 1965; Naylor, 1972). Lavin suggests that this relationship is reflective of the way one presents oneself to others, and in turn affects how others respond. For example, the student who thinks he or she is not very intelligent will probably participate less in class discussion and be less persistent in working on difficult problems. As a result, others may respond to such a student as if he or she were in fact rather incompetent, which might then lead to poorer classroom performance.

One other personality dimension, introversion/extraversion, deserves consideration. Introversion refers to a tendency to be withdrawn from social contact; extraversion refers to the opposite tendency toward sociability. Research with college students consistently shows that measures of introversion are positively related to academic performance (Butcher, 1968; Lavin, 1965; Naylor, 1972). This relationship, though small, occurs when ability is controlled. The scholastic advantage shown by introverts may reflect the relatively little time spent in social activities that frees them to concentrate on their academic pursuits (Lavin, 1965).

Summary of Single-Variable Studies. Research on motivational and personality variables indicates that the student whose school achievement is high tends to have better study habits and more positive attitudes toward school than the student whose school achievement is low. The high-achieving student is also likely to have a greater interest in the areas in which he or she takes courses and to be more certain of his or her educational and occupational goals. Furthermore, in contrast to the low-achieving student, the high-achieving student is more likely to have a higher achievement motive, a higher expectancy of success, less anxiety in test-taking situations, a more positive self-concept, and a more introverted orientation. In general, since most of the research has been at the college level, these conclusions are especially relevant to college students. Finally, as Lavin (1965) emphasizes, the relationships between specific motivational/personality variables and school achievement are, for the most part, rather low (correlations of about .30). For practical purposes, such as making decisions regarding college admissions, little confidence can be attached to specific motivational or personality predictors.

Multivariate Studies. Considerable variation exists in the kinds of multidimensional nonintellective measures and concepts that have been used as predictors of school achievement. Lavin (1965) has summarized the results of studies using multidimensional measures by categorizing the variables according to their conceptual similarity. The results of this "intuitive" factor analysis are presented in Table 6-4. Lavin singles out the following 6 dimensions: (1) social maturity in the student role, (2) emotional stability, (3) achievement motivation syndrome, (4) cognitive style, (5) achievement via conformance, and (6) achievement via independence. These dimensions are generally consistent with the kinds of motivational/personality predictors identified in single-variable studies. For example, social maturity in the student role seems congruent with good study habits and positive attitudes toward school, emotional stability with low test anxiety, achievement motivation syndrome with high achievement motivation, and achievement via independence with introversion (low dependence on social support). On the other hand, cognitive style and achievement via conformance tend to emerge only in multivariate approaches, because of the wide variety of variables considered in these studies. Achievement via conformance and achievement via independence seem to be directly opposite characteristics, yet each is related to high academic performance. Lavin suggests that this can occur because each set of characteristics may operate within a unique social context. In some school environments independence may be rewarded more highly than conformity, while in others the opposite may be true.

In a large-scale multivariate study, not included in Lavin's review, Nichols and Holland (1963) studied a national sample of about 1700 high ability first-year college students (recipients of the National Merit Scholarship). Two nonintellective clusters—perseverance and motivation to achieve, and conformity and socialization—were significant predictors of first-year college grades. Cattell (1971)

Table 6-4. Dimensions and Sample Items of Motivational and Personality Variables
Associated with Academic Performance in Multivariate Studies

Dimension 1:
Social Maturity in the
    Student Role
greater social
    presence*
responsibility
greater social
    maturity
greater socialization
restraint in social
    behavior
	Dimension 4:
	Cognitive Style
	greater curiosity
	greater flexibility
	greater originality
	greater ability to
	    visualize a configuration
	    when moved
	more relevant thinking in
	    class
	more class participation
	    (quality and frequency)

Dimension 2:
Emotional Stability
higher morale
greater stability
greater freedom from
    neurotic orientation to
    study
	greater liking for thinking
	less difficulty with tasks
	    involving ambiguity and
	    spontaneity
	
	Dimension 5:
	Achievement via Conformance
	higher need for order
	greater passivity
	higher conformance

Dimension 3:
Achievement Motivation
    Syndrome
higher achievement
    motivation
higher activity level
more endurance
	Dimension 6:
	Achievement via Independence
	lower need for affiliation
	greater independence
	low conformity to peer
	    group standards
	moderate impulsivity
	    (lack of constrictedness)

*Multivariate study items describe characteristics of the high achiever.
Adapted from *The Prediction of Academic Performance: A Theoretical Analysis and Review
of Research,* by David E. Lavin. © 1965 Russell Sage Foundation, New York. Used by permission
of Basic Books, Inc.

reports the results of several multivariate studies with junior high school and
high school students. Conscientiousness and persistence, self-sufficiency, need
achievement, and submissiveness were the highest nonintellective predictors
of school achievement (correlations of about .30). In general, the variables
identified in these more recent studies are consistent with those presented
in Lavin's summary.

Both ability and motivational/personality variables are important in the
prediction of school achievement. Ability alone is the best single type of predictive variable, but it only accounts for about 25% to 40% of the variance in
achievement. Cattell (1971) estimates that when motivational and personality
characteristics are added to ability, as much as 60% of the variance can be
accounted for (a correlation of about .78). Thus, when personality and motivational variables are added to ability, a considerably higher level of prediction

is attained than when ability alone is considered. Furthermore, Cattell points out that, if the reliability and validity of ability, motivational, and personality measures were improved, as much as 75% of the variance in school achievement could be explained.

What about the remaining 25% to 40% of unaccounted variance? Individual differences among students cannot totally account for the variation in school achievement even with the most reliable and valid predictive measures. We must consider the nature of the situational or environmental context in order to obtain a complete picture of the factors underlying individual differences in school achievement.

Situational Variables

One type of situational variable is the role relationships that exist within the educational context; namely, the student/student relationship, the student/ teacher relationship, and the student/family relationship. The major findings on role relationships are summarized by Lavin (1965). Peer-group norms can influence academic performance. For example, if the peer-group values school achievement, its norms may serve as an incentive to perform well. With respect to the student/teacher relationship, the more similar the student's attitudes and values are to those of the teacher, the higher the student's academic performance. Studies dealing with the effects of family relationships upon student performance indicate that the successful student is likely to come from a family where the parents exhibit warmth and interest, where the child has a relatively strong input in decision making, and where family members tend to agree on issues they regard as important.

Since situational factors are pertinent to the prediction of school achievement, it is possible that academic performance is influenced by particular combinations of situational and individual difference variables. Certain personality characteristics have been found to relate significantly to achievement in some school settings but not in others (Lavin, 1965). A study by Beach (1960) is a good illustration of the interactive role of personality and situational variables. The relationship between sociability and academic achievement was studied in four different kinds of learning situation—a lecture class, a discussion group with instructor, a leaderless discussion group, and an independent study group. Students low on sociability performed better in the lecture class and in instructor-led groups, while more sociable students performed better in the leaderless discussion groups. Further evidence of the importance of an interactionist approach in predicting school achievement is indicated in recent research on the previously mentioned dimension of internal/external attribution (Crandall et al., 1965). Gilmor (1978), in summarizing this research, concludes that students who attribute their success and failure to environmental factors (external attribution) perform better in structured than in nonstructured learning situations, whereas students who attribute their success and failure to personal effort (internal attribution) are better able to adjust to any type of classroom structure. Finally, school achievement as a function of the interaction of individual difference variables (ability, motivation, and personality) and situational variables (instructional methods) has been demonstrated in several research programs reviewed by Cronbach (1975) and Cronbach and Snow (1975).

Conclusions

What are the practical implications of the research findings on predicting school achievement? For one thing, in counseling students about various educational programs or selecting students for higher education, it is clear that we cannot rely on ability measures alone. Motivation, personality, and situational characteristics also need to be taken into consideration. Unfortunately, our knowledge of these nonintellective variables is still at too rudimentary a stage to be of much practical use. One promising lead is research on the interaction between motivational/personality variables and situational variables. In general, educational goals may best be attained if we consider not only the individual differences among our students, but also if we can adapt the environments of our schools to more closely match the students' varied abilities, interests, motives, values, and personalities.

The prediction of achievement should further be examined in the context of achievement in later life. We will now consider the relationship between school achievement and life achievement.

SCHOOL ACHIEVEMENT AND SUCCESS IN LATER LIFE

Both standardized achievement tests and student grades can be used to predict achievement in later life. However, only grades have been typically used for such predictive purposes.

How valuable are grades in predicting achievement after schooling has been completed? This question cannot be answered easily because of the many criteria used as indexes of life achievement. The prestige or status of one's occupation is often used as an index of occupational achievement, but such an index is influenced to a considerable extent by opportunities. The chances of becoming a banker or corporate director are negligible if one is Black or female. Amount of money earned is another available measure of occupational achievement, but confounded with wide discrepancies in average earnings across different occupations. Reputation within one's chosen field is still another index of occupational achievement. However, at what point in one's career should "reputation" be assessed? Some of Mendel's most significant writings were ignored for several decades. The brilliance of Van Gogh was not recognized until some time after his death.

Despite the difficulties involved in evaluating occupational achievement, it is still important to know the predictive power of grades and other related indexes of academic performance. Several reviews have revealed that grades are generally unrelated to occupational success (Berg, 1970; McClelland, 1973).

For instance, in one study, Taylor, Smith, and Ghiselin (1963) found no relationship between college grades and the success of research scientists. The average college grade for the top third in research success was 2.73 (about B–), while the average for the bottom third was 2.69 (also B–). Other findings show that college grades are unrelated to income (Tyler, 1965) and creative achievement (MacKinnon, 1960). On the other hand, the case appears to be different if we predict on the basis of high school grades. In a large-scale study, Sewell, Haller, and Ohlendorf (1970) found a small, but significant, positive correlation of .38 between senior-class ranking and occupational status seven years later. As previously indicated, with more heterogeneity in ability among high school students than among college students, we should expect high school grades to be somewhat more successful predictors than college grades.

Overall, however, grades are not good predictors of occupational success. The poor predictive power of grades enhances the importance of considering other kinds of student characteristics. Nonintellective characteristics, such as leadership abilities, social maturity, wide-ranging interests, and communication skills, may be important prerequisites for personal and social success once school is completed.

SUMMARY

School achievement can be assessed by teacher-assigned grades or by the use of achievement tests. In order to overcome teacher and school variations in achievement standards, standardized achievement tests have been developed. Such tests are constructed for use in a wide variety of schools and consist of content in several basic academic subject-areas. Test performance is interpreted in terms of norms based on representative national samples. Achievement-test norms reveal a wide range of individual differences within given grade levels. Much controversy exists regarding the effectiveness of public education. A current nationwide program (the National Assessment of Educational Progress) will provide comparative data about the achievement level of different generations of students. Such data should indicate whether any historical trends exist in the level of student achievement.

The prediction of school achievement is based on three types of variables: ability, motivational and personality characteristics, and situational characteristics. In general, ability level is a more effective predictor of overall school achievement than achievement in specific content areas. A battery of ability measures is a more successful predictor than a single index of ability. Ability accounts for about 25% to 40% of the variation in school achievement, and is the best single type of predictive characteristic. When motivational and personality variables are added to ability, a considerably higher level of prediction is attained. However, the relationships between specific motivational/personality variables and school achievement are, for the most part, not supported by high correlations. Situational variables appear to be especially pertinent to the prediction of school achievement when they are interacting with individual difference characteristics. Thus, educational goals may best be attained by adapting our school environment to match the various abilities, interests, motives, values, and personalities of our students.

To be useful, school achievement should be an effective predictor of success in later life. However, it is difficult to study the relationship between school achievement and life accomplishment, because in the latter case no clearly defined criteria presently exist. In general, the limited evidence indicates that school grades are poor predictors of occupational success. The poor predictive power of grades suggests that more attention should be paid to the possible relevance of nonintellective student characteristics to personal and social success in later life.

REFERENCES

Anastasi, A. *Psychological testing* (4th ed.). New York: Macmillan, 1976.

Ausubel, D. P., & Robinson, F. G. *School learning: An introduction to educational psychology.* New York: Holt, Rinehart & Winston, 1969.

Beach, L. R. Sociability and academic achievement in various types of learning situations. *Journal of Educational Psychology,* 1960, *51,* 208–212.

Berg, I. E. *Education and jobs: The great training robbery.* New York: Praeger, 1970.

Beshoar, B. B. NAEP's second round with science. *American Education,* 1975, *11*(5), 6–11.

Bloom, B. S. Time and learning. *American Psychologist,* 1974, *29,* 682–688.

Butcher, H. J. *Human intelligence: Its nature and assessment.* London: Methuen, 1968.

Carnett, G. S. Is our mathematics inferior? *Mathematics Teacher,* 1967, *60,* 582–587.

Carver, R. P. Two dimensions of tests: Psychometric and edumetric. *American Psychologist,* 1974, *29,* 512–518.

Cattell, R. B. *Abilities: Their structure, growth, and action.* Boston: Houghton Mifflin, 1971.

Chissom, B. S., & Lanier, D. Prediction of 1st quarter freshman GPA using SAT scores and high school grades. *Educational and Psychological Measurement,* 1975, *35,* 461–463.

Clifford, M. M., & Cleary, T. A. The relationship between children's academic performance and achievement accountability. *Child Development,* 1972, *43,* 647–655.

Coleman, J. C. *The adolescent society.* New York: Free Press, 1961.

Comber, L. C., & Keeves, J. P. *Science education in nineteen countries: International studies in evaluation: I.* New York. Wiley, 1973.

Crandall, V. C. Sex differences in expectancy of intellectual and academic reinforcement. In C. P. Smith (Ed.), *Achievement related motives in children.* New York: Russell Sage Foundation, 1969.

Crandall, V. C., Katkovsky, W., & Crandall, V. J. Children's beliefs in their own control of reinforcements in intellectual-academic achievement situations. *Child Development,* 1965, *36,* 91–109.

Cronbach, L. J. Beyond the two disciplines of scientific psychology. *American Psychologist,* 1975, *30,* 116–127.

Cronbach, L. J., & Snow, R. E. *Aptitudes and instructional methods.* New York: Irvington, 1975.

Edwards, A. L. *Edwards Personal Preference Schedule.* New York: Psychological Corporation, 1953.

Entwisle, D. R. To dispel fantasies about fantasy-based measures of achievement motivation. *Psychological Bulletin,* 1972, *77,* 377–390.

Gilmor, T. M. Locus of control as a mediator of adaptive behavior in children and adolescents. *Canadian Psychological Review,* 1978, *19,* 1–26.

Harper, F. B. The validity of some alternative measures of achievement motivation. *Educational and Psychological Measurement,* 1975, *35,* 905–909.

Harris, W. U. The SAT score decline: Facts, figures and emotions. *Educational Technology,* June 1976, 15–20.

Hill, K. T., & Sarason, S. B. The relation of test anxiety and defensiveness to test and school performance over the elementary school years. *Monographs of the Society for Research in Child Development,* 1966, *31*(2, Serial No. 104).

Hoffman, B. *The tyranny of testing.* New York: Macmillan, 1962.

Husen, T. (Ed.). *International study of achievement in mathematics: A comparison of twelve countries* (Vols. 1 & 2). New York: Wiley, 1967.

Jackson, D. N. *Personality Research Form Manual.* Goshen, N.Y.: Research Psychologists Press, 1967.

Justus, H. Focusing on the states. *American Education,* 1973, *9* (10), 4–9.

Kagan, J., & Kogan, N. Individual variation in cognitive processes. In P. H. Mussen (Ed.), *Carmichael's manual of child psychology* (Vol. 1). New York: Wiley, 1970.

Kline, M. *Why Johnny can't add.* New York: Vintage, 1974.

Klinger, E. Fantasy need achievement as a motivational construct. *Psychological Bulletin,* 1966, *66,* 291–308.

Krathwohl, D. R., & Payne, D. A. Defining and assessing educational objectives. In R. L. Thorndike (Ed.), *Educational measurement* (2nd ed.). Washington, D.C.: American Council of Education, 1971.

Larson, J. R., & Scontrino, M. P. The consistency of high school grade point average and of the verbal and mathematical portions of the Scholastic Aptitude Test of the College Entrance Examination Board, as predictors of college performance: An eight year study. *Educational and Psychological Measurement,* 1976, *36,* 439–443.

Lavin, D. E. *The prediction of academic performance: A theoretical analysis and review of research.* New York: Russell Sage Foundation, 1965.

Levine, M. The academic achievement test: Its historical context and social functions. *American Psychologist,* 1976, *31,* 228–238.

MacKinnon, D. W. What do we mean by talent and how do we test for it? In *The search for talent.* New York: College Entrance Examination Board, 1960.

McClelland, D. C. Testing for competence rather than for "intelligence." *American Psychologist,* 1973, *28,* 1–14.

McClelland, D. C., Atkinson, J. W., Clark, R. A., & Lowell, E. L. *The achievement motive.* New York: Appleton-Century-Crofts, 1953.

McGhee, P. E., & Crandall, V. C. Beliefs in internal-external control of reinforcements and academic performance. *Child Development,* 1968, *39,* 91–102.

Messer, S. B. The relation of internal-external control to academic performance. *Child Development,* 1972, *43,* 1456–1462.

Miller, V. V. Reading achievement of school children, then and now. *Elementary English,* 1956, *33,* 91–97.

Naylor, F. D. *Personality and educational achievement.* New York: Wiley, 1972.

Nichols, R. C., & Holland, J. L. Prediction of the first-year college performance of high-aptitude students. *Psychological Monographs,* 1963, *77* (7, Whole No. 570).

Phillips, B. N., Hindsman, E., & McGuire, C. Factors associated with anxiety and their relation to the school achievement of adolescents. *Psychological Reports*, 1960, 7, 365–372.

Purves, A. C. *Literature education in ten countries: International studies in evaluation: II.* New York: Wiley, 1973.

Sequential Tests of Educational Progress: Handbook for STEP Series II. Princeton, N.J.: Educational Testing Service, 1971.

Sewell, W. H., Haller, A. O., & Ohlendorf, G. W. The educational and early occupational status attainment process: Replication and revision. *American Sociological Review*, 1970, 35, 1014–1027.

Tavris, C. The end of the IQ slump. *Psychology Today*, 1976, 9(11), 69–74.

Taylor, C., Smith, W. R., & Ghiselin, B. The creative and other contributions of one sample of research scientists. In C. W. Taylor & F. Barron (Eds.), *Scientific creativity: Its recognition and development.* New York: Wiley, 1963.

Thorndike, R. L. *Reading comprehension education in fifteen countries: International studies in evaluation: III.* New York: Wiley, 1973.

Tolman, R. R. A look at achievement test score declines. *Biological Sciences Curriculum Study Newsletter*, 1976, No. 65.

Tyler, L. E. *The psychology of human differences* (3rd ed.). New York: Appleton-Century-Crofts, 1965.

Tyler, R. W., Merwin, J. C., & Ebel, R. L. Symposium: A national assessment of educational progress. *Journal of Educational Measurement*, 1966, 3, 1–17.

Walberg, H. J. Changing IQ and family context. *Educational Technology*, June 1976, p. 42.

Willingham, W. W. Predicting success in graduate education. *Science*, 1974, *183*, 273–278.

Zajonc, R. B. Family configuration and intelligence. *Science*, 1976, *192*, 227–236.

Special Aptitudes and Abilities

7

What does it mean when we say that Johnny has a mechanical aptitude or that Sally has an aptitude for music? An *aptitude* refers to the potential to acquire particular behaviors or skills given the appropriate opportunity (Brown, 1976). The frame of reference is toward future performance. Through genetically based dispositions and broad learning experiences in the past, such as working on carpentry as a child, a person can develop the potential to profit from training in a particular area. In contrast to the future orientation of aptitude, *ability* refers to a person's present competence to perform a task (Brown, 1976). Both aptitude and ability are products of genetic influences and general learning experiences. Recall that *achievement* (which like ability refers to present competence) refers to performance that reflects specific learning experiences, such as school instruction (see Chapter 6).

The labeling of a particular measure as "aptitude" or "ability" depends upon its time emphasis. For example, general ability or intelligence tests assess a person's present overall intellectual functioning, whereas tests assessing scholastic aptitude also assess a person's present general ability, but are specifically designed to predict future academic performance.

Our concern in this chapter is with special aptitudes and abilities. In Chapter 4, when we discussed the factor analytic investigations of intelligence, we noted that the various abilities are related to one another in a hierarchical arrangement. The most general abilities (for example, the general intelligence factor, and the verbal/education and spatial/mechanical factors) are at the top of the hierarchy, and the most specific abilities at the bottom. Our interest now is to take a look at some of the more specialized abilities and aptitudes that have been identified. We will first consider two kinds of special aptitudes, and then go on to consider two kinds of special abilities—creativity and cognitive styles.

SPECIAL APTITUDES

Aptitude testing began during the 1920s when vocational psychologists, in both England and the United States, initiated research programs on mechanical aptitude (Tyler, 1965). Tests devised from this research produced moderately high correlations with various criteria of success in mechanical activities. The pattern was set for developing aptitude tests in other work-related areas.

As suggested in the preceding paragraph, the goal in developing vocational aptitude tests is to establish predictive validity. A prospective test is given to a group of trainees or workers prior to the actual training or job experience. When criterion evaluations of performance (for example, supervisor's ratings) become available, a correlation is obtained between the test scores and the criterion measure. The validity of the test is established if the correlation is statistically significant and reasonably high.[1] Such a test can then be confidently used in personnel decisions, such as selection and placement, as well as in vocational counseling.

While aptitude testing progressed in terms of predicting occupational criteria, it was also influenced in the 1940s by the factor analytic research on the structure of intelligence. Factor analysis was used in the development of aptitude test batteries. Tests of specific aptitudes and multiaptitude batteries have been developed primarily in two broad areas—vocational and artistic. We shall first consider vocational aptitudes.

Vocational Aptitudes

Assessments of vocational aptitudes have concentrated on the following areas: (1) mechanical, (2) motor functions, and (3) clerical.

---

[1]Generally, researchers draw a second sample from the same population and repeat the validation procedure used with the original sample to insure that validity data are not influenced by chance factors operating in the sample originally tested.

Mechanical Aptitude. Two types of tests have been used successfully to predict competence in mechanical work: (1) mechanical comprehension and (2) spatial relations. A mechanical comprehension test (for example, the Bennett Mechanical Comprehension Tests) measures the ability to understand physical principles reflected in practical situations, such as in the use of tools. Such tests are used to predict success in training programs and jobs that involve working with complex machinery.

Measures of spatial relations, like the Minnesota Paper Form Board, assess the ability to visualize and manipulate objects in space, such as how parts of a figure fit together to form a complete figure. Spatial relations tests are used to predict performance in occupations such as art, engineering, and tool-making.

Motor Functions. A variety of tests has been developed to assess psycho-motor abilities such as manual dexterity, reaction time, and body coordination. These tests (for example, the Purdue Pegboard) require the person to perform specific motor tasks and are used to predict performance in routine industrial jobs. Because of the great diversity of motor tests, factor analytic research has been used to identify underlying dimensions. This research has revealed that motor abilities are highly specific. Fleishman's (1954, 1972) extensive factor-analytic investigation has identified the following perceptual/motor factors:

Multilimb Coordination: Ability to coordinate the movements of a number of limbs simultaneously.
Control Precision: Ability to make highly controlled and precise muscular adjustments.
Response Orientation: Ability to select the appropriate response under highly speeded conditions.
Reaction Time: Speed with which a person is able to respond to a stimulus when it appears.
Speed of Arm Movement: Speed with which gross arm movements can be made, regardless of accuracy.
Rate Control: Ability to make continuous anticipatory motor adjustments relative to changes in speed and direction of a moving target.
Manual Dexterity: Ability to make skillful, well-directed arm/hand movements in manipulating fairly large objects under speed conditions.
Finger Dexterity: Ability to make skillful, well-directed manipulations of small objects.
Arm/Hand Steadiness: Ability to make precise arm/hand positioning movements where strength and speed are minimized.
Wrist/Finger Speed: Measured by paper-and-pencil tests requiring rapid tapping of a pencil (in relatively large areas; for example, large circles).
Aim: Measured by paper-and-pencil tests that require the person to place a dot accurately and rapidly in each of a series of small circles.

In addition, Fleishman (1964, 1972) has delineated several physical proficiency factors that emerged in factor analyses of tests of physical fitness. They are:

Static Strength: Maximum force that can be exerted against external objects.
Dynamic Strength: Muscular endurance in exerting force continuously and repeatedly.
Explosive Strength: Mobilization of energy for bursts of muscular effort, as in sprints and jumps.
Trunk Strength: Muscular endurance involving trunk muscles, as in leg lifts and sit-ups.
Extent Flexibility: Ability to flex or stretch trunk and back muscles.
Dynamic Flexibility: Repeated, rapid flexing movements.
Gross Body Coordination: Ability to coordinate action of several parts of the body while body is in motion.
Gross Body Equilibrium: Ability to maintain balance with nonvisual cues.
Stamina: Capacity to sustain maximum effort.

Clerical Aptitude. Tests of clerical aptitude assess perceptual speed and accuracy. In the most frequently used test, the Minnesota Clerical Test, the subject is required to rapidly compare pairs of names or numbers and indicate whether the members of each pair are identical or different. Such a task is quite simple, but people are differentiated on the basis of speed and accuracy. Clerical aptitude tests are used to predict successful performance in routine clerical and inspection jobs.

Aptitude Test Batteries. Vocational aptitudes have been assessed by multiaptitude batteries as well as by specific tests. Two vocationally oriented batteries are the General Aptitude Test Battery and the Flanagan Aptitude Classification Test. These batteries, which are based on factor analysis, consist of vocational aptitude measures as well as measures of verbal, numerical, and spatial abilities. The vocationally oriented subtests are similar to those we have just surveyed. Multiaptitude batteries are particularly useful for vocational counseling because they provide for the identification of patterns of strengths and weaknesses.

The Validity of Vocational Aptitude Measures. It is generally difficult to determine the validity of vocational aptitude measures because validity coefficients (correlations between aptitude and criterion) are highly situation-specific (Ghiselli, 1966; Super & Crites, 1962). Wide discrepancies emerge when the validity coefficients for a given test are compared across the various validity studies using the test. Such conflicting evidence is illustrated in Figure 7-1, which shows the range of validity coefficients for each of three jobs. At the top of the figure the validity coefficients involve training criteria, that is, assessments of performance in job training programs for mechanical repairmen. The validity coefficients for the other two jobs (bench workers and machine tenders) are based on proficiency criteria, that is, assessments of on-the-job performance. In all three instances there is a wide variation in the validity coefficients for the given tests. For example, in the case of machine tenders (at the bottom of Figure 7-1) the correlations range from about −.55 to .52. While most of these correlations are positive, many are very low and some are negative. This means that in some studies high scores on the aptitude measure were associated with poor performance on the job.

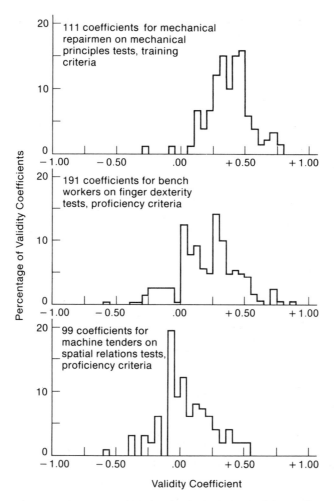

Figure 7-1. Examples of variation in validity coefficients of given tests for particular jobs. Adapted from *The Validity of Occupational Aptitude Tests,* by E. E. Ghiselli. Copyright 1966 by John Wiley & Sons, Inc. Used by permission.

A summary of the general predictive power of a variety of vocational aptitude tests is provided by Ghiselli (1966, 1973) and is shown in Table 7-1. The validity coefficients for motor abilities are, for the most part, lower than those for spatial and mechanical abilities and those for perceptual accuracy (which largely relate to clerical skills). A clear trend exists for higher validity when the criterion is performance in a training program rather than job proficiency. Apparently, the skills required for successful performance in training programs are not necessarily consistent with those required for on-the-job proficiency. The higher correlations for training criteria than for proficiency criteria probably also reflect differences in the two types of samples. Not everyone in a vocational training program will meet the requirements necessary for being selected for a job in the given vocational area; thus on-the-job

Table 7-1. Mean Validity Coefficients of Each Type of
Test for All Jobs

Type of Test	Type of Criterion	
	Training	Proficiency on the Job
Spatial and Mechanical Abilities		
Spatial Relations	.39	.17
Location	.24	.16
Mechanical Principles	.39	.24
Perceptual Accuracy		
Number Comparison	.28	.22
Name Comparison	.26	.21
Cancellation	.30	.20
Pursuit	.17	.16
Perceptual Speed	.39	.30
Motor Abilities		
Tracing	.19	.17
Tapping	.12	.14
Dotting	.15	.14
Finger Dexterity	.22	.19
Hand Dexterity	.38	.15
Arm Dexterity	.29	.17

Adapted from *The Validity of Occupational Aptitude Tests,*
by E. E. Ghiselli. Copyright 1966 by John Wiley & Sons, Inc. Used
by permission.

samples would tend to be more restricted in the range of ability than training
samples. As previously mentioned, a restricted range tends to lower correlation
coefficients.

Overall, the predictive power of vocational aptitude tests is not very high.
How can the predictive validity of vocational aptitude tests be improved? Three
approaches to validation research are relevant: (1) incremental validity, (2)
moderator variables, and (3) decision theory.

Incremental validity involves the use of multiple predictors (Sechrest,
1963). As we learned in the case of predicting school achievement, any one
type of predictor is less successful than a combination of predictors. Other
factors besides special aptitudes determine training and job performance. For
instance, measures of a person's intelligence and motivation correlate positively
with training and job performance. The incremental validity of a vocational
aptitude test is determined by the improvement such a test adds to the predictive validity of a combination of tests. Thus, for example, support for the
incremental validity of a spatial relations test would be indicated if the correlation between a battery of tests (such as intelligence and achievement motivation
tests) and grades in engineering is raised from .50 to .65 when the spatial
relations test is added to the test battery.

Moderator variables refer to the influence some variables have on other
variables used in prediction (Ghiselli, 1963). For example, among factory

workers, age could be a moderating variable. For younger workers finger dexterity might be more important than spatial ability in predicting rate of production on the job, while the reverse might be true for older workers. Thus, age influences the relative weights of finger dexterity and spatial ability in predicting rate of production.

The use of vocational aptitude tests in *decision theory* involves evaluating tests according to their contribution to a decision-making process, such as that involved in personnel selection (Cronbach & Gleser, 1965; Dunnette, 1963, 1966). For example, if a test of mechanical aptitude is introduced as a selection instrument in an industrial organization, the predictive value of the test can be determined by comparing the percentage of workers who are successful on the job when the test is used in the selection decision with the percentage of successful workers when the test is not used. Figure 7-2 illustrates this comparison. Job success is defined by a minimum score on a criterion measure of on-the-job performance (for example, ratings by supervisors). If the test administered to all of the applicants for the job is not actually used to screen out those who score below a cutoff score, then, as the figure shows, 60 of the 100 applicants, or 60%, are successful according to the criterion measure of on-the-job performance. If the test is used to screen out those applicants who fall below the cutoff score, then 38 out of 45 applicants (those who are located on the right side of the figure), or 84%, are successful on the job. The increase in the proportion of "successes" (60% to 84%) when the test is used to make selection decisions provides evidence of the test's predictive validity.

In this section we have considered vocational aptitude measures as predictors of future performance. These same measures can also be used to assess past training and job experience. Research, particularly in the area of motor skills (Fleishman, 1972), reveals that aptitude-test performance is affected by training. As our earlier differentiation between aptitudes and abilities would suggest, when vocational tests are used to assess skills developed from past experience, they are measuring abilities (present competence or proficiency) rather than aptitudes (potential for future training and job performance). Even though two persons may have the same test score, one person's score may reflect the limits of his or her ability while the other's score may reflect a still-developing ability (Brown, 1976).

Artistic Aptitudes

Aptitude measures in the *visual arts* are of two types: (1) aesthetic appreciation and (2) productive skills. The two types are not necessarily related to each other. Many people may develop a sophisticated appreciation of various art forms and remain unable to produce creative works of art.

On visual arts tests of aesthetic appreciation, like the Meier Art Judgment Test, the person taking the test is asked to choose between two artistic representations. One of the representations is the original, whereas the other has been altered in some aesthetic characteristic, such as balance or rhythm.

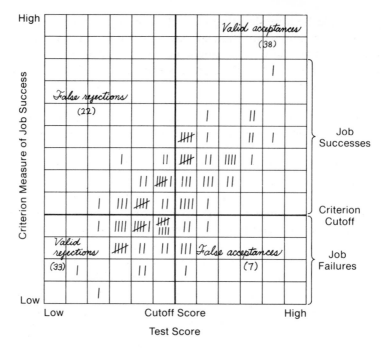

Figure 7-2. Increase in the proportion of "successes" resulting from the use of a selection test. From *Psychological Testing* (4th Ed.), by A. Anastasi. Copyright © 1976 by Anne Anastasi. Reprinted by permission of Macmillan Publishing Co., Inc.

Aesthetic appreciation tests effectively discriminate between contrasting groups of subjects, such as art students versus nonart students (Anastasi, 1976). The Horn Art Aptitude Inventory is an example of a test of productive skills in the visual arts and involves the production of original drawings. The test is used as a selection instrument for admission to art schools, but at present no systematic validation research has been undertaken (Anastasi, 1976).

The major approach to the assessment of *musical aptitude* has been the work of Seashore (1939). The Seashore tests emphasize the measurement of various skills, including pitch, rhythm, timbre, loudness discrimination, time, and tonal memory. Evidence of predictive validity with various criteria of performance in music training is rather limited. Validity coefficients are generally below .30 (Anastasi, 1976).

It is difficult to validate measures of artistic aptitude. For measures of aesthetic appreciation in the visual arts, the major problem is the unreliability of criterion measures—experts often disagree about the aesthetic quality of a given work of art. For measures of productive skills in art and music, the major problem is the complexity of factors that determine one's career success. While talent is obviously important, other factors, such as personality, opportunities, audience appeal, and even luck, appear to affect one's success as an artist or musician. Tests of artistic aptitude are best interpreted in terms of a minimal-level approach (Brown, 1976). A person who achieves a high score may be viewed as possessing at least the minimal level of necessary ability to profit from training in the particular art form assessed.

Now that we have looked at special aptitudes, which refer to a person's potential strengths for future training and job performance, we will move on to consider special abilities, which refer to a person's present competencies. We will examine two kinds of special ability—creativity and cognitive styles.

SPECIAL ABILITIES

Creativity

Creativity can be defined as the production of something—whether it be a work of art, a scientific theory, or the solution to an organizational problem— that is judged to be relatively novel or original. Research interest in creativity is of rather recent origin. In the early 1950s, some psychologists and educators began to question the commonly held view that whatever is described as "creativity" is largely accounted for by existing measures of ability (Butcher, 1968). At the same time, the growing demand for research scientists stimulated interest in the identification and encouragement of creativity in the sciences. Creativity is now recognized as an important aspect of both scientific and artistic achievement.

Two general research strategies have been used to investigate creativity. One approach has focused on the background and personality characteristics that distinguish creative persons. The other has been concerned with the creative process, that is, the thinking processes that are involved in creativity. This focus on the creative process has led to the development of specific measures of creativity.

The Measurement of Creativity. The pioneering work in assessing creativity emerged in Guilford's (1957, 1967) factor analytic research on the structure of intelligence (see Chapter 4). Recall that one of the factors identified was "divergent production." Measures of divergent production call for the generation of multiple solutions to a given problem and are contrasted with measures of "convergent production," which involve processing information in a way that leads to one correct answer. Achievement tests, aptitude tests, and ability tests (including intelligence tests) emphasize the measurement of convergent production. In Guilford's view, divergent production represents the special thinking processes relevant to creative achievement. Among Guilford's tests of divergent production are:

Word Fluency: Rapid listing of words containing a specific letter.
Ideational Fluency: Naming things or objects that fit relatively broad categories (for example, "Fluids that will burn": gasoline, kerosene, alcohol . . .).
Alternate Uses: Listing possible uses for an object, other than its normal uses (for example, "Newspaper, used for reading": to start a fire, as stuffing to pack boxes . . .).

Decorations: Adding different designs to outline drawings of common objects.
Possible Jobs: Listing jobs that might be symbolized by a given emblem (for example, "Light bulb": electrical engineer, light-bulb manufacturer, advertising copywriter . . .).

Another series of divergent production tests, similar to that of Guilford, has been developed by Torrance (1962, 1964, 1965). The Torrance Tests of Creative Thinking were devised within an educational context and are grouped into a verbal, a pictorial, and an auditory battery. They are structured as games and activities. For example, an item from the verbal battery asks the person to think of the ways in which a toy can be improved so children will have more fun playing with it. These tests are suitable from kindergarten through graduate school. For younger children the tests are given to each individual orally, whereas for older groups they are read by the person taking the test.

Information on the predictive validity of the Guilford and Torrance measures is lacking except for a few scattered studies (Anastasi, 1976). Systematic validation research is needed relating these creativity measures to criteria of creative achievement, that is, original and useful contributions in real-life situations. We should also be aware of the possibility that divergent production is only one of several abilities involved in creativity. It seems reasonable to believe that other abilities, including comprehension, memory, and critical evaluation, are essential to the creative process.[2]

Creativity and Intelligence. Are measures of creativity and measures of intelligence relatively independent from each other, and if so, are they predictive of different criteria? The relationship between creativity and intelligence was investigated by Getzels and Jackson (1962). A series of divergent production tests, some of which were based on the Guilford tests, were given to 533 students in grades 6 through 12 of a private school. The average IQ of the children was 132. The correlations between each of the creativity tests and IQ were relatively low, and Wallach and Kogan (1965) in analyzing these data reported an average correlation of approximately .27.

Getzels and Jackson divided the students into two groups: (1) those who scored very high on measures of creativity (in the top 20% of the students in the school compared with the general level of the school) but relatively low on intelligence (below the top 20%) and (2) those who scored very high on intelligence but relatively low on creativity. Getzels and Jackson discovered that the more creative students, despite having somewhat lower IQs, equalled the more intelligent students in scholastic achievement (based on a composite score on several standardized achievement tests). The creative students had an average IQ of 127, compared with the intelligent students, whose average IQ was 150. Other results revealed striking differences between the two groups

---

[2]A convergent-production measure of creativity, the Remote Associates Test, has been developed by Mednick (1962, 1967). However, evidence indicates that this test is heavily weighted with verbal intelligence, and its validity in predicting real-life accomplishments and creativity ratings is generally low (see Buros, 1972).

in measures of values and personality. The creative students tended to have more unconventional values. They placed less value on personal characteristics associated with professional success and expressed greater interest in unusual careers. Furthermore, in open-ended personality measures (story telling and picture completions) the creative students revealed freer fantasy, more humor, and more violence.

The research of Getzels and Jackson aroused much interest in the psychological community and considerable controversy. Other writers pointed to methodological problems in their study, indicating that their findings should be viewed as inconclusive. One problem is that the intercorrelations among the tests of creativity, which averaged .32, are similar to the average correlation of .27 between the creativity and intelligence measures (Wallach & Kogan, 1965). If creativity is relatively distinct from intelligence, the intercorrelations among creativity measures should be much higher than those between creativity and intelligence measures. Another problem is that the findings are based on a highly selective sample of children. Recall that the two extreme groups were drawn from an initial sample whose mean IQ was 132. To what extent can results based on such a selective group of children be generalized? In a fairly close replication of the Getzels and Jackson study, Hasan and Butcher (1966) worked with a group of 175 Scottish children whose mean IQ was 102. In contrast to the low creativity/intelligence correlations reported in the original study, Hasan and Butcher reported a correlation of .74 between a composite creativity measure and intelligence.[3]

How can we account for the discrepant research findings on the relationship between creativity and intelligence? The "threshold theory" of the relation of these two abilities provides some clarification (Barron, 1963; Yamamoto, 1964, 1965). Central to this theory is that intelligence is a necessary but not a sufficient condition of creativity. That is, above a certain level of intelligence, variations in intelligence tend to be unrelated to creativity. Yamamoto's (1965) findings provide support for this view. Using divergent-production measures of creativity and a measure of intelligence, he obtained correlations (corrected for restriction of range) of .88 for subjects with IQs below 90, .69 for subjects with IQs between 90 and 110, −.30 for subjects with IQs between 110 and 130, and −.09 for subjects with IQs above 130. In a subsequent study Yamamoto and Chimbidis (1966) found a correlation of .50 between divergent production and intelligence for subjects with IQs below 120 and a correlation of .20 for subjects with IQs above 120. All of this evidence indicates that creativity is dependent on at least a slightly better than average level of intelligence (an IQ of about 120). Apparently, creative ability builds on general intelligence. It would seem that individuals within the upper range of intelligence have the potential to develop creative ability. We need to learn more about the training conditions that could foster creativity in this group.

---

[3]The range of variation in IQs in both the Getzels/Jackson and Hasan/Butcher samples was equivalent. Thus, the higher correlation for the latter study was not due to the statistical effect of a wider range of ability (Butcher, 1968).

Aside from the question of the relationship between creativity and intelligence, is it possible to make differential predictions about the personal characteristics of those who are highly creative and those who are highly intelligent? A tentative answer was suggested by the Getzels and Jackson study, which indicated value and personality differences between creative and intelligent children. A similar study by Wallach and Kogan (1965) involved 10- to 11-year-old children who were given measures of divergent production and intelligence. The sample of 151 children was divided into four groups.[4] Two groups included children who were high on one characteristic (creativity or intelligence) and low on the other (as in the Getzels and Jackson study). A third group was made up of children who were high on both characteristics, and the fourth was made up of those who were low on both. The four groups were compared on a variety of personality characteristics. Major characteristics that distinguished the groups were as follows: The high creativity/high intelligence children revealed an ability to exercise within themselves both control and freedom. The high creativity/low intelligence children were in angry conflict with both themselves and the school environment and beset by feelings of unworthiness and inadequacy; however, they could excel cognitively in a stress-free context. The low creativity/high intelligence children were highly achievement oriented and perceived the possibility of academic failure as catastrophic. The low creativity/low intelligence children were described as basically bewildered and engaged in various defensive behaviors.

The results of the Wallach and Kogan study suggest the different kinds of environmental conditions that might be beneficial to groups of children who vary in creativity and intelligence. Apparently, highly creative children who are not high in intelligence fare best in relatively free or nonstructured environments; highly intelligent children who are not high in creativity profit from more structured and competitive environments; while those children who are both creative and intelligent have the flexibility to adapt to different kinds of environment. However, we should exercise caution in considering the implications of such results until further replications are available. Furthermore, in a reanalysis of the Wallach and Kogan data, Cronbach (1968) showed that the measures of creativity accounted for only a small proportion (4%) of the variation in the personality measures; whereas, the intelligence measures accounted for a much higher proportion (around 44%) of the variation on some of the personality measures (those indicating adjustment to the school situation).

Perhaps, the study most relevant to the question of differential prediction is an investigation by Wallach and Wing (1969). They worked with a group of first-year college students and related measures of intelligence (the Scholastic Aptitude Test) and divergent production to indexes of creative achievement. Subjects scoring in the top and bottom thirds of each of two creativity measures were compared, and a similar comparison was made between the top and

---

[4]Separate groups were formed for boys and girls. The results revealed little evidence of sex differences, so the major findings can be summarized for the total sample.

bottom third on the intelligence measure. Creative achievement was defined in terms of talented accomplishments outside the classroom, such as painting, creative writing, and the exercise of social leadership. The results showed that highly creative students achieved significantly more talented accomplishments than noncreative students. In contrast, differences in talented accomplishments were negligible between high and low scorers in intelligence. These results clearly show that creativity measures, but not intelligence measures, are predictive of talented accomplishments. That talented accomplishment is equivalent to creative achievement is, however, questionable. Brody (1972) has pointed out that most of the listed accomplishments in the self-descriptive questionnaire used by Wallach and Wing did not refer to the actual production of something that was judged to have creative value. Playing a musical instrument, painting, or being a social leader do not necessarily imply that one is creative. Regarding the few accomplishments that did reflect creative achievement (for example, winning a prize in an art contest), Brody's reanalysis revealed that those who scored high on the intelligence measure were just as likely to be creative as those who scored high on the creativity measures.

In considering the array of evidence from the studies on creativity and intelligence, we can reach two conclusions. First, intelligence is a necessary but not a sufficient condition of creativity. Within the range of high intelligence (IQs above approximately 120), little relationship exists between IQ and creativity, whereas within the lower IQ range, IQ and creativity are directly related. The second conclusion is that measures of creativity, as distinct from measures of intelligence, tend to be related to unconventional interests and values. Related to this pattern is the suggestion that some highly creative children, especially those who are relatively lower in intelligence than creativity, may have difficulty adjusting to an achievement-oriented school environment.

Studies of Creative Persons. Are there particular personality characteristics associated with people who are judged to be creative? This question has been investigated by comparing individuals who have and have not achieved eminence in creative fields, such as art, literature, and science. An example of this type of research is MacKinnon's (1964) study of architects. The architects were given a wide variety of tests and questionnaires. One group included individuals who were judged by professors of architecture to be among the most creative American architects. Another group was made up of "ordinary" architects who were neither known for their creativity nor associated with creative architects. The most striking personality differences appeared on the Judgment-Perception index of the Myers-Briggs test, a measure of personality types (see Chapter 8 for a more extensive discussion of this test). The Judgment-Perception index indicates whether an individual prefers to take a judgmental attitude or an understanding and perceptive attitude toward people and situations. Among the creative architects, 58% were placed in the Perception as opposed to the Judgment category of the Myers-Briggs test, whereas only 17% of the low-creativity group of architects were placed in the Perception category.

A series of studies by Cattell and his collaborators (see Cattell, 1971) involved groups of creative research scientists, artists, and writers who filled out Cattell's 16 Personality Factor questionnaire. Their responses were compared with the general population norms. The creative groups were significantly more withdrawn, introspective, sensitive, radical, and self-sufficient. The high sensitivity among Cattell's creative groups is consistent with the high degree of perceptiveness among MacKinnon's creative architects. However, unlike the introverted pattern (withdrawn, introspective, self-sufficient) among Cattell's groups, no relationship between creativity and introversion was found among MacKinnon's architects.

Three other investigations of creative individuals have involved small groups of eminent scientists or artists who were interviewed as well as given open-ended (projective) personality measures. The studies of scientists by Roe (1953) and Eiduson (1962) generally have indicated a great diversity of personality patterns among the groups studied. One relatively common thread among the scientists was a pattern of social isolation in childhood, although this pattern was much more pronounced among biological and physical scientists than among social scientists (Roe, 1953). In the third study, a study of eminent artists from the fields of painting, music, literature, and theater, Eiduson (1958) also found a pattern of childhood isolation. In addition, the artists, while diverse in needs and defense mechanisms, were characteristically sensitive and perceptive.

The overall results of studies investigating the association of particular personality characteristics with creative ability show that considerable variation appears among groups of creative persons. One characteristic that tends to be consistent in these groups is sensitivity or perceptiveness. One problem with the research in this area is that the few relevant studies have used different methods, preventing generalization across studies. Furthermore, those traits that tend to be associated with creativity may not be intrinsic to creative achievement but may reflect the social role assigned to those in a particular occupation (Brody, 1972). For instance, in the future, introversion, a trait often associated with eminent scientists, may not continue to be related to creativity in scientific fields because of the increasing demand for research scientists to work closely with one another.

Cognitive Styles

Cognitive styles refer to individual differences in modes of perceiving, remembering, and thinking (Kogan, 1971). The implication is that we develop distinctive ways of apprehending, storing, transforming, and utilizing information. Cognitive styles differ from other special abilities in that they involve the manner and form of cognition rather than the level of demonstrated skill. In fact, these stylistic variables are sometimes categorized as personality dimensions (see Chapter 8) because they involve aspects of motivation and temperament.

The investigation of cognitive styles started in the late 1940s and was influenced in part by psychoanalytic ego psychology (Kagan & Kogan, 1970). Psychoanalytic ego psychology (see Hartmann, 1958; Rapaport, 1959), in contrast to orthodox (Freudian) psychoanalytic theory, emphasizes the nondefensive functions of the ego that, in essence, are the cognitive processes of perception, memory, and thinking. Another point emphasized by the ego psychologists is that cognition involves motivational and emotional processes.

The basic principles of ego psychology were translated into a conceptualization of cognitive styles by workers at the Menninger Foundation (Klein, 1954, 1958; Gardner, 1962). According to the Menninger group, cognitive styles represent strategies or approaches that individuals use to gain an understanding of the various situations they have to deal with. Individuals vary in the kinds of cognitive styles that work best for them. The Menninger group has identified several cognitive style dimensions (which they refer to as "cognitive controls"), including leveling-sharpening (individual differences in memory assimilation), constricted-flexible control (individual differences in susceptibility to distraction), and tolerance for unrealistic experience (individual differences in accepting perceptions at variance with conventional experience).

Research on cognitive styles was also influenced by theories of cognitive development, including those of Lewin (1951), Piaget (1954), and Werner (1948). Common to the approaches of these theorists is the notion that in the course of development cognitive structures become more differentiated and hierarchically integrated. Differentiation refers to the growing variety in a person's behaviors and the increasing tendency for the person to function more independently from the environment (Lewin, 1951). As the person becomes more differentiated, a complementary process of hierarchic integration is needed to unify or organize the differentiated aspects of the person's functioning. Individual differences in the extent to which the person becomes differentiated and integrated represent a central theme in the work on "field dependence/independence" by Witkin and associates (1954, 1962) and on "conceptual systems" by Harvey, Hunt, and Schroder (1961). We shall focus our attention on these two cognitive styles as they appear to be the most thoroughly studied and widely known. Research on other cognitive styles, including the cognitive control dimensions, cognitive complexity, reflexivity/impulsivity, and risk-taking, is reviewed by Kagan and Kogan (1970) and Kogan (1971).

Field Dependence/Independence. Individual differences in field dependence/independence represent the extent to which a person can function independently (that is, is differentiated) from his or her environmental context. A relatively low degree of such differentiation is located toward the field-dependence end of the continuum; a relatively high degree of such differentiation is located toward the field-independence end of the continuum.

Witkin and his colleagues (1954, 1962) have developed three measures of field independence: (1) the Body Adjustment Test, (2) The Rod and Frame Test, and (3) the Embedded Figures Test. The Body Adjustment Test, which is illustrated in Figure 7-3, involves a tilting chair within a tilting room. On each of several trials the seated person is given the task of adjusting his or her chair to the true vertical position while the room remains tilted. The Rod and Frame Test consists of a luminous rod within a luminous frame in a completely darkened room. The person's task on each of several trials is to adjust the rod to the true vertical when the rod and frame are tilted in the same or opposite directions. On both the Body Adjustment Test and the Rod and Frame Test a field-independent response is one in which the person's vertical adjustment closely corresponds with the true upright position. That is, the individual is making a vertical adjustment that is relatively independent or differentiated from the external field (the tilted room or tilted frame). The field-dependent person, on the other hand, makes responses that correspond to the vertical position as defined by the tilt of the external-field stimulus (the tilt of the room or the frame). The Embedded Figures Test consists of a set of complex geometric figures in which simple figures are embedded. Field independence on this test is reflected by the person's ability to quickly locate the simple figures without being distracted by the context of the other figures.

Intercorrelations among the three measures of field independence indicate a high level of intertest consistency for groups ranging in age from 8 to 21 (Witkin, Goodenough, & Karp, 1967). Witkin and his colleagues therefore combine scores on the three measures to form a composite perceptual index. What the three tests appear to measure in common is the ability to overcome an embedded context. For instance, in the Rod and Frame Test, if a person adjusts the rod to the true upright position, he or she has overcome the embedded context of the tilted frame.

Groups of young people have been given a series of repeated testings with the field-independence measures (Witkin et al., 1967). One group was tested at ages 8 and 13, and another group at ages 10, 14, 17, and 24. These data revealed progressive increases in field independence up to the age of 17 for boys and 15 for girls. Such data, therefore, support the notion that differentiation in the form of field independence is an ability that increases with age, at least up to the adolescent years. In addition, the longitudinal data showed that the relative position of the subjects on the field dependence/field independence dimension remained fairly constant over a time period of as much as 14 years. Those children who were identified as field independent (relative to their own age group) at age 10 were likely to be so identified at age 24.

As in the case of creativity, it is important to establish that a special ability like field independence is relatively independent of intelligence. However, research generally does not support such independence. Field independence and total IQ scores on the Stanford-Binet and the Wechsler Intelligence Scale for Children (WISC) significantly correlate for 10- and 12-year-old children (Witkin et al., 1962). A factor analytic study by Goodenough and Karp (1961) investigated the relationship between the WISC subtests and measures of field independence. Three identical factors emerged for a sample of 10-year-olds and a sample of 12-year-olds. The first factor, verbal comprehension, was composed of high loadings for the Vocabulary, Information, and

Figure 7-3. The Body Adjustment Test. From *Psychological Differentiation*, by H. A. Witkin, R. B. Dyk, H. F. Faterson, D. R. Goodenough, and S. A. Karp. Copyright 1962. Reprinted by permission of Lawrence Erlbaum Associates, Inc., Publishers. (Photo by David Linton)

Comprehension subtests. The second factor, attention/concentration, was composed of high loadings for Digit Span, Arithmetic, and Coding. The third factor, analytic field approach, was composed of high loadings for the three field-independence measures and for the Picture Completion, Block Design, and Object Assembly subtests of the WISC. Witkin and his associates interpreted this third factor as comprising the common element of an analytical ability to overcome an embedded context. However, it is important to recognize that, if tests of field independence and intelligence are measuring different phenomena, the former would have loaded on a separate factor rather than the same factor as some of the WISC performance subtests. In fact, Zigler (1963) points out that the loading of the field-independence tests with some of the WISC performance subtests indicates that the field-independence measures are primarily nonverbal measures of intelligence.

Furthermore, evidence has not supported the independence of Witkin's measures from measures of verbal and mathematical skills (Kogan, 1971). In addition, research has shown that field independence is related to measures of spatial ability (Gardner, Jackson, & Messick, 1960). All of the foregoing evidence indicates the importance of applying statistical controls for verbal, mathematical, and spatial abilities as well as general intelligence when relating field independence to other variables (Kogan, 1971).

Witkin and his associates have carried out considerable research relating field independence to personality characteristics and social behavior. In a study of 10-year-old boys, which involved clinical ratings of human figure drawings and story completion tests, Witkin and his colleagues (1962) discovered that boys who were relatively high in field independence tended to rely on the use of complex, specialized defense mechanisms, such as intellectualization—a defense that artificially separates emotional content from intellectual content when both are associated with an underlying feeling or impulse, as in the case of describing an act of aggression. On the other hand, the boys who were relatively high in field dependence tended to rely on simple, primitive defenses, such as repression—a defense that blocks off an unconscious impulse (for example, an aggressive or sexual impulse) from conscious awareness. These findings were consistent with Witkin's theoretically based prediction that highly structured defenses, such as intellectualization, contribute to impulse control, which, in turn, is consistent with the kinds of attention regulation necessary to perform in an analytic, field-independent manner (Kagan & Kogan, 1970). However, according to Kagan and Kogan, defense mechanisms assessed by clinical ratings of open-ended, projective test responses (drawings and stories) may not, in fact, validly reflect children's defensive behaviors.

Another problem with the Witkin and associates (1962) study of field independence and defense mechanisms is that measures of general intelligence were not employed as a statistical control, and thus it is not clear to what extent a relationship between field independence and defense mechanisms is affected by differences in general intelligence.

Studies of social behavior with both children and adults reveal that field-dependent individuals are more attentive to social cues, such as the face of the person with whom they are interacting, than are field-independent individuals (Witkin & Goodenough, 1977). Furthermore, field-dependent individuals have an interpersonal orientation—that is, they show strong interest in people, prefer to be physically close to others, are emotionally open, and are attracted to social situations. On the other hand, field-independent individuals have an impersonal orientation—that is, they are not very interested in people, show both physical and psychological distancing from others, and prefer nonsocial situations. In general, the studies of field independence and social behavior have controlled for intelligence.

Some investigations have been concerned with the similarity between parents and children on field-independence measures. If a high correspondence exists, it would be consistent with the idea that parents have some influence in the development of field independence in their children. When field-independence measures are given to both parents and children, correlational analyses interestingly reveal positive and significant relationships between mothers and sons, and fathers and daughters (Kagan & Kogan, 1970). This cross-sex pattern in parent/child similarity has yet to be clearly explained.

Conceptual Systems. A conceptual system refers to a mode of cognitive functioning "that provides the basis by which the individual relates to the environmental events he experiences" (Harvey et al., 1961, pp. 244–245). Individual differences in conceptual systems may be viewed as varying along a dimension of "abstractness/concreteness." A person who experiences the environment at an abstract level is able to discriminate or differentiate between different situational requirements and therefore adapts his or her responses according to the demands of a given situation. On the other hand, a person who experiences the environment at a concrete level tends to see various situations as generally similar in nature and therefore responds in a generalized, rigid way to different situations.

Harvey and associates delineate four levels of cognitive functioning along this abstractness/concreteness continuum (also called a continuum of "integrative complexity"). The particular level of abstractness/concreteness attained by an individual is conceived as a reflection of his or her developmental history of interactions with significant child-training agents, such as parents and teachers. Four "systems" ranging from the most concrete to the most abstract are identified. *System I* functioning (the most concrete level) is characterized by conformity to external, absolute standards and presumably results from an authoritarian training pattern in which exploration and deviation from norms are not tolerated. *System II* functioning is characterized by rebellion from externally imposed standards and is thought to be the consequence of permissive or "laissez-faire" training conditions. *System III* functioning is marked by the individual's use of dependency as a means of manipulating others and presumably reflects exposure to a training pattern of overprotection and overindulgence. Finally, *System IV* functioning (the most abstract level) is marked by the individual's independence of judgment and is viewed as a consequence of optimal training conditions in which the child is encouraged to develop his or her own standards based on personal experience.

The measurement of conceptual systems by Harvey and his colleagues is based on paragraph completion instruments. In the version developed by Harvey (1966), the paragraphs begin with phrases in the form of "This I believe about . . . " followed by referents, such as friendship, guilt, marriage, myself, religion, sin, people, and compromise. The respondent is asked to complete the paragraph with two or three sentences reflecting the theme expressed in the phrase. Another version by Schroder, Driver, and Streufert (1967) contains such phrases as "Rules . . . ," "When I am criticized . . . ," and "When I am in doubt . . . ." Scoring manuals for these paragraph-completion measures contain examples of the kinds of responses that reflect the varying levels of abstractness/concreteness. A relatively high level of abstractness of integrative complexity is reflected in paragraph completions that emphasize criteria such as independence of judgment, flexibility as opposed to rigidity of personal beliefs, and a complex as opposed to a simple interpretation of the world.

An example of a response reflecting a high level of integrative complexity is as follows: "Rules are made for everyone but are interpreted in many ways. It depends on the point of view of the interpreter [independence of judgment and flexibility of beliefs]. It is in this very process of interpretation that a society stays dynamic and changes and grows [a complex interpretation of the world]" (Schroder et al., 1967, p. 192). In contrast, the following response reflects a low level of integrative complexity: "Rules are made to be followed [conformity and rigidity of beliefs]. They give direction to a project or life or anything. They should not be broken except in extreme circumstances [conformity and a simple interpretation of the world]" (Schroder et al., 1967, p. 190).

The paragraph-completion measures are significantly related to measures of verbal intelligence. A correlation of .40 has been reported between a high level of integrative complexity and verbal intelligence (Schroder et al., 1967), meaning that it is necessary to control for intelligence when relating conceptual systems to other variables.

Little research has dealt with the central thesis that child-training experiences affect current conceptual functioning (Kagan & Kogan, 1970). One of the few studies relevant to the developmental antecedents of the level of integrative complexity has been carried out by Cross (1966). He worked with eighth- to twelfth-grade boys and selected those who scored at the opposite extremes of the integrative complexity dimension. Parents of the high- and low-complexity boys were interviewed regarding such matters as their ideas about disciplining their child, how they handle their child when he states an opinion different from their own, and what they think are the most important things for a child to learn while growing up. The interview responses were analyzed according to the degree of parental control exercised, ranging from complete parental control, which compels the child to conform to externally imposed standards of behavior (high unilaterality), to "parent influences only through dissemination of factual information," which allows the child to learn from parental feedback and therefore develop internally based standards of behavior (high interdependence). The findings were consistent with the developmental postulates of conceptual systems theory. Both mothers and fathers of high-complexity boys were more interdependent than parents of low-complexity boys. Thus, parents who allow a relatively high degree of autonomy for their sons are likely to have sons who function at relatively high levels of integrative complexity. The results of the Cross study, however, are open to the criticism of investigator bias (Kagan & Kogan, 1970). During the course of the parental interviews, the interviewers may have been able to infer the levels of the sons' integrative complexity from the parental feedback of how dependent or independent their sons were, which, in turn, could have affected the interviewers' ratings of the parents.

A number of investigations have considered relationships of individual differences in conceptual systems to variations in environmental characteristics. Laboratory studies with college students reported by Schroder and associates (1967) indicate that high-complexity subjects function optimally under conditions of high informational complexity, whereas low-complexity subjects function optimally under conditions of low informational complexity. For instance, in a game modeled on the stock market, groups composed of high-complexity individuals performed better in a situation calling for the integration of a number of indexes, such as the sales index and dividend rate for each stock. On the other hand, low-complexity groups performed better in a situation that was heavily dependent on information handed down by an external authority (a stock-analyst's report). Other evidence of an interaction between conceptual systems and environmental characteristics is contained in a study of academic performance by Pohl and Pervin (1968). Male undergraduates enrolled in engineering, natural sciences, social sciences, and humanities were given a measure of conceptual systems. With intelligence statistically controlled, level of integrative complexity related to grades attained in three of the four fields of study. Among engineering students high grades were associated with low complexity, while among students in the humanities and social sciences high grades were associated with high complexity. These relationships logically follow from an understanding of the task requirements of the various academic areas. If we assume that work in the humanities and social sciences usually involves a greater degree of conceptual integration than is the case in engineering, high-complexity individuals should excel in the first two fields but not in the latter.

Also relevant to the conceptual systems/environment interaction is Hunt's (1966) research with adolescents. Working in a junior high school setting, Hunt grouped students on the basis of their level of integrative complexity. Three homogeneous groups were formed, ranging from a markedly low-complexity group to a group characterized by a moderate level of complexity. The groups were exposed to the same teachers for purposes of later comparison. Classroom observations were carried out on each group for six weeks. The most striking findings were the teachers' statements about which instructional procedures were most effective for each group. The most concrete group (lowest on integrative complexity) required the greatest degree of classroom structure and control. On the other hand, the group highest on complexity required the least amount of structure, working best under relatively nonstructured conditions in which individual activities were encouraged. Thus, the most effective instructional method for each group reflected a match between the complexity level of the students and the degree of classroom structure with which they could best cope. Subsequent studies with high school students have provided further support for the relationship between students' complexity level and degree of classroom structure—that is, low-complexity students require more structure than high-complexity students (Hunt, 1975).

The identification of cognitive styles, such as field independence and conceptual systems, has expanded our awareness of the range of special abilities. Abilities involve not only the level of demonstrated skill but also the manner or style in which problems are solved. Research on cognitive styles is relatively new, and many issues regarding the validity of these constructs still need to be resolved.

SUMMARY

An aptitude refers to the potential to acquire particular behaviors or skills given appropriate opportunity. Aptitudes, therefore, imply future performance. Aptitude tests have typically been developed on the basis of predictive validity, that is, comparing test performance with future criterion performance. Factor analysis has also contributed to the development of aptitude tests. In the area of vocational aptitudes, specific tests and test batteries have been constructed to assess mechanical aptitude, motor functions, and clerical aptitude. The validity coefficients for particular vocational aptitude tests vary widely because they are highly situation-specific. In general, the predictive power of vocational aptitude tests is not very high, though it is somewhat better for training criteria than for proficiency criteria. The validity of vocational aptitude tests can be improved by the research strategies of incremental validity, moderator variables, and decision theory. Artistic aptitude tests assess either aesthetic appreciation or productive skills. Such tests are very difficult to validate.

In contrast to aptitude, ability refers to a person's current level of demonstrated skill. In this chapter two special abilities were considered—creativity and cognitive styles. Creativity signifies the production of something that is judged to be relatively novel or original and has been assessed by measures of divergent production—that is, the generation of multiple solutions to a given problem. Creativity is conceived to be relatively independent of intelligence. Research indicates that intelligence is a necessary but not a sufficient condition of creativity. Within a range of high intelligence little relation exists between IQ and creativity. Within a range of moderate to low intelligence, IQ and creativity are related. Creativity measures, as distinct from intelligence measures, tend to be related to unconventional interests and values and talented accomplishments outside the classroom. Studies of creative persons reveal a considerable diversity of personality characteristics among such people. Where traits have been associated with creative achievement, such as introversion with scientific eminence, it appears they reflect the social role assigned to those in a particular occupation.

Cognitive styles refer to individual differences in modes of perceiving, remembering, and thinking. The investigation of cognitive styles was influenced by psychoanalytic ego psychology and theories of cognitive development. Field dependence/independence represents individual differences in the extent to which a person is differentiated from his or her environment. Field independence refers to a high degree of such differentiation. Measures of field independence appear to assess an analytical ability to overcome an embedded context. In relating field independence to other variables, statistical control for verbal, mathematical, and spatial abilities as well as general intelligence is desirable. Field independence is associated with the use of complex as opposed to simple defensive behaviors and an impersonal as opposed to interpersonal orientation. Conceptual systems reflect individual differences in integrative complexity, ranging from conformity to external, absolute standards (low complexity) to independence of judgment (high complexity). Limited evidence reveals that a parental-training orientation of high interdependence fosters the development of high levels of integrative complexity in children. Other evidence demonstrates an interaction between level of integrative complexity and variations in environmental characteristics, such as informational complexity and structure.

REFERENCES

Anastasi, A. *Psychological testing* (4th ed.). New York: Macmillan, 1976.

Barron, F. *Creativity and psychological health.* Princeton, N.J.: Van Nostrand-Reinhold, 1963.

Brody, N. *Personality: Research and theory.* New York: Academic Press, 1972.

Brown, F. G. *Principles of educational and psychological testing* (2nd ed.). New York: Holt, Rinehart & Winston, 1976.

Buros, O. K. (Ed.). *The seventh mental measurements yearbook* (Vol. 1). Highland Park, N.J.: Gryphon Press, 1972.

Butcher, H. J. *Human intelligence: Its nature and assessment.* London: Methuen, 1968.

Cattell, R. B. *Abilities: Their structure, growth, and action.* Boston: Houghton Mifflin, 1971.

Cronbach, L. J. Intelligence? Creativity? A parsimonious reinterpretation of the Wallach & Kogan data. *American Educational Research Journal,* 1968, *5,* 491–511.

Cronbach, L. J., & Gleser, G. C. *Psychological tests and personnel decisions* (2nd ed.). Urbana, Ill.: University of Illinois Press, 1965.

Cross, H. J. The relation of parental training conditions to conceptual level in adolescent boys. *Journal of Personality,* 1966, *34,* 348–365.

Dunnette, M. D. A modified model for test validation and selection research. *Journal of Applied Psychology,* 1963, *47,* 317–323.

Dunnette, M. D. *Personnel selection and placement.* Belmont, Calif.: Wadsworth, 1966.

Eiduson, B. T. Artist and nonartist: A comparative study. *Journal of Personality,* 1958, *26,* 13–28.

Eiduson, B. T. *Scientists: Their psychological world.* New York: Basic Books, 1962.

Fleishman, E. A. Dimensional analysis of psychomotor abilities. *Journal of Experimental Psychology,* 1954, *48,* 437–454.

Fleishman, E. A. *The structure and measurement of physical fitness.* Englewood Cliffs, N.J.: Prentice-Hall, 1964.

Fleishman, E. A. On the relation between abilities, learning, and human performance. *American Psychologist,* 1972, *27,* 1017–1032.

Gardner, R. W. Cognitive controls in adaptation: Research and measurement. In S. Messick & J. Ross (Eds.), *Measurement in personality and cognition.* New York: Wiley, 1962.

Gardner, R. W., Jackson, D. N., & Messick, S. J. Personality organization in cognitive controls and intellectual abilities. *Psychological Issues,* 1960, *2,* No.4(Monograph 8).

Getzels, J. W., & Jackson, P. W. *Creativity and intelligence.* New York: Wiley, 1962.

Ghiselli, E. E. Moderating effects and differential reliability and validity. *Journal of Applied Psychology,* 1963, *47,* 81–86.

Ghiselli, E. E. *The validity of occupational aptitude tests.* New York: Wiley, 1966.

Ghiselli, E. E. The validity of aptitude tests in personnel selection. *Personnel Psychology,* 1973, *26,* 461–477.

Goodenough, D. R., & Karp, S. A. Field dependence and intellectual functioning. *Journal of Abnormal and Social Psychology*, 1961, *63*, 241–246.

Guilford, J. P. Creative abilities in the arts. *Psychological Review*, 1957, *64*, 110–118.

Guilford, J. P. *The nature of human intelligence.* New York: McGraw-Hill, 1967.

Hartmann, H. *Ego psychology and the problem of adaptation.* New York: International Universities Press, 1958.

Harvey, O. J. System structure, flexibility and creativity. In O. J. Harvey (Ed.), *Experience, structure and adaptability.* New York: Springer, 1966.

Harvey, O. J., Hunt, D. E., & Schroder, H. M. *Conceptual systems and personality organization.* New York: Wiley, 1961.

Hasan, P., & Butcher, H. J. Creativity and intelligence: A partial replication with Scottish children of Getzels and Jackson's study. *British Journal of Psychology*, 1966, *57*, 129–135.

Hunt, D. E. A conceptual systems change model and its application to education. In O. J. Harvey (Ed.), *Experience, structure and adaptability.* New York: Springer, 1966.

Hunt, D. E. The B-P-E paradigm for theory, research and practice. *Canadian Psychological Review*, 1975, *16*, 185–197.

Kagan, J., & Kogan, N. Individual variation in cognitive processes. In P. Mussen (Ed.), *Carmichael's manual of child psychology* (Vol. 1) (3rd ed.). New York: Wiley, 1970.

Klein, G. S. Need and regulation. In M. R. Jones (Ed.), *Nebraska symposium on motivation.* Lincoln: University of Nebraska Press, 1954.

Klein, G. S. Cognitive control and motivation. In G. Lindzey (Ed.), *Assessment of human motives.* New York: Rinehart, 1958.

Kogan, N. Educational implications of cognitive styles. In G. S. Lesser (Ed.), *Psychology and educational practice.* Glenview, Ill.: Scott, Foresman, 1971.

Lewin, K. *Field theory in social science.* New York: Harper & Row, 1951.

MacKinnon, D. W. Creativity of architects. In C. W. Taylor (Ed.), *Widening horizons in creativity.* New York: Wiley, 1964.

Mednick, S. A. The associative basis of the creative process. *Psychological Review*, 1962, *69*, 220–232.

Mednick, S. A. *Remote Associates Test.* Boston: Houghton Mifflin, 1967.

Piaget, J. *The construction of reality in the child.* New York: Basic Books, 1954.

Pohl, R. L., & Pervin, L. A. Academic performance as a function of task requirements and cognitive style. *Psychological Reports*, 1968, *22*, 1017–1020.

Rapaport, D. The structure of psychoanalytic theory: A systemizing attempt. In S. Koch (Ed.), *Psychology: A study of a science* (Vol. 3). New York: McGraw-Hill, 1959.

Roe, A. A psychological study of eminent psychologists and anthropologists, and a comparison with biological and physical scientists. *Psychological Monographs*, 1953, *67*(Whole No. 352).

Schroder, H. M., Driver, M. J., & Streufert, S. *Human information processing.* New York: Holt, Rinehart & Winston, 1967.

Seashore, C. E. *Psychology of music.* New York: McGraw-Hill, 1939.

Sechrest, L. Incremental validity: A recommendation. *Educational and Psychological Measurement*, 1963, *23*, 153–158.

Super, D. E., & Crites, J. O. *Appraising vocational fitness.* New York: Harper & Row, 1962.

Torrance, E. P. *Guiding creative talent.* Englewood Cliffs, N.J.: Prentice-Hall, 1962.

Torrance, E. P. Education and creativity. In C. W. Taylor (Ed.), *Creativity: Progress and potential.* New York: McGraw-Hill, 1964.

Torrance, E. P. *Rewarding creative behavior.* Englewood Cliffs, N.J.: Prentice-Hall, 1965.

Tyler, L. E. *The psychology of human differences* (3rd ed.). New York: Appleton-Century-Crofts, 1965.

Wallach, M. A., & Kogan, N. *Modes of thinking in young children.* New York: Holt, Rinehart & Winston, 1965.

Wallach, M. A., & Wing, C. W., Jr. *The talented student.* New York: Holt, Rinehart & Winston, 1969.

Werner, H. *Comparative psychology of mental development* (rev. ed.). Chicago: Follett, 1948.

Witkin, H. A., Dyk, R. B., Faterson, H. F., Goodenough, D. R., & Karp, S. A. *Psychological differentiation.* New York: Erlbaum, 1962.

Witkin, H. A., & Goodenough, D. R. Field dependence and interpersonal behavior. *Psychological Bulletin,* 1977, *84,* 661–689.

Witkin, H. A., Goodenough, D. R., & Karp, S. A. Stability of cognitive style from childhood to young adulthood. *Journal of Personality and Social Psychology,* 1967, *7,* 291–300.

Witkin, H. A., Lewis, H. B., Hertzman, M., Machover, K., Meissner, P. B., & Wapner, S. *Personality through perception.* New York: Harper, 1954.

Yamamoto, K. Threshold of intelligence in academic achievement of highly creative students. *Journal of Experimental Education,* 1964, *32,* 401–404.

Yamamoto, K. Effects of restriction of range and test unreliability on correlation between measures of intelligence and creative thinking. *British Journal of Educational Psychology,* 1965, *35,* 300–305.

Yamamoto, K., & Chimbidis, M. E. Achievement, intelligence, and creative thinking in fifth grade children: A correlational study. *Merrill-Palmer Quarterly,* 1966, *13,* 233–241.

Zigler, E. A measure in search of a theory. *Contemporary Psychology,* 1963, *8,* 133–135.

Personality

8

We often hear personal descriptions like the following: "Mary Jones has so much personality. She's lively, outgoing, confident, and generous. On the other hand, Mary's sister, Sally, doesn't seem to have much personality at all. Sally is so shy, one hardly notices her." Such statements imply a commonly shared understanding of the meaning of personality, and in fact are not incompatible with our own view of personality. The term, *personality*, refers to observed characteristics that are relatively distinctive and enduring. Such characteristics are called *traits*.

A broad conception of personality denotes all of the various traits that differentiate people from one another. Guilford (1959) categorizes personality traits into four classes: (1) somatic, (2) ability, (3) temperament, and (4) motivation. Somatic traits include both physical (morphological) characteristics, such as body structure, height, and weight, and physiological characteristics, such as heart rate, basal metabolic rate, and body temperature. Ability traits refer to the level of competency in performing tasks and include general ability, achievement, special abilities, and aptitudes (see Chapters 4, 6, and 7). Temperament traits signify the style or manner of behaving and include such characteristics as confidence, sociability, emotionality, and objectivity. Motivational traits involve some aspect of goal directedness and include needs or motives, interests, attitudes, and values.

Many researchers and textbook writers limit the meaning of "personality" to temperament and motivational traits. Furthermore, in the category of motivational traits, some tend to consider only needs as reflecting an aspect of personality. In this chapter we will focus only on the temperament and need aspects of personality. Interests, attitudes, and values will be considered in Chapter 9.

Historically, the first personality characteristics were identified within the realm of temperament. As we pointed out in Chapter 1, the early Greek physicians Hippocrates and Galen designated four temperaments: (1) sanguine (hopeful), (2) melancholic (sad), (3) choleric (irascible), and (4) phlegmatic (apathetic). Hippocrates and Galen believed that the regulation of each of these temperaments was based on particular liquid substances within the body, known as "humors." The four humors of blood, black bile, yellow bile, and phlegm were respectively associated with the sanguine, melancholic, choleric, and phlegmatic temperaments. Presumably, each individual had a predominant humor that would be reflected in the individual's temperament. For instance, people who were observed to be primarily phlegmatic (apathetic) in temperament were assumed to have a predominance of phlegm in their body makeup. This point of view represented a system of classifying people into one of four mutually exclusive temperament categories or types.

Various other personality classification schemes were subsequently introduced, most notably William James's tender-minded versus tough-minded and C. G. Jung's introversion versus extraversion. As personality measurement progressed, narrowly defined traits came to be preferred over broad typologies. As earlier noted, a given trait can be easily quantified in terms of a dimension ranging from low to high. On the other hand, it is difficult to meet the criterion of mutual exclusiveness required by typological categories; that is, according to the classic view of types, the characteristics that describe one type cannot be used to describe another type. Let us now consider the various ways in which personality can be measured.

THE MEASUREMENT OF PERSONALITY

Personality measurement is accomplished using four major methods: (1) rating scales, (2) questionnaires, (3) projective techniques, and (4) behavioral methods.

Rating Methods

In everyday situations we ascribe traits to people we observe. A teacher in a classroom develops impressions concerning each pupil's level of sociability and independence. A hairstylist can differentiate the friendliness of customers.

Similar processes are applied when using rating methods. Ratings may involve assigning a particular numeric value. For example, we could construct a scale of dependency ranging from 1 (extremely dependent) to 5 (extremely independent). Instead of numerical values, ratings may consist of a series of descriptive statements. An illustration of this would be making a choice between one of the following statements: always friendly to others, often friendly to others, sometimes friendly to others, rarely friendly to others, and never friendly to others. Such scales might be used by teachers to rate their students or by psychiatric staff members to rate ward patients.

Sir Francis Galton is credited with initiating rating scales. He used ratings of physical variables in his investigations of individual differences in intelligence (see Chapter 4). However, predating Galton's work, an early 19th-century utopian community in Indiana, known as the New Harmony Colony, made use of trait ratings (see Guilford, 1959). Rating scales were constructed for traits, such as judgment, imagination, excitability, courage, and strength, and apparently used to assess the character development of children.

A problem with the use of ratings is their susceptibility to systematic errors by the rater. For example, some raters may generally be very "hard" on people they rate and give unfavorable ratings, while others may have a tendency to be lenient and give favorable ratings. Another systematic error is a positive "halo effect," which exists if the rater's generally favorable impression of the person being rated influences the ratings. Ratings can also be influenced by negative "halos." Rating errors can be reduced somewhat by devising rating forms that are less susceptible to bias, such as forms that provide for the rating of all persons on a given trait before going on to another trait. This procedure should lessen the occurrence of a halo effect. Training raters to be aware of rating biases can also reduce errors. Even when rating errors are controlled, different raters rating the same person may not agree. It is advisable to have at least two raters making independent judgments, so that interrater reliability can be assessed.

Ratings are especially useful when we wish to observe people in naturalistic settings, such as children in the classroom or psychiatric patients on the ward. Generally, ratings are used when more rigorous measures of personality traits are not available (Guilford, 1959; Kleinmuntz, 1967).

Questionnaires

The self-report personality questionnaire or inventory instructs the respondent to indicate which statements are self-descriptive. The most common response format is a true/false or yes/no dichotomy. Some questionnaires require the respondent to make a choice from among two or more statements (a forced-choice format). Questionnaires may consist of items measuring one particular trait or of items measuring several different traits. The latter may be referred to as multidimensional inventories.

The first personality inventory was introduced during World War I. Robert Woodworth, an experimental psychologist, was asked by the U.S. government to devise a procedure that would screen out psychiatrically unfit recruits for the armed forces. Woodworth constructed a series of questions describing psychiatric symptoms, for example, "Do you daydream frequently?" and "Have you ever been afraid of going insane?" The person responding to Woodworth's questionnaire indicated "Yes" or "No" to each item. Woodworth's inventory served as a model for the development of subsequent personality inventories in the 1920s and 1930s. Mostly aimed at the college student, these inventories purportedly identified students who might have adjustment problems during their college careers.

The most influential personality questionnaire has been the Minnesota Multiphasic Personality Inventory (MMPI), which was developed in the early 1940s. This multidimensional inventory is composed of scales that assess a variety of psychiatric syndromes, including depression, hysteria, paranoia, and schizophrenia. An innovative feature of the MMPI was the inclusion of "validation" scales. These scales assess tendencies on the part of respondents to distort their answers due to carelessness or attempts to present a highly favorable or unfavorable image. Some means of assessing or controlling for such undesirable test-taking attitudes has since become a standard feature in personality inventories.

By the 1950s, a number of multidimensional inventories assessing non-pathological temperament and motivational traits were introduced, such as the California Psychological Inventory and the Edwards Personal Preference Schedule. Also, starting in the 1950s, research with personality questionnaires led to the identification of *response sets*, which refer to tendencies to answer questions in certain ways, independent of item content. For example, responding to items on the basis of their perceived "social desirability" (that is, a person choosing a response because it conveys a favorable image) was found to be a factor influencing personality test scores (Edwards, 1957). Another response set affecting test scores was "acquiescence," the tendency to agree with items, regardless of their content (Messick & Jackson, 1961). As in the case of test-taking attitudes, controls for response sets are usually built into personality inventories when they are constructed.

In general, the self-report questionnaire has proved to be a useful and rigorous method of personality measurement. Early criticism about the ease with which respondents can distort or fake their answers has been overcome by the development of built-in controls. Questionnaires, however, are limited to the assessment of the individual's conscious awareness. Unconscious feelings and frustrated and conflicting needs are difficult to identify through the use of questionnaires. Furthermore, the way people describe themselves on paper-and-pencil tests may be quite different from their actual behaviors. Questionnaires, then, are useful in measuring personality, but need to be supplemented by other methods for a more complete assessment.

Projective Techniques

Projective techniques involve the use of relatively ambiguous stimulus materials, such as ink blots, drawings, and incomplete sentences. The respondents are asked to provide their impressions of or associations with the stimuli.

The rationale for projective techniques is that the ambiguous nature of the stimulus materials enables the respondent to "project" himself or herself into the situation. In this way, the person should reveal unconscious aspects of his or her personality. Because of the focus on unconscious processes, projective techniques have been favored by supporters of a psychoanalytic view of personality.

The oldest and best-known projective measure of personality is the Rorschach Inkblots. This technique was developed by Hermann Rorschach, a Swiss psychiatrist, and first published in 1921. It became very popular in both Europe and North America during the 1920s and 1930s. As psychologists began to work in psychiatric settings, the Rorschach was virtually the only personality assessment tool available. It appeared to be especially useful for determining the degree of reality contact among psychiatric patients. After World War II, a considerable amount of research was directed at investigating the validity of the Rorschach. In general, this research has not been favorable to the Rorschach (see Kleinmuntz, 1967). We should point out, however, that it is very difficult to test the validity of the Rorschach because it is used in an intuitive manner. The same difficulty applies in evaluating other projective techniques, such as the Thematic Apperception Test (TAT), developed by Henry Murray (1938), in which the respondent makes up stories about a series of drawings.

One improvement in projective testing is the attempt to provide population norms when particular instruments are constructed. When the Rorschach was introduced, normative comparisons of the responses of psychiatric and non-psychiatric populations were not carried out. The Holtzman Inkblot Technique, introduced in 1961, included examples of responses given by psychiatric patients and examples of responses given by nonpsychiatric individuals. Using projective techniques as supplements to other personality measures is probably more appropriate than relying on projective techniques as the only method of measuring personality. They should add information not yielded by other methods.

Behavioral Methods

Behavioral methods involve the recording of behavior in standardized and controlled situations. Behavioral methods are often referred to as "objective," because assessment is based on what the person is observed doing. Personality characteristics may be derived from direct laboratory observation, such as in the case of individual differences in conformity under various experimentally manipulated situations, or from specially contrived situational tests, such as observing the responses of armed forces personnel to controlled field situations involving stress. We should note that behavioral assessments of personality are not limited to overt behaviors. Physiological measures can also be used as indexes of personality characteristics. For example, heart rate and sweating in the palms are sometimes used as measures of situational anxiety.

One of the earliest examples of the use of the behavioral method of measuring personality is the investigation of honesty in children carried out by Hartshorne and May (1928). They devised a series of situational tests that were administered in the form of regular classroom examinations, so that the children were unaware of being tested for honesty. With one measure of cheating, children were allowed to grade their own vocabulary and arithmetic tests when supplied with the correct answers. The teachers had records of the children's original answers, making it possible to measure cheating by noting the number of changes in the children's answers. Other measures of honesty included children's susceptibility to stealing and lying when given the appropriate opportunities, as exemplified by not returning all the coins passed out for arithmetic "exercises," or exaggerating the number of chin-ups when making "unobserved" self-recordings.

Behavioral methods are particularly useful in assessing the effects of different situations on personality functioning. "Aggressive" people are not aggressive in all situations. The measurement of personality characteristics, such as aggression or honesty, becomes more accurate when we can specify under what conditions these characteristics are manifested. A problem that may arise with behavioral methods is that, if contrived situations are used, they may not accurately reflect what happens in "real-life" situations. "Stress" that is experimentally manipulated in the laboratory or contrived in the field may be quite different from "stress" in natural conditions. Thus, although people conform to a group's pressure or cope successfully in the research context, they may not necessarily do so under more naturalistic circumstances. Another limitation of behavioral methods is the considerable amount of time needed to assess each individual. A behavioral measure of aggression might take about 30 minutes to complete for each experimental subject. In contrast, a questionnaire measure of aggression can be given to several hundred respondents within a 10-minute period.

Given the variety of methods available for measuring personality, how do we actually determine the basic trait dimensions? We shall now consider the kinds of procedures that have been used in the identification of personality traits.

THE IDENTIFICATION OF PERSONALITY TRAITS

In a pioneering study, Allport and Odbert (1936) examined approximately 18,000 terms, primarily adjectives, that had been used to describe personal characteristics. Their objective was to determine exactly which terms were appropriate as labels for traits. A large proportion of these terms were considered to be unsuitable as trait names because they referred to temporary states of mind (for example, rejoicing or agitated), or they were evaluative and, therefore, described a person's effect on other people (for example, worthy or dependable). Allport and Odbert (1936) concluded that as many as 4500 terms can be used to designate relatively consistent and generalized personal qualities. Needless to say, such a large number of possible terms cannot be applied to the description of personality in any manageable and meaningful way. With the richness of our language, we may be dealing with relatively distinct trait names or several trait names virtually synonymous with one another. When we devise a questionnaire to measure "aggression" how certain can we be that it measures something different from another questionnaire that is purported to measure "hostility"? Furthermore, can we be sure that two "aggression" questionnaires are actually measuring the same trait?

To answer such questions, psychologists have developed procedures aimed at identifying traits that can be measured and shown to be relatively distinct from one another. There are three approaches to trait identification: (1) empirical group comparisons, (2) factor analysis, and (3) the use of a theoretical rationale.

Empirical Group Comparisons

Probably the most direct way of demonstrating that a personality trait can be measured is to compare two groups of people who are known to differ on the characteristic in question. For example, if we want to measure how depressed people are, we can construct a questionnaire composed of items that describe symptoms of depression. We should expect that a group of hospitalized depressive patients would endorse self-descriptive statements of depression to a much greater extent than a group of nonhospitalized people who were matched with the hospitalized patients for demographic factors such as age and social class. In this way we would establish that depression is a measurable trait.[1]

The above example was the procedure followed in constructing the MMPI (Hathaway & McKinley, 1967). Items describing various psychiatric symptoms were administered to groups of patients representing standard psychiatric categories, such as hysteria, depression, paranoia, and schizophrenia. The same items also were administered to a group of visitors to the University of Minnesota Hospital. Scales reflecting the various psychiatric syndromes were constructed on the basis of those items that best discriminated the appropriate psychiatric group from the group of hospital visitors. Thus, the hysteria scale is made up of those items that discriminated the group of diagnosed hysterics from hospital visitors.

In the construction of the MMPI, items selected for inclusion in a particular trait scale were chosen strictly on the basis of the empirical comparison between groups. An item that on the basis of content may have appeared to measure depression would not actually have been selected unless it discriminated depressive patients from the nonpsychiatric group (see Meehl, 1945).

The considerable data that have been gathered on the application of the MMPI indicate that the individual scales have not been successful predictors of specific psychiatric syndromes (Butcher, 1969; Dahlstrom & Welsh, 1960).

---

[1]Empirical group comparisons are also used in the area of aptitudes. Recall in Chapter 7 that contrasting groups of art students and nonart students responded differently to a measure of artistic aptitude.

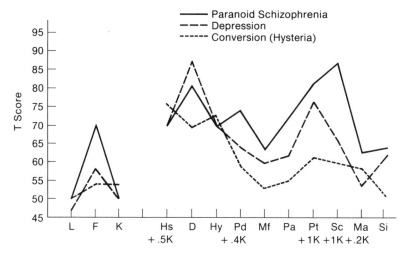

Figure 8-1. Mean *T*-scores for three diagnostic groups on each MMPI scale. The three scales on the left (*L,F,K*) are validation scales. The MMPI clinical scales are: *Hs*-Hypochondriasis, *D*-Depression, *Hy*-Hysteria, *Pd*-Psychopathic deviate, *Mf*-Masculinity-femininity, *Pa*-Paranoia, *Pt*-Psychasthenia, *Sc*-Schizophrenia, *Ma*-Hypomania, *Si*-Social introversion. From "Differentiation of Diagnostic Groups by Individual MMPI Scales," by A. Rosen, *Journal of Consulting Psychology*, 1958, *22*, 453–457. Copyright 1958 by the American Psychological Association. Reprinted by permission.

Rather, particular patterns of scores across the various trait scales have proved the most useful indexes. The profile patterns of MMPI scale scores for three psychiatric groups are shown in Figure 8-1. The raw scores for the scales have been converted to *T*-scores (standard scores with a mean of 50 and a standard deviation of 10; see Chapter 2). As you may have noted, the mean scores for psychiatric groups on most of the scales are at least one standard deviation (10 points) above the mean score of 50, which is the mean for nonpsychiatric individuals.

Another example of an instrument developed by means of empirical group comparisons is the California Psychological Inventory (CPI). The CPI is a multidimensional questionnaire assessing nonpathological personality characteristics. Most of the scales assess temperament dimensions, such as dominance, sociability, social presence, and self-acceptance. Two need traits are also included—achievement via conformance and achievement via independence. In constructing the CPI, items were administered to groups of high school and college students (Gough, 1964). Contrasting groups of students on a given trait were selected on the basis of peer ratings.[2] For example, students were asked to rate their acquaintances on dominance. The item responses of

[2]Eleven of the 15 CPI scales were constructed on the basis of contrasted group responses. Items for the other 4 scales were selected by subjective criteria and then checked for internal consistency (interitem correlations) (see Anastasi, 1976).

those students who were rated very high on dominance were compared with the item responses of those students who were rated very low on dominance. The items finally included in the Dominance scale were those that discriminated between the two contrasting groups. CPI scales have been used to successfully predict various criteria, including delinquency, high school and college grades, and the probability of high school dropout (Anastasi, 1976).

Identifying personality traits by empirical group comparisons is a straightforward and efficient procedure. However, contrasting groups are not always available. Furthermore, psychiatric ratings and peer ratings, which are used as sources for defining groups, are subject to the general weaknesses of other rating methods, such as systematic errors and the possibility of low interrater reliability. Nevertheless, the overall success of the MMPI and CPI attests to the valuable contribution of the contrasted-group method in the identification of traits.

Factor-Analytic Approaches

As in the case of intelligence (see Chapter 4), factor analysis can be used to identify personality trait dimensions. J. P. Guilford, Raymond B. Cattell, and H. J. Eysenck have each independently derived factor structures of temperament. In addition, Cattell has investigated the factor structure of motivation.

Guilford's Structure of Temperament. Guilford's (1959, 1975) factor-analytic investigations, covering a span of 40 years, have been based on questionnaire data obtained primarily from samples of college students. The earliest studies involved factor analyses of questionnaire items purportedly measuring introversion/extraversion. Several factors were identified, including Sociability, Emotional Stability, and Masculinity/Femininity. Over the years other sets of items reflecting various domains of temperament were factor analyzed yielding several additional factors. In all, Guilford and his associates have identified the following 13 temperament factors:

G. *General Activity*: Energetic, rapid-working, lively.
A. *Ascendance*: Upholding one's rights, leadership, not fearful of social contacts.
S. *Sociability*: Likes social activity, not shy or seclusive.
R. *Restraint versus Rhathymia:* Self-restrained and self-controlled versus a happy-go-lucky disposition.
T. *Reflectiveness*: Given to meditative and reflective thinking, philosophically inclined.
C. *Emotionality*: Emotions easily aroused, yet shallow and childish.
D. *Depression*: Emotionally and physically depressed, worried.
N. *Calmness versus Nervousness*: Calm and relaxed rather than nervous and jumpy.
I. *Confidence versus Inferiority Feelings*: Feels accepted by others, socially poised.
O. *Objectivity*: Takes an objective, realistic view of things, alert to one's environment.

F. *Friendliness*: Agreeable, compliant, respect for others.
P. *Good Personal Relations*: Tolerance of people, trust in others.
M. *Masculinity versus Femininity*: Masculine versus feminine interests and emotions.

The Guilford-Zimmerman Temperament Survey (GZTS) (Guilford & Zimmerman, 1949) consists of scales that assess the above 13 factors. The GZTS is actually made up of 10 scales because in earlier Guilford inventories some rather high intercorrelations were found among scales measuring emotionality, depression, nervousness, and inferiority. Scale E (Emotional Stability) was therefore based on a combination of items from these four scales.

Attempts to replicate the Guilford temperament factors have been generally successful (French, 1973; Guilford, 1975; Sells, Demaree, & Will, 1970, 1971). For example, French reviewed available factor analyses of personality items for the purpose of deriving a list of "established factors." An established factor was defined as one appearing in at least three factor analyses conducted in at least two different laboratories. Eleven of the 13 Guilford factors satisfied this criterion.

As we pointed out in considering the structure of intelligence (see Chapter 4), second-order factors can be derived from a set of factors that are correlated with one another. Factor analyses of the GZTS scale scores (each scale represents a factor) typically yield three second-order factors (Guilford, 1975). These are: (1) Social Activity (*SA*), based on scores for Ascendance (*A*), Sociability (*S*), and sometimes General Activity (*G*); (2) Introversion/Extraversion (*IE*), based on Restraint (*R*) and Reflectiveness (*T*); and (3) a third factor based on Emotional Stability (*E*), Objectivity (*O*), Friendliness (*F*), and Cooperativeness (*P*). The third factor in some analyses has been based only on *E* and *O*. In such cases a fourth factor has appeared based on *O*, *F*, and *P*. The third and fourth factors are labeled Emotional Stability (*E*) and Paranoid Disposition (*Pa*), respectively. The Masculinity/Femininity scale (*M*) usually is not included in any higher order factor.

Guilford (1975) has summarized the results of the factor analyses of the GZTS scales in the model shown in Figure 8-2. Each of the 13 first-order factors (based on item intercorrelations) appears on the bottom row. The second row consists of the four second-order factors (based on scale/score intercorrelations). The various clusters of first-order factors in relation to second-order factors are shown by the connecting lines. The dotted line between *G* and *SA* indicates a weaker connection. Guilford also suggests a third-order factor, Emotional Health (*EH*), based on second-order factors *E* and *Pa*. However, no actual factor-analytic evidence supports such a third-order factor.

Cattell's Structure of Temperament. Like Guilford, Cattell (1965; Cattell & Kline, 1977) began his factor-analytic investigations of personality in the 1930s. Cattell, however, did not restrict his data base to questionnaires. He also used ratings carried out by observers and objective tests involving the recording of behavior in standardized and controlled situations. Cattell found

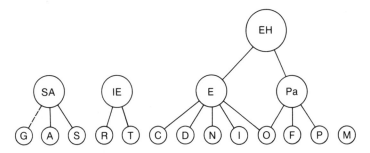

Figure 8-2. A proposed hierarchical model for some of Guilford's factors of personality, showing four second-order factors: *SA* (Social Activity), *IE* (Introversion/Extraversion), *E* (Emotional Stability), and *Pa* (Paranoid disposition); also a third-order factor, *EH* (Emotional Health). See text for labels of factors on the bottom row. From "Factors and Factors of Personality," by J. P. Guilford, *Psychological Bulletin*, 1975, *82*, 802–814. Copyright 1975 by the American Psychological Association. Reprinted by permission.

a close correspondence between the factors emerging from questionnaires and ratings. On the other hand, his more recent work with objective tests has produced little correspondence, possibly because this research is still at an undeveloped stage (Buss & Poley, 1976).

In his factor-analytic research, Cattell attempted to work within the "whole personality sphere" by utilizing Allport and Odbert's (1936) list of about 4500 trait names. He reduced this list to under 200 terms by grouping synonymous terms and eliminating rare terms. Ratings on each of the terms in the shortened list were obtained for a sample of adults and then intercorrelated, yielding a set of 35 clusters. The initial factor analysis was based on ratings obtained from another adult sample for each of the 35 trait clusters. This analysis produced 12 factors that were later confirmed in factor analyses of questionnaire data. The questionnaire data also revealed four additional factors. The total set of 16 factors is represented in Cattell's 16 Personality Factor Inventory (16 PF). These factors, or "source traits," are shown in Table 8-1. The last four factors were identified only through questionnaire data. Of the 16 factors, 15 are temperament factors and one is an ability factor (the second one).

How valid are the temperament factors? Cattell and Gibbons (1968) factor analyzed a combination of Cattell and Guilford questionnaire items. This analysis replicated all of the 14 Cattell factors used (Intelligence and Shrewdness were not used), while 9 of the 15 Guilford factors used (Aesthetic Appreciation and Cultural Conformity were added to the 13 GZTS temperament factors) were replicated. The results of the Cattell and Gibbons study therefore confirm the identification of Cattell's factors. However, these factors have not been well replicated outside of Cattell's laboratory. Howarth and Browne (1971) analyzed a combination of Cattell and Guilford items and replicated 8 Guilford factors, but only 2 Cattell factors. French's (1973) study, which we previously discussed, replicated only 4 Cattell factors. A related problem concerns the unidimensionality of each of the factor scales comprising the 16 PF. Unidimen-

Table 8-1. Technical and Popular Labels for Cattell's Personality Factors

Low Score Description	Factor		Factor	High Score Description
Reserved (Sizothymia)	A–	vs	A+	Outgoing (Affectothymia)
Less intelligent (Low "g")	B–	vs	B+	More intelligent (High "g")
Emotional (Low ego strength)	C–	vs	C+	Stable (High ego strength)
Humble (Submissiveness)	E–	vs	E+	Assertive (Dominance)
Sober (Desurgency)	F–	vs	F+	Happy-go-lucky (Surgency)
Expedient (Low super-ego)	G–	vs	G+	Conscientious (High super-ego)
Shy (Threctia)	H–	vs	H+	Venturesome (Parmia)
Tough-minded (Harria)	I–	vs	I+	Tender-minded (Premsia)
Trusting (Alaxia)	L–	vs	L+	Suspicious (Protension)
Practical (Praxernia)	M–	vs	M+	Imaginative (Autia)
Forthright (Artlessness)	N–	vs	N+	Shrewd (Shrewdness)
Placid (Assurance)	O–	vs	O+	Apprehensive (Guilt-proneness)
Conservative (Conservatism)	Q_1–	vs	Q_1+	Experimenting (Radicalism)
Group-tied (Group adherence)	Q_2–	vs	Q_2+	Self-sufficient (Self-sufficiency)
Casual (Low integration)	Q_3–	vs	Q_3+	Controlled (High self-concept)
Relaxed (Low ergic tension)	Q_4–	vs	Q_4+	Tense (Ergic tension)

From *The Scientific Analysis of Personality,* by R. B. Cattell. Copyright 1965 by Penguin Books, Ltd. Reprinted by permission of the author.

sionality should be demonstrated to support Cattell's factors. However, Levonian (1961), in analyzing the item intercorrelations on the 16 PF, reported that the items representing each factor dimension were highly heterogeneous (that is, the item intercorrelations were low), thus contra-indicative of Cattell's factor structure.

Factor analyses of the 16 PF test have yielded four major second-order factors: (1) Extraversion, (2) Anxiety, (3) Cortertia (cortical alertness), and (4) Independence (Cattell, 1973; Cattell, Eber, & Tatsuoka, 1970). The first-order factors that primarily contribute to each of the second-order factors are shown in Table 8-2. Cattell's second-order factor structure has been replicated on a separate population by Hundleby and Connor (1968). Further confirmation of the second-order factors emerges from factor analyses of objective-test data (Cattell & Warburton, 1967).

Table 8-2. Second-Order Factors Based on the 16 PF Test

Second-Order Factors		First-Order Factors Involved
Extraversion	A+	Outgoing (Affectothymia)
	F+	Happy-go-lucky (Surgency)
	H+	Venturesome (Parmia)
	Q_2-	Group-tied (Group adherence)
Anxiety	C-	Emotional (Low ego strength)
	L+	Suspicious (Protension)
	O+	Apprehensive (Guilt-proneness)
	Q_3-	Casual (Low integration)
	Q_4+	Tense (Ergic tension)
Cortertia	A-	Reserved (Sizothymia)
	I-	Tough-minded (Harria)
	M-	Practical (Praxernia)
Independence	E+	Assertive (Dominance)
	M+	Imaginative (Autia)
	Q_1+	Experimenting (Radicalism)
	Q_2+	Self-sufficient (Self-sufficiency)

Eysenck's Structure of Temperament. Eysenck (1947) started his factor-analytic investigations by using psychiatrists' ratings of patients. From intercorrelations of these ratings he identified two major dimensions: (1) Extraversion/Introversion (E) and (2) Neuroticism/Stability (N). Subsequent analyses conducted on questionnaire and behavioral (objective) test data replicated the two temperament factors (Eysenck, 1952; 1959). Eysenck (1952) also used empirical group comparisons to further delineate his factors. For example, he compared samples of neurotic patients and normal subjects on a variety of personality tests. The Neuroticism factor as finally defined was adjusted to provide the maximum degree of distinctiveness between the two contrasting groups.

Extraversion/Introversion (E) and Neuroticism (N) are assessed on the Eysenck Personality Inventory (EPI) (Eysenck, 1964). High E scores (extraversion) are indicative of a person who is outgoing, impulsive, uninhibited, and socially active, whereas low E scores (introversion) reflect a person who is quiet, socially retiring, and introspective. High N scores are indicative of a person who is emotionally overresponsive and moody, whereas low N scores reflect a person who has good control over his or her emotions. Extraversion/Introversion and Neuroticism/Stability are independent from one other (zero correlation), and it is therefore possible to derive a typology that classes individuals into one of four categories: (1) Extraversion/Neuroticism, (2) Extraversion/Stability, (3) Introversion/Neuroticism, and (4) Introversion/Stability.

Eysenck's two factors appear to correspond to some of the second-order factors identified by Guilford and Cattell. A correlational analysis by Hundleby and Connor (1968) showed considerable agreement between Eysenck's Extraversion and Neuroticism and Cattell's Extraversion and Anxiety, respectively.

Guilford (1975) analyzed the item content of the Eysenck Personality Inventory and concluded that Eysenck's Neuroticism is almost identical to Guilford's Emotional Stability and that Eysenck's Extraversion has some communality with aspects of Guilford's Social Activity and Extraversion (specifically Sociability and Rhathymia).

Eysenck theorizes that his two broad temperament factors reflect individual differences in physiological functioning. For example, he posits that introversion is produced by high arousal levels in the cortex. According to Eysenck, introverts, because they are more aroused, should condition and learn more easily than extraverts. He has conducted a program of research showing that introverts do learn better than extraverts, which therefore provides some support for his hypotheses about the biological basis of temperament (see Eysenck, 1967).

Conclusions about Temperament Factors. How much agreement is there among the factor-analytic results of Guilford, Cattell, and Eysenck? At the lowest level of identifying factors (from intercorrelations among questionnaire items or ratings), the results of Guilford and Cattell essentially overlap. The two factor systems seem to reflect the same temperament realm, and about half of the primary or first-order factors directly match up with each other (Cattell & Gibbons, 1968).

At the level of identifying more general or second-order factors, the results of Guilford, Cattell, and Eysenck show considerable overlap, especially in the delineation of a neuroticism dimension, and to a lesser extent an extraversion dimension.

While the overall results show agreement, why do discrepancies exist in the differentiation of temperament factors? Recall from our discussion in Chapter 4 that the results of any specific factor analysis are affected by a number of conditions. These include the kinds of variables used (such as the particular group of items and tests selected), the samples of subjects involved, and the particular kinds of factor-analytic procedures used. Guilford, Cattell, and Eysenck have used different data sources, samples, and procedures, and such differences should contribute to the discrepancies found in the differentiation of temperament factors. Finally, as we pointed out, Eysenck prefers to first identify the more general factors (which correspond to second-order Guilford and Cattell factors).

In summary, despite some variation in the specific traits that are identified, factor-analytic results provide us with temperament trait dimensions that can be used in investigating individual differences. Eysenck's measures of extraversion and neuroticism have been used to make predictions of individual differences in learning in his previously mentioned work on the biological basis of temperament. The Guilford and Cattell inventories show distinct patterns of scores on the various trait dimensions for people engaged in particular occupations, such as librarians, nurses, teachers, engineers, and airline pilots (see Anastasi, 1976; Kleinmuntz, 1967). Cattell's 16 PF also has been used with psychiatric groups, and, like the MMPI, shows distinct patterns of scores for

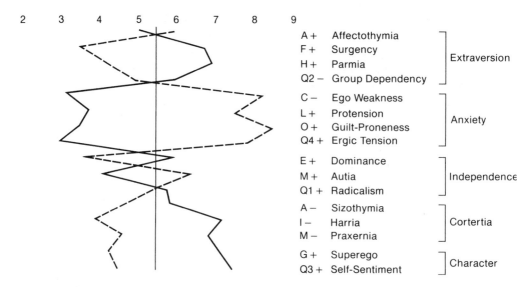

2	3	4	5	6	7	8	9			

A +	Affectothymia	⎤
F +	Surgency	
H +	Parmia	Extraversion
Q2 –	Group Dependency	⎦
C –	Ego Weakness	⎤
L +	Protension	
O +	Guilt-Proneness	Anxiety
Q4 +	Ergic Tension	⎦
E +	Dominance	⎤
M +	Autia	Independence
Q1 +	Radicalism	⎦
A –	Sizothymia	⎤
I –	Harria	Cortertia
M –	Praxernia	⎦
G +	Superego	⎤ Character
Q3 +	Self-Sentiment	⎦

Figure 8-3. Mean profiles for 360 airline pilots (—) and 80 patients with anxiety reaction (– –): 16 PF. The list to the right of the figure shows the first-order and second-order factor measures. In addition to the four major second-order factors, a fifth factor—character—is included. See Table 8-2 for common names for Cattell's factors. From *Introduction to Personality,* by D. S. Cartwright. © 1974 by Rand McNally & Company. Based on data from *Handbook for the Sixteen Personality Factor Questionnaire,* by R. B. Cattell, H. W. Eber, and M. Tatsuoka. Copyright 1970 by R. B. Cattell. Reprinted by permission of Rand McNally College Publishing Company and R. B. Cattell.

various psychiatric categories. An example of two mean profiles on the 16 PF, one for a group of airline pilots and the other for a group of psychiatric patients, is shown in Figure 8-3. Notice the striking differences on the scales related to anxiety. The airline pilots are on the average relatively low on anxiety, which should be reassuring to airline passengers, whereas the patients diagnosed with an anxiety reaction are, as we would expect, relatively high on anxiety.

Cattell's Structure of Motivation. Cattell (1965; Cattell & Kline, 1977) is the only factor-analytic investigator to study the structure of motivational traits. He has focused on two issues: (1) what are the factor components of a single need or motive? and (2) how many different needs or motives can be identified? Let us first consider the components of a given need. One of the needs Cattell has identified is a mating need—that is, the desire to develop an intimate and loving relationship with another person. The strength of such a need can be assessed in a variety of ways. For example, we could assess a young man's physiological reactions (for example, degree of muscle tension or level of blood pressure) when he is shown a picture of a beautiful woman, or we could determine how much information he has acquired about the nature of marital relationships. Cattell has used several methods, including the above-mentioned physiological measures and information tests. When responses to these various measures for a given need are factor-analyzed, two factors emerge—integrated expression and unintegrated expression.[3] *Integrated expression* refers to realistic and socially approved ways of satisfying a need, whereas *unintegrated expression* refers to physiological reactions, unconscious memories, and conscious desires and wishes that are guided by a person's emotions rather than reality-based perceptions.

The strength of a person's need is determined by adding up the scores he or she obtains on measures of integrated expression and unintegrated expression. For instance, a young man with a strong mating need would have a high degree of realistic information about marital relationships and be aware of the social expectations about courtship (integrated expression). He would also have fantasized wishes about marriage, unconscious memories about previous dating experiences, and a heightened physiological reaction when his mating need is aroused (unintegrated expression).

To answer the question of how many different needs exist, Cattell and his associates sampled a wide variety of goal-directed activities. More specifically, the strength of interest in pursuing each of various courses of action was assessed, such as wanting to be with other people, increasing one's salary, and seeing a handsome face in the mirror. Cattell uses the term *attitude* to refer to a person's readiness to act. The use of measures of a wide variety of attitudes has resulted in the identification of two kinds of needs. One group, labeled *ergs*, reflects innate biological needs or drives. The other group, labeled *sentiments*, reflects learned patterns of behavior that are organized around cultural objects or characteristics, such as other persons or social institutions (for example, an organized religion).

Eleven ergs have been identified: curiosity, mating (sex), gregariousness, protection, self-assertion, security, hunger, anger, disgust, appeal, and self-submission. Each erg reflects several attitudes (readiness to act), as illustrated by the mating and security ergs:

> Mating Erg Attitudes
> > I want to love a person I find attractive.
> > I want to see movies, TV shows, and so on with love interest.
> > I want to satisfy mating needs.
> Security Erg Attitudes
> > I want more protection from nuclear weapons.
> > I want to reduce accidents and diseases.
> > I want to stop powers that threaten our nation.

The major *sentiments* (that is, learned patterns of behavior) that have been identified are religious sentiment ("I want to worship God"), career sentiment ("I want to learn skills required for a job"), superego sentiment ("I

---

[3]Integrated expression and unintegrated expression are second-order factors that have been derived from five first-order factors (see Horn, 1966).

want to satisfy sense of duty to church, parents, and so on"), and self-sentiment ("I want to control impulses and mental processes").

Cattell has devised a "dynamic lattice" model that interrelates attitudes, sentiments, and ergs. The *dynamic lattice* is illustrated in Figure 8-4. Attitudes, which represent the starting point of the model, are subsidiary to sentiments, which in turn are subsidiary to ergs. Attitudes and sentiments are therefore viewed as the means to satisfying the biologically rooted needs or ergs. For example, at the top of Figure 8-4, a person's interest in films and plays (attitude level) is a part of his or her involvement with the hobby of photography (sentiment level) which, in turn, satisfies his or her needs for curiosity, sex, and gregariousness (ergic level).

Because of its recency, Cattell's factor-analytic research in motivation is difficult to evaluate. But Cattell's work seems an important step in identifying motivational traits and their relationships to one another.

Theoretical Bases

Theories of personality can serve as guidelines for trait identification because they involve proposed concepts or constructs of temperament and motivation differences. For example, Jung (1923) postulated that people differ in the way they orient themselves to the environment. Some people tend to be outgoing, active, and sensitive to what's happening around them, whereas others are more withdrawn and more concerned with subjective experience. Jung proposed a typology of extraversion/introversion to refer to these differences in orientation.

Once theoretical constructs are introduced, how do we go about measuring them? The rationale of "construct validity" is useful for this purpose (Cronbach & Meehl, 1955; see also Chapter 2). The measure of a given construct should reflect its underlying theoretical definition, and it should also be predictive of theoretically expected relationships.

The process of construct validation was utilized in the development of the Myers-Briggs Type Indicator (Myers, 1962), a self-report questionnaire based on Jung's theory of types. The Myers-Briggs test assesses Extraversion/Introversion as well as three other of Jung's dichotomous type categories: (1) Sensing/Intuition (perceiving directly in a factual way versus indirectly through associated ideas), (2) Thinking/Feeling (judging in a logical way versus judging according to personal and interpersonal values), and (3) Judgment/Perception (an evaluative, judgmental attitude versus an understanding, perceptive attitude). Myers (1962) reports that scores on the Myers-Briggs test are related to a number of theoretically derived criteria. For example, introverts tend to have the highest rate of job turnover in active jobs, extraverts the highest rate in clerical jobs, and thinking types the highest rate in sales jobs.

Another example of the use of construct validity in personality measurement is the Personality Research Form (PRF) developed by Jackson (1967). The PRF is a self-report questionnaire measuring a series of need-trait dimensions. Jackson's starting point was Henry Murray's (1938) theory of personality.

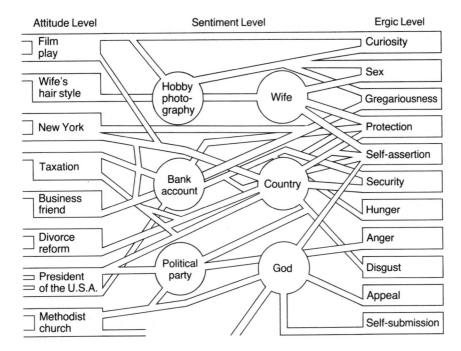

Figure 8-4. A portion of the dynamic lattice, showing the relationship between ergs, attitudes, and sentiments. From *The Scientific Analysis of Personality*, by R. B. Cattell. Copyright 1965 by Penguin Books, Ltd. Reprinted by permission of the author.

Murray had developed a classification of needs based on clinical observation. Jackson selected 20 of Murray's needs, including needs for achievement, affiliation, aggression, autonomy, dominance, and nurturance. On the basis of a review of the relevant theory and research, Jackson developed definitions for each of the 20 needs. Items were then written for each need trait. The PRF scales have been correlated with nontest criteria, such as self-ratings and peer ratings. In general the correlations between the PRF scales and corresponding rating scales show a high level of agreement (Wiggins, 1973).

Murray's classification of needs has also served as the basis for another self-report questionnaire, the Edwards Personal Preference Schedule (EPPS) (Edwards, 1953). On the EPPS, questions concerning the needs are paired and the respondent checks the one that is more self-descriptive. This "forced-choice" procedure was developed as a means of controlling for social desirability.

The theoretical approach to trait identification has been particularly useful in researching single-trait dimensions. Two examples are achievement motivation (Klinger, 1966; McClelland, Atkinson, Clark, & Lowell, 1953) and locus of control (Lefcourt, 1976; Phares, 1976; Rotter, 1966). Locus of control refers to the distinction between those who believe that their own actions are in large measure responsible for what happens to them (internal control) and those who see themselves at the mercy of others: the government, bosses, luck, and fate (external control). The trait is on a continuum and is measured by questionnaires, such as the Internal/External Control Scale.[4]

Now that we have considered the ways to identify personality traits we will examine the influence of genetic and environmental factors on the development of traits.

THE DETERMINANTS OF PERSONALITY

Most theorists of personality have emphasized the role of the social environment in shaping personality characteristics. The traits that children develop are typically explained in terms of the effect parents and other socialization agents have upon the child. This social environmental explanation, however, may not fully account for the development of personality traits. The child's genetic makeup as well as prenatal and perinatal (at birth) experiences conceivably affect the manner in which he or she is treated by socialization agents (Bell, 1968). An infant who tends to be hyperactive may elicit parental reactions that are quite different from those elicited by an infant who tends to be placid.

What evidence is there that "constitutional differences" (differences present at birth) influence the development of personality traits? Twin and adoption studies involving personality characteristics have revealed information about the role of heredity. Also, theory and research exist concerning the relationship between constitutionally based body build and temperament. We will first consider the evidence regarding hereditary influences, then look at constitutional body types, and finally examine the role of the social environment.

Hereditary Influences

The majority of the genetic-design studies (that is, family, twin, and adoption studies) of personality involve comparisons between identical twins and same-sex fraternal twins. Recall that identical twins have the same genetic characteristics, whereas fraternal twins have about half of their genetic characteristics in common. Therefore, if fraternal twin pairs show more phenotypical (observable) diversity than identical twin pairs, this difference can be attributed to the greater genetic difference between fraternal twins. Such a conclusion assumes that identical and same-sex fraternal twins are treated by others in about the same way, otherwise environmental differences could also account for any observed differences between the two types of twins. As we pointed out in our consideration of the determinants of intelligence (see Chapter 5), evidence generally indicates that identical twins are treated more alike than fraternal twins (Bronfenbrenner, 1975). The more similar social reactions iden-

---

[4]Locus of control is similar to the generalized expectancy of success (Crandall, Katkovsky, & Crandall, 1965) discussed in Chapter 6. Unlike the Crandall et al. questionnaire, measures of locus of control are not limited to situations involving intellectual achievement.

tical twins receive, however, do suggest a genetic/environment interaction—because identical twins are genetically equivalent and therefore look alike, they should be treated more alike than fraternal twins.

In interpreting the results of studies that compare identical and fraternal twins, a genetic/environment interaction seems more plausible than attributing observed differences solely to the genetic diversity of fraternal twins. Twin studies relevant to personality have involved either trait dimensions or abnormal personality patterns. The few adoption studies pertain only to the latter.

Trait Dimensions. The hereditary basis of extraversion/introversion has been investigated by Eysenck (1956), who used a sample of same-sex twins born in London between 1935 and 1937. An extraversion/introversion factor was extracted from a battery of tests. Evidence of a hereditary basis for this factor was indicated by the greater similarity in factor scores for identical twin pairs (a correlation of .50) than for fraternal twin pairs (a correlation of –.33). However, these results should be accepted with some caution, because it is difficult to account for the unexpected negative correlation for the fraternal twins. The idea that fraternal twins tend to polarize—that is, one becomes more dominant, the other more submissive—has been proposed, but it is not clear why this should not occur for identical twins. Other evidence supportive of a genetic influence on extraversion/introversion is indicated in a study by Scarr (1969), who used a sample of twin girls with an average age of 97 months. Working with several rating-scale measures of extraversion/introversion, Scarr obtained higher correlations for identical twin pairs (ranging from .56 to .93) than for fraternal twin pairs (ranging from .03 to .83).

Several studies of twin comparisons have been based on the California Psychological Inventory (CPI). Gottesman (1966) used a sample of 147 high school age same-sex twin pairs. Evidence of significant genetic variance (heritability) was obtained for 6 of the 18 CPI scales. These 6 scales related to sociability or extraversion, thus the results are consistent with Eysenck's (1956) previous findings. Similar results for the CPI were reported by Nichols (1966) and Loehlin and Nichols (1976) with a sample of adolescent twins.

A longitudinal follow up of the Gottesman twin sample has been reported by Dworkin, Burke, Maher, and Gottesman (1976). A subsample of 42 twin pairs (25 identical and 17 fraternal) was retested with the CPI 12 years after the original testing. The average age of this group at the time of the follow up was 28 years. The initial scale scores for the retested sample were very similar to those for the total sample, which indicates that the retested sample was a representative one. The results showed different patterns of significant heritability for the two ages studied. The scales related to sociability showed significant heritability in adolescence but not in adulthood, whereas scales reflecting emotional stability and self-confidence showed significant heritability in adulthood but not in adolescence.

What do these changes in heritability from adolescence to adulthood mean? One interpretation, offered by Dworkin and associates, is that the age changes are due to differences in the rate of development. It seems likely that genetic influences are greater in periods of accelerated physical development such as adolescence, and overall a greater number of specific trait measures were found to be more heritable in adolescence than in adulthood. A second possible explanation the investigators point out is that the lower heritability in adulthood could be a function of relaxing environmental controls. The shared environment of identical twins during adolescence appears to be more similar than that of fraternal twins, but by adulthood such a difference would be less likely to occur. More longitudinal research with twin samples is needed to clarify the role of genetic and environmental factors affecting personality traits. As Dworkin and associates (1976) maintain: "age is a variable that must be considered in future research on the genetics of personality" (p. 517).[5]

Abnormal Personality Patterns. The previously cited twin study by Gottesman (1966) also included the administration of the MMPI. The adolescent sample showed significant heritability for six of the ten scales assessing psychopathology. When part of the sample was retested as adults, significant heritability did not appear for any of these six scales (Dworkin et al., 1976). Significance was obtained for one of the other four scales assessing pathological trends. Thus, the MMPI, like the CPI, shows age changes in heritability that are not as yet explicable.

Investigations dealing specifically with the inheritance of neuroticism have produced mixed results. Eysenck and Prell (1951), using a London twin sample, reported a correlation of .85 for identical twins on the neuroticism factor extracted from a battery of tests. The corresponding correlation for fraternal twins was .22. In contrast to this evidence of a strong genetic determination for neuroticism, studies by Cattell and his associates using questionnaires and objective tests with adolescent samples, including identical and fraternal twins, showed a predominantly environmental influence for a neuroticism factor (Cattell, Blewett, & Beloff, 1955; Cattell, Stice, & Kristy, 1957).

Considerable evidence has been obtained supporting a genetic basis for schizophrenia. In extensive reviews of twin studies, Gottesman and Shields (1972, 1976) reported much higher concordance (similarity) rates for schizophrenia among identical twin pairs than among fraternal twin pairs. These results are shown in Table 8-3. As can be seen in the table, the extent of the difference in concordance rates between identical and fraternal twins varied somewhat across the different studies. Establishing precise concordance rates for schizophrenia is particularly difficult because samples tend to differ with respect to age, length of hospitalization, and diagnostic procedures (Rosenthal, 1970).

Adoption studies are also supportive of a genetic contribution to schizophrenia. Heston (1966) studied a group of 47 children who had been separated from their hospitalized schizophrenic mothers at birth. By the time this group

---

[5]For further data about genetic factors in nonpathological personality traits see Vandenberg (1967).

Table 8-3. Concordance Rates from Twin Studies of Schizophrenia

Investigator	Date	Location	Monozygotic Pairs		Dizygotic Pairs	
			Number	Percent Concordant	Number	Percent Concordant
Luxenburger	1928	Germany	19	58	13	0
Rosanoff et al.	1934	U.S.	41	61	53	13
Essen-Möller	1941	Sweden	11	64	27	15
Kallmann	1946	U.S.	174	69	296	11
Slater	1953	U.K.	37	65	58	14
Inouye	1961	Japan	55	60	11	18
Kringlen	1967	Norway	55	45	90	15
Pollin et al.*	1969	U.S.	95	43	125	9
Tienari*	1971	Finland	17	35	20	13
Gottesman & Shields	1972	U.K.	22	58	33	12
Fischer	1973	Denmark	21	56	41	26

*Males only.

Adapted from *Schizophrenia and Genetics: A Twin Study Vantage Point,* by I. I. Gottesman and J. Shields, copyright 1972 (New York: Academic Press); and from "A Critical Review of Recent Adoption, Twin, and Family Studies of Schizophrenia: Behavioral Genetics Perspectives," by I. I. Gottesman and J. Shields, *Schizophrenia Bulletin,* 1976, 2, 360–401. Used by permission of Academic Press and I. I. Gottesman.

reached adulthood, 5 were diagnosed as schizophrenic. A control group of 50 children from the same foundling home, matched for age, sex, length of institutionalization, and type of foster placement, contained no one who was diagnosed as schizophrenic. Furthermore, in addition to those diagnosed as schizophrenic, 13 of the 47 children with schizophrenic mothers were judged to have a neurotic personality disorder, as compared with 7 of the 50 control children. Group differences for both schizophrenia and neurosis were statistically significant. In other adoption studies a higher rate of schizophrenia has been found among natural than among adoptive parents of schizophrenics (see Gottesman & Shields, 1976; Rosenthal & Kety, 1968).

Twin and adoption studies appear to clearly indicate a genetic influence in the development of schizophrenia.[6] What, then, is the role of the environment? Several investigators take the position that environmental influences interact with genetic influences—that is, schizophrenia results from the effects of environmental stressors upon a genetically determined predisposition (Meehl, 1962; Rosenthal, 1970; Sameroff & Zax, 1973). For example, the child of a schizophrenic parent has a high genetic risk for schizophrenia. This risk is likely to be compounded environmentally by the parent's poor caretaking abilities and high anxiety level. Psychologically healthy environments, on the other hand, should act to offset the effects of a high genetic risk for schizophrenia. Evidence needs to be obtained regarding the kinds of positive environmental influences that can inhibit the development of schizophrenia (Wahl, 1976).

Constitutional Body Types

The term *constitutional* refers to characteristics that are present at birth and thus includes genetic and prenatal factors as well as experiences encountered in the birth process (perinatal experiences). Psychologists interested in these constitutional factors have theorized that personality differences can in large part be accounted for on the basis of constitutional differences. A person's constitutional makeup is reflected in his or her physical (morphological) and physiological characteristics. Since it is easier to observe and measure overt physical traits, especially one's general body build or physique, greater emphasis has been placed on physical than on physiological characteristics. Constitutional theorists tend to view postnatal environmental experiences as of less importance than genetic factors and prenatal and perinatal experiences in the development of personality differences. Proponents of this viewpoint also tend not to separate the particular effects of genes from prenatal and perinatal experiences.

Historically, interest in the relationship between physique and behavior can be traced at least as far back as Greek civilization (Hall & Lindzey, 1978). As noted in Chapter 1, Hippocrates devised a typology of physique consisting

---

[6]Twin studies also indicate a rather strong genetic contribution to manic-depressive psychosis, criminality, alcoholism, and smoking (see Chapter 3, Figure 3-4).

of two categories, those people who were long and thin and those who were short and thick. He suggested that these body types were associated with characteristic physical diseases—the long and thin type with tuberculosis and the short and thick type with apoplexy. In the early 19th century, a French investigator, Rostan, suggested a fourfold typology of physique consisting of digestive, muscular, cerebral, and respiratory. The first three of these categories represent the core of most modern-day schemes for typing physiques.

The first empirical studies of the relationship between physique and behavior were conducted by Kretschmer (1925), a German psychiatrist. Based on extensive observations and measurement of psychiatric patients, he devised a threefold classification scheme of physique. This typology consists of the following: (1) "asthenic," a frail, linear physique; (2) "athletic," a well-developed, muscular physique; and (3) "pyknic," a broad, plump physique. Kretschmer was interested in the possible relationship between physique and manifestations of psychotic behavior. He worked with a sample of psychiatric patients who were diagnosed either as schizophrenic or manic-depressive. The results of this investigation showed that schizophrenia was associated with the asthenic physique and manic-depressive psychosis with the pyknic physique. These results, however, appear to have been confounded with age, since Kretschmer did not control for differences in age between the two diagnostic groups (Hall & Lindzey, 1978). Manic-depressive psychosis generally occurs later in life than schizophrenia, and an older age group would tend toward a pyknic or plump body build.

Kretschmer also posited the existence of certain relationships between physique and personality patterns within the normal population. He distinguished between the schizothymic type of temperament (reserved, sensitive) and the cyclothymic type (outgoing, emotionally labile). In line with his psychiatric data, he predicted that the schizothyme would be associated with asthenic physique and the cyclothyme with pyknic physique. In general, little support exists for these relationships (Guilford, 1959). A major problem with Kretschmer's work has been the difficulty of obtaining reliable measurements using his classification scheme of physique.

The investigations carried out by Kretschmer influenced the work of William Sheldon, an American psychologist who also obtained a medical degree. Sheldon and his collaborators (Sheldon & Stevens, 1942; Sheldon, Stevens, & Tucker, 1940) developed typological schemes for both physique and temperament and then investigated the relationship between these two typologies.

The classification of physique was based on photographs of individuals posed in three standard positions: front view, side view, and rear view. Photographs of several thousand male college students were examined by judges in order to determine the principal variables contributing to variations in physique. By this process three primary components of physique were identified: "endomorphy," "mesomorphy," and "ectomorphy." *Endomorphy* is characterized by softness, roundness, and underdevelopment of bone and muscle. *Mesomorphy* represents a firm, hard physique with well-developed bone and muscle. *Ectomorphy* refers to a slender, flat-chested, lightly muscled build.[7] Seventeen measurements are obtained for a given individual's set of photographs by rating different areas of the body, such as head-neck and chest-trunk, as well as ratios, such as height to cube root of weight. These measurements are then used to determine the individual's rating on each of three seven-point scales that correspond to the three components of physique. Ratings follow the order of endomorphy, mesomorphy, and ectomorphy. Thus, an extreme endomorph would be reflected by a profile of 7-1-1, an extreme mesomorph by 1-7-1, an extreme ectomorph by 1-1-7, and a person with moderate ratings on all three components by 4-4-4. An example of each of these profiles is shown in Figure 8-5. Ratings of physique profiles of "somatotypes" show high interrater reliability (correlations of .90 or above). Longitudinal data involving ratings on successive photographs for given individuals suggest that a person's somatotype remains relatively stable from early childhood through late middle life even with weight changes (Sheldon, Lewis, & Tenney, 1969).

Sheldon's typology of temperament was based on observational ratings of a group of 33 young men (mostly graduate students and instructors) over the course of one year. Each of the men was rated on a series of 50 traits. These trait ratings were then intercorrelated, resulting in three major clusters of traits: "viscerotonia," "somatotonia," and "cerebrotonia." *Viscerotonia* is characterized by a relaxed, sociable, enjoying, loving mode of living. A viscerotonic person is drawn to food and people. *Somatotonia* is associated with risk-taking, activity, aggression, and dominance. *Cerebrotonia* implies restraint, inhibition, secrecy, and social withdrawal. These three components make up the "Scale for Temperament," which is a rating procedure. In this way, a person observed by a rater is given a score of 1 to 7 for each of the three temperament components.

The association between physique and temperament was investigated in a five-year study of 200 males who were either college students or college graduates (Sheldon & Stevens, 1942). Temperament ratings were first obtained after a long period of observation, followed by physique ratings. Intercorrelations among these sets of ratings showed a very marked relationship between type of temperament and somatotype. Viscerotonia was associated with endomorphy ($r = .79$), somatotonia with mesomorphy ($r = .82$), and cerebrotonia with ectomorphy ($r = .83$). These findings of an unusually high level of association must be tempered by the criticism of possible rater bias, because Sheldon used the same raters for both the temperament and physique assessments. When rating a person's physique, the rater may have recalled the temperament rating that had already been given. This awareness may have biased the results in favor of high correlation coefficients. Other investigators, controlling for this kind of bias (by using independent raters

---

[7]Sheldon has subsequently examined physique using female samples. He reports that the same components of physique occur in women as in men, but with somewhat different frequencies. Endomorphy is more common among women, whereas mesomorphy is more common among men (see Sheldon, Dupertuis, & McDermott, 1954).

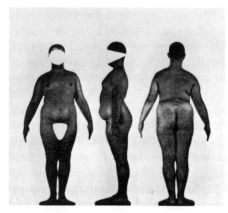

Predominant Endomorphy: 7–1–1

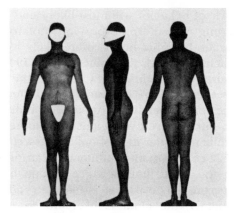

Predominant Mesomorphy: 1–7–1

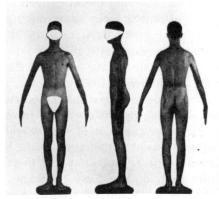

Predominant Ectomorphy: 1–1–7

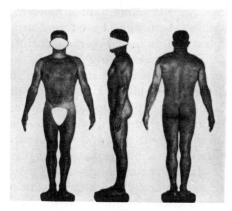

A Balanced Physique: 4–4–4

Figure 8-5. Four examples of Sheldon's body types. From *Atlas of Men: A Guide for Somatotyping the Adult Male at All Ages,* by W. H. Sheldon, C. W. Dupertuis, and E. McDermott. Copyright 1954 by Harper & Row, Publishers, Inc. Reprinted by permission of the executor of the estate of the late W. H. Sheldon, Ph.D., M.D.

for each type of rating or having subjects respond to self-report measures of temperament) have replicated Sheldon's findings; but the correlations, although significant, have been of much smaller magnitude (Child, 1950; Cortes & Gatti, 1972; Walker, 1962). For example, with a sample of 73 boys, Cortes and Gatti, using self-report measures of temperament, obtained the following correlations: viscerotonia and endomorphy ($r = .32$); somatotonia and mesomorphy ($r = .42$); and cerebrotonia and ectomorphy ($r = .31$).

Although it probably is not as strong as Sheldon originally believed, we can conclude that a better-than-chance relationship exists between physique and temperament. What factors account for such a relationship? Hall and Lindzey (1978) suggest four mediating factors. First, particular kinds of behaviors are likely to be associated with particular kinds of physique. An aggressive style of behavior will most likely lead to positive consequences for a physically strong mesomorphic boy, but not for a fragile ectomorphic boy. Therefore, a mesomorphic boy is more likely to engage in aggressive activities. In fact, Sheldon, Hartl, and McDermott (1949) report a relationship between meso- morphy and delinquency. Second, the physique/temperament relationship may be mediated by commonly held stereotypes or the social-stimulus value of the sort of behavior expected of individuals with different kinds of physique. In our culture overweight people are expected to be jolly and good-natured, while muscular men should be assertive (see Lerner, 1969). Third, it is possible that environmental influences can produce particular kinds of physique and at the same time produce certain behavioral dispositions. For example, an overprotective parent is likely to indulge his or her child with food (conse- quently, the child is likely to be overweight) as well as encouraging the child to be dependent. Finally genetic influences may determine both the physique and temperament patterns. Twin studies involving the investigation of physical attributes have found strong evidence of genetic factors determining physique (Newman, Freeman, & Holzinger, 1937; Osborne & De George, 1959).

Before completing our discussion of the relationship between body type and temperament we should note that some investigators have criticized the nature of Sheldon's typology (Ekman, 1951; Humphreys, 1957). The three components of physique are negatively correlated (around –.50) with each other. This means that the three dimensions of physique are not independent from one another—if they were, the correlations between each set of two would be zero. The same holds true for the three dimensions of temperament, which are also correlated at about –.50. It has therefore been suggested that there are two rather than three dimensions within each of Sheldon's typologies. Ekman (1951) recommends that a person's body build can be described in terms of just endomorphy and mesomorphy because extreme ectomorphy rep- resents the absence of the other two somatotypes. Similarly, temperament can be represented simply in terms of somatotonia and viscerotonia because ex- treme cerebrotonia represents the absence of the other two temperament types. Within the realm of physique, factor-analytic research has supported Ekman's two dimensions (Heath, 1952; Sills, 1950).

The Role of the Social Environment

The evidence we have reviewed supports the theory that genetic factors can affect personality. This statement seems especially true in the case of the trait dimension of extraversion/introversion (sociability) and in the case of the pathological syndrome of schizophrenia. In addition, the demonstrated relationship between patterns of physique and temperament suggests the influ- ence of constitutional factors.

If we can assume that genetic and constitutional differences contribute to the development of at least certain personality characteristics, what is the effect of the social environment, especially parental influence? It seems most likely that a complex relationship exists in which genetic and constitutionally based characteristics in children affect parental responses that in turn shape children's developing personality patterns. First of all, we have already mentioned the limitation of studies comparing identical and fraternal twins. Results showing greater similarity for identical twins cannot be accounted for solely in terms of genetic factors, because their environments probably are also more similar than those of fraternal twins. A second point consistent with an interactive interpretation is the evidence of longitudinal changes in the heritability of personality traits. While more data are needed, the observed changes from adolescence to adulthood suggest that environmental experiences can modify traits that have a significant genetic basis.

Further support for an interaction between genetic/constitutional influences and social environmental influences underlying personality is contained in a study conducted by Thomas and associates (Thomas, Chess, & Birch, 1968; Thomas & Chess, 1977). These investigators worked with a sample of 136 newborn infants who were subsequently observed from early infancy through adolescence. The children's characteristic patterns of temperament were derived from parental interviews, which began when the children were about 3 months of age. Among the temperament characteristics rated were activity level, approach versus withdrawal reactions to new stimuli, mood (amount of pleasant versus unpleasant behavior), distractibility, and persistence. These temperament characteristics were judged to be constitutionally determined because they were first identified in early infancy and remained relatively consistent in successive ratings obtained during the first 5 years of life. Of the 136 children, 14 were classified as temperamentally difficult because they were irregular in their biological functioning (sleeping, feeding, and elimination patterns), irritable and negative in mood, and slow to adapt to change. During the course of the study 10 of these 14 children developed behavior problems, such as learning difficulties, inadequate peer relationships, and disciplinary problems. Thomas and his associates suggest that such temperamentally difficult children (who are difficult because of constitutional factors) place great demands on their parents and that the parents respond with resentment and hostility as well as experiencing feelings of anxiety and guilt. These parental reactions in turn add to the child's temperamental difficulties, resulting in overt behavioral problems. Within the framework of an interactive model, the negative spiraling effect just described could be avoided by parents who are able to provide a very secure and supportive environment for a child with temperamentally difficult tendencies.

THE INTERACTION BETWEEN TRAITS AND SITUATIONS

Up to this point, we have concluded that personality traits are generally the joint product of genetic/constitutional and social environmental factors. We have also indicated that traits, once developed, are relatively enduring. It does seem reasonable, however, to expect that personality traits may be

subject to change at different stages of one's life because of marked environmental changes. We will deal with the issue of the stability of personality over
the life-span in Chapter 11.

One further question needs to be considered; namely, how general is
the expression of personality traits across different situations? If one is anxious
in social situations, is one necessarily anxious in achievement situations? If
one's anxiety is confined to social situations, is this anxiety expressed only
in the presence of authority figures? And if so, is anxiety expressed with authority figures of both sexes? If we continue to restrict the environmental conditions
under which a given trait is expressed, we might question the need for using
a concept of trait at all. Would not situational characteristics alone account
for a person's behaviors? This extreme position, which has been labeled *situationism*, is a challenge to the position taken by trait theorists such as Guilford
and Cattell who hold that traits are relatively consistent across situations. Trait
theorists, however, have not completely ignored the influence of situational
characteristics. Cattell (1965) does acknowledge that behavior is in part determined by situational factors, but he has tended to pay little attention to these
factors in his empirical research (Endler & Magnusson, 1976).

The trait/situationism controversy is highlighted by Mischel's (1968) conclusion that little evidence exists to support the trait position of cross-situational
consistency. On the other hand, Bowers (1973) has concluded that there is
little substantiation for the situationist point of view. Both Mischel (1973) and
Bowers (1973), as well as others (Argyle & Little, 1972; Endler & Magnusson,
1976), have resolved the trait versus situation issue by adopting a *person/situa-
tion interactional model*. In contrast to the trait position, which stresses the
person as the major determinant of behavior, and the situationist position,
which stresses the situation as the major determinant of behavior, the interactionist viewpoint implies that behavior is a joint function of the person and
the situation. Furthermore, the interactionist model emphasizes a reciprocal
causal link between the person and the situation. The person is not only influenced by the situation he or she encounters but also actively selects and
modifies the situation in which he or she performs. For example, a teacher
who is forced to teach in an open-concept school, but is used to a structured
style of teaching, may try to impose structure and therefore change the situation. Such an interactionist conception is not new to personality theorizing.
Ekehammer (1974) reviews the earlier versions of interactionism by personality
theorists, such as Kurt Lewin, Henry Murray, and Gardner Murphy.

How valid is the person/situation model of personality? Should it replace
a trait model, which tends to emphasize the stable characteristics of the person
as determinants of behavior? Let us consider the evidence relevant to these
questions.

Empirical Approaches and Results

There are three major empirical approaches relevant to the trait/situa-
tionism issue: (1) correlational research, (2) comparison of variance components, and (3) personality-by-situation experimental design.

Correlational Research. The correlational approach directly assesses the degree to which traits are consistent across situations. Measures of a personality trait are obtained for a sample of individuals across a variety of different situations. An early example of this type of study was the previously mentioned investigation by Hartshorne and May (1928), which showed that honesty was not very consistent across different situations. Reviews of subsequent research have shown that cross-situational correlation coefficients do not generally exceed .30, thus indicating that trait measures at best show only a modest degree of consistency across different situations (Ekehammer, 1974; Endler & Magnusson, 1976; Mischel, 1968). A more recent example of this research is a series of studies by Magnusson and his coworkers (Magnusson, Gerzén, & Nyman, 1968; Magnusson & Heffler, 1969; Magnusson, Heffler, & Nyman, 1968), who investigated the cross-situational consistency of a sample of individuals observed in each of two group situations. Ratings were obtained for each person on cooperative ability, self-confidence, and leadership. When the group situations were similar in terms of group composition (nature of membership) and the nature of the group task, the correlations between the ratings for each personality characteristic were high (around .70). However, when the situation differed in group composition and group task, the correlations between the ratings approached zero—a finding that demonstrates minimal trait consistency across different situations.

One notable exception to the overall findings of low trait consistency across different situations is a study by Bem and Allen (1974). Bem and Allen asked a group of college students to indicate the degree to which they were consistent on the traits of friendliness and conscientiousness. Those individuals who identified themselves as being highly consistent on the traits were, in fact, significantly more consistent across different situations than those who identified themselves as being highly variable. The mean correlations for the highly consistent group were .57 for friendliness and .45 for conscientiousness; the mean correlations for the highly variable group were .27 for friendliness and .09 for conscientiousness. Bem and Allen emphasize the importance of directly asking people about their level of consistency for various traits (an approach that was not employed in previous studies). With such a procedure people are likely to indicate what they consider to be their most distinctive traits, and, according to Bem and Allen, it is with these personally defined traits that we are more likely to find instances of cross-situational consistency. More data are needed to appropriately assess this expectation.

Comparison of Variance Components. It is possible through the use of statistical methods to determine the sources of variance that contribute to a given distribution of responses (see Vaughan & Corballis, 1969; Winer, 1971). This approach was used by Endler, Hunt, and Rosenstein (1962), who constructed a questionnaire of anxiousness in which respondents indicated how anxious they would feel if placed in a number of (verbally described) situations, such as starting off on a long auto trip, going to meet a new date, and getting up to give a speech before a large group. Endler and Hunt (1966, 1969) analyzed these questionnaire data to determine the relative contributions of both individual differences in the degree of anxiousness across situations and the type of anxiety-arousing situation. The results showed that the interaction between individual differences and situations accounted for a larger proportion of the variance in the questionnaire responses than either individual differences or situations. Similar results were obtained by Endler and Hunt (1968) using a questionnaire of hostility.

The results of the Endler/Hunt studies seem to demonstrate that person/situation interactions are more important sources of variation than either persons or situations alone. These studies show that responses, such as anxiety and hostility, are significantly determined by a combination of individual difference characteristics and situational variables. However, these studies and others that involve an analysis of the sources of variance underlying a given distribution of responses do not deal with the reciprocal give-and-take between the person and the situation, a feature also emphasized in the person/situational model. The reason for this limitation is that at the present time our statistical methods have not been fully developed to examine the reciprocal causal relations between the person and the situation (Endler & Magnusson, 1976; Overton & Reese, 1973). This is an important point to keep in mind as we review other interaction studies in both this and the next section.

A series of studies by Moos (1968, 1969, 1970) also demonstrates the importance of the person/situation interaction. Moos obtained self-ratings from psychiatric patients and also made observations of their social behavior (for example, talking, smiling, and smoking). The situations studied were different types of psychiatric ward settings, including individual therapy sessions, group therapy sessions, and community meetings. The results showed that the person/situation interaction was an important source of variance for both self-ratings and observations of social behavior; that is, different patients were differentially affected by different ward settings. For instance, one patient reported a greater decrease in anxiety over a 3-month period in group therapy sessions than in community meetings, whereas another patient reported a greater decrease in anxiety over the same period in community meetings than in group therapy sessions.

Personality-by-Situation Experimental Design. While variance components studies point to the importance of interactions, they do not necessarily tell us how individual differences and situations interact in producing behavior (Endler, 1973). Studies involving an experimental design in which both individual differences (personality) and situations are systematically varied by the investigator can show the effect of particular personality variables, particular situations, and their interactions on behavior.

Many examples of the personality-by-situation experimental design exist. As a matter of fact, there has been an upsurge in personality research that incorporates this kind of design because it provides more information than separate manipulations of only personality or situational variables. One personality variable that has been investigated by means of the personality-by-situation experimental design is locus of control. Recall that locus of control refers to a continuum that varies from a generalized belief that one's own actions are personally controlled (internal control) to a generalized belief that one's own actions are controlled by external forces, such as luck, fate, or powerful others (external control).

Locus of control has been found to interact in a theoretically consistent way with several situational variables. For example, internally controlled children perform better under conditions of intrinsic feedback (self-discovery of success), while externally controlled children perform better under conditions of extrinsic feedback (verbal praise from another person) (Baron, Cowen, Ganz, & McDonald, 1974; Baron & Ganz, 1972). These results reflect a person/situation interaction because, under one type of situation (intrinsic feedback), internally-controlled children outperformed externally-controlled children, whereas, under the opposite type of situation (extrinsic feedback), externally-controlled children outperformed internally-controlled children. Other evidence indicates that, when placed in a performance situation in which they either succeed or fail, college students who are internal tend to attribute their successes to ability (an internal factor) significantly more than do externals. Externals, on the other hand, tend to attribute their failures to luck (an external factor) more than do internals (Gilmor & Minton, 1974). The results of a study in which power position was varied showed that internal male college students were more satisfied in carrying out a communication task when they possessed a high degree of power, whereas external males were more satisfied when they possessed a low degree of power (Hrycenko & Minton, 1974).[8]

Another personality variable that has been studied in relation to situational variables is leadership style; that is, whether a person, when in a leadership position, operates primarily as a taskmaster (task-oriented leader) or as someone who sees to it that good interpersonal relations are maintained within the group (relationship-oriented leader). Fiedler (1971) has conducted a series of studies on leadership effectiveness that generally shows that task-oriented leaders are most effective in two extreme types of situations—when the situation provides the leader with either a very high degree of power and influence over the group's behavior (for example, having the power to hire and fire group members) or a very low degree of power and influence over the group's behavior. On the other hand, relationship-oriented leaders are most effective in situations that provide the leader with a moderate degree of power and influence.

Conclusions

Considerable evidence exists supporting person/situation interaction. This evidence, therefore, does raise questions about the validity of simple trait hypotheses that predict that people tend to be consistent across different situations. An interactional approach that identifies the particular situational characteristics that interact with the particular trait dispositions of the person to

---

[8]This study also included female subjects, who showed a nonsignificant locus of control-by-power position trend in the opposite direction from that shown by males.

produce observed differences in behavior seems more valid. More research is needed to determine which kinds of situations interact with various trait dimensions. Furthermore, as we have already noted, it is important to develop statistical methods that will provide the basis for analyzing the reciprocal give-and-take between the person and the situation. At present, empirical evidence is limited to supporting a unidirectional type of interaction in which behavior is codetermined by the person and situation. In future, we need to gather evidence relevant to the reciprocal interaction between the person and situation (Buss, 1977).

The reciprocal person/situation interaction seems consistent with our previous consideration of a constitutional/environment interaction underlying the development of personality characteristics. A reciprocal causal link between the disposition of the person (shaped by constitutional and previous environmental influences) and the perceived characteristics of the current environmental situation is common to both sets of interactions. The person is both affected by and has an effect upon the situation.

SUMMARY

Personality refers to the observed characteristics of people that are relatively distinctive and enduring. Such characteristics are called traits. In a broad sense, personality denotes all of the various traits that differentiate people from one another. However, the term *personality* is often limited to temperament and need traits. Personality can be measured through the use of rating methods, questionnaires, projective techniques, and behavioral methods.

The identification of personality trait dimensions can be obtained through empirical group comparisons, factor analysis, or a theoretical frame of reference. In empirical group comparisons, two contrasted groups respond to a personality measure. Those items that best differentiate the two groups are used to form a trait scale. Factor analysis has been used to identify traits in both the temperament and motivation domains. The factor structures of temperament identified by Guilford, Cattell, and Eysenck show considerable overlap. Specifically, at the level of first-order factors the results of Guilford and Cattell essentially overlap. At the level of second-order factors considerable correspondence is demonstrated among all three investigators. Cattell's work on the structure of motivation has involved both the factor components of a single need and how many different needs can be identified. Theories of personality can serve as guidelines for trait identification because they involve constructs of temperament and motivation differences. Trait measures of a given construct should reflect the underlying theoretical definition as well as be predictive of theoretically expected relationships.

While the role of the social environment is important in shaping personality traits, the child's genetic makeup as well as prenatal and birth experiences affect the manner in which he or she is treated by socializing agents. Evidence of these constitutional differences (that is, differences present at birth) influencing the development of personality traits is contained in twin and adoption studies as well as research on the relationship between physique and temperament. Constitutional factors appear to be particularly influential with respect to the trait dimension of extraversion/introversion and the pathological syndrome of schizophrenia. However, even when evidence exists supporting the contribution of genetic and other constitutional factors to the development of personality characteristics, the influence of the social environment cannot be disregarded. Apparently, a complex interactive relationship exists in which constitutionally based characteristics in children affect parental responses that in turn shape children's developing personality patterns.

Several theorists and researchers have questioned the assumption that traits are relatively consistent across different situations. Evidence from correlational studies, comparisons of variance components, and personality-by-situation experimental design studies point to the importance of a person/situation interaction. Such evidence suggests that traits should be conceptualized as interacting with situational characteristics.

REFERENCES

Allport, G. W., & Odbert, H. S. Trait-names: A psycho-lexical study. *Psychological Monographs*, 1936, *47*(Whole No. 211).

Anastasi, A. *Psychological testing* (4th ed.). New York: Macmillan, 1976.

Argyle, M., & Little, B. R. Do personality traits apply to social behaviour? *Journal for the Theory of Social Behaviour*, 1972, *2*, 1–35.

Baron, R. M., Cowen, G., Ganz, R. L., & McDonald, M. Interaction of locus of control and type of performance feedback: Considerations of external validity. *Journal of Personality and Social Psychology*, 1974, *30*, 285–292.

Baron, R. M., & Ganz, R. L. Effects of locus of control and type of feedback on the task performance of lower-class black children. *Journal of Personality and Social Psychology*, 1972, *21*, 124–130.

Bell, R. Q. A reinterpretation of the direction of effects in studies of socialization. *Psychological Review*, 1968, *75*, 81–95.

Bem, D. J., & Allen, A. On predicting some of the people some of the time: The search for cross-situational consistencies in behavior. *Psychological Review*, 1974, *81*, 506–520.

Bowers, K. S. Situationism in psychology: An analysis and a critique. *Psychological Review*, 1973, *80*, 307–336.

Bronfenbrenner, U. Nature with nurture: A reinterpretation of the evidence. In A. Montagu (Ed.), *Race and IQ*. New York: Oxford University Press, 1975.

Buss, A. R. The trait-situation controversy and the concept of interaction. *Personality and Social Psychology Bulletin*, 1977, *3*, 196–201.

Buss, A. R., & Poley, W. *Individual differences: Traits and factors*. New York: Gardner Press, 1976.

Butcher, J. N. (Ed.). *MMPI: Research developments in clinical applications*. New York: McGraw-Hill, 1969.

Cartwright, D. S. *Introduction to personality*. Chicago: Rand McNally, 1974.

Cattell, R. B. *The scientific analysis of personality*. London: Penguin, 1965.

Cattell, R. B. *Personality and mood by questionnaire*. San Francisco: Jossey-Bass, 1973.

Cattell, R. B., Blewett, D. B., & Beloff, J. R. The inheritance of personality. *American Journal of Human Genetics*, 1955, 7, 122–146.

Cattell, R. B., Eber, H. W., & Tatsuoka, M. *Handbook for the sixteen personality factor questionnaire.* Champaign, Ill.: Institute for Personality and Ability Testing, 1970.

Cattell, R. B., & Gibbons, B. D. Personality factor structure of the combined Guilford and Cattell personality questionnaires. *Journal of Personality and Social Psychology*, 1968, 9, 107–120.

Cattell, R. B., & Kline, P. *The scientific analysis of personality and motivation.* London: Academic Press, 1977.

Cattell, R. B., Stice, G. F., & Kristy, N. F. A first approximation to nature-nurture ratios for eleven primary personality factors in objective tests. *Journal of Abnormal and Social Psychology*, 1957, 54, 143–159.

Cattell, R. B., & Warburton, F. W. *Objective personality and motivation tests.* Champaign, Ill.: University of Illinois Press, 1967.

Child, I. L. The relation of somatotype to self-rating on Sheldon's temperamental traits. *Journal of Personality*, 1950, 18, 440–453.

Cortes, J. B., & Gatti, F. M. *Delinquency and crime: A biopsychosocial approach.* New York: Seminar Press, 1972.

Crandall, V. C., Katkovsky, W., & Crandall, V. J. Children's beliefs in their own control of reinforcements in intellectual-academic achievement situations. *Child Development*, 1965, 36, 91–109.

Cronbach, L. J., & Meehl, P. E. Construct validity in psychological tests. *Psychological Bulletin*, 1955, 52, 281–302.

Dahlstrom, W. G., & Welsh, G. S. *An MMPI handbook: A guide to use in clinical practice and research.* Minneapolis: University of Minnesota Press, 1960.

Dworkin, R. H., Burke, B. W., Maher, B. A., & Gottesman, I. I. A longitudinal study of the genetics of personality. *Journal of Personality and Social Psychology*, 1976, 34, 510–518.

Edwards, A. L. *Edwards Personal Preference Schedule.* New York: Psychological Corporation, 1953.

Edwards, A. L. *The social desirability variable in personality assessment and research.* New York: Holt, Rinehart & Winston, 1957.

Ekehammer, B. Interactionism in personality from a historical perspective. *Psychological Bulletin*, 1974, 81, 1026–1048.

Ekman, G. On the number and definition of dimensions in Kretschmer's and Sheldon's constitutional types. In *Essays in psychology dedicated to David Katz.* Uppsala: Almquist & Wiksells, 1951.

Endler, N. S. The person versus the situation—A pseudo issue? A response to Alker. *Journal of Personality*, 1973, 41, 287–303.

Endler, N. S., & Hunt, J. McV. Sources of behavioral variance as measured by the S-R Inventory of Anxiousness. *Psychological Bulletin*, 1966, 65, 336–346.

Endler, N. S., & Hunt, J. McV. S-R inventories of hostility and comparisons of the proportions of variance from persons, responses, and situations for hostility and anxiousness. *Journal of Personality and Social Psychology*, 1968, 9, 309–315.

Endler, N. S., & Hunt, J. McV. Generalizability of contributions from sources of variance in the S-R inventories of anxiousness. *Journal of Personality*, 1969, 37, 1–24.

Endler, N. S., Hunt, J. McV., & Rosenstein, A. J. An S-R inventory of anxiousness. *Psychological Monographs*, 1962, 76(Whole No. 536).

Endler, N. S., & Magnusson, D. Toward an interactional psychology of personality. *Psychological Bulletin*, 1976, 83, 956–974.

Eysenck, H. J. *Dimensions of personality*. London: Routledge & Kegan Paul, 1947.

Eysenck, H. J. *The scientific study of personality*. London: Routledge & Kegan Paul, 1952.

Eysenck, H. J. The inheritance of extraversion-introversion. *Acta Psychologica*, 1956, *12*, 95–110.

Eysenck, H. J. *Manual for the Maudsley Personality Inventory*. London: University of London Press, 1959.

Eysenck, H. J. *Manual of the Eysenck Personality Inventory*. London: University of London Press, 1964.

Eysenck, H. J. *The biological basis of personality*. Springfield, Ill.: Charles C Thomas, 1967.

Eysenck, H. J., & Prell, D. B. The inheritance of neuroticism: An experimental study. *The Journal of Mental Science*, 1951, *97*, 441–463.

Fiedler, F. E. Validation and extension of the contingency model of leadership effectiveness: A review of empirical findings. *Psychological Bulletin*, 1971, *76*, 128–148.

French, J. W. *Toward the establishment of noncognitive factors through literature search and interpretation*. Princeton, N. J.: Educational Testing Service, 1973.

Gilmor, T. M., & Minton, H. L. Internal versus external attribution of task performance as a function of locus of control, initial confidence and success-failure outcome. *Journal of Personality*, 1974, *42*, 159–174.

Gottesman, I. I. Genetic variance in adaptive personality traits. *Journal of Child Psychology and Psychiatry*, 1966, *7*, 199–208.

Gottesman, I. I., & Shields, J. *Schizophrenia and genetics: A twin study vantage point*. New York: Academic Press, 1972.

Gottesman, I. I., & Shields, J. A critical review of recent adoption, twin, and family studies of schizophrenia: Behavioral genetics perspectives. *Schizophrenia Bulletin*, 1976, *2*, 360–401.

Gough, H. G. *Manual for the California Psychological Inventory* (Rev. ed.). Palo Alto, Calif.: Consulting Psychologists Press, 1964.

Guilford, J. P. *Personality*. New York: McGraw-Hill, 1959.

Guilford, J. P. Factors and factors of personality. *Psychological Bulletin*, 1975, *82*, 802–814.

Guilford, J. P., & Zimmerman, W. S. *The Guilford-Zimmerman Temperament Survey: Manual*. Beverly Hills, Calif.: Sheridan Supply, 1949.

Hall, C. S., & Lindzey, G. *Theories of personality* (3rd ed.). New York: Wiley, 1978.

Hartshorne, H., & May, M. A. *Studies in the nature of character: Studies in deceit*. New York: Macmillan, 1928.

Hathaway, S. R., & McKinley, J. C. *Minnesota Multiphasic Personality Inventory: Manual for administration and scoring*. New York: Psychological Corporation, 1967.

Heath, H. A factor analysis of women's measurements taken for garment and pattern construction. *Psychometrika*, 1952, *17*, 87–100.

Heston, L. L. Psychiatric disorders in foster home reared children of schizophrenic mothers. *British Journal of Psychiatry*, 1966, *112*, 819–825.

Horn, J. L. Motivation and dynamic calculus concepts from multivariate experiment. In R. B. Cattell (Ed.), *Handbook of multivariate experimental psychology*. Chicago: Rand McNally, 1966.

Howarth, E., & Browne, J. A. Investigation of personality factors in a Canadian context: I. Marker structure in personality questionnaire items. *Canadian Journal of Behavioral Science*, 1971, *3*, 161–173.

Hrycenko, I., & Minton, H. L. Internal-external control, power position, and satisfaction in task-oriented groups. *Journal of Personality and Social Psychology*, 1974, *30*, 871–878.

Humphreys, L. G. Characteristics of type concepts with special reference to Sheldon's typology. *Psychological Bulletin*, 1957, *54*, 218–228.

Hundleby, J. D., & Connor, W. H. Inter-relationships between personality inventories: The 16 P.F., the MMPI, and the MPI. *Journal of Consulting and Clinical Psychology*, 1968, *32*, 152–157.

Jackson, D. N. *Personality Research Form Manual*. Goshen, N.Y.: Research Psychologists Press, 1967.

Jung, C. G. *Psychological types*. London: Routledge & Kegan Paul, 1923.

Kleinmuntz, B. *Personality measurement: An introduction*. Homewood, Ill.: Dorsey Press, 1967.

Klinger, E. Fantasy need achievement as a motivational construct. *Psychological Bulletin*, 1966, *66*, 291–308.

Kretschmer, E. *Physique and character*. New York: Harcourt, 1925.

Lefcourt, H. M. *Locus of control: Current trends in theory and research*. Hillsdale, N.J.: Lawrence Erlbaum Associates, 1976.

Lerner, R. M. The development of stereotyped expectancies of body build-behavior relations. *Child Development*, 1969, *40*, 137–141.

Levonian, E. A statistical analysis of the 16 Personality Factor Questionnaire. *Educational and Psychological Measurement*, 1961, *21*, 589–596.

Loehlin, J. C., & Nichols, R. C. *Heredity, environment, and personality: A study of 850 sets of twins*. Austin: University of Texas Press, 1976.

Magnusson, D., Gerzén, M., & Nyman, B. The generality of behavioral data: I. Generalization from observation on one occasion. *Multivariate Behavioral Research*, 1968, *3*, 295–320.

Magnusson, D., & Heffler, B. The generality of behavioral data: III. Generalization potential as a function of the number of observation instances. *Multivariate Behavioral Research*, 1969, *4*, 29–42.

Magnusson, D., Heffler, B., & Nyman, B. The generality of behavioral data: II. Replication of an experiment on generalization from observation on one occasion. *Multivariate Behavioral Research*, 1968, *3*, 415–422.

McClelland, D. C., Atkinson, J. W., Clark, R. A., & Lowell, E. L. *The achievement motive*. New York: Appleton-Century-Crofts, 1953.

Meehl, P. E. The dynamics of "structured" personality tests. *Journal of Clinical Psychology*, 1945, *1*, 296–303.

Meehl, P. E. Schizotaxia, schizotypy, schizophrenia. *American Psychologist*, 1962, *17*, 827–838.

Messick, S. J., & Jackson, D. N. Acquiescence and the factorial interpretation of the MMPI. *Psychological Bulletin*, 1961, *58*, 299–304.

Mischel, W. *Personality and assessment*. New York: Wiley, 1968.

Mischel, W. Toward a cognitive social learning reconceptualization of personality. *Psychological Review*, 1973, *80*, 252–283.

Moos, R. H. Situational analysis of a therapeutic community milieu. *Journal of Abnormal Psychology*, 1968, *73*, 49–61.

Moos, R. H. Sources of variance in response to questionnaires and in behavior. *Journal of Abnormal Psychology*, 1969, *74*, 405–412.

Moos, R. H. Differential effects of psychiatric ward settings on patient change. *Journal of Nervous and Mental Disease*, 1970, *151*, 316–321.

Murray, H. A. *Explorations in personality*. New York: Oxford University Press, 1938.

Myers, I. B. *The Myers-Briggs Type Indicator: Manual.* Princeton, N.J.: Educational Testing Service, 1962.

Newman, H. H., Freeman, F. N., & Holzinger, K. J. *Twins: A study of heredity and environment.* Chicago: University of Chicago Press, 1937.

Nichols, R. C. The resemblance of twins in personality and interests. *National Merit Scholarship Corporation Research Reports,* 1966, *2,* 1–23.

Osborne, R. H., & De George, F. V. *Genetic basis of morphological variations.* Cambridge, Mass.: Harvard University Press, 1959.

Overton, W. F., & Reese, H. W. Models of development: Methodological implications. In J. R. Nesselroade & H. W. Reese (Eds.), *Life-span developmental psychology: Methodological issues.* New York: Academic Press, 1973.

Phares, E. J. *Locus of control in personality.* Morristown, N.J.: General Learning Press, 1976.

Rosen, A. Differentiation of diagnostic groups by individual MMPI scales. *Journal of Consulting Psychology,* 1958, *22,* 453–457.

Rosenthal, D. *Genetic theory and abnormal behavior.* New York: McGraw-Hill, 1970.

Rosenthal, D., & Kety, S. S. (Eds.). *The transmission of schizophrenia.* Elmsford, N.Y.: Pergamon Press, 1968.

Rotter, J. B. Generalized expectancies for internal versus external control of reinforcement. *Psychological Monographs,* 1966, *80*(Whole No. 609).

Sameroff, A., & Zax, M. Schizotaxia revisited: Model issues in the etiology of schizophrenia. *American Journal of Orthopsychiatry,* 1973, *43,* 744–754.

Scarr, S. Social introversion-extraversion as a heritable response. *Child Development,* 1969, *40,* 823–832.

Sells, S. B., Demaree, R. G., & Will, D. P. Dimensions of personality: I. Conjoint factor structure of Guilford and Cattell trait markers. *Multivariate Behavioral Research,* 1970, *5,* 391–422.

Sells, S. B., Demaree, R. G., & Will, D. P. Dimensions of personality: II. Separate factor structures in Guilford and Cattell trait markers. *Multivariate Behavioral Research,* 1971, *6,* 136–165.

Sheldon, W. H., Dupertuis, C. W., & McDermott, E. *Atlas of men: A guide for somatotyping the adult male at all ages.* New York: Harper, 1954.

Sheldon, W. H., Hartl, E. M., & McDermott, E. *Varieties of delinquent youth: An introduction to constitutional psychiatry.* New York: Harper, 1949.

Sheldon, W. H., Lewis, N. D. C., & Tenney, A. M. Psychotic patterns and physical constitution: A thirty-year follow-up of thirty-eight hundred psychiatric patients in New York State. In D. V. Siva Sankar (Ed.), *Schizophrenia: Current concepts and research.* New York: PJD Publications, 1969.

Sheldon, W. H., & Stevens, S. S. *The varieties of temperament.* New York: Harper, 1942.

Sheldon, W. H., Stevens, S. S., & Tucker, W. B. *The varieties of human physique.* New York: Harper, 1940.

Sills, F. D. A factor analysis of somatotypes and of their relationship to achievement in motor skills. *Research Quarterly of the American Association of Health and Physical Education,* 1950, *21,* 424–437.

Thomas, A., & Chess, S. *Temperament and development.* New York: Brunner/Mazel, 1977.

Thomas, A., Chess, S., & Birch, H. G. *Temperament and behavior disorders in children.* New York: New York University Press, 1968.

Vandenberg, S. G. Hereditary factors in normal personality traits (as measured by inventories). In J. Wortis (Ed.), *Recent advances in biological psychiatry* (Vol. 9). New York: Plenum Press, 1967.

Vaughan, G. M., & Corballis, M. C. Beyond tests of significance: Estimating strength of effects in selected ANOVA designs. *Psychological Bulletin*, 1969, *72*, 204–213.

Wahl, O. F. Monozygotic twins discordant for schizophrenia: A review. *Psychological Bulletin*, 1976, *83*, 91–106.

Walker, R. N. Body build and behavior in young children, I: Body build and nursery school teachers' ratings. *Monographs of the Society for Research in Child Development*, 1962, *27* (3, Serial No. 84).

Wiggins, J. S. *Personality and prediction: Principles of personality assessment.* Reading, Mass.: Addison-Wesley, 1973.

Winer, B. J. *Statistical principles in experimental designs* (2nd ed.). New York: McGraw-Hill, 1971.

Interests and Values

9

We, your authors, differ concerning the kinds of things we like to do and don't like to do. Henry Minton's major likes include playing the piano, attending concerts, and reading about social history and politics. In the psychology department he gains satisfaction from assuming various administrative responsibilities. On the other hand, Frank Schneider is an outdoors-sports enthusiast and likes to spend much of his leisure time sailing, camping, and hiking, as well as playing ice hockey and tennis. On the job he prefers to get administrative responsibilities out of the way in order to engage in other preferred activities. But we also like doing some of the same things. For example, both of us like to teach, conduct research, dine out, travel, and attend movies and the theatre.

The above are examples of what psychologists refer to as similarities and dissimilarities of interests. Although there is no complete consensus regarding a definition of interests, one idea that is common to most definitions is that interests refer to a person's likes and dislikes for various ideas, activities, and objects (Hanson, 1974; Super & Bohn, 1970). To this we add, as has Hanson (1974), that interests lead a person to behave in a consistent way; therefore, interests may be conceived as possessing motivational properties. Tyler (1974) has referred to interests as a category of "motivational directions."

People's interests may be seen as falling into several different categories. There are, for example, vocational interests, educational interests, social interests, and recreational interests. However, although all these kinds of interest are relevant to our personal lives, it is the first category, vocational interests, that has really engaged the attention of psychologists. Because the preponderance of research and practical application has been concentrated on vocational interests, these will be the focus of our attention in this chapter.

The impetus for the study of interests came primarily from the areas of vocational psychology and vocational guidance. The appraisal of the individual's vocational interests is of considerable value to both employer and employee. A worker's on-the-job performance may be conceived as being a function of nonintellective factors as well as job-related aptitudes. The extent to which an individual is interested in his job certainly is one nonintellective factor that may have an important effect on his occupational performance. It is the uninterested worker who is apt to be "turned off" by his job and show low morale and productivity, as well as a high rate of absenteeism and change of job. Thus, both the employer and employee suffer if the latter is not interested in his or her job—for the employer there is a loss in productivity, and for the employee there is the frustration that inevitably accompanies job dissatisfaction and inefficiency.

Vocational development may be described as a sequence of decisions about one's vocational goals and the intermediary steps involved in reaching those goals. Many people, unfortunately, make occupational decisions on the basis of limited or fragmentary information. As a consequence, it is not uncommon to find a person/occupation mismatch in which there is an incompatibility between the requirements of the job and the worker's aptitudes, temperament, or interests. Thus, if we were able to accurately appraise a person's pattern of interests, such information should prove useful in the career development decision process. As suggested by David Campbell (1977), the two principal functions, broadly conceived, of interest measures are:

(1) telling people something about themselves and their relationship to the working world that will lead them to greater self-understanding and to better decisions about the course of their lives; and

(2) providing information to people who must make decisions about others—counselors, teachers, administrators, admissions committees, personnel managers, supervisors—so that their decisions and dispositions might better consider the unique qualities of each individual [p. 1].

Of course, the use of interest measures in vocational development presupposes that job-relevant interests exist prior to entry into a given vocational field and such interests affect job performance and satisfaction. As we will discover in the following sections, this is in fact the case, at least as far as job satisfaction is concerned.

INTERPRETATIONS OF INTERESTS

Super and Crites (1962) distinguish among four methods of obtaining information about a person's interests. On the basis of these methods they derive four "interpretations" of interests. An *expressed interest* merely refers to the pronouncement of interest in some object, activity, task, or occupation. The expressed interest is treated at face value. If you say you like cultivating a garden or would like to be a social worker, these are expressed interests. A *manifest interest* is defined by your overt participation in some activity, regardless of your motives or intentions. Your taking a course in psychology and our being employed as psychology professors are manifestations of an interest in the field of psychology. *Tested interests* are defined in terms of what a person knows about a given endeavor or occupation. If by means of an information test we discover that a person is knowledgeable about political events, then we infer that he is interested in politics.

Last are *inventoried interests*. In this case the individual indicates likes and dislikes for a number of items, and these are summed to yield a composite score reflecting interest in a given kind of activity or occupation. By far the greatest progress in interest measurement, research, and application has been made with respect to inventoried vocational interests, and for this reason we will restrict our attention to their study. Because of the tremendous amount of research that has been carried out on inventoried vocational interests, probably more is known about this particular individual difference dimension than any other dimension with the exception of general intelligence.

We should note that in the case of a given individual, inconsistencies may exist among the four types of interest—expressed, manifest, tested, and inventoried. For example, a student who says he is interested in psychology but rarely attends class or seldom picks up a book to read about psychology may be said to have an expressed interest in psychology but certainly not a strong manifest interest and probably not strong tested and inventoried interests.

VOCATIONAL INTERESTS

More than any other person, Edward K. Strong Jr. has made the greatest contribution to the study and measurement of vocational interests. His impact was felt primarily through his work on the Strong Vocational Interest Blank (SVIB). The original version of the SVIB was published in 1927 and was designed as a measure of men's interests. A women's form of the SVIB was published in 1933. During the 50-odd years since its origin a tremendous

Table 9-1. The Seven Parts and Sample Items from the Strong-Campbell Interest Inventory

Part I	*Occupations* (131 items): actor/actress, building contractor, dentist, hospital records clerk, mechanical engineer, statistician, toolmaker.
Part II	*School Subjects* (36 items): agriculture, calculus, English composition, mechanical drawing, philosophy, psychology, home economics.
Part III	*Activities* (51 items): making a speech, going to church, teaching adults, sewing, drilling soldiers, cabinetmaking, saving money.
Part IV	*Amusements* (39 items): golf, bridge, religious music, formal dress affairs, poetry, popular mechanics magazines, camping.
Part V	*Types of People* (24 items): highway construction workers, foreigners, aggressive people, babies, emotional people, musical geniuses, athletic persons.
Part VI	*Preference Between Two Activities* (30 items): airline pilot and airline ticket agent, taxicab driver and police officer, doing a job yourself and telling somebody else to do the job, outside work and inside work.
Part VII	*Your Characteristics* (14 items): win friends easily, usually start activities of my group, have mechanical ingenuity, have patience when teaching others.

amount of work has been done on establishing the SVIB's reliability and validity and expanding its scope. Over the years both the men's and women's forms have undergone three major revisions. In the most recent, 1974, version (Campbell, 1977) the male and female forms have been merged. Also, the name of the inventory has been changed to the Strong-Campbell Interest Inventory (SCII) in order to give credit to David P. Campbell, who took charge of the work on the instrument after Strong's death in 1963. Today the Strong-Campbell is the most widely used interest inventory in North America.[1]

Strong-Campbell Interest Inventory

The SCII consists of 325 items broken down into seven parts. The name of each part and several sample items are listed in Table 9-1. For Parts I through V the individual responds by selecting either "Like," "Indifferent," or "Dislike" for each item. For Part VI the respondent chooses which activity (the "left" or "right" one) of each pair he or she likes better or, if it can't be decided, marks an "equals." For Part VII the person marks a "yes," "no," or "?" (for can't decide) to indicate whether or not the statement describes him or her.

The SCII derives three major sets of scales from the individual's responses to the above items: (1) occupational scales, (2) basic interest scales, and (3) general occupational themes.

Occupational Scales. The occupational scales are essentially the same kind of scales that comprised the original SVIB and are based on Strong's important discovery that the interests of men working successfully in specific occupations tend to be similar to each other and to differ from those of both men-in-general

---

[1]In 1971 Campbell estimated that every year 300,000 to 500,000 men complete the SVIB.

and men working in various other occupations. This "birds of a feather flock together" finding became the foundation of the development of the Strong inventories. Thus, the principal feature of an SCII item is that it has been empirically shown to elicit a widely different response rate across a variety of occupational groups. The majority of some groups will respond that they like the item, whereas the majority of some other groups will indicate a dislike for the same item. Interestingly (to us anyway), the item "college professor" yields one of the widest ranges of responses, with only 5% of farmers and skilled craftsmen indicating that they would like the work of a college professor but 99% of political scientists, psychologists, and anthropologists indicating so. Table 9-2 shows the percentage of men-in-general and women-in-general who indicated "like" for the occupations covered in the most recent versions of the SVIB.

To construct a specific occupational scale the responses of members of the occupational category are compared with those of a sample of people representing the general population. The occupational sample typically consists of people of the same sex between the age of 25 and 55 who have been on the job for at least three years and have been both satisfied with their job and successful at it. If the occupational sample is of men, then their responses are compared with men-in-general, whereas a female occupational sample is compared with women-in-general. The final occupational scale includes only items about which the occupational sample and sex-appropriate general reference sample differed substantially in their percentage of like/dislike responses.

It is important to emphasize that the occupational scales are empirically derived; that is, they consist of items that differentiate the occupational group from the general reference group. As an *empirical scale* (sometimes called a *normative scale*), the items constituting it tend to be heterogeneous in content, often bearing little apparent relationship to each other. For example, people who receive a high score on the flight attendant scale tend to indicate a liking for the following items from that scale: dental assistant, airplane pilot, buyer of merchandise, costume designer, employment manager, and foreign correspondent (Harmon, 1973). Yet these items seem to bear little intuitive or rational association with each other. Thus a person's score on an occupational scale does not necessarily tell us how interested he or she is in carrying out the actual activities involved in that specific occupation; rather it conveys the extent to which the person's likes and dislikes (that is, interests) are similar to those of people who are successfully engaged in the occupation. The assumption is that, if our general interests parallel those held by members of an occupational group, then it is likely that we would find satisfaction in that occupation (Clark, 1961).

The current SCII includes 124 Occupational Scales. These are listed in Figure 9-1. Of the scales 67 were derived from male criterion samples (for example, artists, army officers, and priests) and 57 from female criterion samples (for example, artists, accountants, and airline stewardesses). Recall that a criterion group refers to people who are working successfully in the given occupation. The sex on which a scale was normed is noted to the right of the scale

Table 9-2. Base Rate Popularity of the 25 Most Liked and 25 Least Liked SVIB Occupational Items*

Males		Females	
Item	Percent Responding "Like"	Item	Percent Responding "Like
Most Liked Occupation			
Inventor	61	Interior decorator	69
Airplane pilot	58	Artist	62
College professor	58	Musician	60
Architect	55	Costume designer	55
Rancher	52	Author of novel	54
Author of novel	51	College professor	54
Foreign service man	51	Foreign correspondent	53
Photographer	49	Author of children's books	52
Foreign correspondent	48	Architect	50
Judge	48	Buyer of merchandise	50
Physician	46	Children's clothes designer	49
Psychologist	45	Interpreter	49
Editor	44	Psychiatrist	49
School teacher	44	Psychologist	49
Actor	43	Vocational counselor	49
Governor of a state	43	Florist	47
Musician	43	Magazine writer	47
Geologist	42	News photographer	47
Lawyer, criminal	42	Travel bureau manager	47
Scientific research worker	42	Hostess	46
Artist	41	Landscape gardener	45
Public relations man	41	Social worker	45
Secret Service man	41	High school teacher	44
Surgeon	41	Inventor	44
Carpenter	40	Editor	43

name. For illustrative purposes, we have each filled out a Strong-Campbell form, and our scores have been profiled. The profile on the left is Henry Minton's; the one on the right is Frank Schneider's. The raw scores on each scale have been converted to a standard score (mean = 50; standard deviation = 10) based on the data from the appropriate criterion group. Moreover, the scores have been plotted for those scales on which the criterion sample was comprised of men. Thus, for example, Henry Minton received a score of 50 on both the college professor scale and advertising executive scale, meaning that his responses to the items were very similar to the average member of both the college professor and advertising executive criterion samples. A score between 26 and 44 on a specific scale indicates he responded to the items on the scale the way people-in-general respond. All scores from 26 to 44 are placed under the "average" column and should be seen as relatively uninformative about his interests; that is, they suggest that he neither responded differently from the criterion sample (that is, scores less than 26) nor like the

Table 9-2. Base Rate Popularity of the 25 Most Liked and 25 Least Liked SVIB Occupational Items* *(continued)*

Males		Females	
Item	Percent Responding "Like"	Item	Percent Responding "Like"
Least Liked Occupation			
Mining superintendent	17	Politician	19
Shop foreman	17	Specialty saleswoman	19
Statistician	17	Hospital records clerk	18
Pharmacist	16	Courtroom stenographer	18
Wholesaler	16	Nurse's aide	18
Worker in YMCA	16	Draftsman	17
Auto salesman	15	Lawyer, corporation	17
City or state employee	15	Scientific illustrator	17
Laboratory technician	15	Stenographer	17
Librarian	14	Business teacher	17
Computer operator	14	Typist	17
Auctioneer	13	Weather forecaster	17
Dentist	12	Real estate saleswoman	16
Music teacher	12	Statistician	16
Specialty salesman	12	Income tax accountant	15
Cashier in bank	11	Artist's model	14
Income tax accountant	11	Office clerk	14
Printer	11	Supervisor in telephone office	14
Watchmaker	11	Mechanical engineer	13
Traveling salesman	10	Electronics technician	11
Labor union official	9	Railroad reservations clerk	11
Bank teller	8	Dentist	9
Life insurance salesman	8	Waitress	8
Private secretary	5	Supermarket checkout clerk	7
Funeral director	5	Life insurance saleswoman	6

*Data are based on the 1969 men-in-general sample (SVIB form T399) and the 1969 women-in-general sample (SVIB form TW398).

Adapted from *Handbook for the Strong Vocational Interest Blank,* by David P. Campbell, with the permission of the publishers, Stanford University Press. © 1971 by the Board of Trustees of the Leland Stanford Junior University.

criterion sample (that is, scores above 44). Of course, the more extreme the score, the more similar (or dissimilar) he is to the criterion sample. Figure 9-1 indicates, as suggested at the outset of this chapter, that the authors do show somewhat different interest patterns.

Basic Interest Scales. In 1969 the Basic Interest Scales were added to the SVIB in order to overcome some of the limitations of the occupational scales (Campbell, 1971). One of the limitations is that scores on such scales are often difficult to interpret because of the heterogeneous item content. It is hard to know exactly what we mean when we say, for instance, that one's interests are similar to a psychologist's. This is because the psychologist scale

Occupational Scales

Code	Scale	Sex Norm	Std Score	Very Dissimilar	Dissimilar	Ave	Similar	Very Similar
RC	Farmer	m	0	☆				
RC	Instrum. Assembl.	f	5					
RCE	Voc. Agric. Tchr.	m−	16	☆				
REC	Dietitian	m	29			☆		
RES	Police Officer	m	6	☆				
RSE	Hwy. Patrol Off.	m	−7	☆				
RE	Army Officer	f	54					
RS	Phys. Ed. Teacher	f	0					
R	Skilled Crafts	m	3	☆				
RI	Forester	m	3	☆				
RI	Rad. Tech. (X-ray)	m	13					
RI	Merch. Mar. Off.	m	19		☆			
RI	Navy Officer	m	17	☆				
RI	Nurse, Registered	m	22		☆			
RI	Veterinarian	m	−1	☆	15	25	45	55
RIC	Cartographer	m	23		☆			
RIC	Army Officer	m	17	☆				
RIE	Air Force Officer	m	12	☆				
RIA	Occup. Therapist	f	30					
IR	Engineer	f	17					
IR	Engineer	m	16	☆				
IR	Chemist	m	10					
IR	Physical Scientist	m	15	☆				
IR	Medical Tech.	f	9					
IR	Pharmacist	f	10					
IR	Dentist	f	19					
IR	Dentist	m	23	15	☆25	45	55	
IR	Dental Hygienist	f	9					
IRS	Phys. Therapist	f	16					
IRS	Physician	m	22		☆			
IRS	Math-Sci. Teacher	m	19		☆			
ICR	Math-Sci. Teacher	f	13					
IC	Dietitian	f	16					
IRC	Medical Tech.	m	5	☆				
IRC	Optometrist	m	26			☆		
IRC	Computer Progr.	f	17					
IRC	Computer Progr.	m	20		☆			
I	Mathematician	f	29					
I	Mathematician	m	32	15	25	☆45	55	
I	Physicist	f	13					
I	Biologist	m	19		☆			
I	Veterinarian	f	2					
I	Optometrist	f	26					
I	Physician	f	28					
I	Social Scientist	m	43			☆		
IA	College Professor	f	43					
IA	College Professor	m	43			☆		
IS	Speech Pathol.	f	53					
IS	Speech Pathol.	m	57				☆	
IAS	Psychologist	f	50					
IAS	Psychologist	m	55	15	25	45	☆	
IA	Language Interpr.	f	52					
ARI	Architect	m	40			☆		
A	Advertising Exec.	f	50					
A	Artist	f	42					
A	Artist	m	41			☆		
A	Art Teacher	f	34					
A	Photographer	m	46			☆		
A	Musician	f	49					
A	Musician	m	54				‡	
A	Entertainer	f	50					
AE	Int. Decorator	f	42					

Code	Scale	Sex Norm	Std Score	Very Dissimilar	Dissimilar	Ave	Similar	Very Similar
AE	Int. Decorator	m	42				☆	
AE	Advertising Exec.	m	51				☆	
A	Language Teacher	f	50					
A	Librarian	f	54					
A	Librarian	m	47				☆	
A	Reporter	f	52					
A	Reporter	m	44				☆	
AS	English Teacher	f	46					
AS	English Teacher	m	49				☆	
SI	Nurse, Registered	f	19					
SIR	Phys. Therapist	m	11	☆				
SRC	Nurse, Lic. Pract.	f	30		☆			
S	Social Worker	f	52					
S	Social Worker	m	40				☆	
S	Priest	m	42	15	25	☆45	55	
S	Dir., Christian Ed.	f	29					
SE	YWCA Staff	f	49					
SIE	Minister	m	34			☆		
SEA	Elem. Teacher	m	33			☆		
SC	Elem. Teacher	f	20					
SCE	Sch. Superintend.	m	36			☆		
SCE	Public Administr.	m	37			☆		
SCE	Guidance Couns.	m	30			☆		
SER	Recreation Leader	f	36					
SEC	Recreation Leader	m	27			☆		
SEC	Guidance Couns.	f	38					
SEC	Soc. Sci. Teacher	f	41	15	25	45	55	
SEC	Soc. Sci. Teacher	m	41				☆	
SEC	Personnel Dir.	m	36			☆		
ESC	Dept. Store Mgr.	m	15	☆				
ESC	Home Econ. Tchr.	f	5					
ESA	Flight Attendant	f	22					
ES	Ch. of Comm. Exec.	m	38			☆		
ES	Sales Manager	m	29			☆		
ES	Life Ins. Agent	m	22		☆			
E	Life Ins. Agent	f	34					
E	Lawyer	f	50					
E	Lawyer	m	41			☆		
EI	Computer Sales	m	18	15 ☆	25	45	55	
EI	Investm. Fund Mgr.	m	44				☆	
EIC	Pharmacist	m	15	☆				
EC	Buyer	f	19					
ECS	Buyer	m	20		☆			
ECS	Credit Manager	m	28			☆		
ECS	Funeral Director	m	19		☆			
ECR	Realtor	m	22		☆			
ERC	Agribusiness Mgr.	m	0	☆				
ERC	Purchasing Agent	m	19		☆			
ESR	Chiropractor	m	30			☆		
CE	Accountant	m	14	☆				
CE	Banker	f	22	15	25	45	55	
CE	Banker	f	26		☆			
CE	Credit Manager	f	27					
CE	Dept. Store Sales	f	4					
CE	Business Ed. Tchr.	f	12					
CES	Business Ed. Tchr.	m	25			☆		
CSE	Exec. Housekeeper	f	13					
C	Accountant	f	24					
C	Secretary	f	22					
CR	Dental Assistant	f	4					
CRI	Nurse, Lic. Pract.	f	2					
CRE	Beautician	f	17					

Figure 9-1. The Strong-Campbell Interest Inventory profile for the occupational scales. The profile on the left was done for Henry Minton; the one on the right was done for Frank Schneider. The forms are reprinted from the *Strong-Campbell Interest Inventory,* Form T325 of the STRONG VOCA-

Occupational Scales

Code	Scale	Sex	Std Norm Score	Very Dissimilar	Dissimilar	Ave	Similar	Very Similar
RC	FARMER	m	29			✳		
RC	INSTRUM. ASSEMBL.	f	27					
RCE	VOC. AGRIC. TCHR.	m	8	✳				
REC	DIETITIAN	m	31			✳		
RES	POLICE-OFFICER	m	22		✳			
RSE	HWY. PATROL OFF.	m	17	✳				
RE	ARMY OFFICER	f	28					
RS	PHYS. ED. TEACHER	f	43					
R	SKILLED CRAFTS	m	17	✳				
RI	FORESTER	m	33			✳		
RI	RAD. TECH. (X-RAY)	f	21					
RI	MERCH. MAR. OFF.	m	28			✳		
RI	NAVY OFFICER	m	17	✳				
RI	NURSE, REGISTERED	m	32			✳		
RI	VETERINARIAN	m	41			✳		
RIC	CARTOGRAPHER	m	23		✳			
RIC	ARMY OFFICER	m	21		✳			
RIE	AIR FORCE OFFICER	m	10	✳				
RIA	OCCUP. THERAPIST	f	20					
IR	ENGINEER	f	17					
IR	ENGINEER	m	19		✳			
IR	CHEMIST	f	12					
IR	PHYSICAL SCIENTIST	m	17	✳				
IR	MEDICAL TECH.	f	26					
IR	PHARMACIST	f	26					
IR	DENTIST	f	25					
IR	DENTIST	m	32			✳		
IR	DENTAL HYGIENIST	f	32					
IRS	PHYS. THERAPIST	f	28					
IRS	PHYSICIAN	m	24		✳			
IRS	MATH-SCI. TEACHER	m	27			✳		
ICR	MATH-SCI. TEACHER	f	33					
IC	DIETITIAN	f	29					
IRC	MEDICAL TECH.	m	23		✳			
IRC	OPTOMETRIST	m	17	✳				
IRC	COMPUTER PROGR.	f	30					
IRC	COMPUTER PROGR.	m	20		✳			
I	MATHEMATICIAN	f	27					
I	MATHEMATICIAN	m	23		✳			
I	PHYSICIST	f	12					
I	BIOLOGIST	m	28			✳		
I	VETERINARIAN	f	35					
I	OPTOMETRIST	f	24					
I	PHYSICIAN	f	33					
I	SOCIAL SCIENTIST	m	33			✳		
IA	COLLEGE PROFESSOR	f	34					
IA	COLLEGE PROFESSOR	m	43			✳		
IS	SPEECH PATHOL.	f	36					
IS	SPEECH PATHOL.	m	41			✳		
IAS	PSYCHOLOGIST	f	33					
IAS	PSYCHOLOGIST	m	32			✳		
IA	LANGUAGE INTERPR.	f	25					
ARI	ARCHITECT	m	11	✳				
A	ADVERTISING EXEC.	f	30					
A	ARTIST	f	28					
A	ARTIST	m	27			✳		
A	ART TEACHER	f	3					
A	PHOTOGRAPHER	f	21		✳			
A	MUSICIAN	f	29					
A	MUSICIAN	m	34			✳		
A	ENTERTAINER	f	28					
AE	INT. DECORATOR	f	-3					
AE	INT. DECORATOR	m	27			✳		
AE	ADVERTISING EXEC.	m	29			✳		
A	LANGUAGE TEACHER	f	24					
A	LIBRARIAN	f	22					
A	LIBRARIAN	m	21		✳			
A	REPORTER	f	31					
A	REPORTER	m	39				✳	
AS	ENGLISH TEACHER	f	25					
AS	ENGLISH TEACHER	m	36				✳	
SI	NURSE, REGISTERED	f	25					
SIR	PHYS. THERAPIST	m	31				✳	
SRC	NURSE, LIC. PRACT.	m	34				✳	
S	SOCIAL WORKER	f	12					
S	SOCIAL WORKER	m	21			✳		
S	PRIEST	m	18		✳			
S	DIR., CHRISTIAN ED.	f	19					
SE	YWCA STAFF	f	34					
SIE	MINISTER	m	10	✳				
SEA	ELEM. TEACHER	m	38				✳	
SC	ELEM. TEACHER	f	24					
SCE	SCH. SUPERINTEND.	m	19		✳			
SCE	PUBLIC ADMINISTR.	m	25			✳		
SCE	GUIDANCE COUNS.	m	22		✳			
SER	RECREATION LEADER	f	31					
SEC	RECREATION LEADER	m	28			✳		
SEC	GUIDANCE COUNS.	f	24					
SEC	SOC. SCI. TEACHER	m	26			✳		
SEC	SOC. SCI. TEACHER	f	36				✳	
SEC	PERSONNEL DIR.	m	23		✳			
ESC	DEPT. STORE MGR.	m	20		✳			
ESC	HOME ECON. TCHR.	f	11					
ESA	FLIGHT ATTENDANT	f	22					
ES	CH. OF COMM. EXEC.	m	16	✳				
ES	SALES MANAGER	m	13	✳				
ES	LIFE INS. AGENT	m	14	✳				
E	LIFE INS. AGENT	f	13					
E	LAWYER	f	22					
E	LAWYER	m	23		✳			
EI	COMPUTER SALES	m	3	✳				
EI	INVESTM. FUND MGR.	m	27			✳		
EIC	PHARMACIST	m	25		✳			
EC	BUYER	f	12					
ECS	BUYER	m	5	✳				
ECS	CREDIT MANAGER	m	20		✳			
ECS	FUNERAL DIRECTOR	m	19		✳			
ECR	REALTOR	m	18		✳			
ERC	AGRIBUSINESS MGR.	m	16	✳				
ERC	PURCHASING AGENT	m	25			✳		
ESR	CHIROPRACTOR	m	26			✳		
CE	ACCOUNTANT	m	5	✳				
CE	BANKER	f	22					
CE	BANKER	m	15	✳				
CE	CREDIT MANAGER	f	16					
CE	DEPT. STORE SALES	f	4					
CE	BUSINESS ED. TCHR.	f	6					
CES	BUSINESS ED. TCHR.	m	23		✳			
CSE	EXEC. HOUSEKEEPER	f	6					
C	ACCOUNTANT	f	12					
C	SECRETARY	f	20					
CR	DENTAL ASSISTANT	f	21					
CRI	NURSE, LIC. PRACT.	f	7					
CRE	BEAUTICIAN	f	33					

General Occupational Themes

Theme	Std Score	Result
R-Theme	34	THIS IS A VERY LOW SCORE.
I-Theme	51	THIS IS AN AVERAGE SCORE.
A-Theme	66	THIS IS A VERY HIGH SCORE.
S-Theme	49	THIS IS AN AVERAGE SCORE.
E-Theme	52	THIS IS AN AVERAGE SCORE.
C-Theme	36	THIS IS A VERY LOW SCORE.

Basic Interest Scales

	Scale	Std Score	Very Low	Low	Average	High	Very High
R-THEME	AGRICULTURE	33					
	NATURE	40	30 · 35 · 45 · 50 · 55 · 60 · 65 · 70				
	ADVENTURE	44					
	MILITARY ACTIVITIES	41					
	MECHANICAL	36					
I-THEME	SCIENCE	49					
	MATHEMATICS	43					
	MEDICAL SCIENCE	41					
	MEDICAL SERVICE	35					
A-THEME	MUSIC/ DRAMATICS	64	30 · 35 · 40 · 45 · 50 · 55 · 60 · 65 · 70				
	ART	64					
	WRITING	62					
S-THEME	TEACHING	57					
	SOCIAL SERVICE	57					
	ATHLETICS	45					
	DOMESTIC ARTS	41					
	RELIGIOUS ACTIVITIES	33					
E-THEME	PUBLIC SPEAKING	61					
	LAW/ POLITICS	58					
	MERCHAND'NG	51					
	SALES	52					
C-TH	BUSINESS MGMT.	52	30 · 35 · 40 · 45 · 50 · 55 · 60 · 65 · 70				
	OFFICE PRACTICES	41					

Figure 9-2. The Strong-Campbell Interest Inventory profile for the general occupational themes and basic interest scales. The form on the left is for Henry Minton; the one on the right is for Frank Schneider. Reprinted from the *Strong-Campbell Interest Inventory*, Form T325 of the STRONG VOCA-

General Occupational Themes

Theme	Std Score	Result
R-Theme	44	THIS IS A LOW SCORE.
I-Theme	46	THIS IS A MODERATELY LOW SCORE.
A-Theme	52	THIS IS AN AVERAGE SCORE.
S-Theme	49	THIS IS AN AVERAGE SCORE.
E-Theme	45	THIS IS A MODERATELY LOW SCORE.
C-Theme	37	THIS IS A LOW SCORE.

Basic Interest Scales

	Scale	Std Score	Very Low	Low	Average	High	Very High
R-THEME	AGRICULTURE	58					
	NATURE	58	30 35 40	45 50 55	60 65 70		
	ADVENTURE	44					
	MILITARY ACTIVITIES	59					
	MECHANICAL	39					
I-THEME	SCIENCE	49					
	MATHEMATICS	43					
	MEDICAL SCIENCE	46					
	MEDICAL SERVICE	40					
A-THEME	MUSIC/ DRAMATICS	52	30 35 40	45 50 55	60 65 70		
	ART	41					
	WRITING	43					
S-THEME	TEACHING	55					
	SOCIAL SERVICE	49					
	ATHLETICS	64					
	DOMESTIC ARTS	53					
	RELIGIOUS ACTIVITIES	44					
E-THEME	PUBLIC SPEAKING	45					
	LAW/ POLITICS	43					
	MERCHAND'NG	45					
	SALES	46					
C-TH	BUSINESS MGMT.	44	30 35 40	45 50 55	60 65 70		
	OFFICE PRACTICES	39					

TIONAL INTEREST BLANK, by Edward K. Strong, Jr., and David P. Campbell, with the permission of the publishers, Stanford University Press. Copyright © 1976 by the Board of Trustees of the Leland Stanford Junior University.

consists of a large number of items (men's = 49, women's = 53) reflecting likes and dislikes regarding a diversity of areas (for example, science, social service, religion, and business), and a high score on the scale can be achieved by multiple combinations of likes and dislikes. A second problem is that there are practical limitations imposed on the use of empirical scales because in theory such a scale could be developed for each of the thousands of occupations in existence. Furthermore, the addition of the Basic Interest Scales probably was encouraged by the successful use of a similarly developed set of scales, the Kuder Preference Record (which is described later).

The basic interest scales complement the occupational scales by providing a limited number of scales that permit one to generalize beyond a specific occupational group. They are *homogeneous scales* in that they consist of items that significantly correlate with each other statistically and that are conceptually similar (that is, alike in content). In contrast to the heterogeneous occupational scales, the items of a basic interest scale focus on a single interest area and consequently are psychologically more meaningful.[2] For example, the Business Management Scale includes such items as "office manager," "sales manager," "meeting and directing people," "interviewing men for a job," and "business methods magazines."

The basic interest scales of the SCII are presented in Figure 9-2. The scales have been standardized on the combined male and female general reference samples (mean = 50 and standard deviation = 10). Thus, a person's score can be compared with the general reference sample. Or, it can be compared with the sex-appropriate reference sample. The unshaded bars in Figure 9-2 reflect the middle 50% of the women's sample; the shaded bars reflect the middle 50% of the men's sample. The thin line extensions signify the middle 80%. Scores of 58 or above are considered to reflect high interest in the area. Once again our scores have been profiled; Henry Minton's profile is on the left, and Frank Schneider's profile is on the right.

Using the basic interest scales in conjunction with the occupational scales provides more information about a person's pattern of interests than if only one kind of scale were available. If a person scores high on an occupational scale such as the psychologist scale, we can look at the basic interest profile to see which combination of interests is primarily responsible—science, writing, teaching, social service, and so on. Table 9-3 lists some occupational groups that score high and low on the basic interest scales.

General Occupational Themes. Throughout the main course of their development, the Strong inventories have been largely empirical, atheoretical instruments (Campbell, 1977). In an attempt to provide a theoretical structure, the 1974 SCII revision includes a set of six scales, the general occupational themes, which is based on John Holland's (1966, 1973) *theory of career develop-*

---

[2]Clark (1961) was the first to differentiate between empirical and homogeneous scales with respect to the measurement of interests; he incorporated both types of scale into the Minnesota Vocational Interest Inventory.

Table 9-3. Some Occupational Groups Scoring High and Low on Each Basic Interest Scale of the Strong-Campbell Interest Inventory

Scale	Some Occupations Scoring High	Some Occupations Scoring Low
Adventure	Astronauts Military officers Police officers Sales personnel	Bankers Judges Physicists School superintendents
Agriculture	Farmers Foresters Veterinarians Vocational agriculture teachers	Accountants Political scientists Sociologists Psychologists Writers
Art	Actors Architects Artists Photographers	Accountants Bankers Farmers Veterinarians
Athletics	Football coaches Physical education teachers Recreation leaders YMCA/YWCA staff	Artists Interior decorators Mathematicians Social scientists
Business Management	Business education teachers Credit managers Sales managers Sales personnel	Anthropologists Artists Scientists Writers
Domestic Arts	Dietitians Executive housekeepers Home economics teachers	Artists Military officers Scientists Writers
Law/Politics	Judges Lawyers Sales personnel State legislators	Architects Artists Farmers Sewing machine operators
Mathematics	Astronauts Astronomers Engineers Math/science teachers	Artists Fashion models Interior decorators Reporters
Public Speaking	Lawyers Ministers Speech pathologists State governors	Artists Beauticians Farmers Laboratory technicians
Religious Activities	Ministers Priests Nuns YMCA/YWCA staff	Artists Chemists Physicians Psychologists

Table 9-3. Some Occupational Groups Scoring High and Low on Each Basic Interest Scale of the Strong-Campbell Interest Inventory *(continued)*

Scale	Some Occupations Scoring High	Some Occupations Scoring Low
Sales	Business education teachers Buyers Sales managers Sales personnel	Anthropologists Artists Scientists Writers
Science	Astronomers Chemists College professors Physicians	Artists Beauticians Business executives Interior decorators Sales personnel
Mechanical Activities	Carpenters Chemists Engineers Machinists	English teachers Lawyers Sales personnel Writers
Medical Science	Dentists Medical technologists Physicians Veterinarians	Artists Farmers Sewing machine operators Writers
Medical Service	Dentists Nurses Physical therapists Physicians	Artists Farmers Writers
Merchandising	Buyers Department store managers Sales personnel Flight attendants	Artists Photographers Scientists Writers
Military Activities	Airplane pilots Military officers Police officers	Actors Musicians Psychologists Sociologists
Music/ Dramatics	Actresses Librarians Music teachers Nightclub entertainers	Beauticians Factory workers Military personnel
Nature	Animal husbandry professors Biologists Farmers Foresters	Business executives Fashion models Nightclub entertainers Sales personnel
Office Practices	Accountants Bankers Office workers Telephone operators	Anthropologists Architects Artists Photographers

Table 9-3. Some Occupational Groups Scoring High and Low on Each Basic
Interest Scale of the Strong-Campbell Interest Inventory *(continued)*

Scale	Some Occupations Scoring High	Some Occupations Scoring Low
Social Service	Guidance counselors Ministers Priests Social workers	Architects Artists Chemists Military officers
Teaching	Elementary teachers Guidance counselors Music teachers School superindendents	Farmers Laboratory technicians Sales personnel Skilled trades workers
Writing	English teachers Ministers Reporters Writers	Beauticians Carpenters Factory workers Farmers

Adapted from *Manual for the Strong-Campbell Interest Inventory*, Form T325 of the *Strong Vocational Interest Blank*, Second Edition, by David P. Campbell, with the permission of the publishers, Stanford University Press. © 1974, 1977 by the Board of Trustees of the Leland Stanford Junior University.

ment. Before we consider the SCII scales let us first review Holland's theory. Holland (1973) makes four major assumptions.

1. "In our culture, most persons can be categorized as one of six types: realistic, investigative, artistic, social, enterprising, or conventional" (p. 2). The types are described in Table 9-4. According to Holland, the description of each type essentially summarizes what is known about the people in a given occupational cluster. As a result of a person's unique heredity and socializing experiences he or she develops preferences for certain activities (interests) that lead him or her to develop related occupational skills. These interests and skills are accompanied by and influence the development of other aspects of the individual's personality. We should note that Holland refers to his types as both interest types and personality types and in so doing affirms his conviction that interests represent a major dimension of personality (see the introductory section of Chapter 8). In fact, he favors the use of the more inclusive term, *personality type*. (We will explore the relation of interests to personality in a later section.)

2. "There are six kinds of environments: realistic, investigative, artistic, social, enterprising, and conventional" (p. 3). Thus for each interest type there is an analogous occupational environment, and each environment is dominated by its own type of individual. For example, an artistic occupational environment is comprised primarily of artistic people who in turn, because of their special interests, competencies, and dispositions, help to create the working atmosphere of their occupation.

Table 9-4. Description of Holland's Six Interest Types

Realistic (R): Realistic people are oriented toward activities that call for motor coordination and the manipulation of objects, tools, and machines. They prefer to deal with concrete rather than abstract problems and to avoid situations requiring verbal and interpersonal skills. They perceive themselves as possessing mechanical and athletic ability and may be described as conforming, frank, natural, practical, stable, thrifty, and uninvolved.

Investigative (I): Investigative individuals prefer activities that require a lot of thinking and understanding and tend to have a scientific orientation. They shy away from interpersonal and persuasive activities. They are confident about their scholarly or intellectual abilities and may be described as analytical, cautious, curious, independent, introspective, and reserved.

Artistic (A): Artistic people prefer free and unstructured situations that maximize opportunities for creative self-expression. They value esthetic qualities and perceive themselves as expressive, original, instructive, nonconforming, and as having artistic ability of some kind. Characteristic traits include complexity, disorderliness, emotionality, idealism, impulsiveness, introspection, and independence.

Social (S): Social people prefer situations calling for interpersonal skills required in manipulating people in order to support them and help them improve their status; that is, they prefer activities that involve informing, training, developing, enlightening, or helping others. They value social and ethical concerns and view themselves as being humanistic, empathetic, having teaching ability, and lacking scientific and mechanical competence. Characteristic traits include cooperativeness, friendliness, helpfulness, persuasiveness, tactfulness, and understanding.

Enterprising (E): Enterprising people are oriented toward the manipulation of others in order to achieve their own organizational or economic objectives. They value power and status, including political and economic achievement, and perceive themselves as aggressive, self-confident, sociable, and having leadership and oral skills. They may be described as adventurous, ambitious, domineering, energetic, exhibitionistic, optimistic, and sociable.

Conventional (C): Conventional people prefer well-structured environments in which their task involves handling numerical or verbal data such as in filing materials, keeping records, or operating data processing machines. They value business and economic achievement and view themselves as being orderly and conforming and high in clerical and numerical skills. Characteristic traits include conscientiousness, efficiency, inflexibility, obedience, practicality, and self-control.

3. "People search for environments that will let them exercise their skills and abilities, express their attitudes and values, and take on agreeable problems and roles" (p. 4). In other words, realistic types search for realistic environments, conventional types seek conventional environments, and so forth.

4. "A person's behavior is determined by an interaction between his personality and the characteristics of his environment" (p. 4). Some of the behavior or personal outcomes that can be predicted from an understanding of the interactive relationship include the person's educational choice and achievement, as well as his or her vocational choice, job satisfaction, and job performance.

Several methods of assessing a person's interest type exist (Holland, 1973).[3] Qualitative methods involve ascertaining the individual's educational or vocational preferences or the educational training or occupation in which he or she is engaged and then classifying him or her according to the corresponding interest type. For example, a physics student would be designated as an investigative type. Holland has also initiated the development of several quantitative measures, including the Vocational Preference Inventory (Holland, 1965) and the Self-directed Search (Holland, 1970). On the former, for instance, the respondent selects from a list of 84 occupations (14 related to each interest type) those that are and are not of interest to him. Then the person's responses are scored for each interest type and profiled.

The interest types also are measured by means of the general occupational themes in the SCII. These themes are based directly on Holland's types, and, in fact, Holland was instrumental in their development (Campbell & Holland, 1972). The themes are listed in their SCII profile in Figure 9-2. Each of the six scales consists of 20 items selected on the basis of Holland's description. The standard score (mean = 50; standard deviation = 10) is based on the general reference sample (males and females combined); however, the brief interpretative comment is based on the distribution of scores for the respondent's sex. The general occupational themes give a general overview of the individual's occupational orientation in contrast to the more specific views offered by the basic interest scales and, especially, the occupational scales (Campbell, 1977).

The basic interest scales and the occupational scales have been categorized according to the appropriate general occupational themes. This information is provided in the left-hand column of the respondent's profiles (see Figures 9-1 and 9-2).

Holland (1973) suggests that the relationship among the six interest types may be depicted in a hexagon as presented in Figure 9-3. According to this *hexagonal model,* the closer the distance between two types, the greater the psychological resemblance. Inspection of Figure 9-3 shows that this does seem to be the case on intuitive grounds. Furthermore, research indicates that the correlations between types tend to be higher the less the distance separating them; for example, the conventional/realistic correlation is larger than the conventional/investigative correlation, which in turn is larger than the conventional/artistic correlation (Campbell, 1977; Holland, 1973; Nafziger & Helms, 1974).

---

[3]In addition to the work of Holland (1966, 1973), there have been numerous attempts to identify the major dimensions of vocational interests. One major approach is factor analysis, with perhaps the most significant contribution being made by Guilford and his colleagues (Guilford, Christensen, Bond, & Sutton, 1954). The second major approach involves grouping occupations together on the basis of the finding that members of the different occupations display similar interest patterns (Super & Crites, 1962). This second approach essentially was the one used by Holland (1966, 1973). Of particular significance is that the findings from all of this research indicate that vocational interests can be described by a relatively small number of dimensions, somewhere between 5 and 8 (Holland found 6 dimensions); also, there is considerable similarity among the dimensions yielded by the various investigations (Hanson, 1974).

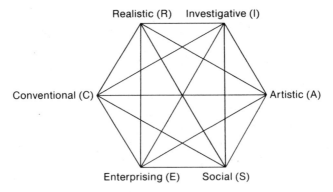

Figure 9-3. The hexagonal model showing the psychological relationships among Holland's interest types.

The hexagonal model helps to explain the concept of *consistency* that is basic to Holland's theory. A person's interest pattern is consistent to the extent that the interest types on which he or she scores highest are close to each other, preferably adjacent, on the hexagon (for example, realistic and investigative). A consistent pattern increases our ability to predict the individual's vocational behavior. Another key concept is *differentiation*. A differentiated person is one who clearly resembles a single interest type and shows little resemblance to the others; an undifferentiated person resembles several or many types. Like consistency, differentiation also increases predictability. According to Osipow (1976), consistency and differentiation are two of the "more promising diagnostic signs," with research showing that "people with sharp, well-defined profiles appear to cope with their vocational problems more effectively than people with ill-defined or flat profiles" (p. 136).

The concepts of differentiation and consistency suggest that in describing a person (also an occupation or environment) we may use more than one interest type. Thus a person may be described as an *S*, an *SA*, an *SAE*, and so on. Notice that in Figure 9-1 some of the occupations are described by a combination of two or three themes (types). Although a combination of all six types (for example, RAISEC) is possible, the use of the strongest one, two, or three types probably is adequate for most purposes. Combining types increases the flexibility of Holland's scheme and helps to account for a greater diversity of individual differences.

Other Vocational-Interest Inventories

Besides the SVIB and SCII, about a dozen measures of vocational interests are in regular use today. Of these, two of the more important ones are the Minnesota Vocational Interest Inventory and the Kuder inventories.

As you may have noted from inspection of Figure 9-1, most of the SCII occupational scales involve white-collar, professional occupations and as such are aimed at the college-educated population. The Minnesota Vocational Interest Inventory (Clark, 1961; Clark & Campbell, 1965) was developed in order to measure the interests of men who are not college oriented and emphasizes nonprofessional occupations, mostly skilled trades but some semiskilled ones. Modeled after the Strong, it is comprised of 21 occupational scales (for example, plumber, carpenter, and truck driver) and 9 interest-area scales (for example, mechanical, electronics, and food service).

Next to the Strong measures, the most widely used interest inventories were developed by G. Frederick Kuder. The best known one is the Kuder Preference Record (Kuder, 1960), the first form of which was published in 1939. The Preference Record consists of homogeneous scales measuring a person's interests in a relatively small number of interest areas. The most recent form has 10 interest scales (for example, outdoor, mechanical, persuasive, and artistic), which are not unlike the basic interest scales of the SCII. As an instrument consisting of homogeneous scales that deal with broad interest areas, the Preference Record complemented Strong's normatively developed occupational scales during the earlier years of interest measurement. The Kuder General Interest Survey (Kuder, 1975a) was developed in the 1960s for use with younger people (grades 6–12). It consists of the same 10 scales as in the Preference Record. The Kuder Occupational Interest Survey (Kuder, 1975b) consists of scales similar to the SCII occupational scales in that they are normatively developed (although in a different manner) and measure the degree to which the respondent's interests agree with those of each of 114 occupational groups. Whereas the Minnesota Vocational Interest Inventory concentrates on blue-collar occupations and the SCII on white-collar occupations, the Occupational Interest Survey tends to cover both occupational domains. Also, the Occupational Interest Survey has scales indicating the similarity between the person's interests and those of students in 48 college-major groups.

Up until now we have been concerned primarily with the theory and methods underlying the measurement of vocational interests. In the next few sections we shift our attention to several important issues relevant to the study of interests: predictability of vocational behavior, sex bias in interest measurement, relationship between interests and personality, and the determinants of interests.

Prediction of Vocational Behavior

The predictive validity of an interest measure refers to its ability to anticipate the interest-related behavior that an individual will display in the future, such as the occupation he or she will pursue or his or her degree of job satisfaction. Of course, in order to be able to predict such behavior it is important that the person's interests, as measured by the inventory, demonstrate a reasonable degree of stability. At one time it was thought that the interests of the typical person were rather capricious phenomena, changing from one time to another. Today, however, we have ample evidence of the satisfactory test/retest reliability of inventoried interests, especially on a short-term basis (Barnette, 1973; Campbell, 1977; Kuder, 1975a, 1975b). For example, on all three kinds of scale on the SCII, the test/retest correlations average in the low .90s for a 2-week interval and in the lower to middle .80s for a 3-year interval (Campbell, 1977). Naturally, the magnitude of the correlation continues to drop off as the test/restest interval increases, but even for adults who have been retested after a 20- or 30-year interval the correlations tend to fall in the .50s and .60s (Campbell, 1971). Not unexpectedly, the interests of adolescents generally show much more fluctuation than those of adults. Thus, we find that when interests are measured at age 16 and then 36 years or so later, the correlations typically drop to around .40 for both the basic interest scales and occupational scales (Campbell, 1971).

The usual paradigm for estimating predictive accuracy is to measure the interests of a group of people, set aside their data, several years later reestablish contact with them, and then ascertain if there is a correspondence between their previously measured interests and their current status. The criterion that has received the most attention is occupational membership. There have been many attempts to determine how well inventoried interests presage eventual vocational choice. The classic study is the one by Strong (1955), who followed up 663 Stanford University men who had taken the SVIB 18 years earlier. He found that a significant percentage of men were in occupations directly related to their earlier occupational-scale scores. For example, one of the better predictor scales was the physician scale. Of the students with high scores (*A* ratings[4]) on that scale, 53% became physicians, and another 5% were engaged in closely allied fields such as dentistry and biology. After completing their own investigation and reviewing the results of earlier ones, Dolliver, Irvin, and Bigley (1972) concluded that an *A* score on a SVIB occupational scale generally means that a person's chances of ending up in that occupation or a closely related one are somewhat less than 50% (nearer 40%), whereas a *C* score means that his chances of being in that occupation are only about 12% (see also Worthington & Dolliver, 1977). Zytowski (1976) reached a similar conclusion in his 12-19 year follow-up study of the Kuder Occupational Interest Survey. About 50% of his subjects were employed in a field that would have been suggested as meriting consideration if their interest scores had been interpreted at the time of testing. Zytowski also found that the college-major scales of the Kuder Occupational Interest Survey predicted college-major choice. We might add that it appears that low scores on an interest inventory seem to predict better which occupations a person won't enter than high scores predict which occupations he or she will enter.

Occupational membership has also been successfully predicted by means of homogeneous scales such as the basic interest scales (Campbell, 1971; Kuder, 1975a; Zytowski, 1976). It appears, in fact, that their predictive accuracy may be slightly superior to that of heterogeneous scales (Zytowski, 1974). However, as noted earlier, combining the information garnered from both kinds of scale

---

[4]A system of letter ratings (viz, *A, B+, B, B–, C+,* and *C*) was employed with the earlier, pre-1974, occupational scales wherein an *A* designated a standard score of 45 and above. Two-thirds of the criterion group scored 45 or higher.

seems to produce the best predictive accuracy. For example, Johnson and Johansson (1972) showed that a person is more likely to enter the sales field if he or she scores high on both the sales area occupational interest scales and the sales basic interest scale. Perhaps because of its more recent development, less research has been carried out on predicting occupational membership using Holland's classification of interest types, but that which exists does demonstrate its value (Holland, 1973).

The above evidence suggests that interest inventories are moderately effective in predicting the general occupational area in which a person eventually will work. Campbell (1971) suggests two reasons why interests are not more highly correlated with occupational membership. One is that people have a variety of reasons for choosing an occupation, only one of which is their interests. For instance, inventories are less accurate with the offspring of the wealthy, presumably because family fortunes and tradition greatly influence career decisions. A second reason is that some people select an occupational area, then discover they don't like it. If such people had taken an interest inventory and scored low on that particular interest area, their membership in the area might seem to document the poor predictive validity of the inventory when, in fact, the inventory did accurately forecast their eventual dissatisfaction.

There are other aspects of vocational behavior that on logical grounds might be expected to be predicted by inventoried interests. Three of these include a person's success on the job, satisfaction with the job, and tenure (length of time) on the job. Probably the weakest relationship is between interests and success. How well one achieves in school or on the job seems to hinge less on one's interest in work-relevant activities than on one's ability and motivation (Super & Bohn, 1970). Interests may tell us a lot about the direction an individual may head, but very little about his or her level of attainment. They do provide information regarding the probability that people will like their work and consequently the chances that they will complete their education (or training) or remain on the job. Thus, interests do seem to be related to job satisfaction (Zytowski, 1976) and tenure (Porter & Steers, 1973), but the relationships are not very strong ones. Campbell (1971), for instance, reports that the correlations between satisfaction on a given job and the relevant SVIB occupational-scale score typically fall in the .20-.30 range.

Sex Bias in Interest Measurement

Since the early 1920s and 30s, when Strong first provided different forms of the SVIB to men and women, the vocational interests of the sexes have been measured, for the most part, by means of separate inventories, scales, and norms. One reason for treating the sexes differently is that males and females respond differently to many interest items (Campbell, 1977). On the SCII, for example, there is a substantial sex difference in response to 50% of the items, and these item differences are further reflected in the sex differences found on all three kinds of scale (general occupational, basic interest, and occupational). In fact, Campbell has found that by using the responses to just 41 items (the "male/female index") the sex of the respondent can be estimated with 90% accuracy. On the Kuder General Interest Survey, sex differences occur on all ten scales, with the highest differences falling on the mechanical scale (boys are higher) and social service scale (girls are higher) (Kuder, 1975a). Another reason for separate inventories is that traditionally there has been a great deal of difference in the employment patterns of men and women, with men gravitating toward certain occupations and women toward others (Campbell, 1977).

In recent years, however, interest inventories have come under attack as being sex-biased, particularly against women (Birk, 1974; Peoples, 1975). According to the Commission on Sex Bias in Measurement of the Association for Measurement and Evaluation in Guidance (Harmon, Cole, Wysong, & Zytowski, 1973), sex bias "within the context of career guidance . . . is that condition or provision which influences a person to limit his or her consideration of career opportunities solely on the basis of that person's sex" (p. 172). The major argument is that the content of interest inventories, including items and scales, encourages women to concentrate on the traditional stereotyped occupations (for example, nurse and elementary school teacher) to the neglect of other occupations that potentially may be of interest to them but that by tradition are considered inappropriate for women to enter. Moreover, it is pointed out that the occupations covered on women's forms generally are lower in status and less financially rewarding than those on men's forms. Also, some titles (for example, sales lady and policeman) imply that certain jobs may be more suitable for one sex than the other. In addition to these factors, the mere use of separate forms, norms, and profiles reinforces the view that some occupations are more appropriate to one sex than the other.

In reply to such allegations against the SVIB, Campbell (1977) wrote:

> Strong would have been offended by the current charge of sex discrimination. He probably felt, as I have, that the provision of a separate system for women was a rational reflection of statistical and social realities; to have thrown men and women into the same norming tables would have reduced the usefulness of the inventory for both sexes [pp. vi–vii].

Yet Campbell did relent, and, just a few years after undertaking the major and costly revision of the SVIB (men's: 1966; women's: 1969), merged the women's and men's forms into the SCII. Some of the changes that were made in an effort to develop a "unisex" interest inventory were: (1) men and women use the same form and profile; (2) the wording has been sex-neutralized (for example, police officer instead of policeman);[5] and (3) males and females are scored and profiled on all of the scales.

---

[5]More recent studies indicate that the use of gender-neutral wording in interest inventories does not alter the interest scores of females (Boyd, 1976; Gottfredson, 1976).

However, the SCII stops short of treating the sexes identically. Because males and females respond differently on so many items and scales, separate occupational scales for men and women are maintained, although a respondent's score on all scales is made available. The basic interest scales and general occupational themes, unlike the occupational scales, are normed on the general reference sample (combined males and females), but the profile (for the basic interest scales) and interpretative comments (for the general occupational themes) are geared to the respondent's sex group. Despite the retention of separate occupational scales and profile norms, the SCII undeniably is a step in the right direction and should influence the neutralization of other interest inventories.

It is worth noting that evidence from research does lead us to question the necessity of using different occupational (empirical) scales for the sexes (Osipow, 1976). These studies generally indicate that men's occupational scales may be valid (for example, in terms of predicting career choices) for women as well as men. More importantly, Hanson and Rayman (1976) administered two interest inventories to college-bound students who expressed different vocational preferences. One inventory, the Unisex Interest Inventory, was sex balanced; that is, it contained only items that are equally popular among the sexes. The other inventory, the ACT Interest Inventory, contained the usual number of items showing sex differences. Hanson and Rayman demonstrated that the balanced inventory was just as effective as the standard inventory in differentiating among the vocational preference groups (that is, the students with different vocational choices had different interest profiles). Also, unlike when other interest inventories are used, with the sex-balanced one, the distributions of scores for males and females on nearly all of the interest scales were essentially the same. According to Hanson and Rayman, this means that sex balancing obviates the problem of deciding whether to use separate or combined sex groups as the normative sample. Moreover, sex-balanced scales would mean that men and women with the same vocational aspirations, educational majors, and in the same occupations should have similar interest profiles.

PERSONALITY AND INTERESTS

It is not uncommon for many of us to assume that if we know a person's occupation then we know what kind of person he or she is. We may perceive salespeople as persuasive and aggressive, office clerks as neat and orderly, and so on. While such occupational stereotypes undoubtedly represent overgeneralizations and in many instances erroneous ones, there is evidence that different occupational groups do show systematic personality differences. For example, Super and Bohn (1970) report that, in line with the cultural stereotype, salespeople are above average in aggressiveness.

If there is a connection between an occupation and the typical personality characteristics of its members, it would seem that the vocational interests of people also would be related to their personalities. Indeed, since the early days of research on interests, many investigators have explored the interrelationships among interests and various personality factors, and often with positive results (Darley & Hagenah, 1955). One of the most consistent relationships that emerged from this research is between interests and psychological adjustment. For instance, it appears that less well-adjusted individuals tend to have aesthetic interests; that is, they express an above average interest in artistic, literary, and musical careers (Osipow, 1973). Another apparently reliable finding is that certain occupational groups (for example, social scientists) show a greater concern for involvement with others than do other occupational groups (for example, biological and physical scientists) (Darley & Hagenah, 1955).

Implicit in the attempt to determine the relationship between vocational interests and personality is the assumption that these two facets of the individual are separate and independent factors. Recall from our discussion in Chapter 8, however, that a broader conceptualization of personality views interests (and also values; see the next section) as just one of many dimensions of personality (see also Anastasi, 1976; Super & Bohn, 1970). Holland's (1973) typology epitomizes this viewpoint in providing a synthesis of vocational psychology and personality psychology:

> What we have called "vocational interests" are simply another aspect of personality. Just as we have developed theories of personality from our knowledge of sex and parental relationships, so we can construct theories of personality from our knowledge of vocational life. We can then reinterpret vocational interests as an expression of personality [p. 7].

In line with this thinking, Holland (1973) argues both that "the choice of a vocation is an expression of personality" and "interest inventories are personality inventories" (pp. 6, 7).

Remember that Holland uses the terms *interest type* and *personality type* interchangeably. He is able to do so because he views vocational interests as an important dimension of personality and the development of the two as inextricably intertwined. Thus, as the six types were described earlier (see Table 9-4), the individual who has a certain pattern of vocational interests is viewed as possessing an interrelated cluster of characteristics. Stimulated by Holland's theory and research, many researchers have set out to test the hypothesized connection between one's vocational orientation and one's personality. By and large the existing research confirms Holland's theorizing (see Holland, 1973; Johnson, Flammer, & Nelson, 1975; Utz & Korben, 1976). For example, Utz and Korben (1976) found that among college students the relationships between scores on the SCII occupational themes and the Edwards Personal Preference Schedule (EPPS) were as Holland would predict. Subjects, especially males, with high scores on the conventional theme, for instance, were also high on the EPPS needs for endurance, order, and dominance and low on the need for autonomy.

DETERMINANTS OF INTERESTS

As we would expect, if we are to account for the development of interests we must recognize the interactive roles of heredity and environment. The evidence concerning the role of heredity stems primarily from studies involving identical and fraternal twins. The interests of identical twins are correlated and compared with the correlations for fraternal twins. A genetic influence is suggested by the finding that the identical twins correlations prove to be significantly greater than the fraternal twins correlations, with the former consistently falling around .50 and the latter in the .20s. These results have been found with the Strong occupational scales, basic interest scales, and general occupational themes (Roberts & Johansson, 1974), as well as other interest measures, including, for example, the Minnesota Vocational Interest Inventory (Grotevant, Scarr, & Weinberg, 1977; Vandenberg & Stafford, 1967). In addition, a study of biologically related families and adoptive families indicated that biologically related family members (for example, child and natural parent) modestly resembled each other on the general occupational themes, whereas unrelated family members (for example, child and adoptive parent) did not significantly resemble each other (Grotevant et al., 1977). It is likely that the genetic contribution to interests is channeled indirectly through the development of an individual's abilities and personality orientations. It seems reasonable to believe that people come to prefer activities which they do well at, and, therefore, some writers have suggested that interests are in part a function of the extent to which abilities have a genetic component (Super & Crites, 1962). Moreover, personality guides the interests of an individual by influencing the kinds of activities he or she chooses to engage in or avoid (Grotevant, et al., 1977). For instance, a highly routinized occupation such as a keypunch operator probably would not be very appealing to an outgoing person with a high activity level.

Holland's (1973) view concerning the development of his personality types is one illustration of the possible role of environmental variables. While acknowledging the role of heredity, Holland proposes that each interest type is to a considerable extent the product of its characteristic environment. Holland says that "types produce types." Accordingly, parents representing a given interest type create a special environment—one that involves activities, experiences, and reinforcements—that fosters in their children the development of their own type and discourages the development of other types. Thus, the artistic parent emphasizes artistic pursuits to the neglect or rejection of, for instance, social (person-oriented) endeavors.

THE NATURE OF VALUES

What is the difference between interests and values? This question has perplexed many psychologists. In the field of vocational psychology, for instance, the two terms often are used interchangeably. As a case in point, in his book on interest measurement, Zytowski (1973) lists the Work Values Inventory (Super, 1969) as an interest inventory. The confusion between the terms is also exemplified by the title of perhaps the best known value inventory, "Study of Values: A Scale for Measuring the Dominant Interests in Personality" (Allport, Vernon, & Lindzey, 1951). Those who treat interests and values as synonymous may justify their view by pointing to the fact that conceptually similar vocational interests and vocational values frequently are statistically correlated with each other. However, most studies indicate that there are only modest correlations between vocational interests and values, supporting the conclusion that it is appropriate to make a distinction between the two (Breme & Cockriel, 1975; Super, 1973). Values refer to goals or objectives that people strive to attain in order to satisfy a need; interests reflect the activities and objects by means of which the goals are achieved (Breme & Cockriel, 1975; Super, 1973). Thus, it seems that interests are preferences for those things that are perceived as leading to the desired goals.

Whereas some investigators are primarily concerned with the meaning of vocational values, others have focused on more general "life" values. One of the most comprehensive analyses has been made by Milton Rokeach (1973). Rokeach, probably more than any other contemporary psychologist, has argued that the concept of values cuts across all of the social sciences—sociology, anthropology, psychology, education, political science, economics, and history—and as such should represent a focal point in the understanding of human behavior. According to Rokeach, the relationship between values and interests is similar to the way values and attitudes are related. Attitudes and interests, both of which entail a strong evaluative component, are directed toward specific objects, people, or activities. Therefore, a person is apt to have a great number of interests and attitudes.[6] On the other hand, Rokeach sees values as transcending the specific, representing standards that guide a person's attitudes, interests, and behavior. Rokeach affirms that there is a limited number of values, and, relative to interests and attitudes, values occupy a more central position in the organization of an individual's personality.

Rokeach defines a value as "an enduring belief that a specific mode of conduct or end-state of existence is personally or socially preferable to an opposite or converse mode of conduct or end-state of existence" (p. 5). As this definition indicates, Rokeach distinguishes between two basic kinds of value. First, values may be beliefs regarding desirable and undesirable modes of conduct. These modes of conduct include, for example, being ambitious, clean, honest, and obedient. Rokeach prefers to call such modes of conduct *instrumental values*. The second kind of value pertains to desirable and undesirable end-states of existence. These include, for example, a comfortable life, a world at peace, happiness, and salvation. Rokeach calls these *terminal values*. Although instrumental and terminal values are conceived as separate

---

[6]We develop attitudes (evaluative reactions) about a great diversity of things, as attested by the fact that over 170 attitude measures are listed in one encyclopedia of attitude scales (Shaw & Wright, 1967). Likewise we have many interests; note the number of occupational scales on the SCII.

systems, they are considered to be interrelated in the sense that the former are considered to be instrumental to the attainment of the latter. We might note that in differentiating between "means" values (instrumental) and "ends" values (terminal) Rokeach has gone beyond the workers in the field of vocational psychology, who have restricted their attention to the latter.

Rokeach further notes that there are two types of instrumental value. Moral values are interpersonal modes of conduct (for example, being honest and loving) that when violated induce feelings of guilt. Competence values are self-actualizing, intrapersonal modes of conduct (for example, being capable and logical) that when violated produce feelings of personal inadequacy. In addition, terminal values are broken down into those that are personal and those that are social. The former are self-centered values and include salvation and peace of mind; the latter are society-centered and include world peace and equality. Rokeach suggests that there may be individual differences in the importance placed on the various types of value. For some people moral instrumental values and personal terminal values take precedence over other values, whereas for others different priorities may exist.

Now we will turn our attention to how both occupational values and more general values are measured and at the same time review some of the evidence concerning how they are manifested.

VOCATIONAL VALUES

A good example of a measure of vocational values is the Work Values Inventory developed by Super (1969). This inventory was designed to measure the kinds of goals that motivate people in their work. The inventory consists of 45 items, each of which is rated for its importance on a 5-point scale. A respondent receives scores on the following 15 value scales: altruism, esthetics, creativity, intellectual stimulation, independence, achievement, prestige, management, economic returns, security, surroundings, supervisory relations, associates, variety, and way of life. Note that some of the valued goals are intrinsic to work (for example, creativity and intellectual stimulation), whereas others are essentially by-products of work (for example, prestige and economic returns).

Super (1973) reports that people working in upper-level occupations are inclined to be motivated by intrinsic goals, those that meet their needs for self-actualization; on the other hand, people in lower level jobs—blue-collar and semiskilled occupations—are apt to be more concerned with extrinsic goals. Research employing the Work Values Inventory and other measures does indicate that people in different occupations and college students in different programs do display distinctive value patterns (Osipow, 1973; Super & Bohn, 1970). For instance, Super and Bohn (1970) cite a dissertation by Normile (1967) in which the Work Values Inventory was given to members of seven occupational groups: psychiatrists, psychologists, teachers, priests, lawyers, CPAs, and engineers. Significant differences were found among the groups. For example, priests scored higher than the other groups on altruism and lower on economic returns, and teachers placed a higher value on security than did psychologists and psychiatrists.

GENERAL LIFE VALUES

Study of Values

As mentioned, the Study of Values by Allport and his colleagues (Allport et al., 1951) seems to be the most widely known values inventory. Like the Strong inventories its usefulness has displayed remarkable longevity, dating back to the first edition in 1931. The Survey contains 45 items, each involving a forced-choice format. A sample item is "Which of the following branches of study do you expect ultimately will prove more important for mankind? (a) mathematics; (b) theology." Six values are assessed by the Survey: (1) theoretical (concern with the discovery of truth), (2) aesthetic (concern with form and harmony), (3) economic (concern with what is useful), (4) social (concern with altruistic love), (5) political (concern with power), and (6) religious (concern with unity). These values were originally based on Spranger's (1928) six-fold typology of ideal values and also seem to bear some resemblance to Holland's (1973) six interest types (review Table 9-4 and see later section on interpersonal values).

As do vocational values, more general values differentiate between various occupational and educational samples (Allport, 1961; Allport et al., 1951). For example, business administration students score high on economic values and engineers on theoretical values. Although the Study of Values continues to be widely used, its critics, including Allport himself (Allport, 1961), observe that one of its major limitations is that by restricting its coverage to a relatively small number of values, it neglects other important ones. The Value Survey, which Rokeach (1973) has developed, endeavors to overcome this problem.

Rokeach's Value Survey

Rokeach's (1973) Value Survey measures 18 terminal values and 18 instrumental values. The two lists of values are presented in Table 9-5. The process of selecting these 36 values was largely an intuitive one, and Rokeach acknowledges that other workers might settle on somewhat different lists. However, he feels confident that they are relatively comprehensive, especially the list of terminal values. Rokeach estimates that each person possesses approximately 18 terminal values and several times that number of instrumental values. In taking the Value Survey, a person is merely asked to review each list at a time and to rank the values "in order of their importance to YOU, as guiding principles in YOUR life." The task takes only a few minutes. You might give it a try; however, be sure to do so without first inspecting the data presented in Table 9-5.

Table 9-5. Value Medians and Composite Rank Orders for
American Men and Women*

Terminal Values			
	Male	Female	p
A comfortable life	7.8(4)	10.0(13)	.001
An exciting life	14.6(18)	15.8(18)	.001
A sense of accomplishment	8.3(7)	9.4(10)	.01
A world at peace	3.8(1)	3.0(1)	.001
A world of beauty	13.6(15)	13.5(15)	—
Equality	8.9(9)	8.3(8)	—
Family security	3.8(2)	3.8(2)	—
Freedom	4.9(3)	6.1(3)	.01
Happiness	7.9(5)	7.4(5)	.05
Inner harmony	11.1(13)	9.8(12)	.001
Mature love	12.6(14)	12.3(14)	—
National security	9.2(10)	9.8(11)	—
Pleasure	14.1(17)	15.0(16)	.01
Salvation	9.9(12)	7.3(4)	.001
Self-respect	8.2(6)	7.4(6)	.01
Social recognition	13.8(16)	15.0(17)	.001
True friendship	9.6(11)	9.1(9)	—
Wisdom	8.5(8)	7.7(7)	.05

Instrumental Values			
	Male	Female	p
Ambitious	5.6(2)	7.4(4)	.001
Broadminded	7.2(4)	7.7(5)	—
Capable	8.9(8)	10.1(12)	.001
Cheerful	10.4(12)	9.4(10)	.05
Clean	9.4(9)	8.1(8)	.01
Courageous	7.5(5)	8.1(6)	—
Forgiving	8.2(6)	6.4(2)	.001
Helpful	8.3(7)	8.1(7)	—
Honest	3.4(1)	3.2(1)	—
Imaginative	14.3(18)	16.1(18)	.001
Independent	10.2(11)	10.7(14)	—
Intellectual	12.8(15)	13.2(16)	—
Logical	13.5(16)	14.7(17)	.001
Loving	10.9(14)	8.6(9)	.001
Obedient	13.5(17)	13.1(15)	—
Polite	10.9(13)	10.7(13)	—
Responsible	6.6(3)	6.8(3)	—
Self-controlled	9.7(10)	9.5(11)	—

*Figures shown are median rankings and, in parentheses, composite rank
orders. The level of significance is indicated when there is a statistically significant difference between the median rankings of the males and the median
rankings of the females. The data are based on 665 males and 744 females.

Adapted from *The Nature of Human Values,* by Milton Rokeach. Copyright © 1973 by The Free Press, a division of Macmillan Publishing Co., Inc.
Used with the permission of Macmillan Publishing Co., Inc.

Rokeach sees values as being organized into a value system that he defines as "an enduring organization of beliefs concerning preferable modes of conduct or end-states of existence along a continuum of relative importance" (p. 5). Thus, in the framework of the Value Survey, each one of us is thought to have a system of terminal values and a system of instrumental values, each consisting of 18 values ordered in terms of their personal importance. Rokeach views one's value system as being strongly dependent on one's culture, society, and idiosyncratic personal history and because of these influences, believes a system is relatively stable. The test/retest correlations of college students' rankings do show a fairly satisfactory degree of stability. Over a 3 to 12 week period the correlations average in the high .70s for terminal values and low .70s for instrumental values. After a 14 to 16 month interval they fall into the .60s.

In 1968 the National Opinion Research Center administered the Value Survey to an American sample of 1400 adults selected so as to be representative of all strata of society. On the basis of these data, Rokeach has been able to describe the values of Americans in general, as well as make comparisons among various demographic groups such as men and women, rich and poor, and Black and White.

Values of Adult Americans. Table 9-5 lists the median rankings of the values of American women and men. Also indicated are the composite rank orders of each value (in parentheses) and the corresponding probability level in those instances in which there is a statistically significant difference between the median rankings of the males and females. It is interesting to take note of those values that on the average have the highest and lowest priorities among Americans. Ranked as the most important terminal values are "a world at peace," "family security," and "freedom," whereas ranked lowest are "an exciting life," "pleasure," "social recognition," and "a world of beauty." Among the instrumental values, American adults ranked "honest," "ambitious," and "responsible" as most important, whereas at the bottom of their value hierarchies were "imaginative," "obedient," "intellectual," and "logical." Do these results agree with what you would have anticipated? How close do your instrumental and terminal value systems approximate those of the typical American?

As was the case with interests, there is ample evidence of sex differences, with men and women differentially evaluating the importance of more than half the values. At the risk of getting ahead of ourselves (sex differences are dealt with in the next chapter), we should observe that Rokeach (1973) interprets the pattern of differences as being consistent with "much that is intuitively known about differences in the ways men and women are socialized in Western industrial societies" (p. 59). He also emphasizes, however, that the sexes are similar on a good many values.

Some Cross-Cultural Value Comparisons. The values of male college students from four countries—the United States, Australia, Israel, and Canada—have also been compared by Rokeach. These data are shown in Table 9-6.

Table 9-6. Value Averages and Composite Rank Orders for College Men from Four Different Countries*

	Terminal Values			
	United States	*Australia*	*Israel*	*Canada*
A comfortable life	10.3(11)	12.6(13)	12.8(15)	11.6(13)
An exciting life	10.8(12)	9.2(11)	8.7(9)	9.8(11)
A sense of accomplishment	7.1(5)	6.3(4)	7.5(7)	9.2(9)
A world at peace	9.3(10)	8.2(9)	4.7(1)	10.0(12)
A world of beauty	14.4(18)	13.0(15)	14.5(17)	12.3(15)
Equality	12.3(13)	9.0(10)	9.3(10)	9.7(10)
Family security	8.1(7)	9.5(12)	7.9(8)	7.5(7)
Freedom	4.7(1)	4.9(3)	6.5(4)	4.5(1)
Happiness	6.2(2)	7.5(7)	6.0(3)	4.7(2)
Inner harmony	8.8(9)	7.7(8)	10.9(13)	7.4(6)
Mature love	7.4(6)	6.6(5)	6.5(5)	5.6(3)
National security	13.8(17)	13.9(17)	5.6(2)	16.6(17)
Pleasure	13.1(15)	12.7(14)	11.2(14)	12.3(14)
Salvation	13.4(16)	15.9(18)	15.9(18)	17.6(18)
Self-respect	7.0(4)	7.5(6)	9.7(11)	6.9(4)
Social recognition	12.9(14)	13.7(16)	13.5(16)	13.9(16)
True friendship	8.7(8)	4.9(2)	10.1(12)	7.3(5)
Wisdom	6.8(3)	4.7(1)	7.3(6)	8.3(8)

	Instrumental Values			
	United States	*Australia*	*Israel*	*Canada*
Ambitious	6.4(3)	7.8(6)	8.7(7)	9.4(11)
Broadminded	6.7(4)	4.6(2)	9.2(9)	6.4(4)
Capable	7.5(5)	8.2(8)	6.5(4)	9.9(12)
Cheerful	12.0(15)	8.5(9)	12.2(14)	8.8(6)
Clean	14.1(17)	13.9(17)	12.6(15)	15.4(17)
Courageous	8.4(8)	8.7(10)	9.8(12)	9.1(8)
Forgiving	10.5(12)	9.3(11)	14.3(18)	9.1(10)
Helpful	11.9(14)	10.2(13)	9.3(10)	9.1(9)
Honest	5.2(1)	4.0(1)	5.1(1)	3.0(1)
Imaginative	10.8(13)	11.5(15)	13.1(16)	10.6(15)
Independent	7.7(6)	7.9(7)	9.9(13)	6.9(5)
Intellectual	8.5(9)	10.6(14)	7.7(6)	8.9(7)
Logical	8.3(7)	9.9(12)	5.9(3)	10.5(14)
Loving	9.1(11)	7.5(4)	9.1(8)	6.4(3)
Obedient	15.0(18)	15.3(18)	13.6(17)	16.6(18)
Polite	13.2(16)	12.1(16)	9.7(11)	14.6(16)
Responsible	5.9(2)	5.2(3)	5.2(2)	5.6(2)
Self-controlled	8.6(10)	7.7(5)	7.6(5)	10.2(13)

*Figures shown are median rankings for U.S., Australian, and Canadian samples, mean rankings for Israeli sample, and, in parentheses, the composite rank orders. They are based on 169 Americans, 279 Australians, 71 Israelis, and 125 Canadians.

Adapted from *The Nature of Human Values*, by Milton Rokeach. Copyright © 1973 by The Free Press, a division of Macmillan Publishing Co., Inc. Used with the permission of Macmillan Publishing Co., Inc.

Although these samples can by no means be viewed as nationally representative (each consists of 71 to 279 students from a single university), Rokeach observes that the findings indicate the kinds of cross-cultural comparisons that are feasible using the Value Survey and bear on the tenability of some hypothesized value differences between the various countries. For instance, the largest terminal value differences pertain to the one-two ranking that Israeli students gave to "a world at peace" and "national security" in contrast to the much lower rankings given those values by the students from the United States, Canada, and Australia. These differences clearly reflect the relatively insecure and vulnerable status held by Israel among her neighboring countries. Moreover, Rokeach suggests that American students' greater emphasis on "a comfortable life" and "ambitious" accords with the stereotype that Americans are oriented toward materialism and achievement; however, he notes that the belief that Americans are egalitarian oriented (Lipset, 1963) is not evident in their ranking of "equality."[7]

Values and Attitudes. Because of his view that values are more central to one's personality than attitudes and thus are seen as underlying the display of attitudes, Rokeach hypothesizes that a person's attitudes should be significantly associated with theoretically related values. In his book, Rokeach provides an impressive amount of evidence to document the tie-in between values and attitudes.

In the survey conducted by the National Opinion Research Center, data were also collected on a variety of attitudinal issues. For instance, several questions elicited opinions regarding civil rights for Black Americans (for example, school desegregation and interracial marriage), on the basis of which an index of prejudice toward Blacks was computed. Whites classified as racists and antiracists differed on many values. The biggest discrepancy was that the antiracists ranked "equality" fourth, whereas the racists ranked it fourteenth. We trust that the differentiating power of "equality" requires no explanatory comment. Rokeach further points out that the system of values characterizing the racist sample was very consistent with accepted descriptions of the racially prejudiced person (Allport, 1954) and authoritarian personality (Adorno, Frenkel-Brunswick, Levinson, & Sanford, 1950). Relative to the nonracist sample, the racists stressed "a comfortable life," "family security," "happiness," "national security," "pleasure," "salvation," being "ambitious," "clean," "obedient," and "polite," and placed less importance on "an exciting life," "a sense of accomplishment," "a world of beauty," "equality," "inner harmony," "wisdom," being "broadminded," "imaginative," "intellectual," and "logical."

Other theoretically meaningful relationships were also found between values and attitudes concerning such diverse matters as the assassination of Dr. Martin Luther King, poor people, student protests, communism, and church activism.

---

[7]More recently, Feather (1975) studied the values of people from the newly independent, developing country of Papua New Guinea and found, as he had predicted, that they stressed values related to a high concern with security (for example, "national security"), material comfort (for example, "comfortable life"), and religion (for example, "salvation").

Values and Behavior. Rokeach's conceptualization predicts that a person's values guide his or her actions as well as his or her attitudes. Accordingly, differences in a given kind of behavior (for example, political behavior) should be directly related to differences in theoretically related values (for example, political values). One type of support for Rokeach's view stems from value comparisons of participants and nonparticipants in various activities such as civil rights demonstrations, church, and antiwar protests. For instance, more than any other value, "salvation" discriminated between churchgoers and non-churchgoers.

The link between values and behavior is also manifested in comparisons of preexisting groups such as various occupational groupings, hippies versus nonhippies, homosexuals versus heterosexuals, and police versus civilians. For instance, the largest terminal value difference between hippies and nonhippies was "a world of beauty" (hippies rated it higher) and the largest instrumental value difference was "responsible" (hippies rated it lower). Also, the instrumental value rankings of police and citizens seem to suggest that the former are characterized by a greater degree of rigidity and authoritarianism (Griffeth & Cafferty, 1977; Rokeach, Miller, & Snyder, 1971). Police tend to rank "obedient" and "self-controlled" higher than citizens, while ranking "cheerful," "forgiving," and "helpful" lower. Finally, the correspondence between values and behavior has been experimentally observed. Rokeach reports a study by Penner (1971) in which it was found that Whites who minimized eye contact with a Black person ranked "equality" lower in importance than did other Whites. In a second study (Homant & Rokeach, 1970), grade 12 students who cheated on a task had previously ranked "honest" lower than did those who did not cheat.

The Two-Value Model of Political Ideology. Perhaps Rokeach's most stimulating contribution to the study of values is his value-based two-dimensional model of political ideology. Rokeach contends that the four major political ideologies of the world—socialism, capitalism, communism, and fascism—are basically reducible to pro or con stances concerning the two political values, freedom and equality. Figure 9-4 shows Rokeach's two-dimensional model of equality and freedom, in which each ideology is located in a separate quadrant. Thus, because socialists are judged to value both freedom and equality, socialism falls in the upper right-hand quadrant; capitalists are thought to show much more concern for freedom than for equality, and, therefore, capitalism is placed on the lower right-hand quadrant, and so forth. Rokeach (1973) notes the resemblance between his model and a two-dimensional model of social attitudes that Eysenck (1954) earlier developed. Eysenck's model consists of a tough-minded/tender-minded dimension and a radicalism/conservatism dimension. Eysenck's data suggested that, as in Rokeach's scheme, certain groups—communists, socialists, fascists, conservatives, liberals—can be located within his two-coordinate model.

Rokeach validated his model by content analyzing writings representative of the four political orientations (for example, Hitler's *Mein Kampf* and Goldwater's *The Conscience of a Conservative*). This involved counting in each set

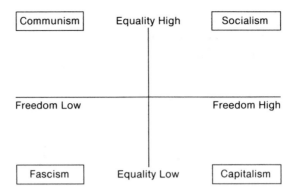

Figure 9-4. Rokeach's freedom-equality model of political variations. Adapted from *The Nature of Human Values*, by Milton Rokeach. Copyright © 1973 by The Free Press, a division of Macmillan Publishing Co., Inc. Used with permission of Macmillan Publishing Co., Inc.

of writings the number of positive references (actually positive minus negative) to all terminal and instrumental values. His results showed that equality and freedom were the most frequently mentioned values in all the writings, and, more importantly, the relative frequencies were in perfect agreement with the model. For example, Lenin made the greatest number of positive references to equality and the least number to freedom. Moreover, the model has received support from comparing the Value Survey responses of people representing known political groups. Table 9-7 shows the composite rank orders for equality and freedom for active supporters of the major presidential candidates during the 1968 campaign. From Table 9-7 it is clear that the major value differentiating the major American political groupings is equality; they both value freedom. In the United States the socialistic and capitalistic ideologies predominate.

Thus, we find ample support for the heuristic usefulness of Rokeach's Value Survey. Nevertheless, we should note that it is not without its limitations (Kitwood & Smithers, 1975; Reich & Adcock, 1976). Some problems pointed out by the Value Survey's critics include: (1) It forces one's values into a strict hierarchy when some that are not mutually exclusive may, in fact, fall at a similar level. (2) It requires people to simultaneously rank values that deal with different kinds of questions (for example, What kind of person do you want to be? versus What do you want the world to be like?). Such a task may not be very psychologically meaningful. (3) The rankings signify only the relative degree of importance, not the absolute degree; people may differ in how strongly they feel about a value to which they have given the same rank. (4) Certain important values have been omitted, values such as "truth" and those related to health and vitality. (5) The distinction between some terminal and instrumental values is questionable when we consider certain value pairs, such as "happiness" and "cheerful" or "freedom" and "independent." Notwithstanding its possible limitations, however, Rokeach's Value Survey and related research have contributed substantially to our knowledge about human values.

Table 9-7. Composite Rank Orders for Equality and Freedom Obtained from Active Supporters of Six Presidential Candidates, 1968

	McCarthy	Humphrey	Rockefeller	Nixon	Reagan	Wallace
N =	30	15	30	16	11	19
Equality	1	2	9	9	17	18
Freedom	2	4	2	2	1	1

Adapted from *The Nature of Human Values*, by Milton Rokeach. Copyright © 1973 by The Free Press, a division of Macmillan Publishing Co., Inc. Used with the permission of Macmillan Publishing Co., Inc.

Interpersonal Values

Gordon (1960) has developed an inventory to measure interpersonal values. According to Gordon, interpersonal values are those related specifically to interactions with other people. Such values, for example, would include the value of altruism, in which importance is attached to carrying out activities that benefit others. (Inspection of Rokeach's Value Survey reveals that some of the values from both the instrumental and terminal lists may be viewed as fitting Gordon's definition of interpersonal values.) Gordon's inventory, the Survey of Interpersonal Values (Gordon, 1960, 1975), consists of six factor-analytically derived scales:

> *Support(S)*—being treated with understanding, receiving encouragement from other people, being treated with kindness and consideration.
> *Conformity(C)*—doing what is socially correct, following regulations closely, doing what is accepted and proper, being a conformist.
> *Recognition(R)*—being looked up to and admired, being considered important, attracting favorable notice, achieving recognition.
> *Independence(I)*—having the right to do whatever one wants to do, being free to make one's own decisions, being able to do things in one's own way.
> *Benevolence(B)*—doing things for other people, sharing with others, helping the unfortunate, being generous.
> *Leadership(L)*—being in charge of other people, having authority over others, being in a position of leadership or power [Gordon, 1975, pp. 22–25].

Because the focus is on interaction with others, some of the scales concern "expressive" values (Conformity, Independence, Benevolence, and Leadership), whereas others reflect "receptive" values (Support, Recognition).

Of particular interest to us is the development of a value typology that Gordon (1975) has undertaken. Very briefly, his procedure involved first selecting a large number of groups who had taken the Survey of Interpersonal Values. Each of these groups included people who were either involved in similar occupations (for example, army officers or salesmen), had similar academic status (for example, high school students or college students), or were engaged in similar activities (for example, incarcerated criminals or adults in therapy). Then the six mean scores on the Survey of Interpersonal Values of each of these groups were intercorrelated with those of the other groups, the resultant correlation matrix was factor analyzed, and a technique called cluster analysis applied. Four bipolar factors were suggested that led to the typology presented in Table 9-8.

In considering the question of the generalizability of this typology, Gordon carried out similar analyses with the Study of Values (Allport et al., 1951) and the Edwards Personal Preference Schedule (Edwards, 1953). The analyses of these other inventories likewise yielded four major factors that bore considerable resemblance to Gordon's. Table 9-8 permits a comparison with the types obtained for the Study of Values. Gordon also concluded that his typology is consistent with Holland's (1973) interest types. The parallels may be seen in Table 9-8. In explaining why his reciprocal Support and Institutional Service types have no counterparts in Holland's scheme, Gordon notes that female groups served to define these types, whereas Holland's typology originally was based on male occupations only. Gordon concludes that his analyses suggest the existence of an appreciable degree of consistency in the typologies that emerge from the use of a variety of scales sampling the personality domain.

Determinants of Values

In contrast to most other individual difference dimensions, there apparently has been much less empirical concern regarding the origin and development of values. However, on a theoretical level the usual array of interrelated factors have been implicated—heredity, socialization, group and class membership, and so on (Reich & Adcock, 1976). Furthermore, it is Rokeach's (1973) conviction that culture is a profound shaper of a person's value system (recall the cross-cultural data). He cites as evidence of the influence of socialization pressures the many variables he has shown to be systematically related to values. These include religious upbringing, political identification, sex (see Chapter 11), class (see Chapter 12), and race (see Chapter 13).

SUMMARY

Interests refer to a person's likes and dislikes for various activities and objects. Researchers have distinguished four different interpretations of interests: expressed interests, manifest interests, tested interests, and inventoried interests. Most psychological attention has concentrated on inventoried vocational interests. The greatest contribution to the measurement and study of vocational interests was made by Edward K. Strong Jr. who was responsible for the development of the widely used Strong Vocational Interest Blank. The most recent version of this inventory, the Strong-Campbell Interest Inventory (SCII), consists primarily of three kinds of scale, which are, in order of increasing generality, the occupational scales, basic interest scales, and general occupational themes. The occupational scales are empirically derived in that their items significantly differentiate between members of a designated occupation and those of other occupations. On the other hand, the basic interest scales and general occupational themes are homogeneous scales in that their items

Table 9-8. Comparison of Types Obtained in Three Different Analyses

| | | Results for Survey of Interpersonal Values | | | Types from Other Research | |
| | | | | | Study of Values | Holland |
Factor	Pole	Type	Major Defining Values	Representative Groups		
I	Positive	Control of others	High on leadership; low on support and benevolence	Salesmen (wholesale), aircraft supervisory trainees, and engineering-project directors	Economic, political	Enterprising
	Negative	Reciprocal support	High on support, benevolence, and independence; low on leadership and conformity	Intellectually superior *female* students in high school and college	Warm, supportive	None
II	Positive	Service to others	High on benevolence; low on conformity and recognition	Peace Corps volunteers, guidance counselors, and first-year medical students	Social	Social
	Negative	(Negative) Service to others	High on leadership and recognition; low on benevolence*	No group as yet clearly identified; likely to include groups involved in profit-making transactions with the public	Negative social	None

(Table 9-8 continues.)

Table 9-8. Comparison of Types Obtained in Three Different Analyses *(continued)*

Factor	Pole	Results for Survey of Interpersonal Values			Types from Other Research	
		Type	Major Defining Values	Representative Groups	Study of Values	Holland
III	Positive	Self-determination	High on independence and leadership; low on conformity and support	Psychiatrists, civil engineers, and college students from highly selective institutions	Theoretical	Intellectual
	Negative	Institutional service	High on conformity and benevolence; low on independence and leadership	Female mental-hospital employees, practical-nurse trainees, and student nurses	None	None
IV	Positive	Institutional restraint	High on conformity; low on independence	Prison guards, aircraft assembly workers, and army enlisted men	Christian conservative	Conventional, realistic
	Negative	(Self-expression)	High on independence, recognition, and support; low on conformity and benevolence*	No groups as yet clearly identified; likely to come from world of arts and entertainment	Aesthetic	Artistic

*The major defining values at this negative pole are tentative.

Adapted from *The Measurement of Interpersonal Values*, by Leonard V. Gordon. © 1975, Science Research Associates, Inc. Used by permission of the publisher.

are both conceptually and statistically related. The general occupational themes are based directly on Holland's theory of career development, which views interests as dimensions of personality and posits the existence of six interest or personality types. Vocational interest inventories have proved moderately successful in the prediction of career choice, job satisfaction, and job tenure, and considerably less successful in predicting job success. In recent years efforts have been made, specifically on the SCII, to reduce the amount of sex bias that critics have attributed to interest inventories.

Vocational values are viewed by vocational psychologists as job-related goals that people strive for in order to satisfy a need. More general "life" values have been analyzed by Milton Rokeach into two kinds: instrumental values (modes of conduct) and terminal values (end-states of existence). According to Rokeach, each person has an instrumental value system and a terminal value system that essentially consist of a fixed number of values ordered along a continuum of importance. Various occupational groupings have been shown to differ in terms of both vocational values and general life values. Also, using the Value Survey, Rokeach has shown that value system differences may be directly related to such factors as sex, social class, race, and national identity. Moreover, Rokeach has provided considerable evidence showing a direct relationship between values and both attitudes and behavior. A typology of interpersonal values developed by Gordon shows an appreciable degree of similarity with Holland's interest types as well as with a typology based on the Study of Values.

REFERENCES

Adorno, T. W., Frenkel-Brunswick, E., Levinson, D. J., & Sanford, R. N. *The authoritarian personality*. New York: Harper, 1950.

Allport, G. W. *The nature of prejudice*. Cambridge, Mass.: Addison-Wesley, 1954.

Allport, G. W. *Pattern and growth in personality*. New York: Holt, Rinehart & Winston, 1961.

Allport, G. W., Vernon, P. E., & Lindzey, G. *Study of values: A scale for measuring the dominant interests in personality*. Boston: Houghton Mifflin, 1951.

Anastasi, A. *Psychological testing* (4th ed.). New York: Macmillan, 1976.

Barnette, W. L., Jr. The Minnesota Vocational Interest Inventory. In D. G. Zytowski (Ed.), *Contemporary approaches to interest measurement*. Minneapolis: University of Minnesota Press, 1973.

Birk, J. M. Interest inventories: A mixed blessing. *Vocational Guidance Quarterly*, 1974, 22, 280–286.

Boyd, V. S. Neutralizing sexist titles in Holland's Self-Directed Search: What difference does it make? *Journal of Vocational Behavior*, 1976, 9, 191–199.

Breme, F. J., & Cockriel, I. W. Work values and work interests: Are they the same? *Journal of Vocational Behavior*, 1975, 6, 331–336.

Campbell, D. P. *Handbook for the Strong Vocational Interest Blank*. Stanford, Calif.: Stanford University Press, 1971.

Campbell, D. P. *Manual for the Strong-Campbell Interest Inventory*. Stanford, Calif.: Stanford University Press, 1977.

Campbell, D. P., & Holland, J. L. A merger in vocational interest research: Applying

Holland's theory to Strong's data. *Journal of Vocational Behavior*, 1972, *2*, 353–376.

Clark, K. E. *The vocational interests of nonprofessional men.* Minneapolis: University of Minnesota Press, 1961.

Clark, K. E., & Campbell, D. P. *Manual for the Minnesota Vocational Interest Inventory.* New York: Psychological Corporation, 1965.

Darley, J. G., & Hagenah, T. *Vocational interest measurement: Theory and practice.* Minneapolis: University of Minnesota Press, 1955.

Dolliver, R. H., Irvin, J. A., & Bigley, S. S. Twelve-year follow-up of the Strong Vocational Interest Blank. *Journal of Counseling Psychology*, 1972, *19*, 212–217.

Edwards, A. L. *Edwards Personal Preference Schedule.* New York: Psychological Corporation, 1953.

Eysenck, H. J. *The psychology of politics.* London: Routledge & Kegan Paul, 1954.

Feather, N. T. *Values in education and society.* New York: Free Press, 1975.

Gordon, L. V. *Survey of interpersonal values.* Chicago: Science Research Associates, 1960.

Gordon, L. V. *The measurement of interpersonal values.* Chicago: Science Research Associates, 1975.

Gottfredson, G. D. A note on sexist wording in interest measurement. *Measurement and Evaluation in Guidance*, 1976, *8*, 221–223.

Griffeth, R. W., & Cafferty, T. P. Police and citizen value systems: Some cross-sectional comparisons. *Journal of Applied Social Psychology*, 1977, 7, 191–204.

Grotevant, H. D., Scarr, S., & Weinberg, R. A. Patterns of interest similarity in adoptive and biological families. *Journal of Personality and Social Psychology*, 1977, *35*, 667–676.

Guilford, J. P., Christensen, P. R., Bond, N. A., Jr., & Sutton, M. A. A factor analysis study of human interests. *Psychological Monographs*, 1954, *68* (4, Whole No. 375).

Hanson, G. R. *Assessing the career interests of college youth: Summary of research and applications.* ACT Research Report No. 67. Iowa City: The American College Testing Program, 1974.

Hanson, G. R., & Rayman, J. Validity of sex-balanced interest inventory scales. *Journal of Vocational Behavior*, 1976, *9*, 279–291.

Harmon, L. W. The 1969 revision of the Strong Vocational Interest Blank for Women. In D. G. Zytowski (Ed.), *Contemporary approaches to interest measurement.* Minneapolis: University of Minnesota, 1973.

Harmon, L. W., Cole, N., Wysong, E., & Zytowski, D. G. AMEG commission report on sex bias in interest measurement. *Measurement and Evaluation in Guidance*, 1973, *6*, 171–177.

Holland, J. L. *Manual for the Vocational Preference Inventory.* Palo Alto, Calif.: Consulting Psychologists Press, 1965.

Holland, J. L. *The psychology of vocational choice: A theory of personality types and model environments.* Waltham, Mass.: Blaisdell, 1966.

Holland, J. L. *The self-directed search.* Palo Alto, Calif.: Consulting Psychologists Press, 1970.

Holland, J. L. *Making vocational choices: A theory of careers.* Englewood Cliffs, N.J.: Prentice-Hall, 1973.

Homant, R., & Rokeach, M. Values for honesty and cheating behavior. *Personality*, 1970, *1*, 153–162.

Johnson, R. W., Flammer, D. P., & Nelson, J. G. Multiple correlations between personality factors and SVIB occupational scales. *Journal of Counseling Psychology*, 1975, *22*, 217–223.

Johnson, R. W., & Johansson, C. B. Moderating effect of basic interests on predictive validity of SVIB occupational scales. *Proceedings of the 80th Annual Convention of the American Psychological Association*, 1972, 7, 589–590.

Kitwood, T. M., & Smithers, A. G. Measurement of human values: An appraisal of the work of Milton Rokeach. *Educational Research*, 1975, *17*, 175–179.

Kuder, G. F. *Administrator's manual: Kuder Preference Record*. Chicago: Science Research Associates, 1960.

Kuder, G. F. *Kuder General Interest Survey Manual*. Chicago: Science Research Associates, 1975. (a)

Kuder, G. F. *Kuder Occupational Interest Survey General Manual*. Chicago: Science Research Associates, 1975. (b)

Lipset, S. M. The value patterns of democracy: A case study in comparative analysis. *American Sociological Review*, 1963, *28*, 515–531.

Nafziger, D. H., & Helms, S. T. Cluster analyses of interest inventory scales as tests of Holland's occupational classification. *Journal of Applied Psychology*, 1974, *59*, 344–353.

Normile, R. H. *Differentiating among known occupational groups by means of the Work Values Inventory*. Unpublished doctoral dissertation, Catholic University of America, 1967.

Osipow, S. H. *Theories of career development*. New York: Appleton-Century-Crofts, 1973.

Osipow, S. H. Vocational behavior and career development, 1975: A review. *Journal of Vocational Behavior*, 1976, *9*, 129–145.

Penner, L. A. Interpersonal attraction toward a black person as a function of value importance. *Personality*, 1971, *2*, 175–187.

Peoples, V. Y. Measuring the vocational interest of women. In S. H. Osipow (Ed.), *Emerging woman: Career analysis and outlooks*. Columbus, Ohio: Charles E. Merrill, 1975.

Porter, L. W., & Steers, K. M. Organizational, work, and personal factors in employee turnover and absenteeism. *Psychological Bulletin*, 1973, *80*, 151–176.

Reich, B., & Adcock, C. *Values, attitudes, and behavior change*. London: Methuen, 1976.

Roberts, C. A., & Johansson, C. B. The inheritance of cognitive interest styles among twins. *Journal of Vocational Behavior*, 1974, *4*, 237–243.

Rokeach, M. *The nature of human values*. New York: Free Press, 1973.

Rokeach, M., Miller, M. G., & Snyder, J. A. The value gap between police and policed. *Journal of Social Issues*, 1971, *27*(2) 155–171.

Shaw, M. E., & Wright, J. (Eds.). *Scales for the measurement of attitudes*. New York: McGraw-Hill, 1967.

Spranger, E. [*Types of men.*] (P. J. W. Pigors, trans.). Halle, German Democratic Republic: Niemeyer, 1928.

Strong, E. K., Jr. *Vocational interests 18 years after college*. Minneapolis: University of Minnesota Press, 1955.

Super, D. E. *The Work Values Inventory*. Boston: Houghton Mifflin, 1969.

Super, D. E. The Work Values Inventory. In D. G. Zytowski (Ed.), *Contemporary approaches to interest measurement*. Minneapolis: University of Minnesota Press, 1973.

Super, D. E., & Bohn, M. J., Jr. *Occupational psychology*. Belmont, Calif.: Wadsworth, 1970.

Super, D. E., & Crites, J. O. *Appraising vocational fitness by means of psychological tests*. New York: Harper, 1962.

Tyler, L. E. *Individual differences: Abilities and motivational directions* (3rd ed.). New York: Appleton-Century-Crofts, 1974.

Utz, P., & Korben, D. The construct validity of the occupational themes on the Strong-Campbell Inventory. *Journal of Vocational Behavior*, 1976, *9*, 31–42.

Vandenberg, S. G., & Stafford, R. E. Hereditary influences on vocational preferences as shown by scores of twins on the Minnesota Vocational Interest Inventory. *Journal of Applied Psychology*, 1967, *51*, 17–19.

Worthington, E. L., Jr., & Dolliver, R. H. Validity studies of the Strong Vocational Interest Inventories. *Journal of Counseling Psychology*, 1977, *24*, 208–216.

Zytowski, D. G. (Ed.). *Contemporary approaches to interest measurement.* Minneapolis: University of Minneapolis Press, 1973.

Zytowski, D. G. Predictive validity of the Kuder Preference Record, Form B, over a 25-year span. *Measurement and Evaluation in Guidance*, 1974, *1*, 122–129.

Zytowski, D. G. Predictive validity of the Kuder Occupational Interest Survey: A 12- to 19-year follow-up. *Journal of Counseling Psychology*, 1976, *23*, 221–233.

Part Three

Group Differences

Sex Differences

The differential categorization of males and females is a universal phenomenon. There is no society that does not recognize this dichotimization, and more importantly, there is no society that fails to ascribe different roles to the sexes (Ford, 1970). Throughout history differences between males and females have been taken for granted, and only recently have the nature and extent of the differences come under both public and scientific scrutiny.

We are reminded of the story about the suffragette who concluded a speech by stating that there is only a little difference between men and women and to which a heckler exclaimed, "Vive la petite difference!" Certainly from the perspective of "people watchers" the most salient division is that which separates us into male and female. Yet, in the past the topic of sex differences was pretty well neglected by psychologists, although the tenets of some major theories (for example, Freudian) were based on implicit assumptions about the nature of sex differences. In research, possible sex differences were shunned because they were viewed as a nuisance factor; consequently, re-searchers tended to use only one sex (usually males) in their experiments, to use both sexes without testing for sex differences, or to merely neglect to report the sex of their subjects. Now, however, undoubtedly due in a large part to the impetus of the feminist movement, interest in sex differences is at an all time high, and in fact, the 1970s witnessed a virtual explosion of psychological research and writing on the topic. It is certainly of some social significance that the majority of current researchers and writers on sex dif-ferences are female.

SEX-ROLE STEREOTYPES

Unlike the usually intangible psychological differences between people, one's sex is visible to the senses. The physical differences between males and females make for the immediate identification of a person's sex and, as in the case of skin color, facilitates the development of stereotypes. If there is one fact that is clear, it is that our society is permeated with sex-role stereotypes. Among women and men of all ages there is extensive agreement as to the different traits that are associated with males and females (Broverman, Vogel, Broverman, Clarkson, & Rosenkrantz, 1972). For example, in a widely recog-nized study by Rosenkrantz and his associates (Rosenkrantz, Vogel, Bee, Bro-verman, & Broverman, 1968) a list of bipolar adjectives was administered to college students. An example is shown below:

Not at all   Very
aggressive   aggressive
1. . . . . . . 2. . . . . . . 3. . . . . . . 4. . . . . . . 5. . . . . . . 6. 7

For each trait the students had to mark the point that characterizes an average adult male and the point that describes an average adult female. Stereotypic traits were defined as those about which there was extensive agreement that one pole is more characteristic of one sex than the other sex. In addition, a second sample of subjects rated which pole of each trait represented the more socially desirable behavior.

Table 10-1 shows the stereotypic traits. The top cluster represents the stereotypically male traits that were rated as socially desirable; the bottom cluster includes the socially desirable female traits. Notice that more male traits are perceived as socially desirable than female traits. Evidence from other investigations supports these findings (for example, McKee & Sherriffs, 1957). Furthermore, the male-valued traits have been described as reflecting a compe-tency factor and the female-valued traits a warmth and expressiveness factor (Broverman et al., 1972). That is, men are viewed as self-confident, independent, active, objective, competitive, ambitious, and able to make decisions easily, whereas women are described as gentle, sensitive to the feelings of others, tactful, and able to express tender feelings.

Table 10-1. Stereotypic Traits

Male-Valued Traits

Aggressive	Feelings not easily hurt
Independent	Adventurous
Unemotional	Makes decisions easily
Hides emotions	Never cries
Objective	Acts as a leader
Easily influenced	Self-confident
Dominant	Not uncomfortable about
Likes math and science	being aggressive
Not excitable in a minor	Ambitious
crisis	Able to separate feelings
Active	from ideas
Competitive	Not dependent
Logical	Not conceited about
Worldly	appearance
Skilled in business	Thinks men are superior
Direct	to women
Knows the ways of the	Talks freely about sex
world	with men

Female-Valued Traits

Does not use harsh language	Interested in own appearance
Talkative	Neat in habits
Tactful	Quiet
Gentle	Strong need for security
Aware of feelings of others	Appreciates art and literature
Religious	Expresses tender feelings

Adapted from "Sex-Role Stereotypes and Self-Concepts in College Students," by P. S. Rosenkrantz et al., *Journal of Consulting and Clinical Psychology*, 1968, *32*, 287–295. Copyright 1968 by the American Psychological Association. Used by permission.

We might note that the competence and warmth-expressiveness clusters of stereotypic traits seem to parallel T. Parsons's (1955) distinction between the "instrumental" role of the male and the "expressive" role of the female. In his instrumental role the male is less concerned with his interpersonal relationships than with mastery and control, whereas in her expressive role the female focuses on emotional relationships and is sensitive to affective cues emanating from others, especially family members.

Sex-role stereotypes (in fact, all stereotypes) should not be taken lightly. While stereotyping serves an adaptive function by helping the individual to organize the complexities of the social environment into manageable categories, its limitations include the fact that reality may be inaccurately mirrored. Even when a stereotype shows a general correspondence with observed differences between the sexes, by error of oversimplification it encourages one to gloss over the behavioral overlap between the sexes. Similarly, although in the pages that follow we may report that males and females differ with respect to some dimension of behavior, we are dealing with average differences, and many males and females will fall above the median of the other sex. Thus, for example, while research has established that males are the more aggressive sex, we are well aware that some women are quite capable of committing atrocious acts of violence.

Furthermore, sex-role stereotypes have profound consequences for interpersonal relationships. They implicitly, sometimes quite explicitly, prescribe how males and females are expected to behave, and in so doing serve the uncommendable function of self-fulfilling prophecies. Research on sex differences is not exempt from such undesirable effects of stereotyping. Because we usually cannot be blind to the sexual identity of our subjects, our own assumptions about male/female differences may predispose us to see differences where they actually don't exist. Most assuredly, the question of sex differences is one of the most emotionally charged topics in psychology and, as other writers have observed (Favreau, 1977; Shields, 1975), is especially vulnerable to the pitfalls of investigator bias.

THE ROLE OF BIOLOGY AND ENVIRONMENT

As we consider the topic of sex differences, our interest will focus not only on the nature and extent of the differences but also on their causes. We again emphasize that the issue is not whether nature or nurture is the primary causative factor, because virtually all behavioral differences between the sexes reflect the interplay of both biological and environmental forces (Archer, 1976). Rather, the issue concerns the modus operandi—how do specific biological and environmental factors operate in the development of sex differences?

Some of the most convincing evidence of the importance of environmental factors in the determination of sex differences in behavior is provided by Money's clinical studies of hermaphrodites (Money & Ehrhardt, 1972). Hermaphroditism is a congenital condition in which the reproductive structures are sufficiently ambiguous that a child's sex cannot be readily identified as exclusively male or female. One kind of hermaphrodite is a person with the adrenogenital syndrome, a disorder caused by exposure of the fetus to abnormally high levels of androgens (male hormones). This individual is a genetic female with normal internal reproductive structures but with external genitalia which are partly or completely male in appearance. Thus, at birth these genetic females may be identified as males. In some cases the external genitalia are surgically feminized and the child is raised as a female; in other cases the child is raised as a male. Money's research indicates that the children who are brought up as females make satisfactory adjustments to their gender role: they consider themselves to be females, behave as females (although they may be tomboyish), and are accepted by others as females. Similarly, those reared as males satisfactorily achieve the appropriate gender identity.

In *My Fair Lady* Henry Higgins asked, "Why can't a woman be more like a man?" Drawing on Money's work with hermaphrodites, our answer to

Henry is that females actually can be more like males. Yet, whether he intended it or not, underlying Henry's query was the implicit assumption that there is a biologically based immutability about sex differences in behavior. As the evidence that we will soon review indicates, this assumption has some empirical justification. Biological agents, including hormonal and genetic factors, are being linked to the behavioral variation between the sexes. Even with respect to Money's adrenogenital children, the role of biology cannot be ignored. For example, their sex-role socialization has to be accompanied by hormonal therapy, and they often show traces of behavior that is contrary to their assigned gender role.

In our survey of psychological sex differences, we will look first at how males and females compare with respect to their basic learning and memory processes, general intellectual functioning, and special abilities before moving on to a consideration of the relative accomplishments of the sexes in the educational and vocational worlds. Then we will examine the extent to which differences in motivational and personality attributes characterize the sexes.

COGNITIVE FUNCTIONING

Do the sexes differ with respect to their intellectual processes? The traditional approach to sex differences in intellectual functioning entails a comparison of the performance of males and females on measures of general and special ability. While we too will emphasize this approach, we want to briefly consider a second perspective—the possibility that the sexes differ in terms of the basic learning and memory processes. Recall that there is surprisingly little relationship between general ability and learning ability, unless we consider the mastery of more complex kinds of tasks (see Chapter 4).

Learning and Memory

Our learning and memory processes are closely related. Although researchers tend to treat learning and memory separately, it is not always easy to differentiate one from the other. We cannot reproduce from memory that which hasn't been acquired (learned), nor can we assess learning without tapping memory, because both are measured in similar ways—with tests of retention. Maccoby and Jacklin (1974) have reviewed over 100 studies that compared how effectively males and females learn. Their review covered a variety of areas, including conditioning, paired-associate learning, discrimination learning, and incidental learning. Maccoby and Jacklin conclude that the evidence clearly does not support the existence of sex differences in learning ability.

On the other hand, males and females do manifest some differences in memory. It is commonly found that females have an edge in rote memory, requiring the recall of a series of facts, such as repeating a group of digits or reciting a passage that has been read (Garai & Scheinfeld, 1968; Hutt, 1972). However, whereas female superiority is the general rule, the difference often is nonsignificant or even reversed (that is, in favor of males), especially if the material is of greater interest or relevance to males than females or when it is quantitative in nature (for example, Sommer, 1958).

The significance of the content of the material was discovered by Maccoby and Jacklin (1974) when they split studies into those dealing with memory for verbal content (for example, a list of words or material from a story) and those dealing with memory for objects and digits (for example, pictures of animals or toys seen in a playroom). This division indicates that females display better verbal memory than males, especially after about age 7, whereas there is minimal evidence of a sex difference in object memory. In addition, it appears that females have a stronger propensity for remembering social stimuli. For example, women are better at remembering the names and faces of people. In one study the subjects included nine groups of people who had been out of high school anywhere from 5 months to 40 years or more (Bahrick, Bahrick, & Wittlinger, 1974). Females in all age groups, except the oldest, were better than males at recalling and recognizing the faces and names of their classmates.

General Ability

In tracing the early history of the psychology of women, Shields (1975) notes that, by the 19th century, philosophers had justified the inferior social status of women and that the onus was on the "scientist" to elaborate the biological determinants of their inferiority. Early in the 19th century, Gall, the phrenologist, looked for the mental deficiency of females by examining the external contours of the cranium. Later, presumed sex differences in intelligence were attributed to females' smaller brain size or to the underdevelopment of various centers of the brain.

Although the first intelligence-test developers, such as Binet and Simon, were not originally concerned with sex differences, they were faced with the fact that boys and girls did not perform the same on a variety of tasks. These early sex differences were initially viewed by many as confirming the existence of innate sex differences in cognitive processes (Garai & Scheinfeld, 1968). However, with the rise of equalitarianism and the influence of the behaviorist premise of the almost infinite malleability of man, there was a shift in emphasis from biological and genetic determinants to the role of environmental factors, such as differential socialization experiences and educational opportunities. For a variety of reasons—the environmentalist emphasis, the ease of developing test norms, the assumption of no sex differences, or merely for the sake of the fair and equitable treatment of the sexes—many test developers explicitly set out to circumvent the occurrence of sex differences by eliminating sex-differentiating items or by counterbalancing them.

In view of the fact that intelligence tests were specifically designed to be sex-balanced, we should not be surprised to discover that a reliable sex difference in overall ability has not been found and that many, perhaps most, investigators find no sex differences (Cattell, 1971; Hutt, 1972; Maccoby &

Jacklin, 1974).[1] There is some indication, however, that when sex differences do appear, they are most likely to be found during the earliest years of life (Maccoby, 1966; Maccoby & Jacklin, 1974). For children under 6 to 7 years, a number of studies, though by no means all, show that girls score higher on measures of general ability. Several factors may be posited to account for an early female advantage—a common one is their advanced physical maturation—but the issue is far from resolved.

Special Abilities

We noted that many test developers worked hard at trying to equate the sexes on general ability. The mere fact that such efforts had to be made brings out an especially important point—differences between boys and girls and between men and women were constantly showing up on a wide variety of test items. Wechsler (1958), who in his scales sought to equate the sexes, eventually concluded that:

> The findings on the WAIS suggest that women seemingly call upon different resources or different degrees of like abilities in exercising whatever it is we call intelligence. For the moment one need not be concerned as to which approach is better or "superior." But our findings do confirm what poets and novelists have often asserted, and the average layman long believed, namely, that men not only behave but "think" differently from women [p. 148].[2]

Verbal Ability. Virtually every writer in the area of sex differences points out that when it comes to verbal ability females as a group are superior to males (for example, Hutt, 1972; Maccoby & Jacklin, 1974). While we do not necessarily disagree with this conclusion, we think that a few points should be kept in mind when the evidence is considered. One is that the difference between the sexes tends to be small, and, in fact, many (perhaps most) studies indicate no sex differences. Second, the female advantage seems to be confined to certain verbal skills—to indexes of verbal fluency but not verbal comprehension and reasoning (Garai & Scheinfeld, 1968; Tyler, 1965).

Concerning verbal fluency, research indicates that girls begin to speak earlier than boys (Schachter, Shore, Hodapp, Chalfin, & Bundy, 1978) and thereafter tend to manifest higher verbal fluency (Oetzel, 1966; Garai & Scheinfeld, 1968). For example, relative to boys, girls are found to articulate more clearly, use longer and more complex sentences, and make fewer grammatical and spelling errors. Furthermore, results of national surveys (for example,

---

[1]Actually, because of the selective construction of the measuring instruments, several writers, including Anastasi (1958) and Tyler (1965), have pointed to the futility of searching for sex differences in general ability.

[2]This and all other quotations from this source are from *The Measurement and Appraisal of Adult Intelligence*, by D. Wechsler. Copyright 1958 by The Williams & Wilkins Company. Reprinted by permission.

Hitchcock & Pinder, 1974; Schaie & Roberts, 1970) indicate that in the 6 to 17 year range, females surpass males in reading skills. Females also suffer fewer speech and reading disabilities (Biller, 1974; Garai & Scheinfeld, 1968). However, with respect to vocabulary level, any initial advantage held by girls seems to be shortlived; by school age there are no consistent differences in vocabulary development.

Regarding verbal reasoning and comprehension, the results are mixed. Some writers conclude that males are superior to females in these abilities (Garai & Scheinfeld, 1968), whereas others suggest the evidence favors females (Maccoby & Jacklin, 1974). In view of the inconsistencies in the literature, it is probably safest to say that neither sex reliably demonstrates a superiority in verbal comprehension or reasoning. One exception is that females seem to outperform males on various aspects of reading ability, including reading comprehension (Jantz, 1974; Mullis, 1975).

Mathematical Ability. It is commonly assumed that one of the most firmly established differences between the sexes is that males are superior in mathematical ability. Aiken (1971), for example, states that "sex differences [favoring males] in mathematical abilities are, of course, present at the kindergarten level and undoubtedly earlier" (p. 203). And, a publication from the National Assessment of Educational Progress (Mullis, 1975) proclaims "in the mathematics assessment, the advantage displayed by males, particularly at the older ages, can only be described as overwhelming" (p. 7).

How conclusive is the evidence concerning sex differences in quantitative ability? It is our opinion that sweeping generalizations about sex differences in mathematical ability (about most sex differences, for that matter) are a risky enterprise. For instance, such generalizations gloss over the fact that at least two kinds of quantitative ability may be differentiated: (1) computational skill, requiring speed and accuracy in the mechanics of computation, and (2) mathematical reasoning, requiring the solution of complex mathematical and geometrical problems. References to the masculine superiority in mathematics should be confined only to the reasoning processes.

With respect to computational ability, some evidence exists (contrary to the above opinion of Aiken) that, among preschool children, girls learn to count earlier than boys (Oetzel, 1966) and are better at enumeration tasks in which the child is asked to point once and only once to each item in a group of stimuli (Potter & Levy, 1968). However, the female head start soon disappears; during the school years the large majority of studies reveal negligible sex differences in computational ability (Fennema, 1974; Hitchcock & Pinder, 1974; Schaie & Roberts, 1970). We also might observe that Piagetian conservation tasks, which establish one's level of concept formation, have been used to assess a young child's readiness for math training. Frequently measured concepts include number, mass, length, and volume. For example, the ability to conserve mass requires a child to comprehend that if he or she has two clay balls of equal size and shapes one into a sausage, the sausage contains the same amount of clay as the ball. The large majority of studies indicate a nonexistence of sex differences in level of concept formation (Brekke & Williams, 1973; Maccoby & Jacklin, 1974).

The male advantage on tests of mathematical reasoning does not manifest itself during the early school years. However, at the upper elementary school level, boys begin to forge ahead and apparently remain ahead throughout their secondary school and post-secondary school years (Fennema, 1974; Maccoby & Jacklin, 1974; Mullis, 1975). A similar pattern has been established regarding achievement in science (Mullis, 1975). However, the interpretation of high school data is made especially difficult by at least two potentially confounding factors. One is that boys are more likely than girls to drop out of school. Consequently, comparisons of the sexes on mathematical ability (as well as other kinds of ability) are likely to be biased in favor of boys because dropouts generally are among the less able students. Second, since boys typically take more math courses than girls, observed differences may be the result of differential classroom exposure. One study, which controlled for these factors, supported the picture of a gradual emergence of a masculine advantage in mathematical reasoning. Hilton and Berglund (1974) started with a nationwide sample of fifth graders and followed the development of their math achievement through grade 11. The results indicated that at grade 5, there were no sex differences in mathematics achievement, but at subsequent grade levels (7, 9, and 11) males surpassed females, with the size of the discrepancy increasing with age.

Spatial Ability. Spatial ability essentially entails the judgment and manipulation of space relationships. A variety of visual tasks have been used to measure this ability, including aiming at a target, arranging objects in a certain pattern, and solving mazes. Also, the spatial subtests of the Differential Aptitude Test and the Primary Mental Abilities Test are used. For example, the latter includes a problem involving a standard American flag and four other pictures of it. The subject must select the flags that are the same as the standard rotated in the plane of the page; mirror-reversals are incorrect choices. Another spatial test involves figuring out how one part of a pictured system of gears will move in conjunction with the movement of another part. An example of a measure of visual spatial ability is presented in Figure 10-1. There is considerable consensus that males are superior to females on these kinds of visual spatial tasks, although there is somewhat less consistent evidence of the difference among preadolescents than among adolescents and adults (Garai & Scheinfeld, 1968; Maccoby & Jacklin, 1974; Vandenberg & Kuse, 1979).[3]

Witkin's (Witkin, Dyk, Faterson, Goodenough, & Karp, 1962) measures of field independence, the Rod and Frame Test (RFT) and Embedded Figures

---

[3]Males also surpass females on mechanical aptitude, which is measured by practical tests requiring the assembly of mechanical devices and by paper-and-pencil measures of mechanical reasoning (Anastasi, 1958; Garai & Scheinfeld, 1968). Garai and Scheinfeld report that mechanical aptitude correlates fairly highly with spatial ability.

The test is made up of pictures of blocks turned different ways. The block at the left is the reference block and the five blocks to the right are the answer blocks. One of these five blocks is the same as the reference block except that it has been turned and is seen from a different point of view. The other four blocks could not be obtained by turning the reference block. For example:

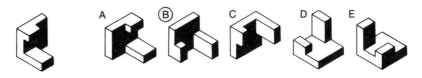

The illustration below shows that "B" is the correct answer.

Figure 10-1. Sample item and solution from a test of spatial ability. From "Identical Blocks, Form AA," by R. E. Stafford and H. Gullikson, 1962. Reprinted by permission of the authors.

Test (EFT), have also been considered as measures of spatial ability (see Chapter 7 for a description of the RFT and EFT). For many years it was assumed that the developmental course for performance on measures of field independence closely parallels that for general measures of visual spatial ability (Maccoby & Jacklin, 1974; Sherman, 1971). However, several more recent studies indicate that, among preschoolers, boys do more poorly than girls on measures of field independence (Coates, 1974). Thus, there seems to be a reversal from the preschool period, when girls are relatively field independent to late childhood/early adolescence when boys become more field independent than girls. Males continue to be more field independent well after adolescence, although their advantage seems to vanish by old age (Markus & Nielsen, 1973).

While successful performance on measures of field independence does require visual spatial skill, it also has been viewed as signifying one's analytical ability. By analytical, in this case, we mean that the task requires one to disembed (differentiate) the element from the background. On the RFT a person must ignore the perceptually misleading cues of the tilted frame, which serves as the background for the rod, and discern when the rod is upright. For the EFT, one must detect simple figures camouflaged in more complex figures.

There is some disagreement as to whether the greater field independence of males (covering most of the life span) is primarily a reflection of the visual spatial component or the analytical component of the tasks. Many writers have interpreted the female's field dependence as a manifestation of her difficulty with the disembedding requirement (for example, Bardwick, 1971; Constantinople, 1974). As Bardwick (1971) states:

In the rod-and-frame test . . . sex differences exist where the task requires analysis, and the female response reveals a passive acceptance of the field rather than an objective analysis of the perceptual problem. Men consistently deal with the field in an active, analytic way—that is, they selectively isolate tasks of different structures and demands [p. 111].

On the other hand, Sherman (1974) and Maccoby and Jacklin (1974) have advanced rather strong evidence in support of the view that it is the greater visual spatial ability of males, not their analytical ability, that accounts for their field independence. These authors point out that both the EFT and RFT have been shown to load on a spatial factor. More importantly, they observe that sex differences primarily are confined to visual tasks of field independence and not to nonvisual tasks. For example, males and females perform similarly on selective listening (auditory disembedding) tests, which require a person to attend to one voice and ignore another; that is, to disembed the correct message from its auditory context. In support of Sherman and Maccoby and Jacklin, one study has indicated that the sex difference in RFT performance is eliminated when differences in spatial ability are statistically controlled (Hyde, Geiringer, & Yen, 1975).[4]

We must add that the aforementioned evidence that preschool girls are more field independent than preschool boys constitutes something of a problem for the view that sex differences in field independence are due to differences in visual spatial ability. If the superior visual spatial ability of males accounts for their field independence, then why are preschool girls more field independent than boys? We cannot offer a satisfactory answer at this time. Part of the answer may lie in the work of Massari and Massari (1973), who found that, among disadvantaged preschoolers, measures of field independence were positively related to intelligence in girls but not in boys. These authors interpret their results as indicating that field dependence/independence is not functionally equivalent for preschool boys and girls, and, extrapolating from the results of other research, suggest that functional equivalency is achieved at later ages.

Analytical Ability. Whether performance on measures of field independence reflects analytical ability or not, it is commonly believed that analytical ability is more characteristic of males than females (Bardwick, 1971; Garai & Scheinfeld, 1968). For instance, Garai and Scheinfeld (1968) suggest that male problem-solving preeminence begins at an early age, with boys more likely than girls to ask "why" and "how" questions. Other writers have strongly countered the claim of a clear-cut male advantage in analytic ability (Maccoby & Jacklin, 1974; Sherman, 1971).

Before proceeding, we should consider further what is meant by *analyti-*

---

[4]This study also indicated that the sex difference in mathematical problem-solving ability disappeared when the difference in spatial ability was removed, thus supporting Sherman's (1967) hypothesis that sex differences in other aspects of cognitive functioning are attributable to differences in space perception.

cal, a term that, unfortunately, has several connotations. When discussing spatial ability we singled out disembedding as one aspect of analytical thinking and noted that there is no evidence of sex differences on nonvisual spatial tasks (for example, selective listening) that require disembedding. On visual spatial tasks requiring disembedding (for example, RFT and EFT), sex differences are found, but they may be attributed to the sexes' differential visual spatial ability rather than to their differential disembedding ability.

Maccoby and Jacklin (1974) distinguish three other aspects of analytical thinking, stipulating, however, that they sometimes are difficult to differentiate from each other and that many analytic tasks involve more than one aspect. One dimension is restructuring or set-breaking, which requires the ability to overcome or break away from an established, yet maladaptive set. The usual procedure is to give a person a series of similar problems, the first few of which are solvable only by a cumbersome and indirect method. However, succeeding problems may be solved either by the indirect, set-induced method or by a simple, more direct procedure. The person with set-breaking ability ignores the initially successful but inefficient strategy and readily adopts the more efficient one. A second dimension of analytic thinking involves inhibiting previously learned or initially probable response tendencies. The Matching Familiar Figures Test (Kagan, Rosman, Day, Albert, & Phillips, 1964), a measure of reflectivity/impulsivity, requires this inhibition ability. On this test a subject has to select a match for a standard figure from a set of six similar figures, some of which are highly similar to the standard; only one is identical to it. An impulsive, nonanalytic person characteristically makes a decision before giving adequate consideration to the alternatives. Third, people can differ in the manner in which they group diverse arrays of objects. Analytical people presumably put together objects on the basis of a particular detail they have in common (for example, a sofa and a child because they both have legs), whereas people who use an inferential strategy tend to group objects that belong to the same more inclusive category (for example, child and dog because they are mammals).

Maccoby and Jacklin's (1974) review of a large number of studies of analytical ability indicates the following: (1) There is evidence that males are superior to females on nonverbal tasks calling for restructuring. However, on verbal restructuring tasks (for example, anagrams) the difference tends to favor females. (2) There is no support for the idea that males are better able to inhibit dominant response tendencies. (3) There is no evidence that males are more likely to use an analytic grouping strategy. In trying to account for the sex differences regarding restructuring, Maccoby and Jacklin (1974) conclude by saying "We cannot feel confident that set-breaking per se is the factor distinguishing the performance of the sexes. There is an elusive element in the sex differences on restructuring that we do not feel has been adequately identified" (p. 105). Thus, according to Maccoby and Jacklin's (1974) examination of the relevant literature, there is insufficient evidence to conclude that males have an across-the-board superiority in analytical ability.

The sexes have also been compared on tests that purportedly tap abstract reasoning. These tests typically measure both inductive and deductive reasoning by calling for the formulation and testing of hypotheses. There is no evidence of consistent sex differences on a variety of tests of abstract reasoning, including Piagetian tests of formal operations and standardized tests such as the reasoning subtest of the Primary Mental Abilities Test (Maccoby & Jacklin, 1974; Oetzel, 1966).

Perceptual Motor Ability. Males surpass females in the speed and coordination of gross bodily movements, and their advantage apparently begins during the first few years of life (Anastasi, 1958; Garai & Scheinfeld, 1968). For example, boys are better than girls at such activities as walking along a narrow board, ascending ladders, and throwing and catching balls. Also, in reaction-time experiments males show faster reaction to visual and auditory stimuli.

On the other hand, girls and women have been reported to excel in manual dexterity, which entails the skillful, rapid movement of the fingers, hands, and wrists (Anastasi, 1958; Garai & Scheinfeld, 1968). However, Maccoby and Jacklin's (1974) analysis indicates that the female advantage is confined to finger dexterity as reflected in such skills as sewing and embroidery. This finding underlines the importance of distinguishing between fine and relatively gross muscle movements. Females are also superior in clerical skills—that is, on tasks requiring the perception of details and frequent shifts of attention. Such tasks include filing, typing, and checking lists for accuracy.

Summary. In summary, we find that males and females do display some differences in their intellectual processes. Females seem to have an edge in memorization, especially of verbal and social material, whereas there are no apparent sex differences in the basic learning processes. There is little indication of sex differences in general ability, except, perhaps, during the first five years or so when girls may have a slight advantage over boys. With respect to special abilities, females tend to surpass males on verbal fluency, reading comprehension, finger dexterity, and clerical skill. Males are superior in mathematical reasoning, visual spatial ability, and speed and coordination of gross motor behaviors. No consistent sex difference occurs for verbal comprehension, computational skill, analytical thinking, and abstract reasoning.

Some Determinants of Sex Differences in Ability

As one might expect, describing how the sexes compare in their intellectual functioning proves a far easier task than trying to account for the apparent dissimilarities. It is not feasible for us to even begin to explore the diverse factors that have been purported to explain the differences in ability. They include, for example, differences between the sexes in genes, hormones, cerebral dominance, rate of maturation, training, cultural practices, and personality structure. In the present discussion we will restrict our attention to the follow-ing sets of variables: genetic factors, hormones, task-relevant experiences, and sex-role expectations.

Biological Factors. In considering the question of whether sex differences in intellectual functioning might possibly be caused by genetic differences, most attention has concentrated on specific abilities, particularly spatial ability (and to a lesser extent, quantitative ability). Up until the mid-1970s it was widely believed that spatial ability has an underlying genetic sex-linkage. The work of several experimenters had suggested that a sex-linked recessive gene is in-volved in the transmission of spatial ability (for example, Bock & Kolakowski, 1973; Stafford, 1961). These researchers hypothesized that the gene for spatial ability is both recessive and located on the X chromosome. On the basis of this hypothesis, they predicted that a specific set of cross-sex correlations should exist between the spatial visualization scores of parents and offspring. For example, because a son receives his X chromosome from his mother and his Y chromosome from his father, assuming that the gene for spatial ability is carried only on the X chromosome, mother/son correlations should show up as positive and significant, whereas father/son correlations should approach zero and be nonsignificant. Especially relevant to the present topic is that, according to this hypothesis, females have a poorer chance of manifesting the spatial ability trait; that is, because the trait is recessive, they must receive the trait carrying X chromosome from both parents, whereas males, possessing only one X chromosome, manifest it as soon as it is present.

While the pattern of correlations discovered in the first few investigations of the hypothesis that spatial ability is sex-linked were generally consistent with the hypothesis, the hypothesis has been undermined by the disconfirma-tory results from a number of more recent studies, including some large-scale ones (Vandenberg & Kuse, 1979).

Whether research eventually confirms or disconfirms the hypothesis that spatial ability is sex-linked, we must emphasize the importance of recognizing that sex-linkage does not imply that a trait is completely missing in one sex and present in the other. If, for example, spatial ability is sex-linked, females who receive two trait-carrying recessive chromosomes will have the trait, whereas males who do not receive the recessive chromosome from their mothers will not have it. Moreover, one may display high spatial ability without possessing the X-linked gene. This is possible both because each of our abilities is influenced by more than a single gene and because experience and training play important roles in the development of any skill. In accord with the second point, there are some data to support the proposition that one reason for the superior spatial skill of males is they are more likely to engage in sensory motor activities that foster its development, including aiming games, model construction, and athletics (Sherman, 1974). Also consistent with the idea that the sex difference in spatial ability is due to an experiential deficit in females is the evidence that the spatial performance of females, but not males, improves after training on a visual spatial test and that training or practice tends to eliminate the sex difference in spatial ability (Connor, Serbin, & Schackman, 1977; see also Vandenberg & Kuse, 1979).

In addition, there is mounting, although complex, evidence of the role of hormonal factors in the development of sex differences in spatial ability and, perhaps, other special abilities (Petersen, 1976; Vandenberg & Kuse, 1979). For instance, in a sample of adolescents, Petersen (1976) related measures of spatial ability to physical manifestations of sex hormone influence (for example, pubic hair distribution, genital/breast size, and body shape). Interestingly, the "masculine" characteristic of superior spatial ability was most likely to occur in less physically masculine males and less physically feminine females.

Sex-Role Expectations. While biological endowment lays the foundation for the development of our abilities, our socialization experiences have an enormous impact on the extent of their development. We focus in particular on the sex-role expectations to which children are exposed. As a case in point, an analysis by Fennema and Sherman (1976) clearly brings forth the way that sex differences in mathematical performance are at least partially determined by sociocultural variables mediated through sex-role expectations.

Fennema and Sherman rely on their own data and the work of others to show that society associates mathematics more closely with the male role than with the female role. Parents apparently consider math more important and appropriate for boys than for girls. For example, parents buy more math-related games and toys for boys and generally provide boys with more encouragement in math. In turn, such sex-typed attitudes become instilled in children, with girls and boys perceiving math as a masculine school subject. Moreover, Fennema and Sherman observe that from the standpoint of role models, most math teachers are male. It is inevitable that the sex-typing of math differentially affects the attitudinal make-up of boys and girls. Fennema and Sherman cite data from several sources showing that girls (1) unrealistically downplay their ability to achieve in math, (2) lose interest in taking math courses as their school years progress, and (3) relative to boys, view math as having less personal relevance and usefulness.

The results of the aforementioned study by Hilton and Berglund (1974) represent an excellent illustration of how the gradual divergence between the sexes in math achievement parallels the emergence of sex-typed interests. Compared with girls, boys found math courses more interesting and less boring and were more likely to read science books and to believe that math courses would help them earn a living. The important point, however, is that at grade 7 the sex differences were negligible, whereas they were significant at grade 9 and more so at grade 11. Moreover, as the boys' interests in math (and science) increased relative to the girls', the sex differences in achievement increased. This is aptly demonstrated in Figure 10-2, which plots on one curve the difference between the boys and girls in math achievement and on a second, parallel curve the difference between them in the percentage who thought

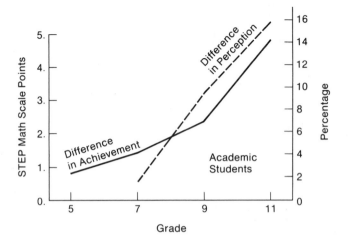

Figure 10-2. Trend lines for mean difference between the sexes in math achievement scores and perception of math as potentially useful. Difference in perception data were unavailable for grade 5 students. Adapted from "Sex Differences in Mathematics Achievement—A Longitudinal Study," by T. L. Hilton and G. W. Berglund, *Journal of Educational Research*, 1974, *67*, 231–237. Copyright 1974 by Heldref Publications. Used by permission.

math courses would help them earn a living. Thus, among students at grade 7 a small difference in favor of boys existed between both the math achievement scores (1.4 achievement points) and the percentage perceiving math as useful (1.7 percentage points), but by the time they reached grade 11 the differences were much larger (4.7 achievement points and 15.7 percentage points).

Needless to say, the impact of sex-role expectations is not restricted to the math/science constellation of abilities. For instance, Dwyer (1973) presents a remarkably similar analysis of girls' superiority in reading during the early school years. Dwyer cites two sets of findings that merit special attention. First, in her doctoral research (Dwyer, 1972), for boys and girls in grades 2-12, there was a direct relationship between reading achievement scores and sex-role standards about reading (the degree to which the child associated reading with his or her sex role). Second, several studies document the extent to which sex-role prescriptions concerning specific achievement areas are rooted in culture. Preston (1962) administered reading achievement tests to German and American fourth and sixth graders and found the common female advantage in the American sample. However, in the German sample, boys outperformed girls. This cross-cultural reversal also pertained to the incidence of reading retardation—it was more characteristic of German girls than boys. Similarly, D. D. Johnson (1973-1974) found that in England and Nigeria boys surpass girls in reading, whereas in the United States and Canada the opposite is the case.

ACHIEVEMENT

Educational Achievement

In the preceding section we found that there is little reason to believe that males and females differ significantly in overall ability. Strictly on the basis of this evidence, we would predict that in school there would not exist an overall sex difference in scholastic performance. In fact, however, what studies consistently show is that throughout their school years girls earn higher grades than boys, with the discrepancy narrowing (perhaps due to higher drop-out rates among males) toward the end of high school, but continuing into college (Garai & Scheinfeld, 1968; Grams & Waetjen, 1975). Furthermore, boys are less likely to be promoted from year to year (Tyler, 1965).

During the primary and secondary school years, then, female students are able to hold their own academically against their male counterparts and are at least as likely to graduate from high school. But what happens after graduation from high school? The answer is that females are less likely than males to continue with their education and attain advanced degrees. The tendency for more boys to further their education contrasts sharply with the evidence that girls have more positive attitudes about school than boys and value their education more highly than boys (P. W. Jackson, 1968; Lueptow, 1975). In one investigation, for instance, high school girls were more likely than high school boys to report that they would be very disappointed if something unexpected caused them to have to drop out of school; yet the boys were more likely to indicate an interest in going on to college after high school (Schneider & Coutts, 1977).

Alexander and Eckland (1974) have shown how sex differences can affect educational attainment. Using longitudinal data from a national sample, with academic ability and socioeconomic status controlled, female high school students received higher grades and possessed more favorable academic self-concepts than their male classmates. Yet, despite their academic advantage, females were less likely than males to be enrolled in a college preparatory curriculum and, notably, to achieve as much post-secondary school education. In addition, the high school grades and amount of education females attained were influenced more by family status factors than by academic ability, whereas for males the reverse was true. Similarly, Epstein and Bronzaft (1974) found that among college freshmen sex differences had a greater influence than ability on career and educational aspirations.

Occupational Achievement

In the vocational world, sex differences in achievement are even more striking. As Tyler (1965) has written, "One set of facts has persistently challenged the investigators. Why have women made so few major contributions to civilization? Why have women ostensibly achieved so much less than men?" (p.

240). For example, Tyler mentions that on J. Cattell's (1903) list of the world's most eminent people, only 32 out of 1000 were women, and only 55 out of 1030 people on Ellis's (1904) list of British geniuses were women. Moreover, little has changed since the beginning of the century. Women comprised only 4.5% of a 1965 sample of people listed in *Who's Who in America*, and this was down from the 1925 figure of 8.5% (Chafetz, 1974). Women are tremendously underrepresented in most of those occupations that offer the greatest financial benefits, social prestige, and self-actualization possibilities. In fact, even in the traditionally feminine domains, such as cooking, fashion design, and the arts, males, rather than females, typically excel.

Several explanations of the sex differences in vocational achievement have been proposed. We will examine the evidence regarding two of them: the variability hypothesis and the role of sociocultural factors.

Variability Hypothesis. Around the turn of the century, a popular explanation of the achievement disparity between the sexes was the variability hypothesis (Ellis, 1894). According to this hypothesis, males and females differ in the range of ability. Females were thought to cluster toward the center of the distribution of intelligence, whereas males deviated more toward both extremes. The potential social and political implications of the variability hypothesis are evident in several of its corollaries:

> (a) genius . . . is a peculiarly male trait; (b) men of genius naturally gravitate to positions of power and prestige (i.e., achieve eminence) by virtue of their talent; (c) an equally high ability level should not be expected of females; and (d) the education of women should, therefore, be consonant with their special talents and special place in society as wives and mothers [Shields, 1975, pp. 744–745].

The variability doctrine, for example, was invoked by those who argued for separate educational programs for the sexes.

To support the variability concept, its proponents pointed to the disproportionately large number of males who were in institutions for the mentally retarded and on the rolls of the eminent. However, most leading differential psychologists, including Anastasi (1958) and Tyler (1965), concluded that this evidence failed to hold up to careful scrutiny. For example, one common argument against the variability hypothesis was that sampling factors were able to account for the higher incidence of males in mental institutions. That is, because of the woman's social role (requiring less initiative and independence), upper-level female retardates have a better chance of getting by in society and avoiding institutionalization.

More recently, the view that greater male variability is a myth has been challenged by Lehrke (1972, 1978), who not only argues persuasively that males do show more variability in intelligence (he makes the strongest case for the low end of the intelligence continuum), but also argues that the greater variability may be caused by the fact that some aspects of intelligence are sex-linked. Lehrke demonstrates that if some genes for intelligence are carried on the

X chromosome, the result would be a situation in which males are disproportionately overrepresented at the extremes of the intelligence distribution. Not
surprisingly, Lehrke's thinking has not gone uncontested (see, for example,
Anastasi, 1972; Nance & Engel, 1972). In view of the controversial status of
the variability hypothesis, as well as its extremely profound social implications,
the most judicious decision at this time appears to be to await the outcome
of more exhaustive analyses of the issue.

Sociocultural Factors. Undoubtedly, the primary causes of the achievement discrepancy lie in the sociocultural forces of our society. The view of
women as an oppressed group has been advanced by writer upon writer both
in academic circles (for example, Andreas, 1971) and in popular literature (for
example, Greer, 1971). Perhaps the most conspicuous and commonly cited
examples of sexism in our society are to be found in the economic sphere,
wherein women must endure a wide range of inequities, including poor salaries,
low promotion rates, and unfair hiring practices (Huber, 1973). In the last few
years a considerable amount of evidence has accrued that supports the feminist
allegation that women aspiring for success in a number of professional areas
are subject to both covert and overt forms of prejudice and discrimination
(Lipman-Blumen & Tickamyer, 1975). For instance, O'Leary (1974) has delineated some of the attitudinal barriers that may interfere with a woman's
chances for promotion into managerial positions. One is the male managerial
model, which equates optimal managerial behavior with male sex-role behavior
and on the basis of which women are judged. A second, related barrier involves
managerial attitudes toward women. It is apparent that many men in managerial positions (that is, potential promoters) hold the opinion that men shun
female bosses and that, relative to men, women are less dependable, less able
to handle emergencies, and less suited temperamentally for management.

The discriminatory attitudes women face in the world of work essentially
mirror the society's sex-role expectations. We have already alluded to the pervasiveness of sex-role stereotypes in our culture (Broverman et al., 1972). Recall
that the traits typically ascribed to females entail a warmth/expressiveness
cluster. On the other hand, males are described by a competency cluster, consisting of such attributes as independence, objectivity, skill in business, self-confidence, ambition, and ease in decision making. Thus, the traits and behaviors
we learn to associate with males and to disassociate with females are the very
ones thought to be conducive to educational and, particularly, vocational
success. Moreover, it appears that people indeed do subscribe to stereotyped
notions of greater male competence when they evaluate the performance of
the sexes. In two studies university students of both sexes were asked to rate
journal articles on their value, scholarliness, writing style, competence, and
so forth (Bem & Bem, 1971; P. H. Goldberg, 1968). Articles attributed to male
authors received more favorable evaluations by both sexes than identical articles attributed to female authors.

Analyses of the content of television programs, children's literature, adver-
tisements, our language, popular music, educational achievement tests, and

curricula have documented how comprehensively our society promotes sex-role stereotyping and sex discrimination (for example, Hillman, 1974; Saario, Jacklin, & Tittle, 1973). For instance, on TV women are portrayed in a smaller variety of roles than men and tend to be depicted as deferent and unproductive, whereas men are depicted as aggressive and constructive; also, on TV fewer working women are married than in actual life, and those who do work have stereotyped traditional jobs and are more likely to have unsuccessful marriages than nonworking women (Kaniuga, Scott, & Gade, 1974; Manes & Melnyk, 1974; Sternglanz & Serbin, 1974).

In light of the pervasiveness of these sex-role stereotypes, it is not surprising that females and males begin to conform to their social sex roles at a very early age. Boys and girls as young as 2-3 years show sex-typed toy and activity preferences; for example, boys play with blocks, guns, and trucks, whereas girls prefer activities involving dolls, artwork, and sewing (Fagot & Patterson, 1969; Fein, Johnson, Kosson, Stork, & Wasserman, 1975).

With respect to occupational and educational goals, children show a similar sex-typed pattern. As possible future jobs boys typically choose traditional male occupations (for example, truck driver and lawyer), and girls pick traditional female occupations (for example, nurse and social worker) (Schlossberg & Goodman, 1972; Siegel, 1973). Of considerable significance is that the range or number of jobs considered by girls is substantially smaller than that for boys (Siegel, 1973). Children are much more likely to believe women should be excluded from men's jobs than vice versa (Schlossberg & Goodman, 1972) and girls show an avoidance of high-prestige occupations (Barnett, 1975). Also, a related and especially important finding is that young girls perform better on a game that is described as being for girls, whereas boys perform better when the same game is described as being for boys (Montemayor, 1974).

We also find that as girls grow older their commitment to future education gradually declines (Rand & Miller, 1972). In fact, Bardwick (1971) proposes that, while discrimination in the marketplace undoubtedly interferes with the career strivings of many working women, the major reason for the lack of occupational accomplishment of women in general is a reluctance to take on a long-term professional commitment. Certainly underlying this reluctance is the female's acceptance of social sex-role prescriptions that stress the adoption of the homemaker/mother role over all other roles.

Taking a strong stand on this matter, Bem and Bem (1971, 1973) contend that American sex-role ideology is primarily responsible for the "homogenization" of women, which involves a subversion of their individuality and capacity for self-fulfillment. To support their argument, Bem and Bem have developed a simple test. They merely ask you to try to predict what a newborn baby girl and newborn baby boy will be doing in 25 years. If you take their test you probably will discover that you feel much more confident about predicting a girl's future than a boy's—a good bet is that the girl will be a homemaker and/or employed in a narrow range of jobs including teaching, nursing, and secretarial work. Furthermore, married women who do choose to work, more so than their working husbands, are apt to experience greater role conflict emanating from the competing demands associated with their dual role responsibilities (O'Leary, 1974).

In sum, we see that, in the post-high school world, men clearly surpass women with respect to both educational and vocational attainment. The inferior achievement of women is mediated by external attitudinal barriers inherent in the sex-role ideology of our society as well as by socialization pressures that compel a woman to accept the self-limiting aspects of her sex role, including lower career aspirations and a preoccupation with her familial obligations.

Before concluding our examination of sex differences in achievement, we should mention that recent years have witnessed some changes in the educational and vocational status of women in American society (Van Dusen & Sheldon, 1976). The percentage of women continuing their education beyond high school is rapidly approaching that of men, and women are beginning to compete for positions that traditionally have been "reserved" for men. For instance, in 1960 women accounted for 4% and 6% of the enrollment in law and medical schools, respectively, whereas in 1974 the corresponding figures were 19% and 18%. Yet, despite such gains, it is likely that the achievement gap will persist well into the future.

> However, despite all these changes, nowhere is it suggested that the pattern of female occupational choices, earnings, or job mobility will approximate that of men, and certainly not in the near future. The reasons have nothing to do with women's skills or aspirations. . . . The reasons have everything to do with the life cycle concerns. . . . Although marital status and parental responsibilities are likely to become less salient in women's career choices, women will continue to bear the major responsibility for children, and it is their career that will continue to be marked by the need to accommodate both parental and occupational roles [Van Dusen & Sheldon, 1976, p. 114].

MOTIVATIONAL AND PERSONALITY ATTRIBUTES

We now will move on to a consideration of sex differences in motivational and personality characteristics. Our review will begin by examining possible differences in the achievement orientation of males and females that may further account for the discrepancy in their educational and vocational attainment. Then we will consider possible sex differences in affiliation orientation and the hypothesis that females are more person oriented than males whereas males are more task oriented than females. Finally, we will take up such potentially differentiating factors as dependency, nurturance, cooperation/competition, aggression, susceptibility to social influence, and psychological adjustment.

Achievement Orientation

Achievement Motivation. For early workers interested in the psychology of sex differences achievement motivation proved to be a particularly perplexing topic. The crux of the problem was that while consistent results were found when projective measures of achievement motivation were used with males, they seldom could be replicated with females. For instance, achievement-motivation scores seemed to predict achievement-related behaviors (for example, effort on laboratory tasks and academic achievement) in males but not females (Klinger, 1966). Also, when given achievement-oriented instructions (the subjects were told their leadership capacity and intelligence were being evaluated), males responded with an increase in the number of achievement themes (McClelland, Atkinson, Clark, & Lowell, 1953), whereas females displayed the same levels of achievement imagery to both achievement-oriented and neutral instructions (Veroff, Wilcox, & Atkinson, 1953). Females, however, did show a tendency to increase their achievement-motivation scores under conditions that aroused concern about their degree of social acceptability, a finding that led McClelland and associates (1953) to suggest that the achievement motive is central to males and the affiliative motive is central to females.

Thus, discouraged by the ambiguous and unreliable research findings with females and the evidence suggesting that for females affiliative concerns are more salient than achievement concerns, early researchers studied achievement motivation in its "pure form" by concentrating virtually all of their effort on male subjects. For instance, in the 873-page *Motives in Fantasy, Action, and Society* (Atkinson, 1958), which covered the literature on the achievement motive and related motives, research on females was relegated to a single footnote. We should add that the imbalance appears to have been reversed in the 1970s; as Deaux (1976) points out, research on achievement behavior in females is at the forefront of the "feminist boom period."

Do males and females differ in their scores on standard measures of achievement motivation? The failure of females in the McClelland and associates (1953) experiment to respond in the achievement-arousal condition with increased achievement imagery led some early writers, as well as some contemporary ones, to conclude that females have lower achievement motivation than males. However, it should be recognized that in that study the females' achievement motivation scores were higher than those of the males under neutral instructions, and the achievement arousal merely elevated the males' scores to the level of the females. Apparently, there have been relatively few direct sex comparisons employing projective measures—for example, TAT and Test of Insight (French, 1958). What evidence there is gives us little reason to believe that one sex is more achievement motivated than the other (Maccoby & Jacklin, 1974; Oetzel, 1966). Similarly, the sexes do not tend to score differently on questionnaire measures of achievement motivation (for example, D. N. Jackson, 1967; Sampson & Hancock, 1967), which incidentally are better predictors of academic achievement than projective measures (Lavin, 1965) and predict achievement for males as well as females (Harper, 1975; Schneider & Green, 1977).

Self-Confidence about Achievement. While males and females may not differ in measured achievement motivation, there is a difference in at least one aspect of their achievement orientations—from school age through adulthood, males tend to express more self-confidence, a greater expectancy of success, in their approach to many performance situations. In the typical study, subjects are given a description of a task and then asked to estimate how well they will perform on it. In a majority of studies, men and boys predict they will do better than women and girls predict they will do regarding a variety of performance measures, including solving anagrams, judging the timing of light flashes, earning grades in school, helping in an emergency, and working in a variety of professions (Maccoby & Jacklin, 1974; J. E. Parsons, Ruble, Hodges, & Small, 1976).

The existence of low self-confidence most assuredly is a matter of considerable concern because it has been tied directly to decrements in both a person's initiative and performance (Lenney, 1977). However, a review by Lenney (1977) indicates that, while males usually express more confidence than females, such is not always the case. Lenney delineated three situational variables that influence whether or not sex differences in self-confidence occur: (1) On tasks defined as female appropriate (that is, on which females are expected to do well, such as ones measuring social skills) as opposed to male appropriate, women are likely to express as much, if not more, self-confidence than men. (2) Women are less self-confident than men if given minimal or ambiguous feedback about their abilities or performances, whereas a sex difference is unlikely to occur if explicit feedback is provided. Thus, college women may be less confident than college men about passing the first exam in a course but not necessarily less confident about passing the final exam (that is, after having received feedback from the instructor about their performance on earlier course assignments and exams). (3) The self-confidence of women is lower than that of men if they are aware that their performance may be evaluated or compared with that of others (for example, under competitive conditions or when informed of some standard of performance), but not lower when such social cues are minimized.

How do we interpret the generally lower expectancies of females? We suggest that it is likely that the differential expectations are at least partially a result of the incorporation of sex-role definitions of greater masculine competence. Consistent with this interpretation is the previously noted evidence that females, as well as males, are apt to evaluate the performance of females less favorably than that of males. Furthermore, males, even during the early school years, are more likely than females to believe they have performed well once a job is done (Deaux, 1976; J. E. Parsons et al., 1976). It seems that, in particular, females are more likely than males to disparage their performance after they have done poorly. Moreover, several studies have involved asking people to provide reasons for their success or failure on a given task (Deaux, 1976). Men tend to attribute a successful performance to their ability, whereas women attribute it to luck. When they fail, women are more likely than men to suggest lack of ability as the cause. Thus it appears that women tend to disclaim responsibility for favorable outcomes and assume responsibility for unfavorable outcomes.

The above findings may be used to support two, not necessarily incompatible, interpretations of male/female differences in achievement orientation. First, Maccoby and Jacklin (1974) suggest that the greater self-confidence of males supports the view that males experience greater feelings of power and control over the events in their lives, including their achievement endeavors. Also consistent with this view is the evidence that among adults, although not necessarily younger people, males tend to score more toward the internal end of locus of control scales than females and that boys and men rate themselves higher on power and dominance than do girls and women (Maccoby & Jacklin, 1974; Palmore & Luikart, 1972). Maccoby and Jacklin suggest the possibility that the females' relatively low feelings of control and potency may partially account for their inferior achievement in the post-school world. Second, Stein and Bailey (1973) affirm that many of the above findings are consistent with the evidence that, relative to males, females suffer more anxiety about the possibility of failure. From an early age on, girls generally score higher on questionnaire measures of test anxiety (Maccoby & Jacklin, 1974; Stein & Bailey, 1973).

Not only do females report more anxiety in test situations than males, but many studies indicate that they manifest a higher degree of generalized anxiety (Maccoby & Jacklin, 1974; Oetzel, 1966). The incidence of anxiety in females has served as a focal point for many researchers trying to come to grips with sex differences in achievement behavior. The basic thesis is that, because of the obligations attached to their social sex role, females in our society are subject to a number of potentially anxiety-arousing conflicts. O'Leary (1974) asserts that "women are caught in a double bind, unable to optimally fulfill the role requirements for the more socially desirable achieving individual and those for the ideal woman simultaneously" (p. 815). And, Hyde and Rosenberg (1976) say:

> Certainly the origin of the *double-bind* for females, probably the single most important influence on female personality, lies in this conflict between achievement and femininity. . . . The adolescent girl is caught in a classic double-bind situation, in which she wants . . . both to be feminine and to achieve, but the two are perceived as being incompatible. Certainly here would appear to be the origins of much of the ambivalence and conflict in female personality, the adolescent girl finding it difficult to combine, because of imposed cultural contingencies, being a worthwhile individual and a proper female [p. 67].

Fear of Success. A provocative thesis of how females and males differ in achievement orientation has been advanced by Horner (1968, 1972), who proposes that many females are motivated to avoid success. Horner suggests that females manifest more anxiety than males in many achievement situations, not only because of the threat of failure, but because they are afraid of the many negative consequences potentially attached to success. Such negative consequences include both a feeling of lessened femininity and the possibility of social rejection, particularly by men. Horner says that men, too, can fear success, but the motive is more likely to characterize women because of the different socialization pressures males and females experience. She suggests that recognition of the operation of the motive to avoid success should help to resolve many of the aforementioned problems related to sex differences in achievement motivation because most of the research is based on the assumption that people are motivated to approach success.

In order to measure the motive to avoid success, Horner asked university students to write stories based on the following verbal lead: "After first-term finals, Anne (John) finds herself (himself) at the top of her (his) medical school class." Females responded to the Anne cue and males to the John cue. Assuming that people project their own feelings into such stories, Horner scored the stories for fear-of-success imagery. Fear of success is considered present if Anne (John), for example, is portrayed as being unhappy about the success, tries to deny the success, or experiences (or anticipates) unfavorable consequences because of success, such as losing friends and dating partners. The stories of 62% of the women, but only 9% of the men, were scored as manifesting fear-of-success imagery. Horner hypothesized that the motive to avoid success is most likely to be aroused (and thus adversely influence performance) in achievement-oriented situations, particularly those involving competition with males. In accord with her hypothesis, she found that high fear-of-success females showed a performance decrement when they performed in a mixed-sex competitive situation, whereas low fear-of-success females performed better in a competitive situation than when alone.

Horner's work on fear of success was met with considerable enthusiasm and was followed by a plethora of experiments aimed at testing and/or expanding her thinking. Unfortunately, the results of this research have not been as encouraging as Horner's original study promised. A number of problems associated with either the concept of fear of success or the measurement of it have been uncovered (Condry & Dyer, 1976; Zuckerman & Wheeler, 1975). One is that, because fear of success is a learned disposition, it should be shown to increase with age. The data do not show such an increase. A second problem, and one particularly damaging to Horner's view, is that males frequently respond to the John cue with more fear-of-success imagery than that with which females respond to the Anne cue. Serious difficulties also reside in the apparent low reliability of the fear-of-success measure and most critically its questionable predictive validity (for example, regarding the performance of high and low fear-of-success females when in competitive versus noncompetitive situations with males). Also, scores on Horner's fear-of-success measure do not correlate significantly with career aspirations and other theoretically related variables.

In view of such limitations, it certainly is appropriate to question the idea that Horner's projective measure taps a motive, an enduring and stable personality trait, and that such a motive primarily characterizes females. A more plausible interpretation is that the negative stories to the Anne cue reflect a social awareness that negative consequence can result when females deviate from sex-role appropriate behavior (Condry & Dyer, 1976). According to this view, successful competition with males in a traditionally male achievement area, such as medicine, is perceived as antithetical to the female role, and consequently such behavior invites negative social sanctions. Consistent with this social awareness interpretation, the results of several studies show that *both* sexes write more fear-of-success stories to the Anne cue than to the John cue. Condry and Dyer (1976) suggest that, while not necessarily possessing an underlying motive to avoid success, the achievement behavior of many females may be seriously inhibited as a result of a realistic recognition of the social penalties that may accompany successful achievement. They further posit that the most severe penalties emanate from males rather than other females. Support for this idea stems from evidence such as that males seem to write more negative stories to the Anne cue than do females (Zuckerman & Wheeler, 1975), and males evaluate successful females (for example, in law school) less favorably than do females (Condry & Dyer, 1976).

We should recognize that males likewise are susceptible to negative consequences for deviation from the culturally defined male role. This is apparent in a study by Cherry and Deaux (1975) who found that more males wrote fear-of-success stories when John was described as being at the top of his nursing school class than at the top of his medical school class. Moreover, as we would expect, females wrote fewer negative stories when Anne excelled in nursing school than in medical school.

These data seem to indicate that, depending on the sex-appropriateness of the circumstances, both males and females recognize that negative consequences may follow success and, therefore, may express anxiety over potential success. However, it also is likely that females may be at a distinct disadvantage in terms of the number (and status value) of the achievement areas in which female success is considered more appropriate than male success.

In conclusion, while the early work on fear of success has been disappointing, it has helped to generate an intensive examination of the factors underlying the achievement behaviors of the sexes. As Condry and Dyer (1976) say,

> ... although there may be conflicting evidence concerning the validity of Horner's FOS [fear of success] measure and its usefulness in the achievement motivation research, a careful analysis is obviously needed of attitudes toward sex roles and how these attitudes affect people's interpersonal interactions. Horner's concept seems not to represent a fear of success but rather a fear of negative consequences incumbent upon deviating from traditional sex-role standards in *certain situations* [p. 75].

Sex-Role Attitudes. In the above passage Condry and Dyer stress the possible influence of sex-role attitudes on achievement behavior. It certainly is reasonable to expect that females who have traditional sex-role attitudes (they accept the traditional female sex role—for example, let one's husband make the major decisions) would be most inclined to conform to cultural sex-role standards, which would serve to channel their achievement strivings into "female appropriate" areas of endeavor and to minimize the expression of stereotypically male achievement characteristics (for example, assertiveness and competitiveness). Research has begun to document the importance of sex-role attitudes. For instance, Peplau (1976) found that college females with traditional sex-role attitudes had lower career aspirations than females with more liberal sex-role attitudes. Moreover, females with nontraditional sex-role attitudes performed better on a task when competing against a boyfriend than when working as a team with their boyfriends; on the other hand, the traditional females performed better when not in competition with a boyfriend. In fact, in this study, whereas sex-role attitudes were consistently related to achievement behavior, fear of success was not. Thus, it appears that we can improve our ability to understand and predict achievement behavior of females (and males) if we have information about their attitudes and personal conceptions of appropriate sex-role behavior.

The Task-versus-Person Orientation Hypothesis. We want to take a look at a few other positions regarding sex differences in achievement orientation. One view, proposed by Hoffman (1972) and others (for example, Crandall, 1964), centers on the idea that, while males are motivated primarily by their achievement needs, for females affiliation needs are more important. Female achievement behavior is geared toward attaining social approval, whereas males strive for mastery and the attainment of standards of excellence.

A second view of sex differences in achievement behavior, offered by Stein and Bailey (1973), holds that males and females have similar levels of achievement motivation, but their achievement strivings are directed toward different goals. Females strive for achievement in areas consistent with their social sex role; in particular, they concentrate on succeeding in interpersonal relations. Males, on the other hand, are supposed to stress achievement on impersonal tasks. This interpretation resembles the aforementioned view of Hoffman in that according to both viewpoints females are conceived as being particularly concerned with social relations. However, Stein and Bailey maintain that it is one's achievement motivation that is being satisfied, whereas for Hoffman, the emphasis is on satisfying one's needs for affiliation and social approval.

At the risk of oversimplification, we will follow Maccoby and Jacklin's (1974) lead and suggest that the views of Stein and Bailey (1973) and Hoffman (1972) may be reduced to the idea that females are person oriented and males are task oriented. Although it is not within the scope of this chapter to provide an in-depth evaluation of the tenability of this distinction, in this and subsequent sections of this chapter, we will examine some of the relevant evidence on which we may begin to formulate an opinion.

Are females less task oriented than males? In trying to answer this question we may look at the research in which males and females are compared on their willingness to devote time to the completion or solution of a task or to return to an unfinished task. The vast majority of these studies indicate that females show at least as much task persistence and involvement as males (Maccoby & Jacklin, 1974; Oetzel, 1966). Therefore, the sex-linked task-versus-person orientation distinction seems to break down when we look at the research on task persistence. However, the possibility remains that males and females differ with respect to other indexes of task orientation. Furthermore, the absence of a sex difference on task orientation would not preclude the existence of a difference in social orientation. We will return to the task orientation versus person orientation issue after we have had a chance to consider additional evidence concerning the respective orientations of the sexes.

Self-Presentation Styles and Task-Appropriateness. Before concluding our discussion of achievement orientation, let us consider a two-part conceptual analysis, proposed by Deaux (1977), that should help facilitate our organization and understanding of sex differences in achievement behavior, as well as other social behaviors. First, Deaux suggests that males and females differ in their self-presentation styles (or strategies). The basic male strategy entails a status-assertive mode of presenting oneself in which strength, dominance, and competence are communicated. Females employ an affiliative strategy wherein the objective is to neutralize status, establish relationships with others, and present oneself as typical in ability and performance. The obvious correspondence between the presentation styles and the social sex-role stereotypes is acknowledged by Deaux, who suggests that the styles are reinforced by socialization practices. Second, Deaux stresses the importance of sex-linked task characteristics. She maintains that the way the sexes behave is greatly influenced by whether the task is more familiar to or appropriate for males or females.

Deaux's analysis is confirmed by many of the findings we have considered. Regarding self-presentation styles, in contrast to females, males express greater feelings of power and control, have more positive expectancies about their performances, evaluate their performances more favorably, and are more likely to attribute their successes to their ability and their failures to external causes. The importance of the sex-appropriateness of the situation has been aptly illustrated in several places, including, for instance, the study that showed the performance of boys and girls varied depending on whether a game was described as for boys or for girls (Montemayor, 1974). Another excellent example is found in the as yet unmentioned work of Stein (Stein, 1971; Stein, Pohly, & Mueller, 1971). In one study, Stein (1971) had sixth and ninth graders rate certain achievement areas according to whether they were more appropriate to boys or girls. Regarding areas deemed as male appropriate (for example, mechanical and athletic), compared with girls, boys generally had higher attainment values (how important they felt it is to be competent in the area) and higher personal standards of performance. A similar pattern was found for girls in the female-appropriate areas (for example, artistic and social).

A brief review of the section on achievement orientation is in order. Whereas males and females tend not to differ on measures of achievement motivation, differences on a number of indexes (for example, expectancies of success and evaluation of own performance) suggest that females are less self-confident about their abilities to achieve. The evidence is against the idea that a motive to avoid success is an important attribute that distinguishes females from males. However, members of both sexes seem to be cognizant of social penalties that may accompany successful achievement in culturally defined sex-inappropriate areas of endeavor. Moreover, the extent to which people have incorporated traditional sex-role attitudes may play an important part in how their achievement strivings are channeled. The hypothesis that males are more task oriented than females and females more person oriented than males has been proposed, and relevant evidence will be examined in the remainder of the chapter. Last, Deaux (1977) has suggested that our understanding of sex differences will be enhanced by recognizing (1) that males tend to manifest a status-assertive self-presentation style, whereas females display a more affiliative style, and (2) that whether males and females manifest behavioral differences or not depends largely on the degree to which the task (or situation) is sex linked.

Affiliative Orientation

We often tend to think that females are the more affiliative, more sociable sex. This idea was suggested in the section on achievement orientation when we entertained the hypothesis that females are person oriented and males are task oriented. The greater sociability of females has been the conviction of many writers interested in the psychology of sex differences (for example, Garai & Scheinfeld, 1968; Hutt, 1972). Let us consider the evidence. Under affiliation orientation we will consider several areas of behavior, including self-report indications of affiliativeness, how infants respond to social stimuli, the quantitative and qualitative nature of social interaction, social sensitivity (in which we differentiate between social insight and empathy), and nonverbal behavior.

Self-Report Indicators of Affiliativeness. If we ask people about how much they value their interpersonal relationships, about their feelings for others and their interest in socializing with others, females tend to give more "affiliative" answers. Females score higher on both projective and questionnaire measures of affiliation motivation, evaluate others more favorably, and express greater liking for them (Maccoby & Jacklin, 1974; Oetzel, 1966). Furthermore, the expression of greater liking by females extends to romantic relationships (Dion & Dion, 1973, 1975). For instance, among university students females are more likely than males to report having been in love with a member of the opposite sex and to describe their romantic experiences as more rewarding; they also report feeling greater liking, love, and trust toward their romantic partners.

Infant Orientations to Social Stimuli. Does the more positive social orientation of females reflected in self-report measures manifest itself in overt behavior? Probably the earliest indication of whether or not one sex is more strongly socially oriented than the other is how infants react to social stimuli. For example, we can compare baby girls and boys on how long they look at a live or representational human face or how much their heartbeats decelerate or their heads turn in response to the sound of a human voice. In the extensive literature on this topic there is little evidence that either sex during the first year or two of life consistently shows more interest in social stimuli than the other (Maccoby & Jacklin, 1974).

Social Interaction. Similarly, Maccoby and Jacklin's (1974) review shows that during early childhood girls and boys are equally friendly in their interactions with nonfamily adults, although there is an indication that little girls learn a fear response to strangers earlier than little boys. Interestingly, when we consider direct interaction with peers, Maccoby and Jacklin's survey shows that, if anything, the edge in sociability favors boys. For example, McIntyre (1972) found that preschool boys engaged in more verbal and nonverbal activity with their peers. Feshbach and Sones (1971) had same-sex pairs of friends (12 to 13 years) work together on the solution of social problems, and then they were joined by a slightly younger newcomer. Girls took longer to speak to the newcomer, were less likely to incorporate the newcomer's ideas, and evaluated the newcomer less favorably.

Thus a somewhat puzzling pattern emerges. On the one hand, observational studies indicate that boys engage in more positive social interaction with their peers; on the other hand, girls express more positive feelings about others and seem more concerned about their social relations. How can this apparent discrepancy be reconciled? The observational studies deal primarily with young subjects (up to early adolescence), whereas most of the self-report studies involved older subjects. It is possible that observational research with older subjects would reveal that, in accordance with the evidence from self-report measures, females are more socially active than males. However, contrary to this, one of us recently had several thousand high school students estimate the number of hours they spend socializing with friends after school and found no significant sex difference (Schneider & Coutts, 1976).

Also, it is possible that females feel more affiliative than males but that social role prescriptions place greater restrictions on their autonomous social activity. This second possibility is consistent with some evidence suggesting that there may be both quantitative and qualitative differences in the friendship patterns of boys and girls. What several investigations have found is that by primary school boys play in larger groups than do girls (Laosa & Brophy, 1972; Waldrop & Halverson, 1975). Girls seem to engage in "intensive" peer relationships, associating with one or two best friends, whereas boys tend to be involved in "extensive" relationships, playing with a larger number of companions.

Several reasons for boys playing with more friends may be suggested. For instance, girls may be prohibited, for protective purposes, from roaming far afield, and this may restrict the number of children with whom they can play. Differential play interests also may be a factor. Boys' games (for example, football, baseball, and cowboys) typically require more participants than girls' games (for example, dolls, house, and hopscotch).

Moreover, it is likely that the *quality* of peer relations is influenced by the different kinds of activity in which the sexes engage and by the sheer number of playmates. Maccoby and Jacklin (1974) propose that interpersonal attraction is a more important factor in the companionship choices of girls. For boys, the game (for example, team sports) needs participants and its enactment takes precedence over the likeability of one's playmates. Moreover, by their very nature (the numbers involved and their action orientation), boys' games militate against the development of intimacy and interpersonal involvement, two factors likely to characterize the intensive two-person or three-person relationships of girls. In accord with this notion of greater intimacy in female peer groups, Littlefield (1974), with ninth graders, and Rivenbark (1971), with 9- to 17-year-olds, found females reported they disclose more personal information to their female friends than do males to their male friends.

With respect to adulthood, the results of many investigations also indicate a higher propensity for self-disclosure among females than males (Cozby, 1973). In addition, an investigation by Booth (1972) indicates that there is a general correspondence between the nature of children's friendship relations and those of adults. Booth interviewed 800 people who were at least 45 years old. While men and women reported having a similar number of close friends, several indicators suggested that the friendship relations of the women were affectively stronger (more intensive) than those of the men. The women saw their friends more frequently, engaged in more spontaneous activities with them, and were more inclined to confide in them regarding personal difficulties. Also, women maintained more kinship ties than men.

Social Sensitivity. Is there any evidence of greater social sensitivity among females? Before considering this question, let us distinguish between two aspects of social sensitivity: social insight and empathy. A person with social insight has the ability to accurately perceive how other people feel. A person with empathy has the capacity to vicariously experience how others feel.

One procedure for measuring *social insight* has been devised by Feshbach and Roe (1968). A child is shown a sequence of slides, accompanied by narrative material, that depicts children in different affective states (for example, happiness and anger). Social insight is measured by asking the child to describe the feelings of the central child in each sequence. When this technique is used with young children (4 to 7 years), boys and girls do not differ in social insight (Feshbach & Roe, 1968; Hoffman & Levine, 1976).

On the other hand, Hall (1978) came to a different conclusion upon reviewing 75 studies that compared the abilities of males and females to accurately judge the emotions or states communicated by nonverbal cues. The stimuli involved face, body, or vocal cues (shown separately or in combination) and were presented by a variety of media (for example, photos, films, and electronically filtered speech). Hall did not consider the results of studies whose procedures included informative verbal cues among the stimuli to be judged; thus, because the Feshbach and Roe procedure involves the use of accompanying narrative material, studies employing it were omitted. Hall found that the proportion of studies showing a female advantage in judging nonverbal cues exceeded that which would be expected by chance—of those 61 studies for which the direction of the difference was known (some merely reported nonsignificance), 84% favored females. The sex difference pertained to both children and adults. We should also allude to one related set of findings. Research on observational accuracy suggests that females have a slight edge in accuracy when it comes to observing others—for example, as when asked to describe the appearance, conversation, or actions of someone whom they recently encountered (Mazanec & McCall, 1975).

The Feshbach and Roe (1968) procedure also has been used to measure the *empathy* aspect of social sensitivity. To measure empathy the child is merely asked to describe how he or she personally feels after viewing each slide story sequence. Research with this technique shows that young girls score higher on empathy than young boys (Feshbach & Roe, 1968; Hoffman & Levine, 1976). There is a paucity of additional research bearing on the question of sex differences in empathy, although college females apparently score higher on questionnaire measures of empathy (Mehrabian & Epstein, 1972). The lack of research is particularly unfortunate because it is not entirely clear whether the results using the Feshbach and Roe technique do, in fact, reflect a sex difference in empathy or merely the greater willingness of females to express their feelings.

The possibility of sex differences in emotional expressiveness actually was suggested by Feshbach and Roe (1968) and receives support from the work of Zaidel and Mehrabian (1969) and Buck and his coworkers (Buck, Miller, & Caul, 1974). This research indicates that adult females are superior in giving nonverbal expression to their feelings. For instance, in a cleverly designed study with college students, Buck and associates (1974) had one subject (the sender) view slides designed to elicit an emotional reaction. A second subject (the observer), who could not see the slides, had to categorize the emotional response of the first subject merely by observing the subject's facial reaction. In contrast to male senders, female senders more effectively communicated their emotions to their observers and were rated by the experimenter as being more facially expressive.

Buck and his colleagues also measured changes in their subjects' skin conductance and heart rate. There was a tendency for males to be internalizers and females externalizers with respect to their reactions to emotion-arousing slides. An internalizer is one who shows a strong physiological response (for example, change in skin conductance) but little overt emotional expression; an externalizer is low in physiological response but high in overt emotional expression. Buck and associates interpret their finding as consistent with the view that in our culture males are encouraged more than females to suppress the expression of their emotions. Subsequent research by Buck (1977) is consistent with the idea that the sex difference in emotional expressiveness only emerges as the result of a long process of social learning. Among preschoolers there is little evidence of sex differences in the communication of emotions and the tendency for males to be internalizers and females externalizers; moreover, overt emotional expressiveness declines with age (from age 4 to 6) in boys, but not in girls.

In sum, the research on social sensitivity suggests that females are superior to males on measures of social insight involving the recognition of affect as communicated by nonverbal cues and also that females may be better social observers than males. Since research has demonstrated that sensitivity to non-verbal cues is related positively to several indexes of individual competence, including those reflecting maturity, teaching ability, and clinical ability (Hall, 1978), the findings regarding social insight certainly seem to have significant interpersonal implications for the sexes. With respect to empathy, we cannot safely say that females are more empathic than males, because existing measures do not differentiate between what people feel and what they say they feel or the overt manifestation of their feelings. It does appear that as they grow into adulthood females become more expressive nonverbally than males.

Nonverbal Behavior. In addition to their overt emotionality, males and females differ in other aspects of nonverbal behavior, and these differences give us further insight into the respective orientations of the sexes. The existence of sex differences in patterns of nonverbal behavior is widely recognized (Deaux, 1976; Ickes & Barnes, 1977; Mehrabian, 1972). For instance, compared with males, females generally engage in more eye contact, prefer to interact at closer distances, and face their coactors more directly. It appears that the differences in nonverbal behavior are apt to characterize children as well as adults, although there is some evidence that, at least for visual behavior (Russo, 1975) and interpersonal distance (Tennis & Dabbs, 1975), the size of the discrepancy increases from childhood to adulthood.

The female pattern of nonverbal behavior—involving more intimate distances, both spatially and visually—has been interpreted as reflecting greater affiliativeness, interpersonal involvement, and warmth than the male pattern of nonverbal behavior (Frieze & Ramsey, 1976; Ickes & Barnes, 1977). On the other hand, males may be perceived as displaying by their nonverbal cues more status and dominance (Frieze & Ramsey, 1976). For example, males require more physical space (territory) than females, which frequently is a concomitant of high status and dominance in primates, including humans. While it does seem to be true that females are nonverbally more affiliative than males, we cannot be sure about how much their affiliativeness reflects a genuine desire to affiliate and to be emotionally involved with others and how much it reflects an outward conformity to societal sex-role expectations, which permit greater physical closeness among females than males.

We also want to mention some other research on interpersonal distance that is not only relevant to our discussion but also interesting in its own right. Several experiments have indicated that men and women respond quite differently to the experience of being in a crowded situation with strangers of the same sex. Males, as we might expect, react more negatively to a crowded situation than an uncrowded one; females, however, seem to prefer the more crowded context (for example, Freedman, Levy, Buchanan, & Price, 1972; Ross, Layton, Erickson, & Schopler, 1973). For example, in a mock jury experiment, Freedman and his colleagues placed six to ten subjects in either a small or relatively large room. The subjects had to listen to tape recorded condensations of courtroom cases (for example, a rape and a hit-and-run accident), give a verdict of guilty or not guilty, and decide the severity of the sentence if the defendant was found guilty. The groups of women responded more positively in the crowded situation than in the uncrowded situation: they gave less severe sentences, reported that they liked each other more, and found each other more interesting and the experimental session more interesting and pleasant. The men, on the other hand, showed the opposite pattern of behavior, reacting more positively under the less crowded conditions. In a second study, Freedman and associates found that males were more competitive when crowded than not crowded, whereas females were more competitive when uncrowded than crowded.

Several attempts have been made to explain the interaction between sex and crowding. One of the more promising ones is Freedman's (1975) hypothesis that crowding intensifies a person's typical reaction to a situation. That is, according to Freedman, the effects of crowding are not inevitably bad. Rather if one normally associates positive feelings with a given situation (for example, a cocktail party) then crowding may serve to enhance those positive feelings. To account for the experimental findings Freedman suggests that the men in these experiments may have perceived the experimental interaction in competitive terms and reacted to the other males with some degree of suspiciousness, defensiveness, and/or mild dislike. On the other hand, the females probably were less threatened by the situation and anticipated a more friendly and interesting interaction. Thus, according to the theory, the generally negative responses of the males and the generally positive responses of the females were accentuated under the high density condition.[5]

As indicated, Freedman (1975) argues that sex differences in proxemic orientation may be accounted for in terms of the female's greater affiliativeness and the male's greater competitiveness. As we have seen, according to a number of indicators, females do seem to be the more affiliative sex. Relative to males, females give more affiliative answers on self-report measures, engage in more intensive peer interactions, are given a slight edge in terms of being more socially perceptive and, perhaps, more empathic, and show more affiliativeness and interpersonal involvement in their nonverbal behavior. Yet some indicators of affiliation orientation fail to reveal a difference in favor of females, including infant responsiveness to social stimuli and the absolute number of friends a person has. If females tend to be more affiliative than males, are they, as Freedman suggests, less competitive than males? This is the question to which we now will address ourselves.

Cooperation and Competition

The everyday activities of males tend to have a stronger competitive element than those of females. This certainly is true if we consider the play behavior of males; for example, their gravitation toward competitive sports.

---

[5]The reader is referred to Freedman's (1975) book for the experimental evidence he provides in support of this theory.

Also, it is probably the case with respect to the vocational world, wherein men seem to be under more pressure to successfully compete with others for jobs, promotions, and occupational recognition.

Research with Young Children. Several experiments have been conducted which involved a comparison of the behavior of young boys and girls in activities calling for either a cooperative response or a competitive response. Szal (1972), for instance, had 4- and 5-year-olds play a two-person marble-pull game in which cooperative behavior was adaptive and competitive behavior maladaptive regarding the goal of winning marbles. Each child stood at the end of a table and held a string which was connected to a marble holder. By pulling the string a child could draw the holder toward him and the marble would drop in his cup; however, if both children pulled the string simultaneously, the marble fell into neither player's cup. In the Szal study, pairs of boys were more competitive than pairs of girls; the girls obtained more marbles because they more frequently developed a turn-taking strategy.

Maccoby and Jacklin (1974) reviewed roughly a dozen experiments involving children (ages 3 to 9) and concluded that, although half showed no sex difference, the remainder tended to confirm the view that boys are more competitive than girls. However, Maccoby and Jacklin made a procedural criticism of the studies for failing to permit one to distinguish between the possible motives underlying the subjects' actions. For example, in the Szal experiment the "competitive" choice of pulling against the other player may reflect a desire to maximize one's own gains (individualistic orientation) or a desire to deprive or defeat the other person (competitive orientation). In a more recent experiment, which enabled a differentiation between individualistic, competitive, and cooperative orientations, McClintock and Moskowitz (1976) found among 5- to 8-year-olds a small, although significant, tendency for boys to be more competitive than girls.

Research with the Prisoner's Dilemma Game. With older children and adults the Prisoner's Dilemma Game is most frequently used to study cooperation and competition. In this two-person game, each player has two choices, A and B. Choice A is the cooperative one because, if selected by both players, each receives a relatively high and equal outcome (for example, 5 points). Choice B is competitive because it allows the player who selects it to earn the largest possible gain (10 points) and the player who doesn't select it to earn the lowest possible outcome (1 point). If both players act competitively by choosing B, each receives the minimal outcome (1 point). In most cases the game is played over a large number of trials; the two players cannot speak to each other and alternate between making the first choice.

Prisoner's Dilemma research presents an unexpected picture as far as sex differences are concerned. It appears that males are more likely than females to adopt a cooperative strategy, although this difference typically emerges only after the game has been played for a number of trials (Carment, 1974; van de Sande, 1973). Taken at face value, these findings should be a bit surprising to us in light of the results of the research on competition in children, as well as our stereotyped assumptions that women are less competitive than men. How can we resolve this apparent discrepancy? For one thing, several writers have criticized the suitability of the Prisoner's Dilemma paradigm for studying individual differences in competition and cooperation (Deaux, 1976; Maccoby & Jacklin, 1974). Maccoby and Jacklin (1974), for instance, note the dissimilarity between the occurrences in the Prisoner's Dilemma Game and real life competition and cooperation. They also point out that, in the Prisoner's Dilemma Game and the experiments conducted with younger children, competitive behavior usually is maladaptive, whereas outside the laboratory it often leads to individual gain. Maccoby and Jacklin further observe that it often is difficult to separate a person's cooperative orientation from his competitive orientation because successful competition frequently requires within-group (within-team) cooperation.

Perhaps the most important information from the research on the Prisoner's Dilemma Game pertains to what we can learn about differences in the interaction styles of the two sexes. According to several analysts (for example, van de Sande, 1973; Vinacke, Mogy, Powers, Langan, & Beck, 1974), the primary emphasis of male participants is to successfully play the game. Their strategy is an opportunistic one whereby they concentrate on developing tactics (that is, cooperation) that will insure that their outcomes are maximized. Females, on the other hand, display an accommodative strategy, being less concerned with the game per se than with the interpersonal aspects of the situation. That is, the goals of playing the game well and maximizing rewards are secondary to engaging in social interaction and achieving a pleasant social situation. In fact, the play of females often appears "irrational" vis-à-vis the way males play the game.

The results from several studies support the idea that males and females employ different interaction strategies (for example, Hottes & Kahn, 1974; Kahn, Hottes, & Davis, 1971). In one study male pairs and female pairs played the Prisoner's Dilemma Game for 31 trials, during which the members of each pair were not allowed to communicate (Hottes & Kahn, 1974). Then they were given a break. During the break most male dyads discussed how to improve their game strategy, whereas the female dyads almost never talked strategy, tending to discuss such topics as roommates, common friends, and their general interest (or lack of it) in the game. After the break, male dyads showed a marked increase in cooperation (and thus earnings), whereas there was no change in the performance of the female dyads. Similar sex differences in interaction strategies have been observed in experimental studies of coalition formation (Vinacke et al., 1974).

In sum, both the complexity of the nature of competition and cooperation and the related methodological shortcomings of the empirical research make it difficult to arrive at hard and fast conclusions about sex differences in competitiveness. The research with children does demonstrate that boys are somewhat more competitive than girls. On the other hand, the immediate relevance of Prisoner's Dilemma research would seem to be the evidence that males are motivated primarily out of a concern for mastering the task, whereas females are less concerned with their task performance than with fostering a satisfactory social situation.

Aggression

There is nearly unanimous agreement that males, as a group, are more aggressive than females (Mischel, 1970; Moyer, 1974). For one thing, the statistics on crime speak for themselves—the overwhelming majority of violent crimes are committed by males (National Commission on Violence, 1969). For example, during 1968 in the United States males committed five times as many homicides as did females. Psychological evidence likewise suggests that males are the more aggressive sex. If we combine the 100 plus studies surveyed by Oetzel (1966) and Maccoby and Jacklin (1974), we find that whereas roughly 70% provided some evidence of more aggression in males than females, only about 5% provided the reverse (the remainder showed no sex difference).

The greater aggressiveness of the male has been documented by experimenters using a wide variety of measurement strategies, including self-report measures, projective tests, rating scales, naturalistic observations, and experimental procedures. The sex difference has been found in children as young as 2 to 3 years, as well as in people up through college age. Boys, relative to girls, imitate more readily an aggressive model, are rated by peers, teachers, and parents as more aggressive, and have been observed to engage in more "negativistic" behavior, rough-and-tumble play (mock fighting), quarrels, and physical aggression (for example, hitting and pushing). In experimental situations boys and men are more willing to deliver an aversive stimulus (for example, shock or loud noise) to another person. Moreover, males score higher on projective and self-report measures of aggressiveness and hostility. Males also seem to be more perceptually attuned to aggressive stimuli. For example, they have been found to have better memories for the aggressive content of films (Maccoby & Wilson, 1957), to require less exposure time in order to identify aggressive scenes presented visually by means of a tachistoscope (Kagan & Moss, 1962), and to more often report seeing a violent scene when it and a nonviolent one are simultaneously presented, each to a different eye, by means of a stereoscope (Moore, 1966).

Before considering some factors that may contribute to the male's greater aggressiveness, we should note that Frodi, Macaulay, and Thome (1977) have examined the literature on adult aggression in terms of the studies in which males were more aggressive than females across *all* experimental conditions and found that less than half met this criterion. The authors used this evidence to argue against the view that women are almost always less aggressive than men. Frodi and associates' point is well taken. Their analysis indicates that the sex difference in aggression is not as dependable as may be commonly assumed and further underlines the fact that even with respect to a dimension of behavior that is widely acknowledged as showing a sex difference, the overlap between the groups is appreciable.

Biological Bases of Aggression. A number of writers have argued that there is a biological basis to the sex differences in aggression; that is, constitutional factors predispose males to be more aggressive (R. N. Johnson, 1972; Moyer, 1974, 1976). Maccoby and Jacklin (1974) offer four reasons for advocating the biological viewpoint. Below we list each reason and briefly entertain some of the supportive evidence.

1. "The sex differences are found early in life, at a time when there is no evidence that differential socialization pressures have been brought to bear by adults to 'shape' aggression differently in the two sexes" (p. 242). As we mentioned before, sex differences in aggression appear as early as 2 to 3 years (for example, Pedersen & Bell, 1970). Maccoby and Jacklin (1974) have reviewed studies that are concerned with parental reactions to aggressive behavior in young children and found no consistent support for the belief that aggression toward parents and siblings by boys is met with greater permissiveness than similar aggression by girls. Thus, they affirm that it is unlikely that differential sex-role socialization can account for the early sex differences in aggression.

2. "Males are more aggressive than females in all human societies for which evidence is available" (p. 242). Maccoby and Jacklin (1974) cite two observational studies that indicate more aggression in boys than girls: one by Whiting and Edwards (1973), involving six cultures, and a second by Omark, Omark, and Edelman (1973), involving three cultures. However, it should be pointed out that in the Whiting and Edwards study, the sex difference was significant only for the six cultures combined, and in at least one culture there was a tendency (nonsignificant) for girls to engage in more aggressive behavior than boys.

3. "Similar sex differences are found in man and subhuman primates" pp. 242–243). Nonhuman primates, such as rhesus monkeys, chimpanzees, and baboons, and most other mammalian species for that matter, conform to the picture of greater intraspecies aggression among males (Gray, 1971; Moyer, 1974). And, as with human children, the sex difference initially appears in subhuman primates as a predisposition for immature males to engage in rough-and-tumble play that apparently represents a simulation of adult aggressive behavior. In addition, among subhuman primates aggression predominantly occurs between males, and the same pattern, although to a lesser extent, prevails among humans—girls and women are.less frequently the targets of aggression than boys and men (Maccoby & Jacklin, 1974; Frodi et al., 1977).

4. "Aggression is related to levels of sex hormones and can be changed by experimental administrations of these hormones" (p. 243). Research on several animal species indicates that the intermale aggression of prepubescent males is considerably subdued relative to the aggression displayed by adult males; however, injections of testosterone produce a significant increase in their level of aggression (Moyer, 1974, 1976). Furthermore, both prenatal and postnatal exposure to abnormally high amounts of androgens can produce increased aggression in subhuman primate females. For instance, Joslyn (1973) found that testosterone-treated female rhesus monkeys showed marked increases in aggressiveness, even to the point of attacking and subduing dominant males.

With respect to humans, Ehrhardt and Baker (1974) report that, if females are exposed to abnormally high levels of androgens as a fetus (for example, adrenogenital syndrome), they display masculine behavior patterns and interests, including a higher degree of rough-and-tumble outdoor play and a tendency (nonsignificant) to initiate more fighting than their normal sisters. Also, therapeutic castrations of sex offenders, which incidentally are legal in some European countries, have been found to be effective in reducing the rate of recidivism, especially for offenders committing violent crimes (R. N. Johnson, 1972; Moyer, 1976). Moyer (1976) reports a study in which testosterone injections of castrates increased their general level of destructiveness (for example, fighting and destroying furniture); termination of the hormone administrations resulted in a return to an initial low level of distructiveness. A number of studies indicate that administration of female hormones to males, including highly dangerous individuals, may greatly curb their aggressive tendencies (Moyer, 1976). Moreover, there is some evidence linking testosterone levels in human males with aggressiveness (Moyer, 1974). For example, in a study by Persky, Smith, and Basu (1971) testosterone production rate was significantly correlated with scores on a self-report measure of hostility and aggression. In another study, whereas the amount of plasma testosterone was not related to scores on the same self-report measure of aggression used by Persky and associates (1971) nor to ongoing physical aggression in young prisoners, it was directly associated with the incidence of violent crimes during their adolescence (Kreuz & Rose, 1972).[6] While the above findings are suggestive of a causal link between sex hormones and aggressiveness, Meyer-Bahlburg (1974) cautions that the hormone/aggression association has not been unquestionably established in humans.

Female Attitudes about Aggression. Notwithstanding the possible role of biological factors, sociocultural factors undoubtedly contribute to the sex differences in aggression. Deaux (1976) observes that from 1960 to 1970 there was a 69% increase in violent crimes by women. She suggests that the biological makeup of women certainly could not have changed in just 10 years; thus women either must have learned to be more aggressive in that period or to become less inhibited about displaying aggressive behavior. The second possibility is the likelier of the two. Several writers have suggested that females are socialized to associate negative consequences with aggressive behavior and consequently are less likely to perform aggressive acts (for example, Bandura, 1965; Mischel, 1970). Indeed, research does indicate that women are more apt than men to experience anxiety or guilt over aggression (Frodi et al., 1977).

It is partly on the basis of the evidence that females possess greater conflict and anxiety over aggression that some writers (for example, Feshbach,

---

[6]In women the premenstrual/menstrual period has been associated with an increase in irritability and aggressiveness. For example, according to reviews by R. N. Johnson (1972) and Moyer (1974), women are much more likely to commit crimes, including violent ones, during this period. In fact, criminal law in some countries recognizes menstruation as an extenuating circumstance. The "premenstrual syndrome" is generally attributed to a fall in the level of progesterone.

1970) have proposed that females tend to inhibit overt expressions of aggression, with the result that their aggressive impulses find a release in less physical, more indirect or disguised ways. A parallel hypothesis is that society tolerates, perhaps reinforces, physical forms of aggression in males but nonphysical forms of aggression in females. While these hypotheses have intuitive appeal, there is minimal empirical support for them. As we noted earlier, there is little indication that females are more aggressive than males on any of a variety of indexes, including verbal, fantasy, and mock aggression, as well as physical aggression.

When Do Males and Females Show Similar Levels of Aggression? To conclude our discussion of aggression we wish to consider some of the conditions under which females may be as aggressive as males. The analysis of this question by Frodi and her associates (Frodi et al., 1977) suggests that if the circumstances minimize the opportunity for the arousal of empathy (for the potential target of aggression) and aggression anxiety, sex differences are unlikely to occur. An important means of reducing or avoiding aggression anxiety is to provide the individual with justification for his or her aggression (for example, the aggressive behavior is necessary for scientific research).

Moreover, Deaux (1976) has made an interesting observation. She distinguishes between the initiation of aggression and reaction to aggression, and she proposes that the sex difference lies primarily with the former. That is, Deaux interprets the experimental research as demonstrating that males exceed females only with respect to the initiation of aggressive acts and that as targets of aggression females tend to counter-aggress as willfully as males.

Among the evidence cited by Deaux is an experiment by Taylor and Epstein (1967). In that study subjects were told they were competing with another person on a reaction time task. Whenever the subject won a given trial he or she could shock the opponent at one of five intensities; however, when the opponent had a faster reaction time, the opponent could shock the subject. Initially, males chose more severe shocks for their opponents than did females. However, as the trials progressed and the opponent became more aggressive, the females responded in kind, so that by the end of the experiment they were administering slightly stronger shocks than the males. This kind of "tit for tat" similarity between the sexes leads Deaux to speculate that in a long-term relationship involving members of each sex, differences in level of aggression are minimized. Consistent with Deaux's thinking is the evidence that a sex difference in physical aggressiveness less frequently occurs in studies in which subjects have been provoked (angered) than in those in which there is no provocation (Frodi et al., 1977).

Dependency and Nurturance

Dependency. One of the so-called truisms in research on sex differences is the greater dependency of females. This view is held by nearly every writer in the area (for example, Hutt, 1972; Hyde & Rosenberg, 1976). Bardwick (1971), for instance, says:

Since we know that girls are socialized to be dependent in comparison with boys, we expect to find that many dependent behaviors in girls are not only common but normal and adaptive, and our evaluation of the level of dependency in girls depends upon the appropriateness of the behavior, or, conversely, upon a generalized inability to be independent [p. 116].

We are aware that according to the cultural stereotype, females are supposed to be dependent and males independent, but we may also feel a little unsure of ourselves if asked to stipulate exactly what dependency means. Sears, Rau, and Alpert (1965) define dependency as "an action system in which another person's nurturant, helping, and caretaking activities are the rewarding environmental events" (p. 27). According to this definition, a number of different behaviors can be classified as dependent, including seeking another person's attention, reassurance, assistance, comfort, or protection. Also, merely remaining close to or in physical contact with a person may reflect dependency. Before we look at the evidence on dependency, we should be aware of the fact that the many behavioral indicators of dependency often are not significantly intercorrelated, suggesting that we are not dealing with a unidimensional concept (Maccoby & Jacklin, 1974).

Whether we find sex differences in dependency or not seems to depend on the method of measurement employed. If we wish to confirm the belief that females are the more dependent sex, we should look at the research in which either observer (for example, teacher or parent) ratings, projective tests, or self-report scales were used (Maccoby & Jacklin, 1974). On the other hand, if we have an equalitarian bias, we should restrict our attention to research that relies on the observational method that entails the counting and categorizing of directly observed behavioral events (see Oetzel, 1966). In accounting for the discrepant evidence from the different research methods, Edwards and Whiting (1972) contend that the observational method is a more valid means of measuring dependency than the other techniques, which are more susceptible to many forms of investigator bias. For instance, Mischel (1970) persuasively argues that observer ratings of people's personality attributes are likely to reflect characteristics of the rater (for example, his or her stereotypic view that females are dependent) as much as those of the ratee. Thus, because the observational method seems to be less susceptible to bias and because it unexpectedly yields data that call into question the assumed sex differences in dependency, we will confine our discussion to the results derived from it.

As mentioned, the amount of distance a young child maintains between him- or herself and an adult frequently is considered an indication of his or her degree of dependence on that person. A 3-year-old who regularly clings to his or her mother, plays right beside her, looks in her direction, or follows her about is thought to be behaving in a dependent manner. Also, dependent children are apt to cry and discontinue their play activity when their mothers leave their presence. A lot of research has been done on these "attachment" behaviors. Naturally, almost all of it involves infants and preschoolers. In Maccoby and Jacklin's (1974) review, the large majority of studies revealed no sex differences in attachment behavior (to nonfamily adults as well as parents).

However, an interesting pattern emerged in the few studies showing differences. Girls seem to display more attachment than boys when their parent is in the room with them; on the other hand, boys seem to be more likely to resist separation from their parents. On the whole, however, the attachment measure of dependency shows the sexes to be quite similar.

The other observational evidence of sex differences in dependency stems from the research tradition of Whiting and Edwards (1973) and Sears, Whiting, Nowlis, and Sears (1953). As in the research on attachment, certain behavioral units are designated as exemplifying dependency. These categories of dependent behavior essentially represent "seeking behaviors" whereby the child endeavors to have his or her needs met by adults or older children (see Table 10-2). An investigator observes a child and simply records how often each behavior occurs. Edwards and Whiting (1972) collated the significant and nonsignificant findings from 17 investigations of children ranging in age from 3 to 16. The results for children under 6 are summarized in Table 10-2, which indicates a preponderance of nonsignificant differences and a nearly even split between the sexes in amount of dependency when differences are found. The data for children aged 6 to 16 show essentially the same pattern; in fact, in no instance are girls found to be more dependent than boys (13 differences were nonsignificant and 4 favored boys). We should point out that most of the findings regarding the older children are based on cross-cultural research. Nevertheless, both sets of research are consistent in showing that girls are not more likely to rely on others for the gratification of their needs. Edwards and Whiting do interpret the data as suggesting that boys and girls tend to display different styles of dependency. Little girls seem to be more likely to seek help from older people and to maintain close contact with them (which is consistent with the trend noted in the attachment behavior research). Little boys seem to devote more effort to attention-getting, both in terms of looking for approval and in more negative forms of behavior such as boasting and being interruptive and annoying.

Thus, we find two sets of reviewers who independently have adduced evidence that contests the widely held belief tying dependency and femaleness. However, we also should acknowledge that Maccoby and Jacklin's (1974) review has been criticized by Block (1976) for failing to include several studies that indicate greater dependency in girls than boys. Yet, despite these omissions, the amount of observational evidence that disconfirms the stereotype of the dependent female certainly is noteworthy.

We confess that even your liberated authors experience (for the first time?) a twinge of dissonance when considering the results of dependency research. Perhaps there are other dimensions of dependency the above review fails to cover and on which people typically focus when assigning the trait to females. One possibility is that people are concentrating on the woman's dependency that is manifested during and immediately following the period of pregnancy. Another possibility is that females are more likely to lean on the advice of others when making decisions about their lives. Also, as early adulthood approaches, males may be more inclined than females to break their

Table 10-2. Relation of Sex to Dependent Behavior in Children under Six: Number of Studies Showing Significant Sex Differences versus the Number Showing No Sex Differences

Dependent Behavior	Significant Difference Boys Higher	Girls Higher	No Significant Difference
Seeks proximity	0	1	5
Touches, clings, holds	1	3	5
Seeks help	1	2	4
Seeks praise, approval	0	0	8
Seeks negative attention	2	0	2
Seeks comfort, affection	0	0	6
Seeks information	0	1	2
Seeks permission	0	0	2
Sociability	1	0	3
TOTAL	5	7	37

Adapted from "Women and Dependency," by C. P. Edwards and B. B. Whiting, *Politics and Society*, 1972, *4*, 343–355. Copyright 1972 by Geron-X Inc., Publications. Used by permission.

ties with their parents by assuming financial independence and moving out of the home.

Nurturance. In addition to their purported dependency, females are often regarded as the more nurturant sex. However, these two characteristics, dependence and nurturance, would seem to be incompatible with each other if expressed in the same person. If we are dependent, we seek nurturance from other people, whereas, if we are nurturant, we seek to nurture those who are dependent, although it is conceivable that we can be high in both.

In the minds of many people the most convincing evidence of the female's greater capacity for nurturance lies in her propensity to love and care for children. However, although in virtually all cultures women fulfill the role of caretaker for the young and sick, still at issue is whether or not their nurturant behavior has a biological basis to it. As Shields (1975) notes, most early psychologists were convinced of the existence of a maternal instinct, and some believed that men also possess a parental instinct, although it was usually regarded as a protective attitude over those for whom they feel responsible. Evidence from animal and human studies has begun to point to the importance of sex hormones in the development of maternal behavior. For example, nonpregnant or virgin animals, such as rats and rabbits, display an increase in maternal behavior (for example, nest building and licking infants) soon after they receive an injection of female hormones (Moltz, Lubin, Leon, & Numan, 1970). Regarding humans, Ehrhardt (Ehrhardt, 1973; Ehrhardt & Baker, 1974) provides some evidence that fetally androgenized girls (adrenogenital syndrome) display less interest in a variety of maternal behaviors. Relative to a matched normal control group, adrenogenital girls (ages 4 to 16) reported being totally indifferent to infants and having fewer fantasies about being pregnant and bearing children; they were also less interested in playing with dolls and caring for young siblings. Ehrhardt cautions us, however, about overemphasizing the role of hormonal factors and disregarding the importance of social environmental forces. The viewpoint that parental nurturance is entirely an outcome of social forces is expressed by Chafetz (1974):

> Myth has it that the process of being pregnant and giving birth magically results in instant "mother love," namely, an overwhelming desire to nurture and care for all the needs of her offspring for the next 15 to 20 years of life. If, indeed, "nature" provided such an urge we could scarcely account for the large numbers of mothers who neglect, abuse, and abandon their children, not to mention the even larger number who perform their maternal tasks poorly. Nor could we account for the deep "maternal" love people of both genders often develop for children they did not physically conceive. The fact of the matter is that a *social* injunction is placed on virtually all females to be mothers, to do the required types of things and develop the "appropriate" emotions [p. 174].

All of us have seen instances in which males display a high level of nurturance towards infants. Actually, research on responsiveness to babies (for example, holding, touching, looking at, and kissing) has suggested that in most instances males are just as nurturant as females. Studies have been done on the behavior of 8- to 9-year-olds and 14- to 15-year-olds (Feldman, Nash, & Cutrona, 1977), as well as that of several categories of adults: cohabiting couples, childless married couples, couples expecting their first child, parents of infants, parents of 8- to 9-year-olds, and parents of adolescents (Feldman & Nash, 1978; Nash & Feldman, 1977). Only among adolescents and parents of infants did females display significantly more interest and involvement with babies. While it is possible that this interesting pattern of differences and similarities may be reflective of biological (for example, hormonal) determinants, it is even more compatible with an explanation based on sex-role related considerations. That is, the sex difference in adolescence may well reflect a conformity to the appropriate sex-role stereotype during the period of intensified striving for sex-role identity. By adulthood the sex difference generally disappears because males and females feel secure in their sex-role identities and emerges only when the role demands concerning babies are appreciably different for males and females (that is, when they have an infant under their care).

Is there any corroboration of these findings in other studies of nurturant behavior? A consideration of several surveys on nurturance reveals the same methodological pattern that we observed regarding dependency (Maccoby & Jacklin, 1974; Oetzel, 1966). Studies employing self-report and rating measures consistently indicate that females are more nurturant than males, whereas those using observational procedures are less likely to uncover sex differences.

As in the observational research on dependency, the bulk of the investigations of nurturance were concerned with the behavior of small children. However, the results of these studies have been bolstered by the evidence from research on altruism, which may be conceived as a form of nurturant behavior. Experimenters interested in altruism have used a wide variety and often highly imaginative set of procedures to measure a person's response to a situation in which he or she has the capacity to benefit another person through his or her actions. Sometimes a subject is given a chance to offer physical assistance (for example, picking up dropped items, helping another finish a task, or intervening in an emergency), whereas in other experiments the subject must decide whether or not he or she wants to donate money to a needy cause or to share a valued item with someone. Sex differences are not usually found, either in young children or adults (Krebs, 1970; Rushton, 1976).[7]

The studies that show sex differences in altruism are fairly divided between those favoring males and those favoring females. Deaux (1976, 1977) provides an analysis of altruistic behavior in which she demonstrates how knowledge of the sex-linkage of the situation helps to predict when differences in altruism will favor one sex or the other. In a situation in which males typically are more knowledgeable than females (for example, repairing a disabled vehicle) we surely expect males to be more helpful; on the other hand, females might be more inclined to help in other settings (for example, responding to a crying child who is alone in a department store). Many situations tend to be sex neutral in character and, consequently, fail to elicit sex differences in response.

Responsiveness to Social Influence

In considering whether there are sex differences in responsiveness to social influence we must distinguish between several kinds of influence. We may be concerned with the extent to which a person complies with another's demands or requests, complies in a group-pressure situation, or changes his or her opinion as a result of a persuasive communication. Also under the rubric of social influence we may include the propensity to respond to social reinforcement (for example, praise) with an increment in learning or performance and to modeling (the tendency for an observer to imitate the behavior of another). Indeed, as we shall discover, whether or not sex differences are found does depend on the category of social influence.

Compliance with the Directives of Adults. Minton, Kagan, and Levine (1971) made in-home observations of the interactions between 2-year-old children and their mothers. One category of interaction involved maternal commands (for example, pertaining to dressing, eating, helping mother, and picking up toys). Boys were less likely than girls to comply immediately with their mother's commands; that is, they would resist initially and then comply or be forced to comply. The results of most other studies likewise show that,

[7]Moral behavior, including altruism, has been conceptually and empirically linked to moral judgment. In view of the absence of a sex difference in altruism, we should not be surprised by the evidence that males and females follow a similar pattern of development with respect to Kohlberg's (1964) stages of moral reasoning (Maccoby & Jacklin, 1974).

among children of preschool age or younger, girls are more likely than boys to comply with directives from adults such as parents and teachers (Maccoby & Jacklin, 1974). The same conclusion applies to the research on resistance to temptation that has been carried out with children in the 5- to 8-year range (Maccoby & Jacklin, 1974). The typical procedure in this research is to have an adult instruct a child not to touch a group of attractive toys and then to determine whether or not the child complies with the directive during the adult's absence.

A dearth of experimental information exists regarding how older boys and girls respond to influence attempts from adults. However, in a recent questionnaire study (Schneider & Coutts, 1976), high school students were asked how they would react if they were invited to join a highly attractive group of which their parents disapproved. Boys were more likely than girls to indicate that they probably would join the group over their parents' objections. The above findings certainly coincide with the stereotype of the submissive, conforming female and independent, self-reliant male, and they are also consistent with the finding that males score higher on self-report measures of independence.

Conformity Behavior. For many years the extensive research on conformity behavior has been cited as further proof of the females' greater susceptibility to social influence. Most experiments on conformity involve the procedure (or some variation of it) originally employed by Asch (1956). The subject has to make a decision in the presence of other people, but the situation is so contrived that before stating the decision, he or she discovers that the decision is not the same as the one held by most or all of the other people. Under these kinds of circumstance many investigators have found that females, children and adults alike, are more likely than males to "conform" by making a decision that is consistent with the majority's opinion (although that opinion may clearly be erroneous) (Eagly, 1978; Maccoby & Jacklin, 1974). Nord (1969), for example, concluded "It has also been well established, at least in our culture, that females supply greater amounts of conformity under almost all conditions than males" (p. 198). We should add that exceptions to the finding of sex differences in conformity are not uncommon. In fact, a majority of researchers have reported negligible sex differences, although instances of males conforming more than females are rare (Eagly, 1978). However, enough studies have had significant results to lead to the conclusion that a sex difference in conformity to group pressure does exist.

An experiment by Sistrunk and McDavid (1971; replicated by C. Goldberg, 1974) indicates a methodological factor that at least partially accounts for the higher female conformity in laboratory settings. Sistrunk and McDavid noted that in most conformity experiments the stimuli about which subjects have to make judgments are biased in the direction of male interests and abilities (the task-appropriateness variable surfaces once again). Most studies, in fact, involve making decisions on a visual-spatial task (for example, judging the sizes of geometric figures). Sistrunk and McDavid used three kinds of items: those that were likely to be of more interest to or more accurately judged by (1) males, (2) females, and (3) both sexes equally. The overall results of four separate studies by Sistrunk and McDavid indicated that females conformed more than males on the masculine topics and, most importantly, males conformed more than females on the feminine topics. No sex differences occurred on the sex-neutral topics. Thus, it appears that we have to be cautious about overgeneralizing concerning the conformist tendencies of the female. However, the possibility remains that males feel more confident than females on a greater variety of issues (recall the findings on task confidence), and thus usually are less influenceable in group-pressure situations.

Susceptibility to Persuasion. In the experiments on conformity behavior individuals are not actually subjected to conformity pressure in the sense that others actively try to influence their judgments. Rather, subjects are merely made aware that others disagree with them. More direct efforts to influence often are employed in the area of attitude or opinion change. Here subjects are exposed to a communication, typically a written one, intended to persuade them to change their opinion on some issue. It should be noted, however, the source of the persuasive communication usually is not present (for example, the communication is attributed to an expert on the topic); thus the situation lacks the face-to-face impact of most conformity studies. In the pioneering research in the 1950s (Janis & Field, 1959), females were found to be more persuasible than males. However, subsequent research reveals that greater persuasibility of females is anything but a reliable finding—the preponderance of studies (over 80%) show an absence of sex differences (Eagly, 1978; Maccoby & Jacklin, 1974).

Imitation and Social Reinforcement. The extensive research on social learning and reinforcement provides little indication of sex differences. The vast majority of experiments on modeling reveal no differences between males and females in their tendency to imitate the actions of others (Maccoby & Jacklin, 1974), although differences may occur if the behavior in question is sex-typed (for example, boys imitating an aggressive model). Likewise, according to Maccoby and Jacklin's (1974) review of research on social reinforcement, there appears to be no consistent tendency for one sex to learn or perform better than the other sex when, for example, they are exposed to praise versus no reinforcement or to verbal feedback versus nonhuman feedback (for example, buzzer).

Let us briefly recapitulate what we have discovered about the susceptibility of males and females to social influence. Among children there is a sex difference concerning compliance to authority—boys are less responsive to influence attempts from adults, especially their parents. On the other hand, research on persuasion, imitation, and social reinforcement shows no sex differences and that on conformity indicates that whereas many studies denote greater conformity in females, the relative conformity level of the sexes can be manipulated by altering the sex-appropriateness of the task. Certainly this evidence suggests that we should be wary about unequivocally endorsing the stereotypic notion that females are more submissive than males. In fact, as in the case of conformity, sometimes females are more independent than males. Also, a study by Hollander and Marcia (1970) suggests that in some ways boys may be more influenced than girls by their peers. They asked 10-year-olds to resolve dilemma situations by choosing between peer values or their own values. One dilemma, for example, required the child to choose between going to a highly desirable summer camp or a less desirable one to which his or her friends were going. Boys were more likely than girls to make the peer-oriented decision. Similarly, boys are less likely to report that they would resist an attempt by peers to get them to engage in misbehavior (Bixenstine, DeCorte, & Bixenstine, 1976).

Eagly (1978) concludes that the evidence indicates that the sex difference in influenceability most readily emerges in social influence situations involving group pressure—where the individual recognizes that the other people who are present will (may) be informed of his or her response. Eagly notes that the most popular explanation of the female tendency to yield to social influence is that submissiveness is part of the culturally defined female role. However, she rejects this explanation because of its failure to adequately account for the data. For instance, according to the submissiveness interpretation, the greater female influenceability should generalize across many (most) situations; yet, as we have seen, it does not. Eagly forms an explanation that posits that females may be more likely to yield to social influence because they are more concerned than males with the interpersonal aspects of group interactions and, therefore, with maintaining harmonious relationships (that is, to disagree is to increase interpersonal conflict). According to Eagly, this interpersonal-orientation explanation accounts for the fact that the sex difference in conformity most reliably occurs in group-pressure situations.

Moreover, Eagly makes the interesting point that, in line with our sex-role stereotypes, the incidence of female influenceability in the everyday world probably is greater than that which psychological research seems to indicate. One reason for suggesting this is that many situations in the everyday world possess the ingredients that in the laboratory seem to maximize sex differences—the individual's behavior is under the scrutiny of the source of influence. More importantly, in real life the behavior of males and females is strongly governed by role expectations and institutional constraints based on sex, whereas in psychological research males and females share the same role—that of a subject. Therefore, in everyday life the culturally prescribed power differences inherent in the social structure (between husband and wife, doctor and nurse, and so on) dictate a sex-linked pattern of social influence that is much less apparent in the psychological laboratory.

As you probably noted, our discussion of social influence, particularly Eagly's interpersonal-orientation explanation of existing sex differences, bears directly upon the tenability of the hypothesis, mentioned in our consideration of achievement motivation, that females are person oriented and males are task oriented. Let us return to our examination of that hypothesis.

The Task-versus-Person-Orientation Hypothesis Revisited

In the section on achievement orientation we noted that research on task persistence and involvement revealed no consistent sex differences, thus failing to support the proposition that males are more task oriented than females. Furthermore, in the section on responsiveness to social influence we discovered that research on sensitivity to social reinforcement provides no support for the idea that females are more person oriented than males. Maccoby and Jacklin (1974) relied heavily on these two sets of results in arguing against the viability of the task-orientation-versus-person-orientation distinction.

Many other topics we have considered in this chapter bear on the viability of this distinction. However, before we review them, we want to discuss two experiments by Harter (1975a, 1975b) in which the relative strength of mastery motivation and need for approval in children were examined. Harter defined *mastery motivation* as the desire to solve complex problems merely for the sake of discovering the solution, and she assesses it by measuring how long a child spends on one of two discrimination tasks: an unsolvable (challenging) one and an easily solvable one. Need for social approval is inferred by comparing how long children spend on a task while working alone versus while working in the presence of an adult who verbally reinforces their correct choices. Harter's results clearly corroborate the task-orientation-versus-person-orientation distinction. Among 10- and 11-year-olds, boys spent more time than girls trying to solve the unsolvable problem, whereas there was no sex difference on the solvable problem. On the other hand, only the performance of the girls was influenced by whether an approving adult was present or absent. Girls worked longer on both solvable and unsolvable problems when the adult was present than when there was no adult.

The significant effect of Harter's social-reinforcement manipulation may help to account for the failure of earlier studies to show sex differences in both task persistence and sensitivity to social reinforcement. In the research showing no sex differences in task persistence the experimenter typically is present during the subject's performance. The presence of the experimenter may very well act as a motivating factor for females but not for males and consequently serve to reduce the possibility of discovering sex differences in persistence. Furthermore, in research on social reinforcement, the reinforcement manipulation typically is not as strong as Harter's approving adult-present-versus-adult-absent manipulation; rather the reinforcements (for example, praise or criticism) are administered by the always present experimenter.

With respect to the other relevant findings covered in this chapter, it is our impression that the general picture they present does indicate that females are more person oriented than males. While in some instances no sex differences are in evidence, when they are found, with few exceptions, the difference favors females. The negative evidence regarding person orientation includes the following findings: females and males display fairly similar amounts of dependent and nurturant behavior; baby boys and girls are equally responsive to social stimuli; males have as many, if not more, friends than females; and males are as likely as females to be influenced by a persuasive communication and to imitate the behavior of a model. The positive evidence includes: females have better memories for the names and faces of others; females give more affiliative responses on self-report scales; female friendship relations are more "intensive"; females show some evidence of being more socially insightful and, perhaps, more empathic; females show greater nonverbal involvement with others; females' proxemic reactions and game strategies are reflective of an emphasis on promoting positive interpersonal relations; little girls are more likely to comply with an adult's directives; and females display somewhat more conformity behavior. Furthermore, females have been found to express greater preference for person-oriented occupations (Weller, Shlomi, & Zimont, 1976) and to score higher on self-report measures of social interest (Greever, Tseng, & Friedland, 1973).

Substantially less information is available regarding the idea that males are higher on task orientation. However, consistent with this view, Prisoner's Dilemma research suggests that males are primarily motivated by a concern with successful performance of the game, and a similar orientation was noted regarding coalition-formation experiments. Furthermore, Landau and Leventhal (1976) report a simulation of administrative decision making in which college students assumed the part of an administrator who had to make counteroffers to employees who received job offers from another company. When following their own discretion, males acted as though they wanted to get rid of nonproductive employees (that is, gave them poor counteroffers), whereas females acted as though they wished to retain nonproductive employees (that is, gave them more generous counteroffers) and, therefore, preserve ongoing social relationships.

We might add that the person-orientation-versus-task-orientation distinction also accords with the way males and females describe themselves. Carlson (1971) finds that females represent themselves as interpersonally oriented, whereas males depict themselves in impersonal, individualistic terms. For example, females select social adjectives to describe themselves (compassionate, cooperative, and friendly), whereas males select personal adjectives (imaginative, optimistic, and practical).

Therefore, we must disagree with Maccoby and Jacklin and conclude that the data generally support the sex-linked person-orientation-versus-task-orientation differentiation, and as such, are consistent with T. Parsons' (1955) distinction between the expressive role of women and the instrumental role of men. However, we hasten to reaffirm that the task-orientation-versus-person-orientation distinction undeniably represents an oversimplification of a highly complex matter. Surely, as our review indicates, we cannot conclude that males are less person oriented than females and females less task oriented than males with respect to all dimensions of behavior and all areas of concern.

Adjustment

As we noted earlier, there is a great deal of evidence that stereotypically masculine attributes are more socially desirable and more highly valued in our culture than are stereotypically feminine attributes (Broverman et al., 1972). Furthermore, it appears that feminine characteristics are perceived as less healthy than masculine characteristics. This is aptly demonstrated in a study by Broverman and associates (1970) in which mental-health clinicians (for example, clinical psychologists and psychiatrists) had to describe either a mature, healthy, and socially competent adult woman, adult man, or an adult person (of unspecified sex). The clinicians' concepts of a healthy man more closely approximated their concepts of a healthy adult person than did their concepts of a healthy woman. Apparently, if we apply adult standards of health, females are perceived by mental health professionals as being significantly less healthy than males.

In this section we will consider the question of whether or not there are, in fact, any differences between the sexes in psychological adjustment. As we consider the evidence, we should keep in mind the fact that sex-role stereotypes may affect the judgments and definitions of mental health. Also, we should recognize the possibility that stereotypes are incorporated into the personalities of the targets of the stereotypes.

Self-Concept and Anxiety in the Nonclinical Population. In this vein, we might expect that the negative aspects of the female stereotype would show up in the self-images of females, thus producing a general lowering of their self-esteem. Consistent with this possibility is the aforementioned evidence that, relative to males, females express less self-confidence regarding their performance on a variety of tasks and feel in less control of the events in their lives (that is, females have a less potent self-concept). Is this apparent low regard for her personal efficacy reflective of the female's self-regard in general? The answer appears to be "no." According to Maccoby and Jacklin's (1974) review of studies employing questionnaire measures of self-esteem, males and females report similar levels of self-esteem from the early school years throughout adulthood.

A positive self-concept, including a moderately high level of self-esteem, is generally viewed as a defining quality of a psychologically healthy person. We have found that males and females do not differ in the healthiness of their self-concepts. One's level of anxiety is another index of adjustment. As we noted earlier, girls and women report more anxiety than boys and men on both general-anxiety and test-anxiety scales. As we soon will see, further confirmation of the difference in anxiety is found among clinical populations.

Mental Illness. Until now, we have been considering people who are drawn pretty much at random from the normal population. While females report having more anxiety than males, the level of anxiety is not, for the most part, sufficiently debilitating to interfere with their ability to adequately adjust to their environment. It is the debilitating form of anxiety that is the primary symptom of psychoneuroses. We now turn to a comparison of the sexes with respect to the incidence of neurotic disorders, as well as other forms of mental illness. Gove and Tudor (1973) completed a comprehensive review of United States data on mental illness among adults for the period of the 1950s and 1960s. The review covered community surveys of mental illness, psychiatric hospital admissions, psychiatric care in general hospitals and outpatient clinics, private outpatient psychiatric care, and psychiatric treatment given by general practitioners. The categories of illness included neurotic disorders, functional psychoses, transient situational disorders, and psychosomatic disorders. Gove and Tudor concluded that *"all* of the information on persons in psychiatric treatment indicates that more women are mentally ill" (p. 61). Inspection of Gove and Tudor's summary tables does indeed indicate a remarkably consistent difference between men and women in the prevalence of mental illness.[8] Furthermore, although men are more likely to commit suicide, females are much more likely to attempt suicide.

In noting the results of Gove and Tudor's survey and earlier reviews that led to the same conclusion, Nathanson (1975) has pointed out that the statistics regarding physical illness parallel those for mental illness. Using data from the National Health Survey, Nathanson shows that females surpass males on most indexes of physical illness, including the incidence of acute (but not chronic) conditions, days of restricted activity and bed disability, and physician visits. Thus, it appears that women manifest a greater vulnerability to physical illness as well as mental illness. Incidentally, as Nathanson notes, these sex differences in morbidity (incidence of disease) stand in sharp contrast to the evidence that the life expectancy of a woman continues to exceed that of a man by a good margin, a fact that can be accounted for by the females' greater resistance to infectious and degenerative diseases.

Nathanson describes three not necessarily incompatible explanations for the higher morbidity rates among females. One is that emotional problems are more socially acceptable in women, and, thus, they more readily acknowledge their problems and seek out professional assistance. According to this view, sickness is more stigmatizing for males. The Broverman and associates (1970) finding that society applies a less adult standard of health to women fits nicely with this viewpoint. The second explanation is that the sick role is more compatible with a woman's role obligations than with those of a man. For example, one variant of this position is that women have more time to

---

[8]We should note that although the sex difference in mental illness rates has been found to apply to many Western nations, we must be careful not to overgeneralize, even within North America. The existing evidence on mental-illness rates in Canada fails to indicate a higher incidence in females (Luce & Wand, 1977).

be sick because the female role, especially that of the housewife, is less demanding than the male role.

Notice that the first two explanations essentially deny the existence of sex differences in illness rates. The third position accepts the sex difference as factual and focuses on the idea that the source of the difference lies in the greater stress and frustration associated with the woman's social role. Aspects of the woman's role that conceivably facilitate the development of emotional problems include the idea that being a housewife involves unskilled, low-prestige work with few alternative sources of gratification, that working wives tend to have low status jobs, and that women are subjected to unclear and diffuse sex-role expectations. The stress interpretation is the one given by Gove and Tudor (1973) to account for the evidence that mental illness is more common in women than men. Gove and Tudor particularly emphasize the evidence that the sex difference in mental illness characterizes only those who are married; that is, it exists among those for whom the stress differential should be at a maximum. Among single people, females do not show a higher incidence of mental illness (Gove, 1972). As additional support for the stress interpretation, Gove presents United States data on psychiatric treatment and shows that during adolescence males have higher mental illness rates than females; however, by late adolescence females have at least as high, if not higher, rates of mental illness than males (Gove & Herb, 1974). Gove and Herb suggest that this reversal accords with the view that the early years of life are more stressful for boys than girls (perhaps due to their generally slower rate of development), but at the onset of adolescence and during the transition to adulthood, girls begin to experience the stresses associated with their adult sex role.

Nathanson (1975) has appraised the three explanatory models with respect to their ability to account for differences in rates of illness among certain critical groups of women (for example, married versus single women and married women with children versus those without). According to Nathanson, the role compatibility explanation fares the best under this kind of scrutiny. The supportive evidence she cites suggests, for instance, that women with young children are particularly disinclined to adopt the sick role, presumably because sickness is incompatible with their maternal obligations, which are at peak at this period of time.

It appears that there is evidence in support of each of the explanations for the observed sex differences in mental illness. We repeat that it is possible all three are determining factors. Only further research will tell.

The Androgynous Personality. Sandra Bem (in press) proposes a conception of mental health that involves the integration of the positive aspects of masculinity and femininity. Bem cites evidence that indicates that both high femininity in adult females and high masculinity in adult males are associated with poor psychological adjustment. According to Bem, for completely effective and healthy functioning an individual must be freed from the restrictions of social sex roles. The androgynous person, either male or female, is one who combines the best of femininity and masculinity, including, for example, the instrumental attributes of the male role and the expressive attributes of the female role (T. Parsons, 1955). This person does not eschew certain behaviors because society has defined them as more appropriate for the other sex. Rather, the androgynous person is nurturant, socially sensitive, and responsive to the needs of others as well as self-reliant, independent, and achievement oriented.

In her research, Bem employs a sex-role inventory that ascertains whether the respondent endorses as self-descriptive both stereotypically feminine and masculine traits (the androgynous profile) or endorses primarily feminine or masculine traits. Bem finds that sex-typing does impose constraints on the behavior of people. In a series of experiments, masculine persons of both sexes were high in independence (in an Asch conformity situation) but low in nurturance (regarding their interaction with a baby and a lonely, disheartened peer), whereas feminine males and females were low in independence but high in nurturance. On the other hand, androgynous people were both independent and nurturant.

THE FINAL CONSIDERATION: SEX DIFFERENTIATION IN THE SOCIALIZATION BEHAVIORS OF PARENTS

Our review has underscored the importance of both biological/genetic and social/environmental factors in the etiology of sex differences. Yet, one of the major issues that we have barely touched on is the question of the extent to which socializing agents, in particular parents, shape boys and girls toward sex-appropriate behaviors and away from sex-inappropriate behaviors. After reviewing the literature on parental socialization practices, Maccoby and Jacklin (1974) surprised the psychological community by interpreting it as showing very little evidence of differential parental treatment of boys and girls. They point out that parents do encourage the adoption of sex-typed interests (for example, through the provision of "appropriate" toys and clothing) and that sex-inappropriate behavior,. especially in boys, is frowned on. However, Maccoby and Jacklin conclude that parents show little difference in the way they socialize their sons and daughters concerning aggression, dependency, achievement strivings, and sexual behavior. Nor are they convinced that children learn very much sex-role behavior by imitating same-sex models, including their parents. They note that children do not closely resemble their same-sex parent and do not show a preference for imitating same-sex models.

In light of the fact that Maccoby and Jacklin's conclusions attack a long-standing psychological "truism"—that females and males are socialized differently—it is not surprising that counterarguments were soon to follow. For example, Block (1975) has ardently contested their conclusions. One of Block's arguments is that most of the studies (77%) reviewed by Maccoby and Jacklin concerned the socialization of preschool chilren and, if the remaining studies are examined, there is a greater evidence of sex-differentiating parental behaviors. Thus, Block maintains that the amount of emphasis that parents place on sex-appropriate behavior in their children may increase considerably as children become older. This accords with the evidence that sex differences in behavior are more commonly found as the age of the sample increases from preschool through college (Block, 1976). Block also points out that most socialization research has concentrated on the behavior of the mother and that there is evidence suggesting that fathers are more sex-differentiating than mothers in their treatment of their children.

Block also integrated the results from several samples each of mothers, fathers, and college students who completed a socialization practices questionnaire. The mothers and fathers reported about their own child-rearing practices, whereas the college students reported about those of their parents. Contrary to Maccoby and Jacklin, Block's analysis provided substantial support for the view that parents do socialize their sons and daughters differently. For example, a few of Block's findings were that mothers and fathers emphasize in their sons more than their daughters achievement, competition, control of the expression of emotion, and independence. Fathers are stricter and less tolerant of aggression directed toward themselves by their sons than by their daughters.

Thus, the extent to which sex differences are traceable directly to sex-differentiated parental socialization practices remains an unresolved question. Although we are inclined to favor Block's position, we recognize that the process of sex-role socialization is exceedingly complex and requires a great deal of additional attention.

SUMMARY

Our survey has indicated that there is little evidence to suggest that the sexes differ in general ability, except, perhaps, during the first five years or so, when girls may have a slight lead. However, the sexes do differ regarding certain specific abilities. Females generally surpass males in verbal fluency, reading comprehension, finger dexterity, and clerical skills, whereas males are superior in mathematical reasoning, visual spatial ability, and speed and coordination of large bodily movements. Moreover, females are better at rote memory, especially of verbal and social material. Despite displaying no apparent advantage in global intelligence and scholastic performance, history documents an overwhelming male advantage with respect to educational attainment and vocational accomplishment.

Some differences in the achievement orientation of the sexes may help to account for the achievement discrepancy. While males and females score similarly on measures of achievement motivation, females feel less confident about their ability, less in control of environmental events, and more anxious about the possibility of failure; also, females are more likely to denigrate their own performances and attribute their successes to luck and failures to personal limitations. Whereas the evidence does not support the idea that females are especially likely to be characterized by a motive to avoid success, it does suggest that both sexes are aware of negative consequences accruing from successful performance in sex-inappropriate areas of achievement. Considerable attention was devoted to the proposition that males tend to be task oriented and females person oriented. We concluded that there is enough support for this hypothesis to warrant its tentative acceptance (the relevant findings are summarized in the section specifically devoted to the hypothesis).

Research does corroborate the idea that females are less aggressive than males, but the difference apparently isn't as reliably found as is commonly assumed. Regarding cooperation and competition, methodological problems force us to restrict our conclusion about the greater competitiveness of males to young children. Last, mental illness is reported to occur more frequently in women than in men.

Thus, males and females do differ along a number of dimensions of behavior. But the differences are not categorical. In fact, one might easily be more impressed with the similarities between the sexes than the differences. The importance of the sex appropriateness of the task further accentuates the fact that in many cases the direction of the sex difference is situationally contingent. Furthermore, we should note that most of the evidence considered was drawn from White middle-class samples and that direct inferences about other populations in most instances would be unwarranted.

REFERENCES

Aiken, L. R. Jr. Intellective variables and mathematics achievement: Directions for research. *Journal of School Psychology*, 1971, *9*, 201–212.

Alexander, K. L., & Eckland, B. K. Sex differences in the educational attainment process. *American Sociological Review*, 1974, *39*, 668–682.

Anastasi, A. *Differential psychology: Individual and group differences in behavior* (3rd ed.). New York: Macmillan, 1958.

Anastasi, A. Four hypotheses with a dearth of data: Response to Lehrke's "A theory of X-linkage of major intellectual traits." *American Journal of Mental Deficiency*, 1972, *76*, 620–622.

Andreas, C. *Sex and caste in America.* Englewood Cliffs, N.J.: Prentice-Hall, 1971.

Archer, J. Biological explanations of psychological sex differences. In B. Lloyd & J. Archer (Eds.), *Exploring sex differences.* New York: Academic Press, 1976.

Asch, S. E. Studies of independence and conformity: A minority of one against a unanimous majority. *Psychological Monographs*, 1956, *70*(9, Whole No. 416).

Atkinson, J. W. (Ed.). *Motives in fantasy, action, and society.* Princeton, N.J.: Van Nostrand, 1958.

Bahrick, H. P., Bahrick, P. O., & Wittlinger, R. P. Long-term memory: Those unforgettable high-school days. *Psychology Today*, 1974, *8*(7), 50–56.

Bandura, A. Influence of models reinforcement contingencies on the acquisition of imitative responses. *Journal of Personality and Social Psychology*, 1965, *1*, 589–595.

Bardwick, J. M. *Psychology of women: A study of bio-cultural conflicts.* New York: Harper & Row, 1971.

Barnett, R. C. Sex differences and age trends in occupational preference and occupational prestige. *Journal of Counseling Psychology*, 1975, *22*, 35–38.

Bem, S. L. Beyond androgyny: Some presumptuous prescriptions for a liberated sexual identity. In J. Sherman & F. Denmark (Eds.), *Psychology of women: Future directions of research.* Psychological Dimensions, in press.

Bem, S. L., & Bem, D. J. Training the woman to know her place: The power of a nonconscious ideology. In M. H. Garskof (Ed.), *Roles women play: Readings toward women's liberation.* Belmont, Calif.: Wadsworth, 1971.

Bem, S. L., & Bem, D. J. On liberating the female student. *School Psychology Digest,* 1973, *2*(3), 10–18.

Biller, H. B. Paternal deprivation, cognitive functioning, and the feminized classroom. In A. Davids (Ed.), *Child personality and psychopathology: Current topics.* New York: Wiley, 1974.

Bixenstine, V. E., DeCorte, M. S., & Bixenstine, B. A. Conformity to peer-sponsored misconduct at four grade levels. *Developmental Psychology,* 1976, *12*, 226–236.

Block, J. H. *Another look at sex differentiation in the socialization behaviors of mothers and fathers.* Paper presented at the Conference on New Directions for Research on Women, Madison, Wisconsin, May 1975.

Block, J. H. Assessing sex differences: Issues, problems, and pitfalls. *Merrill-Palmer Quarterly,* 1976, *22*, 283–308.

Bock, D. R., & Kolakowski, D. Further evidence of sex-linked major-gene influence on human spatial visualizing ability. *American Journal of Human Genetics,* 1973, *25*, 1–14.

Booth, A. Sex and social participation. *American Sociological Review,* 1972, *37*, 183–193.

Brekke, B., & Williams, J. D. Conservation and sex. *Perceptual and Motor Skills,* 1973, *37*, 14.

Broverman, D. M., Clarkson, F. E., Rosenkrantz, P. S., & Vogel, S. R. Sex-role stereotypes and clinical judgments of mental health. *Journal of Consulting and Clinical Psychology,* 1970, *34*, 1–7.

Broverman, I. K., Vogel, S. R., Broverman, D. M., Clarkson, F. E., & Rosenkrantz, P. S. Sex role stereotypes: A current appraisal. *Journal of Social Issues,* 1972, *28*(2), 59–78.

Buck, R. Nonverbal communication of affect in preschool children: Relationships with personality and skin conductance. *Journal of Personality and Social Psychology,* 1977, *35*, 225–236.

Buck, R., Miller, R. E., & Caul, W. F. Sex, personality, and physiological variables in the communication of affect via facial expression. *Journal of Personality and Social Psychology,* 1974, *30*, 587–596.

Carlson, R. Sex differences in ego functioning: Exploratory studies of agency and communion. *Journal of Consulting and Clinical Psychology,* 1971, *37*, 267–277.

Carment, D. W. Effects of sex role in a maximizing difference game. *Journal of Conflict Resolution,* 1974, *18*, 461–472.

Cattell, J. A statistical study of eminent men. *Popular Science Monthly,* 1903, *62*, 359–377.

Cattell, R. B. *Abilities: Their structure, growth, and action.* New York: Houghton Mifflin, 1971.

Chafetz, J. S. *Masculine/feminine or human? An overview of the sociology of sex roles.* Itasca, Ill.: F. E. Peacock, 1974.

Cherry, F., & Deaux, K. *Fear of success versus fear of gender-inconsistent behavior: A sex similarity.* Paper presented at the meeting of the Midwestern Psychological Association, Chicago, 1975.

Coates, S. Sex differences in field independence among preschool children. In R. C. Friedman, R. M. Richart, & R. L. Vande Wiele (Eds.), *Sex differences in behavior.* New York: Wiley, 1974.

Condry, J., & Dyer, S. Fear of success: Attribution of cause to the victim. *Journal of Social Issues*, 1976, *32*(3), 63–83.

Connor, J. M., Serbin, L. A., & Schackman, M. Sex differences in children's response to training on a visual-spatial test. *Developmental Psychology*, 1977, *13*, 293–294.

Constantinople, A. Analytical ability and perceived similarity to parents. *Psychological Reports*, 1974, *35*, 1335–1345.

Cozby, P. C. Self-disclosure: A literature review. *Psychological Bulletin*, 1973, *79*, 73–91.

Crandall, V. C. Achievement behavior in young children. *Young Children*, 1964, *20*, 77–90.

Deaux, K. *The behavior of women and men.* Monterey, Calif.: Brooks/Cole, 1976.

Deaux, K. Sex differences in social behavior. In T. Blass (Ed.), *Personality variables in social behavior.* New York: Halsted Press, 1977.

Dion, K. K., & Dion, K. L. Self-esteem and romantic love. *Journal of Personality*, 1975, *43*, 39–57.

Dion, K. L., & Dion, K. K. Correlates of romantic love. *Journal of Consulting and Clinical Psychology*, 1973, *41*, 51–56.

Dwyer, C. A. *Children's sex-role standards and sex-role identification and their relationship to achievement.* Unpublished doctoral dissertation, University of California, Berkeley, 1972.

Dwyer, C. A. Sex differences in reading: An evaluation and a critique of current theories. *Review of Educational Research*, 1973, *43*, 455–468.

Eagly, A. H. Sex differences in influenceability. *Psychological Bulletin*, 1978, *85*, 86–116.

Edwards, C. P., & Whiting, B. B. Women and dependency. *Politics and Society*, 1972, *4*, 343–355.

Ehrhardt, A. A. Maternalism in fetal hormonal and related syndromes. In J. Zubin & J. Money (Eds.), *Contemporary sexual behavior: Critical issues in the 1970s.* Baltimore: Johns Hopkins University Press, 1973.

Ehrhardt, A. A., & Baker, S. W. Fetal androgens, human central nervous system differentiation, and behavior sex differences. In R. C. Friedman, R. M. Richart, & R. L. Vande Wiele (Eds.), *Sex differences in behavior.* New York: Wiley, 1974.

Ellis, H. A. *Man and woman: A study of human secondary sexual characteristics.* New York: Scribner's, 1894.

Ellis, H. A. *A study of British genius.* London: Hurst, 1904.

Epstein, G. F., & Bronzaft, A. L. Female modesty in aspiration level. *Journal of Counseling Psychology*, 1974, *21*, 57–60.

Fagot, B. I., & Patterson, G. R. An in vivo analysis of reinforcing contingencies for sex-role behaviors in the preschool child. *Developmental Psychology*, 1969, *1*, 563–568.

Favreau, O. E. Sex bias in psychological research. *Canadian Psychological Review*, 1977, *18*, 56–65.

Fein, G., Johnson, D., Kosson, N., Stork, L., & Wasserman, L. Sex stereotypes and preferences in the toy choices of 20-month-old boys and girls. *Developmental Psychology*, 1975, *11*, 527–528.

Feldman, S. S., & Nash, S. C. Interest in babies during young adulthood. *Child Development*, 1978, *49*, 617–622.

Feldman, S. S., Nash, S. C., & Cutrona, C. The influence of age and sex on responsiveness to babies. *Developmental Psychology*, 1977, *13*, 675–676.

Fennema, E. Mathematics learning and the sexes: A review. *Journal for Research in Mathematics Education*, 1974, *5*, 126–139.

Fennema, E., & Sherman, J. A. *Sex-related differences in mathematics learning: Myths, realities and related factors.* Paper presented at the meeting of the American Association for the Advancement of Science, Boston, 1976.

Feshbach, N. D., & Roe, K. Empathy in six- and seven-year-olds. *Child Development,* 1968, *39*, 133–145.

Feshbach, N. D., & Sones, G. Sex differences in adolescent reactions toward newcomers. *Developmental Psychology,* 1971, *4*, 381–386.

Feshbach, S. Aggression. In P. H. Mussen (Ed.), *Carmichael's manual of child psychology.* New York: Wiley, 1970.

Ford, C. S. Some primitive societies. In G. H. Seward & R. C. Williamson (Eds.), *Sex roles in changing society.* New York: Random House, 1970.

Freedman, J. L. *Crowding and behavior.* New York: Viking, 1975.

Freedman, J. L., Levy, A. S., Buchanan, R. W., & Price, J. Crowding and human aggressiveness. *Journal of Experimental Social Psychology,* 1972, *8*, 528–548.

French, E. Effects of the interaction of motivation and feedback on task performance. In J. Atkinson (Ed.), *Motives in fantasy, action, and society.* Princeton, N.J.: Van Nostrand, 1958.

Frieze, I. H., & Ramsey, S. J. Nonverbal maintenance of traditional sex roles. *Journal of Social Issues,* 1976, *32*(3), 133–141.

Frodi, A., Macaulay, J., & Thome, P. R. Are women always less aggressive than men? A review of the experimental literature. *Psychological Bulletin,* 1977, *84*, 634–660.

Garai, J. E., & Scheinfeld, A. Sex differences in mental and behavioral traits. *Genetic Psychology Monographs,* 1968, *77*, 169–299.

Goldberg, C. Sex roles, task competence, and conformity. *The Journal of Psychology,* 1974, *86*, 157–164.

Goldberg, P. H. Are women prejudicial against women? *Transaction,* 1968, *5*, 28–30.

Gove, W. R. The relationship between sex roles, marital status, and mental illness. *Social Forces,* 1972, *51*, 34–44.

Gove, W. R., & Herb, T. R. Stress and mental illness among the young: A comparison of the sexes. *Social Forces,* 1974, *53*, 256–265.

Gove, W. R., & Tudor, J. F. Adult sex roles and mental illness. In J. Huber (Ed.), *Changing women in a changing society.* Chicago: University of Chicago Press, 1973.

Grams, J. D., & Waetjen, W. B. *Sex: Does it make a difference?* North Scituate, Mass.: Duxbury, 1975.

Gray, J. A. Sex differences in emotional behaviour in mammals including man: Endocrine bases. *Acta Psychologica,* 1971, *35*, 29–46.

Greer, G. *The female eunuch.* New York: McGraw-Hill, 1971.

Greever, K. B., Tseng, M. S., & Friedland, B. U. Development of the social interest index. *Journal of Consulting and Clinical Psychology,* 1973, *41*, 454–458.

Hall, J. A. Gender effects in decoding nonverbal cues. *Psychological Bulletin,* 1978, *85*, 845–857.

Harper, F. B. The validity of some alternative measures of achievement motivation. *Educational and Psychological Measurement,* 1975, *35*, 905–909.

Harter, S. Developmental differences in the manifestation of mastery motivation on problem-solving tasks. *Child Development,* 1975, *46*, 370–378. (a)

Harter, S. Mastery motivation and the need for approval in older children and their relationship to social desirability response tendencies. *Developmental Psychology,* 1975, *11*, 186–196. (b)

Hillman, J. S. An analysis of male and female roles in two periods of children's literature. *Journal of Educational Research,* 1974, *68*, 84–88.

Hilton, T. L., & Berglund, G. W. Sex differences in mathematics achievement—A longitudinal study. *Journal of Educational Research,* 1974, *67*, 231–237.

Hitchcock, D. C., & Pinder, G. D. *Reading and arithmetic achievement among youths*

12-17 years as measured by the Wide Range Achievement Test. (Vital and Health Statistics—Series 11—No. 136.) Washington, D.C.: U.S. Government Printing Office, 1974.

Hoffman, L. W. Early childhood experiences and women's achievement motives. *Journal of Social Issues,* 1972, *28*(2), 129–155.

Hoffman, M. L., & Levine, L. E. Early sex differences in empathy. *Developmental Psychology,* 1976, *12,* 557–558.

Hollander, E. P., & Marcia, J. E. Parental determinants of peer-orientation and self-orientation among preadolescents. *Developmental Psychology,* 1970, *2,* 292–302.

Horner, M. S. *Sex differences in achievement motivation and performance.* Unpublished doctoral dissertation, University of Michigan, 1968.

Horner, M. S. Toward an understanding of achievement-related conflicts in women. *Journal of Social Issues,* 1972, *28*(2), 157–175.

Hottes, J. H., & Kahn, A. Sex differences in a mixed-motive conflict situation. *Journal of Personality,* 1974, *42,* 260–275.

Huber, J. (Ed.). *Changing women in a changing society.* Chicago: University of Chicago Press, 1973.

Hutt, C. *Males and females.* Middlesex, England: Penguin Books, 1972.

Hyde, J. S., Geiringer, E. R., & Yen, W. M. On the empirical relation between spatial ability and sex differences in other aspects of cognitive performance. *Multivariate Behavioral Research,* 1975, *10,* 289–310.

Hyde, J. S., & Rosenberg, B. G. *Half the human experience: The psychology of women.* Lexington, Mass.: D. C. Heath, 1976.

Ickes, W., & Barnes, R. D. The role of sex and self-monitoring in unstructured dyadic interactions. *Journal of Personality and Social Psychology,* 1977, *35,* 315–330.

Jackson, D. N. *Personality Research Form manual.* New York: Research Psychologists Press, 1967.

Jackson, P. W. *Life in classrooms.* New York: Holt, Rinehart & Winston, 1968.

Janis, I. L., & Field, P. B. Sex differences and personality factors related to persuasibility. In C. I. Hovland & I. L. Janis (Eds.), *Personality and persuasibility.* New Haven: Yale University Press, 1959.

Jantz, R. K. The effects of sex, race, IQ and SES on the reading scores of sixth graders for both levels and gains in performance. *Psychology in the Schools,* 1974, *11*(1), 90–94.

Johnson, D. D. Sex differences in reading across cultures. *Reading Research Quarterly,* 1973–1974, *9*(1), 67–86.

Johnson, R. N. *Aggression in man and animals.* Philadelphia: Saunders, 1972.

Joslyn, W. D. Androgen-induced social dominance in infant female rhesus monkeys. *Journal of Child Psychology and Psychiatry,* 1973, *14,* 137–145.

Kagan, J., & Moss, H. A. *Birth to maturity: A study in psychological development.* New York: Wiley, 1962.

Kagan, J., Rosman, B. L., Day, D., Albert, J., & Phillips, W. Information processing in the child: Significance of analytic and reflective attitudes. *Psychological Monographs: General and Applied,* 1964, *78*(Whole No. 578).

Kahn, A., Hottes, J. H., & Davis, W. L. Cooperation and optimal responding in the Prisoner's Dilemma Game: Effects of sex and physical attractiveness. *Journal of Personality and Social Psychology,* 1971, *17,* 267–279.

Kaniuga, N., Scott, T., & Gade, E. Working women portrayed on evening television programs. *Vocational Guidance Quarterly,* 1974, *23*(2), 134–137.

Klinger, E. Fantasy need achievement as a motivational construct. *Psychological Bulletin,* 1966, *66,* 291–308.

Kohlberg, L. Development of moral character and moral ideology. In M. L. Hoffman & L. W. Hoffman (Eds.), *Review of child development research.* (Vol. 1). New York: Russell Sage Foundation, 1964.

Krebs, D. L. Altruism—an examination of the concept and a review of the literature. *Psychological Bulletin,* 1970, *73,* 258–302.

Kreuz, L. E., & Rose, R. M. Assessment of aggressive behavior and plasma testosterone in a young criminal population. *Psychosomatic Medicine,* 1972, *34,* 321–332.

Landau, S. B., & Leventhal, G. S. A simulation study of administrators' behavior toward employees who receive job offers. *Journal of Applied Social Psychology,* 1976, *6,* 291–306.

Laosa, L. M., & Brophy, J. E. Effects of sex and birth order on sex-role development and intelligence among kindergarten children. *Developmental Psychology,* 1972, *6,* 409–415.

Lavin, D. E. *The prediction of academic performance: A theoretical analysis and review of research.* New York: Russell Sage, 1965.

Lehrke, R. G. A theory of X-linkage of major intellectual traits. *American Journal of Mental Deficiency,* 1972, *76,* 611–619.

Lehrke, R. G. Sex linkage: A biological basis for greater male variability in intelligence. In R. T. Osborne, C. E. Noble, & N. Weyl (Eds.), *Human variation: The biopsychology of age, race, and sex.* New York: Academic Press, 1978.

Lenney, E. Women's self-confidence in achievement settings. *Psychological Bulletin,* 1977, *84,* 1–13.

Lipman-Blumen, J., & Tickamyer, A. R. Sex roles in transition: A ten-year perspective. *Annual review of sociology.* Palo Alto, Calif.: Annual Reviews, Inc., 1975.

Littlefield, R. P. Self-disclosure among some Negro, White and Mexican-American adolescents. *Journal of Counseling Psychology,* 1974, *21,* 133–136.

Luce, S. R., & Wand, B. Sex differences in health and illness. *Canadian Psychological Review,* 1977, *18,* 79–91.

Lueptow, L. B. Parental status and influence and the achievement orientations of high school seniors. *Sociology of Education,* 1975, *48,* 91–110.

McClelland, D. C., Atkinson, J. W., Clark, R. A., & Lowell, E. L. *The achievement motive.* New York: Appleton-Century-Crofts, 1953.

McClintock, C. G., & Moskowitz, J. M. Children's preferences for individualistic, cooperative and competitive outcomes. *Journal of Personality and Social Psychology,* 1976, *34,* 543–555.

McIntyre, A. Sex differences in children's aggression. *Proceedings of the 80th Annual Convention of the American Psychological Association,* 1972, *7,* 93–94.

McKee, J. P., & Sherriffs, A. C. The differential evaluation of males and females. *Journal of Personality,* 1957, *25,* 356–371.

Maccoby, E. E. Sex differences in intellectual functioning. In E. E. Maccoby (Ed.), *The development of sex differences.* Stanford, Calif.: Stanford University Press, 1966.

Maccoby, E. E., & Jacklin, C. N. *The psychology of sex differences.* Stanford, Calif.: Stanford University Press, 1974.

Maccoby, E. E., & Wilson, W. C. Identification and observational learning from films. *Journal of Abnormal and Social Psychology,* 1957, *55,* 76–87.

Manes, A. L., & Melnyk, P. Televised models of female achievement. *Journal of Applied Social Psychology,* 1974, *4,* 365–374.

Markus, E. J., & Nielsen, M. Embedded-Figures Test scores among five samples of aged persons. *Perceptual and Motor Skills,* 1973, *36,* 455–459.

Massari, D. J., & Massari, J. A. Sex differences in the relationship of cognitive style and intellectual functioning in disadvantaged preschool children. *Journal of Genetic Psychology,* 1973, *122,* 175–181.

Mazanec, N., & McCall, G. J. Sex, cognitive categories, and observational accuracy. *Psychological Reports,* 1975, *37,* 987–990.

Mehrabian, A. *Nonverbal communication.* Chicago: Aldine-Atherton, 1972.

Mehrabian, A., & Epstein, N. A measure of emotional empathy. *Journal of Personality,* 1972, *40,* 525–543.

Meyer-Bahlburg, H. F. L. Aggression, androgens, and the XYY syndrome. In R. C. Friedman, R. M. Richart, & R. L. Vande Wiele (Eds.), *Sex differences in behavior.* New York: Wiley, 1974.

Minton, C., Kagan, J., & Levine, J. A. Maternal control and obedience in the two-year-old. *Child Development,* 1971, *42,* 1873–1894.

Mischel, W. Sex-typing and socialization. In P. H. Mussen (Ed.), *Carmichael's manual of child psychology.* New York: Wiley, 1970.

Moltz, H., Lubin, M., Leon, M., & Numan, M. Hormonal induction of maternal behavior in the ovariectomized nulliparous rat. *Physiology and Behavior,* 1970, *5,* 1373–1377.

Money, J., & Ehrhardt, A. A. *Man and woman, boy and girl.* Baltimore: Johns Hopkins University Press, 1972.

Montemayor, R. Children's performance in a game and their attraction to it as a function of sex-typed labels. *Child Development,* 1974, *45,* 152–156.

Moore, M. Aggressive themes in a binocular rivalry situation. *Journal of Personality and Social Psychology,* 1966, *3,* 685–688.

Moyer, K. E. Sex differences in aggression. In R. C. Friedman, R. M. Richart, & R. L. Vande Wiele (Eds.), *Sex differences in behavior.* New York: Wiley, 1974.

Moyer, K. E. *The psychobiology of aggression.* New York: Harper & Row, 1976.

Mullis, I. V. S. *Educational achievement and sex discrimination.* Denver: National Assessment of Educational Progress, 1975.

Nance, W. E., & Engel, E. One X and four hypotheses: Response to Lehrke's "A theory of X-linkage of major intellectual traits." *American Journal of Mental Deficiency,* 1972, *76,* 623–625.

Nash, S. C., & Feldman, S. S. *Responsiveness to babies: Life-situation specific sex differences in adulthood.* Manuscript submitted for publication, 1977.

Nathanson, C. A. Illness and the feminine role: A theoretical review. *Social Science & Medicine,* 1975, *9*(2), 57–62.

National Commission on the Causes and Prevention of Violence. *To establish justice, to insure domestic tranquility.* Washington, D.C.: U.S. Government Printing Office, 1969.

Nord, W. R. Social exchange theory: An integrative approach to social conformity. *Psychological Bulletin,* 1969, *71,* 174–208.

Oetzel, R. M. Classified summary of research in sex differences. In E. E. Maccoby (Ed.), *The development of sex differences.* Stanford, Calif.: Stanford University Press, 1966.

O'Leary, V. E. Some attitudinal barriers to occupational aspirations in women. *Psychological Bulletin,* 1974, *81,* 809–826.

Omark, D. R., Omark, M., & Edelman, M. *Dominance hierarchies in young children.* Paper presented at the meeting of the International Congress of Anthropological and Ethnological Sciences, Chicago, 1973.

Palmore, E., & Luikart, C. Health and social factors related to life satisfaction. *Journal of Health and Social Behavior,* 1972, *13,* 68–80.

Parsons, J. E., Ruble, D. N., Hodges, K. L., & Small, A. W. Cognitive developmental factors in emerging sex differences in achievement-related expectancies. *Journal of Social Issues,* 1976, *32*(3), 47–61.

Parsons, T. The American family: Its relations to personality and to the social structure. In T. Parsons & R. F. Bales (Eds.), *Family, socialization and interaction process.* New York: Free Press, 1955.

Pedersen, F. A., & Bell, R. Q. Sex differences in preschool children without histories of complications of pregnancy and delivery. *Developmental Psychology,* 1970, *3,* 10–15.

Peplau, L. A. Impact of fear of success and sex-role attitudes on women's competitive achievement. *Journal of Personality and Social Psychology,* 1976, *34,* 561–568.

Persky, H., Smith, K. D., & Basu, G. K. Relation of psychologic measures of aggression and hostility to testosterone production in man. *Psychosomatic Medicine,* 1971, *33,* 265–277.

Petersen, A. C. Physical androgyny and cognitive functioning in adolescence. *Developmental Psychology,* 1976, *12,* 524–533.

Potter, M. C., & Levy, E. Spatial enumeration without counting. *Child Development,* 1968, *39,* 265–272.

Preston, R. C. Reading achievement of German and American children. *School and Society,* 1962, *90,* 350–354.

Rand, L. M., & Miller, A. L. A developmental cross-sectioning of women's careers and marriage attitudes and life plans. *Journal of Vocational Behavior,* 1972, *2,* 317–331.

Rivenbark, W. H. Self-disclosure among adolescents. *Psychological Reports,* 1971, *28,* 35–42.

Rosenkrantz, P. S., Vogel, S. R., Bee, H., Broverman, I. K., & Broverman, D. M. Sex-role stereotypes and self-concepts in college students. *Journal of Consulting and Clinical Psychology,* 1968, *32,* 287–295.

Ross, M., Layton, B., Erickson, B., & Schopler, J. Affect, facial regard, and reactions to crowding. *Journal of Personality and Social Psychology,* 1973, *28,* 68–76.

Rushton, J. P. Socialization and the altruistic behavior of children. *Psychological Bulletin,* 1976, *83,* 898–913.

Russo, N. F. Eye contact, interpersonal distance, and the equilibrium theory. *Journal of Personality and Social Psychology,* 1975, *31,* 497–502.

Saario, T. N., Jacklin, C. N., & Tittle, K. Sex role stereotyping in the public schools. *Harvard Educational Review,* 1973, *43,* 386–416.

Sampson, E. E., & Hancock, F. T. An examination of the relationship between ordinal position, personality, and conformity. *Journal of Personality and Social Psychology,* 1967, *5,* 398–407.

Schachter, F. F., Shore, E., Hodapp, R., Chalfin, S., & Bundy, C. Do girls talk earlier? Mean length of utterance in toddlers. *Developmental Psychology,* 1978, *14,* 388–392.

Schaie, K. W., & Roberts, J. *School achievement of children as measured by the reading and arithmetic subtests of the Wide Range Achievement Test.* (Vital and Health Statistics—Series 11—No. 103.) Washington, D.C.: U.S. Government Printing Office, 1970.

Schlossberg, N. K., & Goodman, J. A. Children's sex stereotyping of occupations. *Vocational Guidance Quarterly,* 1972, *20,* 266–270.

Schneider, F. W., & Coutts, L. M. Unpublished data, 1976.

Schneider, F. W., & Coutts, L. M. Educational orientation of students in coeducational and single-sex high schools. Research report to Canada Council, 1977.

Schneider, F. W., & Green, J. E. Need for affiliation and sex as moderators of the relationship between need for achievement and academic performance. *Journal of School Psychology*, 1977, *15*, 269–277.

Sears, R. R., Rau, L., & Alpert, R. *Identification and child rearing.* Stanford, Calif.: Stanford University Press, 1965.

Sears, R. R., Whiting, J., Nowlis, V., & Sears, P. S. Some child rearing antecedents of aggression and dependency in young children. *Psychology Monographs*, 1953, *67*, 135–234.

Sherman, J. A. Problem of sex differences in space perception and aspects of intellectual functioning. *Psychological Review*, 1967, *74*, 290–299.

Sherman, J. A. *On the psychology of women.* Springfield, Ill.: Charles C Thomas, 1971.

Sherman, J. A. Field articulation, sex, spatial visualization, dependency, practice, laterality of the brain and birth order. *Perceptual and Motor Skills*, 1974, *38*, 1223–1235.

Shields, S. A. Functionalism, Darwinism, and the psychology of women: A study in social myth. *American Psychologist*, 1975, *30*, 739–754.

Siegel, C. L. F. Sex differences in the occupational choices of second graders. *Journal of Vocational Behavior*, 1973, *3*, 15–19.

Sistrunk, F., & McDavid, J. W. Sex variable in conforming behavior. *Journal of Personality and Social Psychology*, 1971, *17*, 200–207.

Sommer, R. Sex differences in the retention of quantitative information. *Journal of Educational Psychology*, 1958, *49*, 187–192.

Stafford, R. E. Sex differences in spatial visualization as evidence of sex-linked inheritance. *Perceptual and Motor Skills*, 1961, *13*, 428.

Stein, A. H. The effects of sex role standards for achievement and sex role preference on three determinants of achievement motivation. *Developmental Psychology*, 1971, *4*, 219–231.

Stein, A. H., & Bailey, M. M. The socialization of achievement orientation in females. *Psychological Bulletin*, 1973, *80*, 345–366.

Stein, A. H., Pohly, S. R., & Mueller, E. The influence of masculine, feminine, and neutral tasks on children's achievement behavior, expectancies of success, and attainment values. *Child Development*, 1971, *42*, 195–207.

Sternglanz, S. H., & Serbin, L. A. Sex role stereotyping in children's television programs. *Developmental Psychology*, 1974, *10*, 710–715.

Szal, J. A. *Sex differences in the cooperative and competitive behaviors of nursery school children.* Unpublished master's thesis, Stanford University, 1972.

Taylor, S. P., & Epstein, S. Aggression as a function of the interaction between sex of the aggressor and the sex of the victim. *Journal of Personality*, 1967, *35*, 474–486.

Tennis, G. H., & Dabbs, J. M. Sex, setting and personal space: First grade through college. *Sociometry*, 1975, *38*, 385–394.

Tyler, L. E. *The psychology of human differences* (3rd ed.). New York: Appleton-Century-Crofts, 1965.

Vandenberg, S. G., & Kuse, A. R. Spatial ability: A critical review of the sex-linked major-gene hypothesis. In M. Wittig & A. Petersen (Eds.), *Determinants of sex-related differences in cognitive functioning.* New York: Academic Press, 1979.

van de Sande, J. P. An investigation of the behavioral differences between men and women with regard to game theory. *Nederlands Tijdschrift voor de Psychologie en haar Grensgebieden*, 1973, *28*, 327–341.

Van Dusen, R. A., & Sheldon, E. B. The changing status of American women: A life cycle perspective. *American Psychologist*, 1976, *31*, 106–116.

Veroff, J., Wilcox, S., & Atkinson, J. W. The achievement motive in high school and college age women. *Journal of Abnormal and Social Psychology,* 1953, *48,* 108–119.

Vinacke, W. E., Mogy, R., Powers, W., Langan, C., & Beck, R. Accommodative strategy and communication in a three-person matrix game. *Journal of Personality and Social Psychology,* 1974, *29,* 509–525.

Waldrop, M. F., & Halverson, C. F., Jr. Intensive and extensive peer behavior: Longitudinal and cross-sectional analyses. *Child Development,* 1975, *46,* 19–26.

Wechsler, D. *The measurement and appraisal of adult intelligence.* Baltimore: Williams & Wilkins, 1958.

Weller, L., Shlomi, A., & Zimont, G. Birth order, sex, and occupational interest. *Journal of Vocational Behavior,* 1976, *8,* 45–50.

Whiting, B. B., & Edwards, C. P. A cross-cultural analysis of sex differences in the behavior of children aged three through eleven. *Journal of Social Psychology,* 1973, *91,* 171–188.

Witkin, H. A., Dyk, R. B., Faterson, H. F., Goodenough, D. R., & Karp, S. A. (Eds.). *Psychological differentiation: Studies of development.* New York: Wiley, 1962.

Zaidel, S. F., & Mehrabian, A. The ability to communicate and infer positive and negative attitudes facially and vocally. *Journal of Experimental Research in Personality,* 1969, *3,* 233–241.

Zuckerman, M., & Wheeler, L. To dispel fantasies about the fantasy-based measure of fear of success. *Psychological Bulletin,* 1975, *82,* 932–946.

———————————————————————— **II**

Age Differences

In this chapter we have elected to restrict our attention to age differences in adulthood instead of dealing with the entire life span. One reason for concentrating on the adult period is the disproportionately high amount of attention childhood and adolescence have traditionally received in psychology curricula. We also believe that embarking on an exploration of age differences in adulthood should be anticipated with special interest by every person who has recently, or fairly recently, entered adulthood. Such an endeavor provides a unique opportunity for a person to glimpse into his or her own future development. Indeed, the tremendous popularity of Gail Sheehy's *Passages* (1976) exemplifies the current upsurge of interest in the psychology of adulthood.

Our perspective stems from the field of life-span developmental psychology, the area of psychology "concerned with the description and explication of ontogenetic (age-related) behavioral change from birth to death" (Baltes & Goulet, 1970, p. 12). It is important to point out that the emphasis is on *age-related behavioral changes* as opposed to age differences per se. The distinction between age changes and age differences is a critical one. As we will discover, age differences may be the outcome of changes that are systematically related to the aging process or they may be due to factors that are not necessarily tied to aging. For example, suppose that the political views of your parents are more conservative than yours. The question remains whether the difference is due to the fact that when they were your age your parents held similar views to your present ones but became progressively more conservative as they aged or whether they always have held the same views but that their generation is just more conservative than your generation. Only in the former instance does the age difference reflect an age-related behavioral change. Indeed one of the life-span developmental psychologist's most challenging tasks is to disentangle those factors that are and are not responsible for existing age differences.

Several assumptions underlie a life-span developmental approach (Kimmel, 1974): (1) The individual's characteristics (both intellective and nonintellective) are not permanently fixed before reaching adulthood; development—change and growth—is a life-long process. (2) Adult development is a "sequential orderly progression." (3) The developmental psychology of adulthood is not simply an extension of the developmental psychology of childhood. The salient issues during childhood and adolescence (for example, achieving in school, becoming independent from parents, and developing a sex-role identity) generally differ from those in adulthood (for example, adapting successfully to marriage, parenting, one's job, menopause, retirement, decline in bodily function, and impending death). In a similar vein, Rabbitt (1977) says, with reference to changes in problem-solving ability that occur from young adulthood to old age, "we must never uncritically agree . . . that the relationships between processes mediating problem solving in young adults are *necessarily* the same as those in the old" (p. 606).

When the subjects of aging, age differences, or age changes are brought up, we usually assume that it is chronological age that is under consideration. Nevertheless, some investigators distinguish among several meanings of age (Birren & Renner, 1977). *Biological age* refers to a person's position in relation to his or her potential life span. Measurements of vital life-limiting organ systems presumably could be used to determine which of two individuals with the same birth date is biologically younger than the other. *Psychological age* refers to how successfully the individual, as compared with others, is able to adapt to the demands of his or her environment. Finally *social age* pertains to the extent to which a person's roles and behavior correspond with the societal expectations for his or her chronological age group.

However, while different conceptions of age may have heuristic merit, it is very unlikely that any of them will soon become more commonly used than the much more objective and widely understood concept of *chronological age* (Neugarten, 1977). Yet chronological age, by itself, is an empty variable—it is merely an index of the passage of time. Changes that occur as a person grows older are not caused by age; they are caused by the biological and social influences that coincide with the passage of time. It is this limitation of chronological age as an explanatory variable that led to the advocacy of other definitions of age.

In trying to account for existing differences between age groups we must look to the effects of both inner biological processes and outer sociological conditions. Biological decline occurs—a decline in vision and hearing, slowing of central nervous system functioning, loss of physical strength, and so on—and these changes undoubtedly influence behavior. Also, since socialization is a lifelong process, age differences and changes reflect the impact of a continuously changing social/cultural context, including being socialized into new social positions with their attendant age norms and age constraints.

People of all ages experience the constraining influence of society's age norms. As people advance in age, they encounter shifting expectations concerning age-appropriate behavior. It has been suggested that people are cognizant of "social clocks" that help to define for them appropriate and inappropriate times for engaging in various activities and behaviors (Neugarten, Moore, & Lowe, 1968). Research by Neugarten and associates (1968) indicates that there is consensus concerning the age limits for various activities, such as the "best time" for getting married, for finishing school, and for retiring. These investigators gave descriptions of a variety of behaviors to a group of adults and asked them to indicate their degree of approval given that people of different ages engaged in each of the behaviors. For example, one item was, "A woman who feels it's all right at her age to wear a two-piece bathing suit to the beach: When she's 45. When she's 30. When she's 18." The most important finding was that the older the subjects the more likely were they to attach constraints to behavior simply on the basis of a person's age. These results suggest that the adult socialization process leads to an increased acceptance of age norms and, presumably, to an internalization of these norms as moderators of personal behavior.

In addition to the imposition of age norms and related constraints, people are subjected to prevailing age stereotypes. In view of the fact that aging is negatively viewed by most members of society, it should not be a surprise that the least favorable stereotypes are those about older people. Some of the less positive characteristics commonly ascribed to older persons include: ill, tired, uninterested in sex, grouchy, withdrawn, mentally slower, forgetful, less able to learn new things, and unproductive. More positive attributes include being wise from experience, friendly, and warm (Harris et al., 1975; McTavish, 1971).

The possibility that individual differences decrease with age would seem to be suggested by the above evidence that as people grow older they place increasing emphasis on age norms and the evidence of the existence of age stereotypes that foster the impression that older people share a highly similar cluster of characteristics. Yet there is little empirical basis for this impression. Older people are not a homogeneous lot. Controlled studies of a variety of psychological variables (for example, depression, reaction time, and intellectual ability) and physiological variables (for example, cardiovascular status, weight, and blood cholesterol) show that variability among people remains the same or even increases with age (Maddox & Douglass, 1974; Schonfield, 1974). An excellent example of older people showing greater variability than younger people may be found in Figure 2-7 in Chapter 2. Let us now turn to a consideration of age-related variability in cognitive functioning.

COGNITIVE FUNCTIONING AND RELATED VARIABLES

In this section we will first consider the relationship between global indexes of intelligence and age, directing particular attention to the fact that the nature of the research findings varies somewhat depending on whether the cross-sectional method or longitudinal method is employed. Then we will consider research on special abilities, learning and memory, problem solving, response speed, and motivation.

Intelligence

For years most psychologists had little doubt about the course of mental development during adulthood—they believed aging is accompanied by a decline in intellectual ability. Wechsler (1958), the developer of the WAIS and Wechsler-Bellevue, asserted that:

> Beginning with the investigation by Galton in 1883 and continuing up to and including the most recent studies of Pacaud, nearly all studies dealing with the age factor in adult performance have shown that most human abilities, insofar as they are measurable, decline progressively, after reaching a peak somewhere between the ages of 18 and 25. . . . the decline occurs in all mental measures of ability, including those employed in tests of intelligence [p. 135].

Such a view undoubtedly was reinforced by the common stereotype of the older person. In 1967 Jack Botwinick introduced his book *Cognitive Processes in Maturity and Old Age* by asking, "Does intelligence decline in old age?" At the time Botwinick meant his question largely as a rhetorical one because the evidence he subsequently presented favored the decremental hypothesis, at least with respect to many aspects of cognitive functioning. Yet just one decade later, in the *Handbook of the Psychology of Aging*, he no longer viewed the question as rhetorical, suggesting that there may be some plausible reasons for challenging the decremental hypothesis (Botwinick, 1977). In fact, during the 1970s the question of the age-intelligence relationship developed into quite a controversial topic, and the *American Psychologist* served as a forum for a running debate (for example, Baltes & Schaie, 1976; Horn & Donaldson, 1977).

What events have transpired in recent years to undermine confidence in the widely embraced decremental model of aging? At the heart of the matter were important methodological issues, particularly those centering on the distinction between the two main research strategies—the cross-sectional method and the longitudinal method.

Cross-Sectional Investigations. In a cross-sectional study, at a single point in time some characteristic of two or more age groups is measured and compared. For instance, in 1980 we might measure and then compare the intelligence-test scores of samples of 30-, 50-, and 70-year-olds. If the results of such a study reveal intelligence differences between the age groups, we might infer that these reflect age changes in intelligence. That is, we might conclude that when the 70-year-olds were 50 years old they had the same level of intelligence as the 50-year-old sample, and by the year 2000 the 50-year-olds will be like the 70-year-olds were in 1980. This kind of inference, however, reflects the major pitfall of the cross-sectional method. We simply cannot assume that the three samples differ only with respect to age and that it is only a matter of time before the younger groups become like the older ones. The three samples also differ in their years of birth, which means that a difference in intelligence may be the consequence of any cultural and historical differences to which the samples were exposed. Suppose that the oldest group scored lower in intelligence than the younger groups. Would it merely be due to the fact that they are older, or could it be due to the fact that, because they were raised in a different era, they received less and/or poorer formal education? In addition to possible differences in education, the three groups were exposed to a number of other differences—historical events, socialization practices, health care—any of which might contribute to age differences in intelligence.

An early example of the possible confounding influence of sociohistorical factors occurred when the performances of World War I and World War II recruits on similar intelligence tests were compared. The median (50th percentile) of the World War II recruits was above the 84th percentile of the World War I recruits (Tuddenham, 1948). The superior performance of the World War II men was apparently attributable to improvements in such areas as amount and quality of education, communication, public health, and welfare.

A group of people who were born at or about the same time and consequently have been exposed to similar cultural and historical factors is often called a *cohort*. A *cohort effect* is when part or all of an age difference is traceable to cultural/historical influences associated with the year of birth. The important point is that the cross-sectional method does not permit the investigator to separate age effects and cohort effects. Thus cross-sectional studies are useful in the analysis of age differences, but are deficient for appraising age changes.

Earlier in this century (in the 1930s, 40s, and 50s) the great majority of investigators of the age-intelligence relationship relied entirely on the cross-sectional method. Using a variety of measures of global intelligence, most investigations revealed that intelligence peaked early in adulthood (often during the 20s), and then, perhaps after a short leveling-off period, declined steadily into old age (Botwinick, 1967; Troll, 1975). The early researchers relied on these cross-sectional data to bolster their conviction about the validity of the decremental hypothesis. However, with the passing years, the disenchantment with these findings began to mount (Botwinick, 1977). For one thing, there was an increasing awareness of the confounding of age and cohort effects. It was discovered that if different age groups are equated for educational level, a "decline" in intelligence is much less apparent. Second, a few of the later cross-sectional studies indicated that intelligence does not begin to decline until the late 40s or early 50s. Thirdly, and most importantly, there was an increasing number of longitudinal studies, and the longitudinal data did not agree with the cross-sectional data.

Longitudinal Investigations. With the longitudinal method, the intelligence of one age cohort is measured at one point in time and is measured again on one or more subsequent occasions. Thus, if our earlier mentioned group of 70-year-olds had been participants in a longitudinal study, their intelligence would have been measured when they were ages 30 and 50, as well as when they were 70. This is a repeated measure or within-cohort design. Although longitudinal studies have some practical disadvantages relative to cross-sectional studies—they require a longer time (often decades) to complete and are costlier in terms of money and effort—they do overcome the problem of cohort effects because all of the subjects were born about the same time. Moreover, it isn't necessary to assume the subjects in one age group are similar to those in another; they are the same people.

The decremental hypothesis receives much less support when we look at the results of longitudinal investigations (for example, Owens, 1953). Contrary to the early decline found in most cross-sectional studies, longitudinal studies consistently show that intelligence-test scores remain stable from early adulthood up to the age of 50 or so. In fact, what is frequently found before the 50s is that change does occur, but it is in a slightly upward direction. In the 50s intelligence scores typically show a gradual decline and the decline continues into old age.

Thus longitudinal research provides a much more optimistic view of development of general intelligence during adulthood. However, while the longitudinal method is generally accepted as preferable to the cross-sectional method, it, too, has limitations that diminish our confidence in the data it provides. In longitudinal research, time of measurement is a serious potentially confounding factor (Botwinick, 1973). *Time of measurement* refers to "that state of the environment within which a given set of data were obtained, ... changes in the state of the environment may contribute to the effects noted in an aging study" (Schaie, 1967, p. 129). Time-of-measurement variables may be broadly conceived as including states of the subject as well as states of the experiment and the wider sociocultural milieu.

Let us consider a few time-of-measurement effects. The very act of measuring a person's intelligence on one occasion may affect his or her response on the next occasion. For one thing, a subject's familiarity with the test and testing situation may help improve his or her performance on subsequent testings (that is, a "practice effect"). The testing situation also may change from one period of measurement to the next. One change that often occurs is that the experimenter is an entirely different person at one measurement occasion than at another or, if the same person, may have undergone some personal change of his or her own. At the very least, the experimenter has become more experienced with the test materials and somewhat older. Also, if a group of people is tested on two occasions, cultural and historical events (for example, upsurge in adult education or interruption of education by a war) during the interval between testings may moderate the age/intelligence pattern. Thus the age-intelligence function may be peculiar to a given time period and not representative of a more general pattern reflecting ontogenetic change. Time-of-measurement effects often occur in subtle ways that are hard to detect.

But the most serious problem of longitudinal research is that of *selective dropout.* Some subjects inevitably drop out as a longitudinal project progresses from one testing to the next. They may drop out for psychological and social reasons (for example, they become uninterested or dissatisfied with the experiment or move away) or for biological reasons (for example, ill health or death). In research on intelligence, such attrition is especially problematic because there is strong evidence that the initially more competent participants tend to remain in the project, whereas the initially less competent tend to drop out. Furthermore, dropping out is most likely to occur with the approach and onset of old age. Thus, as a longitudinal study progresses from initial testing through retestings, the survivors become an increasingly "elite" group. Needless to say, as a result of selective dropout, there is an inherent methodological bias against finding a decline in intelligence with age. In cross-sectional research a kind of attrition also occurs; among the older groups it is the healthy and able person who is most likely to volunteer for research, but the bias is not believed to be as acute as in longitudinal research.

Thus, as Botwinick (1977) has observed, while the cross-sectional method seems to spuriously *magnify* an age-related decrement in intelligence, the longitudinal method may spuriously *minimize* the decline. Actually, Botwinick further suggests that the age patterns revealed in cross-sectional and longitudinal studies differ only in a quantitative sense and not in a qualitative sense. Botwinick illustrates this by examining the results of Schaie's research, which involves the use of both cross-sectional and longitudinal techniques (Schaie, 1959; Schaie & Labouvie-Vief, 1974; Schaie, Labouvie, & Buech, 1973). In 1956 Schaie administered the Primary Mental Abilities test to 500 people, 50 in each 5-year interval from ages 20-25 to 66-70. This constituted a cross-sectional sample. Then, the subjects were retested in 1963 and again in 1970, providing longitudinal data spanning 14 years for each age cohort. Schaie's cross-sectional results are depicted in Figure 11-1, and the longitudinal results are portrayed in Figure 11-2.

First, look at Figure 11-1, and notice that up to age 50 the curve suggests stability of intellectual performance. The scores of the 36-50 year-olds approximated those of the 20-25 year-old group, with a slight bump in the 26-35 age range. An appreciable decline first shows up after age 46-50, but it is not until age 61-65 that the scores are more than a standard deviation below those of the highest group. This pattern definitely conflicts with the early cross-sectional

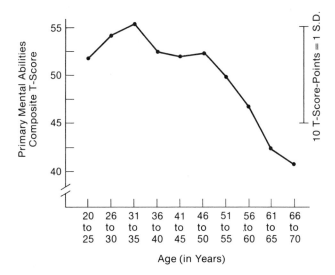

Figure 11-1. Cross-sectional analysis of composite Primary Mental Abilities. From "Cross-Sectional Methods in the Psychological Aspects of Aging," by K. W. Schaie, *Journal of Gerontology,* 1959, *14,* 208–215. Copyright 1959 by the Gerontological Society. Reprinted by permission.

studies, many of which, if you recall, indicated declining intelligence beginning early in adulthood.

Figure 11-2, which reports the longitudinal data, needs some clarification. There is a separate curve for each of the seven age cohorts. For example, cohort I was first tested in 1956 at the age of 25, then tested in 1963 at the age of 32, and in 1970 at the age of 39. Likewise, the oldest cohort, cohort VII, began testing in 1956 at the age of 67 and completed the third testing in 1970 when they were 81. Looking at the individual curves we can see that none of the youngest cohorts showed a decline in their ability scores over a 14-year interval. A decline was in evidence in cohorts V, VI, and VII, but statistically significant only in the oldest two.

Now the really important question is whether Figures 11-1 and 11-2 reflect the same age/intelligence pattern. Inspection indicates that indeed there is a strong similarity between the longitudinal and cross-sectional data. Both indicate little or no decrease before age 50 and then sometime after 50 a decline begins to occur. Botwinick's analyses of the relative rates of decline among the older subjects do indicate that the cross-sectional method showed sharper decline rates than the longitudinal method. It was on the basis of these analyses and his review of other relevant research that Botwinick (1977) concluded, "When the limitations of the cohort effect in cross-sectional research and the selective subject dropout effect in longitudinal research are recognized, the two methods may provide similar interpretations: differences are quantitative, not qualitative" (p. 603). In other words, it seems that the shape of the general

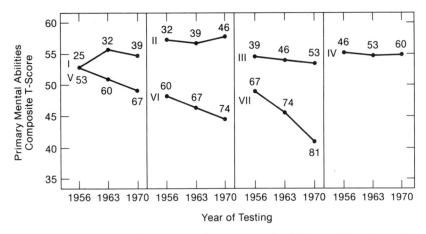

Figure 11-2. Longitudinal analysis of composite Primary Mental Abilities. Roman numerals refer to age cohorts and Arabic numbers refer to mean age at testing (see text). Adapted from "Intellectual Abilities," by J. Botwinick. In J. E. Birren and K. W. Schaie (Eds.), *Handbook of the Psychology of Aging.* © 1977 by Litton Educational Publishing, Inc. Based on data from K. W. Schaie and Labouvie-Vief (1974) and Schaie, Labouvie, and Buech (1973). Used by permission of Van Nostrand Reinhold Company and the American Psychological Association.

intelligence/age function is basically the same for both cross-sectional data and longitudinal data—relative stability of intelligence until around the 50s and then a gradual decline. The only difference is that the cross-sectional method suggests a sharper decline than the longitudinal method.

Special Abilities

Up to this point we have been considering the evidence concerning the association between aging and global indexes of intelligence. Yet, as we have discovered, intelligence may be conceived as consisting of a number of specific abilities. If we recognize that intelligence is not a purely unitary construct, it makes sense to examine the age pattern for each kind of ability separately.

Classic Aging Pattern. It will be recalled that as well as yielding an overall IQ score the Wechsler Adult Intelligence Scale (WAIS) yields a Verbal IQ and a Performance IQ. The Performance subtests (for example, block design and digit symbol) seem to have in common an emphasis on speed of response and perceptual integration in the solution of novel problems, whereas the Verbal subtests (for example, information and vocabulary) reflect verbal skills and the use of information acquired from one's previous experiences. Scores on the two kinds of test display different age functions (Botwinick, 1967, 1977). The Verbal score shows little or no decline, whereas the Performance score does decline. This pattern has emerged so consistently that it has come to be known as a "classic aging pattern." The classic pattern has been found both in cross-sectional studies and longitudinal studies, although there is some longitudinal evidence suggesting that very late in life (after age 70) the Performance and Verbal functions merge into a general decline (for example, Eisdorfer & Wilkie, 1973).

Although the verbal scores have repeatedly been found to hold up well in the face of advancing age, a study by Botwinick and Storandt (1974) gives us some reason to question the validity of this generalization. These researchers first matched samples of older and younger people (mean ages = 71 and 18) on the WAIS vocabulary subtest using the standard quantitative scoring procedure. Then they deviated from the traditional scoring procedure by evaluating the quality of the subjects' responses. Botwinick and Storandt found that the most superior kind of response—an excellent synonym—was less frequently given by the older group than the younger group. The older subjects were able to score as well as the younger ones by giving lower quality, although correct, answers (for example, a good explanation of the word's meaning). Botwinick and Storandt speculated that if qualitative analyses of other kinds of verbal function (for example, information and comprehension) were implemented, the stable verbal portion of the class aging pattern might disappear.

Crystallized and Fluid Intelligence. In considering the possibility that the nature of the age pattern varies with the kind of ability being measured, the distinction between crystallized intelligence and fluid intelligence also is relevant (Horn, 1970, 1975; Horn & Cattell, 1967). As discussed in Chapter 4, crystallized intelligence involves such abilities as verbal comprehension, vocabulary, knowledge about academic subject matter (for example, science and literature), general factual information, and social awareness. Fluid intelligence involves such abilities as associative memory (as measured, for example, by recall in paired associate learning), inductive reasoning, and memory span. Crystallized intelligence is thought to be strongly dependent on a person's previous experiences. Therefore, with the advancement of age it should hold up well because of practice, increased learning, and the consolidation of knowledge. On the other hand, fluid intelligence is largely independent of experience and is presumed to have a strong neurophysiological basis (and thus a greater genetic element than crystallized intelligence). Fluid abilities are perceived as declining with age because of possible physiological degeneration and such things as rigid habits built up over the years.

Horn (1975) has summarized the results of both cross-sectional and longitudinal research pertaining to both kinds of intelligence. Starting early in adulthood, measures of fluid intelligence show a steady decline, whereas measures of crystallized intelligence increase or remain constant across adulthood.[1]

---

[1]Horn (1977) makes the point that virtually every task has both a fluid component and a crystallized component to it, although many are more heavily weighted with one than the other. One person may successfully cope with a task by relying on his or her fluid abilities, whereas a second may use his or her crystallized abilities.

These findings concerning fluid and crystallized intelligence are entirely compatible with the classic aging pattern, and, in fact, you may have detected a similarity between the fluid and crystallized abilities, on the one hand, and the Performance and Verbal subtests of the WAIS, on the other hand.

We should also refer to the accumulating cross-sectional evidence indicating the existence of a curvilinear relationship between age and performance on Piagetian measures of cognitive functioning. Contrary to Piaget's formulation that cognitive development is unidirectional and that little cognitive change occurs during adulthood, the elderly display lower levels of cognitive ability than younger adults (and sometimes as low as children) on measures of moral judgment and egocentrism, and certain logical operations tasks, such as those requiring conservation ability (Papalia & Bielby, 1974). Some writers have suggested that the tasks used by Piaget and those used to measure fluid ability reflect similar underlying cognitive processes. Although this would account for the decline in old age which is suggested when both kinds of measure are used, the evidence to date concerning their degree of similarity has been inconclusive (Clayton & Overton, 1976).

Thus, it seems that some of the confusion concerning the age/intelligence relationship is lessened by recognizing that intelligence is not necessarily a unitary construct. As Horn and Donaldson (1976) have noted, when the results concerning the decremental hypothesis conflict, it often may be due to the fact that the investigators have employed tests with different concentrations of fluid and crystallized abilities. When the former predominate, a downward trend is found; when the latter predominate, no such trend is observed.

Terminal Decline

Apparently there is a period in one's life cycle when even those abilities most resistant to decline (for example, verbal skill) begin to wane. A number of investigators have provided support for what has become known as the terminal drop (for example, Kleemeier, 1962; Riegel & Riegel, 1972). This phenomenon refers to the fact that human cognitive functioning shows a marked decrement during the period (months or few years) immediately preceding death. The theory is that those factors, both genetic and environmental, that are responsible for death also cause the drop in cognitive performance. We might note that an analysis by Palmore and Cleveland (1976) suggests that what may be more likely to occur is a terminal decline rather than a terminal drop. The former refers to a steady linear decline that begins at some point preceding death, whereas the latter signifies a curvilinear (increasingly rapid) fall off before death.

Although the theory of terminal drop (decline) presumably relates to all aspects of human functioning, possible terminal drops in noncognitive functioning have received little attention. One study did show, as might be expected, substantial declines with the advancement of age on measures of both physical functioning (for example, health ratings by physicians and tests of vision and hearing) and social functioning (for example, number of intimate contacts and leisure activities), and small declines with age on indicators of psychological functioning (for example, feelings of happiness and satisfaction with work and friendships) (Palmore & Cleveland, 1976). However, with the exception of a terminal decline in physical functioning as rated by a physician, there was little evidence of significant terminal declines or terminal drops.

Learning and Memory

As indicated in the preceding section, at least some aspects of intelligence apparently decline with advancing age. It seems reasonable, then, to expect that such decrements would be associated with corresponding changes in the learning and memory processes. Older people themselves are often heard to worry about their failing ability to remember things. In fact, we should recall that Horn (1975) reports fluid intelligence, which is most apt to reveal an age decrement, involves at least two memory factors—span memory and associative memory.[2]

The laboratory evidence does indeed indicate that a decline in verbal learning ability accompanies the advancement of age (Arenberg & Robertson-Tchabo, 1977). The most commonly used measures of verbal learning involve serial learning tasks (that is, learning of a list of items, such as words, in correct order) and paired-associate learning tasks (that is, learning associations between pairs of items, such as dog/cat).

The evidence also suggests that memory capacity declines with age (Craik, 1977; Reese, 1976). However, in considering the relationship between age and memory, it is important to distinguish between primary memory and secondary memory (Craik, 1977). *Primary memory* is when the material is in conscious awareness—that is, still being rehearsed by the individual. Only a few (2-4) verbal items can be maintained in primary memory. *Secondary memory* is the main memory system in which information is stored and from which it may be retrieved. Research suggests that there is negligible decline in primary memory with age, whereas substantial decrements seem to occur with respect to secondary memory processes (Craik, 1977; Reese, 1976). This difference is illustrated when people are presented with a list of 15-20 words and asked to recall them in any order. Older subjects recall just as many of the last few words as the younger subjects, suggesting no differences in primary memory (that is, these are the words still in conscious awareness). However, they recall fewer of the earlier presented words, which suggests impairment in secondary memory. Slight decrements are even found in a memory-span task calling for the retention of a short series of 6 or 7 items because, here, too, the primary memory capacity of 2 to 4 items has been exceeded, and some information must be retrieved from secondary memory. Older people are especially likely to encounter difficulty when a memory-span test calls for them to recall the items in reverse serial order. This backward span measure

---

[2]We should again point out that it is difficult, if not impossible, to deal with learning and memory separately because of the integral connection between the two.

requires that the content of the memory be reorganized. As we will see below, an older person is especially handicapped when his or her organizational abilities are tested.

The belief is often expressed that older people have a remarkable ability to remember things from far back into their past. Yet, such ability entails the secondary memory processes which, as we have seen, have been found to decrease in proficiency when measured in the laboratory on a relatively short-term basis. Several studies of long-term memory confirm the laboratory data, showing that older people are, in fact, less able to recall and recognize events and people from the past (for example, Bahrick, Bahrick, & Wittlinger, 1975).

Memory ability requires both acquisition and retrieval. *Acquisition* refers to the process of getting the information into storage, and *retrieval* refers to the process of getting the information out of storage. If there is little difference in primary memory capacity between older and younger people, it suggests that the memory deficit results not from a failure to perceive the material but from limitations in the acquisition of it, the retrieval of it, or both. And it appears that older people have difficulties with both acquisition and retrieval. An acquisition deficit essentially means that information in the primary memory is inadequately transferred to secondary memory. The central problem for older people seems to be a difficiency in the *organizational processes*, wherein there is a failure to spontaneously make use of efficient strategies in organizing the material to be learned and retained. Such strategies include using mediational techniques, as well as organizing the information into semantic categories, conceptual categories, and hierarchical groupings (Arenberg & Robertson-Tchabo, 1977; Craik, 1977; Elias, Elias, & Elias, 1977). For instance, several studies show that older persons are less apt to employ mnemonics—techniques that make the information easier to remember by adding to it additional information such as a visual image or verbal association. As an illustration, suppose in a paired associate task you have to learn which nouns are associated with each other, including the pair "girl" and "candle." To facilitate learning this association, you might employ a visual mediator (for example, you imagine a girl lighting a candle) or a verbal mediator (for example, you verbalize "girl lights candle"). It seems that older people are less likely to employ such strategies and when they do, often use inappropriate or confusing ones.

Furthermore, there is evidence that older people suffer from deficits in their ability to retrieve (recover) information that has been stored in memory (Craik, 1977; Reese, 1976). Apparently, when it is time to recall information, older people are less able, or at least less likely, to generate their own effective retrieval cues or strategies. Thus, compared with younger adults, their performance improves disproportionately more if they are provided with information to help them remember. For example, recognition tests (as in a multiple-choice exam wherein the to-be-remembered information is presented along with incorrect information) produce a greater improvement over recall performance for older adults than younger adults. Arenberg and Robertson-Tchabo (1977) and Horn (1976) also suggest that another thing that underlies the older person's retrieval difficulties is the inadequate organization he or she imposes on the material during acquisition; information that is poorly organized is harder to retrieve. Horn (1976) has argued persuasively that it is the declining ability to give some meaningful organization to the material to be learned and retrieved that is at least partly responsible for the decrements in intellectual abilities found in old age.

The point should be underscored that current evidence emphasizes the significance of the acquisition and retrieval processes and not what occurs while the information is stored in memory. That is, there is less support for the idea that older people lose information that is stored in memory due to the effects of such factors as interference or decay processes (Craik, 1977; Reese, 1976).

We have seen that situations that demand the manipulation and organization (or reorganization) of material to be learned and retained seem to penalize the older person. In addition, older people apparently are apt to encounter particular difficulty relative to younger adults in situations that require the division of their attention—for example, when they must learn both visual and auditory stimuli presented simultaneously (Craik, 1977). Older people apparently tend to focus on one set of stimuli to the neglect of the other stimuli, and, consequently, there is a deficit in the acquisition of the nonattended material.

In sum, the evidence on learning and memory suggests that older persons are handicapped by deficits in learning ability and memory ability. The memory deficit, however, apparently resides in secondary memory rather than in primary memory. Older people encounter particular difficulty when their organizational (or reorganizational) capacities are challenged. They seem to employ less efficient strategies in organizing the to-be-remembered material during the acquisition process and also generate less effective retrieval strategies when required to get the information out of storage.

Problem Solving

Not surprisingly, older people perform more poorly than younger adults on laboratory tests of problem-solving ability (Botwinick, 1973; Rabbitt, 1977). Part of their problem-solving difficulty is traceable to the same kinds of factors underlying their diminished learning and memory performance. As Rabbitt (1977) says:

> For problem solving . . . in so far as the ability to store new information in a "current" store is important, old people may be disadvantaged because their ability to *perceptually organize* and *encode* new information when *presented* makes storage (and perhaps retrieval) of current data more difficult, and successive decisions taken on the basis of such information are correspondingly less reliable [p. 621].

A study by Denney and Denney (1973) is an interesting illustration of the kinds of difficulty older persons have in directing their intellectual processes in a problem-solving situation. Middle-aged and elderly women were given a task in which they had to "guess" which of several pictures the experimenter was thinking about. In this "20 questions" kind of game, compared with the older subjects, younger subjects used more constraint-seeking questions that helped them to deduce that the picture belonged to one or another of several categories (for example, "Is it something that flies?"). On the other hand, older subjects asked more irrelevant and redundant questions (for example, "Is it a car?" after receiving a negative answer to "Is it something mechanical?") and consequently needed many more questions to arrive at a solution. The findings were viewed as reflecting an age-related decrement in the use of classification strategies.

Speed of Response

One of the more firmly established findings is that older people experience a slowing down of their speed in performing various motor tasks (Bischof, 1976; Welford, 1977). This slowing may be seen in their ability to make simple movements (for example, shifting a lever back and forth in a slot) and even more so in complex movements (for example, writing or tracing). Also showing an age decrement is reaction time, the interval between the appearance of a stimulus and the beginning of one's motor response to it. Simple reaction time (when there is one signal and one response) shows some age decrement, but older people have particular difficulty with measures of choice reaction time (when there are several signals and a separate response to each). The more complex the reaction-time task—that is, the more choices available—the greater the age decrement. An everyday example of simple reaction time is beginning to accelerate when a traffic light turns from red to green; sorting playing cards into the four suits is an example of choice reaction time.

According to a review by Welford (1977), the slowing is much less due to muscular limitations than to the increased time needed both to make the decision concerning which movements are required and to monitor the sequence of movements. Thus, Welford notes that on relatively simple tasks, the decrement in response speed often may be offset considerably if the task is a familiar one or if the individual has a chance to prepare for it or to practice it. But if the task is quite complex, calling for a series of responses that is difficult to program ahead of time, familiarity and practice have much less benefit. Consequently, older people may continue to write their own names quickly but may need extra time to trace over a very complex pattern.

The evidence concerning response speed leads us back to the controversy over whether intelligence declines with age or not. Recall that those abilities most likely to decline with age (for example, the Performance subtests of the WAIS) are also the measures that call for quickness of perceptual/motor response. Some workers, such as Lorge (1936) and, more recently, Green (1969), have argued that the age-related decline in such abilities is primarily a consequence of slowing in response speed and not the manifestation of an intellectual deficit per se. Those who take this viewpoint maintain that the Performance tests of the WAIS and many of the measures of fluid intelligence are, because of the speed requirement, clearly unsuitable, and consequently unfair, to use for measuring intelligence in older people. They suggest that, if the abilities of older people are tested under untimed conditions, age differences in ability tend to vanish.

While the "unsuitability" position may seem to have some compelling aspects, it has been seriously weakened by the arguments presented by those who hold it in disfavor (for example, Botwinick, 1977; Elias et al., 1977; Horn, 1975, 1977). One argument (see Elias et al., 1977) is that, if a person can complete an intellectual task more rapidly than another person, then regardless of the cause of the difference in performance, the faster person is more capable than the slower person, at least with respect to that particular task. Also, a strong argument against the "unsuitability" position is that, when speed requirements are reduced or even eliminated so that people can complete tasks at their own rate, age differences, although smaller, still remain. For example, when given ample time to complete the various WAIS subtests, the classic aging pattern tends to be reduced but not eliminated—older people continue to show a decrement on the Performance tests. Similarly, Horn (1977) reports that fluid intelligence shows a decline even when motor speed and reaction time are statistically controlled. Botwinick (1977) also reviews evidence that indicates that those subtests of the WAIS requiring speed tend to be more highly related to scores on measures of verbal ability than to tests of pure speed. For example, Botwinick and Storandt (1973) found that performance on the digit symbol subtest (the closest "pure speed" test on the WAIS) correlated around .50 with the vocabulary subtest and negligibly with two speed tests.

Motivation and Arousal

One nonintellective factor that has been mentioned as helping to account for age differences in intellectual performance is differences in motivation. It is suggested that older people simply are not sufficiently motivated to perform well on the low relevance tasks administered in the typical testing situation and would improve considerably if adequately motivated. However, verbal learning research by Eisdorfer and his coworkers (for example, Eisdorfer, Nowlin, & Wilkie, 1970) suggests that the truth of the matter may be just the opposite—that older people may find the task demands overly stressful; that is, they become too anxious or aroused, and the heightened arousal interferes with optimal performance (for a review see Elias & Elias, 1977).

Eisdorfer has found that, when involved in a verbal learning task, older subjects exhibit higher levels of autonomic nervous system arousal than younger subjects and significantly improve their performance if they receive a drug that blocks autonomic arousal. Moreover, it is possible that a vicious cycle develops wherein the high arousal state of older people causes them to perform below their capabilities, their subsequent feeling (and fear) of failure further enhances their level of arousal, and so forth. On the basis of Eisdorfer's findings, Arenberg and Robertson-Tchabo (1977) suggest that special care should be taken to minimize the stressfulness of testing situations involving older persons; they also report studies that indicate that older people do respond with improved performance to supportive instructions.

Accounting for the Decrement in Cognitive Performance

How can we account for the decrement in cognitive performance that accompanies advancing age? The decrement is usually attributed to neurophysiological changes (that is, to biological deterioration). In theory such changes can either be the natural, inevitable concomitant of the basic aging process or they may be the result of disease, the incidence of which tends to increase with age. We should note that changes resulting from the basic aging process and those caused by disease are often difficult to disentangle.

The terminal decline phenomenon in which intelligence drops significantly during the period immediately preceding death is consistent with the view that biological deterioration underlies cognitive decline. Research does show that health status affects intellectual performance. An example of a particular health factor that influences an individual's cognitive performance is his or her cardiovascular status. Certain cardiovascular diseases, such as arteriosclerosis (characterized by hardening of the blood vessel walls) and hypertension (abnormally high blood pressure), increase in frequency with age and are associated with deficits in cognitive functioning (Elias et al., 1977).

On the other hand, some workers have suggested that there is a tendency to infer a biological cause of a cognitive deficit when at least part of the cause may reside in the environment (for example, Labouvie-Vief & Gonda, 1976). The possibility that the decrement in cognitive performance reflects a deficit in environmental stimulation, perhaps even to a greater extent than a biological deficit, has received increasing emphasis. According to Baltes and Labouvie (1973), the environment of older people is deficient in several ways that may restrict the development and maintenance of cognitive skills. For instance, they note that very few older persons take advantage of adult education courses, that family settings and institutions for the elderly often are both intellectually and socially impoverished, and that societal expectations do not emphasize the importance of intellectual competence in the older person.

This is a positive or optimistic perspective because the decline in intelligence among older people is not perceived as inevitable or irreversible. (Of course, we can also be optimistic about retarding some aspects of biological decline.) Proponents of this view advocate that educational and social intervention programs can be employed to retard and even reverse the decline in cognitive performance. Moreover, there is evidence that the intellectual performance of older persons can be improved by the provision of appropriate experiences. A good demonstration of this is a study by Labouvie-Vief and Gonda (1976) in which the inductive reasoning ability of older persons (mean age of 76) was improved by both training and practice, and furthermore, the

improvement was shown to maintain itself over a two-week interval and generalize to other inductive reasoning tasks. Labouvie-Vief and Gonda, while not
denying the role of biological change, interpret their results as suggesting
greater plasticity of intelligence in old age than most psychologists presently
appear ready to acknowledge.

We also want to report that a note of optimism has come from research
on the neuroanatomy of aging. Evidence stemming primarily from neuroana-
tomical experiments on animals suggests that the nervous system, including
the brain, has the potential to resist substantial deterioration with aging if
there is an absence of disease and if the organism is exposed to a stimulating
environment (Diamond, 1978).

Conclusion

Our examination of the evidence concerning the course of cognitive development across adulthood leads us to an overriding impression—the apparent
futility of searching for *one* "normal" or "true" relationship between intelligence and age. The question is much more complex than trying to pin it down
to a single age function. It is true that our review has revealed that, in general,
performance on global indexes of intelligence begins to manifest a gradual
decline sometime after the 40s. However, we must recognize that focusing
solely on general intelligence tends to be misleading because it masks the fact
that most measures of general intelligence tap a variety of special abilities,
and such abilities seem to be differentially influenced by the aging process.
That is, what seems to be the case is that whether we find a decline in intelligence or not depends on what aspects of intelligence, which abilities, we
are dealing with. If we measure abilities such as those that require swiftness
of response, perceptual/motor coordination, and the solution of novel problems, then a decline is likely to be in evidence. On the other hand, if we
emphasize performance that relies largely on the use of acquired information
and skills, then a decline is much less likely to occur. In fact, some individuals
may even show continued improvement, thus adding further testimony to the
view that there is no universal aging pattern. We should be especially careful,
however, about unquestioningly accepting this last conclusion because of the
previously mentioned finding of Botwinick and Storandt (1974) of a qualitative
decrement (as opposed to a quantitative one) in vocabulary ability among the
elderly.

The development of cognitive functioning varies greatly depending on
the individuals concerned. We have noted that good health is important in
the maintenance of cognitive abilities and that the cognitive performance of
older people can be improved via training and practice. Thus, it appears that
in many instances, the older person who has good health and continues to
exercise his or her mind may continue to maintain the same or nearly the
same degree of intellectual competence well into old age. On the other hand,
poor health, including nearness to death, and the lack of intellectual stimulation
may have a detrimental impact on an individual's mental vigor. A discussion

by Baltes and Labouvie (1973) further amplifies the futility of seeking a universal age function for intelligence. They note that not only do age functions
vary from one kind of ability to another, but also that the functions may be
influenced by (and thus vary with) such factors as a person's level of ability,
social-class level, and generation (cohort).

The issue regarding the nature of intelligence seems to be particularly
germane to the present discussion. A number of writers have questioned the
appropriateness of applying the same conceptualization of intelligence to older
people and younger people (for example, Bischof, 1976; Kalish, 1975). In
considering an older person's intelligence, should we focus on the ability to
succeed on perceptual/motor tasks, to define difficult words, to solve abstract
mathematical problems, to learn the associations between a series of paired
items, and so forth? Should we rely on his or her performance on a standard
intelligence test, an instrument that emphasizes abilities needed to succeed
in an academic setting? Or should we endorse a view similar to Wechsler's
(1958)?

> In the case of older people it seems that the one thing we wish most to
> include under the term intelligence, is what William James long ago referred
> to as *sagacity*, a trait which may be broadly defined as the ability to deal with
> life's situations in terms of past experience [p. 143].

We believe there may be merit to the idea that somewhat different criteria
should be used to compare the intelligence of the young and the old. Perhaps
what is more important than whether one age group is higher or lower than
another with respect to a specific ability is how successfully the individuals
bring their available repertoires of skills to bear in adapting to the demands
of their everyday environments. (Recall Horn's view that the same kinds of
problems may be dealt with successfully by emphasizing different abilities,
either crystallized or fluid.) In line with this thinking, then, we agree with
Wechsler's proposition that something like sagacity may represent an important, albeit difficult to measure, dimension of intelligence.

Also it is important to acknowledge that age accounts for only a small
part of the variance in intelligence-test scores; one estimate is 25% of the
variance (Elias et al., 1977). Another important consideration is that there is
a tremendous amount of overlap between older and younger people. As Elias
and associates note, many older people can run "intellectual circles" around
their younger contemporaries.

Clearly the above considerations have significant implications for social
policy vis-à-vis the older person. Schaie (1974) has explored some of the implications, making major policy recommendations concerning adult education
and employer retirement practices. In view of the evidence that older people
can function at a high intellectual level and can benefit from educational intervention strategies, he advocates the continuance of education into old age and
"the development of specific educational programs designed to reverse the
cultural and technological obsolescence of the aged" (p. 805). Furthermore,

given the great variability in intellectual development, Schaie contends that age is an inappropriate criterion on which to base a decision regarding a person's vocational competence. Thus, Schaie argues for the abolishment of mandatory age-based retirement policies and the application of criteria that emphasize the individual's ability to do the job. This second recommendation by Schaie brings us to our next topic, which concerns the level of vocational accomplishment people maintain as they move from early adulthood into middle and late adulthood.

ACHIEVEMENT

Upon resigning as professor of clinical medicine at Johns Hopkins University in 1905 at the age of 56, Sir William Osler assured his colleagues that his leaving was inconsequential:

> I have two fixed ideas well known to my friends. . . . The first is the comparative uselessness of men over forty years of age. . . . Take the sum of human achievement in action, in science, in art, in literature—subtract the work of men above forty, and while we should miss great treasures, even priceless treasures, we would practically be where we are today. . . . My second fixed idea is the uselessness of men above sixty years of age, and the incalculable benefit it would be in commercial, political, and in professional life if, as a matter of course, men stopped work at this age [Lambert & Goodwin, 1929, pp. 326–327].

This is certainly a pessimistic view of our potential to make significant contributions as we grow older. Although the statement was made some years ago, its essence continues to be reflected in age-role stereotypes and incorporated into the hiring, promotional, and retirement policies of many business, educational, and governmental organizations. In 1972, for instance, approximately 2000 companies were found guilty of violating federal laws against age discrimination ("Thinking Young," 1974).

Quality of Achievement

Was Osler correct? Does the quality of a person's work decline as he or she moves through middle age and into old age? You may be inclined to answer "no," because you can cite several examples of individuals who have made outstanding contributions during their later years. Yet these may be rare exceptions, and Osler may have been right with respect to the general population.

Undoubtedly the most extensive analysis of the association between age and achievement has been made by Harvey Lehman (1953, 1960). In his work, Lehman was particularly interested in discovering when men are likely to make their *most outstanding contributions.* His basic method involved using standard reference books (for example, historical surveys and encyclopedias) and to a lesser extent the opinion of present-day authorities to determine at what age men in a great many fields of endeavor were recognized as demonstrating their highest achievement. Lehman found a marked similarity among most of the fields he looked at. His results show that the apex of distinctive achievement typically occurs sometime between 30 and 39 years of age. Some of the fields that peaked in the 30s include: physical sciences (chemistry, physics, geology), biological sciences (botany, genetics, psychology, medicine), mathematics, practical inventions, music (vocal solos, symphonies, chamber, grand opera), literature (short stories, comedies, tragedies), philosophy (logic, ethics, aethestics, general), educational theory and practice, economics and political science, and art (oil paintings, sculpture). In relatively few areas did the high point of outstanding achievement fail to occur between 30 and 39. Certain kinds of poetry (pastoral elegies, sonnets, lyric) peaked in the middle to late 20s, and several areas peaked in the early 40s, including music (cantatas, light opera, musical comedy), literature (novels), and modern architecture.

Thus, Lehman's data would seem to confirm Sir William's contention about the meritorious accomplishments of younger adults in contrast to older adults. Yet further consideration of his data suggests that, while individuals are most likely to make their best contributions during young adulthood, many do their most significant work at later ages. In Figure 11-3 is a generalized curve of the relationship between achievement and age that Lehman found. This curve represents a composite of the age/achievement function across a number of fields of endeavor. The *general* picture that emerges is that the rate of creative output increases sharply from the 20s to the 30s and then from a high point in the 30s declines steadily into old age.[3]

While Lehman's data convincingly indicate that the highest rate of outstanding achievement occurs in the 30s, they also show that outstanding contributions can be made throughout adulthood. Clearly there is no age limit to creative achievement. For example, a look at Lehman's results for contributions to psychology indicates (to the consolation of your middle-aged authors) that many psychologists make significant contributions well into old age (Lehman, 1953, 1966). Wilhelm Wundt, for instance, wrote six volumes about his work on social psychology when he was between the ages of 82 and 88. Freud was 44 when his first great work, *The Interpretation of Dreams* (1923/ 1955), was published. In fact, Lehman was able to produce a long list of people who demonstrated outstanding achievement before they reached 22 years (Marconi had transmitted radio signals) and after age 70 (Galileo Galilei discovered the diurnal and monthly oscillations of the moon).

Quantity of Achievement

While Lehman was mainly concerned with individuals' most superior accomplishments, he did look at the association between age and contributions of lesser merit. He found that for virtually all areas of endeavor the curve

[3]A major exception to the general age/achievement relationship pertained to the attainment of leadership. As we would expect, Lehman's data indicate that people who achieve important leadership positions—heads of state, congressmen, Supreme Court justices—usually are in their 50s, 60s, or 70s.

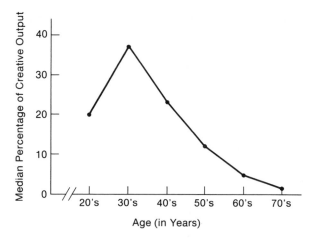

Figure 11-3. Percentage of creative output as a function of age. This shows a generalized curve representing a combination of various fields of endeavor and various estimates of quality. From *Cognitive Processes in Maturity and Old Age*, by Jack Botwinick. Copyright © 1967 by Springer Publishing Company, Inc., New York. Based on data from *Age and Achievement*, by Harvey C. Lehman. Copyright 1953 by the American Philosophical Society. Reprinted by permission of Springer Publishing Company, Inc., and Princeton University Press.

for contributions of lesser quality declined less rapidly than that for those of higher quality. In fact when Lehman considered the total output of an individual, ignoring its quality, he found that a relatively high rate of productivity well into old age characterized many areas. In some areas (for example, philosophy and orchestral music) quantity of output sustained itself at a constant level into the 70s.

That quantity of output (in contrast to quality of output) is likely to be sustained into the later years is further confirmed by a study by Dennis (1966). Dennis looked at the total works produced in each decade of adulthood by individuals who lived to be at least 80 years old. He subdivided them into three categories: scholars (for example, historians and philosophers), scientists (for example, biologists, geologists, and mathematicians), and artists (for example, architects, novelists, chamber music composers). Dennis's data are depicted in Figure 11-4. This figure shows that scholars (that is, the humanities) maintained a constant level of productivity from the 30s into the 70s, and scientists maintained a constant level through the 60s, then declined in the 70s to about 68% of their peak decade. The artists displayed the greatest fall off—in the 60s they produced 54% of their peak decade, and in the 70s they produced 23% of it.

Thus the picture that emerges is that although individuals may make significant contributions during their later years, they are most likely to make them during the early stages of their careers. However, whereas qualitative output generally declines substantially with age, quantitative output displays a much more gradual decline, and, in fact, many people maintain the same

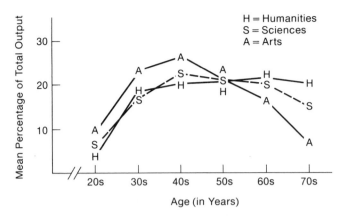

Figure 11-4. Percentage of total output as a function of age for the humanities, sciences, and arts. Each curve is based on the means of several specific disciplines. From *Cognitive Processes in Maturity and Old Age*, by Jack Botwinick. Copyright © 1967 by Springer Publishing Company, Inc., New York. Based on data from "Creative Productivity Between the Ages of Twenty and Eighty Years," by W. Dennis, *Journal of Gerontology*, 1966, *21*, 1–8. Copyright 1966 by Gerontological Society. Reprinted by permission of Springer Publishing Company, Inc., and the Gerontological Society.

level of productivity throughout their lives. One cautionary note is warranted. We have been considering, for the most part, the performance of individuals who are recognized for their achievement in their respective fields and we can't be certain concerning the generalizability of these findings to less distinguished persons. However, a review of research on workers in a variety of manufacturing and service industries indicates that in most occupations there are no or only minor differences in job effectiveness between older and younger workers (Meier & Kerr, 1976).

Accounting for the Age/Achievement Relationship

How can we account for the age-related decline in superior achievement? It is doubtful that one factor alone is chiefly responsible. Lehman listed 16 possible causes of the decrease, including decline in motivation, vigor, and good health, and the encroachment of administrative responsibilities. However, it is difficult to see how such factors would severely interfere with the quality of one's work but have much less impact on the quantity (recall that quality declines more rapidly than quantity). A more plausible explanation offered by Lehman is that, compared with younger people, older people may experience more positive and negative transfer (transfer refers to the effect that learning one thing has on the learning of another). Positive transfer insures a greater store of knowledge, and, thus, may facilitate productivity, whereas negative transfer makes it difficult to unlearn the old and, as a consequence, may inhibit creative thinking. In line with Lehman's thinking, there is some evidence that when well-established habits are conducive to learning, older persons benefit disproportionately more than younger people; on the other hand, if such habits are apt to interfere with learning, they do more so in the old than the young (Arenberg & Robertson-Tchabo, 1977).

Except for his observation about negative transfer, Lehman is noticeably reluctant to acknowledge the possible role of waning intellectual ability. However, as Bromley (1966) argues, this should not be dismissed as a possibility. Those abilities most likely to decline with age, namely fluid abilities, may indeed be the ones that contribute the most to creative thinking. Moreover, Bromley adds that older people may show less creative achievement because they essentially rest on their laurels and devote their energies to elaborating their original contribution(s). Newcomers to a field seek out the original in order to make names for themselves.

In addition, older workers in many fields may be able to sustain a relatively high rate of productivity because they can benefit from the work of collaborators or assistants, draw on data and materials that have been collected and stored for years, and/or receive credit for extending or modifying their earlier contributions. In the arts, where one's contribution is supposed to be both individual and original, such is not the case. This may account for the fact that total output shows a sharper drop in the later years for those engaged in the arts than for scholars and scientists (see Figure 11-4).

In the conclusion to our section on intellectual functioning, we considered Schaie's (1974) recommendations pertaining to the inadvisability of mandatory retirement practices and the need for sustaining educational experiences for the old. The evidence on achievement does not contradict Schaie. Outstanding achievement and high levels of productivity *can* accompany one's later years and might well be lost if age-based employment policies prevented the older person from working. With respect to education, Botwinick draws an interesting implication of the data on achievement. Because the peak of creative achievement occurs for most people and most fields early in adulthood, Botwinick (1967) suggests that the individual's potential to achieve is effectively reduced by current trends to prolong his or her education and training. According to Botwinick, "means must be found to start young people on their creative careers early in life" (p. 182).

We have considered the evidence concerning possible age-related changes in cognitive functioning and vocational achievement. Now we will turn our attention to personality and explore the possibility that, as in the case of cognition and achievement, changes in personality do occur as we grow older.

PERSONALITY

Is your personality at this moment in time the same as it was at an earlier period in your life, say, when you were a young child or adolescent? It is quite likely that your answer is a hedging "yes and no"; yes, you are essentially the same person that you were then, but no, you have changed since then.

Would your prediction of the course of your personality through the remainder of adulthood parallel your perception of its earlier course? Will your personality change at all, or has it largely stabilized?

It has long been recognized that during childhood and adolescence many aspects of personality undergo change (Mussen, 1970). However, until fairly recently the adult personality was generally neglected by developmental psychologists. This lack of attention was partly because of the domination of such orientations as psychoanalytic theory, which holds that personality characteristics are established during a person's early childhood and only modifications of such characteristics occur in adulthood, and the biological growth/maturity/decline model, which assumes that, except for the later years, adulthood is marked by little behavior change. Today, however, as the subsequent review will make clear, personality change must be recognized as a salient aspect of adulthood. An individual's personality is by no means permanently established at some early stage of life.

One consequence of developmental psychology's fixation on the first two decades of life has been the relative dearth of useful psychological theories relevant to the total life span. There are a few exceptions. The most noteworthy is Erikson's (1963) conceptualization of eight stages of development, each of which entails a crisis for the developing ego. Three of the crises occur in adulthood. After the adolescent crisis of ego identity (that is, self-identification), the crisis of early adulthood is concerned with the development of intimacy: ability to commit oneself to and develop an intimate relationship with others. In middle adulthood the crisis focuses on generativity: investment in the products of one's own creation, usually through parenthood and work, and achieving a sense of continuity with the future. And late adulthood is marked by the crisis of ego integrity: acceptance of the meaningfulness of and the responsibility for one's life and the inevitability of life and death. Failure to successfully pass through one stage jeopardizes successful passage through later stages.

Neugarten (1977), while acknowledging the need for progress in theory development, advises us that the most pressing problem for those interested in studying the adult personality is not the formulation and testing of theories. Rather she argues that our present body of knowledge does not even permit the determination of whether or not those personality changes that do occur follow an orderly and sequential course with the passage of time. Neugarten stresses that the current emphasis should be on carrying out descriptive studies, those which are concerned with ascertaining the course of personality development. She also stresses the importance of theory generated on the basis of descriptive research instead of theory that precedes such research. In line with Neugarten's call for an empirical orientation, our coverage of personality emphasizes description—what is known about personality development—rather than theory.

As in the area of intellectual functioning, the preponderance of studies of personality and aging have been cross-sectional. Most of the methodological concerns discussed in the section on intelligence are equally relevant to the question of age changes in personality. The primary concern again is the problem of determining the source of age differences. Do personality differences between age groups reflect cohort factors—that is, are they due to social and historical differences—or do they reflect orderly age changes that are independent of cohort differences? The confounding influence of cohort factors is illustrated by research on field independence (see Chapter 7). Cross-sectional data indicate that field independence decreases with age, whereas longitudinal data indicate the absence of change. In a study by Gruenfeld and MacEachron (1975), older adults were less field independent than younger adults, but as so often happens, they also had less formal education. When educational background was statistically controlled, the relationship between age and field independence disappeared.

Furthermore, for both cross-sectional and longitudinal research, personality change may be precipitated by a variety of life events or crises, including marriage, pregnancy, divorce, illness, and job loss. Yet there is a tendency to treat age-related changes in personality as a function of the aging process per se as if they were independent of such intervening events.

Neugarten (1977) reviews some of the other conceptual and methodological problems that contribute to a prevalence of inconsistent findings. One salient difficulty resides in the area of standardization; that is, few, if any, personality measures have been developed that are appropriate to all age groups. For example, most personality measures initially were designed for and standardized on young adults (typically college students). It is questionable how reliable and valid such measures are for older adults. A related difficulty concerns the purpose for which a personality measure was originally constructed. Is one that has been developed to measure psychopathology, for example, necessarily sensitive to personality changes that accompany the normal aging process? Another concern is the comparability of personality constructs from one age group to another. Do dependency and aggressiveness in the 30-year-old denote the same things as dependency and aggressiveness in the 70-year-old? Or should our conceptualization of various personality constructs vary from one age to another?

Serious problems are involved in the study of personality and age, problems that can lead to spurious conclusions about the development of personality. The area of personality and aging is just as complex as that of intelligence, if not more so. The existing evidence is, at best, tentative. We will first consider the cross-sectional data and then shift our focus to longitudinal investigations.

Multitrait Cross-Sectional Investigations: The Kansas City Study of Aging

The vast majority of the literally hundreds of cross-sectional studies of personality and aging have focused on a single trait. There have been only a handful of multidimensional investigations, those that look at changes in the interrelated aspects of personality instead of emphasizing specific personality characteristics. The multidimensional investigation that has had the greatest impact is the Kansas City study of aging, headed by a team of researchers from the University of Chicago (Neugarten & Associates, 1964). This research program involved a sample that was fairly representative of all noninstitutionalized people 40 years and older who were living in Kansas City during the 1950s and early 1960s. Cross-sectional data were obtained on 700 men and women, and a second set of longitudinal data over a 6-year period were obtained on 300 people. Most of the discussion that follows is based on the results from the cross-sectional part of the investigation.

Extensive information on each participant was collected using a variety of measures, including projective tests, questionnaires, and in-depth interviews. The results of this work indicated both stability and change in personality. Stability or consistency occurred with respect to what Neugarten (1964) calls socioadaptational characteristics of personality, whereas change was evident in intrapsychic processes.

Socioadaptational Characteristics. Socioadaptational dimensions refer to the "adaptive, goal-directed, and purposive qualities of personality" (Neugarten, 1964, p. 192). For example, in one segment of the research, factor-analytic procedures identified several personality types (see descriptions in later section on personality and successful aging) that were seen as varying in terms of the individual's ability to adapt to his or her environment (Neugarten, Crotty, & Tobin, 1964). There were no consistent age differences with respect to the various personality types. Especially relevant was that they found little evidence to indicate a higher incidence of less adaptive personalities among older adults and a higher incidence of more adaptive personalities among younger adults. Similar results have been reported by Reichard, Livson, and Petersen (1962). Other data from the Kansas City investigation indicated no significant relationship between age and adjustment as measured by an index of life satisfaction (Havighurst, Neugarten, & Tobin, 1968). We will return to the issues of successful adaptation and life satisfaction in later sections.

Intrapsychic Processes. As noted, in contrast to the apparent stability of socioadaptational characteristics, the Kansas City study revealed that the intrapsychic processes were marked by change. Intrapsychic processes are less readily available to conscious awareness and control than other aspects of personality. The Kansas City researchers relied primarily on the analysis of projective data, specifically TAT stories, to study the intrapsychic processes.

Two of the most salient features of the participants' intrapsychic processes involved an increase in interiority with age (Rosen & Neugarten, 1964) and a related shift in ego style from active mastery to passive mastery (Gutmann, 1964). Movement toward *interiority* was viewed as meaning an increased preoccupation with the self and one's inner life (Neugarten, 1964). This change was seen as being manifested, for example, by a decrease in an individual's tendency to deal with the outer world. The greater tendency in the younger subjects was indicated by the fact that they were more likely than older subjects to introduce new (nonpictured) characters into their TAT stories, to complicate their stories with conflict, and to ascribe to the characters high levels of energy. Rosen and Neugarten (1964) suggest "The implication is that the older person tends to respond to inner rather than to outer stimuli, to withdraw emotional investments, to give up self-assertiveness, and to avoid rather than embrace challenge" (p. 99). A five-year follow up of some of the participants provided longitudinal confirmation of a decline in ego energy with age (Lubin, 1964).

The transition toward greater interiority is entirely congruent with the evidence on introversion/extraversion. Studies employing self-report inventories suggest that older adults are more introverted than younger adults (Chown, 1968). As Chown (1968) concludes: "Introversion in all its manifestations increases with age" (p. 157). Also, in describing the current status of cross-sectional investigations of age differences in personality traits, Neugarten (1977) paints a rather bleak picture of a pool of knowledge beset by inconsistencies. But she adds that one major exception is introversion. She expresses confidence that, despite the methodological limitations of the research, the force of the evidence leads to the conclusion that an increase in introversion or interiority occurs during the later years of life.

As noted, the other salient personality change discovered in the Kansas City investigation was Gutmann's (1964) finding of a shift in ego style from *active mastery* to *passive mastery*. This change was in terms of the person's perception of the self in relation to the environment. As the age of the subjects increased from the 40s into the 50s and then the 60s, there was a decline in the number of people who projected active mastery (an assertive orientation to the external world) into their TAT stories and a corresponding increase in those projecting passive mastery (a defensive tendency to passively withdraw from contact with the external world). According to Neugarten (1964):

> Forty-year-olds seem to see the environment as one that rewards boldness and risk-taking and to see themselves possessing energy congruent with the opportunities presented in the outer world. Sixty-year-olds seem to see the environment as complex and dangerous, no longer to be reformed in line with one's own wishes, and to see the self as conforming and accommodating to outer-world demands [p. 189].

This change from active to passive mastery was stronger in the men than the women. Also, many of Gutmann's (1964) older subjects expressed what he called "a magical style of mastery" (a reliance on primitive defense mechanisms such as denial and projection, as well as the use of ritual, magic, and meditation as means for coping with the perceived demands of the world).

Gutmann (1977) has followed up his Kansas City findings with extensive cross-cultural analyses. Drawing on his own interviews and projective testing with the Navajo of Arizona, Maya of Mexico, and the Druze of Israel, as well as the work of many others, he has concluded that the movement from active to passive and/or magical mastery in men has universal aspects to it. Gutmann contends, on the other hand, that women move in the opposite direction—from a passive mode, as characterized by a dependent and deferential relationship to their husbands, to a more active one in which they become more assertive and domineering and less concerned with their security needs. He further states that this sex-related reversal fits a broader pattern wherein during the latter half of life there is a general convergence on the part of both sexes toward a more androgynous personality—a feminization of men and a masculinization of women. Both sexes move in the direction of less sex-stereotypical values, interests, and behaviors. For example, with regard to the United States culture (as well as other cultures), Gutmann cites evidence that, with the advance of age, men express increased interest in family-oriented values, domestic activities, and gardening, as well as showing an increase in such qualities as need for affiliation and sensitivity to interpersonal relationships. Women, on the other hand, seem to become less concerned about socio-emotional ties, more interpersonally aggressive, more concerned with practical affairs, and more dominant in family relationships. This change on the part of women may very likely be related to the fact that because women tend to live and maintain their health longer than men, many are essentially forced into a situation wherein they must assume the traditionally masculine instrumental role.

Interestingly, such a unisex trend was apparent in the sex-role perceptions the Kansas City sample expressed in their TAT stories (Neugarten & Gutmann, 1964). Relative to younger subjects (age 40-54), older subjects (age 55-70) were more likely to describe older story characters in terms of a role reversal regarding authority in the family: older men were perceived as submissive and older women as dominant. Moreover, Neugarten (1964) described the findings as suggesting that "Older men seem to be more receptive than younger men of their affiliative, nurturant, and sensual promptings; older women, more receptive than younger women of their aggressive and egocentric inpulses" (pp. 189–190).

As mentioned, cross-sectional studies tend to focus on one or just a few dimensions of personality. The findings related to many of these dimensions are fraught with inconsistency (Neugarten, 1977). We have selected four traits which it seems plausible are linked to the process of aging—cautiousness, rigidity, locus of control, and life satisfaction—and in the next few pages have tried to make sense out of the existing evidence concerning them.

Single Trait Cross-Sectional Investigations

Cautiousness. Undoubtedly one of the most widely held age stereotypes is that older people are more cautious and conservative than younger people. Early appraisals—in the 1920s through the 1940s—of age-related differences in values, attitudes, and interests corroborated this belief, although the differences were relatively small in magnitude and were seen as having little practical significance (Pressey & Kuhlen, 1957). Since then investigators have switched their attention to the manifestation of cautiousness in a variety of laboratory performance situations.

Botwinick (1973) reviewed the evidence concerning the performance of young and old adults on various psychomotor, perceptual judgment, and learning tasks and concluded that older people do employ more cautious strategies in dealing with problems that confront them. For one thing, they seem to place a greater value on accuracy of performance than speed of performance. Also, during intelligence testing and on serial learning and paired-associate learning tasks, older people are more likely than younger people to make errors of omission, meaning they tend to refrain from answering a question or responding on a given trial. Botwinick hypothesizes, and presents supporting evidence, that the propensity to sacrifice speed for accuracy and the related tendency to display omission errors signify a lack of self-confidence, a need for greater certainty before committing oneself. Botwinick views cautiousness as serving an ego-defensive function by helping the individual to avoid making mistakes.

In the studies reviewed by Botwinick, the greater cautiousness in older persons was inferred from their task-performing strategies. A more direct test of the hypothesized association between age and cautiousness entails the analysis of behavior in actual risk-taking situations. Okun and Di Vesta (1976) had two groups of men (ages 18-30 and 60-76) complete a vocabulary test that was divided into items comprising six levels of difficulty. Then, in a second testing, the participants undertook a similar task and were told their goal was to earn as many points as possible. The number of points that would be awarded for correctly answering items at each difficulty level was scaled according to each person's previous performance at that level. That is, if a man earlier had done well (or poorly) at a given difficulty level, he was told he would receive a relatively small (or large) number of points for items answered correctly. The participants had to choose which difficulty level they wished to work at in order to try to accumulate points. Degree of cautiousness was reflected directly in the objective probability of success at which the person decided to work. The older men did make more cautious decisions than the younger men, selecting tasks at which they had higher probabilities of success.

Okun (1976; Okun & Di Vesta, 1976) agrees with Botwinick's (1973) thesis that the cautiousness of older people helps to protect their egos from possible insult. He further draws on Atkinson's (1957) motivational theory of risk taking to account for the older person's cautious behavior and suggests that older people experience an increase in fear of failure and a concomitant decline in need for achievement (fear of failure is viewed as a primary component of need for achievement). In Okun's study, as well as others (for example, Veroff, Atkinson, Feld, & Gurin, 1960), males over 50 do tend to score lower than younger men on various measures of need for achievement. Therefore, Okun suggests that instead of reacting as a person with high need for achievement and selecting the challenging, more risky tasks, the older men acted as people who are low in need for achievement and cautiously opted for tasks that were more in line with their abilities and less likely to result in failure experience. Also, of those men who had successfully answered all of the items at a given difficulty level, younger men were more likely than older men to select more difficult levels on subsequent trials. This lower level of aspiration set by the older men is another indication of their greater need for certainty.

Rigidity. Rigidity is a trait that is often thought to go hand-in-hand with cautiousness. Rigidity refers to a resistance to change, a tendency to persist with one mode of behavior when other modes may be more appropriate or rewarding. A great variety of tasks have been used to measure rigidity/flexibility, including those that seem to tap a person's set-breaking ability (see the section on analytical thinking in Chapter 10). Rigidity appears to be a multidimensional concept. A factor-analytic study by Schaie (1958) uncovered three types of rigidity: motor/cognitive (inability to shift from one activity to another), personality/perceptual (inability to adjust readily to changing surroundings), and psychomotor speed (inability to rapidly emit familiar cognitive responses).

Also, a study by Chown (1961) revealed five kinds of rigidity (spontaneous flexibility, personality, speed, alphabet, and two factors of dispositional). The age/rigidity association seems to change depending on the dimension of rigidity under examination. For instance, two of the patterns found by Chown (1961) were: spontaneous flexibility (for example, listing as many possible uses of an object such as a brick) increased from the 20s to the 40s and showed a decrease after the late 50s; and personality rigidity (for example, "I dislike having to learn new ways of doing things.") showed a slight decline across age. Therefore instead of asking, "Do people become more rigid as they age?", which may be an oversimplification of the issue, it may be more appropriate to ask "In what ways, if any, does rigidity increase with age?"

Yet, notwithstanding the complexity of the rigidity concept, the cross-sectional evidence for the most part suggests that older people are somewhat more rigid than younger people. However, the age differences may not necessarily be intrinsic to maturational age changes (Botwinick, 1973). Schaie has found that the age/rigidity relationship emerges when cross-sectional analyses are employed, but largely disappears when subjected to longitudinal analyses (Schaie & Strother, 1968). This suggests that the differences between age groups commonly found in cross-sectional studies could very well be due to cohort effects (that is, cultural and experiential differences between generations). Moreover, as Botwinick (1973) points out, it is difficult, if not impossible, to determine whether observed decrements in performance on measures of rigidity are a function of chronological age per se or a result of the decreases in intellectual abilities and response speed that typically coincide with increasing chronological age. The important question remains—which is the primary factor? While declining response speed and cognitive ability may produce rigid behavior, rigidity may be responsible for their decline as well.

Locus of Control. Rotter's (1954) social learning theory posits that an individual's feeling of personal efficacy increases as he or she experiences greater mastery and control over his or her environment. Thus we would expect that as people mature into adulthood, they might develop an increasing sense of internal control and a diminished feeling of external control. We might also expect that sometime during their later years older people may begin to lose a sense of internal control as a consequence of possible reductions in their autonomy and physical and cognitive abilities. The first expectation has for the most part been confirmed, but the second expectation has not. According to research, internal locus of control seems to increase from adolescence into early adulthood (the 20s or 30s) and then stabilize. However, there is little indication of a decline in old age (Lao, 1974; Ryckman & Malikiosi, 1975). In fact, some studies suggest that internal control continues to rise up to at least age 60 (for example, Staats, 1974). As in all cross-sectional research there is a possibility that the results (in this case an apparent lack of decline in locus of control) reflect a cohort confound. However, in this particular instance the possibility is reduced because poorer educated people (usually the older groups) typically score lower on internal locus of control than better educated people (usually the younger groups) and, thus, existing educational differences would be biased against finding a lack of differences between age groups in locus of control.

We should note, however, that when we assess feelings of control with respect to different areas of achievement, there is evidence in older people of heightened feelings of external control. Compared with younger adults, people aged 60-90 have been found to feel more externally controlled with respect to social and physical areas of achievement, but not with respect to intellectual areas (Bradley & Webb, 1976).

Life Satisfaction. Do a person's feelings of satisfaction with life change as he or she ages? Given a host of interrelated factors—the existence of negative stereotypes concerning old age, the apprehension that most people feel about growing old, the increasing imminence of death, the likely decline in physical health, the loss of friends and loved ones—it is not unreasonable to expect a drop in life satisfaction with age. Indeed, the results of most early investigations pointed to such a conclusion (Riley, Foner, Moore, Hess, & Roth, 1968). However, the results were far from consistent, one noteworthy exception being the previously mentioned Kansas City study by Neugarten, Havighurst, and Tobin (1961). Also, the age/satisfaction relationship seemed to depend on the particular dimension of satisfaction being studied. For example, older people were viewed as being less likely than younger people to express feelings of happiness and morale but to be no more likely to admit to worries and insecurities (Riley et al., 1968).

More recently, this research has been criticized for its failure to employ a multivariate approach to evaluate the determinants of life satisfaction. This approach examines the relative influence of several variables that would seem to be related to life satisfaction (for example, socioeconomic status, social participation, and health status, as well as age) and the relationship of each variable to life satisfaction when the other variables have been statistically controlled. When a multivariate approach is applied, the negative association between age and life satisfaction essentially disappears (Edwards & Klemmack, 1973; Palmore & Luikart, 1972) or even becomes positive (Clemente & Sauer, 1976). For example, Palmore and Luikart (1972) found a −.04 correlation between age (range from 45 to 69 years) and a person's standing on a life satisfaction ladder, a measure which requires a respondent to indicate on which rung of the ladder he or she currently stands (top rung = best possible life; bottom rung = worst possible life). Also, Clemente and Sauer (1976) divided a national sample of American adults into three age groups (18-39, 40-59, 60 and up) and found the two older groups were higher on a composite measure of satisfaction regarding place of residence, family life, friendships, and activities.

Therefore, recent evidence casts considerable doubt on the commonly accepted view that the average older person is less satisfied with his or her life than is a younger counterpart. Of all the factors that do seem to moderate one's level of satisfaction, physical health as perceived by the individual is the one that stands out from one study to the next (Clemente & Sauer, 1976; Palmore & Luikart, 1972). A feeling of good health at any age helps to maintain a sense of life satisfaction.

A rather interesting technique for examining the relationship between age and "happiness" has been proposed by Back and Bourque (1970). It is called "draw-a-graph" and involves having respondents draw a graph of their life as they see it, including their anticipation of the future as well as their perception of the present and past. The underlying assumption is that the relative height of the curve at different age periods reflects the individual's level of happiness. According to the authors, by using different age groups but obtaining a life curve for each person, the technique represents an integration of both cross-sectional and longitudinal methods. Using a sample aged 20 to 80, Back and Bourque found that all age groups tended to agree that life gradually improves from childhood until a peak at around age 55 and then begins a gradual decline. The life curve for all age groups combined is portrayed in Figure 11-5. One optimistic finding was that, for every age level, the anticipated portion of life was higher than the experienced portion (that is, the average of the entire part of the future end of the curve was higher than the average of the entire part of the past end).

Before leaving the topic of life satisfaction, we should note that the sources of satisfaction, and accordingly a person's definition of satisfaction, may change as he or she moves across the life span. One study indicates that among men the correlates of overall happiness (for example, financial status, friendships, and physical health) change as they pass through various stages of the life cycle. In this particular study, men with young children seemed to define happiness in terms of family life, whereas men at other stages were apt to emphasize sources of satisfaction outside of the family (Harry, 1976).

Longitudinal Investigations

As noted earlier, considerably fewer longitudinal investigations of personality have been conducted than cross-sectional investigations. The imbalance in the number of cross-sectional and longitudinal studies is regrettable, not only because the latter are preferred from a methodological standpoint, but because, as in the area of cognitive functioning, the two strategies typically lead to different conclusions regarding personality development. Longitudinal

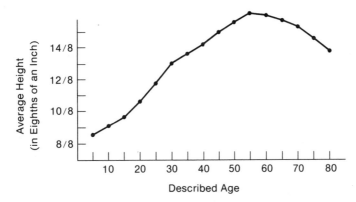

Figure 11-5. Life graph showing average height of life curve at described ages for sample as a whole. From "Life Graphs: Aging and Cohort Effect," by K. W. Back and L. B. Bourque, *Journal of Gerontology,* 1970, *25,* 249–255. Copyright 1970 by the Gerontological Society. Reprinted by permission.

studies are less likely than cross-sectional studies to support the notion that personality changes during adulthood.

In an effort to separate age-related change from generational change, Woodruff and Birren (1972) conducted a study involving both longitudinal and cross-sectional comparisons. One group of subjects completed the California Test of Personality (measuring personal and social adjustment) in 1944 as university students and again in 1969. A longitudinal comparison of their 1944 and 1969 scores suggested no change in mean level of adjustment over the 25-year span. However, cohort differences appeared when the 1969 scores from these subjects who were born around 1924 (1924 cohort) were compared with the scores of two younger groups of subjects who likewise were tested in 1969. One group consisted of college students who were born in 1948 (1948 cohort), and the second group consisted of high school students who were born in 1953 (1953 cohort).

When tested in 1969 at the mean age of 44.5, the 1924 cohort scored higher on adjustment than did the two younger cohorts. In addition, and importantly, the adjustment level of the older cohort in 1944, when their mean age was 19.5, exceeded that of the comparably aged younger cohorts in 1969. Thus, a possible inference that age differences existing in 1969 (cross-sectional evidence) signify age changes—that is, the older subjects were lower in adjustment in 1944 than in 1969—would have been grossly incorrect. This set of results provides rather compelling verification that the sociocultural milieu of the era in which one is socialized may have a profound impact on personality development and may in some instances be chiefly responsible for age differences found in cross-sectional research. Woodruff and Birren conclude that their finding of greater cohort differences than age changes "confirmed in the domain of personality what previous investigations demonstrated in the area of cognition" (p. 252).

Another interesting finding emerged when the older subjects were asked in 1969 to fill out the adjustment inventory as they thought they had completed it 25 years earlier. These people believed that their level of adjustment had been lower during their late teens or early 20s; they perceived themselves to have experienced an increase in adjustment with maturation, an increase that objectively was nonexistent. This projection into the past of a less positive status parallels, in an interesting way, the subjective reports of life satisfaction in the aforementioned Back and Bourque (1970) study.

Probably the most extensive set of investigations of personality has been carried out by a group of researchers from the Institute of Human Development at the University of California at Berkeley (Block, 1971; Maas & Kuypers, 1974). We will give this program of research primary consideration in our review of longitudinal studies of personality. The subjects for this research were initially participants in two separate longitudinal studies—the Oakland Growth Study and the Guidance Study—but eventually were merged into a single sample. Originally the number of subjects exceeded 450, but in the longitudinal followups the numbers inevitably were smaller.

The Berkeley Studies: Adolescence through Early Adulthood. Jack Block, in his book *Lives Through Time* (1971), examines the development of personality from early adolescence (junior high school) through middle adolescence (senior high school) to early adulthood (the 30s). His sample consisted of 84 males and 87 females. The personalities were analyzed by means of the Q-sort procedure. This procedure involves brief descriptions of a large number of personality characteristics that are printed on cards. The descriptions are used by judges to rate a person's personality. The judges, who in Block's study were clinical psychologists, arrange the cards into nine categories, ranging from those that are most characteristic of the person to those that are least characteristic. The judgments of the subjects' personalities in adulthood were based on data from intensive interviews (averaging 12 hours in length), whereas several kinds of information were used in making the judgments about adolescence, including teacher evaluations, ratings of social and interview behavior, projective measures, self-reports, and peer sociometric ratings. In order to study the development of personality, Block subjected the Q-sort data to several kinds of analysis. In the following paragraphs we will review each set of analyses in turn.

In the first set of analyses, *the subjects' standings on each personality characteristic at one time period were correlated with their standings at the next time period.* For females and males, respectively, 96% and 89% of the early adolescence/middle adolescence correlations were significant, while 59% and 60% of the middle adolescence/early adulthood correlations were significant. Thus, the findings concerning the majority of the second set of correlations do suggest consistency of personality from middle adolescence into middle adulthood—the ranking of people on many of the descriptive characteristics tended to remain at the same level from one period to the next. Yet although many correlations were significant the majority were only slight to moderate in magnitude (seldom exceeding +.50).

In trying to explain why the correlations between adolescence and adulthood were not higher, Block reasoned that it may be because the degree of personality stability may vary from one person to the next—some people change considerably, whereas others do not. Moreover, he suggested the possibility that characteristic differences might be found in the personalities of those who do change and those who do not.

Block applied this thinking by means of a second set of analyses. Rather than looking at the across-time correlations for each personality variable, as was done in the first set of analyses, Block computed the across-time correlations for each person, that is, the *correlation between all of a person's Q-sort ratings at one age and those at a later age.* The resulting correlation provided an index of the overall stability of the person's personality. The distributions of adolescence/adulthood correlations for each sex are presented in Figure 11-6. The mean correlations for the females and males were .54 and .56, respectively, suggesting an appreciable degree of personality consistency from late adolescence into early adulthood. (As would be expected, the corresponding early adolescence/middle adolescence correlations were substantially higher—.75 and .77.) However, the most striking feature of the two distributions is the extraordinary variation in the amount of personality consistency, with correlations ranging from –.30 to .97 for the females and from –.40 to .99 for the males. What this wide range of individual differences means is that the adolescent personalities of some individuals were highly reliable predictors of the nature of their adult personalities a generation later, whereas, for other individuals, information about their earlier personalities was valueless—even detrimental—for making predictions.

Then, Block compared the people whose personalities showed substantial change with those whose personalities showed little change. He divided his sample, separately for each sex, into those whose adolescence/adulthood correlations were above the mean correlation, calling them "nonchangers," and those whose correlations fell below the mean, the "changers." When the Q-sort descriptions of the changers and nonchangers were compared, marked differences were found. The emergent picture of the males is one in which at each age period, from adolescence into adulthood, the nonchangers were higher in IQ and possessed greater maturity and psychological adjustment than the changers. The changers were described as:

> Prototypical adolescents wallowing in the culturally given and culturally indulged role of the "adolescent." . . . intensely peer-oriented, they are interpersonally fitful, they are sly, they are hedonistic. Adrift without the rudder of character to give them direction, their pleasures are immediate and easily knowable; their fears distant and unrecognized. At adulthood, these male changers still appear comparatively adolescent . . . ill-prepared for the second half of life that has begun. They have matured to some degree [p. 101].[4]

The nonchangers, on the other hand, were:

[4]This and all other quotations from this source are from *Lives Through Time*, by J. Block. Copyright 1971 by Bancroft Books. Reprinted by permission.

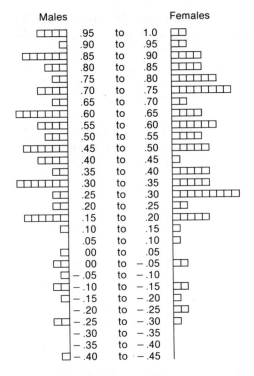

Each block represents one person.

Figure 11-6. Distribution of across-time correlations, showing the correlation between each person's overall Q-sort description in adolescence and the person's description in adulthood. The correlations have been statistically corrected for attentuation due to measurement error; they represent estimates of what the "true" correlation would be if fallible measures were not used. Data on eight males and three females were missing. Adapted from *Lives through Time*, by J. Block. Copyright 1971 by Bancroft Books. Used by permission.

Impressive for their compassionate, informed maturity even during adolescence. They are reaching out for experience also but where the Changers seek gratification and self-reinforcement, the Nonchangers seek growth into competence and a self-differentiation . . . are alert, diligent, and parent respecting. . . . At adulthood, the Nonchangers continue with their maturity [pp. 101, 102].

Among the females, as with the males, the nonchangers were judged higher in maturity and psychological adjustment than the changers, although the differences were only characteristic of the adolescent period and not adulthood. In adolescence the changers were viewed as being relatively high on such traits as brittle, self-defensive, withdraws when frustrated, self-indulgent, negativistic, deceitful, distrustful, and attention-getting behaviors with peers; in adulthood they were described as "cognitively more interesting people, still somewhat rebellious but now more relaxed with themselves and with their place in life" (p. 106). During adolescence the nonchangers were seen as standing relatively high on such traits as dependable, productive, high aspiration level, giving, arouses liking, insightful, submissive, wide interests, values intellectual matters, and satisfied with self; however, in adulthood, the nonchangers "have not shown psychological maturation beyond what was to be observed in their adolescent years. . . . although reasonably adaptable [they] may not be evaluated as more suitable than the Changers for the rigors and flux of life" (p. 107).

Thus, Block's second set of analyses suggests two important aspects related to personality and aging during the second, third, and fourth decades of life: (1) a tremendous amount of individual variation in the degree to which personality is consistent and (2) the existence of readily discernible personality differences between those demonstrating relatively high and low degrees of consistency.

Block believed these findings were also consistent with an approach that emphasizes patterns of personality—homogeneous personality types—and which recognizes that different subgroups of people may show different, albeit orderly, patterns of personality development. Consequently, Block's third approach to the study of personality development entailed *deriving personality types from a factor analysis of the combined early adolescent and adult Q-sort data.* Each of the resulting factors or personality types encompassed the way the type was both in adolescence and adulthood, as well as parallels in the way the members of the type evolved across time. In Block's view, individuals comprising a given personality type have in common an interrelated set of personality traits; yet over time, the personality types may evolve and, therefore, demonstrate major, although orderly, changes. He says that "a personality type early is a personality type later, albeit a different one perhaps" (p. 113).

Five male types and six female types were derived. The Q-sort items and a variety of other sources of information about the subjects' personalities and family environment were used as a basis for determining the similarities and differences between each personality type and all of the remaining subjects. In accordance with Block's conceptualization of personality development, high, moderate, and low levels of personality continuity were found depending on the type under consideration. For example, one male personality type, the "ego resilients" (described as possessing "long-standing characterological integrity and resourcefulness" [pp. 150, 151]), and one female type, the "female prototypes" (conveying "the exemplary way in which these individuals . . . have manifested the qualities our culture prescribes as appropriate for its females" [p. 202]), both showed high relative personality continuity from adolescence to adulthood and consistently high psychological adjustment. On the other hand, the male "anomic extraverts" (conveying the "valuelessness and the absence of inner life that has so essentially characterized them" [p. 177]) displayed a comparatively high level of personality change from adolescence to adulthood and a progressive decline in psychological adjustment from a high level in early adolescence to a low level in adulthood. Moreover, female "cognitive copers" (signifying the "essentially intellectual way they have applied throughout life as a means of processing encounters with the world" [p. 211]) displayed average continuity of personality and a progressive increase in psychological adjustment from a low level in early adolescence to a high level in adulthood. Thus Block's typological analyses provide evidence of personality coherence and both personality consistency and change during the time span studied.

Berkeley Studies: Early Adulthood through Old Age. The course of personality development spanning the interval from early adulthood to old age was explored by a second set of investigators from the Institute of Human Development. Maas and Kuypers (1974) undertook a follow-up investigation of 142 parents (95 mothers and 47 fathers) of the Berkeley sample. They had access to information that was gathered when the parents were in their thirties and interview material collected in the late 1960s, when the parents averaged approximately 70 years of age.

First, looking at old age, the investigators factor analyzed 88 measures of life-style that had been derived from interview data and observations made during home visits. According to Maas and Kuypers, *life-style* refers to the patterned manner in which a person lives from day to day. They viewed a person's life-style as being manifested in 12 areas of life (for example, home and visiting, work and leisure, parenting, friendships, church, and politics) and with respect to each area as varying along the following four dimensions: interactive, involvement, satisfaction, and perception of change. The fathers could be characterized by four different life-styles whose titles are relatively self-explanatory: family-centered, hobbyists, remotely sociable, and unwell/ disengaged. The mothers fit into one of six life-styles: husband-centered, visiting, work-centered, group-centered, uncentered, and disabled/disengaging. Also, factor analyses of Q-sort personality data yielded three *personality types* among the fathers: person-oriented, conservative/ordering, and active/competent; and four types among the mothers: person-oriented, autonomous, fearful/ordering, and anxious/asserting. The high level of diversity represented by the variety of personality types and life-styles, as well as the individual uniqueness existing within these clusters, is highlighted by Maas and Kuypers as documenting the perpetuation of individual differences into old age and as underscoring the inadequacies of social stereotypes that emphasize the sameness of the elderly.

Maas and Kuypers also measured continuity of life-style and personality by ascertaining if the information gathered early in adulthood was predictive of life-styles and personality types in old age. Because of insufficient data from early adulthood the analyses could be done on only slightly more than half of the parents (26 men and 53 women). Continuity was apparent, but change was also. The degree of continuity depended on the sex of the parent and the specific life-style and personality type. Life-style continuity was more characteristic of the fathers than the mothers. In fact, the women in four of the six mothers' groups—the work-centered, group-centered, uncentered, and disabled/disengaging—seemed to have manifested considerable discontinuity in their style of living from early to late adulthood. However, the discontinuity did reflect constancy in the sense of a shared change from an earlier life-style to a later one. For many mothers old age presented opportunities for a transition to different life-styles, some of which were very gratifying and others that were much less so. A positive instance is the work-centered mothers, who earlier had been trapped in unsatisfying marriages and were shy, withdrawn, and low in self-esteem, but later in life found liberation in divorce or widowhood and gratification in a style of life centering on their employment and newly found network of social relationships.

Maas and Kuypers presented evidence suggesting that the greater discontinuity of life-style in the mothers was due in part to a greater responsiveness to change in their environments and life circumstances. These "contextual" factors were found to differentiate among the six mother life-style groups to a much greater degree than among the four father life-style groups. For example, compared with the contexts of the other mothers, those of the visiting mothers were defined by a number of factors that foster the development of a life-style centering on visiting family and/or friends and being visited by them. These factors included a high proportion of working husbands, stable, long-lasting marriages, few divorced offspring, many children and grandchildren, geographic closeness to children, sizeable social network, and many long-standing friends. Maas and Kuypers posit that women are more influenced by context and contextual alterations because they have had less freedom to exercise control over their environmental circumstances than men and, in fact, may have experienced greater contextual change during adulthood (for example, transition from work to housewife and then back to work). Thus, the women are viewed as having experienced greater pressure to be adaptive. The continuity in the men's life-styles was epitomized by the apparently minimal impact that retirement seemed to have on the core of their life-styles.

Moving from life-style to the realm of personality, the converse occurred—the mothers displayed more continuity than the fathers. Actually, a strong connection between personality in early and late adulthood was found with respect to just two personality types, the fearful/ordering mothers and the anxious/asserting mothers. These women displayed low adaptive qualities across the span of adulthood, including anxiety, depression, low self-esteem, and high self-doubt. From this Maas and Kuypers speculated that " 'pathology' in old age has more visible roots in early adulthood than does 'strength' " (p. 199).

Berkeley Studies: Summary and Conclusions. The Berkeley studies provide us with the most comprehensive package of longitudinal data to date. Let us briefly review the major findings. In Block's (1971) investigation, when the correlations between adolescence and middle adulthood were calculated on each of the individual personality characteristics (first of Block's analyses), more than half were significant (indicating continuity), but most were low in magnitude and many were not significant (indicating the presence of an appreciable degree of change). When each subject's Q-sort description for adolescence was correlated with the description for adulthood (Block's second analysis), the resultant correlations were high positive for some subjects (non-changers) but low positive or even negative for other subjects (changers). And clearly discernible personality differences characterized the changers and non-changers. Factor analyses of the combined adolescence/adulthood Q-sort data (Block's third analysis) revealed several coherent personality types, some of which manifested relatively high continuity from adolescence into adulthood and others relatively low continuity. The Maas and Kuypers (1974) follow-up study of the parents identified several different life-styles and personality types, some of which manifested considerable change from early adulthood to late adulthood, whereas others displayed little change. Thus the picture that emerges from the Berkeley research is that *both* personality continuity and personality change occur from adolescence through late adulthood. Clearly our personalities are not necessarily permanently fixed by the time we reach adulthood; nor are they necessarily subject to continuous alteration.

Other Longitudinal Investigations. Several other longitudinal investigations, all of less magnitude, have been reported. These studies are consistent with the Berkeley series in upholding the notion that personality through the life span is marked by both continuity and change (Bischof, 1976; Bengtson, 1973). Of course, two very important questions that remain to be answered are who—which kinds of personality—are most and least likely to change, and what are the determinants of personality continuity and discontinuity?

Perhaps one underlying principle is that the continuities and discontinuities of personality are tied directly to the process of adapting to the constancies and changes of life's circumstances (Bengtson, 1973). The conditions of our lives inevitably change as we grow older; we encounter changes in our physical status, move into new social positions, come under the influence of the norms and constraints that are attendant to those positions and to our constantly changing age status, experience alterations in our social milieu, and pass through some of the major events and crises that demarcate life. All of these experiences require adaptation, and it is reasonable to expect such adaptation may be the source of personality change. On the other hand, there are environmental constancies in our lives and each of us has a uniquely personal history of adaptation, and these constancies serve to maintain personality continuity. Moreover, it is quite conceivable that change becomes more difficult with the passage of time, although it can occur well into old age.

The possible impact of contextual changes was aptly exemplified when we considered life-style changes in the Berkeley mothers. Other investigators likewise have stressed adaptation to contextual change. In a 9-year longitudinal study of elderly people, Britton and Britton (1972) found some evidence for continuity but emphasized the amount of negative change in personality and adjustment that occurred. They stressed the importance of situational factors in accounting for both stability and change.

Conceivably there are many modes of adapting to the events and stages of one's life, although there is a noticeable lack of theory pertaining to adaptation across the span of adulthood. One notable exception is disengagement theory, which was advanced to account for successful adjustment to old age.

Disengagement

On the basis of the early cross-sectional data from the Kansas City study of aging, Cumming and Henry (1961) developed a theory of disengagement. This theory posits that as people move into their later years a process of mutual withdrawal occurs, one in which society withdraws from the individual and the individual from society. Society's disengagement from the individual may be seen in the gradual reduction in role obligations, including, for example, that which accompanies such events as widowhood and retirement. The individual disengages both socially and psychologically from society. In socially disengaging the person reduces the number of his or her role relationships and his or her general level of social interaction, whereas in psychologically disengaging he or she becomes more involved with the self and his or her own satisfactions and less involved and committed to his or her social relationships and the world in general. Psychological disengagement is virtually synonymous with the notion of interiority that we discussed earlier. Psychological disengagement is conceived as preceding or at least coinciding with social disengagement. According to the early formulation of disengagement theory, disengagement is a developmental phenomenon, an inevitable and natural process, that is inherent in the individual. Moreover, and this is the most controversial aspect of the theory, disengagement was thought to facilitate successful aging; the disengaged older person is considered most likely to sustain a high level of morale and life satisfaction.

Pitted against the proponents of disengagement theory were those who favored what is known as "activity theory" (for example, Maddox, 1963). Activity theory is the view that any reduction in social involvement that occurs with old age is largely due to the withdrawal of society from the individual and is contrary to the wishes of most older people. Therefore, optimal aging, including high morale and life satisfaction, characterizes the individual who successfully resists the contraction of his or her social world and is able to maintain many of the activities and role relationships of middle age and/or replace them with similarly satisfying activities (for example, hobbies) and relationships (for example, new friendships).

The initial formulation of disengagement theory by Cumming and Henry (1961) generated a lively controversy and a large quantity of research. One particularly noteworthy research contribution was made by several other Kansas City investigators who had the benefit of longitudinal data and more complex measures of disengagement and adaptation (Havighurst, Neugarten, & Tobin, 1968). These investigators studied people ranging in age from 54 to 94 years and found evidence for the occurrence of both psychological and social disengagement. Psychological disengagement tended to occur earlier than social disengagement (in the 50s versus the 60s and 70s) as if it foreshadowed the latter. Neugarten (1973) suggests that the fact that psychological withdrawal precedes social withdrawal supports the view that movement toward interiority is a developmental phenomenon and not merely a pattern of reaction to the decline in social interaction that occurs.

However, contrary to disengagement theory, the data did not confirm the hypothesized connection between disengagement and morale. For instance, they found that an index of the extent and intensity of present role activity[5] was positively related to both how favorably the sample felt about their present role activities ($r = .73$) and their feelings of life satisfaction ($r = .46$). Thus, the results generally supported activity theory. Other studies likewise have indicated that activity is directly related to morale among older people. Maddox (1963), for instance, found that increases and decreases in activity (involvement with the environment) were in general accompanied by corresponding increases and decreases in morale. Nevertheless, Havighurst and his colleagues emphasize that their data reveal diversity rather than singularity in the patterns of aging. They note that the correlations were only moderate in size and that within their sample were persons typifying all four combinations of high and low activity and high and low morale, including the disengagement pattern of low activity and high morale. Thus, they argue that neither theory can adequately explain all of the patterns of aging. Moreover, from their data Havighurst and his associates postulate the presence of two concurrent value systems in the majority of their sample—one emphasizing the importance of remaining involved in order to retain a feeling of self-worth and the second pressing for withdrawal and concentration on a more leisurely and contemplative manner of existence. They suggest that neither activity theory nor disengagement theory can account for the synchronous operation of these value patterns.

Neugarten (1973) succinctly expresses the case for and against disengagement theory: "As a description of social and psychological processes, it appears to be accurate. Psychological disengagement seems to precede social disengagement and seems to have developmental properties" (p. 330). But she adds that it is inadequate as a description of optimal aging: "In short disengagement proceeds at different rates and different patterns in different people in different places and has different outcomes with regard to psychological well-being" (p. 330).

Personality and Successful Aging

Given the diversity in the aging patterns they found, the Kansas City team began to explore the possibility that the relationship between level of disengagement and morale might be mediated by the personality of the individual. This research, which we will now describe, led to the conclusion that personality is the "pivotal" factor underlying patterns of aging.

---

[5]Role activity score was based on the composite involvement in 11 different social roles: parent, spouse, grandparent, kin-group member, worker, homemaker, citizen, friend, neighbor, club-and-association member, and church member. For instance, a man was rated high in his role of spouse if he carried out many of his daily activities with his wife but low on the spouse role if he primarily shared with her only perfunctory routines such as dining.

By means of factor analysis of various personality variables, the researchers derived several personality types (Neugarten, Crotty, & Tobin, 1964). Then they interrelated four major personality types to indexes of social-role activity and life satisfaction in a sample of 59 women and men who were in their seventies (Neugarten, Havighurst, & Tobin, 1961). The four personality types are defined as follows:

1. *integrated*: "well-functioning persons who have a complex inner life and at the same time, intact cognitive abilities and competent egos" (p. 175).
2. *armored-defended*: "striving, ambitious, achievement-oriented personalities, with high defenses against anxiety and with the need to maintain tight controls over impulse life" (pp. 175–176).
3. *passive/dependent*: "those who have strong dependency needs and who seek responsiveness from others" or those "in whom passivity is a striking feature" (p. 176).
4. *unintegrated*: "personalities who showed a *disorganized* pattern of aging. . . . persons who had gross defects in psychological functions, loss of control over emotions and deterioration in thought processes" (p. 176).

When level of role activity and life satisfaction were also taken into consideration, the investigators were able to delineate eight different aging patterns. These patterns are listed in Table 11-1. As indicated in Table 11-1, the relationship between role activity and life satisfaction appears to depend on the type of personality involved. For instance all three of the integrated types (that is, the reorganizers, focused, and disengaged) are high on life satisfaction, regardless of their level of role activity. On the other hand, of the passive/ dependent types who engage in a relatively high degree of activity only the succorance-seeking (that is, those who have strong dependency needs and need others to respond to them) seem to be able to achieve a high level of satisfaction.

The results of other investigations have also indicated that successful aging is characteristic of more than one personality type. For instance, Reichard and her colleagues (1962) studied a group of 87 men and discovered three personality types who were high on life satisfaction and two who were low. We should also mention that if an individual has the benefit of a close, intimate relationship with another person (someone to confide in), the presence of such a confidant can help the individual considerably in maintaining his or her morale and mental stability in the face of the various social losses associated with aging (Lowenthal & Haven, 1968).

Thus, it appears that personality has a definite influence on how adequately the individual adapts to old age. While there seems to be a general tendency toward increased interiority of personality (psychological disengagement), people maintain their individuality. As Neugarten (1973) says,

> There is no single social-psychological pattern by which people grow old
> . . . persons age in ways that are consistent with their earlier life histories
> . . . older persons like younger ones will choose the combinations of activities
> that offer them the most ego involvement and that are most consonant with

Table 11-1. Relation of Personality Types to Role Activity and Life Satisfaction*

	Personality Type	Role Activity	Life Satisfaction	Number of Subjects
A.	Integrated (reorganizers)	High	High	9
B.	Integrated (focused)	Medium	High	5
C.	Integrated (disengaged)	Low	High	3
D.	Armored-defended (holding on)	High or medium	High	11
E.	Armored-defended (constricted)	Low or medium	High or medium	4
F.	Passive/dependent (succorance-seeking)	High or medium	High or medium	6
G.	Passive/dependent (apathetic)	Low	Medium or low	5
H.	Unintegrated (disorganized)	Low	Medium or low	7

*The number of subjects is less than the total of 59 because some of the subjects did not fit into one of the four major personality types.

From "Personality and Patterns of Aging," by R. J. Havighurst, *Gerontologist*, 1968, *8*, 20–23. Copyright 1968 by the Gerontological Society. Reprinted by permission.

their long-established value patterns and self-concepts. Aging is not a leveler of individual differences except, perhaps, at the very end of life [p. 329].

The above discussion centered on the relationship between personality and adaptation during late adulthood, leaving unanswered the question concerning the earlier years of adulthood. As Neugarten (1977) points out, while personality seems to be a strong predictor of adjustment during adulthood, those aspects of personality that predict well during one age period may be less useful during another. According to Neugarten, the picture is complicated by the fact that different social and psychological issues may be critical in successive age periods. As we pass from early adulthood through middle adulthood to old age, the occurrence of certain life events places different demands on our coping abilities. We will not undertake a review of personality and adaptation in earlier adulthood but merely indicate that Neugarten (1977) notes that the evidence suggests that personality is related to adaptation in middle life, just as it is related in old age.

In conclusion, it is apparent that one's pattern of personality characteristics influences how successfully one adapts to different periods of life. We now turn our attention to the association between age and the likelihood of experiencing severe problems of adaptation—the incidence of mental illness.

Mental Illness

We have found that, although their styles of adaptation may vary considerably, many people seem to make satisfactory adjustments to the process of aging. For instance, with such factors as physical health and socioeconomic status controlled, there is no appreciable relationship between age and feelings of life satisfaction. Yet we can think of reasons that would suggest that the incidence of mental illness might fluctuate during the span of adulthood. For instance, stressful events or crises may be more likely to severely tax a person's adaptive capacities at some age periods than at others. Also, as a person's age increases, so does the opportunity to contract various maladaptive modes of behavior. Furthermore, conditions connected with degeneration of the central nervous system, such as cerebral arteriosclerosis and senile brain disease, are likely to increase with age.

A precautionary note seems warranted concerning the problem of obtaining accurate information on the incidence of mental illness in the general population. Statistics on mental illness typically are based on institutionalized populations, despite the fact that a large proportion of the mentally ill, perhaps a majority, live at home. Moreover, psychiatric help may be disproportionately available to some age groups.

Figures 11-7 and 11-8 give us some indication of how the incidence of psychopathology relates to age. Both figures summarize data on the use of psychiatric care facilities. Figure 11-7 shows that the frequency of admissions to psychiatric institutions peaks in the 25-44 age group and falls off thereafter. On the other hand, Figure 11-8 gives a much different picture, indicating that the number of people receiving treatment from psychiatric facilities increases fairly steadily until the late 30s, levels off during middle age, and then increases after the early 60s. The discrepancy between the curves in Figures 11-7 and 11-8 apparently is due to the fact that, while more people during early adulthood seek (or are referred for) psychiatric help than people during later adulthood, their treatment is more likely to be short-term. Notice that in Figure 11-7 the high point of admissions is disproportionately determined by admissions to outpatient clinics and general hospitals, both of which are less likely than mental hospitals to maintain patients on a long-term treatment basis. If the two figures are combined—admissions plus patients at beginning of year—we still have a curvilinear relationship but the decline in the older age groups is not nearly as sharp as the one in Figure 11-7.

Some comment is needed concerning the increasing numbers of older people in residence in mental institutions. At least two factors contribute to this state of affairs. One is that there is a gradual increase with age in the size of the hard-core chronic population, patients with functional psychoses who grow old in hospitals. Functional psychoses refer to disorders that have no apparent physical cause and are presumed to have primarily psychological and/or socioenvironmental origins (for example, schizophrenia and manic-depression). A second reason is that the prevalence of organic brain syndrome increases across adulthood, and beginning in the fifties there is a tremendous upsurge in its incidence, and hence in hospital cases (Kramer, Taube, & Redick, 1973; Riley et al., 1968). In fact, among the mentally ill who are 65 years of age and older, roughly half suffer from organic brain syndromes and the percentage increases with each year. A person with organic brain disease may display a diversity of psychiatric symptoms, including depression, euphoria, hallucinations, delusions, withdrawal, and violent outbursts; however, the major constellation of symptoms involves breakdowns in various aspects of cognitive functioning.

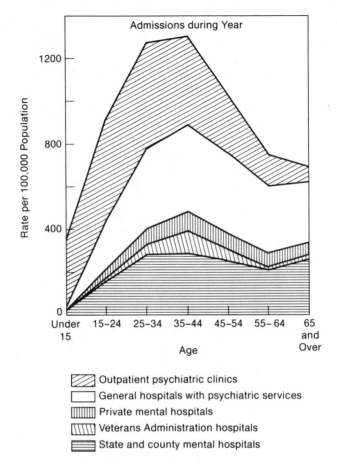

Figure 11-7. Number of patients per 100,000 at each age level who were admitted to various types of psychiatric facility, United States, 1966. From "Patterns of Use of Psychiatric Facilities by the Aged: Past, Present, and Future," by M. Kramer, C. A. Taube, and R. W. Redick. In C. Eisdorfer and M. P. Lawton (Eds.), *The Psychology of Adult Development and Aging.* Copyright 1973 by the American Psychological Association. Reprinted by permission.

Suicide is one other psychological disturbance that shows a striking association with age, although the relationship is confounded by several factors, including sex and marital status (Riley et al., 1968). As Figure 11-9 indicates, the incidence of suicide among White males in the United States rises quite steadily across the life span, whereas White females and non-Whites of both sexes show a fairly constant level across most of adulthood and some decline in the later years. In 1970 the suicide rate for the entire U.S. population was 11.6 per 100,000 people, whereas for those over 64 it was 36.9 per 100,000 (Pfeiffer, 1977). Married people are much less likely to take their own lives than unmarried people. Deletion of the data from divorced and single groups nearly flattens the suicide-age curve for men. It is worth noting that, although

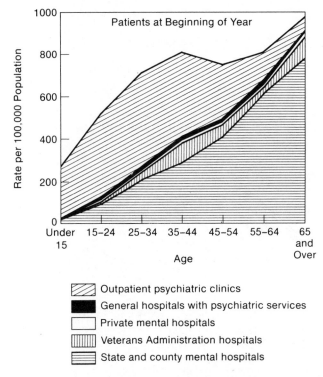

Figure 11-8. Legend:

- ▨ Outpatient psychiatric clinics
- ■ General hospitals with psychiatric services
- ☐ Private mental hospitals
- ▥ Veterans Administration hospitals
- ▤ State and county mental hospitals

Figure 11-8. Number of patients per 100,000 at each age level who were residents in inpatient psychiatric facilities or on the rolls of outpatient psychiatric clinics at the beginning of year, United States, 1966. From "Patterns of Use of Psychiatric Facilities by the Aged: Past, Present, and Future," by M. Kramer, C. A. Taube, and R. W. Redick. In C. Eisdorfer and M. P. Lawton (Eds.), *The Psychology of Adult Development and Aging.* Copyright 1973 by the American Psychological Association. Reprinted by permission.

higher in absolute terms in older people, suicide rates in the younger population are more outstanding in light of the fact that the mortality rate is so much lower; suicide ranks about thirty-fifth among the causes of death for men 85 or older but sixth for men 15 to 24. Many more younger people attempt suicide than successfully commit it, whereas among older people roughly the same number attempt it and fail as attempt it and succeed. Older people who try suicide do so because they want to die. Depression seems to be the precipitating factor in the majority of older suicides. On the other hand, in younger people, but rarely older people, suicide often serves as an expression of hostility toward others or as a strategy to manipulate others (Pfeiffer, 1977). The rise in suicide, at least in males, parallels the fact that depression is the most frequent form of functional psychoses in the later years (Pfeiffer, 1977). Although depression may result from a variety of aversive circumstances, it is basically a maladaptive reaction to loss—of loved ones, self-esteem, bodily health, money, and so forth.

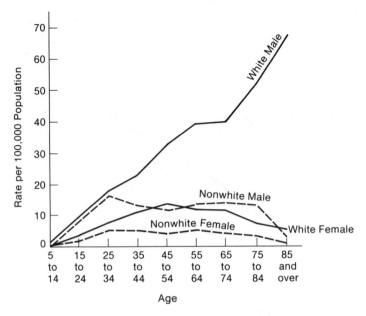

Figure 11-9. Number of suicides per 100,000 at each age level by sex and race, United States, 1964. From *Vital Health Statistics,* 1967, Series 20, No. 5. National Center for Health Statistics.

INTERESTS AND VALUES

Do our interests change much as we age? The answer is yes if we can rely on the judgment of Alvin Toffler (1970), the author of *Future Shock.* Toffler says "in a society caught in the throes of the most rapid change in history, it would be astonishing if the interests of individuals did not change kaleido-scopically" (p. 119). On the other hand, if we recall the evidence regarding the long-term stability of vocational interests (see Chapter 9), the answer is no—once people reach adulthood their vocational interests are not likely to change very much at all. Longitudinal investigations of the interests of people in various occupational groups, such as bankers (Campbell, 1966) and psychologists (Campbell & Soliman, 1968; Vinitsky, 1973), have revealed a remarkable degree of similarity between their early Strong occupational scale profiles and their profiles 24 to 40 years later. That is, when in their 60s and 70s bankers continue to peak on the banker scale and psychologists on the psychologist scale. Moreover, their general pattern of lows and highs is virtually identical to that which they manifested many years earlier. For instance, in Vinitsky's (1973) 35-45 year follow up of the interests of male psychologists, their mean scores were initially highest on science occupations and lowest on skilled trades, business, and social service occupations, and they remained so throughout their careers. Despite the indication of some change, Campbell (1971) concluded, "stability, almost to the point of rigidity, is the dominant feature" (p.

130). Thus, the existing evidence contradicts Toffler's belief in "kaleidoscopically" changing interests, at least in the area of vocational interests.

The major longitudinal contribution to the study of value change has been made by Hoge and Bender (1974). They integrated the results from three samples of Dartmouth College men who had taken the Allport-Vernon Study of Values on either two or three occasions: (1) 1931-1952, (2) 1940-1955-1969, and (3) 1956-1969. Also they had available information concerning Dartmouth seniors at three points in time: 1940, 1956, and 1968. The results are graphically summarized in Figure 11-10.

Each of the three longitudinal samples is depicted by the lines, and the three independent samples are represented by the separate solid circles. Value change is clearly apparent in the longitudinal data. While economic, social, and political values changed little, theoretical values increased in strength and aesthetic and religious values shifted in a back-and-forth pattern.[6] Hoge and Bender apply the data in Figure 11-10 to an evaluation of three, by now familiar, explanatory models of age differences. The first one is the "standard life cycle" model, which posits that value change is a natural concomitant of the aging process. A person's values change as he or she passes from one stage of the life cycle to another. Figure 11-10 reveals little support for the "standard life cycle" model. It predicts that, for a given value, any change would be in the same direction for men of similar ages but different cohorts. Yet for both aesthetic and religious values, two groups changed in one direction during the years following college, whereas the third group changed in the opposite direction. The second model is the "cohort" model, which assumes that value systems are firmly established during the individual's formative years and rooted in the sociohistorical conditions of the period. This model predicts little value change. That is, the lines in Figure 11-10 should be horizontal; however, the only instance of this is with political values. The third model, the "current experiences" model, receives the greatest support. According to this model, the ongoing social and historical events that people experience determine the extent and direction of value change. (Thus, we find more support for Toffler in the realm of values than interests.) All age groups are affected in the same manner. Notice in the right-hand side of the graphs for aesthetic and religious values that the 1940-1955-1969 sample shifted in the 1955-1969 period in precisely the direction of the younger 1956-1969 sample. Also, note that the curves follow the same pattern as the separate circles, which depict the values of college seniors at each point in time. Two other findings lend some support to the cohort explanation. One is that value changes during the lifetimes of

[6]It is important to recognize that the format for responding to the Allport-Vernon Study of Values necessarily limits the sum of scores on all six values to a constant. This means that if the importance a person (or group) attaches to a given value increases (decreases) over time, there must be a concomitant decrease (increase) in the measured importance of one or more of the other values. This "ipsative" nature of the scale is a definite drawback because it does not allow for the possibility that a person's other values can remain at the same level of strength when a change in the strength of one value takes place. The Rokeach Value Survey has similar properties.

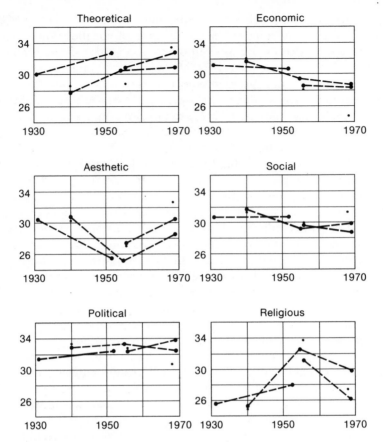

Figure 11-10. Mean Allport-Vernon Value Survey scores for various groups of Dartmouth men. From "Factors Influencing Value Change Among College Graduates in Adult Life," by D. R. Hoge and I. E. Bender, *Journal of Personality and Social Psychology*, 1974, *29*, 572–585. Copyright 1974 by the American Psychological Association. Reprinted by permission.

the alumni were less than the differences among the 1940, 1956, and 1968 seniors (note the pattern of separate circles). The other is that the alumni showed more change during the 15 years immediately following college than during their later years. Thus the values developed in the college years did display some degree of permanence as suggested by the cohort model. Hoge and Bender conclude that the most promising explanation of their results is one that entails an integration of the current experiences model and cohort model, with a recognition that less change occurs as people age.

Rokeach's (1973) analysis of the national sample provided by the National Opinion Research Center (see Chapter 9) provides some cross-sectional data. Rokeach was impressed with the amount of value differences that he found among his age groups. He identified a number of developmental patterns based on various clusters of values. A few of the more interesting and/or striking patterns were: The sharpest age trend occurred with respect to love, with both the terminal value "mature love" and instrumental value "loving" declining steadily in importance from young adulthood through old age. Somewhat surprisingly the value denoting a sense of responsibility ("responsible") also declined with age. On the other hand, several values showed substantial increases in the hierarchy of importance, including "obedient" and those emphasizing economic security ("a comfortable life") and religion ("salvation"). Some values displayed a consistently high level of importance across all age groups, including "a world at peace," "honest," "freedom," "family security," and "ambitious."

One recent study looked at a different issue. Ryff and Baltes (1976) hypothesized that as people move from middle age into old age they begin to place greater importance on terminal values and less importance on instrumental values. Their hypothesis was based on both empirical and theoretical grounds (Ryff, 1977). An increasing emphasis on terminal values in late adulthood is congruent with the evidence of a movement toward interiority (a heightened concern with the self) and a shift from active to passive mastery (an accommodative rather than instrumental attitude toward the external world). At a theoretical level the hypothesis accords with Erikson's (1963) proposition that adults move from the seventh stage of ego development, generativity, in which instrumental values have priority, to the final stage, integrity, in which instrumentality is deemphasized. In support of their hypothesis, Ryff and Baltes found that middle-aged women (mean age = 43) ranked instrumental values (on the Rokeach Value Survey) more important than did older women (mean age = 70), whereas they ranked terminal values as less important.

Finally, the evidence that values fluctuate more with increasing age than do interests is somewhat difficult to reconcile with Rokeach's (1973) view (see Chapter 9) that values, as more central components of personality, underlie the display of interests. One possible explanation stems from Hoge and Bender's findings that only certain values show significant change—those dealing with theoretical, aesthetic, and religious areas, but not economic, social, and political areas. Research on interests has concentrated strongly on vocational interests, which may become firmly entrenched as an outcome of continued involvement in one's work. Perhaps if other interest domains were sampled, greater change would be apparent.

SUMMARY

An important distinction is made between age differences and age-related behavioral changes. The former may reflect the latter or they may be due to factors that are unrelated to the aging process per se, such as cohort effects (that is, differences resulting from cultural/historical influences). The major limitation of the cross-sectional research method is that it does not permit a separation of age effects and cohort effects. One outcome is that the cross-sectional method tends to spuriously magnify the extent to which intelligence declines with age. On the other hand, because of other methodological problems (most notably, selective dropout), the longitudinal method spuriously minimizes the decline. Both methods suggest that general intelligence remains relatively stable across much of adulthood and begins to show some decline after age 50.

Learning, memory, and problem-solving deficits tend to accompany advanced age. The memory deficits occur in the secondary memory processes but not in the primary memory processes and seem to be largely the result of deficiencies in the person's organizational capacities. Older people experience a slowing in response speed, especially on complex and unfamiliar kinds of motor tasks, but existing evidence fails to support the idea that slowing of response speed accounts for the intellectual deficit in abilities requiring quickness of perceptual/motor response. Some evidence does suggest that high levels of arousal may interfere with the performance of older persons on measures of intellectual functioning.

It is concluded that it is futile to search for a single, correct age/intelligence function because different special abilities show different relationships with age. Abilities involving response speed, perceptual/motor coordination, and novel problem solving are more apt to show a decline than abilities emphasizing acquired information and skills (for example, many verbal abilities). Furthermore, a person who is in good health and continues to exercise his or her cognitive capacities may maintain a relatively constant level of intellectual functioning well into old age.

Research on occupational achievement indicates that in most fields of endeavor the peak of outstanding achievement tends to occur when people are in their thirties. On the other hand, quantity of output (in contrast to quality) shows no such early peak and is likely to be sustained into the later years.

The most important multitrait cross-sectional investigation of personality and age has been the Kansas City study of aging. This research indicated no appreciable differences across age in the socioadaptational characteristics of personality, whereas differences in intrapsychic processes were in evidence—an increase in interiority with age and a shift from an ego style of active mastery to one of passive mastery. The results from single-trait cross-sectional investigations of four traits—cautiousness, rigidity, locus of control, and life satisfaction—were reviewed. Although the probable multidimensionality of most of these traits advises against looking for a single age function, the evidence generally suggests that with advancing age cautiousness and rigidity tend to increase, whereas feelings of personal control and life satisfaction remain stable. The results from the Berkeley studies of aging, the most extensive longitudinal research on personality and age, indicated the following: (1) some people show considerable personality change from middle adolescence to the middle 30s, whereas other people evince little change; (2) from adolescence to the 30s coherent personality types are in evidence, some of which display high personality continuity and others relatively low continuity; and (3) from early adulthood to old age several distinct life styles and personality types are detectable, and these likewise show varying degrees of change.

Neither a process of gradual disengagement nor one of sustained activity appears to be the "best" way to adjust to old age. Successful aging is an individual matter, with both high and low morale characterizing people who disengage and those who remain active. Moreover, personality seems to be the pivotal factor underlying successful aging—whether or not a person's degree of role activity correlates directly with his or her level of life satisfaction depends on the nature of the person's personality.

Evidence on psychopathology shows that the frequency of psychiatric admissions peaks in the 25-44 age group, whereas the frequency of people receiving treatment from psychiatric facilities is constant during middle age and then begins to rise in the 60s. The increasing number of the aged in mental institutions is associated with an increase in the hard-core chronic population and the incidence of those with organic brain syndrome. Suicide increases steadily across the life span for White males but remains at a constant level for other groups. Last, little change occurs across adulthood with respect to vocational interests, whereas certain kinds of values do show a greater likelihood of change.

REFERENCES

Arenberg, D., & Robertson-Tchabo, E. A. Learning and aging. In J. E. Birren & K. W. Schaie (Eds.), *Handbook of the psychology of aging.* New York: Van Nostrand Reinhold, 1977.

Atkinson, J. W. Motivational determinants of risk-taking behavior. *Psychological Review,* 1957, *64,* 359–372.

Back, K. W., & Bourque, L. B. Life graphs: Aging and cohort effect. *Journal of Gerontology,* 1970, *25,* 249–255.

Bahrick, H. P., Bahrick, P. O., & Wittlinger, R. P. Fifty years of memory for names and faces: A cross-sectional approach. *Journal of Experimental Psychology: General,* 1975, *104,* 54–75.

Baltes, P. B., & Goulet, L. R. Status and issues of a life-span developmental psychology. In L. R. Goulet & P. B. Baltes (Eds.), *Life-span developmental psychology: Research and theory.* New York: Academic Press, 1970.

Baltes, P. B., & Labouvie, G. V. Adult development of intellectual performance: Description, explanation, and modification. In C. Eisdorfer & M. P. Lawton (Eds.), *The psychology of adult development and aging.* Washington, D.C.: American Psychological Association, 1973.

Baltes, P. B., & Schaie, K. W. On the plasticity of intelligence in adulthood and old age: Where Horn and Donaldson fail. *American Psychologist,* 1976, *31,* 720–725.

Bengtson, V. L. *The social psychology of aging.* New York: Bobbs-Merrill, 1973.

Birren, J. E., & Renner, V. J. Research on the psychology of aging: Principles and experimentation. In J. E. Birren & K. W. Schaie (Eds.), *Handbook of the psychology of aging.* New York: Van Nostrand Reinhold, 1977.

Bischof, J. *Adult psychology* (2nd ed.). New York: Harper & Row, 1976.

Block, J. *Lives through time.* Berkeley, Calif.: Bancroft Books, 1971.

Botwinick, J. *Cognitive processes in maturity and old age.* New York: Springer, 1967.

Botwinick, J. *Aging and behavior.* New York: Springer, 1973.

Botwinick, J. Intellectual abilities. In J. E. Birren & K. W. Schaie (Eds.), *Handbook of the psychology of aging.* New York: Van Nostrand Reinhold, 1977.

Botwinick, J., & Storandt, M. Speed functions, vocabulary ability, and age. *Perceptual and Motor Skills,* 1973, *36,* 1123–1128.

Botwinick, J., & Storandt, M. Vocabulary ability in later life. *Journal of Genetic Psychology,* 1974, *125,* 303–308.

Bradley, R. H., & Webb, R. Age-related differences in locus of control orientation in three behavior domains. *Human Development,* 1976, *19,* 49–55.

Britton, J. H., & Britton, J. O. *Personality changes in aging.* New York: Springer, 1972.

Bromley, D. B. *The psychology of aging.* Baltimore: Penguin, 1966.

Campbell, D. P. The stability of vocational interests within occupations over long time spans. *Personnel and Guidance Journal,* 1966, *44,* 1012–1019.

Campbell, D. P. *Handbook for the Strong Vocational Interest Blank.* Stanford, Calif.: Stanford University Press, 1971.

Campbell, D. P., & Soliman, A. M. The vocational interests of women in psychology: 1942–66. *American Psychologist,* 1968, *23,* 158–163.

Chown, S. M. Age and the rigidities. *Journal of Gerontology,* 1961, *16,* 353–362.

Chown, S. M. Personality and aging. In K. W. Schaie (Ed.), *Theory and methods of research on aging.* Morgantown, West Virginia: West Virginia University, 1968.

Clayton, V., & Overton, W. F. Concrete and formal operational thought processes in young adulthood and old age. *International Journal of Aging and Human Development,* 1976, *7,* 237–245.

Clemente, F., & Sauer, W. J. Life satisfaction in the United States. *Social Forces,* 1976, *54,* 621–631.

Craik, F. I. M. Age differences in human memory. In J. E. Birren & K. W. Schaie (Eds.), *Handbook of the psychology of aging.* New York: Van Nostrand Reinhold, 1977.

Cumming, E., & Henry, W. E. *Growing old.* New York: Basic Books, 1961.

Denney, D. R., & Denney, N. W. The use of classification for problem solving: A comparison of middle and old age. *Developmental Psychology,* 1973, *9,* 275–278.

Dennis, W. Creative productivity between the ages of twenty and eighty years. *Journal of Gerontology,* 1966, *21,* 1–8.

Diamond, M. C. The aging brain: Some enlightening and optimistic results. *American Scientist,* 1978, *66,* 66–71.

Edwards, J. N., & Klemmack, L. Correlates of life satisfaction: A re-examination. *Journal of Gerontology,* 1973, *28,* 497–502.

Eisdorfer, C., Nowlin, J., & Wilkie, F. Improvement of learning in the aged by modification of autonomic nervous system activity. *Science,* 1970, *170,* 1327–1329.

Eisdorfer, C., & Wilkie, F. Intellectual changes with advancing age. In L. F. Jarvik, C. Eisdorfer, & J. E. Blum (Eds.), *Intellectual functioning in adults.* New York: Springer, 1973.

Elias, M. F., & Elias, P. K. Motivation and activity. In J. E. Birren & K. W. Schaie (Eds.), *Handbook of the psychology of aging.* New York: Van Nostrand Reinhold, 1977.

Elias, M. F., Elias, P. K., & Elias, J. W. *Basic processes in adult developmental psychology.* St. Louis: Mosby, 1977.

Erikson, E. H. *Childhood and society* (2nd ed.). New York: W. W. Norton, 1963.

Freud, S. [*The interpretation of dreams*] (J. Strachey, Ed. and trans.). New York: Basic Books, 1955. (Originally published, 1923.)

Green, R. F. Age-intelligence relationship between ages sixteen and sixty-four: A rising trend. *Developmental Psychology*, 1969, *1*, 618–627.

Gruenfeld, L. W., & MacEachron, A. E. *Perceptual and Motor Skills*, 1975, *41*, 449–450.

Gutmann, D. L. An exploration of ego configurations in middle and later life. In B. L. Neugarten, H. Berkowitz, W. J. Crotty, W. Gruen, D. L. Gutmann, M. I. Lubin, D. L. Miller, R. F. Peck, J. L. Rosen, A. Shukin, and S. S. Tobin, *Personality in middle and late life*. New York: Atherton, 1964.

Gutmann, D. L. The cross-cultural perspective: Notes toward a comparative psychology of aging. In J. E. Birren & K. W. Schaie (Eds.), *Handbook of the psychology of aging*. New York: Van Nostrand Reinhold, 1977.

Harris, L., & Associates. *The myth and reality of aging in America*. New York: National Council on the Aging, 1975.

Harry, J. Evolving sources of happiness for men over the life cycle: A structural analysis. *Journal of Marriage and the Family*, 1976, *38* (2), 289–296.

Havighurst, R. J. Personality and patterns of aging. *Gerontologist*, 1968, *8*, 20–23.

Havighurst, R. J., Neugarten, B. L., & Tobin, S. S. Disengagement and patterns of aging. In B. L. Neugarten (Ed.), *Middle age and aging*. Chicago: University of Chicago Press, 1968.

Hoge, D. R., & Bender, I. E. Factors influencing value change among college graduates in adult life. *Journal of Personality and Social Psychology*, 1974, *29*, 572–585.

Horn, J. L. Organization of data on life-span development of human abilities. In L. R. Goulet & P. B. Baltes (Eds.), *Life-span developmental psychology*. New York: Academic Press, 1970.

Horn, J. L. Psychometric studies of aging and intelligence. In S. Gershon & A. Raskin (Eds.), *Genesis and treatment of psychological disorders in the elderly* (Vol. 2). New York: Raven, 1975.

Horn, J. L. Human abilities: A review of research and theory in the early 1970s. In M. R. Rosenzweig & L. W. Porter (Eds.), *Annual review of psychology* (Vol. 27). Palo Alto, Calif.: Annual Reviews, 1976.

Horn, J. L. Human ability systems. In P. B. Baltes (Ed.), *Life-span development and behavior*. New York: Academic Press, 1977.

Horn, J. L., & Cattell, R. B. Age differences in fluid and crystallized intelligence. *Acta Psychologica*, 1967, *26*, 107–129.

Horn, J. L., & Donaldson, G. On the myth of intellectual decline in adulthood. *American Psychologist*, 1976, *31*, 701–719.

Horn, J. L., & Donaldson, G. Faith is not enough: A response to the Baltes-Schaie claim that intelligence does not wane. *American Psychologist*, 1977, *32*, 369–373.

Kalish, R. A. *Late adulthood: Perspectives on human development*. Monterey, Calif.: Brooks/Cole, 1975.

Kimmel, D. C. *Adulthood and aging*. New York: Wiley, 1974.

Kleemeier, R. W. Intellectual changes in the senium. *Proceedings of the American Statistical Association*, 1962, *1*, 290–295.

Kramer, M., Taube, C. A., & Redick, R. W. Patterns of use of psychiatric facilities by the aged: Past, present, and future. In C. Eisdorfer & M. P. Lawton (Eds.), *The psychology of adult development and aging*. Washington, D.C.: American Psychological Association, 1973.

Labouvie-Vief, G., & Gonda, J. N. Cognitive strategy training and intellectual performance in the elderly. *Journal of Gerontology*, 1976, *31*, 327–332.

Lambert, S. W., & Goodwin, G. M. *Medical leaders from Hippocrates to Osler*. Indianapolis: Bobbs-Merrill, 1929.

Lao, R. C. The developmental trend of the locus of control. *Personality and Social Psychology Bulletin*, 1974, *1*, 348–350.

Lehman, H. C. *Age and achievement.* Princeton, N.J.: Princeton University Press, 1953.

Lehman, H. C. The age decrement in outstanding scientific creativity. *American Psychologist*, 1960, *15*, 128–134.

Lehman, H. C. The psychologist's most creative years. *American Psychologist*, 1966, *21*, 363–369.

Lorge, I. The influence of the test upon the nature of mental decline as a function of age. *Journal of Educational Psychology*, 1936, *27*, 100–110.

Lowenthal, M. F., & Haven, C. Interaction and adaptation intimacy as a critical variable. *American Sociological Review*, 1968, *33*, 20–30.

Lubin, M. I. Addendum to chapter 4. In B. L. Neugarten, H. Berkowitz, W. J. Crotty, W. Gruen, D. L. Gutmann, M. I. Lubin, D. L. Miller, R. F. Peck, J. L. Rosen, A. Shukin, and S. S. Tobin, *Personality in middle and late life.* New York: Atherton, 1964.

Maas, H. S., & Kuypers, J. A. *From thirty to seventy.* San Francisco: Jossey-Bass, 1974.

Maddox, G. L. Activity and morale: A longitudinal study of selected elderly subjects. *Social Forces*, 1963, *42*, 195–204.

Maddox, G. L., & Douglass, E. B. Aging and individual differences: A longitudinal analysis of social, psychological, and physiological indicators. *Journal of Gerontology*, 1974, *29*, 555–563.

McTavish, D. G. Perceptions of old people: A review of research methodologies and findings. *The Gerontologist*, 1971, *11* (4, Pt. 2), 90–102.

Meier, E. L., & Kerr, E. A. Capabilities of middle-aged and older workers: A survey of the literature. *Industrial Gerontology*, 1976, *3*(3), 147–156.

Mussen, P. H. *Carmichael's manual of child psychology* (3rd ed.) (Vol. 2). New York: Wiley, 1970.

National Center for Health Statistics, 1967, *Vital and Health Statistics*, Series 20, No. 5.

Neugarten, B. L. Summary and implications. In B. L. Neugarten, H. Berkowitz, W. J. Crotty, W. Gruen, D. L. Gutmann, M. I. Lubin, D. L. Miller, R. F. Peck, J. L. Rosen, A. Shukin, and S. S. Tobin, *Personality in middle and late life.* New York: Atherton, 1964.

Neugarten, B. L. Personality change in late life: A developmental perspective. In C. Eisdorfer & M. P. Lawton (Eds.), *The psychology of adult development and aging.* Washington, D.C.: American Psychological Association, 1973.

Neugarten, B. L. Personality and aging. In J. E. Birren & K. W. Schaie (Eds.), *Handbook of the psychology of aging.* New York: Van Nostrand Reinhold, 1977.

Neugarten, B. L., Berkowitz, H., Crotty, W. J., Gruen, W., Gutmann, D. L., Lubin, M. I., Miller, D. L., Peck, R. F., Rosen, J. L., Shukin, A., & Tobin, S. S. *Personality in middle and late life.* New York: Atherton, 1964.

Neugarten, B. L., Crotty, W. J., & Tobin, S. S. Personality types in an aged population. In B. L. Neugarten, H. Berkowitz, W. J. Crotty, W. Gruen, D. L. Gutmann, M. I. Lubin, D. L. Miller, R. F. Peck, J. L. Rosen, A. Shukin, & S. S. Tobin, *Personality in middle and late life.* New York: Atherton, 1964.

Neugarten, B. L., & Gutmann, D. L. Age-sex roles and personality in middle age: A thematic apperception study. In B. L. Neugarten & Associates, *Personality in middle and late life.* New York: Atherton, 1964.

Neugarten, B. L., Havighurst, R. J., & Tobin, S. S. The measurement of life satisfaction. *Journal of Gerontology*, 1961, *16*, 134–143.

Neugarten, B. L., Moore, J. W., & Lowe, J. C. Age norms, age constraints, and adult socialization. In B. L. Neugarten (Ed.), *Middle age and aging.* Chicago: University of Chicago Press, 1968.

Okun, M. A. Adult age and cautiousness in decision: A review of the literature. *Human Development,* 1976, *19,* 220–233.

Okun, M. A., & Di Vesta, F. J. Cautiousness in adulthood as a function of age and instructions. *Journal of Gerontology,* 1976, *31,* 571–576.

Owens, W. A., Jr. Age and mental abilities: A longitudinal study. *Genetic Psychology Monographs,* 1953, *48,* 3–54.

Palmore, E., & Cleveland, W. Aging, terminal decline, and terminal drop. *Journal of Gerontology,* 1976, *31,* 76–81.

Palmore, E., & Luikart, C. Health and social factors related to life satisfaction. *Journal of Health and Social Behavior,* 1972, *13,* 68–80.

Papalia, D. E., & Bielby, D. D. Cognitive functioning in middle and old age adults: A review of research based on Piaget's theory. *Human Development,* 1974, *17,* 424–443.

Pfeiffer, E. Psychopathology and social psychopathology. In J. W. Birren & K. W. Schaie (Eds.), *Handbook of the psychology of aging.* New York: Van Nostrand Reinhold, 1977.

Pressey, S. L., & Kuhlen, R. G. *Psychological development through the life span.* New York: Harper, 1957.

Rabbitt, P. Changes in problem solving ability in old age. In J. E. Birren & K. W. Schaie (Eds.), *Handbook of the psychology of aging.* New York: Van Nostrand Reinhold, 1977.

Reese, H. W. The development of memory: Life-span perspectives. In H. W. Reese (Ed.), *Advances in child development and behavior* (Vol. 2). New York: Academic Press, 1976.

Reichard, S., Livson, F., & Petersen, P. G. *Aging and personality.* New York: Wiley, 1962.

Riegel, K. F., & Riegel, R. M. Development, drop, and death. *Developmental Psychology,* 1972, *6,* 306–319.

Riley, M. W., Foner, A., Moore, M. E., Hess, B., & Roth, B. K. *Aging and society. Volume one: An inventory of research findings.* New York: Russell Sage, 1968.

Rokeach, M. *The nature of human values.* New York: Free Press, 1973.

Rosen, J. L., & Neugarten, B. L. Ego functions in the middle and later years: A thematic apperception study. In B. L. Neugarten, H. Berkowitz, W. J. Crotty, W. Gruen, D. L. Gutmann, M. I. Lubin, D. L. Miller, R. F. Peck, J. L. Rosen, A. Shukin, & S. S. Tobin, *Personality in middle and late life.* New York: Atherton, 1964.

Rotter, J. B. *Social learning and clinical psychology.* New York: Prentice-Hall, 1954.

Ryckman, R. M., & Malikiosi, M. X. Relationship between locus of control and chronological age. *Psychological Reports,* 1975, *36,* 655–658.

Ryff, C. D. Personal communication, August 3, 1977.

Ryff, C. D., & Baltes, P. B. Value transition and adult development in women: The instrumentality-terminality sequence hypothesis. *Developmental Psychology,* 1976, *12,* 567–568.

Schaie, K. W. Rigidity-flexibility and intelligence: A cross-sectional study of the adult life span from 20 to 70 years. *Psychological Monographs: General and Applied,* 1958, *72* (9, Whole No. 462).

Schaie, K. W. Cross-sectional methods in the psychological aspects of aging. *Journal of Gerontology,* 1959, *14,* 208–215.

Schaie, K. W. Age changes and age differences. *Gerontologist,* 1967, *7,* 128–132.

Schaie, K. W. Translations to gerontology—from lab to life. *American Psychologist,* 1974, *29,* 802–807.

Schaie, K. W., Labouvie, G. V., & Buech, B. U. Generational and cohort-specific differences in adult cognitive functioning: A fourteen-year study of independent samples. *Developmental Psychology,* 1973, *9,* 151–166.

Schaie, K. W., & Labouvie, G. V. Generational versus ontogenetic components of change in adult cognitive behavior: A fourteen-year cross-sequential study. *Developmental Psychology,* 1974, *10,* 305–320.

Schaie, K. W., & Strother, C. R. A cross-sequential study of age changes in cognitive behavior. *Psychological Bulletin,* 1968, *70,* 671–680.

Schonfield, D. Translations to gerontology—from lab to life: Utilizing information. *American Psychologist,* 1974, *29,* 796–801.

Sheehy, G. *Passages.* New York: Dutton, 1976.

Staats, S. Internal versus external locus of control for three age groups. *International Journal of Aging and Human Development,* 1974, *5,* 7–10.

Thinking young. *Newsweek,* April 29, 1974, p. 80.

Toffler, A. *Future shock.* New York: Random House, 1970.

Troll, L. E. *Early and middle adulthood.* Monterey, Calif.: Brooks/Cole, 1975.

Tuddenham, R. D. Soldier intelligence in World Wars I and II. *American Psychologist,* 1948, *3,* 54–56.

Veroff, J., Atkinson, J. W., Feld, S. C., & Gurin, G. The use of thematic apperception to assess motivation in a nationwide sample. *Psychological Monographs,* 1960, *74* (12, Whole No. 499).

Vinitsky, M. A forty-year follow-up on the vocational interests of psychologists and their relationship to career development. *American Psychologist,* 1973, *28,* 1000–1009.

Wechsler, D. *The measurement and appraisal of adult intelligence* (4th ed.). Baltimore: Williams & Wilkins, 1958.

Welford, A. T. Motor performance. In J. E. Birren & K. W. Schaie (Eds.), *Handbook of the psychology of aging.* New York: Van Nostrand Reinhold, 1977.

Woodruff, D. S., & Birren, J. E. Age changes and cohort differences in personality. *Developmental Psychology,* 1972, *6,* 252–259.

Social Class Differences

Each one of us comes from a different social background. Our parents have certain amounts of formal education, work at specific kinds of jobs, and earn particular incomes. We have grown up in a certain neighborhood on the right or wrong "side of the tracks," and we have been used to a particular level of material comfort, such as sharing a room with one or more siblings or having a room of our own. How does our social background affect us? This is what we want to determine in the present chapter. We'll start off with a consideration of what is meant by social class.

THE CONCEPT OF SOCIAL CLASS

The social background characteristics we mentioned above each reflect a hierarchy of status positions. For example, the greater a person's income or the more education completed the higher his or her social status. Some degree of status differentiation seems to be present in all societies. Tumin (1967) has noted that stratification occurred even in the small wandering bands in the earliest days of human existence. Among such primitive groups, "women and children last" appears to have been the dominant rule of order. Records of ancient peoples, such as the Persians, Hebrews, and Greeks, indicate that hierarchical arrangements based on property, power, and prestige were very much a part of their societies. Today, some form of stratification can be found in societies ranging from technologically advanced nations, socialist as well as capitalist, to nonliterate groups, such as the Bushmen of Australia with their socially prescribed inequalities between men and women and between adults and children.

The modern study of social class began in the latter half of the 19th century with the highly influential writings of Karl Marx. Marx believed that human history is primarily shaped by economic conditions. He conceived of social classes as developing from different roles individuals carry out in the productive scheme of a society. In an industrialized society one class, the bourgeoisie, owns the means of production, while another class, the proletariat, provides the labor to carry out the production. For Marx the concept of social class was not merely an abstract representation of objective economic conditions. He believed that class members can develop a class consciousness—that is, a subjective awareness of their position in the productive system and a sense of their common interests. Once class consciousness develops among the proletariat, it serves as the basis for the class struggle, which should ultimately lead to the overthrow of those who control the means of production, the bourgeoisie.

In addition to Marx, the study of social class has been guided by the writings of Max Weber in the early part of the 20th century (see Gerth & Mills, 1946). In contrast to Marx, Weber conceived of stratification as multidimensional. Besides the economic sphere, there are the political sphere of power and the social sphere of prestige or status. For Weber, the political and social dimensions of stratification were not mere extensions of the economic. Weber also did not accept the Marxian belief that people's primary identification and consciousness emanated from class.

Weber's ideas, rather than those of Marx, have had a significant influence on contemporary American sociologists. For example, Nisbet (1970) observes that economic class, although a reality and a very important element in present-day American society, is not the primary and controlling force that Marxism contends. Over the years American sociologists have focused on the prestige dimension of stratification, particularly as exemplified in the work of W. Lloyd Warner. Warner studied a New England community, which he called "Yankee City" (see Warner & Lunt, 1941), and set the example for a series of subsequent community studies, including "Oldtown" (Davis, Gardner, & Gardner, 1941), "Midwest" (Warner, Havighurst, & Loeb, 1944), and "Plainville" (West, 1945). Warner attempted to analyze the varied associations among the many segments within the New England community through subjective perception of its inhabitants.

To characterize American society on the basis of a single dimension of stratification, whether it be the Marxist emphasis on economic class or the Warnerian emphasis on social prestige, oversimplifies the social structure. According to Nisbet (1970), the contemporary realities of stratification in the United States require the adoption of a multidimensional perspective. He states that the picture of American stratification "is rich in thrusts of political power, in spheres as well as levels of wealth, in variety of life-style, in degrees of education, in varying emphasis placed on family, religion, and ethnicity, and perhaps above all, in diversity of occupation" (p. 204).

Contrary to the Marxist emphasis of class consciousness and the Warnerian emphasis of group identity based on prestige, social classes in America are not distinct social groups. Several social scientists, including Rodman (1968), Nisbet (1970), and Berkowitz (1975), have therefore argued that the idea of gradations in status level should be substituted for the concept of "class." As Berkowitz (1975) points out:

> The social hierarchy existing in contemporary society consists of various status levels, with each rank having only a vague border between it and the strata just above and below it. When people classify themselves hierarchically, chances are they think of themselves as being at a certain level in the social order rather than as belonging to a distinct group with common attitudes and shared norms [p. 519].

Although the term *social class* is still commonly used, most of the recent work on social stratification is consistent with the notion of a continuum of status levels. When we refer to social-class differences, we imply that individuals have been differentiated according to various status levels in the social hierarchy.

The Measurement of Social Class

There are three methods of measuring social class: (1) the reputational approach, (2) the objective approach, and (3) the subjective approach. In the community studies by Warner and others, social stratification was assessed by the *reputational approach*, which involves determining a person's social-class standing on the basis of other people's perceptions. Individuals were chosen from the community who were known to have extensive knowledge about many of the other residents in the community. These informants were asked about which people in the community associated with one another—that is, who visited one another's homes, who got together at social functions, who married into each other's families, and so forth. Based on the informants' responses, the investigators determined to which class an individual belonged according to the particular group of people he or she normally associated with. People usually formed associations with others who were similar to themselves in terms of such factors as income, occupation, type of residence, religious affiliation, and political attitudes. In the established Eastern and Southern communities studied, six social classes were identified: upper-upper, lower-upper, upper-middle, lower-middle, upper-lower, and lower-lower. In the newer communities in the Midwest no division appeared within the upper class.

The major problem with the reputational approach is that it can be carried out only in relatively small communities where people know each other. It is therefore not surprising that in these communities social class may be defined in terms of social groups that vary in prestige. However, it is difficult to make any generalizations about social stratification in American society using a method limited to small communities. Indeed, as we have pointed out, social class on a national level is not based on distinct social groups.

In response to the limited application of the reputational approach, Warner and his associates eventually developed the *objective approach*. This method takes into account objective criteria for social-class placement, as exemplified by the "Index of Status Characteristics" (ISC) (Warner, Meeker, & Eells, 1949). The ISC is based on the following four factors: (1) occupation (ranked according to level of skill and prestige value), (2) source of income (inherited wealth, salaries, welfare, and so on), (3) house type (the size and condition of dwelling unit), and (4) location of dwelling area (the general quality and reputation). Each of these factors is weighted, with occupational level receiving the largest weighting. Other objective indexes have also been developed, including Hollingshead's "Index of Social Position," which is based on level of occupation and amount of education (Hollingshead & Redlich, 1958).

Instead of employing a composite index of social class, many investigations make use of the single factor of occupational level because it is moderately correlated with other stratification dimensions, such as amount of education, source of income, and type and location of housing. Thus, for example, a person's social position can be determined by using the rank-order classification scheme for occupations developed by the U.S. Bureau of the Census:

1. Professional persons
2. Proprietors, managers, and officials
3. Clerks and kindred workers
4. Skilled workers and foremen
5. Semiskilled workers
6. Unskilled workers

This rank-order classification is based on how experts view the level of skill and prestige value attached to the various occupations. It is highly consistent with the results of two national surveys that have ascertained the opinions of representative samples of adult Americans regarding the social standing (that is, prestige value) of each of 90 occupations (Hodge, Siegel, & Rossi, 1964; North & Hatt, 1953). The two surveys included the same set of 90 occupations, and these occupations were ranked similarly on both occasions. The prestige rankings for some of the occupations are shown in Table 12-1. As can be seen in the table, professions (for example, physician and lawyer) are ranked at the top, whereas semiskilled vocations (for example, store clerk) and unskilled vocations (for example, shoe shiner) are ranked at the bottom.

Table 12-1. Prestige Scores and Ranks for Some Occupations

	Score*	Rank
Supreme Court justice	94	1
Physician	93	2
Scientist	92	3.5
College professor	90	8
Lawyer	89	11
Dentist	88	14
Civil engineer	86	21.5
Accountant—large business	81	29.5
Public school teacher	81	29.5
Building contractor	80	31.5
Artist (painter)	78	34.5
Electrician	76	39
Police officer	72	47
Insurance agent	69	51.5
Carpenter	68	53
Plumber	65	59
Auto repairman	64	60
Truck driver	59	67
Store clerk	56	70
Farmhand	48	83
Shoe shiner	34	90

*In this table a score of 100 = "excellent social standing"; 80 = "good"; 60 = "average"; 40 = "somewhat below average"; and 20 = "poor social standing."

Adapted from *A Survey of Social Psychology,* by Leonard Berkowitz. Copyright © 1975 by The Dryden Press, a division of Holt, Rinehart and Winston, Publishers. Based on data from "Occupational Prestige in the United States: 1925-1963," by R. W. Hodge, P. M. Siegel, and P. H. Rossi, *American Journal of Sociology,* 1964, *70,* 286–302. Copyright 1964 by The University of Chicago Press. Used by permission of Holt, Rinehart and Winston and The University of Chicago Press.

Now that we have looked at the reputational and objective methods of assessing social class, let's move on to the *subjective approach.* This approach involves asking people to classify themselves on the social hierarchy. Centers (1949) conducted a national survey of adult males to determine how they identified themselves according to social class. He asked the following question: "If you were asked to use one of these four names for your social class, which would you say you belonged in: the middle class, lower class, working class, or upper class?" The survey results yielded the following: (1) upper class (3%), (2) middle class (43%), (3) working class (51%), and (4) lower class (1%). The remaining 2% indicated they either didn't know what class they belonged to or didn't believe in classes. Similar results have been obtained in more recent surveys (Hardert, Parker, Pfuhl, & Anderson, 1974). Thus, a majority of Americans identify themselves as "working class."

When we look at the actual kinds of occupations these working-class people are engaged in, we find that slightly over 50% of them have manual jobs, such as factory work or farm work. Surprisingly, about 20% of those who classify themselves as working class are business owners, and about another 20% are factory managers. As Hardert and associates point out, the fact that both owners and laborers identify themselves as working class is a far cry from Marx's idea of a working class composed exclusively of the proletariat. Another interesting finding in these surveys is that when the choice is limited to upper, middle, or lower class (that is, when the working-class label is omitted) about 75% to 85% designate themselves as middle class.

The most frequently used method of assessing social class is the objective approach. This is because it overcomes the observer biases inherent in both rating others (the reputational approach) and in self-ratings (the subjective approach). In addition, as we noted, the objective approach can be used widely (for example, at a local or national level). Unlike the reputational approach it is not limited to small communities where people know each other.

Based on objective indexes let us take a look at the major characteristics that distinguish the various social-class levels. In studies of stratification in the United States (see Roach, Gross, & Gursslin, 1969), the *upper class* typically constitutes from 1% to 3% of the population. In some communities, a division exists within the upper class between those who have possessed wealth for several generations (the upper-upper class) and those who have only recently come into wealth (the lower-upper class or "nouveau riche").

Middle-class persons are distinguished from upper-class persons primarily on the basis of their more limited wealth and power and from lower-class persons primarily by their occupational endeavors. The size of the middle class is generally estimated to be between 40% and 50% of the population. Middle-class people tend to have occupations that require verbal skills rather than manual labor; their work is concentrated mainly in professional, technical, administrative, sales, and clerical areas. Usually a distinction is made between those who have a high degree of training and responsibility over others (upper-middle class) and those with less training and responsibility (lower-middle class). A much larger percentage of people fall within the lower-middle than the upper-middle category.

The *lower class* consists of two categories. The upper-lower class, often labeled "working class," is composed of skilled and semiskilled manual workers and is estimated to comprise between 30% and 40% of the population. In many cases the income of working-class people is equal to or greater than that of many lower-middle class people.[1] However, they are classed as lower because their work is at a lower prestige rank than middle-class occupations. The lower-lower class is made up of unskilled workers and the unemployed, and comprises from 15% to 20% of the population. Lower-lower class persons live at or below an economic subsistence level (the poverty line).

In many analyses of stratification, broad categories (for example, "middle class" and "lower class") often are used causing difficulties when attempts are made to compare categories across different studies. For instance, when the "middle class" label is used, it may not be clear whether this refers to professional or clerical workers. A similar ambiguity exists with the "lower

---

[1] A recent study also indicates that on the basis of intergenerational mobility and residential patterns most white-collar workers (clerical workers and technicians) are more similar to manual workers (working-class) than to workers in middle-class occupations (Vanneman, 1977).

class" label regarding the distinction between skilled and semiskilled workers, on the one hand, and unskilled workers and the unemployed, on the other. Most of the research on lower-class persons has actually dealt with the working class rather than those at the poverty level, but often this fact is not made explicit.

VALUES

We begin our consideration of social-class differences with a look at values, because they can be viewed as important factors underlying social-class differences in intelligence, achievement, and personality.

Do people at the lower end of the social order have a different set of general life values than people at the upper end of the social order? Rokeach's (1973) investigation of the general life values of a sample of adult Americans included comparisons based on level of income and amount of education. The pattern of results for income and education was essentially the same so we will concern ourselves with the findings for income.

As we noted in Chapter 9, Rokeach's Value Survey includes lists of both instrumental values (modes of conduct) and terminal values (end-states of existence). Tables 12-2 and 12-3 show the median rankings and composite rank orders of the values for groups varying in income. Significant differences (represented by the probability levels in the last columns) are indicated for 9 of the 18 terminal values and 11 of the 18 instrumental values. The greatest distinction occurs with the instrumental value "clean," which decreases as income increases. (It is ranked second for the lowest income group and 17th for the highest income group.) According to Rokeach the low ranking of "clean" by the rich suggests that the affluent take cleanliness for granted. On the other hand, the high ranking of cleanliness by the poor suggests that this is a very salient issue for people forced to live under squalid conditions. Another value that shows a marked contrast between high and low income groups is "a comfortable life." (Its rank for the lowest income group is sixth and for the highest, 15th.) As in the case of cleanliness, a comfortable life is something the affluent already experience, whereas it is something the poor lack.

Other terminal and instrumental values that distinguish the poor from the rich are not necessarily based on which conditions people experience or do not experience. For instance, "salvation," "true friendship," being "cheerful," "helpful," "obedient," and "polite" are valued more by low-income groups than high-income groups. In contrast, "a sense of accomplishment," "family security," "inner harmony," "mature love," "wisdom," being "capable," "imaginative," "intellectual," and "logical" are valued more by high-income groups.

Overall, as Rokeach points out, the value differences found between low-income and high-income groups seem to suggest that they come from different cultures. Rokeach (1973) states:

> The poor are more religious than the rich, more other-directed and conforming to traditional values, less concerned with taking responsibility and with

Table 12-2. Terminal Value Medians and Composite Rank Orders for Groups Varying in Income (N = 1325)

Value	Under $2,000	$2,000 to 3,999	$4,000 to 5,999	$6,000 to 7,999	$8,000 to 9,999	$10,000 to 14,999	$15,000 and over	p
N =	139	239	217	249	178	208	95	
A comfortable life	7.2(6)*	8.5(7)	8.4(7)	8.1(6)	10.0(11)	11.0(13)	13.4(15)	.001
An exciting life	15.3(18)	15.4(18)	15.6(18)	15.4(18)	15.4(18)	15.2(18)	14.3(16)	—
A sense of accomplishment	10.4(12)	10.3(12)	9.1(9)	9.4(10)	8.4(8)	7.6(6)	6.1(5)	.001
A world at peace	2.7(1)	3.1(1)	3.2(1)	3.4(2)	3.9(2)	3.8(2)	3.5(1)	—
A world of beauty	13.6(14)	12.7(14)	13.5(15)	14.0(15)	13.8(15)	13.7(15)	12.6(13)	—
Equality	7.0(5)	8.5(8)	8.3(6)	9.0(9)	7.8(5)	9.7(9)	7.5(6)	.01
Family security	5.6(2)	4.6(2)	3.6(2)	3.2(1)	3.2(1)	3.6(1)	4.1(2)	.001
Freedom	6.8(4)	5.2(3)	5.2(3)	5.4(3)	5.9(3)	5.9(3)	5.0(3)	—
Happiness	7.7(7)	8.0(6)	7.1(4)	6.9(4)	7.6(4)	8.1(7)	9.2(8)	—
Inner harmony	11.6(13)	10.9(13)	10.8(13)	10.5(13)	10.2(13)	9.9(11)	9.2(9)	.01
Mature love	14.4(17)	14.0(16)	12.3(14)	12.2(14)	10.8(14)	11.5(14)	11.8(12)	.001
National security	8.9(11)	9.5(11)	9.7(12)	9.5(11)	9.3(10)	9.4(8)	11.3(11)	—
Pleasure	13.6(16)	14.5(17)	14.7(16)	14.7(17)	15.1(17)	15.0(16)	15.2(18)	—
Salvation	6.6(3)	7.3(5)	9.4(11)	8.4(8)	8.6(9)	10.1(12)	13.3(14)	.001
Self-respect	7.9(8)	7.2(4)	7.6(5)	8.4(7)	7.9(6)	7.2(4)	7.8(7)	—
Social recognition	13.6(15)	13.9(15)	14.8(17)	14.6(16)	14.2(16)	15.1(17)	14.6(17)	—
True friendship	7.9(9)	8.5(10)	9.2(10)	9.9(12)	10.1(12)	9.7(10)	9.4(10)	.01
Wisdom	8.7(10)	8.5(9)	8.8(8)	7.0(5)	8.1(7)	7.4(5)	5.6(4)	.01

*Figures shown are median rankings and, in parentheses, composite rank orders.

From *The Nature of Human Values*, by M. Rokeach. Copyright © 1973 by The Free Press, a division of Macmillan Publishing Co., Inc. Reprinted by permission.

Table 12-3. Instrumental Value Medians and Composite Rank Orders for Groups Varying in Income (N = 1325)

Value	N =	Under $2,000 139	$2,000 to 3,999 239	$4,000 to 5,999 217	$6,000 to 7,999 249	$8,000 to 9,999 178	$10,000 to 14,999 208	$15,000 and over 95	p
Ambitious		8.0(6)*	6.9(3)	6.1(2)	6.8(3)	6.6(3)	5.8(2)	6.4(3)	—
Broadminded		8.6(8)	7.2(4)	8.1(8)	8.1(6)	7.1(4)	6.4(4)	7.0(4)	—
Capable		9.5(10)	10.5(14)	9.8(11)	9.3(11)	9.8(11)	8.4(7)	8.8(8)	.05
Cheerful		9.0(9)	8.6(9)	10.6(14)	10.3(12)	10.7(12)	10.2(11)	11.3(14)	.01
Clean		6.4(2)	7.3(5)	8.0(7)	8.6(8)	9.3(10)	10.4(12)	14.4(17)	.001
Courageous		7.5(5)	8.1(8)	8.0(5)	7.5(5)	7.4(6)	8.0(5)	7.2(5)	—
Forgiving		6.4(3)	6.5(2)	7.3(4)	6.8(4)	7.4(5)	8.1(6)	10.7(12)	.01
Helpful		7.1(4)	7.4(6)	8.0(6)	8.2(7)	8.9(8)	9.3(8)	9.1(9)	.01
Honest		3.3(1)	3.7(1)	3.4(1)	3.0(1)	3.0(1)	3.4(1)	3.0(1)	—
Imaginative		15.2(18)	15.8(18)	15.6(18)	15.9(18)	15.0(18)	14.6(18)	11.4(15)	.001
Independent		10.5(14)	10.3(12)	10.0(12)	10.7(14)	11.4(13)	11.0(13)	8.3(6)	—
Intellectual		13.9(16)	13.4(16)	13.3(16)	13.6(16)	13.1(15)	12.1(15)	8.6(7)	.001
Logical		15.2(17)	14.8(17)	14.7(17)	14.1(17)	14.0(16)	12.8(16)	10.9(13)	.001
Loving		10.0(11)	10.3(13)	9.5(10)	9.1(10)	8.8(7)	10.2(10)	9.8(10)	—
Obedient		12.0(15)	12.4(15)	13.3(15)	13.2(15)	14.2(17)	14.3(17)	15.3(18)	.001
Polite		10.4(13)	10.2(11)	10.2(13)	10.4(13)	11.4(14)	11.2(14)	13.2(16)	.001
Responsible		8.2(7)	7.8(7)	7.1(3)	5.8(2)	6.0(2)	6.0(3)	5.9(2)	.001
Self-controlled		10.2(12)	9.9(10)	9.2(9)	9.0(9)	9.0(9)	9.7(9)	9.9(11)	—

*Figures shown are median rankings and, in parentheses, composite rank orders.

From *The Nature of Human Values*, by M. Rokeach. Copyright © 1973 by The Free Press, a division of Macmillan Publishing Co., Inc. Reprinted by permission.

the security of the family, and more motivated by a desire for affiliation with members of one's own sex than a desire for love with members of the opposite sex. Finally, the poor differ from the rich by placing a lower value on competence, intellectual, and self-actualization values [pp. 62–63].

The emphasis that individuals at the lower end of the social order place on conformity in contrast to the emphasis on self-direction found among higher status individuals is also revealed in a study conducted by Kohn (1969). Kohn investigated the relationship between social class and parental values—that is, the values that parents would most like to see embodied in their children's behavior. He interviewed samples of middle- and working-class parents in the Washington, D.C., area and asked them to select from a list of characteristics the three qualities they believed most important for their children. Although both groups of parents believed that happiness, honesty, consideration, obedience, dependability, and self-control were important, differences were revealed by the fact that middle-class parents gave higher priority than working-class parents to those values that reflected self-direction and an understanding of other people's feelings. Specifically, middle-class parents emphasized self-control, curiosity, and consideration. In contrast, working-class parents emphasized those values that reflected conformity to externally defined standards—obedience and neatness. These class differences were replicated with samples of middle- and working-class parents in Turin, Italy.

Because middle-class parents value self-direction in their children and working-class parents value conformity, it is reasonable to expect that these class differences in values would be reflected by differences in child-rearing practices. This expectation is generally confirmed by the evidence that middle- and working-class parents do differ in their child-rearing practices (Bronfenbrenner, 1958; Hess, 1970). In particular, class differences in discipline seem to reflect the differences in parental values. This is suggested by Kohn's (1969) finding of class differences in the kinds of situation in which mothers use physical punishment. His results indicated that working-class mothers are more likely to use physical punishment when the consequences of their children's misbehavior are serious, such as those which may happen in aggressive play. In contrast, middle-class mothers are more likely to use physical punishment in reaction to what they view as negative feelings on the part of their children, such as a violent or aggressive outburst of temper. These results appear to be related to Kohn's findings of class differences in parental values. Since working-class mothers value conformity, they would be more concerned with their children's misbehavior if external standards are transgressed. Middle-class mothers, who value self-direction, would be more sensitive toward their children's showing loss of self-control, as in temper outbursts.

Kohn did not find any differences in the overall frequency with which middle- and working-class mothers administered physical punishment. Erlanger (1974) in reviewing the research on parental discipline concluded that there is only a slight (although statistically significant) tendency for working-class parents to use physical punishment more frequently than middle-class parents.

Other class differences in child-rearing practices also may be related to differences in parental values. The high priority middle-class mothers place on self-direction for their children may be reflected in the fact that middle-class mothers, as opposed to working-class mothers, have more tolerance for their children's expression of various drives and impulses, such as toilet accidents, sex, and aggression (Bronfenbrenner, 1958; Hess, 1970). Also indicative of self-direction values is the finding that middle-class mothers emphasize independence training; that is, they expect their children to be self-reliant at earlier ages than do working-class mothers.

In summary, class differences exist in many of the general life values identified by Rokeach (1973). Lower-class people are more other-directed and conforming to traditional values than middle-class people, and lower-class people place less emphasis on competence, intellectual, and self-actualization values. The middle-class emphasis on self-direction and the working-class emphasis on conformity appear to be especially significant because, as Kohn's (1969) research indicates, middle-class parents place a high priority on their children's self-directedness, whereas working-class parents place a high priority on their children's conformity. These class differences in parental values may be a factor underlying class differences in intelligence, achievement, and personality.

INTELLIGENCE

Social-class differences in intelligence have been consistently exhibited in IQ tests. Evidence of these differences has appeared in adult samples and in samples of children when categorized according to their parents' social-class position.

Social Class and Adult Intelligence

A positive relationship between social status and tested intelligence was demonstrated among servicemen during World War I (Fryer, 1922) and World War II (Harrell & Harrell, 1945; Stewart, 1947). This relationship is illustrated in Figure 12-1, which includes the median score and range of scores on the Army General Classification Test (AGCT) for 15 selected occupations. There is a progressive increase in test scores from the unskilled-labor occupations at the bottom to the professional occupations at the top. An important characteristic of the armed forces data is the considerable variability in test performance for each occupational group (see Figure 12-1). This variability tends to be greater at the lower end of the hierarchy, which most likely reflects the greater heterogeneity of educational level that exists in lower status occupational groups.

One limitation of these armed forces data is that they are restricted to enlisted men and, therefore, underrepresent the occupations at the upper end of the hierarchy. However, studies of civilian samples, where such a bias does

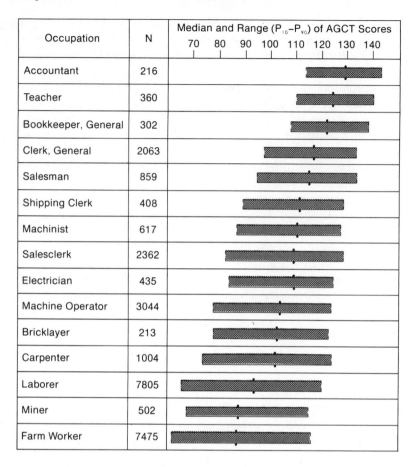

Occupation	N	Median and Range (P₁₀–P₉₀) of AGCT Scores
		70 80 90 100 110 120 130 140
Accountant	216	
Teacher	360	
Bookkeeper, General	302	
Clerk, General	2063	
Salesman	859	
Shipping Clerk	408	
Machinist	617	
Salesclerk	2362	
Electrician	435	
Machine Operator	3044	
Bricklayer	213	
Carpenter	1004	
Laborer	7805	
Miner	502	
Farm Worker	7475	

Figure 12-1. AGCT scores for various civilian occupational groups. The median score is denoted by the vertical line and the range (from the 10th percentile to the 90th percentile) by the shaded bars. From *Differential Psychology,* by A. Anastasi. Copyright © 1958 by Macmillan Publishing Co., Inc. Based on data from "AGCT Scores of Army Personnel Grouped by Occupation," by N. Stewart, *Occupations,* 1947, *26*(1), 5–41. Copyright 1947 by the American Personnel and Guidance Association. Reprinted by permission.

not exist, have also shown a positive relationship between occupational level and tested intelligence (Duncan, Featherman, & Duncan, 1972; Schaie, 1958; Simon & Levitt, 1950).

Social Class and Children's Intelligence

Consistent with the findings for adults, when children are categorized according to their fathers' occupation a positive relationship exists between tested intelligence and occupational level. This is exemplified by the data col-

Table 12-4. Mean Stanford-Binet IQs of Children According to Fathers' Occupations

Fathers' Occupational Classification		Chronological Ages			
		2 to 5½	*6 to 9*	*10 to 14*	*15 to 18*
I	Professional	114.8	114.9	117.5	116.4
II	Semi-professional and Managerial	112.4	107.3	112.2	116.7
III	Clerical, Skilled Trades, and Retail Business	108.0	104.9	107.4	109.6
IV	Rural Owners	97.8	94.6	92.4	94.3
V	Semi-skilled, Minor Clerical and Business	104.3	104.6	103.4	106.7
VI	Slightly Skilled	97.2	100.0	100.6	96.2
VII	Day Labor, Urban and Rural	93.8	96.0	97.2	97.6

Adapted from *Revision of the Stanford-Binet Scale,* by Q. McNemar. Copyright © 1942 by Houghton Mifflin Company. Used by permission.

lected during the standardization of the Stanford-Binet (McNemar, 1942). As Table 12-4 indicates, the average IQs for children with fathers in the professions were about 20 points higher than those for children with fathers in unskilled occupations. The relationship between the tested intelligence of children and fathers' occupational level has been reported in a number of other studies (Anastasi, 1958; Kaufman & Doppelt, 1976).

The intelligence-test scores of children have also been analyzed in relation to parents' social-class rating, as determined by the Warner Index of Status Characteristics. This approach was used in the "Midwest" community study (Havighurst & Breese, 1947; Havighurst & Janke, 1944; Janke & Havighurst, 1945). The investigators administered a battery of tests to nearly all of the 10-, 13-, and 16-year-olds who lived in the community. The test battery given to the 10- and 16-year-olds included several verbal and nonverbal tests of intelligence, as well as special ability tests of reading, spatial relationships, and mechanical assembly. The 13-year-old group was given the Primary Mental Abilities battery. The mean test scores for the 10- and 16-year-olds are indicated in Tables 12-5 and 12-6, respectively. In the younger group, no children appeared from the upper or upper-middle classes, so the social status ranged from lower-middle to lower-lower. In the older group, the small number of children from the two highest social status categories was combined into one category. With the exception of the Mechanical Assembly Test for the 16-year-old boys, the mean test scores for both samples tended to increase with social status. Furthermore, most of the test-score differences among the social-status groups were statistically significant.

Table 12-5. Means of Social Status Groups on Psychological Tests—Ten-Year-Old Children

Social Status	N	Stanford-Binet IQ	Cornell*-Coxe IQ	Goodenough* Draw-A-Person IQ	Iowa Silent Reading Score	Minnesota Paper Form Board Score	Mechanical Assembly T-Score		Porteus* Maze Mental Age
							Boys	Girls	
Lower-Middle	26	114	116	107	99	22.5	52.5	56.0	12.7
Upper-Lower	68	110	110	102	99	21.3	49.2	49.5	12.8
Lower-Lower	16	91	96	91	88	15.7	46.9	41.3	10.4

*Nonverbal tests of intelligence.
Adapted from "Relation between Ability and Social Status in a Midwestern Community: I. Ten-Year-Old Children," by R. J. Havighurst and L. L. Janke, *Journal of Educational Psychology*, 1944, 45, 357–368. Used by permission.

Table 12-6. Means of Social Status Groups on Psychological Tests—Sixteen-Year-Old Children

Social Status	N	Stanford- Binet	Wechsler Bellevue	Iowa Silent Reading	Minnesota Paper Form Board	Mechanical Assembly	
						Boys	Girls
Upper and Upper-Middle	9	128	118	58.0	44	46.8	62.1
Lower-Middle	44	112	108	51.0	40	51.6	52.0
Upper-Lower	49	104	102	48.9	31	48.8	48.5
Lower-Lower	13	89	103	45.6	31	53.0	45.9

Adapted from "Relation between Ability and Social Status in a Midwestern Community: II. Sixteen-Year-Old Boys and Girls," by L. L. Janke and R. J. Havighurst, *Journal of Educational Psychology*, 1945, *36*, 499–509. Used by permission.

The results with the 13-year-old group on the Primary Mental Abilities battery also showed a tendency for higher scores to be associated with higher social status (Havighurst & Breese, 1947). This tendency is reflected in the reported correlations between social status and the ability factors: .42 for Verbal Comprehension, .32 for Number, .30 for Word Fluency, .25 for Space, .23 for Reasoning, and .21 for Memory. The magnitude of these correlations indicates that abilities more closely associated with academic background (for example, Verbal Comprehension and Number) bear a stronger relationship to social class than other abilities (for example, Space and Memory).

The results of the "Midwest" study are limited because they are based on rather small samples. However, other investigations with larger samples have demonstrated the same relationship between children's tested intelligence and family social status. In the "River City" community study (Havighurst, Bowman, Liddle, Mathews, & Pierce, 1962), based on sixth-grade samples of 237 boys and 237 girls, respective correlations of .34 and .28 were reported between a composite measure of average intelligence and social status. Two large-scale studies (Duncan, Haller, & Portes, 1968; Sewell, Haller, & Ohlendorf, 1970) of male high school students have reported correlations of .23 and .29, respectively, between IQ scores and social class.

An important exception to the general finding of a positive relationship between children's intelligence and social class is the evidence for very young children. In reviewing this evidence, Golden and Birns (1976) conclude that social-class differences on intelligence measures do not emerge until about two years of age. However, as we noted in Chapter 5, the infant tests may not be measuring the same kinds of characteristics assessed by intelligence tests at later ages—that is, infant tests tend to focus on sensorimotor abilities while tests for older children stress verbal abilities.

In addition to the investigation of social class and intelligence, there has been some consideration of areas of special ability in relation to social class. We have already discussed the "Midwest" study, which showed that verbal and numerical abilities were more clearly associated with social class than spatial, reasoning, and memory abilities. More recently, Jensen (1969) has looked at social class in relation to two broad ability areas he designates as Level I and Level II abilities. *Level I* refers to associative learning or the capacity to register and recall incoming information that is most directly measured by tests such as memory for digits and serial rote learning. *Level II* involves the ability to abstract as reflected in the concept-learning and problem-solving tasks of general intelligence tests. Jensen reported that lower-class children do as well as middle-class children on Level I tests of associative learning, but lower-class children are at a disadvantage in the more abstract Level II tests. Subsequent research has provided some confirmation of these findings (Loehlin, Lindzey, & Spuhler, 1975). However, many of the studies have involved comparisons between lower-class Black children and middle-class White children so it is not clear whether the Level I/Level II distinction is more pertinent to social class or to racial differences.

Before completing our review of the evidence bearing on social class and intelligence, it is important to emphasize that much overlapping occurs between class levels, and a wide range of individual differences exists within each social-class level. As noted previously, larger numbers of individuals proportionately compose the lower social classes than the higher social classes. Anastasi (1958) suggests the possibility of finding a larger percentage of intellectually superior individuals from the lower than from the upper social classes. She cites, as an example, a survey of Wisconsin high school seniors. Of those scoring above the group median in intelligence test scores, only 7.9% had fathers in the professions, while 17.4% had fathers in skilled-labor occupations. However, the median percentile score for the group with professional fathers was 68.5 as against 51.1 for the group with skilled-labor fathers. Such data indicate that in absolute numbers the lower classes may contribute more intellectually superior individuals. Yet, in terms of relative numbers within each class, the higher classes make the greater contribution.

Urban/Rural Differences

Traditionally, rural background has been judged to be similar to lower social-class background because in both cases people's opportunities for intellectual stimulation have been more limited than the opportunities of people from urban and middle- or upper-class backgrounds. With our increasing urbanization and the impact of mass media, rural residents are no longer as isolated as they once were. It is not surprising then that interest in investigating urban/rural differences in intelligence has been declining.

Both Anastasi (1958) and Tyler (1965) have reviewed many studies that quite consistently show that urban children score significantly higher than rural children in both the United States and several European countries.[2] Repre-

---

[2]The only notable exception has been in Scotland where a 1932 survey (Scottish Council, 1939) revealed no differences between urban and rural children. In a later survey (Scottish Council, 1949) a slight, but significant, difference was found in favor of urban children. These results were interpreted as a reflection of the relative equivalence of educational opportunities throughout Scotland.

Table 12-7. Mean Stanford-Binet IQs of Urban, Suburban, and Rural Children

| Locality | Age Range in Years | | | | | |
| | 2 to 5½ | | 6 to 14 | | 15 to 18 | |
	N	Mean	N	Mean	N	Mean
Urban	354	106.3	864	105.8	204	107.9
Suburban	158	105.0	537	104.5	112	106.9
Rural	144	100.6	422	95.4	103	95.7

Adapted from *Revision of the Stanford-Binet Scale,* By Q. McNemar. Copyright © 1942 by Houghton Mifflin Company. Reprinted by permission.

sentative of the results of these studies are the mean IQs for the standardization sample of the Stanford-Binet (McNemar, 1942). As indicated in Table 12-7, no differences were found between urban and suburban groups, which is not surprising since both are part of a metropolitan environment. On the other hand, the rural children averaged about 5 IQ points lower than the other groups at the youngest age range and about 10 IQ points lower at the other age ranges. Results from the standardization of the Wechsler Intelligence Scale for Children (WISC) show that the difference in favor of urban children is somewhat greater for verbal than for nonverbal tests (Kaufman & Doppelt, 1976; Seashore, Wesman, & Doppelt, 1950). As we mentioned, if the rural environment is less isolated than it once was, we should expect that over the last several years there would have been a decrease in the IQ discrepancy between rural and urban samples. Evidence of such a trend is reported by Kaufman and Doppelt (1976), who found that in the standardization sample for the 1974 WISC there was only a 2-point full-scale IQ difference in favor of urban children compared with a 5½-point full-scale IQ difference in favor of urban children for the 1949 WISC standardization sample (Seashore et al., 1950).

The Interpretation of Social-Class Differences

The evidence quite clearly demonstrates the existence of social-class differences in intelligence. We will consider three basic interpretations which have been offered to account for these differences: (1) the genetic argument, (2) the environmental argument, and (3) the argument that a class bias exists within intelligence tests.

Hereditary Influences. In Chapter 5 we concluded that heredity does contribute to individual differences in intelligence. It therefore seems reasonable to assume, as Loehlin, Lindzey, and Spuhler (1975) do, that people born and reared in a particular social-class subculture not only are exposed to a similar environment but also share in a distinctive gene pool. Furthermore, a person's upward or downward social mobility may also be partly determined by heredity. According to several writers, if a society provides the opportunities for social mobility, we should expect the most able members of a given generation to rise toward the top of the status hierarchy and the least able to move toward the bottom (Burt, 1961; Eckland, 1967; Herrnstein, 1973). In American society, the existing social barriers against minority groups (most notably Blacks, Hispanic Americans, and Native Americans) essentially limit this genetic hypothesis of social mobility to the White majority.

There is evidence of the relationship between social mobility and intelligence that is based on differences in social status between parent and offspring. Waller (1971) predicted that sons who had a considerably higher IQ than their fathers would rise in social status, and sons who had a much lower IQ than their fathers would fall in social status. Waller studied 131 fathers and 170 of their sons. IQ scores for both generations were obtained from school records, and social status was based on educational attainment and occupation. The results supported the predicted differences. Twenty of the 27 sons who surpassed their fathers by 23 or more IQ points moved up in social status, whereas among the sons whose IQs were 23 or more IQ points lower, 9 out of 11 moved down. For the group of fathers and sons with less extreme IQ differences (8 to 22 IQ points), trends in the same direction appeared, but to a lesser degree.

While the results of Waller's study are consistent with a genetic hypothesis, they could also be accounted for by an environmental explanation of differences in early cultural experiences. For example, those sons who surpassed their fathers in IQ could have been encouraged to rise above their fathers' intellectual accomplishments. In contrast, those sons who had lower IQs than their fathers could have been discouraged from attempting to match their fathers' level of accomplishment. It is therefore difficult to ascertain the degree to which social mobility is due to heredity and the degree to which it is due to environment. The fact that genetic differences contribute to individual ability differences suggests that heredity in part underlies the relationship between social class and intelligence.

Environmental Influences. If the early experiences of the lower-class child differ from those of the higher-class child, such differences may help account for social-class differences in intelligence. As we noted in our discussion of values, studies reveal a variety of social-class differences in child-rearing practices.

A number of studies have indicated the existence of class differences in the degree of intellectual stimulation provided by parents (Hess, 1970; Golden & Birns, 1976). For instance, middle-class mothers are generally more responsive, attentive, and helpful than lower-class mothers while interacting with their children in play and problem-solving situations. In this connection, class differences were found in a series of studies conducted by Hess and Shipman (1965, 1967, 1968) in which the interaction between Black mothers and their 4-year-old children was observed. The social status of the mothers varied from upper-middle class to families on public assistance. The mothers were initially taught three simple tasks (for example, sorting a number of plastic toys by color and by function) and were then asked to teach these tasks to their children. Both verbal and nonverbal interactions were recorded. The results revealed that middle-class mothers were more likely than lower-class mothers to define the task for the child, to give specific instructions, to ask the child for verbal feedback rather than physical compliance, and, when necessary, to provide the child with information needed to complete the task. Middle-class mothers were also less likely than lower-class mothers to exercise their control by relying on the power inherent in their parental status. They tended to explain to the child the rationale involved in their requests, thus allowing the child to avoid confrontation with parental power. These class differences in maternal behavior are consistent with the previously mentioned emphasis by lower-class parents on conformist values. The results of the Hess and Shipman studies suggest that social-class differences in the way in which mothers interact with their children in problem-solving situations may be a contributing factor to social-class differences in their children's intelligence.

The evidence concerning the way lower-class mothers relate to their children does not mean that such behavior is resistant to change. In Chapter 5, we discussed the studies by Levenstein (1970) and Heber and his associates (1972). These studies revealed that intervention programs that involve training lower-class mothers to become more responsive to their children's intellectual and educational needs have produced marked IQ gains for the children during their preschool years.

Social-class differences in the use of language may be another environmental variable contributing to class differences in intelligence. For example, Bernstein (1970) proposes that there are social-class differences in the kinds of communication styles used within families, and these differences should have an effect on children's intellectual functioning. According to Bernstein, lower-class families tend to engage in a *restricted style of communication* that is characterized by simple, short, and often unfinished sentences. In addition, lower-class families rarely use subordinate clauses, which would provide an elaboration of the sentence content. Communication within these families therefore lacks specificity and exactness, qualities necessary if children are to develop precise conceptualizations and acquire specific information. In contrast, Bernstein points out that middle-class families tend to engage in an *elaborated style of communication* characterized by the use of a relatively wide variety of words, subordinate clauses, and fairly long sentences. Ideas and intentions on the part of the speaker are therefore carefully spelled out for the listener. Such a specific and exact mode of communication within middle-class families should facilitate intellectual development on the part of the children in these families.

Bernstein's class-related distinction between restricted and elaborated styles of communication has generated much interest among social scientists; however, in a review of the relevant research, Higgins (1976) concludes that as yet little support exists for social-class differences in communication styles. Thus, it remains to be seen whether or not there are consistent class differences in the use of language, and if so whether or not these differences contribute to the relationship between social class and intelligence.

We have looked at the possible influence of parental behaviors and communication styles within families on social-class differences in intelligence.

There is some suggestion that differences in how much intellectual stimulation and encouragement parents provide for their children may help to account for the class differences. There may also be environmental influences of a biological nature that are relevant. Children growing up in poverty are likely to receive poor medical care and have nutritional deficiencies (Birch & Gussow, 1970). In addition, the prenatal care lower-class mothers receive tends to be poorer than that received by middle-class mothers (Broman, Nichols, & Kennedy, 1975). Thus, the relatively inferior physical care that poor children tend to receive could be a deterrent to their intellectual development.

Test Bias. As we pointed out in Chapter 4, the developers of intelligence tests biased their tests in favor of high social status because high educational and occupational levels were viewed as relevant criteria for validating intelligence tests. Their rationale was that, in a society which provides opportunities for social mobility, people who attain the highest level of social status are those who are the most intellectually competent. Obviously, then, test bias must be considered in interpreting social-class differences in intelligence.

An early attempt at investigating test bias was carried out by Shimberg (1929). She was concerned with possible sources of bias in the commonly used intelligence tests, which favored children with urban as opposed to rural backgrounds. She constructed two tests of equal difficulty, one reflecting the particular cultural background of urban children and the other the background of rural children. The tests were composed of general information items (for example, "What are the colors in the American flag?" and "Of what is butter made?"), and for each test the items were selected according to the rate of success for respective samples of urban and rural school children. When the tests were administered to new samples, urban children performed significantly better on the urban test, and rural children performed significantly better on the rural test. While there is some question about how much Shimberg's results can be generalized to standard intelligence tests, they do suggest the possible role of test bias in producing differences between children of varying class levels as well as between urban and rural children.

The contribution of test bias to socioeconomic differences in intelligence was investigated by Eells, Davis, Havighurst, Herrick, and Tyler (1951) at the University of Chicago. Eight widely used intelligence tests were administered to nearly all of the 9-, 10-, 13-, and 14-year-olds in a small midwestern city. High and low social-status children were compared. In general, the high-status group was superior. However, a rather high degree of variability existed across the different items in the extent to which the high-status group excelled. In fact, for a few items no class differences were found. For the most part, the relative superiority of the high-status group was greater for verbal than for nonverbal items. It was argued that the variability in differences between the status groups reflected differences in the degree of familiarity with the test content and, therefore, was evidence of test unfairness.

The Eells and associates study led to the development of a "culture-fair" test of problem-solving ability, the Davis-Eells Games (Davis & Eells, 1953).

A *culture-fair test* is one that is fair to all persons, regardless of their sociocultural background. In the test developed by Davis and Eells the respondent does not have to read. Rather the test involves pictorial items that depict problems children generally experience, such as what is the best way to carry three packages home from the store. The child taking the test chooses the best of three alternative answers provided for each item. The test developers expected that low-status children would perform as well as high-status children, thus validating the notion of a culture-fair test. However, it has been found that although low-status children do somewhat better on the Davis-Eells test than on standard intelligence tests, they still fall significantly below high-status children (Tyler, 1965).

Another culture-fair test that has been developed is R. B. Cattell's Culture Fair Test of Intelligence (Cattell, 1971). The Culture Fair Test of Intelligence is a paper-and-pencil test consisting of simple geometric figures. Items are presented in a multiple-choice response format. For example, one set of items deals with classification in which the respondent indicates which geometric figure does not belong with a group of other geometric figures. It is assumed that such items are relatively independent of a person's particular cultural background. Consistent with this assumption, Cattell (1971) reports that the Culture Fair Test of Intelligence loads highly on the fluid intelligence factor, a factor that reflects content relatively independent of the knowledge a person acquires in school (see Chapter 4).

Do lower-class children perform as well as middle-class children on the Culture Fair Test? An investigation by Willard (1968) suggests that social-class differences are not reduced with the Culture Fair Test of Intelligence. Black lower-class children did no better on the Culture Fair Test than on the Stanford-Binet, meaning that regardless of which intelligence test was used these lower-class children scored below the average level of middle-class children.

The Progressive Matrices, a test developed in Great Britain by Raven, is still another example of a culture-fair intelligence test (see Anastasi, 1976). This test also consists of geometric figures and has a multiple-choice response format. Each matrix or design has a part missing. The respondent chooses the missing part from among six or eight given alternatives. As with other culture-fair tests, the level of performance on the Progressive Matrices is not independent of social class. A large-scale study in Holland with 19-year-old men indicated that performance on the Progressive Matrices was related to social-class background, though the relationship was not as marked as it was on tests of language skills (Belmont & Marolla, 1973).

In conclusion, we find that culture-fair tests of intelligence do not eliminate class differences. Apparently, they can reduce these differences to some extent because culturally based content is minimized. To account for the social-class differences in these tests it seems likely that variables other than test content are involved. For one thing, noncognitive factors may contribute to the poorer performance of lower-class individuals, not only on culture-fair tests but on intelligence tests in general. For example, lower-class individuals may be less motivated in the testing situation. Wrightsman (1977) makes the point that middle-class people tend to react to a testing situation with energy and effort, because they believe more than lower-class people that the results of testing have implications for their future success and achievement. In addition, because lower-class children generally are not as well prepared for the school situation as are middle-class children, they may have anxiety about being tested. Another explanation seems to lie in the kinds of abilities tapped by the culture-fair tests. While verbal skills are minimized, these tests do reflect other abilities including spatial relations, perceptual accuracy, memory, and inductive reasoning (Burke, 1958; Cattell, 1971). Thus, to some extent the class differences obtained in culture-fair tests seem to reflect class differences in the abilities measured by the tests.

From the overall evidence we have reviewed, social-class differences in intelligence cannot be reduced to any one explanation. Along with inherent biases in the measures of intelligence, genetic and environmental influences need to be considered. Our next concern is whether or not social-class differences exist in academic and vocational achievement.

ACHIEVEMENT

As we have noted, a person's social-class position tends to be tied directly to his or her education and occupation. To what extent does the level of education and occupation people attain depend on their social-class background? Because both educational and occupational attainment are related to academic performance and motivational variables (for example, aspirations and needs), we first have to consider the degree to which performance and motivation are associated with social class.

Scholastic Performance

In view of the fact that there are social-class differences in intelligence and intelligence is related to school success, we should not be surprised to find that school achievement is positively related to social class. For example, in a national survey of school children between the ages of 6 and 11, mean scores on the Reading and Arithmetic subtests of the Wide Range Achievement Test increased with the size of family income and the educational level of the parent who was the head of the household (National Center for Health Statistics, 1971). The findings for annual family income, which ranged from less than $3,000 to $15,000 or more, are shown in Figure 12-2. On both subtests significant differences in mean raw scores occurred between successive income levels except for the two highest ($10,000 to $14,999 and $15,000 or more). Other studies have also shown that school achievement is positively related to social class (Hess, 1970).

These social-class differences in scholastic performance appear to be consistent with the class differences in intelligence. On the average, then, lower-class children perform scholastically below the level of middle-class children,

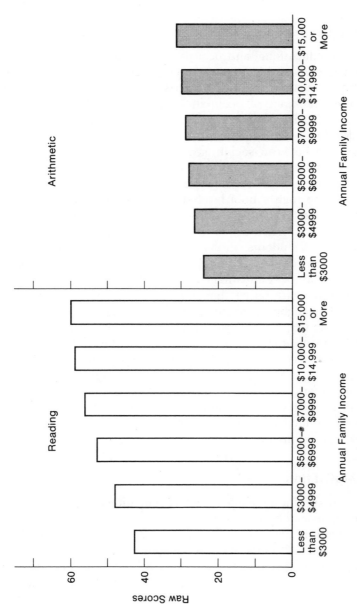

Figure 12-2. Average Reading and Arithmetic raw scores on the Wide Range Achievement Test for children by annual family income, United States. From "School Achievement of Children by Demographic and Socioeconomic Factors," *Vital Health Statistics,* November 1971, National Center for Health Statistics. Public Health Service Publication No. 1000-11/109.

at least in part because of class differences in intelligence. In addition, motivational variables also appear to contribute to class differences in school achievement. As we will see, middle-class students have higher aspirations and achievement motivation than lower-class students.

Educational and Occupational Aspirations

An analysis of educational and occupational aspirations is possible only if there is general agreement that an occupational hierarchy exists in the society (Hess, 1970). As previously mentioned, experts and the general public essentially agree in their rankings of occupations (see Table 12-1). Furthermore, people at different social-class levels generally agree in their rankings of occupations (Inkeles, 1960).

The relationship between social class and aspirations has been investigated at both the elementary and high school levels. Among elementary school children vocational preferences are not generally related to social class (Hess, 1970). However, at the high school level studies indicate that social class is associated with educational and occupational aspirations (Harrison, 1969; Kahl, 1953; Sewell et al., 1970). When asked to state their educational and occupational plans, high school students who are more advantaged in terms of family social-class position expect to attain more schooling and higher-status occupations than those who are less advantaged. Furthermore, when aspirations are assessed according to desire rather than expectation, higher social-class position is also related to higher educational and occupational goals (Harrison, 1969). We should note that social class continues to be significantly associated with educational and occupational aspirations even when IQ and scholastic performance are controlled (Harrison, 1969; Sewell et al., 1970).

What accounts for the social-class differences in aspirations? The influence of significant others, including parents, teachers, and peers, seems important. Sewell and associates (1970) found that higher social-class high school students were more influenced by their parents, teachers, and friends to attend college and seek high occupational status.

Achievement Motivation

In addition to specific educational and occupational aspirations, social-class differences appear in how motivated a person is to achieve. Most studies show that lower-class individuals score significantly lower than middle-class individuals on measures of achievement motivation (Allen, 1970). For example, Rosen (1959) administered the TAT measure of achievement motivation to a sample of 427 boys, aged 8 to 14. Middle-class boys had higher achievement motivation scores than lower-class boys. In addition, as has been reported in studies reviewed by Bronfenbrenner (1958) and Hess (1970), middle-class mothers placed greater emphasis on independence training for their sons, expecting their sons to be self-reliant at earlier ages than did lower-class mothers. This is consistent with the previously mentioned finding that middle-class parents more highly value the development of self-direction in their children. Achievement motivation, then, appears to be related to how much parents encourage their children to be self-directed.

There may also be social-class differences in the kinds of incentives that are effective in motivating children to achieve. Some studies have shown lower-class children perform better when they are given material rewards, such as candy or money, rather than verbal praise, whereas middle-class children perform better when they are given verbal praise rather than material rewards (Terrel, Durkin, & Wiesley, 1959; Zigler & de Labry, 1962). However, these social-class differences have not been found in several other studies (Allen, 1970).

A study by Rosenhan (1966) suggests that the characteristics of who administers the reinforcement may be associated with social-class differences in performance. Rosenhan investigated the reaction of middle-class and lower-class first-grade boys to two types of verbal reinforcement—praise and disapproval. The task the children worked on was learning to make correct responses on an apparatus involving a choice of two levers. Each child received from a male experimenter either verbal praise for making the right choice or verbal disapproval for making the wrong choice. The results showed that under conditions of approval the performance of the lower-class children improved more than that of the middle-class children. Under conditions of disapproval the lower-class children performed more poorly than the middle-class children. The middle-class children performed similarly under both conditions. Rosenhan interprets these results in terms of how comfortable children of varying social-class backgrounds feel in interacting with middle-class people and institutions. Because lower-class children are less familiar than middle-class children with middle-class people and school situations they may be more anxious under such conditions and sensitive to the type of reinforcement—praise or disapproval—they receive. On the other hand, middle-class children who feel comfortable in a middle-class school setting should perform about as well when they receive disapproval for incorrect responses as when they receive approval for correct responses. Rosenhan's study also provides evidence for the point that we made earlier that lower-class children's intelligence-test performance is depressed in part because they feel anxious in the testing situation.

Social-class differences in achievement motivation and the way in which achievement behavior is reinforced may in part contribute to the social-class differences in educational and vocational aspirations. As we have seen from the studies reviewed in this section, class differences in achievement motivation and reactions to reinforcement show up among elementary school children. This suggests that when middle-class children reach high school and begin to develop specific educational and vocational goals they already place a relatively high value on achievement. In fact, a study by Lueptow (1975) with high school seniors indicated that parental socioeconomic status was positively associated with achievement values, such as the importance of individual effort and an orientation towards the future. Therefore, middle-class adolescents should aspire to high-level educational and vocational goals. In contrast, the relatively low levels of aspirations that lower-class adolescents develop are consistent with their lower level of achievement motivation.

Educational and Occupational Attainment

As we have indicated, social class is positively related to academic perfor-mance, educational and occupational aspirations, and achievement motivation. It seems reasonable to expect that educational attainment and occupational attainment are also related to social class. An example of the relationship between social class and educational attainment is found in the Project Talent Study, a large-scale investigation of American high school students (Flanagan & Cooley, 1966). The results showed that the probability of entering college for a grade 11 male student in the top 25% of general academic ability (based on tests of reading comprehension, arithmetic reasoning, and abstract reason-ing) varied from .48 for low socioeconomic status (SES) to .87 for high SES. For grade 11 female students in the top 25% of academic ability, the probability of entering college varied from .34 for low SES to .82 for high SES. The Project Talent data also revealed that for students in the lowest 25% of academic ability, the probabilities of entering college varied for males from .06 (low SES) to .26 (high SES) and from .07 to .20 for females.

Other evidence of the relationship between social class and educational attainment is contained in Sewell and associates' (1970) study of over 4000 male high school seniors from rural and urban areas in Wisconsin. The correla-tion was .42 between family social-class position and educational attainment (varying from no post-high school education to college graduation). We should keep in mind that the social-class difference in educational attainment is partly caused by the fact that the more socioeconomically advantaged adolescents can better afford a college education.

Due to the relationship between social class and educational attainment, an association between social class and occupational attainment is expected. In the study by Sewell and associates, the correlation between social class and occupational status attainment (7 years after high school graduation) was .33. With a national sample of American adult males, an association was also found between a person's family social-class background and the status of his or her occupation (Blau & Duncan, 1967; Duncan, Featherman, & Duncan, 1972).

PERSONALITY

Social-class comparisons of personality questionnaires generally reveal negligible differences (Auld, 1952; Eysenck, 1960). However, social-class dif-ferences do emerge in investigations of aggression and adjustment. We should expect the contrasting life conditions at different levels of the social-status hierarchy to have an effect on the ways in which people channel their aggres-sion and adjust to stress.

Aggression

In reviewing studies involving social-class comparisons of aggression in preschool and elementary school children, Hess (1970) indicates that some studies show lower-class children are more aggressive, while others show middle-class children are more aggressive. One of the problems inherent in the analysis of class-linked aggression is that the definition of aggression is relative to the intent of the aggressor. The middle-class child appears to be more sensitive to the reactions of others and can better anticipate the consequences of an aggressive act. An act of aggression performed by a middle-class child should therefore probably be regarded as more aggressive than if it is performed by a lower-class child (Hess, 1970).

Among adolescents, when aggression is defined according to delinquent behavior, some social-class differences in aggression are revealed. Delinquency can be assessed either through the use of official records or by self-reports, such as asking an adolescent on a questionnaire or in an interview: "How many times have you taken things that didn't belong to you?" Delinquency rates based on official records are not always consistent with those based on self-reports, and it is therefore desirable in any given investigation to include both sources of data. In large cities, evidence based on both official records and self-report indexes indicates that involvement in delinquency is more likely for lower- than for middle-class youths (Short & Strodtbeck, 1965). However, studies conducted in small cities and in rural areas generally do not indicate that lower-class youths have higher delinquency rates than middle-class youths (Hess, 1970). Apparently, the relationship between social class and delinquency is primarily an urban phenomenon.

Sociologists have proposed two major theoretical explanations of lower-class delinquency (see Cohen & Short, 1972). One interpretation offered is that lower-class delinquency may be a product of lower-class values, such as toughness, excitement, and fate, concomitant with concerns about belonging and status (Miller, 1958). These values and concerns are thought to be shared by members of adolescent gangs. Aggressive acts by gang members serve peer-group norms and provide a means of achieving favorable status within the peer-group. Support for this interpretation is found in the Chicago study of delinquency by Short and Strodtbeck (1965). Role relationships and status considerations within gangs greatly influenced the behavior of the boys and their female counterparts. For example, delinquency episodes were often precipitated by status threats, such as when a gang with a reputation for toughness and fighting skills was challenged by a rival group or when the reputation of a gang leader was challenged within the group.

A contrasting explanation views lower-class delinquency as a reflection of status frustration. Lower-class youths who aspire to middle-class goals become frustrated because lack of opportunities, particularly occupational ones, prevent them from achieving such goals (Cloward & Ohlin, 1960; Cohen, 1955). Because opportunities are blocked, delinquent behaviors are viewed by lower-class youths as the most effective means of attaining middle-class goals.

In support of this status-frustration hypothesis, the discrepancy between boys' occupational aspirations and occupational expectations is related to official delinquency rates for samples of lower-class boys (Short, Rivera, & Tennyson, 1964). However, the same discrepancy between aspirations and expectations is also related to delinquency for middle-class boys. Thus the status-frustration theory might apply to middle-class delinquency as well as lower-class delinquency. Needless to say, however, because of existing social conditions, lower-class youths are more likely than their middle-class counterparts to experience status frustration, and this would account for the higher percentage of lower-class youths who engage in delinquency behavior.

Support for the two aforementioned theories indicates that both peer-group interaction and the effects of unequal opportunities in the social structure underlie social-class differences in delinquency. Another factor that appears to contribute to the relationship between social class and delinquency is the tendency on the part of police to perceive and act toward youngsters from different socioeconomic backgrounds in different ways. Youngsters from poor families are more likely to be labeled "delinquent" than are youngsters from middle-class families.

Once youths are socialized into a delinquent subculture, many eventually pass into an adult criminal subculture (Sutherland & Cressey, 1970). This is because a network of bonds exists between age levels. Adolescent delinquents are interpersonally linked with young adult offenders, who in turn are linked with adult criminals. Thus, the higher incidence of criminal offenses among lower-class adults than among middle- or upper-class adults (Quinney, 1970) can be viewed, at least in part, as a product of the social-class differences in delinquency.

Adjustment

Self-Concept and Happiness. Since people at the bottom of the socioeconomic hierarchy possess fewer material comforts than those at the top, we might expect social-class differences in measures of self-concept and happiness. However, differences do not emerge in studies that assess feelings about the self—self-esteem, self-acceptance, or the discrepancy between actual and ideal self (Allen, 1970). Lower-class people are not necessarily discontented about themselves, although a positive self-image may be used by lower-class people as a defense against anxiety and the admission of inadequacy (Allen, 1970).

In contrast to findings about self-feelings, when people are asked to rate their external life conditions, lower social status is consistently associated with greater unhappiness (Cantril, 1965; Easterlin, 1973; Inkeles, 1960). For example, Cantril surveyed nearly 20,000 people in 13 countries, including both Western and non-Western nations. The respondents rated their present life conditions on a scale ranging from the worst possible to the best possible life they could imagine. All the nations showed that higher-status people were more satisfied than lower-status people.

Mental Health. Unhappiness about life conditions is not the only negative concomitant of lower-class existence. Evidence consistently shows that the lower a person's socioeconomic status the greater the probability of poor mental health. This evidence is in part based on large-scale investigations of individuals receiving psychiatric treatment. For example, a psychiatric survey was carried out by Hollingshead and Redlich (1958) in New Haven, Connecticut. All residents in the New Haven area who received psychiatric treatment between May 31 and December 1, 1950, were included. The psychiatric population included persons treated in physicians' offices and patients in private and public hospitals. Psychiatric disorder was most common at the lower social-class levels. Class differences also appeared in type of disorder. Psychoses were more common than neuroses at the lower levels, whereas the reverse was true at the upper levels.

An important limitation exists concerning these findings, however. Evidence based only on persons receiving treatment may not be generalizable to the overall population. People at different social-status levels may differ in their ability to recognize psychiatric symptoms. Indeed, the greater proportion of neuroses among higher-status persons in the New Haven study may have reflected class differences in the sensitivity to neurotic symptoms.

More conclusive evidence of the relationship between social class and mental health is contained in the Midtown Manhattan study (Srole, Langner, Michael, Opler, & Rennie, 1962). Home interviews were conducted with a representative sample of 1660 adults residing in the midtown area of Manhattan. Based on the interview data, a team of psychiatrists rated each respondent on a six-point scale of mental health ranging from "well" to "incapacitated." Mental-health ratings were highly related to both the respondents' social-class origin (parental socioeconomic status) and their own present socioeconomic status. The proportion of "well" ratings decreased from the highest to the lowest status groups, while the proportion of "impaired" ratings (the three lowest categories) increased. The most marked differences in ratings occurred between the highest and lowest groups based on present socioeconomic status. Falling in the impaired categories was 47% of the lowest stratum versus 12.5% of the highest stratum. Falling in the well category was only 5% of the lowest stratum as against 30% of the highest stratum.

Further analyses of the data from the Midtown Manhattan study revealed a relationship between mental health and life stress (Langner & Michael, 1963). Ten stress factors were assessed, including childhood experiences (for example, broken homes and economic deprivation) and adult experiences (for example, poor physical health and concerns about work), and these indexes correlated with mental-health ratings across social-class levels. The greater the number of stress factors, the more negative the mental-health rating. Only slight differences in the frequency of stress factors existed among social-class groups. However, when the number of stress factors was held constant, the low-status group showed a more negative mental-health rating. In other words, as the number of stressors increases, lower-class persons suffer more severe mental-health impairment (psychoses) than do middle- and upper-class persons. When middle- and upper-class persons are faced with stress, they respond in less socially incapacitating ways. Therefore, lower-class people are more likely to develop psychoses and higher-class people to develop neuroses.

SUMMARY

Social class within American society is conceptualized as a series of ranked status levels rather than distinct groups that people identify with. There are three methods of measuring social class: (1) the reputational approach, (2) the objective approach, and (3) the subjective approach. The objective approach is typically used and involves either a single index of occupational level or a combined index of several factors, such as occupation, education, and income.

Social-class comparisons of general life values indicate that higher-status persons tend to emphasize self-direction, whereas lower-status persons stress conformity to external authority. These differences are reflected in child-rearing practices. Middle-class mothers, as opposed to working-class mothers, tolerate more extensive expression of drives and impulses and have greater expectations for their children's independence and achievement. Differences in the use of physical punishment are revealed by middle-class mothers' tendencies to use such disciplinary measures when their children show a loss of self-control. On the other hand, working-class mothers tend to use physical punishment when their children do not conform to external standards.

Intelligence is positively correlated with social class for both adults and children. Social-class differences can be accounted for by three factors: (1) genetic differences between people at various levels of the status hierarchy, (2) environmental experiences that provide greater intellectual stimulation for higher-status children, and (3) test bias that favors higher-status children. While mean IQ differences exist between social-class groups, much overlapping occurs between groups and a wide range of individual differences exists within each social-class level.

Like intelligence, school achievement is positively correlated with social class. Among high school students high socioeconomic status is also associated with high educational and occupational aspirations as well as high achievement motivation. Similarly, high socioeconomic status is associated with high educational and occupational attainment.

Differences are generally not demonstrated in social-class comparisons of personality measures. However, class differences do emerge in studies of aggression and adjustment. Delinquency rates are highest among lower-class youths in large cities, but social-class differences do not generally appear in studies conducted in small cities and in rural areas. Two factors that appear to contribute to lower-class delinquency are peer-group norms and status frustration. When people are asked to rate their external life conditions, lower social status is associated with greater unhappiness. Evidence also shows that the lower a person's socioeconomic status the greater the probability of poor mental health.

REFERENCES

Allen, V. L. Personality correlates of poverty. In V. L. Allen (Ed.), *Psychological factors in poverty*. New York: Academic Press, 1970.

Anastasi, A. *Differential psychology* (3rd ed.). New York: Macmillan, 1958.

Anastasi, A. *Psychological testing* (4th ed.). New York: Macmillan, 1976.

Auld, F. Influence of social class on personality test responses. *Psychological Bulletin*, 1952, *49*, 318–332.

Belmont, L., & Marolla, F. A. Birth order, family size, and intelligence. *Science*, 1973, *182*, 1096–1101.

Berkowitz, L. *A survey of social psychology*. Hinsdale, Ill.: Dryden, 1975.

Bernstein, B. A sociolinguistic approach to socialization: With some reference to educability. In F. Williams (Ed.), *Language and poverty: Perspectives on a theme*. Chicago: Markham, 1970.

Birch, H. G., & Gussow, J. D. *Disadvantaged children: Health, nutrition, and school failure*. New York: Harcourt Brace Jovanovich, 1970.

Blau, P. M., & Duncan, O. D. *The American occupational structure*. New York: Wiley, 1967.

Broman, S. H., Nichols, P. L., & Kennedy, W. A. *Preschool IQ: Prenatal and early developmental correlates*. Hillsdale, N.J.: Lawrence Erlbaum Associates, 1975.

Bronfenbrenner, U. Socialization and social class through time and space. In E. E. Maccoby, T. M. Newcomb, & E. L. Hartly (Eds.), *Readings in social psychology*. New York: Holt, Rinehart & Winston, 1958.

Burke, H. R. Raven's Progressive Matrices: A review and critical evaluation. *Journal of Genetic Psychology*, 1958, *93*, 199–228.

Burt, C. Intelligence and social mobility. *British Journal of Statistical Psychology*, 1961, *14*, 3–24.

Cantril, H. *The pattern of human concerns*. New Brunswick, N.J.: Rutgers University Press, 1965.

Cattell, R. B. *Abilities: Their structure, growth, and action*. Boston: Houghton Mifflin, 1971.

Centers, R. C. *The psychology of social classes*. Princeton, N.J.: Princeton University Press, 1949.

Cloward, R. A., & Ohlin, L. E. *Delinquency and opportunity*. Glencoe, Ill.: Free Press, 1960.

Cohen, A. K. *Delinquent boys*. Glencoe, Ill.: Free Press, 1955.

Cohen, A. K., & Short, J. F., Jr. A survey of delinquency theories. In J. P. Reed & F. Baali (Eds.), *Faces of delinquency*. Englewood Cliffs, N.J.: Prentice-Hall, 1972.

Davis, A., & Eells, K. *Davis-Eells Games: Davis-Eells Test of General Intelligence or Problem-Solving Ability, Manual*. Yonkers-on-Hudson, N.Y.: World Book, 1953.

Davis, A., Gardner, B. B., & Gardner, M. B. *Deep south*. Chicago: University of Chicago Press, 1941.

Duncan, O. D., Featherman, D. L., & Duncan, B. *Socioeconomic background and achievement*. New York: Seminar Press, 1972.

Duncan, O. D., Haller, A. O., & Portes, A. Peer influences on aspirations: A reinterpretation. *American Journal of Sociology*, 1968, *74*, 119–137.

Easterlin, R. A. Does economic growth improve the human lot? Some empirical evidence. In P. A. David & M. W. Reder (Eds.), *Nations and households in economic growth*. Stanford, Calif.: Stanford University Press, 1973.

Eckland, B. K. Genetics and sociology: A reconsideration. *American Sociological Review*, 1967, *32*, 173–194.

Eells, K., Davis, A., Havighurst, R. J., Herrick, V. E., & Tyler, R. W. *Intelligence and cultural differences.* Chicago: University of Chicago Press, 1951.

Erlanger, H. S. Social class and corporal punishment in child-rearing: A reassessment. *American Sociological Review,* 1974, *39,* 68–85.

Eysenck, S. B. G. Social class, sex, and response to a five-part personality inventory. *Educational and Psychological Measurement,* 1960, *20,* 47–54.

Flanagan, J. C., & Cooley, W. W. *Project talent one-year followup studies.* Cooperative Research Project Number 2333, University of Pittsburgh, 1966.

Fryer, D. Occupational-intelligence standards. *School and Society,* 1922, *16,* 273–277.

Gerth, H. H., & Mills, G. W. (Eds.). *From Max Weber: Essays in sociology.* New York: Oxford University Press, 1946.

Golden, M., & Birns, B. Social class and infant intelligence. In M. Lewis (Ed.), *Origins of intelligence: Infancy and early childhood.* New York: Plenum, 1976.

Hardert, R. A., Parker, H. A., Pfuhl, E. H., & Anderson, W. A. *Sociology and social issues.* San Francisco: Rinehart, 1974.

Harrell, T. W., & Harrell, M. S. Army general classification test scores for civilian occupations. *Educational and Psychological Measurement,* 1945, *5,* 229–239.

Harrison, F. Aspirations as related to school performance and socioeconomic status. *Sociometry,* 1969, *32,* 70–79.

Havighurst, R. J., Bowman, P. H., Liddle, G. P., Mathews, C. V., & Pierce, J. V. *Growing up in River City.* New York: Wiley, 1962.

Havighurst, R. J., & Breese, F. H. Relation between ability and social status in a midwestern community: III. Primary Mental Abilities. *Journal of Educational Psychology,* 1947, *38,* 241–247.

Havighurst, R. J., & Janke, L. L. Relation between ability and social status in a midwestern community: I. Ten-year-old children. *Journal of Educational Psychology,* 1944, *35,* 357–368.

Heber, R., Garber, H., Herrington, S., Hoffman, C., & Falender, C. *Rehabilitation of families at risk for mental retardation.* Progress report, December 1972, Rehabilitation Research and Training Center in Mental Retardation, University of Wisconsin, Madison, Wisconsin.

Herrnstein, R. J. *IQ in the meritocracy.* Boston: Little, Brown, 1973.

Hess, R. D. Social class and ethnic differences upon socialization. In P. H. Mussen (Ed.), *Carmichael's manual of child psychology* (Vol. 2) (3rd ed.). New York: Wiley, 1970.

Hess, R. D., & Shipman, V. C. Early experience and the socialization of cognitive modes in children. *Child Development,* 1965, *34,* 869–886.

Hess, R. D., & Shipman, V. C. Cognitive elements in maternal behavior. In J. P. Hill (Ed.), *Minnesota Symposia on Child Psychology* (Vol. I). Minneapolis: University of Minnesota Press, 1967.

Hess, R. D., & Shipman, V. C. Maternal attitudes toward the school and the role of the pupil: Some social class comparisons. In A. H. Passow (Ed.), *Developing programs for the educationally disadvantaged.* New York: Teachers College, Columbia University, 1968.

Higgins, E. T. Social class differences in verbal communicative accuracy: A question of "Which Question?" *Psychological Bulletin,* 1976, *83,* 695–714.

Hodge, R. W., Siegel, P. M., & Rossi, P. H. Occupational prestige in the United States: 1925-1963. *American Journal of Sociology,* 1964, *70,* 286–302.

Hollingshead, A. B., & Redlich, F. C. *Social class and mental illness.* New York: Wiley, 1958.

Inkeles, A. Industrial man: The relation of status to experience, perception, and value. *American Journal of Sociology,* 1960, *66,* 1–31.

Janke, L. L., & Havighurst, R. J. Relation between ability and social status in a midwestern community: II. Sixteen-year-old boys and girls. *Journal of Educational Psychology,* 1945, *36,* 499–509.

Jensen, A. R. How much can we boost IQ and scholastic achievement? *Harvard Educational Review,* 1969, *39,* 1–123.

Kahl, J. A. Educational and occupational aspirations of the "common man" boys. *Harvard Educational Review,* 1953, *23,* 186–203.

Kaufman, A. S., & Doppelt, J. E. Analysis of WISC-R standardization data in terms of the stratification variables. *Child Development,* 1976, *47,* 165–171.

Kohn, M. L. *Class and conformity: A study in values.* Homewood, Ill.: Dorsey Press, 1969.

Langner, T. S., & Michael, S. T. *Life stress and mental health.* Glencoe, Ill.: Free Press, 1963.

Levenstein, P. Cognitive growth in preschoolers through verbal interaction with mothers. *American Journal of Orthopsychiatry,* 1970, *40,* 426–432.

Loehlin, J. C., Lindzey, G., & Spuhler, J. N. *Race differences in intelligence.* San Francisco: Freeman, 1975.

Lueptow, L. B. Parental status and influence and the achievement orientations of high school seniors. *Sociology of Education,* 1975, *48,* 91–110.

McNemar, Q. *The revision of the Stanford-Binet scale.* Boston: Houghton Mifflin, 1942.

Miller, W. B. Lower class culture as a generating milieu of gang delinquency. *Journal of Social Issues,* 1958, *14*(3), 5–19.

National Center for Health Statistics: School achievement of children by demographic and socioeconomic factors. *Vital Health Statistics.* PHS Pub. No. 1000—Series 11—No. 109. Public Health Service. Washington: U.S. Government Printing Office, November 1971.

Nisbet, R. A. *The social bond: An introduction to the study of society.* New York: Knopf, 1970.

North, C. C., & Hatt, P. K. Jobs and occupations: A popular evaluation. In R. Bendix & S. M. Lipset (Eds.), *Class, status, and power.* Glencoe, Ill.: Free Press, 1953.

Quinney, R. *The social reality of crime.* Boston: Little, Brown, 1970.

Roach, J. L., Gross, L., & Gursslin, O. (Eds.). *Social stratification in the United States.* Englewood Cliffs, N.J.: Prentice-Hall, 1969.

Rodman, H. Class culture. In D. L. Sills (Ed.), *International encyclopedia of the social sciences* (Vol. 15). New York: Macmillan, 1968.

Rokeach, M. *The nature of human values.* New York: Free Press, 1973.

Rosen, B. C. Race, ethnicity, and the achievement syndrome. *American Sociological Review,* 1959, *24,* 47–60.

Rosenhan, D. L. Effects of social class and race on responsiveness to approval and disapproval. *Journal of Personality and Social Psychology,* 1966, *4,* 253–259.

Schaie, K. W. Occupational level and the primary mental abilities. *Journal of Educational Psychology,* 1958, *49,* 299–303.

Scottish Council for Research in Education. *The intelligence of a representative group of Scottish children.* London: University of London Press, 1939.

Scottish Council for Research in Education. *The trend of Scottish intelligence.* London: University of London Press, 1949.

Seashore, H., Wesman, A., & Doppelt, J. E. The standardization of the Wechsler Intelligence Scale for Children. *Journal of Consulting Psychology,* 1950, *14,* 99–110.

Sewell, W. H., Haller, A. O., & Ohlendorf, G. W. The educational and early occupational status attainment process: Replication and revision. *American Sociological Review*, 1970, *35*, 1014–1027.

Shimberg, M. E. An investigation into the validity of norms with special reference to urban and rural groups. *Archives of Psychology*, 1929, No. 104.

Short, J. F., Jr., Rivera, R., & Tennyson, R. A. Perceived opportunities, gang membership, and delinquency. *American Sociological Review*, 1964, *30*, 56–67.

Short, J. F., Jr., & Strodtbeck, F. L. *Group process and gang delinquency*. Chicago: University of Chicago Press, 1965.

Simon, L. M., & Levitt, E. A. The relation between Wechsler-Bellevue IQ scores and occupational area. *Occupations*, 1950, *29*, 23–25.

Srole, L., Langner, T. S., Michael, S. T., Opler, M. K., & Rennie, T. A. C. *Mental health in the metropolis*. New York: McGraw-Hill, 1962.

Stewart, N. AGCT scores of Army personnel grouped by occupation. *Occupations*, 1947, *26*(1), 5–41.

Sutherland, E. H., & Cressey, D. R. *Criminology* (8th ed.). Philadelphia: Lippincott, 1970.

Terrel, G., Jr., Durkin, K., & Wiesley, M. Social class and the nature of the incentive in discrimination learning. *Journal of Abnormal and Social Psychology*, 1959, *59*, 270–272.

Tumin, M. M. *Social stratification: The forms and functions of inequality*. Englewood Cliffs, N.J.: Prentice-Hall, 1967.

Tyler, L. E. *The psychology of human differences* (3rd ed.). New York: Appleton-Century-Crofts, 1965.

Vanneman, R. The occupational composition of American classes: Results from cluster analysis. *American Journal of Sociology*, 1977, *82*, 783–807.

Waller, J. H. Achievement and social mobility: Relationships among IQ score, education, and occupation in two generations. *Social Biology*, 1971, *18*, 252–259.

Warner, W. L., Havighurst, R. J., & Loeb, M. B. *Who shall be educated?* New York: Harper & Row, 1944.

Warner, W. L., & Lunt, P. S. *The social life of the modern community*. New Haven: Yale University Press, 1941.

Warner, W. L., Meeker, M., & Eells, K. *Social class in America*. Chicago: Science Research Associates, 1949.

West, J. *Plainville, U.S.A.* New York: Columbia University Press, 1945.

Willard, L. S. A comparison of Culture Fair Test scores with group and individual intelligence test scores of disadvantaged Negro children. *Journal of Learning Disabilities*, 1968, *1*, 584–589.

Wrightsman, L. S. *Social psychology* (2nd ed.). Monterey, Calif.: Brooks/Cole, 1977.

Zigler, E., & de Labry, J. Concept-switching in middle-class, lower-class and retarded children. *Journal of Abnormal and Social Psychology*, 1962, *65*, 267–273.

Race Differences

In the late 19th and early 20th centuries, scientists in America produced an extensive literature that purportedly demonstrated that the Black race was inferior to the White race. The conclusions reached by Robert Bennett Bean, an M.D. and professor of anatomy at the University of Virginia, are illustrative of the scientific thinking of that era:

> The Caucasian and the negro are fundamentally opposite extremes in evolution. Having demonstrated that the negro and the Caucasian are widely different in characteristics, due to a deficiency of gray matter and connecting fibers in the negro brain . . . a deficiency that is hereditary and can be altered only by intermarriage, we are forced to conclude that it is useless to try to elevate the negro by education or otherwise, except in the direction of his natural endowments. The way may be made plain to the black people, and they may be encouraged in the proper direction, but the solution of the [race] question still must come within the race. Let them win their reward by diligent service [Bean, 1906, reprinted in Newby, 1968, p. 53].

The study of race differences has had to overcome its racist origins. Our task in this chapter is to reach an understanding of what the evidence shows about race differences and, therefore, to separate truth from stereotype. The major questions we will deal with are: What is meant by the concept of race? How extensive and how large are race differences? Where differences exist, what accounts for them? We'll start with the first question.

THE CONCEPT OF RACE

The meaning of race varies in different areas of science. In the social sciences, race customarily refers to racial identification—that is, the particular racial group a person identifies with or is categorized into by others. In the biological sciences, races are customarily considered as biological subspecies, defined by gene frequencies (Loehlin, Lindzey, & Spuhler, 1975). The racial category of an individual may, therefore, vary according to which definition is used. From a sociological perspective, children of Black/White marriages in the United States are typically regarded as Black. However, biologically this categorization is not strictly valid because such children have some genetic characteristics of each racial group (Bodmer, 1972). Let us explore the biological aspects of race.

Race as a Biological Concept

According to the biological view, race is a subspecies of individuals who share genetically determined characteristics that make them distinguishable from other subgroups of the species. Relatively distinct races or subgroups develop because members typically find mates from within their own group. Historically, racial groups have been kept physically apart from one another by great distances or geographical barriers, such as mountains, bodies of water, and deserts. With technological advances in transportation, contacts between groups became increasingly possible. Migrations of particular groups led to new mating patterns and the formation of new racial groups. In North America the importation of slaves from different areas of West Africa plus some admixtures of Native American and European genes formed the basis for the American Negro subgroup.

When groups of people are isolated from one another, two processes can contribute to racial differences: (1) genetic drift and (2) natural selection. *Genetic drift* refers to the chance distribution of gene frequencies from generation to generation. This is most likely to occur in small populations because each offspring's genes are a random half from those of his or her parents; Thus, on the basis of chance, appreciable changes in gene frequencies may take place from one generation to the next. On the other hand, in large populations, drift is negligible because individual sampling variations average out, and without selective factors each generation as a whole closely reproduces the genotypic proportions of the previous generation (Loehlin et al., 1975).

The way in which genetic drift can account for racial differences is indicated by Loehlin and his associates (1975) as follows:

> In order to assign a substantial role to drift in accounting for gene-frequency differences among modern major racial groups, one would need to assume that these groups originated at some past time from small populations, which developed distinctive patterns of gene frequencies due to drift, and which then expanded to distribute their characteristic patterns of gene frequencies across wide sections of the globe [p. 42].[1]

Natural selection means that those genes best suited to the environment will be the ones most likely to increase in frequency in succeeding generations. An example of a racial difference based on natural selection is skin pigmentation. An individual's skin color is largely determined by the activity of a single enzyme system within the pigment cells (Pettigrew, 1964). Apparently this enzyme system is genetically independent of other physical characteristics differentiating Negroes and Caucasians (see Stern, 1960). Natural selection for beneficial genes acted differently for Negroes and Caucasians. Dark pigmentation turned out to be an adaptive protection against the intense sunlight of Africa, while light pigmentation proved to be an adaptive means of allowing sufficient penetration of the faint sunlight of Northern Europe (Pettigrew, 1964). Thus, in Africa individuals who were most likely to survive and transmit their genes to future generations were those who were genetically endowed with dark pigmentation, whereas in Northern Europe individuals with a genetic predisposition to light pigmentation were most likely to survive and transmit their genes.

In the present-day world, for the most part racial groups are less isolated than they were in the past, a fact that raises questions about the genetic distinctiveness of modern races. Racial groups can be classified according to characteristics known to have a genetic basis, such as physical appearance and blood type. For example, Boyd (1963) used about a dozen blood-group systems (that is, groups of blood types such as ABO) to distinguish seven principal races: (1) Caucasians, (2) Black Africans, (3) Mongoloids, (4) South Asian Aborigines, (5) Native Americans, (6) Oceanians (Indonesians, Melanesians, and Polynesians), and (7) Australian Aborigines.

However, even on the basis of blood types the differences among racially differing populations are relatively small. For example, Lewontin (1972) studied the gene frequencies for blood-group systems and serum proteins among the aforementioned seven racial groups. He estimates that only about 6% of the genetic diversity of the world population is due to racial membership. About an additional 8% represents genetic differences between local populations within races (for example, English, French, and Italians within the Caucasian

[1]This and all other quotations from this source are from *Race Differences in Intelligence,* by J. C. Loehlin, G. Lindzey, and J. N. Spuhler. Copyright © 1975 by W. H. Freeman and Company. Reprinted by permission.

Table 13-1. Some Gene Frequency Differences between Racial Groups

Blood-Group System	Blood Type	Gene Frequencies		
		Caucasoid	Negroid	Mongoloid
ABO	A_1	.21	.10	.19
	A_2	.07	.08	.00
	B	.06	.11	.17
	O	.66	.71	.64
MNS	MS	.24	.09	.04
	Ms	.31	.49	.57
	NS	.07	.04	.01
	Ns	.39	.38	.38
Rhesus	R_0	.02	.74	.04
	R_1	.40	.03	.76
	R_2	.17	.04	.20
	r	.38	.12	.00
	r′	.00	.07	.00
P	P_1	.52	.89	.17
	P_2	.48	.11	.83

Adapted from *Race Differences in Intelligence,* by J. C. Loehlin, G. Lindzey, and J. N. Spuhler. Copyright © 1975 by W. H. Freeman and Company. Based on data from *The Genetics of Human Populations,* by L. L. Cavalli-Sforza and W. F. Bodmer. Copyright © 1971 by W. H. Freeman and Company. Used by permission.

race). This leaves about 85% of the genetic diversity within populations. Some blood-group systems show greater between-race variation than others. This is illustrated in Table 13-1. The Rhesus (Rh factor) and P blood groups demonstrate marked differences between the Causasoid, Negroid, and Mongoloid groups, whereas the ABO and MNS blood groups show little differentiation. It is important to emphasize, then, that racial differences are not absolute. Rather, they represent varying proportions of biological characteristics, and these characteristics show considerable overlap across different racial groups.

Race Differences in the United States

North and South America are among the most racially heterogeneous regions in the world. While this might surprise you, think of the large waves of migration by Europeans and Africans plus the smaller waves of migration by Asians (to the West Coast of North America) and East Indians (to the Caribbean area)—all of whom joined the Native Americans. The United States itself is as much a biological as a cultural melting pot (Pettigrew, 1964). A fair degree of miscegenation (interbreeding) has taken place between Negroes, Caucasians, and Native Americans, particularly between the first two groups. One estimate, based on modern serological techniques (that is, blood-type analyses), indicates that between 22% and 29% of the Negro American gene pool consists of non-Negroid genes (mostly Caucasian) (Glass, 1955). The considerable interbreeding between Blacks and Whites would account for why it has been possible for some Blacks to pass for Whites (Davie, 1949). Furthermore, it is estimated that about 20% of White Americans have some Black genetic background (Stuckert, 1964). Despite this racial mixture, people are typically identified in an either/or fashion—they are Black or they are White. A person is a Black if any trace of Black ancestry is known. As Pettigrew (1964) comments: "Negroes joke that 'Negro blood' must be powerful stuff if it can overwhelm any amount of 'white blood' " (p. 69).

In studying race differences in the United States, we typically rely on social definitions of race rather than more rigorous biological definitions. The social definition is based either on a person's self-classification of race, or on how other people categorize a person according to race. However, since overt physical features, especially skin color, do provide the basis for racial identification, social classification does take into consideration biological differences between groups. When discrepancies exist between biological and social definitions of race, as in the case of children of Black/White marriages, it is, as we noted earlier, the social classification that typically defines race.

In considering race differences in America we need to be aware of the integral relationship between race and social class. The discrimination that some racial groups have suffered, most notably Blacks and Native Americans, has contributed to a disproportionate representation of these groups at the lower end of the social-status hierarchy. Poverty, regardless of race, is associated with inferior standing on a number of indexes of individual differences, including intelligence-test performance, school achievement, and psychological adjustment (see Chapter 12). If true race differences exist, these differences must be demonstrated independent of social-class differences.

One example of the necessity of separating race and social class is with respect to values. Rokeach (1973) in his national survey of general life values (see Chapter 12) found that Black Americans, more than White Americans, appeared to rank as more important a high standard of living and equality in society and at the same time placed a higher value on conformity. However, when the samples of Whites and Blacks were matched for indexes of social class (that is, income and education), most of the value differences either disappeared or became minimal—the only exception was that Blacks continued to attach much greater importance to equality.

In this chapter, the major interracial comparison will be between Blacks and Whites. Some relevant data are also presented for other racial groups, including Native Americans and Asian Americans. Furthermore, we will consider some groups, such as Spanish Americans and Jews, that are commonly labeled "ethnic" rather than "racial." Unlike the biological variation underlying racial groups, ethnic groups vary in terms of culture and language. However, in a sociological sense the phenomenon of identifying oneself with a given group is the same whether one is Black, Puerto Rican, or Jewish.

INTELLIGENCE

Around 1900, when investigators started to study race differences in abilities, there was a commonly held belief that "primitive" non-White peoples surpassed members of "civilized" societies in their sensory capacities. In 1898, a team of British researchers (the Cambridge Anthropological Expedition) studied the inhabitants of the Torres Straits Islands, which are located between New Guinea and Australia. The Papuan natives were given measures of sensory abilities and their performance was compared with that of European subjects. The findings indicated that while the Papuan natives were generally superior in visual acuity, they were inferior in auditory capacity (*Reports*, 1901; 1903). The results were therefore not entirely consistent with the notion that primitive peoples had superior sensory capacities. A subsequent study by Woodworth (1910) offered even less support for this notion. Various tests of sensory and motor abilities, administered at the 1904 St. Louis World's Fair, showed little differentiation between members of "primitive" racial groups (for example, Native Americans, Africans, and Eskimos) and White subjects.

The investigation of race differences in the United States started again at the time of the First World War, when tests of general intelligence were administered to army inductees. IQ differences were evident between the samples of Black and White adult males. Subsequent studies, involving samples of children as well as adults, have consistently shown IQ differences between Blacks and Whites (Dreger & Miller, 1960, 1968; Shuey, 1966). The common finding is that Black samples generally average about 15 IQ points below White samples. Examples of these differences are shown in Figure 13-1, which presents the percentages of children from two Black and two White samples who obtained various IQ scores on the Stanford-Binet. Curve A represents the Stanford-Binet normative sample of White American schoolchildren, curves B and C represent samples of White and Black schoolchildren, respectively, living in "Millfield," a rural area in central North Carolina, and curve D represents a sample of Black schoolchildren from urban and rural areas in five southeastern states—Alabama, Georgia, Florida, South Carolina, and Tennessee. The mean IQs for the White samples were around 100, while the mean IQs for the Black samples were between 80 and 90. Significantly, as we can see by inspecting Figure 13-1, the curves show considerable overlap between the White and Black samples. This indicates that, despite average differences between the groups, many Black children have higher IQ scores than many White children.

The consistent finding that the average IQ of Blacks falls below that of Whites has raised controversial interpretations of race differences. In the past this finding has been used to support racist arguments (see Chapter 3). More recently, the article by Jensen (1969) has reignited the whole controversy. Jensen (1969) states:

> No one, to my knowledge, questions the role of environmental factors, including influences from past history, in determining at least some of the variance between racial groups in standard measures of intelligence, school

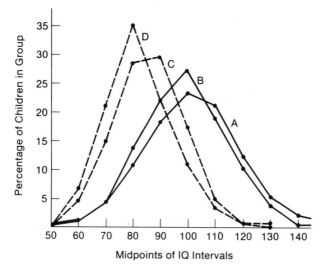

Figure 13-1. Percentages of children from four research groups who earned various IQ scores. A = U.S. White children (*N* = 1419) (Terman & Merrill, 1937). B = Millfield White children (*N* = 464) and C = Millfield Black children (N = 452) (Baughman & Dahlstrom, 1968). D = Southeast U.S. Black children (N = 1630) (Kennedy, Van de Riet, & White, 1963). From *Negro and White Children: A Psychological Study in the Rural South*, by E. E. Baughman and W. G. Dahlstrom. Copyright 1968 by Academic Press, Inc. Reprinted by permission.

performance, and occupational status. . . . But the possible importance of genetic factors in racial behavioral differences has been greatly ignored, almost to the point of being a tabooed subject, just as were the topics of venereal disease and birth control a generation or so ago.

There is an increasing realization among students of the psychology of the disadvantaged that the discrepancy in their performance cannot be completely or directly attributed to discrimination or inequalities in education. It seems not unreasonable, in view of the fact that intelligence variation has a large genetic component, to hypothesize that genetic factors may play a part in this picture. But such an hypothesis is anathema to many social scientists. The idea that the lower average intelligence and scholastic performance of Negroes could involve, not only environmental, but also genetic, factors has indeed been strongly denounced. . . . But it has been neither contradicted nor discredited by evidence.

The fact that a reasonable hypothesis has not been rigorously proved does not mean that it should be summarily dismissed. It only means that we need more appropriate research for putting it to the test. I believe such definitive research is entirely possible, but has not yet been done. So all we are left with are various lines of evidence, no one of which is definitive alone, but which, viewed all together, make it a not unreasonable hypothesis that genetic factors are strongly implicated in the average Negro-white intelligence difference. The preponderancy of the evidence is, in my opinion, less consistent with a strictly environmental hypothesis than with a genetic hypothesis, which of course, does not exclude the influence of environment or its interaction with genetic factors [pp. 79–82].[2]

Jensen believes that social scientists have generally ignored the possible importance of genetic factors underlying racial differences. However, because heredity plays a large role in accounting for individual differences in intelligence, it is not unreasonable according to Jensen to hypothesize that genetic factors are strongly involved in the average Black/White intelligence difference. That is, the average genetic potential of the Black population may be below that of the White population. Is the available evidence consistent with such a hypothesis? To formulate an answer to this question, we will make extensive reference to a recent analysis of the evidence on race differences in intelligence by Loehlin, Lindzey, and Spuhler (1975). The evidence reviewed by Loehlin and his associates is organized into four categories: (1) genetic designs, (2) temporal changes in IQ, (3) cross-group comparisons of intellectual abilities, and (4) nutrition and intellectual performance.

Genetic Designs

Genetic-design studies involve comparisons among individuals who differ in the extent of their genetic similarity, such as between identical and fraternal twins. Studies relevant to race differences in intelligence include twin studies, interracial adoption studies, and studies of race mixture.

Twin Studies. Twin studies that include both Black and White samples make it possible to obtain a racial comparison of the heritability for tested intelligence. Recall that heritability is a population characteristic and refers to the proportion of the total variance of a characteristic (in this case, measured intelligence) that is due to genetic variance (see Chapter 5).

Scarr-Salapatek (1971) studied a group of Black and White twins in the Philadelphia public school system. These children ranged in grades from 2 to 12. Scores for verbal and nonverbal aptitude tests were each intercorrelated for the Black and White twins. Information was not available as to whether twin pairs were identical or fraternal. Each group of twins was divided into same-sex and opposite-sex subgroups. In addition, data were separately reported for a subgroup who were identified as coming from low-socioeconomic status (SES) families. The correlational results are shown in Table 13-2. A consistent trend across the various tests and subgroups shows that the twin correlations are generally lower in the Black sample than they are in the White sample.[3]

If one assumes that environmental factors would contribute equally to

---

[2]From "How Much Can We Boost IQ and Scholastic Achievement?" by A. R. Jensen, *Harvard Educational Review,* 1969, *39,* 1–123. Copyright © 1969 by the President and Fellows of Harvard College. Reprinted by permission.

[3]It is rather surprising that there is little differentiation between the same-sex and opposite-sex groups. It would be expected that the correlations would be higher for the same-sex group, since such a group would contain a large proportion of identical twins.

Table 13-2. Correlations for Black and White Philadelphia Twins

| Test and Sample | Black | | White | |
	Same Sex	Opposite Sex	Same Sex	Opposite Sex
No. pairs in sample				
Low SES	(211)	(107)	(41)	(16)
Total group	(333)	(169)	(192)	(82)
Verbal aptitude				
Low SES	.49	.42	.48	.55
Total group	.54	.44	.67	.59
Nonverbal aptitude				
Low SES	.51	.52	.52	.62
Total group	.54	.49	.63	.66
Combined aptitude				
Low SES	.53	.60	.60	.63
Total group	.57	.58	.75	.69

Adapted from *Race Differences in Intelligence*, by J. C. Loehlin, G. Lindzey, and J. N. Spuhler. Copyright © 1975 by W. H. Freeman and Company. Based on data from "Race, Social Class, and IQ," by S. Scarr-Salapatek, *Science*, 1971, *174*, 1285–1295. Copyright 1971 by the American Association for the Advancement of Science. Used by permission.

twin similarities in Black and White twins, the greater similarity among White twins than among Black twins suggests that heredity plays a greater role in verbal and nonverbal aptitude-test performance for White children than for Black children. It also seems that heredity plays a greater role for higher- than lower-status children, regardless of race, because the twin correlations are generally higher for the total group than for the lower-status group. These results appear to support an environmental interpretation of race differences in measured intelligence. The lower heritability for Black children, which is compounded further by the fact that most of them also fell in the lower social-status group, suggests that it is the relatively restrictive environmental conditions that Black children face that are depressing their intellectual performance. Thus, even if a Black child has the genetic potential for a high level of intellectual performance, the lack of environmental opportunities will suppress that potential. It follows, then, as Scarr-Salapatek points out, that, if Blacks are given more environmental advantage, the heritability underlying their intellectual performance should increase and thus racial differences in the heritability of intelligence would be reduced.

A series of studies by Osborne, Vandenberg, and associates (Osborne & Gregor, 1968; Osborne & Miele, 1969; Vandenberg, 1970), involving a comparison of Black and White identical twins of high school age, replicated the results obtained by Scarr-Salapatek. On a battery of ability tests, including measures of spatial, perceptual, numerical, and verbal ability, the correlations for the Black twins were in general somewhat lower than they were for the White twins. Different results, however, were obtained by Nichols (1970) who studied a sample of Black and White twins who were first given intelligence tests at

8 months of age. Some of these twins were also tested at 4 years of age. In this study, unlike the two previous ones, the correlations for Black and White twins (identical and fraternal twins were included in each group) were generally equivalent. In one case—4-year-old identical twins—the correlation was higher for the sample of Black twins, suggesting higher heritability for Blacks than Whites. These results should be accepted cautiously, however, because intelligence tests at age 4 are not as reliable as those given at later ages (Brody & Brody, 1976). The same caution would apply to the results with infant tests, because they are also not as reliable as intelligence tests given at the school-age level.

In summary, twin studies with Black and White samples suggest that, at least at the elementary and high school levels, racial differences exist in the heritability of abilities—heritability appears to be greater for White children than for Black children. This research has important social implications. It appears that intervention programs that expand environmental opportunities would help Black children achieve their genetic potential for intellectual functioning.

Interracial Adoption Studies. As we noted in Chapter 5, adoption studies provide the opportunity to separate the effects of heredity and environment by comparing the characteristics of adopted children with those of their biological and adoptive parents. When children of one race are adopted by parents of another, it affords an opportunity to investigate racial differences. We have previously discussed the interracial adoption study by Scarr and Weinberg (1976) (see Chapter 5). The results of this study showed that the mean IQ of a sample of Black children who were adopted by White parents was 106, which is more than a standard deviation above 85, the national average IQ of Black children, and slightly higher than 100, the average IQ of White children. Furthermore, when the age of adoption was controlled for, the average IQ of the adopted Black children was comparable to the average IQ for a sample of White children who were adopted by some of the same families who adopted the Black children. These results acknowledge the appreciable influence of environmental conditions in reducing the Black/White IQ gap.

Racial Mixture. Another way of investigating the contribution of genes to Black/White IQ differences is to study individuals of mixed racial background. A genetic argument would be supported if the average IQ of those Blacks with some European ancestry exceeded the average IQ of those Blacks who lacked European ancestry. In studies that have used light skin color as an indicator of mixed racial background in Blacks or Native Americans, the results have generally shown that light-skinned individuals perform somewhat better on intelligence tests than dark-skinned individuals (Loehlin et al., 1975). However, the meaning of these results is difficult to interpret. Physical characteristics, such as skin color, are not particularly reliable indicators of racial ancestry. Furthermore, it is not possible to separate environmental from genetic influences. Light-skinned persons may do better on intelligence tests either because their partial-European ancestry provides a better genetic potential or because they are more integrated into the White culture.

Other evidence on racial mixture and intelligence provides some clarification about the relative contributions of heredity and environment. Loehlin, Vandenberg, and Osborne (1973) investigated the association of blood groups with performance on intellectual tests in samples of Blacks and Whites. The investigators first determined for 16 blood groups the extent to which each was more common in the White than in the Black sample. This made it possible to examine whether those blood groups associated with good intellectual performance among Blacks were also those blood groups found more frequently among Whites—that is, those blood groups most likely to be based on European ancestry. The results showed no association of European blood groups with higher ability in the sample of Blacks and were thus not supportive of a genetic interpretation.

Evidence consistent with an environmental hypothesis emerges from a study by Eyferth (1961) of illegitimate children in Germany who were fathered by American Black and White occupation soldiers. Both groups of children were raised by their German mothers under comparable conditions of social status. If we assume that the group of Black fathers had a lower average IQ than the group of White fathers, then from a genetic viewpoint we would expect the offspring of Black fathers to have a lower average IQ than the offspring of White fathers. However, no overall difference in average IQ was found between the children whose fathers were Black and those whose fathers were White. These results, however, cannot be conclusive because no information was available on the ability level of the fathers.

Evidence concerning racial mixture and intelligence is also available from Scarr and Weinberg's (1976) interracial adoption study. They compared the IQ scores of children who had one Black biological parent with those who had two. The sample of 29 children of two Black parents had an average score of 97, while the sample of 68 with only one Black parent scored 109. The higher average IQ for the racially mixed children is consistent with a genetic interpretation. However, these children were, on the average, adopted at an earlier age than the children who had two Black parents. Hence, the better performance of the racially mixed group might have been attributable to an environmental advantage.

Taken together, the studies of Black and White twins, interracial adoption, and racial mixture provide little conclusive evidence on the determinants of racial differences in intellectual performance. No evidence clearly supports a genetic interpretation. The influence of environmental conditions on Black/White IQ differences is suggested from some of the twin studies and the studies of interracial adoption and interracial mating.

Temporal Changes in IQ

If IQ scores of a particular racial group change substantially over time, perhaps a few generations, it seems likely that they would be traceable to major changes that have taken place in the environment. It is highly unlikely that alterations in the genetic makeup of a given group would be responsible for such IQ changes. Some evidence exists regarding temporal changes in measured intelligence involving racial/ethnic group comparisons, which includes population trends in IQ over time, age trends in the development of intelligence, and the effects of intervention programs ("compensatory education") designed to produce positive changes in intellectual functioning.

Population IQ Trends. The available evidence on racial and ethnic group comparisons in population IQ trends indicates that the magnitude of the difference between groups and the relative position among groups remain stable over a period of several years. A study by Smith (1942) in Hawaii involved two multiracial groups of children, aged 10 to 15. The first group was tested in 1924 and the second group in 1938. The results showed an overall increase of about 13 IQ points on a nonverbal test. Despite this improvement over a 14-year time period, the relative position of the various racial/ethnic groups remained the same. The mean performance of the oriental groups (Korean, Japanese, and Chinese) and a group identified as "white" was highest, followed by that of Filipinos, Hawaiians, Portuguese, and Puerto Ricans. Apparently, the educational changes that had taken place in the 14-year interval between testings were beneficial to about the same extent for each of the racial/ethnic groups.

A review by Shuey (1966) of studies comparing U.S. Black and White IQ trends in children generally showed that the difference between the two groups remained constant over the periods before and after 1945. The majority of these studies were based on elementary school samples, and it was among these that the stability was most noticeable. With preschool children and high school students, Blacks tended to fall further behind the Whites in the later period (1945-1965). However, the composition of the preschool and high school samples possibly restricts the generalizability of these results. The preschool studies involved only those children attending nursery school and kindergarten. The high school studies included samples that averaged somewhat below the respective national averages for Blacks and Whites, and the samples were drawn mostly from the South.

Comparisons in IQ trends between U.S. Black and White adults generally agree with the trends found with preschool and high school children. The data for adults are based on the armed services testing programs conducted during World War I, World War II, and the Vietnam War. Because different tests were used at different times, Loehlin and associates (1975), in their analysis of the testing data, converted percentiles to standard score equivalents. On this basis they estimated that Blacks averaged 17 IQ points below Whites during World War I and 23 IQ points below Whites during World War II and the Vietnam War. As with preschool and high school samples, the samples on which the military data are based present possible difficulties in generalizing to the wider population. Military recruits are not representative of U.S. males in general.

However, despite possible restricted generalizability, the fact that the gap has increased since World War I is surprising, for as Loehlin and associates suggest, the operation of at least two factors should have acted to reduce a Black/White difference. First, by World War II and, especially, the Vietnam War, the Northern urban migration of Blacks would have lowered the Southern rural bias of the World War I Black sample. Since a Southern and rural background is related to lower IQ scores, a reduction in the proportion of Blacks in the army sample who were from the rural South would have been expected to produce a rise in the average IQ level of Black recruits and consequently a reduced Black/White difference. Second, between 1910 and 1960 the Black/White gap in school attendance has been markedly reduced. Forty-five percent of Black children between the ages of 5 and 20 years attended school in 1910 versus 61% of White children, while in 1960 the respective figures were 79% and 82%. Thus closing the education gap between Black and White children should have worked in favor of reducing the IQ discrepancy.

It therefore appears that the increase in the Black/White IQ gap is inconsistent with environmental views and supportive of hereditarian views. However, there may be some social changes that could account for the increase in the Black/White IQ gap shown in the armed forces data and some of the school data. One possibility is that, while more Black children are now attending school, they may not be receiving the same quality of education provided to White children. Perhaps the discrepancy in the quality-of-education between Black and White children has been increasing over the years. For instance, Kenneth B. Clark (1965) pointed out that in contrast to the achievement gap between Black and White students in the 1960s, Black children attending Harlem (New York City) schools in the 1920s and 1930s "had average academic achievement close to, if not equal to, the white norms" (p. 141). He attributed this change to the deterioration of ghetto schools over the years.

Another possible explanation of the increase in the Black/White IQ discrepancy is the occupational changes that have taken place over the years. Loehlin and associates point out that the gap in average occupational status between U.S. Blacks and Whites appears to have increased up until World War II, a trend that parallels the increase in the IQ gap. In the period since World War II the Black/White difference in average occupational status has remained large. Thus, while there has been a progressive increase in the amount of schooling received by the average Black over the last several decades, relative to Whites, Blacks may be falling further behind in terms of the quality of their schooling. Also, the occupational gap between Blacks and Whites appears to have increased in the past and continues to be substantial.

Age and Racial/Ethnic IQ Differences. Intelligence-test comparisons between U.S. Black and White children of various ages quite consistently demonstrate that group differences do not emerge until approximately 3 years of age (Loehlin et al., 1975). Only after the first three years do White children show higher IQ scores than Black children. The results of a recent longitudinal study by Goffeney, Henderson, and Butler (1971) exemplify this age trend. Black and White lower-class children in Oregon were first tested at 8 months

Table 13-3. Average IQs of White and Black Children at 8 Months and at 7 Years

Group	Bayley IQ* at 8 Months	WISC IQ at 7 Years	Number of Children
White males	95	98	208
White females	94	98	189
Black males	93	90	116
Black females	95	91	113

*Raw scores from Bayley Mental Scale converted to IQ equivalents.
Adapted from *Race Differences in Intelligence*, by J. C. Loehlin, G. Lindzey, and J. N. Spuhler. Copyright © 1975 by W. H. Freeman and Company. Based on data from "Negro-White, Male-Female Eight-Month Developmental Scores Compared with Seven-Year WISC and Bender Test Scores," by B. Goffeney, N. B. Henderson, and B. V. Butler, *Child Development*, 1971, *42*, 595–604. Copyright 1971 by The Society for Research in Child Development, Inc. Used by permission.

of age and then retested at age 7. As can be seen in Table 13-3, the Black and White groups are distinguishable only at the later age. Such results are not limited to Black/White comparisons. A longitudinal study in Hawaii by Werner, Simonian, and Smith (1968) shows that the average IQs of children of various ethnic groups were similar at the age of 20 months, but different at the age of 10½ years. The results are presented in Table 13-4.

These developmental results could be explained in terms of the increasing impact of cultural factors that start to affect children around the age of three. It is at this age that the ability for complex cognitive learning begins to expand. However, these results do not necessarily rule out genetic factors, because there could be racial differences in the frequencies of genes that underlie such complex cognitive functioning (Loehlin et al., 1975).

The influence of environmental conditions is clearly indicated by other research that has involved successive testings with school-age Black children. Lee (1951) studied a group of Black children who were tested in the Philadelphia school system. His results showed that IQ scores rise in relation to an improvement in education. Intelligence-test scores (from a test standardized on Philadelphia schoolchildren) were available for Black children who were born in Philadelphia and for children who had lived in Philadelphia for varying lengths of time since migrating from the South. The IQs for the Philadelphia-born children remained stable over a period of years, whereas the IQs for the children who had migrated improved over time. The degree of improvement depended on how long the children lived in Philadelphia. These results are shown in Table 13-5. The presumed reason for the increase in intellectual performance was the transition from the very disadvantaged environment of the rural South to the better environment of the urban North.

Studies by Osborne (1966) and Gray and Klaus (1970) similarly show a relationship between a rise in IQ scores and a change in educational conditions. In both studies, Black children were tested before entering first grade and then retested one year later. The results showed that intelligence-test performance improved on the retest, thus pointing to the positive effect of school experience.

Table 13-4. Average IQs of Children from Five Ethnic Groups in Hawaii at 2 and 10 Years

Group	Cattell IQ at 20 Months	PMA IQ at 10½ Years	Number of Children
Anglo-Saxon Caucasian	98	112	18
Japanese	103	108	253
Filipino	95	101	138
Full- and part-Hawaiian	96	99	180
Portuguese	99	96	46

Adapted from *Race Differences in Intelligence*, by J. C. Loehlin, G. Lindzey, and J. N. Spuhler. Copyright © 1975 by W. H. Freeman and Company. Based on data from "Ethnic and Socio-Economic Status Differences in Abilities and Achievement among Preschool and School Age Children in Hawaii," by E. E. Werner, K. Simonian, and R. S. Smith, *Journal of Social Psychology*, 1968, *75*, 43–59. Copyright 1968 by The Journal Press. Used by permission.

Table 13-5. Mean IQs of Black Children Varying in the Length of Residence in Philadelphia

	IQ[1] in Grade					Number of Children
	1A	2B	4B	6B	9A	
Philadelphia-born, KG[2]	97	96	97	98	97	212
Philadelphia-born, no KG	92	93	95	94	94	424
Southern-born, entered 1A	86	89	92	93	93	182
Southern-born, entered 1B-2B		87	89	91	90	109
Southern-born, entered 3A-4B			86	87	89	199
Southern-born, entered 5A-6B				88	90	221
Southern-born, entered 7A-9A					87	219

[1]From Philadelphia Tests of Mental and Verbal Ability (norm group—all Philadelphia children).

[2]KG means that the children in the sample attended kindergarten.

Adapted from *Race Differences in Intelligence*, by J. C. Loehlin, G. Lindzey, and J. N. Spuhler. Copyright © 1975 by W. H. Freeman and Company. Based on data from "Negro Intelligence & Selective Migration: A Philadelphia Test of the Klineberg Hypothesis," by E. S. Lee, *American Sociological Review*, 1951, *16*, 227–233. Copyright 1951 by the American Sociological Association. Used by permission.

What happens if school-age children are continually exposed to conditions of environmental deprivation? In contrast to the above studies, showing a direct association between IQ improvement and educational improvement, we should expect a progressive decrease in IQ scores when children are exposed to the cumulative effects of a lack of intellectual stimulation in the home and school environments. Recall from our discussion of deprivation in Chapter 5 that IQ decrements with increasing age did occur among culturally isolated canal boat children in England during the 1920s and White children living in remote parts of Appalachia during the 1930s. What about disadvantaged Black children in the 1970s? Evidence of age decrement in IQ for this group is indicated in a recent study by Jensen (1977). This study involved samples of Black and

White school children in rural Georgia, between the ages of 5 and 18. Jensen notes that the Black group as a whole was within the lowest socioeconomic category: "probably as severely disadvantaged, educationally and economically, as can be found anywhere in the United States today" (p. 185). The White children, in contrast, were predominantly in the upper-lower and lower-middle socioeconomic categories. Age decrement in IQ (both verbal and nonverbal) was measured by the average IQ difference between younger and older siblings. To be consistent with the idea that the effect of poor environment is cumulative, the older siblings would have to manifest lower IQs because of their greater exposure to the deficient environment. The results of the study showed that Blacks, but not Whites, had significant and substantial age decrements (from about 5 to 16 points) in verbal and nonverbal IQ scores on a group intelligence test (the California Test of Mental Maturity). Jensen concludes that these results of age decrement in IQ are caused by the environmental effect of cumulative deprivation.[4] However, because these data are cross-sectional rather than longitudinal, the results could alternatively be interpreted as indicating that social and educational changes have taken place and have therefore facilitated IQ development in recently born Black children (Kamin, 1978).

Compensatory Education.   Compensatory education programs and their effectiveness are crucial to the environmentalist interpretation of racial differences in intelligence. Moreover, this research has potential relevance to the more general nature/nurture issue in intelligence (see Chapter 5). These programs were first instituted in the 1960s to raise the academic performance of disadvantaged children of preschool age to the level of middle-class children. Advocates of compensatory education believed that an educationally "enriched" experience for disadvantaged children could remove the cultural and educational disadvantage before school entrance and, consequently, serve to reduce, perhaps even eliminate, the racial difference in intellectual performance. The most common evaluation tool, the IQ test, was used in most studies to assess the effectiveness of compensatory education programs.

Can compensatory education programs reduce racial differences in intelligence? Unfortunately, the nature of the samples that have been studied and the reports evaluating the effectiveness of the programs do not allow suitable comparisons among disadvantaged children of different races. In most of the studies, the samples were predominantly Black, and, when the samples were integrated, separate results for different racial groups were not reported (Loehlin et al., 1975). Conclusions drawn about the effectiveness of compensatory education for the most part pertain to a population of disadvantaged children, a large proportion of whom are Black.

The major finding of the research evaluating compensatory education programs is the lack of any enduring gain in IQ scores. The most common

---

[4]In view of Jensen's (1969) emphasis on a genetic basis for Black/White differences in intelligence, it is noteworthy that he arrived at an environmental interpretation of the results of this study.

pattern has been for treatment groups (the children enrolled in the compensatory programs) to manifest initial IQ gains that disappear on follow up a year or two later (Bronfenbrenner, 1975; Jensen, 1969; Loehlin et al., 1975). Illustrative of this pattern is the Early Training Project in Nashville, Tennessee (Gray & Klaus, 1970; Klaus & Gray, 1968). Two treatment groups of Black preschool-age children attended special training programs for two or three summers. In addition, they had weekly meetings with a trained home visitor during the rest of the year. At the beginning of the program, the mean IQs for the two groups were 88 and 92. When the program was terminated at the time of their entry into first grade, the average IQs had risen to 96 and 97, respectively. However, a follow-up testing after grade three revealed average IQs of 87 and 90, which were comparable to the IQs attained at the beginning of the program. The study also included two control groups who were given only the IQ tests. One group averaged 85 both at the first testing and at the end of grade three. The second group had an initial average IQ of 87 and a final average IQ of 78. Thus, the treatment groups did have an advantage in relation to one of the control groups.

Such results suggest that recent efforts at compensatory education have failed to reduce the IQ gap between advantaged and disadvantaged children. Indeed, this conclusion is the one reached by Jensen (1969). One possible reason for the ineffectiveness of compensatory education is that the treatment variables assumed to be effective in any intervention program may not in fact be the critical variables. Merely providing disadvantaged children with some preschool experience may not be sufficient to produce significant changes. Rather, the effectiveness of a program may depend on the particular methods used. For instance, comparisons have been made between those preschool programs that are traditionally unstructured and those that are highly structured in terms of developing cognitive and academic skills (see Loehlin et al., 1975). The results of these studies have shown that children in structured programs do reveal significant IQ gains. However, at least one study of a traditional program also has shown a comparable gain (Weikart, 1972). Thus, a structured approach may be important, but other factors need to be considered.

A variation of compensatory education for preschool children has been home-based intervention in which specially trained home visitors work with both mother and child. In Chapter 5, we discussed a home-based program in which the children manifested significant IQ gains, and these gains were maintained in follow-up testing (Levenstein, 1970). We also reviewed the study by Heber, Garber, Herrington, Hoffman, and Falender (1972), who evaluated a training program for mothers and their newborn infants that continued until the children reached school age. In this program, the training took place at a neighborhood center. The experimental group of children showed a gradual rise in IQ starting at 12 months, and by age 3 they averaged about 30 points higher than the control group. Several other studies involving training with both mothers and children are reviewed by Bronfenbrenner (1975). Generally the results of these studies point to the importance of involving the parent directly in the activities used to foster the child's intellectual development.

Bronfenbrenner points out that further research is needed before firm conclusions can be drawn; but he submits the following as a guide for successful early intervention programs, not only with respect to intellectual performance, but to the total development of the child:

> [A] long range intervention program may be viewed in terms of five uninterrupted stages:
>
> 1. preparation for parenthood—child care, nutrition and medical training
> 2. before children come—adequate housing, economic security
> 3. the first three years of life—establishment of a child-parent relationship of reciprocal interaction centered around activities which are challenging to the child; home visits, group meetings to establish the parent as the primary agent of intervention
> 4. ages four through six—exposure to a cognitively oriented pre-school program along with a continuation of parent intervention
> 5. ages six through twelve—parental support of the child's educational activities at home and at school; parent remains primary figure responsible for the child's development as a person [Bronfenbrenner, 1975, pp. 316–317].

Bronfenbrenner's guide provides an encompassing prescription for successful intervention. Since piecemeal intervention programs of the past have generally proved unsuccessful, these five steps should facilitate the design of more effective programs.

In general, the evidence on temporal changes in IQ is indicative of the importance of environmental factors underlying racial differences in intelligence. The fact that the IQ gap between Blacks and Whites has not decreased over several decades seems to reflect the continuing restrictions in educational and occupational opportunities that Blacks have endured. There is some evidence that the intellectual performance of Black children improves when educational conditions improve. However, recent research on compensatory education programs suggests that, in order for intervention programs to be effective, parents need to be involved as well as children.

Cross-Group Comparisons of Intellectual Abilities

Comparisons of the intellectual performance of various U.S. subpopulations, such as social-class subgroups in each of several racial/ethnic groups, can provide further insight about the determinants of racial and ethnic differences. For example, some racial/ethnic groups may have less of a social-class difference in measured intelligence than other groups. If a racial group has relatively little social-class differentiation in IQ, it may be that limited environmental opportunities, such as residential and school segregation based on race, generally restrict intellectual development for members of that racial group, regardless of their social-class standing. On the other hand, if we know that the environment is conducive to intellectual development and the group still manifests little social-class differentiation in IQ, then genetic factors would seem to be important. Also, racial/ethnic differences may exist in special abilities as well as in the pattern of relative strengths and weaknesses across special ability areas. It is possible that genetic and environmental determinants can be more clearly identified for special abilities than for general intelligence. We shall first consider the relationship between IQ and social class in different racial/ethnic groups and then look at racial/ethnic differences in special abilities.

IQ and Social Class in Different Racial/Ethnic Groups. In Chapter 12, we reviewed the evidence on social-class differences in general intelligence within the U.S. White population. We concluded that a moderately positive relationship exists between social-status level and intelligence-test scores. Does the same relationship appear in other U.S. racial/ethnic groups?

Considerable data are available for samples of Black children regarding the association of IQ and family social status. Loehlin and associates (1975) report an average correlation of about .30 (based on several recent studies) between Black children's IQs and their family social status, a finding consistent with the general level of correlations reported for samples of White children. In a direct comparison of Black and White children, slightly higher correlations between several WISC subtests and social status were reported for White children (.33) than for Black children (.24) (Nichols, 1970). The Black/White similarity in correlations between social class and IQ that is generally found for children also holds for young adults. Based on extensive Selective Service data, the correlations between Armed Forces Qualifying test scores and level of educational attainment were .59 for Whites and .62 for Blacks (Duncan, 1968).

The relationship between social class and IQ for Black and White children has also been studied in terms of group means. Shuey (1966) has combined the results of six studies involving group means. In each of these studies, the Black and White samples were each divided into a relatively high social-class category and a relatively low one. Within the White samples, the mean IQ of higher social class was 112, while the mean for the lower social class was 94—a difference of 18 points. Within the Black samples, the corresponding mean IQs were 92 and 82—a difference of 10 points. Shuey's analysis, therefore, indicates that social-class differentiation is somewhat greater for White children than for Black children. Similar results are also indicated in Loehlin and associates' review of seven comparable studies carried out since the Shuey report. Five of these studies showed a greater social-class difference for White children, one study showed no group differences, and one study showed a greater social-class difference for Black children. Although the results of these recent studies are not uniform, Shuey's finding of a greater social-class differentiation among White children generally is supported. Loehlin and associates interpret this trend as indicating that a social-mobility mechanism is working more effectively within the White population than within the Black population. Apparently, as we noted when discussing the Black/White twin studies, there are greater opportunities to facilitate intellectual development for Whites than for Blacks, and with such an advantage Whites have more access to higher status levels in society.

Overall, the association between social class and measured intelligence seems to be fairly consistent across Black and White samples. In some studies (mostly those using group means rather than correlations), there is a trend toward greater differentiation among Whites than among Blacks, which may be interpreted as suggesting racial differences in opportunities for social mobility. The evidence on other U.S. minority group children (Asian American, Chicano, Puerto Rican, and Jewish) reveals that the magnitude of association between social class and ability in all of these groups generally corresponds with that which is found in the White majority (Loehlin et al., 1975).

Racial/Ethnic Differences in Ability Profiles. Beginning with the reports of the Torres Straits expedition at the turn of the 20th century, interest was raised in testing the hypothesis that different racial/ethnic groups excel in those particular abilities appropriate to the demands of their environment. As we noted earlier, in the case of the Papuans of the Torres Straits, it was thought, though only partly confirmed, that they would have superior sensory abilities when compared with Europeans. Research on U.S. racial/ethnic groups has focused on differences in the levels of various special abilities. In order to make group comparisons involving a series of ability dimensions, it is important to first establish that the factor structure of abilities is consistent from one group to the next. After reviewing the relevant research, Loehlin and associates (1975) conclude that the same underlying dimensions or factors of ability are generally revealed within the various U.S. racial/ethnic groups.

The relative standings of different groups on several cognitive ability dimensions were investigated by Lesser, Fifer, and Clark (1965). Samples of Chinese-American, Jewish, Black, and Puerto Rican first-grade children of middle- and lower-class backgrounds in New York City were included in the study. The children were given a modified form of the Hunter College Aptitude Scales for Gifted Children, which assess verbal, reasoning, numerical, and spatial abilities. These tests were revised so that they would be fairer to the past experiences of the different groups of children. The ethnic group differences are shown in Figure 13-2. Differences appear both in the overall level of ability scores and in the particular patterning across the four ability scales. The Chinese-American and Jewish groups performed at a considerably higher overall level than the Black and Puerto Rican groups. The Jewish children were strongest on verbal ability, followed by numerical ability and last, spatial ability. Chinese children, in contrast, did poorest on the verbal test. The Black children, like the Jewish children, performed best on the verbal test.

A partial replication of the Lesser and associates study was carried out by Stodolsky and Lesser (1967) in Boston. For the two replicated samples (Chinese-American and Blacks), the results on the four tests were similar to those obtained in the original investigation. Some consistency with the results of Lesser and associates is also indicated in a study by Backman (1972) based on a national sample of twelfth-grade high school students. Jewish students proved best on measures of verbal and math abilities and weakest on a measure of spatial ability. Asian-American students scored exceptionally high on math ability. With respect to Lesser and associates' finding that Blacks do relatively

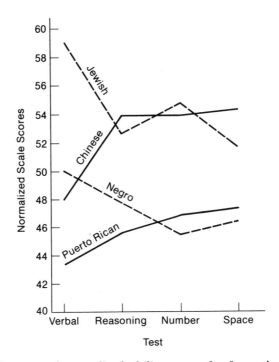

Figure 13-2. Patterns of normalized ability scores for four ethnic groups. From "Mental Abilities of Children from Different Social-Class and Cultural Groups," by G. S. Lesser, G. Fifer, and D. H. Clark, *Monographs of the Society for Research in Child Development,* 1965, *30*(4, Serial No. 102). Copyright 1965 by the Society for Research in Child Development. Reprinted by permission.

better on verbal than nonverbal ability measures, the data from various studies of Black subjects' performance on the verbal and nonverbal scales of the Wechsler tests show the same pattern in most instances (see Loehlin et al., 1975).

Thus some relatively consistent group differences in ability patterns emerge. How do we account for such differences? It seems likely that particular cultural values stressed by a group would have a strong influence. Levinson (1959, 1963) has pointed out that the relatively good performance on verbal tests by Jewish children reflects the emphasis Jews place on verbal learning, because such learning is seen as relevant to the perpetuation of religious and national identity.

While the cultural values of a racial or ethnic group may have some influence on ability patterns, other environmental factors also may be important. Tyler (1965) hypothesizes that the poor perceptual and spatial test performance of Blacks may be due to early environmental deprivation, specifically the meagerness of early childhood surroundings. She believes that such a deficit, if it exists, can be corrected by appropriate early environmental enrichment. In reviewing the research on perceptual performance by Blacks and Whites, Mandler and Stein (1977) concluded that as yet there are no studies that have actually examined whether or not Black/White differences exist in early environmental impoverishment. Thus, Tyler's perceptual-deficit hypothesis has not been directly investigated.

Genetic factors also may underlie differential ability patterns. Loehlin and associates (1975) examined the hypothesis that the deficit in spatial ability among Blacks is substantially influenced by the low frequency of a single gene in populations of West African origin. They referred to the IQ test data from Eyferth's (1961) study of the offspring of German women and Black and White American servicemen and predicted the following:

> If the gene for spatial ability is X-linked, [that is, comes only on the X-chromosome and not the Y-chromosome] and if the gene was more frequent among the white fathers of these children than among the black fathers, but equally frequent among the two sets of German mothers, there is a clear genetic prediction. The Caucasian and mixed-raced girls should show a difference in spatial ability in favor of the Caucasians, since each girl received an X-chromosome from her father, and there should be no such difference among the boys, whose X-chromosomes all came from their German mothers [Loehlin et al., 1975, p. 193].

Using the scores of the Block Design subtest of a German version of the WISC, which measures spatial ability, Loehlin and associates found no support for the genetic prediction. Nor was there any support in the other WISC subtests with a spatial-ability component. In each of these subtests, the girls with Black fathers performed as well as the girls with White fathers. A limitation of this analysis, which Loehlin and associates acknowledge, is that no information was available on the test performance of the parents. Nevertheless, Loehlin and associates conclude these results offer no support for the hypothesis that an X-linked spatial-ability gene is lower in frequency in African than in European populations.

In general, the available evidence is rather inconclusive with respect to the role of environmental and genetic influences on ethnic/racial group differences in ability patterns. Although the role of environmental factors is suggested, gene-based differences cannot be ruled out.

Nutrition and Intellectual Performance

In reviewing the evidence on the nutritional status of American racial/ethnic groups, Loehlin and associates (1975) conclude that Whites are better nourished than Blacks and Spanish Americans who in turn are better nourished than Native Americans. However, instances of severe malnutrition are rare in all American ethnic groups.

Improved nutrition can sometimes lead to rises in IQ test scores (see Chapter 5). It is possible that if nutrition were improved for disadvantaged ethnic groups, their average IQ level would rise. Because the effects of nutritional supplementation on tested intelligence have not as yet been compared across different U.S. racial/ethnic groups, present evidence is limited. There is some evidence concerning the association between four indicators of nutritional status (obesity, blood level of ascorbic acid, birth weight, and head circumference) and IQ scores within racial/ethnic groups (Loehlin et al., 1975). For the most part these nutritional indexes do not offer much promise for modifying existing IQ differences between U.S. Blacks and Whites, although some modest effects (an average rise of 3 or 4 IQ points) may occur if ascorbic acid consumption is increased (for example, in supplemental amounts of orange juice) among low-income Blacks.

Conclusions about the Roles of Heredity and Environment

Any conclusions regarding the genetic and environmental determinants of racial/ethnic differences in intelligence must be viewed as quite tentative because relevant evidence is limited. There is a great need for more research involving samples of different racial/ethnic groups in each of the areas we have considered: genetic-design studies, temporal changes in IQ, cross-group comparisons, and the effects of nutritional supplementation. It is our belief that the existing evidence does not appear to support Jensen's (1969) hypothesis, cited earlier, that genetic factors largely account for racial/ethnic differences in intelligence. No evidence from studies of Black and White twins, interracial adoption, or racial mixture is clearly supportive of genetic influences underlying Black/White differences in intelligence. Nor is there any evidence to suggest that genetic factors underlie differences in special abilities, in particular spatial ability. To the contrary, some studies of interracial adoption, interracial mating, and temporal changes in IQ suggest that environmental factors can reduce the Black/White IQ gap. Studies of compensatory education, however, underscore the difficulty of achieving lasting effects on measured intelligence. Such studies suggest that marked environmental changes have to be introduced in order to achieve significant effects, and, as yet, there is minimal evidence on these kinds of changes. We should note that, although there is no strong evidence favoring a genetic interpretation, neither does the present evidence necessarily exclude the possible influence of genetic factors. Nevertheless, even if evidence supportive of genetic factors in Black/White IQ differences were to be obtained, the role of environmental factors in reducing the IQ gap would not be mitigated. It is important to remember that traits that have a strong genetic basis to them are not necessarily impervious to environmental influences.

Test Bias

In addition to hereditary and environmental influences, test bias is a factor to be considered in accounting for racial/ethnic differences in intelligence. As noted in Chapter 12, lower-class individuals appear to be at some disadvantage on intelligence measures because of their relative lack of familiarity with test content. Because of the disproportionately high representation of lower-class individuals in certain minority-group populations—Blacks, Spanish Americans, and Native Americans—test bias might have an effect of lowering average IQ scores for these groups. Furthermore, many members of these minority groups have a cultural and linguistic disadvantage when compared with Whites.

One way of ascertaining the effect of test bias is to determine whether or not differences exist in the extent to which ability tests are predictive of achievement for various racial/ethnic groups. For example, if a general ability test, such as the Scholastic Aptitude Test, is more accurate in predicting college performance for Whites than for Blacks, its appropriateness for Blacks would be questionable. If, in fact, the test produced a predicted grade point average for Blacks that was too low, a certain proportion of Black high school students could be unfairly rejected for college admission. It is also possible that the reverse situation could occur; that is, if the test produced a predicted grade point average for Blacks that was too high, then a certain proportion of White high school students could be unfairly rejected for college admission. A number of studies have examined the relative predictability of college performance for Blacks and Whites from general ability tests, such as the Scholastic Aptitude Test and the American College Test. In reviewing this research, Cleary, Humphreys, Kendrick, and Wesman (1975) conclude that these standardized tests produce comparable predictions of college performance for Black and White students. Thus, at least with respect to the relative predictability of ability tests for Blacks and Whites, the available evidence is not supportive of test bias.

Another means of assessing test bias, and one we discussed in relation to social class (see Chapter 12), is to determine whether or not any bias exists in the content of test items that would place minority-group individuals at a disadvantage because of their relative lack of familiarity with test content. Samuda (1975), in reviewing the research on test content, points out that many common words do not have the same meanings for Blacks as they have for Whites. Samuda also reports that on scholastic aptitude tests those items dealing with Blacks and modern culture have been shown to be more appropriate for Black students than those relating to the past and to more remote concepts. Not all of the evidence on item content is suggestive of test bias. A study by Quay (1971) with inner-city Black preschool children found no significant difference in performance between two versions of the Stanford-Binet. One group of children was given the standard version of the test while another group of children was given a version that had been translated into the Black English dialect.

It has also been suggested that, aside from biases within tests, minority-group individuals are at a disadvantage with respect to the testing situation. That is, they may be overly anxious about being evaluated, and they may perceive hostility in the test environment (Samuda, 1975). Evidence indicates that one feature of the testing situation may be of considerable importance—the racial identity of the tester. When Black children are tested by a Black examiner, they score higher on intelligence measures than when they are tested by a White examiner (Forrester & Klaus, 1964; Moore & Retish, 1974). These results suggest that Black children generally feel more at ease and secure with a Black examiner. Apparently, care should be taken to insure that when intelligence tests are administered to minority children, they are administered by an examiner who can establish a positive and accepting relationship with the children.

Before completing our discussion of intelligence it is important to emphasize that, as in the case of social-class and other group differences, a wide range of individual differences within racial/ethnic groups appears as well as considerable overlapping between groups (see Figure 13-1 for Black/White comparisons). The most unequivocal conclusion is that differences among individuals within various racial/ethnic groups greatly exceed the average difference between such groups (Loehlin et al., 1975). Unfortunately, this point has tended to be obscured in the controversy surrounding the race and IQ issue. For all practical purposes, the high within-group variability and the overlap between group distributions prevent any meaningful predictions about a particular individual's IQ solely on the basis of his or her racial or ethnic group identity. Baughman's (1971) comment in the case of Blacks is relevant to this point:

> [The] overlap in IQ distributions plotted with respect to the social definition of race ... show[s] that it is impossible to predict an individual's IQ by the color of his skin, and it is unfair to him to make predictions about his intelligence based upon differences in means between racial groups [p. 13].

ACHIEVEMENT

The racial/ethnic differences in intelligence lead us to expect that differences also are likely to be found with respect to achievement. We will first look at educational achievement and then consider occupational achievement.

Educational Achievement

The most comprehensive investigation of racial/ethnic differences in scholastic performance is the study conducted by James Coleman and his associates (1966), widely known as the Coleman Report. This large-scale national survey was based on some 570,000 pupils in about 4000 schools. Six racial/ethnic groups were represented: Native Americans, Chicanos, Asian Americans, Puerto Ricans, Blacks, and a final group, the White majority. The major finding of this study was that, with the exception of Asian Americans, minority-group children score significantly lower on standardized verbal and nonverbal achievement tests than White children. While a difference in performance was present at all grade levels sampled—first, third, sixth, ninth, and twelfth—the magnitude of the differences in performance was greater in the upper grades. For example, Blacks in the metropolitan Northeast were 1.6 years behind Whites at grade 6, 2.4 years behind at grade 9, and 3.3 years behind at grade 12. The fact that the differences increased with grade level led Coleman and associates to conclude that whatever combination of nonschool factors—poverty, family and community attitudes, low educational levels of parents—

contributed to the poorer performance of minority children, the effects of education do not reduce the achievement gap between minority and majority children. The increasing achievement deficit shown by Black children is consistent with the cumulative deficit for Black children on measured intelligence.

Other studies of the scholastic performance of Black and White children agree with the Coleman study in showing that Black pupils perform considerably below the level of White pupils (see Baughman, 1971; Hess, 1970). Some of these studies have also included separate comparisons for boys and girls (Baughman & Dahlstrom, 1968; Deutsch, 1960; Kennedy et al., 1963). These comparisons consistently indicate that Black girls perform better than Black boys, and their superiority tends to increase with age. Among White children girls also perform better scholastically than boys, but the sex differences are greater among Black children. Actually, when looking at the pattern of sex differences, the achievement gap between Black girls and White boys is small, especially beginning around age 12. In fact, in one study it was found that, starting in early adolescence, the spelling performance of Black girls exceeded that of White boys (Baughman & Dahlstrom, 1968).

Because minority and majority children differ in school achievement indexes, we might expect a parallel difference in educational attainment. We should first note, as we pointed out in our discussion of temporal changes in measured intelligence, there has been a marked reduction over the years in the Black/White gap in school attendance so that, by 1960, the percentages of Black and White children attending school were virtually equivalent (79% for Blacks and 82% for Whites). With respect to the amount of schooling completed, Jencks and associates (1972) report that, since 1900, the educational attainment of Blacks has increased faster than that of Whites. Blacks born at the turn of the century averaged 3 years less schooling than Whites, whereas Blacks born during World War II averaged 1 year less than Whites. As a consequence of the civil rights movement, Black enrollment at the college level by the late 1960s rose considerably faster than White enrollment. As Jencks and associates (1972) state: "It therefore seems reasonable to assume that the upcoming generation of blacks will get almost as much schooling as whites get" [p. 142].

The fact that Black children perform significantly below White children on standardized achievement tests and yet attain almost as much schooling as White children suggests that if we hold test scores constant Black children actually have an advantage in amount of schooling. In fact, Jencks and associates indicate that, based on the Armed Forces Qualification Test, Blacks with low scores generally have about one more year of schooling than Whites with similar scores. In the case of high scores, Blacks have had about the same amount of schooling as Whites. Thus we find that the overall difference between Black and White educational attainment is much smaller than the difference between Black and White scholastic performance.

Apparently, scholastic performance is a more significant predictor of educational attainment for Whites than for Blacks. Portes and Wilson (1976) point out that the grades Black students receive, especially those from all-Black high schools, tend to be irrelevant as marks of achievement within schools themselves or as criteria for selection for higher education. This is because educational administrators generally discount the value of inner-city or other Black school grades. On the other hand, grades for White students serve as a sign of differential achievement in high school, and they provide a criterion that counts in college admission.

Now that we have considered the overall pattern of racial/ethnic differences in scholastic performance and educational attainment, we will attempt to reach an understanding of why such marked differences in performance exist between minority and majority children. Because most of the data are based on comparisons between Black and White children, we will focus on the factors that may account for the academic-performance decrement in Black children.

Accounting for the Black/White Difference in Scholastic Performance

The fact that Black children on the average score about one standard deviation below White children on intelligence tests would in part contribute to the finding that they also fall below White children on indexes of school achievement. As we noted in Chapter 6, intelligence measures are related to scholastic performance. However, as we also mentioned, other factors need to be considered in relation to school achievement. We will examine personality and motivational variables, family background, school characteristics, and teacher characteristics as they relate to the Black/White difference in school achievement.

Personality and Motivational Variables. Several writers suggest that early socialization in Black homes creates personality and motivational patterns detrimental to school achievement as well as achievement in later life (for example, Ausubel & Ausubel, 1963; McClelland, 1961). In particular, these writers point to the harsh authoritarian child-rearing practices of many Black parents. Such practices weaken the development of achievement strivings and lead to a general resentment towards authority figures. Indeed, teachers in ghetto schools often point to the rebelliousness and lack of interest in school shown by Black children. Illustrative of this is the following impression of a young teacher in a Harlem school (Levy, 1966):

> What impressed me most was the fact that my children (9-10 years old) are already cynical and disillusioned about school, themselves, and life-in-general. They are hostile, rebellious, and bitter. . . . They are hyper-active and are constantly in motion. In many ways they can be compared with wild horses that are suddenly fenced in [pp. 430–431].

This description does not necessarily apply to all predominantly Black schools. Apparently, in less impoverished neighborhoods, teachers complain less about children's open hostility and rebelliousness, and more about their covert withdrawal into apathy, inattention, and laziness (Katz, 1967).

When story-completion measures of *achievement motivation* (that is, the TAT) are administered to Black children, they generally score lower than White children (Allen, 1970). This racial difference holds when social class is controlled. Yet, despite the apparently lower need for achievement among Black children, there is no direct evidence that this Black/White difference in achievement motivation is related to differences in scholastic performance (Katz, 1973)—most likely a reflection of the fact that projective measures don't consistently correlate with achievement (see Chapter 6). Furthermore, although Black children score lower in achievement motivation than White children, the two racial groups do not differ in their level of aspiration. When Black children are asked about their educational and vocational hopes and plans, they generally have aspirations as high as White children (St. John, 1975). It is difficult to reconcile the high aspirations of Black children with their relatively low achievement motivation. It may be that they do not see their own personal efforts to achieve as having much to do with what happens to them in the future, and so they tend not to be motivated to achieve.

While there is some question as to whether or not achievement motivation is related to Black/White differences in scholastic performance, two other personality characteristics do appear to be associated with these differences —locus of control and test anxiety. Recall that *locus of control* refers to the extent to which an individual feels he or she has control over life events. In one study, when Black and White sixth and eighth graders were given a projective picture test of locus of control, White children displayed a greater belief in internal or personal control (Battle & Rotter, 1963). Similarly in the Coleman Report (Coleman et al., 1966), which included a questionnaire measure of locus of control, White children had a greater sense of personal control than Black children. Within each racial group, those children with a greater sense of personal control had better achievement-test performance. A positive relationship between personal control and achievement has also been reported for a sample of Black college students in the South (Gurin, Gurin, Lao, & Beattie, 1969). A belief in personal control, then, is positively associated with school achievement. The finding that Black children generally have less of a belief in their own personal control than do White children may therefore be a contributing factor to the Black/White gap in school achievement. It is not apparent from the research why Black children have a relatively low sense of personal control. It may be that they feel their lives are externally controlled before they enter the school situation, and this feeling adversely affects their academic performance and, as we previously suggested, their motivation to achieve. It is also possible that because they do not perform well in school they develop a sense of external control.

Another factor that may add to the relatively poor school performance of Black children is their tendency to express more test anxiety than Whites (Katz, 1973). Test anxiety refers to anxiety about being evaluated in testing and school situations (see Chapter 6) and is believed to interfere with a student's performance in the classroom. This is illustrated in a study by Katz (1967), which involved a sample of Black boys in a northern urban school. The results revealed that high levels of test anxiety were associated with poor academic performance. Because of the evidence that Black children, as a group, report experiencing more test anxiety than White children, it is reasonable to conclude that test anxiety contributes to the poor performance of Black students. High anxiety about being evaluated in testing and school situations appears to be especially characteristic of lower-class Black children. According to Katz (1973), the lower-class parents' inability to provide encouragement for their children's intellectual efforts produces anxiety before they reach school. Furthermore, Katz suggests that the lower-class Black child probably develops a relatively high expectation of punishment for failure to meet adult demands, which, combined with little parental encouragement, serves to perpetuate his or her anxiety while in school.

In summary, at least two personality characteristics—locus of control and test anxiety—appear to be related to the Black/White differences in school achievement. It is also possible that the relatively lower achievement motivation of Black children may further contribute to these differences.

Family Background. In the Coleman Report (Coleman et al., 1966), several family-background variables were positively associated with achievement-test performance for each racial/ethnic group. These included parents' education, reading material in the home, and items in the home indicating its economic standing. In other words, for each group there was a positive relationship between social class and school achievement. However, racial/ethnic differences still held when social-class indexes were controlled. The White children exceeded the Black children (as well as the Native American, Chicano, and Puerto Rican children) on the achievement measures at each of three social-class levels—low, medium, and high (Mosteller & Moynihan, 1972).

Nevertheless, when children were matched for social class, there was some reduction in the Black/White achievement gap. For instance, at grade six, Black children averaged 2.1 grade levels behind the White children, but with social class controlled, the difference was 1.8 grade levels. To a small extent, then, the fact that Black families are disproportionately represented at the lower-class level does contribute to the overall differences between Black and White children on school achievement indexes.

School Characteristics. It is commonly suggested that while many Blacks receive as much formal schooling as Whites the quality of that schooling is inferior to that which is afforded White children. One way of assessing the quality of schooling is to look at the quantifiable characteristics of the schools themselves, such as facilities and racial composition. To what extent do school characteristics contribute to the Black/White achievement gap? Several kinds of characteristics have been looked at in relation to racial differences in achievement, including school facilities, desegregation, and community control.

An analysis of *school facilities* was included in the Coleman Report. Information on school facilities was obtained from self-administered questionnaires completed by principals and teachers. Contrary to the popular belief that Black children suffer from inferior schools, Coleman and associates (1966) found that for the most part school facilities in majority-Black schools (that is, more than 50% Black) were as adequate as those in majority-White schools. However, the Black children did appear to be at a disadvantage, albeit a slight one, with respect to those facilities most relevant to academic achievement. As Coleman and associates (1966) state:

> Nationally, Negro pupils have fewer of some of the facilities that seem most related to academic achievement: They have less access to physics, chemistry, and language laboratories; there are fewer books per pupil in their libraries; their textbooks are less often in sufficient supply. To the extent that physical facilities are important to learning, such items appear to be more relevant than some others, such as cafeterias, in which minority groups are at an advantage [pp. 9 and 12].

The finding that there were only slight Black/White differences in school facilities was viewed as misleading by many people who reviewed the Coleman Report (Mosteller & Moynihan, 1972). These reviewers pointed out that the Coleman data may have been biased because of (1) failure to determine whether the facilities in Black and White schools were of equal quality and (2) nonresponse and errors in response to the school-facility questionnaires. Such biases could have made the survey results look fairer than the conditions actually were. It does seem reasonable to conclude from the Coleman Report that by the mid-1960s school facilities for Black and White children were probably more comparable than they had been earlier in the century because of the impetus of the 1954 Supreme Court ruling on school desegregation. That is, even in predominantly Black schools, conditions most likely improved between 1954 and 1966—the time covered by the Coleman Report. Such improvements, however, did not appear to have any appreciable effect on enabling Black children to improve their academic performance in relation to White children.

A matter of deep concern for both Blacks and Whites in recent years has been the effect of *school desegregation* on academic performance. In a review of some 60 studies of the relationship between school racial composition and achievement, St. John (1975) concludes that biracial schooling has been neither a demonstrated success nor a demonstrated failure. She points out that desegregation has not closed the Black/White gap in school achievement, though it has rarely lowered and sometimes raised the achievement-test scores of Black children. When improvement is reported for Black children, it more often occurs in the early grades, in mathematical rather than verbal achievement, and in schools that are over 50% White. These gains, however, have often been intermittent and small. The achievement of White children has not been significantly affected in schools that remained mostly White, but it has been lowered in those schools in which Whites are in the minority.

These overall findings of the relation of desegregation and school achievement are not necessarily conclusive. According to St. John, there are several limitations in the desegregation research. Virtually no long-term longitudinal studies (that is, over several years both before and after desegregation has taken place) have been carried out comparing predesegregation and postdesegregation scores on the same tests. Children have generally not been matched with sufficient care on home background and initial ability when entering school. Also, school quality has not been controlled; that is, segregated and integrated schools often differ in physical plant, equipment, program, and the credentials of teachers. St. John observes that the most serious deficiency in desegregation research has been the inattention to the classroom process. The defensiveness of principals and teachers has interfered with a proper assessment of their role in setting the racial climate of schools.

Besides desegregation, other educational changes have been recommended to raise the achievement level of minority children. At least one study implies that the development of *community-controlled schools,* in which parents and local community people acquire power over the conduct of their schools, shows promise. Guttentag (1972) compared a community-controlled school district with a non-community-controlled district, both of which were in predominantly Black residential areas of New York City. The results showed that achievement-test performance (reading and arithmetic) in the community-controlled schools improved over the three-year period of the study. (Ironically, the study had to end because the community-controlled district was phased out.) No comparable improvement in achievement occurred in the non-community-controlled schools. Guttentag attributed the success of the community-controlled school district to its small size, frequent parent/teacher contacts, and unified social ideology.

Unfortunately, the community-control experiment in New York City was phased out because of the political controversy over who should make decisions about educational policy. It remains to be seen whether community control will be implemented in the future, and if so whether it will have a positive effect on the achievement of minority children.

In general, school characteristics, whether we focus on facilities or racial mix, do not appear to appreciably contribute to the achievement difference between Black and White children. This may be due to the greater significance of what takes place in the classroom, and we will now turn our attention to teacher characteristics.

Teacher Characteristics. We shall consider two teacher characteristics—competence and expectations. The Coleman Report dealt with two general areas of *teaching competence* that may be relevant to student achievement—professional background of the teacher and the teacher's own level of verbal achievement (Armor, 1972). With respect to teacher background (for example, holding a Master's degree or higher, undergraduate major in education, and number of years of teaching experience) majority-Black schools showed a slight advantage over majority-White schools. We should note that this teacher-background advantage for Black schools was confined mostly to the South where the majority of teachers were Black. As Armor (1972) points out, if most of these southern Black teachers attended all-Black colleges in the South, where academic quality is reputed to be very low, their background characteristics may not be comparable to those of White teachers or to northern Black teachers.

The verbal-achievement level of teachers in the Coleman Report was assessed by a short test attached to teacher questionnaires. Armor's analysis of these data indicates that the Black schools were substantially behind White schools in teacher verbal achievement. The largest differences occurred in those regions with the largest percent of Black teachers in Black schools (that is, in southern areas and nonmetropolitan Mid-Atlantic and Great Lakes areas). Thus, Black teachers, in comparison with White teachers, score lower on verbal achievement tests, even though their professional credentials are superior to those of White teachers. As Armor suggests, it may be that Black teachers themselves have been "deprived" at some point in their background, though not necessarily by the schools they attended. It does appear that Black children in majority-Black schools are at a disadvantage in terms of the academic achievement level of their teachers. The lower achievement level of teachers in Black schools therefore seems to be a factor which may contribute to the achievement gap between Black and White children.

A study by Murnane (1975), conducted in an inner-city Black elementary school in New Haven, provides further support for the importance of teacher competency in relation to student performance. Those teachers who received relatively high evaluations in teaching performance from their principals had students who scored higher on standardized achievement tests in reading and arithmetic than those students whose teachers received relatively low teaching evaluations. These findings appear to indicate that the classroom skills of the teacher can be a critical factor in the performance level of Black students, and therefore teachers should be a significant resource in raising the school achievement level of Black students.

Considerable attention has been given to the possibility that the *expectations* teachers have about their pupils' academic performance can, in fact, affect the way the pupils perform. For example, Clark (1965) contends that the massive academic failure of ghetto school children is in large part due to the teachers because they generally do not expect their pupils to learn. In other words, teachers' expectancies may result in a "self-fulfilling prophecy" with respect to student performance.

In an influential study, Rosenthal and Jacobson (1968) studied the effect of teacher expectations in the classroom. They experimentally manipulated teachers' expectations by randomly designating 20% of the students in a class as "academic bloomers." The teachers were told that these students would show a considerable increase in IQ during the coming year. The results showed that the "academic bloomers" performed according to expectation. Subsequent attempts to replicate these findings have produced mixed results (Good & Brophy, 1973). Apparently, IQ scores are not as amenable to change by teacher expectations as the orginal study indicated. However, teacher expectations do seem to have a more consistent effect on academic achievement and interactions in the classroom. Studies have shown that teachers who expect certain pupils in their classes to perform well interact more with those pupils and the pupils themselves perform academically at a level consistent with the teachers' expectations (Firestone & Brody, 1975).

Are teacher expectations influenced by the race of the student? Rubovits and Maehr (1973) studied teacher expectations using both Black and White students. The expectations were experimentally induced by providing the teachers with information about the students. The teachers were White female undergraduates enrolled in a teaching-training course. The students were seventh and eighth graders who were randomly selected from within ability groups. Two White students and two Black students from the same ability level were assigned to each teacher. The teacher was given a seating plan that contained each student's first name, IQ score, and a label indicating whether the student had been chosen from the school's gifted program or from the regular ability track. One Black and one White student were randomly assigned high IQs and the label "gifted"; the other two students were given average IQs and the label "nongifted." The interaction between the teacher and students was observed for a 40-minute session. The results showed that the teachers gave the statements made by Black children less attention, less praise, and more criticism than the statements made by White children. Furthermore, the expectations affected the behavior of teachers in different ways depending upon the race of the student. Among White students those who were identified as "gifted" received more attention and praise from the teachers than those who were identified as "nongifted." On the other hand, among Black students those who were labeled "gifted" received less attention and praise from the teachers than those who were labeled "nongifted."

It is difficult to generalize from this study because of the relatively artificial classroom situation and the inexperience of the teachers. In fact, it is by no means clear that White teachers discriminate against Black pupils by offering them less encouragement and attention than they provide for White students. Byalick and Bersoff (1974) reported that White teachers in several southern elementary schools praised and encouraged Black male students more than White male students and treated female students of both races equivalently.

There is also evidence that suggests that Black teachers have different expectations for Black children depending on the social-class level of the children. In a Black-neighborhood school staffed by Black teachers, Rist (1970) found that family-background factors were related to the teacher's assignment of children in a kindergarten class to one of two ability groups—"slow learners" and "fast learners." The parents of "fast learners" had more formal education and higher incomes than the parents of "slow learners." Classroom observations revealed that the teacher spent more time with the "fast learners," and these children made better progress than the "slow learners" in their reading-readiness material. When the children were followed up in the first and second grades, most were assigned to the same ability groups as in kindergarten because the higher-ability groups did better on reading achievement tests. In the second grade, each ability group read different material, and reading was a group rather than an individual activity. What is significant is that no matter how well a child in the low-ability group read he or she was destined to remain in the same ability track. This study suggests that a social-class bias may operate in ghetto schools, so that those children who come from the poorest families are most likely to be labeled by teachers as poor learners when they first start school, and this label will serve as a continuing restraint to their academic progress. However, we must be cautious in generalizing the results of this study because it is based on only one classroom group of children. Also, teacher social-class biases are not limited to Black classrooms—they also show up in predominantly White classrooms (Friedman, 1976).

In general, the evidence indicates that if teachers have low expectations concerning the performance of certain pupils they tend to give those pupils less attention and less encouragement than they give to pupils they consider to be of high ability. There is some suggestion that teacher expectations are influenced by the race and social class of students, with the consequence that less may be expected of Black students than of White students, and within each racial group less will be expected of children from impoverished families than children from more economically advantaged families. It appears as though the relative lack of teacher encouragement that Black and poor children may receive would adversely affect their academic performance.

Conclusions. The fact that Black children as a group perform academically below the level of White children seems to be due to several factors. First of all, Black children score significantly below White children on intelligence tests, and this contributes to the comparable Black/White difference on indexes of school achievement. Second, Black children generally come from homes that are at a lower social-class level than is the case for White children. As we noted in Chapter 12, social class is positively associated with academic performance. However, when social class is controlled the performance of Black children still falls below that of White children, though the gap is reduced to some extent. The personality characteristics of the children also appear to be related to the Black/White achievement difference. Black children, in comparison with White children, have less of a sense of personal control and more anxiety in testing and school situations—both of which seem to place Black children at a disadvantage in school.

School facilities and racial makeup do not appear to be appreciably related to the achievement difference between Blacks and Whites. On the other hand, the opportunity for Black parents and local community people to have some share in educational policy making may be a factor that could reduce the racial gap in achievement. In fact, the issue of community control may be important when considering desegregation. As St. John (1975) observes:

> A segregated school is . . . not necessarily a symbol of powerlessness, nor is a desegregated school a symbol of powerlessness denied. The essential condi-

tion appears to be self-determination and share in educational decision-making, both on an individual and a community level. The black child who attends a racially mixed school would especially benefit . . . if desegregation were voluntary or achieved through community effort, . . . or if it led to political gains in the control of the mixed school. On the other hand if a black community achieved control of its local school and managed it successfully, and if parents consciously chose that school over an equally available desegregated one, their children might experience a greater sense of power than former classmates who fled the ghetto [pp. 91–92].

Finally, teacher characteristics, including competency and expectations, appear to be important. While there is much debate about the characteristics of the schools Black children attend, it may be more critical to focus on what is happening in the classroom between the teacher and the students.

We should also note that the Black/White gap in school achievement cannot be viewed independently from the racial climate in our society. The fact is, as Pettigrew and Green (1976) point out, residential racial segregation is so massive that school desegregation could have at best a relatively small impact. Furthermore, what are the opportunities for occupational achievement that Black children can look forward to? Let's move on to consider this.

Occupational Achievement

It should come as no surprise to learn that Blacks do not enjoy as high a level of occupational status as Whites. This conclusion has been documented by Duncan, Featherman, and Duncan (1972) in their analysis of U.S. Census information. What is especially noteworthy is that this racial difference holds when social-class background is controlled. Duncan and his associates (1972) state: "For any given level of occupational origin (father's occupation), the black man is less likely to move into a high status occupation than is a white man with the same level of origin" [p. 55]. Thus rather distinct patterns of mobility between generations are present in the two populations. If White men come from low origins, they typically tend to move up to higher status jobs; given high origins they tend to remain at high occupational levels. In contrast, for Blacks, men with low origins tend to remain at low occupational levels, whereas those few with high origins tend to fall to low status jobs.

Not only is there a racial gap in occupational status; Duncan and associates report a discrepancy in income when occupational status is held constant. Based on 1962 statistics Black men earned about 38% less than White men "in the same line of work, with the same amount of education, the same number of siblings, and the same family socioeconomic background" (Duncan et al., 1972, p. 61). Moreover, the income differentials between Blacks and Whites have remained fairly large over a period of years—the average Black income during the decade of the 1960s was about 55% of the average White income (Farley & Hermalin, 1972). As we mentioned in our discussion of racial differences in intelligence, the occupational gap between Blacks and Whites continues to be large. However, the fact that Black educational attainment is approaching that of Whites in recent years is a promising sign that the Black/White occupational discrepancy will be decreased. In fact, starting around 1970 and continuing into the mid-1970s (the most recent data available) there has been something of a reduction in the income differential between racial groups, so that the average Black income in the mid-1970s was about 65% of the average White income (Smith & Welch, 1978).

Yet, until discrimination against Blacks in residential, occupational, and economic spheres is markedly reduced, and eventually eradicated, it is difficult to accomplish an equality of educational opportunity for Black and White children. With limited social and economic opportunities, what is there to motivate the Black child in school and to encourage the Black parent about the future of his or her child?

PERSONALITY

Most of the research on racial/ethnic differences in personality has been restricted to comparisons between Blacks and Whites. We have already considered those personality variables related to Black/White differences in school achievement—that is, achievement motivation, locus of control, and test anxiety. We will now consider whether Blacks and Whites differ with respect to aggression, self-concept, and mental health. We will also examine the relationship between Black family characteristics and Black personality patterns.

Aggression

The ghetto riots of the 1960s undoubtedly alerted White Americans to the deep anger or "rage" of Blacks. Indeed for many Whites the riots may have modified their myths of the "happy nigger" (Baughman, 1971). Historically, Blacks have been extremely hesitant to convert feelings of anger into overt acts of aggression against their White oppressors. The reason for this block against overt aggression has been the realistic fear of White counteraggression. For example, Blacks in the South prior to World War II were confronted with the pervasive threat of lynching by Whites (Hovland & Sears, 1940). While the danger of White retaliation in present-day American society has abated, it has not been eliminated completely. As Baughman (1971) observed in the early 1970s: "Economic reprisals against the 'uppity nigger' are still quite common, for example, and the Black Panther believes that it may not take much provocation—if any at all—for certain policemen to eliminate him as a threat" (p. 57).

Channeling Black Aggression. How do Blacks cope with their anger towards Whites? Hortense Powdermaker (1943), an anthropologist, has described various ways in which Blacks channel their aggressive impulses. Of course, over the three decades since Powdermaker's publication, there has been a change in emphasis on some of these forms of expressing aggression.

The most obvious way for Blacks to express their aggression is to attack the White oppressor. As previously noted, Blacks historically had generally rejected the idea of attacking Whites because they feared White retaliation. Within recent years, however, Blacks' attitudes toward the use of aggression against Whites has varied. In a survey conducted shortly after the Watts riot, Sears and McConahay (1970) found that those who were more active in the riot tended to be young, disaffected politically, and to have high economic aspirations and expectations. Similarly, in a study of Black youths carried out shortly after the 1967 Detroit riot, Forward and Williams (1970) found that persons who reacted most favorably to the riot were those who were most confident of their own ability to shape their future (a high sense of personal control) and simultaneously were most aware of the extensive racial discrimination preventing Black people from achieving their goals. The results of these two studies suggest that Black militancy is highest among those who feel their opportunities are blocked under current societal conditions.

Rather than attacking Whites and running the risk of counteraggression, Blacks may displace their aggression toward other Blacks. This displacement may account in part for the fact that the homicide rate for Blacks against Blacks is much higher than it is for Blacks against Whites (Pettigrew, 1964). Experimental evidence of a displacement of aggression to fellow Blacks is provided by Katz, Robinson, Epps, and Waly (1964). Black male high school students were informally given a questionnaire measure of aggression by a Black adult; the test was disguised as a measure of concept formation. The test was given again at a later time either by a White or a Black adult who described the test either neutrally or as an intelligence test. It was predicted that the intelligence-test instructions, but not the neutral instructions, would arouse hostility toward an adult authority figure because Black students generally expect an unfavorable evaluation in ability-testing situations. Under the neutral conditions, average scores in both the White-tester and Black-tester groups remained the same. However, with intelligence-test instructions the aggression scores increased when the experimenter was Black and decreased when the experimenter was White. These results indicate that once hostile reactions were aroused they could only be safely expressed with the Black experimenter.

A third behavior tactic for Blacks is to avoid contact with Whites. Although it would be difficult to achieve, some Blacks have worked toward the creation of a separate Black society. Such endeavors have included the back-to-Africa movements and the goal of establishing a Black nation within the United States. A survey conducted in a northern city indicated that Blacks who favored separatism tended to be more alienated, fearful of race genocide, race conscious, and supportive of racial violence than those who endorsed interracial cooperation (Turner & Wilson, 1976).

Powdermaker also refers to three other modes of channeling interracial aggression. Blacks may discharge some of their hostility through wit or humor, and a study by Prange and Vitols (1963) showed that a high proportion of jokes told by Blacks to Blacks referred to race relations. Blacks may also "identify with the oppressor," but with the recent rise in Black pride such identification is probably less common than in the past. Finally, Blacks may behave in ways that Whites have traditionally expected of Blacks—that is, as a "good nigger." Grier and Cobbs (1968), two Black psychiatrists, describe this role in their book, *Black Rage:*

> Granting the limitations of stereotypes, we should nevertheless like to sketch a paradigmatic black man. His characteristics seem so connected to employment that we call it "the postal-clerk syndrome." This man is always described as "nice" by white people. In whatever integrated setting he works, he is the standard against whom other blacks are measured. "If they were all only like him, everything would be so much better." He is passive, nonassertive, and nonaggressive. He has made a virtue of identification with the aggressor, and he has adopted an ingratiating and compliant manner. In public his thoughts and feelings are consciously shaped in the direction he thinks white people want them to be. The pattern begins in childhood when the mother may actually say: "You must be this way because this is the only way you will get along with Mr. Charlie."
>
> This man renounces gratifications that are available to others. He assumes a deferential mask. He is always submissive. He must figure out "the man" but keep "the man" from deciphering him. He is prevalent in the middle and upper-middle classes, but is found throughout the social structure. The more closely allied to the white man, the more complete the picture becomes. He is a direct lineal descendant of the "house nigger" who was designed to identify totally with the white master. The danger he poses to himself and others is great, but only the surface of passivity and compliance is visible. The storm below is hidden [pp. 66–67].[5]

The "postal-clerk syndrome" may be the result of socialization practices directed toward the inhibition of aggression (Baughman, 1971).

Black/White Differences. While Blacks express interracial hostility in a variety of ways, they may not be more aggressive than Whites. Evidence on Black/White comparisons of aggression is limited, except for a few studies with children involving projective or questionnaire measures of aggression. Hammer (1953) used a sample of 400 elementary school children who were asked to draw a house, a tree, and a person (the H-T-P test). The results showed that the mean aggression score on the test was significantly higher for Blacks than for Whites. However, the way in which children perform on projective measures, such as drawings, can be influenced by their level of ability. Hammer in his study did not match the Black and White children for IQ nor did he match them for social class, and it is therefore possible that the racial differences in aggression scores could have been due to the intellectual and socioeconomic differences between the two groups (Kuhlman & Bieliauskas, 1976). A more recent study by Baughman and Dahlstrom (1968) involved a projective story-telling measure of aggression and controlled for intelligence though not

---

[5]This and all other quotations from this source are from *Black Rage*, by W. H. Grier and P. M. Cobbs. © 1968 by William H. Grier and Price M. Cobbs. Reprinted by permission of Basic Books, Inc., Publishers, New York, and Jonathan Cape Ltd., London.

social class. No significant differences in aggression were found between Black and White children.

Shaw (1974) used a self-image questionnaire of hostility with Black and White elementary school children. Results showed that Blacks saw themselves as more hostile than did Whites. Shaw indicates that the Blacks were generally disadvantaged and the Whites were generally advantaged, so it is not clear whether the differences in perceived hostility reflected race or social class. Thus, at least based on projective and questionnaire measures, there does not seem to be any conclusive evidence that Black and White children differ in aggression.

The only other available evidence on Black/White differences in aggression resides in the statistics on aggressive crime rates. For crimes of violence, including homicide and aggravated assault, Blacks are disproportionately represented as both offenders and victims (Coleman, 1976; Uniform Crime Reports, 1976). However, these comparisons are certainly confounded to some extent with social-class differences. Compared with White Americans, Blacks are concentrated in those social sectors that exhibit high crime rates regardless of race—they are disproportionately represented among those who are lower class, slum residents, victims of severe family disorganization, young, and unemployed (Coleman, 1976; Pettigrew, 1964).

Adjustment

We might well expect that Blacks in the United States, because of their status as a subjugated minority, would bear a "mark of oppression" (Kardiner & Ovesey, 1951) in terms of a negative concept of self and a high incidence of psychiatric disorders. As Pettigrew (1964) observes:

> The ubiquity of racial prejudice in the United States guarantees that virtually every Negro American faces at some level the impersonal effects of discrimination, the frightening feeling of being a black man in what often appears to him to be a white man's world [p. 3].

One apparent reflection of the effects of racial status is the finding, based on national surveys, that Black adults when compared with White adults are less satisfied with their condition of life, including their place of residence, family life, friendships, and activities (Clemente & Sauer, 1976; Robinson & Shaver, 1970). This difference is revealed even when social class is controlled. Let's go on to consider how Blacks and Whites compare with respect to self-concept and mental health.

Self-Concept. That many Blacks have negative self-concepts is a commonly held notion (Baughman, 1971). Evidence in support of this view is found in a series of studies, carried out several decades ago, of the racial preferences of Black children (for example, Clark & Clark, 1947; Horowitz, 1939; Landreth & Johnson, 1953). The Clarks' study showed that samples of northern and southern Black children (aged 3 to 7) preferred White dolls and rejected Black dolls when asked to choose which were nice, which looked bad, which they would like to play with, and which were a nice color. The studies that included Black and White children indicated both groups prefer White dolls. The preference for White expressed by Black and White children also was indicated when other materials were used, such as puppets and pictures.

More recent studies, however, show that Black children express a greater degree of same-race preference than was characteristic of the earlier research (Brand, Ruiz, & Padilla, 1974). In fact, several recent replications of the Clarks' doll preference study indicate that a majority of Black children prefer Black dolls (Gregor & McPherson, 1966; Guttentag, 1972; Hraba & Grant, 1970), although one study with Canadian Black children still found the White preference (Crooks, 1970). This trend toward same-race preference in all likelihood reflects the changing climate of Black pride—Black children of today are growing up with the sense that "Black is beautiful."

Were the earlier findings of a White preference by Black children really indicative of a negative self-concept? Brand and associates (1974), in their review of the racial preference research, conclude that it is not at all clear that race was the critical stimulus eliciting choice behavior. Black dolls, puppets, and pictures may have differed from White stimuli on several dimensions, such as cleanliness, attractiveness, and novelty. In fact, one study using photographs has shown that children's preferences are based more on the cleanliness than the race of the child pictured (Epstein, Krupat, & Obudho, 1976). Also, Black children are now probably more familiar with Black dolls and other Black representational materials than were previous generations of Black children. While the current climate of Black pride serves as a salient reinforcer for a positive self-concept, it is not known if Blacks maintained a negative self-concept before Black pride emerged. Perhaps being Black is advantageous as far as self-esteem is concerned (Baughman, 1971). The discrimination that Blacks have endured enables a Black person to attribute his or her frustrations and failure to external sources rather than to perceive them as personal deficiencies.

Mental Health. For the most part, poor mental health is more common among Blacks than Whites. Studies of admissions to public hospitals generally show that incidence rates for psychosis are much greater for Blacks than for Whites (Pettigrew, 1964; Warheit, Holzer, & Arey, 1975). Schizophrenia is especially frequent among Black admissions. Two organic disorders, paresis (a consequence of syphilis) and alcoholic psychosis, are also overrepresented among Blacks. However, since Whites can better afford private treatment, data from public institutions underestimate the incidence of White psychoses. Personality measures of psychotic symptoms also show racial differences. Blacks score significantly higher on the Schizophrenia and Paranoia scales of the Minnesota Multiphasic Personality Inventory (MMPI) (Davis & Jones, 1974; Gynther, 1972).

With respect to neurotic symptoms, the evidence on racial differences is less consistent than it is for the psychoses. On the MMPI scales assessing neurotic patterns, such as hysteria, hypochondriasis, and depression, the results of some studies reveal that Blacks score higher than Whites, but in other studies the reverse is true (Davis & Jones, 1974; Gynther, 1972). However, a recent large-scale survey conducted in the South did show that Blacks consistently scored higher than Whites on several scales of neurotic symptoms, including phobic reactions, anxiety, and depression (Warheit et al., 1975). Racial differences have also been reported for the psychosomatic disorder of high blood pressure or "hypertension." The incidence of hypertension is about twice as high among Blacks as it is among Whites (Coleman, 1976).

There is one pathological pattern that has shown a higher incidence rate for Whites than for Blacks—suicide. Whites (especially males; see Chapter 10) commit suicide far more frequently than Blacks (Pettigrew, 1964). The relatively low suicide rate for Blacks has been interpreted as a reflection of the fact that Blacks express their violence outwardly, as exemplified by their high homicide rate. However, the Black/White difference in the incidence of suicide appears to be changing. Coleman (1976) reports that in recent years there has been a marked increase in the suicide rate among Black youths. This group also has a high homicide rate, so, at least for Black youths, it no longer seems to be true that homicide and suicide are inversely related to each other.

What accounts for the Black/White differences in psychopathology? There seem to be two major explanatory factors—social-class differences between the two racial groups and cultural norms indigenous to each group. Let's first consider social class. Recall from Chapter 12 that poor mental health is associated with low social status. The disproportionate representation of Blacks at the lower levels of the social hierarchy would, therefore, appear to be a contributing factor to the racial differences in psychopathology. In fact, in the survey study of neurotic symptoms by Warheit and associates (1975), Black/White differences were largely nonsignificant when social-status indexes were controlled. Another instance of the influence of social class on racial differences in mental health is the suggestion that Blacks suffer more from hypertension than do Whites because of the stresses of ghetto life as well as dietary factors (which in themselves reflect social-class factors) (Coleman, 1976).

However, social class does not appear to completely account for the racial differences. In studies of Black and White performance on the MMPI, Blacks scored higher on many of the scales, especially Schizophrenia, when social class was controlled (Costello, Tiffany, & Gier, 1972; Davis & Jones, 1974). The fact that, at least in some instances, racial differences persist when social class is controlled raises the possibility that psychopathology among Blacks is in part caused by other factors, such as gene-based predispositions or norms and life experiences that are associated with being the object of racial discrimination. Indeed, with respect to racial discrimination, Gynther (1972) believes that Blacks present more pathological appearing MMPI patterns because they feel alienated from the established White society and because they have learned to be suspicious of others as a way of insuring their survival. These pathological tendencies on the MMPI, however, appear to be more characteristic of poorly educated than of well educated Blacks (Davis & Jones, 1974). In other words, it is the particularly disadvantaged Black who must cope with the stresses of racial discrimination, and who therefore needs to develop "adaptive devices" in order to survive. Grier and Cobbs (1968) provide several examples of the adaptive devices that Blacks have learned to use:

> We submit that it is necessary for a black man in America to develop a profound distrust of his white fellow citizens and of the nation. He must be on guard to protect himself against physical hurt. He must cushion himself against cheating, slander, humiliation, and outright mistreatment by the official representatives of society. If he does not so protect himself, he will live a life of such pain and shock as to find life itself unbearable. For his own survival, then, he must develop a *cultural paranoia* in which every white man is a potential enemy unless proved otherwise and every social system is set against him unless he personally finds out differently.
>
> Every black man in America has suffered such injury as to be realistically sad about the hurt done him. He must, however, live in spite of the hurt and so he learns to know his tormentor exceedingly well. He develops a sadness and intimacy with misery which has become a characteristic of black Americans. It is a *cultural depression* and a *cultural masochism*.
>
> He can never quite respect laws which have no respect for him and laws designed to protect white men are viewed as white men's laws. To break another man's law may be inconvenient if one is caught and punished, but it can never have the moral consequences involved in breaking one's own law. The result may be described as a *cultural antisocialism*, but it is simply an accurate reading of one's environment—a gift black people have developed to a high degree, to keep alive.
>
> These and related traits are simply adaptive devices developed in response to a peculiar environment. They are no more pathological than the compulsive manner in which a diver checks his equipment before a dive or a pilot his parachute. They represent normal devices for "making it" in America and clinicians who are interested in the psychological functioning of black people must get acquainted with this body of character traits which we call the *Black Norm*. It is a normal complement of psychological devices, and to find the amount of sickness a black man has, one must first total all that appears to represent illness and then subtract the Black Norm. What remains is illness and a proper subject for therapeutic endeavor. To regard the Black Norm as pathological and attempt to remove such traits by treatment would be akin to analyzing away a hunter's cunning or a banker's prudence. This is a body of characteristics essential to life for black men in America and woe be unto that therapist who does not recognize it [pp. 177–179].

Thus, recognition of existence in a hostile environment is paramount to objective assessment of Black pathology, and according to Grier and Cobbs, those treating pathological behaviors in Blacks must be cognizant of the special problems facing Blacks.

In conclusion, the higher incidence of psychiatric symptoms among Blacks than among Whites is due in part to the lower social-class level of Blacks and in part to the life experiences of Blacks that make it necessary for them to develop various adaptive mechanisms.

Black Family Characteristics and Personality

Historically, the family characteristics of Blacks in America have been quite different from those of Whites. The stability of the White American family was unknown to the great majority of Blacks during slavery (Frazier, 1939). In more recent times, Black families had to cope with the stress of migrating from the rural South to the very different environment of the urban North. Once settled in urban centers, Black family stability suffered because Black women could get employment while their husbands frequently could not (Ten-Houten, 1970).

Baughman (1971) has summarized the evidence on the distinguishing characteristics of Black family structure. He points out that Black family life has been especially vulnerable to urbanization. Evidently, disorganization among Black families is much more prevalent in urban than in rural areas. Also the Black child is more likely to be socialized in a much larger family than is the White child. Among Black families, the number of children is inversely correlated with family income; thus, available monetary resources are very small for training and educating the typical Black child. Furthermore, Black children are more likely to grow up in extended families than are White children. Often, extended family members are relatives, but the Black household may also frequently include nonrelatives, such as roomers or boarders. Hence, the extended family may have a changeable composition adding uncertainty to the child's home environment. The extended family situation may mean that the child's socialization is affected by individuals who are less committed to adequate child rearing than the typical parent.

A particularly critical aspect of Black families, especially those in urban settings, is the high incidence of father absence. Census data show that at any given time approximately one-fourth of Black families are without a male head, and this rate is almost three times that found in the White community. However, according to TenHouten (1970), when social class is controlled the Black/White difference is much smaller. Among low-income families the percentage of female-headed families is 47 for Blacks and 38 for Whites; among middle- and high-income families the percentage is 8 for Blacks and 4 for Whites. As these figures indicate, father absence is much more prevalent among lower-class families, regardless of race.

A commonly held belief is that the Black family is a matriarchy—that is, a family in which the wife plays the dominant role. This is seen as a psychologically unhealthy situation because it implies that the Black male is emasculated. For example, in a widely publicized report on the Black family, sponsored by the U.S. Department of Labor, Daniel P. Moynihan (1965) observed:

> The Negro community has been forced into a matriarchal structure which, because it is so out of line with the rest of American society, seriously retards the progress of the group as a whole, and imposes a crushing burden on the Negro male [p. 29].

In actuality, there does not appear to be any convincing evidence that the Black family can be characterized as a matriarchy, either in fatherless families or in intact families. In the former case, there is no evidence indicating that those Black men who leave their wives do so because they cannot play a dominant role in the family (TenHouten, 1970). With respect to intact families research shows that Black children do not view their fathers as any less dominant in the family than do White children (Baughman, 1971).

Thus the major differences that emerge between Black and White families are the larger size of Black families (that is, number of children and number of extended family members) and the higher incidence of father absence among Black families. There has been considerable research, mostly with White children, on the effects of father absence (Hunt & Hunt, 1975). Studies with White children generally show that, compared with children from intact families, father-absent children, especially boys, have impaired sex-role identification, academic difficulties in school, and low achievement aspirations. On the other hand, research with Black children suggests that father absence may not be detrimental. Kandel (1971) found that father absence was unrelated to the level of school performance among Black high school students. In this study, the lack of a relationship between father absence and school performance also held for White high school students. Hunt and Hunt (1975) studied Black and White male adolescents and reported that father absence had detrimental effects only for the White boys. Among Whites, the father-absent boys had lower self-reported school grades, lower educational aspirations, and lower self-esteem than boys from intact families. In contrast, among Blacks no differences were found between boys whose fathers were absent and those whose fathers were present. These racial differences were also generally revealed within each of three social-class levels—lower, working, and middle.

The results of the research on father absence suggest that for the most part Black children are less affected by family characteristics than are White children. According to Hunt and Hunt (1975), because societal barriers to the attainment of success goals are so pronounced for Blacks, family variation—especially with respect to the father/son connection—has relatively little impact on Black children. Apparently, as for future goals, it matters little for the Black boy whether or not his father is at home. His chances of becoming an economic success are limited by the racism and oppression he perceives and experiences in society. In contrast, the White boy cannot easily identify barriers to success outside of the family. If his father is not at home, he may feel deprived of having a model of successful achievement with whom he can identify.

That societal obstacles, rather than family socialization, are the major problem facing Blacks is also expressed by Liebow (1967). Based on a study of lower-class Black males, he concludes that it is the experiences outside the family—in the spheres of school and work—that lead to difficulties. In particular, it is the poverty wage attached to available jobs that makes it virtually impossible to assume the family provider role. Thus, according to Liebow, family instability and identity problems are not the cause of the Black male's problems; rather, they are the consequence of trying to achieve success in a racially stratified society.

SUMMARY

The concept of race in the social sciences customarily refers to racial identification, while in the biological sciences, races are customarily considered as biological subspecies, defined by gene frequencies. Different racial groups have developed as a result of genetic drift, natural selection, and migration. For the most part, genetic differences among modern races are relatively small. However, for a minority of biological characteristics, different racial populations have markedly different distributions of gene frequencies. Such characteristics include skin color, physical appearance, and some blood-group systems. In the United States, racial mixture exists to a considerable degree, and the way in which an individual is racially categorized is usually based on a social definition. Since race and social class in the United States are highly correlated, racial differences are in many instances largely due to social-class differences.

In comparisons of Black and White groups on tests of general intelligence, Blacks average about one standard deviation below Whites. Explanation of racial differences in intelligence must be tentative because relevant evidence is limited. Evidence does not support the marked contribution of genetic factors to the average Black/White IQ difference nor to Black/White differences in specific abilities, such as spatial ability. If future evidence strongly points to genetic factors underlying racial IQ differences, the IQ gap could still be reduced by environmental intervention. Research findings on interracial adoption, interracial mating, and temporal changes in IQ suggest that environmental factors can reduce the Black/White IQ gap. Evaluations of compensatory education, however, indicate the difficulty of achieving lasting effects on measured intelligence. Such studies suggest that very marked environmental changes need to be introduced in order to achieve significant results. In addition to hereditary and environmental influences, test bias is a factor to be considered in accounting for racial/ethnic differences in intelligence. There is some suggestion that test content is biased against minority-group individuals. While differences in measured intelligence exist between racial/ethnic groups, differences among individuals within these groups greatly exceed the average between-group differences.

In comparisons of achievement-test performance, the average scores attained by Black children are significantly below the average scores attained by White children. Several factors appear to contribute to the Black/White gap in school achievement. Family background is one factor because Black children generally come from homes that are at a lower social-class level than is the case for White children. However, when social class is controlled, Black children still fall below White children, though the gap is reduced to some extent. The personal characteristics of the children also contribute to the Black/White achievement difference. Black children, in comparison with White children, have less of a feeling of personal control, more anxiety in testing and school situations, and as we previously mentioned, lower IQ scores—all of which seem to place Black children at a disadvantage in school achievement.

The characteristics of schools, such as facilities and racial composition, do not appear to be appreciably related to racial achievement differences; however, teacher characteristics, including competency and expectations, appear to be important. A Black/White gap also exists in the area of occupational achievement. Blacks on the average do not have as high a level of occupational status as Whites, and within occupational-status levels Blacks have lower income levels.

Evidence on Black/White differences in aggression is very limited. Based on projective and questionnaire measures there does not seem to be any conclusive evidence that Black and White children differ in aggression. Statistics on crimes involving aggression show much higher rates for Blacks, but these high rates reflect to a considerable extent the fact that Blacks are concentrated in those social sectors with high crime rates regardless of race—they are disproportionately represented among those who are lower class, slum residents, victims of severe family disorganization, young, and unemployed. That Blacks have a negative self-concept has been commonly believed. However, with the new attitude of Black pride, recent studies of racial preference show no evidence of negative self-concept. Methodological problems in studies of racial preferences have also raised questions concerning a negative self-concept among Black children before the days of Black pride. Indications of psychopathology are generally more common among Blacks than Whites. The higher incidence rate for Blacks is not clearly independent of social class, and pathological symptoms among Blacks may be due in part to the experiences of a hostile social environment. Because of historical factors, the family characteristics of Blacks have differed from those of Whites. The major differences between Black and White families are the larger size of Black families and the higher incidence of father absence among Black families. However, father absence appears to have more detrimental effects for White children than for Black children.

REFERENCES

Allen, V. L. Personality correlates of poverty. In V. L. Allen (Ed.), *Psychological factors in poverty*. New York: Academic Press, 1970.

Armor, D. J. School and family effects on black and white achievement: A reexamination of the USOE data. In F. Mosteller & D. P. Moynihan (Eds.), *On equality of educational opportunity*. New York: Random House, 1972.

Ausubel, D. P., & Ausubel, P. Ego development among segregated Negro children. In A. H. Passow (Ed.), *Education in depressed areas*. New York: Bureau of Publications, Teachers College, Columbia University, 1963.

Backman, M. E. Patterns of mental abilities: Ethnic, socioeconomic, and sex differences. *American Educational Research Journal*, 1972, *9*, 1–12.

Battle, E., & Rotter, J. B. Children's feelings of personal control as related to social class and ethnic group. *Journal of Personality*, 1963, *31*, 482–490.

Baughman, E. E. *Black Americans: A psychological analysis*. New York: Academic Press, 1971.

Baughman, E. E., & Dahlstrom, W. G. *Negro and white children: A psychological study in the rural South.* New York: Academic Press, 1968.

Bean, R. B. The Negro brain. *Century Magazine,* October 1906, pp. 778–784. Reprinted in I. A. Newby (Ed.), *The development of segregationist thought.* Homewood, Ill.: Dorsey Press, 1968.

Bodmer, W. F. Race and IQ: The genetic background. In K. Richardson, D. Spears, & M. Richards (Eds.), *Race, culture, and intelligence.* Baltimore: Penguin, 1972.

Boyd, W. C. Genetics and the human race. *Science,* 1963, *140,* 1057–1064.

Brand, E. S., Ruiz, R. A., & Padilla, A. M. Ethnic identification and preference: A review. *Psychological Bulletin,* 1974, *81,* 860–890.

Brody, E. B., & Brody, N. *Intelligence: Nature, determinants, and consequences.* New York: Academic Press, 1976.

Bronfenbrenner, U. Is early intervention effective? Some studies of early education in familial and extra-familial settings. In A. Montagu (Ed.), *Race and IQ.* New York: Oxford University Press, 1975.

Byalick, R., & Bersoff, D. Reinforcement practices of black and white teachers in integrated classrooms. *Journal of Educational Psychology,* 1974, *66,* 473–480.

Cavalli-Sforza, L. L., & Bodmer, W. F. *The genetics of human populations.* San Francisco: Freeman, 1971.

Clark, K. B. *Dark ghetto.* New York: Harper & Row, 1965.

Clark, K. B., & Clark, M. P. Racial identification and preference in Negro children. In T. M. Newcomb & E. L. Hartley (Eds.), *Readings in social psychology.* New York: Holt, 1947.

Cleary, T. A., Humphreys, L. G., Kendrick, S. A., & Wesman, A. Educational uses of tests with disadvantaged students. *American Psychologist,* 1975, *30,* 15–41.

Clemente, F., & Sauer, W. J. Life satisfaction in the United States. *Social Forces,* 1976, *54,* 621–631.

Coleman, J. C. *Abnormal psychology and modern life* (5th ed.). Glenview, Ill.: Scott Foresman, 1976.

Coleman, J. S., Campbell, E. Q., Hobson, C. J., McPartland, J., Mood, A. M., Weinfeld, F. D., & York, R. L. *Equality of educational opportunity.* Washington, D.C.: U.S. Office of Education, 1966.

Costello, R. M., Tiffany, D. W., & Gier, R. H. Methodological issues and racial (black-white) comparisons on the MMPI. *Journal of Consulting and Clinical Psychology,* 1972, *38,* 161–168.

Crooks, R. C. The effects of an interracial preschool program upon racial preference, knowledge of racial differences, and racial identification. *Journal of Social Issues,* 1970, *26*(4), 137–144.

Davie, M. R. *Negroes in American society.* New York: McGraw-Hill, 1949.

Davis, W. E., & Jones, M. H. Negro versus Caucasian psychological test performance revisited. *Journal of Consulting and Clinical Psychology,* 1974, *42,* 675–679.

Deutsch, M. Minority group and class status as related to social and personality factors in scholastic achievement. *Monograph of the Society for Applied Anthropology,* 1960, No. 2, 1–32.

Dreger, R. M., & Miller, K. S. Comparative psychological studies of Negroes and whites in the United States. *Psychological Bulletin,* 1960, *57,* 361–402.

Dreger, R. M., & Miller, K. S. Comparative psychological studies of Negroes and whites in the United States: 1959-1965. *Psychological Bulletin Monograph Supplement,* 1968, *70*(3, pt. 2).

Duncan, O. D. Ability and achievement. *Eugenics Quarterly,* 1968, *15,* 1–11.

Duncan, O. D., Featherman, D. L., & Duncan, B. *Socioeconomic background and achievement.* New York: Seminar Press, 1972.

Epstein, Y. M., Krupat, E., & Obudho, C. Clean is beautiful: Identification and preference as a function of race and cleanliness. *Journal of Social Issues,* 1976, *32*(2), 109–118.

Eyferth, K. Leistungen verschiedener Gruppen von Besatzungskindern in Hamburg-Wechsler Intelligenztest für Kinder (HAWIK). *Archiv für die gesamte Psychologie,* 1961, *113,* 222–241.

Farley, R., & Hermalin, A. The 1960s: A decade of progress for blacks? *Demography,* 1972, *9*(3), 353–370.

Firestone, R., & Brody, N. Longitudinal investigation of teacher-student interactions and their relationship to academic performance. *Journal of Educational Psychology,* 1975, *67,* 544–550.

Forrester, B. J., & Klaus, R. A. The effect of race of the examiner on intelligence test scores of Negro kindergarten children. *Peabody Papers in Human Development,* 1964, *2*(7), 1–7.

Forward, J. R., & Williams, J. R. Internal-external control and black militancy. *Journal of Social Issues,* 1970, *26*(1), 75–92.

Frazier, E. F. *The Negro family in the United States.* Chicago: University of Chicago Press, 1939.

Friedman, P. Comparisons of teacher reinforcement schedules for students with different social class backgrounds. *Journal of Educational Psychology,* 1976, *68,* 286–292.

Glass, B. On the unlikelihood of significant admixture of genes from the North American Indians in the present composition of the Negroes of the United States. *American Journal of Human Genetics,* 1955, *7,* 368–385.

Goffeney, B., Henderson, N. B., & Butler, B. V. Negro-white, male-female eight-month developmental scores compared with seven-year WISC and Bender test scores. *Child Development,* 1971, *42,* 595–604.

Good, T. L., & Brophy, J. E. *Looking in classrooms.* New York: Harper & Row, 1973.

Gray, S. W., & Klaus, R. A. The early training project: A seventh-year report. *Child Development,* 1970, *41,* 909–924.

Gregor, A. J., & McPherson, D. A. Racial attitudes among white and Negro children in a deep South standard metropolitan area. *Journal of Social Psychology,* 1966, *68,* 95–106.

Grier, W. H., & Cobbs, P. M. *Black rage.* New York: Basic Books, 1968.

Gurin, P., Gurin, G., Lao, R. C., & Beattie, M. Internal-external control in the motivational dynamics of Negro youth. *Journal of Social Issues,* 1969, *25*(3), 29–53.

Guttentag, M. Children in Harlem's community controlled schools. *Journal of Social Issues,* 1972, *28*(4), 1–20.

Gynther, M. D. White norms and Black MMPIs: A prescription for discrimination. *Psychological Bulletin,* 1972, *78,* 386–402.

Hammer, E. F. Frustration-aggression hypothesis extended to socio-racial areas: Comparison of Negro and white children's H.T.P.'s. *Psychiatric Quarterly,* 1953, *27,* 597–607.

Heber, R., Garber, H., Herrington, S., Hoffman, C., & Falender, C. *Rehabilitation of families at risk for mental retardation.* Progress report, December 1972. Rehabilitation Research and Training Center in Mental Retardation, University of Wisconsin, Madison, Wisconsin.

Hess, R. D. Social class and ethnic influences upon socialization. In P. H. Mussen (Ed.), *Carmichael's manual of child psychology* (Vol. 2) (3rd ed.). New York: Wiley, 1970.

Horowitz, R. E. Racial aspects of self-identification in nursery school children. *Journal of Psychology*, 1939, *7*, 91–99.

Hovland, C. L., & Sears, R. R. Minor studies in aggression: VI. Correlation of lynchings with economic indices. *Journal of Psychology*, 1940, *9*, 301–310.

Hraba, J., & Grant, G. Black is beautiful: A reexamination of racial preference and identification. *Journal of Personality and Social Psychology*, 1970, *16*, 398–402.

Hunt, L. L., & Hunt, J. G. Race and the father-son connection: The conditional relevance of father absence for the orientations and identities of adolescent boys. *Social Problems*, 1975, *23*, 35–52.

Jencks, C., Smith, M., Acland, H., Bane, M. J., Cohen, D., Gintis, H., Heyns, B., & Michelson, S. *Inequality: A reassessment of the effect of family and schooling in America.* New York: Basic Books, 1972.

Jensen, A. R. How much can we boost IQ and scholastic achievement? *Harvard Educational Review*, 1969, *39*, 1–123.

Jensen, A. R. Cumulative deficit in IQ of blacks in the rural South. *Developmental Psychology*, 1977, *13*, 184–191.

Kamin, L. J. A positive interpretation of apparent "Cumulative Deficit." *Developmental Psychology*, 1978, *14*, 195–196.

Kandel, D. B. Race, maternal authority, and adolescent aspiration. *American Journal of Sociology*, 1971, *76*, 999–1020.

Kardiner, A., & Ovesey, L. *The mark of oppression.* New York: Norton, 1951.

Katz, I. The socialization of academic motivation in minority-group children. In D. Levine (Ed.), *Nebraska Symposium on Motivation.* Lincoln: University of Nebraska Press, 1967.

Katz, I. Alternatives to a personality-deficit interpretation of Negro under-achievement. In P. Watson (Ed.), *Psychology and race.* Baltimore: Penguin Books, 1973.

Katz, I., Robinson, J. M., Epps, E. G., & Waly, P. Race of experimenter and instructions in the expression of hostility by Negro boys. *Journal of Social Issues*, 1964, *20*(2), 54–60.

Kennedy, W. A., Van de Riet, V., & White, J. C., Jr. A normative sample of intelligence and achievement of Negro elementary school children in the southeastern United States. *Monographs of the Society for Research in Child Development*, 1963, *28* (6, Serial No. 90).

Klaus, R. A., & Gray, S. W. The early training project for disadvantaged children: A report after five years. *Monographs of the Society for Research in Child Development*, 1968, *33* (4, Serial No. 120).

Kuhlman, T. L., & Bieliauskas, V. J. A comparison of black and white adolescents on the HTP. *Journal of Clinical Psychology*, 1976, *32*, 728–731.

Landreth, C., & Johnson, B. C. Young children's responses to a picture and inset test designed to reveal reactions to persons of different skin color. *Child Development*, 1953, *24*, 63–79.

Lee, E. S. Negro intelligence and selective migration: A Philadelphia test of the Klineberg hypothesis. *American Sociological Review*, 1951, *16*, 227–233.

Lesser, G. S., Fifer, G., & Clark, D. H. Mental abilities of children from different social-class and cultural groups. *Monographs of the Society for Research in Child Development*, 1965, *30* (4, Serial No. 102).

Levenstein, P. Cognitive growth in preschoolers through verbal interaction with mothers. *American Journal of Orthopsychiatry,* 1970, *40,* 426–432.

Levinson, B. M. Traditional Jewish cultural values and performance on the Wechsler tests. *Journal of Educational Psychology,* 1959, *50,* 177–181.

Levinson, B. M. The WAIS quotient of subcultural deviation. *Journal of Genetic Psychology,* 1963, *103,* 123–131.

Levy, B. An urban teacher speaks out. In S. W. Webster (Ed.), *The disadvantaged learner.* San Francisco: Chandler, 1966.

Lewontin, R. C. The apportionment of human diversity. In T. Dobzhansky, M. K. Hecht, & W. C. Steere (Eds.), *Evolutionary biology* (Vol. 6). New York: Appleton-Century-Crofts, 1972.

Liebow, E. *Tally's corner.* Boston: Little, Brown, 1967.

Loehlin, J. C., Lindzey, G., & Spuhler, J. N. *Race differences in intelligence.* San Francisco: Freeman, 1975.

Loehlin, J. C., Vandenberg, S. G., & Osborne, R. T. Blood group genes and Negro-white ability differences. *Behavior Genetics,* 1973, *3,* 263–270.

Mandler, J. M., & Stein, N. L. The myth of perceptual defect: Sources and evidence. *Psychological Bulletin,* 1977, *84,* 173–192.

McClelland, D. C. *The achieving society.* New York: Van Nostrand, 1961.

Moore, C. L., & Retish, P. M. Effect of the examiner's race on Black children's Wechsler preschool and primary scale of intelligence IQ. *Developmental Psychology,* 1974, *10,* 672–676.

Mosteller, F., & Moynihan, D. P. A pathbreaking report. In F. Mosteller & D. P. Moynihan (Eds.), *On equality of educational opportunity.* New York: Random House, 1972.

Moynihan, D. P. *The Negro family: The case for national action.* U.S. Dept. of Labor. Washington, D.C.: U.S. Government Printing Office, 1965.

Murnane, R. J. *The impact of school resources on the learning of inner city children.* Cambridge, Mass.: Ballinger, 1975.

Nichols, P. L. *The effects of heredity and environment on intelligence test performance in 4 and 7 year white and Negro sibling pairs.* Unpublished doctoral dissertation, University of Minnesota. Ann Arbor, Michigan: University Microfilm, 1970, No. 71–18, 874.

Osborne, R. T. Stability of factor structure of the WISC for normal Negro children from pre-school level to first grade. *Psychological Reports,* 1966, *18,* 655–664.

Osborne, R. T., & Gregor, A. J. Racial differences in heritability estimates for tests of spatial ability. *Perceptual and Motor Skills,* 1968, *27,* 735–739.

Osborne, R. T., & Miele, F. Racial differences in environmental influences on numerical ability as determined by heritability estimates. *Perceptual and Motor Skills,* 1969, *28,* 535–538.

Pettigrew, T. F. *A profile of the Negro American.* Princeton, N.J.: Van Nostrand, 1964.

Pettigrew, T. F., & Green, R. L. School desegregation in large cities: A critique of the Coleman "White Flight" thesis. *Harvard Educational Review,* 1976, *46,* 1–53.

Portes, A., & Wilson, K. L. Black-white differences in educational attainment. *American Sociological Review,* 1976, *41,* 414–431.

Powdermaker, H. The channeling of Negro aggression by the cultural process. *American Journal of Sociology,* 1943, *48,* 750–758.

Prange, A. J., Jr., & Vitols, M. M. Jokes among southern Negroes: The revelation of conflict. *Journal of Nervous and Mental Disease,* 1963, *136,* 162–166.

Quay, L. C. Language dialect, reinforcement, and the intelligence-test performance of Negro children. *Child Development*, 1971, *42*, 5–15.

Reports of the Cambridge anthropological expedition to the Torres Straits (Vol. 2). Cambridge: Cambridge University Press, 1901 and 1903.

Rist, R. Student social class and teacher expectations: The self-fulfilling prophecy in ghetto education. *Harvard Educational Review*, 1970, *40*, 411–451.

Robinson, J. P., & Shaver, P. R. *Measures of social psychological attitudes*. Ann Arbor: Institute for Social Research, University of Michigan, 1970.

Rokeach, M. *The nature of values*. New York: Free Press, 1973.

Rosenthal, R., & Jacobson, L. *Pygmalion in the classroom: Teacher expectation and pupils' intellectual development*. New York: Holt, Rinehart & Winston, 1968.

Rubovits, P. C., & Maehr, M. L. Pygmalion black and white. *Journal of Personality and Social Psychology*, 1973, *25*, 210–218.

Samuda, R. J. *Psychological testing of American minorities: Issues and consequences*. New York: Dodd, Mead, 1975.

Scarr, S., & Weinberg, R. A. IQ test performance of Black children adopted by White families. *American Psychologist*, 1976, *31*, 726–739.

Scarr-Salapatek, S. Race, social class, and IQ. *Science*, 1971, *174*, 1285–1295.

Sears, D. O., & McConahay, J. B. Racial socialization, comparison levels, and the Watts riot. *Journal of Social Issues*, 1970, *26*(1), 121–140.

Shaw, M. E. The self-image of black and white pupils in an integrated school. *Journal of Personality*, 1974, *42*, 12–22.

Shuey, A. M. *The testing of Negro intelligence* (2nd ed.). New York: Social Science Press, 1966.

Smith, J. P., & Welch, F. *Race differences in earnings: A survey and new evidence*. Santa Monica, Calif.: The Rand Corporation, 1978.

Smith, S. Language and non-verbal test performance of racial groups in Honolulu before and after a fourteen-year interval. *Journal of General Psychology*, 1942, *26*, 51–93.

St. John, N. H. *School desegregation outcomes for children*. New York: Wiley, 1975.

Stern, C. *Principles of human genetics* (2nd ed.). San Francisco: Freeman, 1960.

Stodolsky, S. S., & Lesser, G. S. Learning patterns in the disadvantaged. *Harvard Educational Review*, 1967, *37*, 546–593.

Stuckert, R. P. Race mixture: The African ancestry of White Americans. In P. B. Hammond (Ed.), *Physical anthropology and archeology, selected readings*. New York: Macmillan, 1964.

TenHouten, W. D. The Black family: Myth and reality. *Psychiatry*, 1970, *33*, 145–173.

Terman, L. M., & Merrill, M. A. *Measuring intelligence: A guide to the administration of the new revised Stanford-Binet tests of intelligence*. Boston: Houghton Mifflin, 1937.

Turner, C. B., & Wilson, W. J. Dimensions of racial ideology: A study of urban black attitudes. *Journal of Social Issues*, 1976, *32*(2), 139–152.

Tyler, L. E. *The psychology of human differences* (3rd ed.). New York: Appleton-Century-Crofts, 1965.

Uniform Crime Reports. Federal Bureau of Investigation. U.S. Dept. of Justice. Washington, D.C.: U.S. Government Printing Office, 1976.

Vandenberg, S. G. A comparison of heritability estimates of U.S. Negro and white high school students. *Acta Geneticae Medicae et Gemellologiae*, 1970, *19*, 280–284.

Warheit, G. J., Holzer, C. E., III, & Arey, S. A. Race and mental illness: An epidemiologic update. *Journal of Mental and Social Behavior,* 1975, *16*(3), 243–256.

Weikart, D. P. Relationship of curriculum, teaching, and learning in preschool education. In J. C. Stanley (Ed.), *Preschool programs for the disadvantaged.* Baltimore: Johns Hopkins University Press, 1972.

Werner, E. E., Simonian, K., & Smith, R. S. Ethnic and socioeconomic status differences in abilities and achievement among preschool and school age children in Hawaii. *Journal of Social Psychology,* 1968, *75,* 43–59.

Woodworth, R. S. Racial differences in mental traits. *Science,* 1910, *31,* 171–186.

Part Four

Conclusions

Trends
and Implications

What major trends can we identify in the study of human differences? What are the future directions of differential psychology? What social implications can be extracted from our scientific knowledge about human differences? Finally, how can we apply such knowledge to social issues such as equality of educational opportunity, changing sex roles, intergroup relations, and human rights? These are the questions we will try to answer in this closing chapter.

Let us start off by stating that we believe there are at least four major trends now taking place in differential psychology. These are: (1) increased attention to the complex nature of the interaction between hereditary and environmental influences, (2) a focusing on the interaction between the person and situation, (3) a greater recognition of the sociohistorical context of the field, and (4) an examination of the role of the individual in society. Consideration of each of these trends should indicate the future directions and social implications of differential psychology.

THE INTERACTION BETWEEN HEREDITY
AND ENVIRONMENT

We have noted that the study of human differences was initially dominated by a genetic point of view. Starting in the 1930s, the pendulum began
to move in the direction of the environmental position. By the late 1960s,
however, doubts were raised about the overemphasis on environmental influences and neglect of genetic influences. Attention was therefore directed to
the nature of the heredity/environment interaction, the importance of which
Anne Anastasi (1958b) had pointed to in the late 1950s.

An abundance of evidence, primarily based on animal research, exists
demonstrating significant interactions of hereditary and environmental variables (Anastasi, 1972). It has been considerably more difficult to investigate
the interaction between heredity and environment with humans than with
animals because when dealing with humans there are ethical restrictions concerning the extent to which relevant variables can be controlled and manipulated. However, recent developments are beginning to show how the heredity/
environment interaction can be studied at the human level. Some of the most
promising developments stem from research on the etiology of psychopathology (Erlenmeyer-Kimling, 1975). Pathological patterns, such as schizophrenia,
manic-depressive psychosis, alcoholism, and minimal brain damage, appear
to involve a genetic predisposition that is a necessary, though not sufficient,
etiological factor. The critical question for understanding the gene/environ-
ment interaction in the development of psychopathology is: What are the environmental characteristics that interact with the genetic predisposition, and at
what time during the individual's life must they interact to produce the observed psychopathology?

How can we identify the environmental variables in the etiology of psychiatric disorders? A major problem is that such disorders as schizophrenia and
manic-depressive psychosis do not become manifest until early adulthood. Yet,
the roots of these disorders appear to originate sometime earlier in the developmental history of the affected individual. As Erlenmeyer-Kimling (1976) points
out in the case of schizophrenia:

> The problem is that schizophrenologists have backed into the study of
> development. They have examined the childhoods of thousands of schizophrenic
> patients but almost always from a distance, from backward glances long after
> the traces of important formative influences have become obscured and recall—a
> shaky affair at best—has been colored by the knowledge that eventually a failure
> had occurred. . . . Equally capable of misleading are attempts to identify primary
> disturbances in psychological or biological functions from observations of abnor-
> malities in schizophrenic patients. Yet, until comparatively recently, the early
> years of those who would later become schizophrenic, and all the adverse things
> that were supposed to be taking place in those years, were known only from
> retrospective reports [p. 289].

Erlenmeyer-Kimling (1976) indicates that a number of investigators have
begun to turn away from the traditional retrospective approaches to the eti-

ology of schizophrenia. Instead, they have adopted a prospective approach by studying children of schizophrenic mothers who are considered to be at high genetic risk for showing schizophrenia at some time later than the time of initial observation. Careful longitudinal follow ups of such populations afford the opportunity to observe the potential schizophrenic as a developing organism. It should be possible to distinguish those environmental factors that interact with the genetic predisposition to precipitate manifest pathology from those environmental factors that act as deterrents. Furthermore, once vulnerable individuals are identified, it should be possible to provide them access to early preventive intervention. Presently, at least 20 longitudinal studies of populations at high risk for schizophrenia are being carried out (Erlenmeyer-Kimling, 1976). These studies show promise in providing a much greater understanding of how heredity and environment specifically interact with each other to produce (or fail to produce) the schizophrenic personality. Moreover, applying similar methods for studying the interaction between heredity and environment to other characteristics should help further our comprehension of their origins.

THE INTERACTION BETWEEN THE PERSON AND THE SITUATION

In dealing with the dimensions of individual differences, the underlying assumption in differential psychology has traditionally been that such dimensions (or traits) are consistent across situations and enduring over time. This was true of the classic differential psychology texts by Anastasi (1958a) and Tyler (1965), and it is also true, albeit to a lesser extent, of ours. In this book, we have at times acknowledged the importance of the interaction between the person and situation but suggest that increased emphasis must be given to it in future.

The person/situation interaction means that the observable behaviors of an individual in a given situation are the joint product of the characteristics of the individual (that is, individual difference dimensions) and the characteristics of the situation. What this means is that how a given characteristic of an individual is related to that individual's actual behavior varies depending on the nature of the situation. In addition, the interaction between the person and situation may be viewed as implying a reciprocal causal relationship between the person and the situation—the person not only is affected by the situation but can also modify the situation. For example, because of a tendency toward extraversion, a college student may not like the lecture-type teaching style of the instructor of a course he or she is enrolled in. The student may effectively change the situation by generating more group discussion than would normally characterize a class taught by the instructor. This emphasis on the person/situation interaction calls for a fundamental shift in differential psychology from a singular focus on the characteristics of the individual to a concern with situational parameters as well. Thus, while differential psychology will remain the study of individual and group differences, an underlying premise is that an understanding of said differences is facilitated greatly by a situational perspective.

As we noted in Chapter 8, analyzing person/situation interactions is limited by the fact that at the present time our statistical methods are insufficiently developed to permit the examination of the reciprocal causal relations between the person and the situation (Endler & Magnusson, 1976; Overton & Reese, 1973). The greater recognition of the importance of person/situation interactions also calls for changes in research strategies. Rather than the dominant strategy of studying individuals at only one point in time, more longitudinal investigations are needed to gain a better understanding of the reciprocal causal relationship between the person and the situation. For example, we can study the life histories of individuals through the use of the case-study method and biographical and autobiographical data (see Carlson, 1971). We also need more complete information about the nature of situations, such as how they can be classified, how they are perceived by individuals, and the extent to which individual perceptions are congruent with objective measures of the situations (see Moos, 1976). Finally, we need to know more about how individuals perceive their own consistency across situations. There is some suggestion that individuals vary in terms of how consistently they view themselves as manifesting a given trait, and the degree of perceived consistency appears to be directly associated with actual consistency across situations (Bem & Allen, 1974).

A significant implication of the interaction between the person and situation is the idea that people are more versatile than has been commonly believed. This point of view is expressed by Leona Tyler (1978) in her recent book on the nature of individuality:

> An individual is not limited to one way of dealing with any of life's demands. Through encounters with a very large number of situations and persons exemplifying different possibilities for structuring reality, one puts together one's own repertoire of possibility-processing structures [the ways in which the person controls the selection of perceptions, activities, and learning situations]. If we need to predict a person's behavior in some situation and we are familiar with his or her repertoire, we can predict with some certainty what he or she will *not* do, but with much less certainty what he or she *will* do. The more extensive the person's repertoire, the more uncertainty there is about which of the available structures will control the behavior in any one "actual occasion." People are less limited and more versatile than our dominant psychological theories have led us to assume. Individuality is plural, not singular [p. 232].[1]

In conclusion, differential psychology has traditionally focused on the characteristics of the person that were assumed to be relatively stable across situations and enduring over time. However, to gain a more comprehensive

[1]This and all other quotations from this source are from *Individuality: Human Possibilities and Personal Choice in the Psychological Development of Men and Women*, by L. Tyler. Copyright 1978 by Jossey-Bass, Inc., Publishers. Reprinted by permission.

understanding of human differences, we need to know more than just a person's standing on various trait measures; we must assess the reciprocal influences between the person and the situation.

THE SOCIOHISTORICAL CONTEXT OF DIFFERENTIAL PSYCHOLOGY

As we indicated in Chapter 1, the development of differential psychology was related to historical trends in Western European society. Capitalism and Protestantism stressed the importance of individual effort rather than collective effort. In particular, British society, by the latter half of the 19th century, encouraged individual differences, and a scientific differential psychology emerged from the milieu of British individualism.

When we try to relate an area of knowledge, such as psychology, to its historical and social roots, we are working within the realm of the "sociology of knowledge" (see Buss, 1975; Remmling, 1973; Sampson, 1971). The task of the sociologist of knowledge is to analyze how various aspects of knowledge, such as beliefs, values, ideas, philosophy, and science, are related to the historical and societal contexts in which they were formulated. The sociologist of knowledge assumes that, to a considerable degree, our ideas and values are influenced by the kind of society in which we live. For example, Karl Marx held that the nature of a society's economic production system has an extensive influence on its intellectual, social, and political processes.

In psychology, there has been a recent trend to apply the sociology of knowledge to various aspects of psychological thinking, such as to conceptions of human development (Riegel, 1972) and social interaction (Gergen, 1973). Such an approach assumes that the theories and ideas formulated in psychology are affected by conditions in society, and furthermore, that society itself can be affected by psychological theorizing. Differential psychology is an area within psychology that has been particularly sensitive to societal forces. We have already noted that the origins of the study of human differences began in a society that valued individualism. The United States at the turn of the 20th century was ready for pragmatic advantages inherent in the prediction of individual achievement. Psychological tests of various sorts—intelligence, aptitude, scholastic achievement, and personality—were developed and extensively utilized by the 1920s. However, as Tyler (1978) observes: "We are beginning to recognize now . . . that in the years since World War II accelerating social changes have been making our present approaches to the study and utilization of individual differences increasingly obsolete" (p. 235). According to Tyler, 50 years ago it made sense to sort out high scorers from low scorers on tests and select the high scorers for the most desirable jobs and training programs, leaving the low scorers to fill the many unskilled labor jobs that were available. Technological advances, such as automation and power machinery, have strikingly reduced the demand for unskilled workers. Now individuals who are screened out of job training programs or higher education because of low test scores have limited access to the job market. Thus, because of our changing society we need to develop new ways in which to measure and utilize individual differences. Toward this end Tyler suggests that, in addition to the traditional conceptualization of individual differences in terms of a vertical differentiation of individuals, we evolve an approach in which individuals are differentiated in a horizontal, complementary fashion.

Not only are changing social conditions forcing us to reevaluate our conceptualization of individual differences, but they are also having other effects on differential psychology. What we choose to study is very much a reflection of the events occurring in our society. By the 1960s, the civil rights movement had triggered a tremendous upsurge of interest in the study of race differences, and, as changes in the educational system began to take place, including the implementation of school desegregation and compensatory education, a considerable amount of research activity was directed at evaluating the effects of these changes. The decade of the 1960s also was marked by the emergence of other human rights movements, including student power, gray power, the women's movement, and gay liberation. By the late 1960s, differential psychology was taking a new look at generational differences, age differences, sex differences, and alternate life-styles. The particular saliency of racial differences, sex differences, and age differences in contemporary society is reflected in the emphasis given to them in this book.

How we explain human differences is also influenced by the sociohistorical context. As we noted, the pendulum has tended to swing back and forth with respect to the nature/nurture issue. Differential psychology started with a strong hereditary bias. While this hereditarian emphasis was partly due to the impact of Darwin's ideas about evolution, it was also a position that was consistent with the prevalent ideology of British and American societies in the late 19th and early 20th centuries. As Buss (1976) has pointed out, Galton, the British scholar who founded differential psychology, took the position that in a free and democratic society like that of Britain each individual had equal opportunity to be successful. Therefore Galton believed it necessarily followed that individual differences as reflected by people's standing in the social hierarchy of occupations had to be due to innate differences in ability. Galton extended his genetic view of individual differences within British society to racial differences across various societies. The opposing environmental view of human differences, especially of race differences, began to receive added support in the 1930s and was reinforced at least to some extent by the disillusionment and apprehension over highly racist policies, especially those advocated by Nazi Germany. By the early 1960s environmental interpretations of human differences clearly predominated over genetic interpretations. However, the early results from the many environmental intervention programs for disadvantaged children were a source of major disappointment for many people—both scientists and laypersons—who favored the environmentalist explanations. The disenchantment with such programs as well as advances made in the field of behavior genetics made the time ripe for a renewed acceptance of the possible role of heredity in the development of individual and group differences, especially in accounting for racial differences in ability. Arthur Jensen (1969) expressed this view in his controversial article in the *Harvard Educational Review* and therefore reignited the nature/nurture issue. During the 1970s, many investigators of human differences have taken a more careful look at genetic contributions and, as we have noted, particularly at the complex nature of the heredity/environment interaction and its social implications. We should add that, despite the increased emphasis on the role of heredity, a certain reluctance to acknowledge the importance of genetic determinants continues to remain deeply ingrained in many members of society. Many of our students experience considerable consternation when their convictions about the preeminence of the environment are seriously challenged. This resistance to genetic explanations of human differences—especially group differences—undoubtedly reflects the liberal, democratic context in which people are raised. We must also emphasize, as we have at many points in this book, that the role of heredity does not imply an immutability of behavior, and therefore the consideration of genetic influences in accounting for human differences does not run counter to a liberal, democratic perspective.

A greater recognition of the sociohistorical context of differential psychology should provide us with a greater awareness of how we develop and modify our conceptions of human differences.[2] Furthermore, a sensitivity to the social changes that are taking place should alert us to how relevant our methods are for studying and utilizing individual differences. An awareness of societal changes should also alert us to critical issues about human differences that need to be studied. Finally, as we have noted, the application of the sociology of knowledge to psychology is concerned not only with how society influences psychological thinking but also with how psychological thinking can affect society. The last trend we shall consider—the role of the individual in society—points to ways in which the study of human differences can have an influence on society. We will consider the relationship between the individual and society in terms of individualism and collectivism.

INDIVIDUALISM AND COLLECTIVISM

The role of the person in society can be construed in at least two ways—individually and collectively (Parsons & Shils, 1951; Sampson, 1971). Individualism refers to the belief that each person is a separate and self-sufficient entity. The legitimate role of each person is one that emphasizes individual effort for personal gain and prominence. In contrast, collectivism implies common effort. Each individual is an interdependent part of the social system and his or her role is one of cooperative effort for the benefit of all. As capitalism and Protestantism developed in Western society, individualism became the dominant cultural value and has remained a predominant theme of contemporary society (Sampson, 1977).

---

[2]The interested reader is referred to Kuhn's (1970) analysis of how changes in scientific thinking take place (see also Buss, 1975; Cohen, 1973).

As several writers have observed, psychology has, for the most part, taken an individualistic orientation. For example, Hogan (1975, 1976) points out that the major theoretical perspectives on the "whole person" in American psychology are individualistic and hostile to the impact of culture. Hogan (1976) states: "Without exception they take the view that society is an alien intrusion, an exogenous force imposed on people from without that necessarily stultifies and inhibits human development" (p. 364). Pepitone (1976) comments on the inadequacy of a purely individual psychology in which normative aspects of behavior are ignored. He argues for a theoretical and methodological reorientation in psychology (especially social psychology) that will more adequately reflect the collective and normative determinants of behavior. Finally, Sampson (1977) concludes that psychology can no longer follow the American ideal of individualism: "in an era in which collective problem solving is necessary, the perpetuation of self-contained individualistic conceptions can stifle psychology's efforts to contribute to resolving contemporary social issues" (p. 767).

We have already noted that the historical development of differential psychology has been closely linked to the cultural value of individualism. Differential psychology has been traditionally concerned with the identification of individual characteristics, with relatively little attention directed to factors in the social system that might be beneficial or detrimental to human development. However, by the 1960s more emphasis was given to the effects of the environment, such as those aspects of the social structure that foster discrimination and thus impede the development of minority group members.

We believe that differential psychology is now at a critical juncture. Nurtured within the context of individualism, it is facing the challenge of an alternative view of interdependent collectivism. The issue is whether we should continue to focus only on the characteristics of individuals and groups of individuals or move towards a collectivistic orientation in which we direct our attention to the interdependent relationships between individuals and between groups of individuals. Rather than concern ourselves only with what Bill Jones and Mary Smith are each capable of, interested in, and so on, should we also concentrate on what strengths Bill and Mary have as a team and how the assets of each can complement the other for the common good? Rather than concern ourselves only with Black/White differences, should we focus on how the varied cultural backgrounds of Blacks and Whites can complement one another for the common good?

Let us consider two concepts—equality and sex roles—that are particularly relevant to the questions we have raised.

Equality

Equality is a collectivistic concept that can be contrasted with the individualistic concept of equity. Edward Sampson (1975) discusses these concepts within the framework of the distribution of resources, such as income and status. In a system based on equity, resources are divided according to the differential characteristics of persons or groups, such as ability, achievement, and motivation. The more time and effort an individual puts forth and the greater the contributions that he or she makes, the greater is his or her share of the available resources in society. In contrast, a system based on equality rests on the principle that resources are divided equally, and therefore differential investments do not legitimately lead to differential rewards. With regard to individual differences, Sampson (1975) points out:

> Equality does not require a homogenization of persons who may indeed be differentiated in many ways (age, sex, authority, levels of skills, years of training, etc.), but rather argues that these differentiations do not require differential access to resources. All persons deserve much the same [p. 49].

Under a system of equality, individual differences would still exist but each person would be guaranteed the same share of resources.

Social psychological research, especially studies of interpersonal gaming behavior, provides some insight regarding whether an equity or equality principle is followed in interpersonal relations. Sampson, in reviewing this research, points to four factors that influence the choice of equity or equality: (1) the person's interaction goals, such as maximizing one's own personal gains as opposed to creating positive interpersonal relationships, (2) the person's basic orientation (cooperative or competitive), (3) the "situated identity" a person communicates to his or her partner—that is, the personal impressions we give to others as a consequence of our behaviors in a given situation, and (4) sex-role socialization.

The factor of sex-role socialization is especially interesting. As we indicated in Chapter 10, males tend to be competitive and task-oriented, while females tend to be cooperative and concerned with the feelings of others. In other words, males tend to be socialized according to the equity principle, whereas females tend to be socialized according to the equality principle. The equity principle for males is consistent with the economic roles they are trained to carry out. The equality principle for females is consistent with the familial roles they traditionally fulfill. As Sampson suggests, now that women are moving into more economically important roles they may be expected to become more competitive, and as men take on noneconomic roles they should engage in more cooperative relationships. It also appears, however, that our economic system of capitalism will continue to foster individualism and equity as dominant cultural values. Block (1973), in a cross-national comparison, found less of a competitive, individualistic orientation in socialistic Sweden and Denmark than in the United States. She also found fewer sex differences in the socialistic countries, suggesting that capitalism is associated with sharper distinctions between the traditional male economic role and the traditional female familial role.

Should psychology in general, and differential psychology in particular, simply reflect our dominant cultural values of individualism and equity? In our opinion the social changes that have been taking place since World War II, such as the changing labor market and the growing demand for equal rights by minority groups, raise the need for a reorientation of psychological thought towards the cultural values of collectivism and equality. We earlier referred to Tyler's (1978) recommendation in light of the changing labor market that we move away from an approach to individual differences that emphasizes a vertical differentiation—a model of individual differences based on equity—to one that encourages differentiation in terms of complementary role skills—a model of individual differences based on equality. According to Tyler (1978):

> It is true that competition is a salient aspect of our society and that individuals must adapt themselves to it. But it is not the *only* aspect. A psychology of individual differences should recognize *complementarity* as well as competition. It is necessary that individuals play different roles, do different things, and these differences need not be scaled or graded. In schools, teachers are being challenged to find out how each individual learns most readily rather than just how much he or she learns in a standard situation. In work places, new systems of organization are being explored, systems in which individual workers contribute in different ways to the functioning of work groups rather than acting as competitive units in an impersonal machine. Colleges that practice open enrollment must find for each individual who enters some fraction of the world's vast store of knowledge which will contribute to his or her intellectual development [p. 237].

With respect to the issue of equal rights for minority groups, differential psychology should become more concerned with how the social system can provide more equality of opportunities—as in the case of educational opportunity—and how groups can relate to one another on an equal basis. We will briefly look at desired goals for educational opportunity and intergroup relations.

Educational Opportunity. The ideal of universal equalization of educational opportunity became an established goal in the United States by the mid-19th century (Gordon, 1972). However, it took another century for this goal to be meaningfully attended to with the civil rights movement of the 1950s and 1960s. The social and political pressures toward achieving equalization raised questions about how equality of educational opportunity was to be defined. Gordon (1972) reviews the several attempts at reaching a definition and concludes that equality of educational opportunity can best be defined as the opportunity for all learners to acquire the necessary skills and credentials for meaningful participation in the mainstream of society.

Gordon identifies five kinds of prerequisite skills for effective functioning at the level of social survival or participation. These are: (1) mastery of basic communication skills, such as speech, reading, writing, and arithmetic computation; (2) problem-solving, involving competence in problem identification and problem-solving; (3) the management of knowledge, which involves a basic understanding of the principles used in the physical, biological, and social sciences; (4) readiness for continuing education, which reflects the fact that changing technology is increasing the demand for trainability and continuing education throughout one's life span in the labor force; and (5) self-management, involving personal, social, and character development.

Equality of educational opportunity would, according to Gordon, mean the achievement of at least these basic survival skills in all pupils save the small minority who are truly mentally defective. Gordon (1972) states: "To make the opportunity equal, the school would have to develop and use whatever methods, materials, or procedures are required by the special style, special ability, or special background the child may bring" (p. 433). While equalization of educational opportunity implies a parity in achievement at a baseline level of participation or survival skills, it also has to allow for the opportunity and freedom to vary with respect to achievement ceilings. Equality of educational opportunity would thus imply both the equalized opportunity to attain basic educational achievement and freedom of individuals to rise above such a baseline.

Intergroup Relations. How do we achieve a pluralistic society—one of a diversity of groups of peoples—based on egalitarian or interdependent relationships among our component subgroups? This is certainly a critical issue in our contemporary society. The civil rights movement initially sought integration as the solution for a pluralistic society. However, since the 1960s it does not seem apparent that integration is necessarily the most direct pathway to pluralism. Harry Triandis (1976), in an analysis of the future of pluralism, argues for an alternative to integration; namely, what he calls "additive multiculturalism." He states:

> My argument has been that our most current attempts at integration, based on a legal framework, disregard individual differences and are attempts to eliminate cultural differences. I am advocating a shift from that perspective to one that provides for a marriage of the legal framework with our understanding of social psychological principles. Rather than integration, as conceived today, or assimilation, which involves the elimination of cultural differences, I am advocating *additive multiculturalism* where people learn to be effective and to appreciate others who are different in culture. Additive multiculturalism is by its very nature something that needs to be developed in the majority rather than the minority of the population. As more members of the minority learn to integrate in jobs and are given a chance to do so, the majority must learn to relate to the minorities with a perspective of additive multiculturalism. Within that framework and over a period of many years, we should develop a pluralism that gives self-respect to all, appreciation of cultural differences, and social skills leading to interpersonal relationships with more reward than costs [p. 205].[3]

It is noteworthy that Triandis argues for the need of the majority to become knowledgeable about the minority. The inherent social inequities in

[3]From "The Future of Pluralism," by H. C. Triandis, *Journal of Social Issues*, 1976, *32*(4), 179–208. Copyright 1976 by the Society for the Psychological Study of Social Issues. Reprinted by permission.

American society have forced minority groups to become socialized to the norms and values of White Americans. Such a situation does not lead to a sense of mutual respect between majority and minority. To achieve a pluralistic society composed of interdependent cultural subgroups who are equivalent in status, it will become necessary for Whites to learn how to get along with Blacks, Chicanos, and other minority groups. Triandis points out that new techniques for culture learning are becoming available and that what especially needs to be acquired are new interaction skills. For example, the White teacher working with Spanish-American children will not be able to establish close contact with these children unless he or she is knowledgeable about the cultural and familial patterns of Spanish Americans (see Castañada, James, & Robbins, 1974). Additionally, as Triandis indicates, cultural learning techniques should have potential for improving relationships between men and women, old and young, and so on.

Sex Roles

We previously mentioned the significance of sex roles in our discussion of equality. Societal conceptions of masculinity and femininity affect all of us. The 1960s and 1970s have been marked by a profound challenge to our traditional definitions of womanhood. Before the 1960s analyses of women were barely noticeable in the psychological literature. In the past decade we have experienced an explosion of interest and engagement in a "psychology of women." A similar explosion of involvement in a "psychology of men" now seems to be emerging (see Levinson, Darrow, Klein, Levinson, & McKee, 1978; Pleck & Sawyer, 1974). Challenges to our traditional beliefs about women are quite naturally raising challenges about our traditional beliefs about men.

The liberating trend in our conceptions of masculinity and femininity seems desirable. Human development should not be constrained by rigid sex-role definitions. Furthermore, our potential to grow as persons may be greatly facilitated if we are able to adopt, regardless of our biological sex, both traditional masculine and feminine characteristics. Sandra Bem (1974) has labeled the integration of masculine and feminine qualities *androgyny* (see Chapter 10).

But is androgyny the optimal antidote for rigid sex-role norms? If we conclude that collectivism is a more valued cultural ideal than individualism, our answer to this question has to be—no. As Sampson (1977) observes, androgyny is consistent with an individualistic principle. The androgynous person is a self-contained male and female. The synthesis of masculinity and femininity is located within the individual rather than within the interdependent collective system of which the individual is a part.

On the other hand, a collectivistic solution to the opposing characteristics of masculinity and femininity would locate the synthesis within an interdependent system rather than within the individual. Rather than look to the individual as a source for both the masculine quality of task effectiveness and the feminine quality of interpersonal effectiveness, we may foster interdependent relationships between task specialists and interpersonal (or maintenance) specialties (see Bales, 1958). As Sampson (1977) points out, these role specialists need not be associated with sex roles. Regardless of one's biological sex, each individual should have the opportunity to excel either as a task specialist or as an interpersonal specialist. Furthermore, aside from the question of whether collectivism is more desirable than individualism, the synthesis of task effectiveness and interpersonal effectiveness within the individual is a rare and unusual pattern (Bales, 1958; Sampson, 1977). It thus seems more realistic to look for a synthesis of these role functions in the interdependent collectivity, where individuals performing different functions can work together in a cooperative effort.

A FINAL WORD

Our thesis is that knowledge emerges within a historical and social context, and therefore the sociohistorical context has had an impact on our psychological thinking about human differences. In particular, changes in our society over the last several decades have forced us to reexamine basic issues in differential psychology, such as heredity versus environment, the nature of intelligence, the effectiveness of public education, race differences, age and generational differences, and sex differences. This reexamination has indicated that the study of human differences requires a greater sophistication in theory and method than we have been accustomed to. We cannot limit ourselves to the identification of trait dimensions or typological classifications across individuals without also considering the characteristics of the environments within which individuals function. Nor can we limit ourselves to an analysis of the environmental determinants of human differences without also considering the hereditary determinants. Finally, we have to ask ourselves what kind of society is most desirable for the expression of human diversity—for the opportunity for each of us to grow as individuals and at the same time not infringe on the rights of others to develop their own individuality. We have argued that a society based on principles of collectivism is more conducive to this goal than one based on principles of individualism.

But how can we argue for collectivistic solutions to issues of human differences when we are part of an individualistic society? The answer is that our systems of knowledge, our conceptualizations of science, do not merely reflect what currently exists. Our ideas, beliefs, and theories can also contribute to social change. The sociology of knowledge deals not only with society's effect on knowledge; it also deals with the effect of knowledge on society. Marx's ideas and Freud's ideas were not only reflections of their historical and social contexts; Marxism and Freudianism have had profound effects on society. Will differential psychology make meaningful contributions to the ideal of a pluralistic society based on equal rights for all? This is the challenge of the future.

REFERENCES

Anastasi, A. *Differential psychology* (3rd ed.). New York: Macmillan, 1958. (a)

Anastasi, A. Heredity, environment, and the question "How?" *Psychological Review*, 1958, *65*, 197–208. (b)

Anastasi, A. The cultivation of diversity. *American Psychologist*, 1972, *27*, 1091–1099.

Bales, R. F. Task roles and social roles in problem-solving groups. In E. E. Maccoby, T. M. Newcomb, & E. L. Hartley (Eds.), *Readings in social psychology* (3rd ed.). New York: Holt, Rinehart & Winston, 1958.

Bem, D. J., & Allen, A. On predicting some of the people some of the time: The search for cross-situational consistencies in behavior. *Psychological Review*, 1974, *81*, 506–520.

Bem, S. L. The measurement of psychological androgyny. *Journal of Consulting and Clinical Psychology*, 1974, *42*, 155–162.

Block, J. H. Conceptions of sex role: Some cross-cultural and longitudinal perspectives. *American Psychologist*, 1973, *28*, 512–526.

Buss, A. R. The emerging field of the sociology of psychological knowledge. *American Psychologist*, 1975, *30*, 988–1002.

Buss, A. R. Galton and the birth of differential psychology and eugenics: Social, political and economic forces. *Journal of the History of the Behavioral Sciences*, 1976, *12*, 47–58.

Carlson, R. Where is the person in personality research? *Psychological Bulletin*, 1971, *75*, 203–219.

Castañada, A., James, R. L., & Robbins, W. *The educational needs of minority groups.* Lincoln, Neb.: Professional Educators Publishers, 1974.

Cohen, H. R. Dialectics and scientific revolutions. *Science & Society*, 1973, *37*, 326–336.

Endler, N. S., & Magnusson, D. Toward an interactional psychology of personality. *Psychological Bulletin*, 1976, *83*, 956–974.

Erlenmeyer-Kimling, L. Gene-environment interaction in human behavioral development: Commentary. In K. W. Schaie, V. E. Anderson, G. E. McClearn, & J. Money (Eds.), *Developmental human behavior genetics.* Lexington, Mass.: Heath, 1975.

Erlenmeyer-Kimling, L. Discussion of genetics and mental health. *Behavior Genetics*, 1976, *6*, 285–290.

Gergen, K. J. Social psychology as history. *Journal of Personality and Social Psychology*, 1973, *26*, 309–320.

Gordon, E. W. Toward defining equality of educational opportunity. In F. Mosteller & D. P. Moynihan (Eds.), *On equality of educational opportunity.* New York: Random House, 1972.

Hogan, R. Theoretical egocentrism and the problem of compliance. *American Psychologist*, 1975, *30*, 533–540.

Hogan, R. Reply to Campbell. *American Psychologist*, 1976, *31*, 363–366.

Jensen, A. R. How much can we boost IQ and scholastic achievement? *Harvard Educational Review*, 1969, *39*, 1–123.

Kuhn, T. S. *The structure of scientific revolutions* (2nd ed.). Chicago: University of Chicago Press, 1970.

Levinson, D. J., Darrow, C. N., Klein, E. B., Levinson, M. H., & McKee, B. *The seasons of a man's life.* New York: Knopf, 1978.

Moos, R. H. *The human context: Environmental determinants of behavior.* New York: Wiley, 1976.

Overton, W. F., & Reese, H. W. Models of development: Methodological implications. In J. R. Nesselroade & H. W. Reese (Eds.), *Life-span developmental psychology: Methodological issues.* New York: Academic Press, 1973.

Parsons, T., & Shils, E. A. (Eds.). *Towards a general theory of action.* Cambridge, Mass.: Harvard University Press, 1951.

Pepitone, A. Toward a normative and comparative biocultural social psychology. *Journal of Personality and Social Psychology,* 1976, *34,* 641–653.

Pleck, J. H., & Sawyer, J. (Eds.). *Men and masculinity.* Englewood Cliffs, N. J.: Prentice-Hall, 1974.

Remmling, G. W. (Ed.). *Towards the sociology of knowledge: Origins and development of a sociological thought style.* London: Routledge and Kegan Paul, 1973.

Riegel, K. F. Influence of economic and political ideologies on the development of developmental psychology. *Psychological Bulletin,* 1972, *78,* 129–141.

Sampson, E. E. *Social psychology and contemporary society.* New York: Wiley, 1971.

Sampson, E. E. On justice as equality. *Journal of Social Issues,* 1975, *31*(3), 45–64.

Sampson, E. E. Psychology and the American ideal. *Journal of Personality and Social Psychology,* 1977, *35,* 767–782.

Triandis, H. C. The future of pluralism. *Journal of Social Issues,* 1976, *32*(4), 179–208.

Tyler, L. E. *The psychology of human differences* (3rd ed.). New York: Appleton-Century-Crofts, 1965.

Tyler, L. E. *Individuality: Human possibilities and personal choice in the psychological development of men and women.* San Francisco: Jossey-Bass, 1978.

Name Index

Italic numbers refer to the references cited.

Acland, H., *133, 471*
Adams, M. S., 53, *70*
Adcock, C., 254, 256, *261*
Adorno, T. W., 252, *257*
Aiken, L. R., Jr., 272, *320*
Albert, J., 276, *324*
Alexander, K. L., 281, *320*
Allen, A., 211, *215*, 480, *490*
Allen, L., 121, *133*
Allen, V. L., 412–413, 416, *419*, 450, *468*
Allport, G. W., 187, 192, *215*, 246, 248, 252, 256, *257*
Alpert, R., 305, *328*
Anastasi, A., 17–19, 27–29, *41*, 57, 65–68, *70*, 80–81, 89, *101*, 130–131, *132*, 144, *154*, 164, 166, *179*, 189–190, 195, *215*, 244, *257*, 271,

Anastasi, A. *(continued)*
273, 277, 282–283, *320*, 400–401, 404, 409, *419*, 478–479, *490*
Anderson, W. A., 393, *420*
Andreas, C., 283, *320*
Appelbaum, M. L., 121–122, *134*
Archer, J., 268, *320*
Arenberg, D., 341–342, 346, 353, *383*
Arey, S. A., 462, *473*
Argyle, M., 210, *215*
Aristotle, 5
Armor, D. J., 453–545, *468*
Asch, S. E., 310, 318, *320*
Ascher, E. J., 123, *132*
Atkinson, J. W., 147, *155*, 199, *218*, 286, *320*, 325, 329, 359, *383, 388*
Auld, F., 414, *419*

Subject Index